248 - 53 - Brit   286 - 88 German

3 27 - 29 - Austria - Hungry

2 61 - 66 - Russia

The Modern World

The Modern World

16th century to the present

World

HARRIETTE FLORY
SAMUEL JENIKE

Longman

Authors:

Harriette Flory, PhD
is Associate Professor of History and Assistant Dean,
Educational Services, at Raymond Walters College,
University of Cincinnati. She has also taught English
and History at the high school level.

Samuel Jenike
is Social Studies Department Head, Walnut Hills High School,
Cincinnati, Ohio.

Executive Editor   **Lyn McLean**
Developmental Editor   **Anne Jensen**
Production Director   **Eduardo Castillo**
Project Designer   **Gayle Jaeger**
Production Assistant   **Katherine Rangoon**
Photo Researchers   **Katherine Rangoon** and **Barbara Conlon**
Maps by   **J & R Art Services, Inc.**

Typesetter   **Maryland Composition**
Preparation House   **Jay's Publishers Services**
Printer   **Von Hoffman Press**

10   9   8   7   6   5   4   3   2   1

ISBN: 0-582-36756-5

Longman Inc.
95 Church St.
White Plains, New York   10601

Associated Companies:
Longman Group Ltd., London
Longman Cheshire Pty., Melbourne
Longman Paul Pty., Auckland
Copp Clark Pitman, Toronto
Pitman Publishing Inc., New York

Supplementary Materials:
Teacher's Handbook
Worksheet Masters

Contributing Editor:
Dean Moore
Supervisor of Social Studies
Cincinnati Public Schools

Consultants:
Mildred Alpern
History Teacher
Spring Valley Senior High School, New York

Wentworth Clarke
Professor of Social Science Education
University of Central Florida at Orlando

William R. Dunnagan
Social Studies Teacher
Klein Independent School District, Texas

Roy Erickson
Program Specialist for Social Studies
San Juan School District, California

Mary Lauranne Lifka
Professor of History
College of Saint Teresa
Winona, Minnesota

Roy R. Pellicano
Professor of Education, Social Studies Teacher
Brooklyn, New York

Thomas R. Rumsey
History Teacher
Casady School
Oklahoma City, Oklahoma

Denny Schillings
Western Civilization Teacher
Homewood-Flossmoor High School, Illinois

William White
Past Coordinator of Social Sciences
Jefferson County Public Schools, Colorado

Special thanks to:
Dorothy and Thomas Hoobler
for contributing their historical and editorial expertise throughout this project

Contents

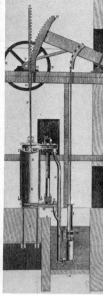

Maps

Glossary

absenteeism one of the Church abuses identified during the Reformation: the holding of offices, or benefices, by persons who do not perform the assigned duties.

absolute monarch a ruler whose authority is unquestioned and unlimited. In an *absolute monarchy*, the ruler's wishes are law.

apartheid the policy of strict racial segregation practiced by the government of South Africa. *Apartheid* applies to all public accommodations—restaurants, beaches, transportation, etc.—and to schools and housing.

capital resources that may be used to create more wealth. Capital may be in the form of money or other assets such as stocks that are accepted as the equivalent.

capitalism the economic system in which *capitalists*—wealthy individuals—own and operate most businesses, factories, and transportation systems. In the advanced stages of a capitalist economy, government regulations restrict the free activity of the marketplace by regulating prices, wages, etc. Also, giant corporations tend to be formed in which ownership is shared by many stockholders.

communism the most radical form of *socialism*. According to the theory outlined by Karl Marx and Friedrich Engels, the workers most exploited in industrialized capitalist societies—the *proletariat*—would rise in revolt, seizing control of factories, transportation systems, etc. They would then operate these facilities for their own benefit, and establish a worker-controlled government. In practice, a communist system has never been established in this way: the term applies instead to states in which most private property has been abolished, and the government controls and operates the economy.

Counter-Reformation the actions taken by the Roman Catholic Church and Catholic monarchs in the 16th and 17th centuries to reduce the influence of Protestantism and assert the universal authority of the pope.

deductive method the use of reasoning to attain knowledge, usually beginning with a premise, or known fact, and using general logical principles to draw new conclusions.

dialectic a method of argumentation and logic, often in question and answer form. Karl Marx and other 19th-century philosophers used *dialectic* to examine social and economic forces, starting from the premise that each event (thesis) leads to its opposite (antithesis).

diet an assembly of princes and other electors. In the Holy Roman Empire, diets convened to elect the Holy Roman emperor and to render opinions on judicial matters.

duma a representative assembly whose function was to advise the government of tsarist Russia; one of the reforms initiated by Alexander I (1801–1825).

economic determinism the belief that the pattern of wealth distribution within a society determines its political, social, and legal institutions, etc.

enclosure movement the consolidation of communal village lands and scattered strips of land in the hands of large landowners. The enclosure movement led to more efficient agriculture methods and created a pool of landless agricultural laborers. During the 19th century, many of these laborers migrated to urban areas to seek employment in factories.

ethnocentrism an attitude or belief that one's own culture is superior to any other.

evolution the theory that plants and animals develop special genetic characteristics to help them adapt to their environment. A corollary theory is that of *natural selection*: those individuals who adapt most successfully are likely to reproduce, and thus pass their special characteristics on to succeeding generations.

extended family a family in which parents, children, and other relatives live together in one household. Such social groupings are especially prevalent in rural areas. See also *nuclear family*.

geocentric centering upon the earth. In a *geocentric* world scheme, the heavenly bodies are thought to revolve around the earth.

heliocentric centering upon the sun. In a *heliocentric* world system, the planetary bodies revolve around the sun.

heresy a religious belief which has been condemned by an established church as a possible threat to the well-being of the faithful.

humanism the secular, or worldly, orientation of philosophers, artists, and writers beginning in the late Middle Ages. Humanists emphasized the potential of man and his works rather than theological doctrines.

individualism a belief that people should be free to pursue their own self-development without conforming to established standards and patterns.

inductive method the listing and categorization of diverse facts in order to arrive at a general conclusion.

indulgence a pardon for sins granted by clergy of the Catholic Church. Usually, the sinner completes the sacrament of penance before an indulgence is granted.

materialist relating to the philosophy that so-cial and political change is caused by economic forces rather than intellectual or spiritual developments.

money crop an agricultural commodity intended for sale rather than for the subsistence of farm workers.

nationalism extreme patriotism; the belief that the interests of one's own nation are more important than international concerns.

nepotism the practice of showing favoritism to relatives, especially in granting jobs or offices.

nuclear family a family in which parents and their children live together apart from other relatives. See also *extended family*.

pluralities one of the Church abuses identified during the Reformation: the holding of more than one office, or benefice, at a time.

proletariat the industrial working class, especially laborers employed in factories.

rationalism the belief that reason, rather than sensory experience, is the source of human knowledge.

Reformation the name given to the movement to reform the Roman Catholic Church and to the Protestant doctrines that subsequently arose.

relativism a recognition that judgments are subjective—based on individual experiences—and do not have absolute or universal validity.

romanticism an artistic and literary movement which began in the early 18th century. *Romantics* emphasized the importance of human emotions—rather than the rational qualities extolled by Enlightenment philosophers—and expressed a new appreciation of nature and of the common man.

simony the sale of Church offices or sacraments for gain.

socialism an economic system in which communities, rather than private individuals, own and operate the means of production—the factories, transportation systems, etc.

soviet a governing council of local leaders. In the Soviet Union, village and town soviets report to the Supreme Soviet composed of top Communist Party leaders.

theocracy a government ruled by a religious authority or authorities in the name of a supreme being.

The Modern World

● *"History is bunk."*
HENRY FORD

Prologue

These three words of the American industrialist Henry Ford are perhaps the most popularly known definition of history. In fact, Henry Ford actually said, "History is more or less bunk." Is there a difference? Let us apply one of the techniques of the historian, and examine the context of the remark.

The statement was made in 1916, one year before the United States entered the first World War. Ford was giving an interview to a reporter from the *Chicago Tribune*, Charles Wheeler, to express his views on disarmament and pacifism. Ford was an ardent pacifist, and opposed the possible entrance of the United States into the war.

Wheeler had just given an example from history to demonstrate how Britain's military preparedness and the strength of its navy prevented Napoleon from crossing the English Channel and invading the British Isles. Henry Ford's response was:

● ● ● *What do I care about Napoleon. It means nothing to me. History is more or less bunk. We want to live in the present and the only history that is worth a tinker's damn is the history we make today. The men who are responsible for the present war in Europe*

knew all about history. Yet they brought on the worst war in the world's history.[1]

What other historiographical methods can we apply to Ford's statement? First, we might ask the question, "Is it true that all the major European leaders knew all about history?" There is no evidence for this in Ford's statement. This raises other questions: Was Ford an expert on history? Did the timing of the interview affect Ford's reply?

Given Henry Ford's pacifistic sentiments and commitment to disarmament, perhaps Wheeler's question received a response that was emotional rather than rational. The same question asked at another time might have evoked a different answer. In addition, Ford, one of the great captains of industry, lived in an era when there was great optimism about the future of the United States. Many Americans had little interest in looking backward.

From his other actions, we know that Ford's attitude toward history was ambivalent. Years later he established a museum in Greenfield Village, near Dearborn, Michigan.

---

[1]John B. Rae, ed., *Henry Ford: Great Lives Observed* (Prentice-Hall, 1969), pp. 53-4.

It is a recreation of artifacts of American life from the 18th century through the early part of the 20th century. It contains a large collection of American tools, agricultural implements, decorative arts, transportation and communication artifacts.

When asked why he had invested so much money in the project, Ford replied that he "wanted to preserve what was the contribution of plain men who never got into history."[2] Ironically, it was the widespread use of the automobile, Ford's contribution to culture, that did much to change the earlier way of life that Ford now sought to preserve.

Moreover, Ford, in an area adjacent to Greenfield Village, set aside land for houses, workshops, and other structures that were significant in American history. At great cost, these were removed from their original locations and transported to Michigan. The area contains the courthouse where Abraham Lincoln practiced law as a circuit rider, the laboratories of Thomas Edison, and birthplaces or homes of such famous Americans as the Wright brothers, Robert Frost, and Noah Webster. So, in spite of his statement, Ford had some sense of the importance of history and the necessity of preserving the past.

WHAT IS HISTORY?

From the example of Henry Ford, it is clear that there is some confusion as to just what the discipline of history is and what its value is. Just what comes to mind when one asks, "What is history?" One of the clearest and simplest definitions of history is that by the American historian Carl Becker: "History is the memory of things said and done."

The historical memory is composed of many types of evidence. There are written records and artifacts that provide clues for the historian. By its nature this evidence is fragmentary. Just imagine how little histo-

rians a thousand years from now could make of the causes and results of World War II, if all they had to go by was the bombed out ruins of London and Hiroshima. Yet this is the detective job necessary for historians who study early societies.

Written records would seem a better historical source than ruins or other archaeological evidence. However, these too can be misleading. If a historian's understanding of the American political system were based solely on a reading of the United States Constitution, most of our political process—such as the role of political parties or the function of the Electoral College—would remain unknown.

Historians studying the recent past face different problems. For some subjects, the amount of primary source material is overwhelming and nearly unmanageable. At other times, crucial pieces of the puzzle are not available because of a government's or individual's need to withhold sensitive information.

Even when the written sources are sufficient and complete, the historian still has the task of interpretation. For the names and dates of events are only the raw materials of history. It is the job of the historian to link together in a meaningful way what we know about the past. The historian's interpretations and re-creations, rather than the data, are what make up what we call history. Because of the historian's role as interpreter, history is an ever-changing field—for the same data will be viewed and evaluated differently by different people. Such factors as the selection of facts, the significance ascribed to them, and the climate of the times in which the historian is writing will affect his or her work.

This does not have to discourage us unduly. When we watch the most recent "history" on the television nightly news, we accept the fact that we are receiving only a minute fraction of the events that have happened that day. We are getting the "news"

---

[2]Michael Kammen, ed., *The Past Before Us: Contemporary Historical Writing in the United States* (Ithaca: Cornell University Press, 1980), p. 24.

that seems important to whomever has prepared the news program. A description of every event that happened that day would not only be impossibly long, but also not digestible. The same is true with history.

In order to make history intelligible, historians choose the items that they believe are significant from the data they have. No one could absorb history from the time of Sumerian civilization to the present if the material were not broken up into understandable periods. For European history, the traditional divisions of classical, medieval, and modern history are instructive for what they say about the study of history.

Obviously all history was originally experienced as contemporary events. No people actually thought of themselves as living in the classical period; they were living in their present. Labels such as these are given to the period by future generations. In addition they are not value-free labels. The implication of the term Middle Ages, for example, is that the events of this era occurred between two periods of greater historical importance. People looked back with admiration to the Greeks and Romans, and felt that it was only with the period of the Renaissance (following the Middle Ages) that Europeans matched the achievements of their classical forebears. Today no historian would agree with that value judgment, but the name has stuck.

In the same way, future historians will have a perspective on the 20th century which we lack. It is interesting to speculate what will be said in the 21st century about the era of the Cold War. Depending on subsequent events, it might be seen as the first hesitant step towards the establishment of a world community—or the first stage of a new era of democratic revolutions throughout the world—or even the major factor in touching off World War III.

Moreover, out of the chaos of events, the historian must fashion order. To do this, he or she looks for patterns of continuity and discontinuity. For some periods of history, certain characteristics that fit the accepted pattern will be stressed; in other periods, alternate characteristics are emphasized. For example, the Renaissance represents a flowering of culture and art, while scientific and intellectual accomplishments are the primary focus of Enlightenment studies.

Perhaps the most important influence on the shaping of history is that each historian by necessity brings to the study of the past the values and questions of his or her own time. This can be useful in that it enables the past to shed light on the present. Indeed many historians believe that this is the primary usefulness of the study of history. Henry T. Buckle, a 19th-century historian, claimed, "There will always be a connection between the way in which men contemplate the past and the way in which they contemplate the present."

However, other historians feel the past should be appreciated for itself. According to this view, the past should be captured as much as possible in its own terms, without attempting to impose modern viewpoints on it. Even if the relevance to the present is slight, there are benefits in understanding earlier societies and the experiences of the people who lived in them.

The degree of accuracy possible is also a topic of debate. Perhaps the Greek historian Herodotus spoke most honestly to this point: "My business is to record what people say. But I am by no means bound to believe it—and that may be taken to apply to this book as a whole."

INTERDISCIPLINARY APPROACHES
In recent years many historians have expanded the definition of history by using data and discoveries from other fields of knowledge. The social sciences—particularly anthropology, archaeology, and social psychology—have been utilized to draw historical conclusions. Psychoanalytic insights have been applied to important historical person-

ages such as Martin Luther and Adolf Hitler. The field of social psychology has been used to explain the rise of totalitarianism, and also to explain the increase in warlike sentiments during certain periods.

The methods developed for the social sciences, such as the use of statistics and other types of analysis, have been useful to the historian. Historians now draw on both the techniques and knowledge of many fields to study the past. For example, the generalization that a martial spirit was in the air in the years preceding World War I can now be verified through empirical evidence found in contemporary music, popular novels, the spoken language, or even clothing styles. And by applying skills learned from the sociologist, the historian can distinguish between a society's "folkways" (standardized practices) and its "mores" (patterns of behavior that are basic to the health and survival of a society).

DIFFERING APPROACHES It was only in the 19th century that history was established as an individual discipline and profession. Previously history was a branch of literature, whose practitioners might be propagandists or those who sacrificed accuracy for literary effect. There was no professional tradition of historical standards.

No country was more important in the birth of modern historical writing than Germany. It was there that history was tied to the growing studies in philology, the history of language. The man who was to become the leading figure in German historical studies was Leopold von Ranke. In his view, no one who could not read the language of the culture should write about it. He believed that only primary sources—evidence, written and otherwise, that dates from the time being studied—should be consulted by an historian, since things written afterwards could not be proved to be accurate.

Von Ranke's ideal was history that only conveyed "what actually happened." Today we know that this is an impossible goal. But von Ranke's recognition of the importance of primary sources has remained to this day as an important part of historical studies.

Another approach to history has been that of the great systematizers. These historians, such as Karl Marx and Arnold Toynbee, believed that they found laws of history that were relevant to all civilizations. Marx believed that the core element of history was the struggle between the various classes of society. Toynbee saw civilizations as following a cycle almost like that of an individual human. In Toynbee's view, each civilization had a developing period, a period of ripeness, and then a decay. A similar idea was expressed by Oswald Spengler, who posited that the West was in a period of decline. Spengler's thesis of the decline of the West was influenced by the disillusionment with western civilization that was an important intellectual current in the years following World War I.

Most historians no longer believe that there are any such grand unifying principles relevant to all civilizations. This mode of historical interpretation is definitely not in favor today.

The professionalization of history in the 19th century led to an increasing specialization among historians. Much of traditional history had primarily concerned itself with political, military, and diplomatic affairs. It made great use of official records and materials. With the specialization of the field, economic history, cultural history, and social history emerged as distinct areas of study and thought. The British historian George Trevelyan offered a definition of one of the new fields: "Social history might be defined negatively as the history of a people with the politics left out."

As historians have benefited from knowledge in other fields, new historical specializations have emerged. Demographics, or population studies, have provided a new way of looking at the past. Geography has been increasingly used in combination with history to find insights into the causes of historical currents. Cliometrics approaches history from the perspective of statistical evidence. (The term combines the name of the muse of history, Clio, with *metrics*, or measurement.) These are just a few of the new fields that are expected to yield new historical insights.

A much-discussed question for historical thinking is whether the historian should be partisan. Some feel that the historian should make every attempt to be a neutral observer. This was the position of von Ranke. But others have claimed that neutrality, or complete objectivity, is neither a realistic possibility nor the responsibility of the historian. In this view, the historian should be open about his or her position on particular issues. The question of integrity for the historian lies not with partisanship but rather in maintaining the integrity of sources and in attempting to get as full a picture as possible.

The question of whether people or events make history has been a point of controversy among historians. It is sometimes called the "great man vs. historical forces" dispute. In the 19th century, Thomas Carlyle was an important proponent of the "great man" theory. Today it is somewhat discredited, and there is more interest in the conditions that lead to change rather than just the biographies and influence of great historical figures.

One of the most exciting developments in today's new approaches to history is the increasing realization that many people have been left out of the history written in the past. Traditional histories stressed the powerful individuals and the great public events. This was natural, as there is more definite information available on political and military leaders. But today there is a realization that there was always more to history than what happened at the top of society.

Historians are now trying to reconstruct the lives of the ordinary people of the day.

Their study begins with records of births and deaths, tax records, and other statistical information. These can give information on life expectancy and the effects of weather and climate on agriculture, as well as other facets of a civilization. Through these techniques it is hoped that more can be gleaned about overall conditions of an era. The historian today does not find it necessary to write in terms of individuals, but rather considers the way groups of people were influenced by long-term trends and economic conditions.

One aspect of this new approach explores the role of women and the position of the family in different societies and times. This emphasis was partly the result of the women's movement. There has been criticism that the only references to women in traditional histories concerned exceptional women who were rulers or able to excel in a man's world. Some people argue that women's role in the past has been a distinct one, separate from that of men, and that efforts to explore it will yield significant historical insights:

• • • *It is not surprising that most women feel that their sex does not have an interesting or significant past. However, like minority groups, women cannot afford to lack a consciousness of a collective identity, one which necessarily involves a shared awareness of the past. Without this, a social group suffers from a kind of collective amnesia, which makes it vulnerable to the impositions of dubious stereotypes, as well as limiting prejudices about what is right and proper for it to do or not to do.*"[3]

To get a truer picture of the recent past, many historians have made extensive use of the technique of recording oral histories. This allows the voices of ordinary people to be part of the record for historians of the future. Oral history has been used very effectively

[3]Sheila R. Johansson, "Herstory as History: A New Field or Another Fad?", in Bernice A. Carroll, ed., *Liberating Women's History* (Illinois University Press, 1976), p. 427.

to document the civil rights movement, the Great Depression in the United States, and the experience of Holocaust survivors.

Moreover, historians today are willing to use literature and myths to deepen their understanding of a period or people. There is a feeling among today's historians that all information is grist for the historical mill. The search for undiscovered historical documents is a growth industry in the profession today. There is also a growing understanding that popular culture is a fertile field for study. Sports, amusements, and popular art forms all have a history, and they tell us something about the society in which they thrived. From this you can see the truth of the Carl Becker dictum: "Everyman is a historian." You already know some pieces of history even if it is only about the recent past.

WHY STUDY HISTORY? The study of history is important for all citizens because knowledge about the past is essential for an understanding of the present. For our own history, a knowledge of how and why our political and social institutions were created deepens our understanding of how they work today and what they mean to the society in which we live.

Similarly, knowledge of European and world history deepens our understanding of our culture, and of the shrinking world in which we live. The achievements of classical Greece and Rome remain relevant today. More than 2300 years ago, Aristotle wrote, "Poverty is the parent of revolution and crime." Philosophers since then have not been able to improve on his observation. Thinkers of the past dealt with questions that people still ask, and we benefit from learning of the answers they found.

Much of the culture of the United States has antecedents in Europe. Thus the study of European history can lead to a greater appreciation of western art and music, which are surely some of the great joys of civilized people. Similarly, learning about European

political institutions can increase our understanding of the American political system that sprang from them.

The study of history enables the student to see how the world came to be what it is today. Because we live in a world in which little-known nations suddenly take on a significant role—as the recent examples of Vietnam, Iran, Afghanistan, and Libya illustrate—it is important to understand the culture and history that have shaped the present. The importance of promoting a mutual understanding between the various peoples of the world has never been as important as it is today. The first step in understanding other people is in comprehending their history.

Furthermore, though history does not repeat itself, the study of past events teaches useful lessons because some characteristics of human nature remain the same. The study of history, if creatively used, can lead to a better understanding of interactions between people or the likely consequences of actions. The following account graphically illustrates how ethnocentrism and ignorance of another society can lead to violence and tragedy:

● ● ● *In the late 19th century a group of European explorers led by Henry M. Stanley, an American reporter and would-be rescuer of Dr. Livingstone, were rounding a bend in the Congo River in Africa when they came face to face with 50 large canoes of militant savages shrieking war chants and brandishing spears. Only quick thinking and the superiority of the rifle prevented disaster. A number of the heathen were killed and the remainder fled into the jungle.*[4]

What you have just read is the European account of what happened. Fortunately, the Africans' perception of the incident was also recorded. Chief Mojimba's account tells an entirely different story:

---

[4]Leften S. Stavrianos, ed., *Readings in World History* (Boston: Allyn and Bacon, 1964), pp. 784-5.

••• *All night long the drums announced the strange news—a man with white flesh [was coming up the river]! . . . We will prepare a feast, I ordered, we will go to meet our brother and escort him into the village with rejoicing! . . . We swept forward, my canoe leading, the others following with songs of joy and with dancing to meet the first white man our eyes beheld, and to do him honor.*

But as we drew near his canoes there were loud reports . . . and fire staves spat bits of iron at us. Several of my men fell down. . . . Some screamed dreadfully—others were silent—they were dead, and blood flowed from little holes in their bodies. "War! That is war!" I yelled. "Go back!" . . . That was no brother! That was the worst enemy our country had ever seen. . . . We fled into the forest and flung ourselves on the ground. When we returned that evening, our eyes beheld fearful things; our brothers dead, dying, bleeding, our village plundered and burned. The robbers and murderers had disappeared.[5]

The consequence of this tragic and unnecessary incident was a generation of bloodshed between African and European in that part of Africa.

Looking at civilizations that are separated from ours by different cultural practices and time is also a refreshing intellectual experience. The history of different cultures is a vast reservoir of possibilities as to how things might be done. Knowledge of other cultures forces an intelligent person to confront his or her own ideas and see that perhaps there are other ways of life that might be as satisfactory as their own.

Knowing history enhances understanding of current events, because many problems have antecedents in the past. Being knowledgeable means that one can make more intelligent judgments about a situation. One is less likely to be swayed by people who oversimplify causes and solutions. Historical understanding makes it easier to form one's own opinions.

Finally, studying history can be fun. Current movies and popular fiction—particularly in the broad genre called "science fiction"—often present imagined cultures. The popular movie sequence *Star Wars* begins with this message on the screen: "A long time ago, in a galaxy far, far away . . ." Substitute "place" for "galaxy," and you begin the study of history. The stories of real people in different times and places can be just as thrilling as any fiction.

Although the various cultures and times we study each have their own flavor, human nature is not so different wherever one looks. History is filled with figures who are villainous, outrageous, and infamous. Edward Gibbon, the English historian, described history as "little more than the crimes, follies and misfortunes of mankind." History is also filled with the good and the ordinary.

The American historian Frederick Jackson Turner summarized the appeal of history this way:

••• *History has been a romance and a tragedy. In it we read the brilliant annals of the few. The intrigues of courts, knightly valor, palaces and pyramids, the loves of ladies, the songs of minstrels, and the chants from cathedrals pass like a pageant, or linger like a strain of music as we turn the pages. But history has its tragedy as well, which tells of the degraded tillers of the soil, toiling that others might dream, the slavery that rendered possible the 'glory that was Greece,' the serfdom into which decayed the 'grandeur that was Rome'—these as well demanded their annals.[6]*

The study of history has the same joys as good literature. It is an attempt to capture the feeling of what is human, what endures. Discovering the past helps one to discover the present.

---

[5]Ibid.

[6]Frederick Jackson Turner, "The Significance of History," in *The Early writings of Frederick Jackson Turner*, ed. F. Mood (Madison, Wis.: Wisconsin University Press, 1938), pp. 47–8.

OECVMENICA SACRO SANCTA SYNODVS TRIDENTI VRBE CELEBRI HABITA, ET PROMVLGATA

The Beginnings of Modern Europe

● *No man shall be blamed for reasoning in the maintenance of his own religion.*

THOMAS MORE

● *In conformity to the clear teaching of scripture we assert that by an eternal and immutable counsel God has once for all determined both whom he would admit to salvation and whom he would condemn to destruction.*

JOHN CALVIN

● *The colony of a civilized nation which takes possession either of a waste country, or of one so thinly inhabited that the natives easily give place to the new settlers, advances more rapidly to wealth and greatness than any other human society.*

ADAM SMITH

● *They saw a great boat appear on the wide sea. This boat had white wings, flashing like knives. White men came out of the water and spoke words no one could understand. Our ancestors were afraid, they said these were "Vumbi," ghosts of the dead. They drove them back to the sea, with flights of arrows. But the "Vumbi" spat fire with a noise of thunder.*

WEST AFRICAN ACCOUNT

● . . . it is not only in individual men that nature has implanted self-love. She implants a kind of it as a common possession in the various races, and even cities. By this token the English claim . . . good looks, music, and the best eating as their special properties. The Scots flatter themselves on the score of high birth and royal blood, not to mention their dialectical skill. Frenchmen have taken all politeness for their province. . . . The Italians . . . flatter themselves upon the fact that they alone, of all mortal men, are not barbarians. . . . The Turks, and that whole rabble of the truly barbarous, claim praise for their religion, laughing at Christians as superstitious. . . . Spaniards yield to no one in martial reputation. Germans take pride in their great stature and their knowledge of magic.

ERASMUS

Europe at the Beginning of the Modern Age (1450 – 1550)

The last half of the 15th century and the beginning of the 16th century were transitional years of great importance in European history. Historians mark this as a dividing line between medieval times and the early modern period. Such a break was not an abrupt one. Elements of medieval civilization, such as feudalism, lingered in many parts of Europe for a long time.

Nor were most people who lived at this time aware that they were at the beginning of a new age. One of their principal concerns was the ever-present threat of the dreaded plague. "How can it even be called a life," asked one person, "which begets so many deaths and plagues?"[1] To those who looked beyond their own village or local area, the greatest concern was the encroachment of the Turks. With their capture of Constantinople in 1453, the infidel Turks were at the eastern gate of Europe—and threatening to progress farther.

From today's vantage point, we can see that things were happening that would have far greater consequences than either the plague or the Turks. In 1454, in the town of Mainz, Germany, Johann Gutenberg produced the first book in Europe printed from movable type. The "invention of printing" was the key event in the dissemination of information that would help bring about the Reformation and the scientific revolution.

Portuguese explorers were making their first tentative voyages outside the sphere of Europe—down the African coast. The Italian Christopher Columbus crossed the Atlantic Ocean with three ships in 1492. From these beginnings, Europeans would go on to reach all parts of the inhabited world, spreading European culture as they went.

In countries such as England, France, and Spain, the new monarchs (Chapter 3) were strengthening their power. The people of

---

[1] Margaret Aston, *The Fifteenth Century* (New York: Harcourt, Brace, 1968), p. 18.

these countries were transferring their loyalty from feudal lords to the monarchy. This too was a beginning—of what would become the predominant political form in Europe, the nation-state.

At the time, however, people still saw the Roman Catholic Church and the Holy Roman Empire as the most important institutions in Europe. In 1517, an Augustinian monk in the German town of Wittenberg would challenge Catholicism's universal hold on European life (Chapter 2). And the power of the Holy Roman Empire was beginning its long decline as well.

In addition, the winds of change that had produced the Renaissance in the Italian city-states would make their way north and enrich the civilization of the northern European countries.

A TRIP THROUGH EUROPE

A traveler visiting Europe about the year 1500 would find a wide variety of conditions and political arrangements. He would observe that some states were consolidating their territory under strong monarchs. Feudalism was on the decline for three major reasons. First, strong monarchs made the protective function of the feudal lords less important. Secondly, the rise of a money economy and the growth of towns decreased the economic power of feudal lords. Finally, new weapons had produced a new kind of warfare that made the knight less powerful.

This was not true of all of Europe, however. In parts of central and northern Europe, no centralized monarchy arose. Yet the cities in these areas flourished, and for a time were economically the most advanced in Europe.

THE IBERIAN PENINSULA

In the second half of the 15th century the Iberian peninsula was divided into the kingdoms of Portugal, Castile, Aragon, Navarre, and at the extreme southeast the Emirate of Granada, the last of the Muslim kingdoms of Spain. With the marriage of Ferdinand of Aragon (1479–1516) to Isabella of Castile (1474–1504) in 1469, the two largest kingdoms in Spain were united under one rule. Their two kingdoms remained theoretically separate, but in the years that followed, many of Spain's institutions would become united under one monarchy.

In most of Europe, the criterion of good order was the ability to travel safely while carrying valuables. Travelers often commented on the lack of this safety in the Iberian peninsula.

• • • *A visit to Castile was like a journey into another world, where reluctant envoys from more civilized centers found themselves reduced to exchanging their horses for mules, killing and skinning their meat, living like gypsies and sleeping in the open.*[2]

Thus, a strengthened monarchy was popular with Isabella and Ferdinand's subjects, because it helped increase the general safety.

Ferdinand and Isabella's greater power meant less power for the Spanish nobility, and for the Cortés, the medieval parliament. In addition, Ferdinand and Isabella took control of the Church within their territory, in order to bring about religious reforms and to eliminate any potential challenge to their power.

The *Inquisition*—which was to wield its power in cruel and ruthless fashion—was established in 1478 to enforce religious uniformity. The first inquisitor general, Tomás de Torquemada, in 1492 persuaded the monarchs to order the expulsion of all Jews who refused to be baptized. The loss of about 170,000 Jews deprived Spain of many of its financiers and businessmen, and helped other areas of Europe to increase their economic power.

In 1492, the same year that Ferdinand and Isabella sponsored Columbus' first voyage to the New World, Spain rounded out its ter-

---

[2] *Ibid.*, p. 21.

EUROPE IN THE MID-16TH CENTURY

Why did the Hapsburgs pose the greatest threat to French interests on the continent of Europe?

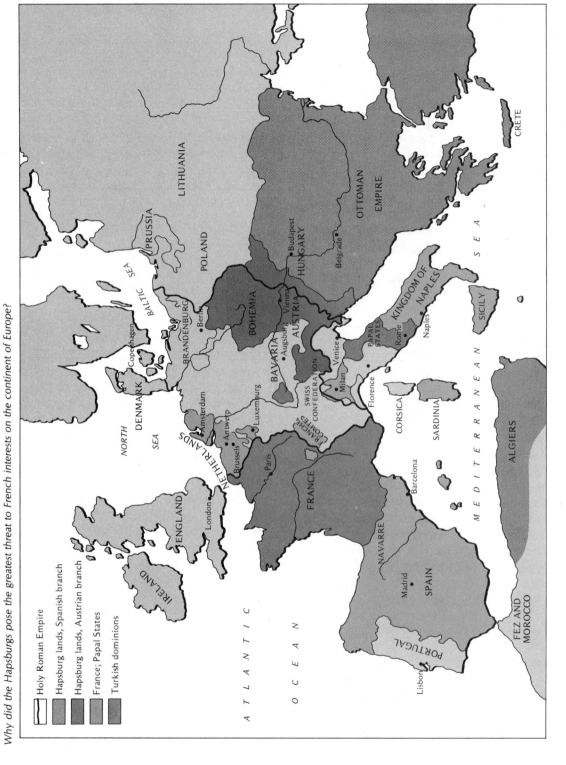

Legend:
- ☐ Holy Roman Empire
- Hapsburg lands, Spanish branch
- Hapsburg lands, Austrian branch
- France; Papal States
- Turkish dominions

ritory by conquering Granada. The expulsion of the Moors soon followed, and Spain lost another economically productive element of society. Ferdinand in 1512 conquered the kingdom of Navarre south of the Pyrenees. Through Ferdinand's participation in the invasion of Italy he also acquired the kingdom of Naples.

Portugal, except for a brief period between 1580 and 1640, was to remain separate from Spain. For its size, it would become unusually important in Europe's economy. This was largely due to the efforts of one man, Prince Henry, who created a school for navigators that provided the impetus for Portuguese exploration and colonization (Chapter 4). Portugal's overseas empire brought great wealth to the country, and helped to strengthen the monarchy.

ENGLAND

When England emerged from the Hundred Years' War with France (1337–1453), it was almost immediately plunged into a civil war known as the *War of the Roses*. The war ended in 1485 when Henry VII (1485–1509), the founder of the Tudor dynasty, defeated Richard III and was crowned king of England. Henry was able to increase the power of the monarchy, in part because many of the members of the old nobility had been killed in the civil war. His task of consolidating the areas under his rule was also made easier by a general desire for the restoration of order.

Henry formed a close alliance with the middle class, and appointed many of its members to government posts. A frugal man, he was careful about government expenses. He encouraged commerce and trade by giving English merchants a monopoly on certain goods carried on English ships, and by reducing the special privileges of foreign merchants in England. He negotiated treaties with foreign powers to protect the rights of English traders in other countries. These efforts increased the size and power of the En-

glish middle class. They also enriched London, the largest city in England, which had a population of about 60,000 in 1500.

Henry curtailed the privileges of the remaining nobles, notably the privileges of maintenance and livery. (Lords at this time still retained followers who could be identified by markings on their clothes, or livery. Often these retainers used their positions to terrorize the countryside.) Henry used the royal council, known as the *Star Chamber*, in its judicial capacity to control the local lords and prevent them from interfering with justice and oppressing those who lived on the land. Over time, the Star Chamber became noted for abuses of power and was abolished by Parliament in 1641.

At the end of Henry VII's reign, there was a surplus of funds. England with its 3.75 million people was more prosperous than before his reign. However, Henry's son and successor, Henry VIII, would soon use up this surplus.

FRANCE

The Hundred Years' War had caused havoc in France. The added destruction brought about by mercenary soldiers almost brought the country to its knees. Poorly paid, often of foreign nationality, and having no feeling of loyalty to the country they served, these soldiers stayed on to loot and devastate the countryside once the organized fighting had ended.

With the victory over the English, there was a rise in nationalistic sentiment in France. However, much of what we know today as France was not under the direct control of the monarch. The task of consolidating and expanding the royal domain fell to Louis XI (1461–1483), known as "the Spider King" for his clever diplomatic machinations. Louis' eye fell on the domain of Charles the Bold, Duke of Burgundy, which included the Netherlands and other territory on the fringes of France in addition to Burgundy. The signal achievement of Louis'

Louis XI, the "Spider King," consolidated and expanded the domain of the monarchy. His efforts were instrumental in building the nation-state of France.

The Holy Roman Empire, established in 962, had been an attempt to hold together the unity of Christian Europe. In its subsequent development, it did not follow the pattern typical in the rest of western Europe, where power had been consolidated by centralized monarchies. Its holdings were mostly in central Europe, comprising over 2500 separate political entities, including ecclesiastical domains, free cities, duchies, and landgravates. Allegiance to the Holy Roman emperor was secondary to that owed to the local prince or city. By the time of Maximilian (1493–1519), the emperor was largely a figurehead. The only portion of his realm that he really controlled was the personal domain of the Hapsburgs. He could neither collect taxes directly nor maintain an army. The real power in the empire was held by the seven Electors—princes and archbishops who ruled important territories and elected the emperor. The diet of the empire was almost

reign was to exploit Charles' mistakes to bring about his downfall. However, Louis did not receive all the spoils from Charles' defeat. Charles' daughter, Mary of Burgundy, was to bring much of his territory, particularly in the Netherlands, to her husband, Maximilian of Austria.

In addition, the Angevin domains in the south of France came under the French king's control. Louis appointed officials from the middle class to help him rule his enlarged domains. He cut the power of the nobles and lessened the political authority of the States General. By the time of his death, much of what we know today as France was under the control of the throne. Louis' two successors, Charles VIII (1483–1498) and Louis XII (1498–1515), did little to enlarge the royal domain. Instead they became embroiled in the invasion of Italy.

Maximilian I failed in his attempts to unify the Holy Roman Empire, but sponsored the development of Renaissance culture in northern Europe. This portrait of the emperor is by Albrecht Dürer.

as powerless as the emperor. It could not secure obedience to the laws that it legislated.

Maximilian, however, had the advantage of territories that had come to him by his marriage to Mary of Burgundy, daughter of Charles the Bold, as well as the ancestral Hapsburg estates. These included the Netherlands, which contained some of the most prosperous areas of Europe. Its cities of Bruges, Antwerp, and Ghent, among others, fueled much of the economic drive of early modern Europe. They were centers of the wool trade and the emerging textile industry.

Maximilian himself was a curious mixture of the medieval and modern. A man who loved medieval display, a skilled knight and huntsman, he was also a military expert on artillery and the organization of the *Landsknechte* (infantry). However, he had other interests in addition to the military. He was a patron of the arts and wrote books on the art of hunting, metallurgy, architecture, and gardening. Many of his books were illustrated by Albrecht Dürer, the great painter and engraver of the Northern Renaissance.

EASTERN EUROPE

For a brief time toward the end of the 15th century, Bohemia, Hungary, Poland, Lithuania, and Pomerania were united into one kingdom under the Jagellonian dynasty, but that unity was not to last. In the next century, Bohemia and Hungary would become part of the Hapsburg domains through a marriage alliance arranged by Maximilian. However, Poland under the Jagellonian dynasty kept control of the large principality of Lithuania. This dynasty did not make an effort to build a unified state. Instead, the country evolved in the opposite direction from much of the rest of Europe. As serfdom was disappearing in western Europe, the nobles' control over the serfs increased in Poland. The Polish nobility also increased their power over the monarchy. The legislature was strengthened and the nobles had veto power over any action of the king.

THE OTTOMAN EMPIRE

The major threat to Europe in the 15th century was the Ottoman Empire. After the taking of Constantinople in 1453, the Ottoman leader Mohammed II was seen as having ambitions to extend his rule over all of Europe. Several projected crusades were called against the Turks to unite Christendom, but they all came to nothing. The Ottomans also conquered to the east, taking over much of the old Arab empire and in the process bringing the *caliphate*, the religious leadership of the Moslem world, to Constantinople.

The Ottoman Empire was strengthened by the arrival of many Jews and Moslems driven from Spain by the Inquisition. The Turkish army was well trained and up-to-date in the use of modern weaponry. The infantry was the strength of the army, particularly an elite group recruited from Christian subjects, known as the *Janissaries.*

The Ottoman conquests continued. Greece fell, and the Turks turned to the rest of the Balkans, where they took Serbia and Bosnia, later adding portions of today's Bulgaria and Rumania. The pope lamented, "The Turks are devastating one country after another."[3] In 1480 the Turks took the city of Otranto in southern Italy, and Rome appeared threatened. But with the death of Mohammed II, the Turks retreated from Italy.

RUSSIA

Prior to the 13th century, Russia had had some trading contacts with the countries of western Europe. However, the Mongol conquest had isolated all of the medieval Russian city-states with the exception of Novgorod, cutting off their contact with the West. The Mongol occupation began in 1223 and lasted for 200 years. Moreover, the fact that the Russians practiced the Orthodox form of Christianity further distanced them from the Latin West. With the fall of Constantinople, the Russian Church became the

---

[3] *Ibid.*, p. 13.

only independent branch of Orthodox Christianity.

Under the leadership of Ivan III (1462–1505), Russia began to consolidate into a nation-state with a strong monarch (Chapter 7). In 1480, the last tribute payment was made to the Mongols. Ivan imported Italian builders to help in the rebuilding of Moscow. Formal relations were established between Moscow and the Vatican, the Holy Roman Empire, and the Ottoman sultan, among others. Count Herberstein, the representative of the Holy Roman Empire, commented on the power of the Russian ruler:

• • • *[He] holds unlimited control over all his subjects' lives and property. None of his Counsellors has sufficient authority to dare oppose him, or even differ from him. . . . They openly proclaim that the Prince's will is God's will.*[4]

ITALY

The Italian city-states were the most advanced part of Europe. They led Europe in economic, intellectual, and artistic achievements. Yet they did not coalesce into a nation in the way the separate domains within Spain, France, and England did. The people of the cities thought of themselves as citizens of their own city, rather than of Italy. The region was divided into five major powers with a host of smaller entities. The major powers were the papal states in the center of the country, the kingdom of Naples in the south, and the city-states of Florence, Milan, and Venice in the north.

The *Lodi Agreement of 1451* established a balance among the five Italian powers, regulating relationships among them. The origins of European diplomatic practices can be traced to the conduct of relations between these five powers. Venice and Rome, in particular, found it necessary to know on a regular basis what the other states were doing.

---

[4] Ronald Hingley, *A Concise History of Russia* (New York: Viking Press, 1972), p. 40.

They sent permanent representatives (ambassadors) to the capitals of other states to collect information. This practice was soon adopted by the other European states.

When the throne of Naples became vacant toward the end of the 15th century, it was claimed by Charles VIII of France on the basis of dynastic ties dating back to the Middle Ages. Charles invaded Italy in 1494. He marched down the peninsula with little opposition and took Naples. Leaving a garrison in Naples he returned home.

Soon after, the French garrison was pushed out, and another king of Naples was installed. However, Charles' invasion was only the beginning of a series of invasions that was to continue until the 19th century.

NEW FORCES IN EUROPE In the 15th century, Europe was finally recovering from the ravages of the Black Death. The depopulation had caused social changes that were irreversible. The price of labor increased due to the shortage of workers. Many of the feudal levies of service and farm produce were replaced by cash payments. All these factors loosened the feudal bonds between lord and serf.

EXPANSION OF THE ECONOMY

At the end of the 15th century, there was an increase in wealth throughout Europe as the result of a dramatic growth in trade and manufacturing. Goods flowed back and forth across Europe, and the Italian city-states of Venice and Genoa served as a marketplace for luxury goods from the East.

The increase in trade brought about changes in financing. It was necessary to develop orderly means of extending credit to promote trade ventures that required extensive financial backing. Many modern banking practices date from this time, and the Italians led the way in the development of a banking system.

The growth of trade and manufacturing meant that agriculture had to become more productive to feed the increasing numbers of people engaged in these occupations. In some areas, traditional subsistence farming gave way to the planting of a **money crop**, a single crop intended for use in trade. By concentrating on a single crop—rather than planting all of the crops needed for subsistence—farmers were able to make better use of their land. Technological advances such as an improved plow and water-powered machinery for milling grain also enabled them to produce food much more efficiently.

In England, the growth in the importance of the wool trade meant that it was more profitable to use land for the raising of sheep than for the growing of food crops. This economic incentive, along with the weakening of feudal ties, led to the **enclosure movement**, in which land formerly used as a common grazing area was divided and enclosed for the purpose of raising sheep. Fewer workers were needed to raise sheep than had been required for farming. The surplus workers often drifted to the cities to find new kinds of work.

In the late Middle Ages, the Netherlands increased in importance as a center of commerce. Their traditionally important role as middlemen in the north-south European trade became more lucrative as that trade increased. In addition, the Netherlands became the trading center for overseas goods. In the markets of Bruges and Antwerp could be found spices from the Orient, furs from Novgorod, and tin from England. This international trade brought wealth to the Netherlands and fostered the growth of a large merchant class.

The prosperity of the Netherlands also rested on industry, particularly the textile industry. This industry was controlled by merchant-employers who bought raw wool and paid wages to workers who turned it into cloth. The workers in the cloth trades of the Netherlands formed the beginnings of a **proletariat**, or industrial working class, that was to grow in size and importance throughout Europe in later times.

Eventually, competition from the emerging English wool industry caused unemployment for the wool workers in the Netherlands. To compensate, new industries were developed: the making of fine lace, tapestries, and linens. In these new industries, the workers had even less protection than they formerly had through their guilds.

Southern Germany experienced an economic boom toward the end of the 15th century. It centered around the cities, such as Nuremberg and Augsburg, and was tied to the mining industry of eastern Europe. The Fugger family of Augsburg played a key role in bringing about this economic growth. They used money earned in textiles to invest and experiment in new methods of mining in Bohemia and Hungary. The shaft-mining techniques they developed replaced the less efficient surface mining that had been practiced by independent operators.

The revival of trade and commerce transformed the values and lifestyles of medieval society. In this Flemish portrait, a wife inattentively turns the pages of her breviary while watching her husband conduct his banking activities.

The Fuggers invested their wealth throughout Europe and became the bankers for the Hapsburgs. By the end of the 15th century, Jacob Fugger (1459–1525) was the wealthiest man in Europe, and his activities helped Augsburg in Germany and the trade cities of the Netherlands to become thriving centers of commerce.

The changes in agriculture and the growing need for non-agricultural labor led to a drastic decrease in serfdom in much of western Europe. However, in eastern Europe, serfdom remained a common way of life. Here, the nobles retained much of their power. Most of the wealth of the nobility depended on agriculture, and thus they made a concerted effort to strengthen the feudal system.

SOCIAL CHANGES

The developing economic wealth in northern Europe brought social changes as well. Although wealth increased, so did the disparity between rich and poor. A contemporary wrote:

● ● ● *O God, see the indigence [poverty] of the common people. Provide for it with all speed: Alas! with hunger, cold, fear and misery they tremble. If they have sinned or are guilty of negligence toward Thee, they beg indulgence.*[5]

For the wealthy, new goods made for a richer life-style than in the past. Clothing was often fashioned in bright colors and rich material such as brocades or velvets embroidered with precious stones. The style of parti-colored clothes swept Europe from the beginning of the 16th century. Governments passed *sumptuary* laws—laws forbidding certain kinds of dress or products to a class of people—but usually they were ignored.

For the aristocrats and the wealthy, amusements included chess, dice, archery, tennis, and playing cards. Hunting as always was the aristocratic sport *par excellence*. For the less well-to-do, there were church festivals and public holidays, particularly May Day festivities which marked the arrival of spring. Rich and poor alike celebrated this holiday by walking into the countryside to pick the spring blossoms.

The early modern period saw a gradual ending of the communal life-style. In medieval times, the **extended family** was important as a work unit as well as a social unit. As the manorial system declined, family life centered more around the **nuclear family**, with father, mother, and children sharing a home, often in an urban environment.

WOMEN OF THE RENAISSANCE

In part because of the influence of humanism, there were more opportunities for Renaissance women to receive an education. The daughters of Thomas More were tutored by the best scholars available, and were renowned for their learning. More wrote to the tutor of his children that "learning and morals go together," and went on to say:

● ● ● *Nor do I think that it affects the harvest, that a man or woman has sown the seed. If they are worthy of being ranked with the human race, if they are distinguished by reason from beasts; then learning, by which the reason is cultivated, is equally suitable to both. Both of them, if the seed of good principles be sown in them, equally produce the germs of virtue.*[6]

However, women educated in academic subjects were a rarity even among the upper classes. One woman of the time wrote, "I cannot but complain of parents in letting the fertile grounds of their daughters lie fallow, and yet send the barren noodles of their sons to the University."[7]

---

[5] Johan Huizinga, *The Waning of the Middle Ages* (New York: Anchor Books, 1954), p. 63.

[6] Jakob Bronowski and Bruce Mazlish, "A Man Out of Season," *Horizon Magazine*, Vol. IV, No. 5, May, 1962, p. 92.

[7] Hannah Woolley, quoted in Mary Cathcart Borer, *Willingly to School: A History of Women's Education* (London: Lutterworth, 1975), p. 108.

The religious life was still an option for many women. During the Renaissance, one reform was the establishment of contemplative orders, in which nuns were enclosed in convents. Members of contemplative orders—there were also such orders for men—were encouraged to maintain a rigorous spiritual life of prayer and meditation.

Renaissance women did work at numerous secular occupations as well. They were employed as weavers, seamstresses, innkeepers, moneylenders, midwives, and teachers. Some wealthy women gave money to create new convents or other charitable projects. Of course, most peasant women worked at the strenuous physical tasks of farming and livestock raising.

A few women, especially daughters who received training from artist-fathers, excelled in the arts. Most women did not have the opportunity to become artists because it was not considered proper for them to become apprenticed to an older male artist. They more often found outlets for their artistic talents in handicrafts such as the making of tapestries.

A notable example of a woman author of the time is Margaret of Navarre (1429–1482), sister of Francis I, king of France. She was the author of the *Heptameron*, a series of 72 tales modeled after Boccaccio's *Decameron*. Her stories celebrate the triumph of virtue, honor, and quick-wittedness over vice and hypocrisy, often represented by grasping monks and clerics. Margaret was an important patron and protector of humanist thinkers and writers.

Margaret of Navarre, sister of Francis I, was noted as an author and as a patron of the arts. One of her protégés was the writer Rabelais.

THE NORTHERN RENAISSANCE

The Italian Renaissance was the most important event of this time. During the period 1450–1550, the rebirth in learning spread north across the Alps, and inspired a Northern Renaissance. But the Renaissance in the north developed differently. It was much more closely tied to religion than the Italian Renaissance had been. Patrons of learning in the north tended to be monarchs or nobles, rather than rich merchants, as in Italy. The character of northern art was different as well.

NORTHERN HUMANISTS

The ideas of *humanism*, which took their inspiration from the authors of classical times, were pursued with the same enthusiasm in northern Europe as they had been in Italy.

Humanism in Germany and France. One of the concerns of humanists in Germany was the desire to study the early works of Christianity to get a deeper understanding of the roots of religion. This necessitated a knowledge of Greek and Hebrew as well as Latin. The most important figure in this movement was Johann Reuchlin (1455–1522), who published the first Hebrew grammar north of the Alps. His study of Hebrew enabled people to widen their understanding of Old Testament texts.

The French king Francis I invited Leonardo da Vinci to France and encouraged him to live out his final years at the French court. Francis became a patron of the arts much like the Medicis or Sforzas.

Francis also encouraged the work of François Rabelais (1494–1553), whose stories on religion and customs of the early 16th century are still admired today. His *Gargantua and Pantagruel* relates the adventures of two giants who revel in all the known pleasures of the world. Rabelais, through the use of sharp wit and satire, attacked the established church and condemned the hypocrisy in the moral standards of the age.

Erasmus. The most important of the northern humanists was Desiderius Erasmus (1466–1536), known as "the Prince of Humanists." Erasmus was born in Rotterdam, the illegitimate son of a priest and a physician's daughter. The circumstances of his birth, and the loss of both parents to the plague when he was 13 years old, had a lasting effect on him.

Erasmus' first formal schooling was with the *Brethren and Sisters of the Common Life*, founded by Gerhard Groote. This was a loosely organized religious group consisting of priests, nuns, and lay persons. In their schools students were introduced to Greek and Latin classics, and the teachers emphasized personal beliefs more than standardized forms or rituals. Erasmus moved on to an Augustinian monastery, where he was ordained a priest. He rarely performed his priestly duties, preferring the life of a classical scholar and writer.

Erasmus escaped from the discipline of the monastery by obtaining the post of secretary to a bishop. He was to spend the rest of his life writing for a living and searching out patrons who would support his scholarly activities. Much of his time was spent in travel between the Netherlands, France, Italy, and England, meeting the great and near-great from all walks of life.

Erasmus wrote both in Latin and Greek,

Erasmus was the most notable scholar of the Northern Renaissance. Although he remained a loyal member of the Church, his writings and translations challenged certain aspects of Church dogma.

primarily on subjects contemporary to the 16th century, and in a prose style that breathed new life into those ancient languages. His wit, style, and perceptive comments earned his writings popularity and acclaim from the literate public of his day.

The *Adages* (1500), his first major work and one of his most popular books, is a collection of clever and discerning remarks from antiquity, supplemented by Erasmus' commentary. His most famous and enduring work is *The Praise of Folly* (1509), *Encomium Moriae* in Latin. It was written one rainy weekend while Erasmus was a guest in the home of Thomas More. The Latin title is a play on words, using More's name. Erasmus tells us through his narrator "Folly" that wisdom and absurdity are interchangeable, and true understanding comes only from experiencing both. "The philosopher with his triangles, quadrangles, circles, and mathematical forms is one of Folly's chief disciples. He knows nothing yet professes to know everything."[8]

Erasmus was particularly adept in the use of satire to condemn religious abuses. His goal was to "humanize" Christianity by purging the Church of abuses. In the *Manual of the Christian Soldier* (1503), Erasmus downplayed the importance of ritual and dogma and stressed ethical concerns. He advocated an end to strife and violence, and an emphasis instead on the use of reason to resolve human problems. In this, he summed up one of the main thrusts of humanism, which held that human life had value in and of itself, rather than being merely a preparation for the life hereafter.

Erasmus' greatest scholarly achievement was his Greek and Latin translation of the New Testament, the first in over a thousand years. Erasmus wisely dedicated his edition of the New Testament to the pope, thereby gaining official sanction. In the preface, Erasmus eloquently expresses his philosophy of Christian humanism with the declaration that the ". . . doctrine of Christ casts aside no age, no sex, no fortune or position in life. . . . It keeps no one at a distance."[9] Erasmus' passion was the pursuit of knowledge, and he unselfishly dedicated his life to nurturing the mind and character of others. He was above all else a teacher.

Thomas More. The great English humanist Thomas More (1478–1535) was knighted by Henry VIII and later executed for refusing to recognize the king as head of the Church of England (Chapter 2). For his martyrdom, he was declared a saint by the Roman Catholic Church. His last words were that he "died the king's good servant but God's first."[10]

In contrast to the secular humanism of Niccolo Machiavelli, the great political writer of

A portrait of Thomas More, the Lord Chancellor and humanist scholar who was martyred for his religious convictions. Compare this portrait to that of Erasmus on facing page, also by Hans Holbein.

the Italian Renaissance, More's writings represent the neo-Platonic or Christian humanism so characteristic of the Northern Renaissance. The neo-Platonists believed that human beings have the capacity to seek out and understand ideal beauty or perfection. The title of More's most famous work, *Utopia* (1516), entered the English language as the name for any ideal political or social system. The Utopia More described was an imaginary island similar in physical character to England. Evil, More believed, is social in origin. All one needs to do to create the ideal society is to change the social structure. Pride, born of greed for material possessions, is the major sin that must be eliminated in any society. More's Utopia has a planned economy; war is outlawed except in self-defense; and there is religious freedom for all except atheists. Every citizen in Utopia has

[8] *Ibid.*, p. 93.

[9] *Ibid.*, p. 92.

[10] *Encyclopedia Britannica*, 1969 ed., Vol. 15, p. 833.

economic security, but only in return for hard work. There are no major differences in social or economic status, and without greed, pride becomes controllable.

More's Utopians did not make a distinction between public and private morality. There is no need for formal alliances and treaties since ". . . men are bound more adequately by good will than by pacts, more strongly by their hearts than by their words."[11]

In contrast to More's ideal Utopia, Machiavelli's great political works, *The Prince* and *The Discourses*, describe the reality of politics in early 16th-century Italy. Machiavelli saw the world as being dangerous and in a constant state of change. Whereas More's

Utopia is a static society where universal laws and timeless rules determine human actions, the success of Machiavelli's Prince depends upon his ability to change with the circumstances. To Machiavelli, success in this world requires a continuous struggle for power among a few leaders who have the ability to create a temporary order out of disorder and peace from conflict. More, on the other hand, believed that power could and should be controlled and made harmless. This debate between two opposing views of human nature and of political realities still goes on today.

THE ARTS OF THE NORTHERN RENAISSANCE

Just as in Italy, the enthusiasm for new learning also sparked artistic activity in the north.

---

[11] Wallace K. Ferguson *et al.*, *Facets of the Renaissance: Essays* (New York: Harper & Row, 1959), p. 61.

Niccolo Machiavelli, a central figure of the Italian Renaissance, expressed a world view that contrasted sharply with that of northern European theorists.

"Knight, Death, and Devil," an engraving by Albrecht Dürer, was probably inspired by a work entitled **Manual of the Christian Soldier,** in which Erasmus used the metaphor of battle to describe the struggle of virtue against temptation.

The rediscovery and development of the techniques of oil painting by the Flemish artist Jan Van Eyck (c. 1390–1441) soon influenced Italian painters. Van Eyck's masterpiece is the Ghent altarpiece. Its many panels depict traditional religious subjects, but the figures have a realistic character, perspective, and detail.

The paintings of another Flemish painter, Pieter Breughel the Elder (c. 1525–1569), often take everyday life and landscapes as their subjects. Sometimes the characters in his paintings are exaggerated, ugly, or distorted, reflecting the influence of the Dutch painter Hieronymus Bosch (c. 1450–1516). Bosch's often fantastic paintings have a frightening, other-worldly quality that resembles some elements of 20th-century surrealism. His canvases are filled with characters from folklore, legend, and his own bizarre imagination. Sometimes half-human, half-animal, even half-plant, the strange figures in Bosch's works have provided material for many later interpreters.

The German Hans Holbein the Younger (1497–1543) fled to England during the Reformation and became court painter for Henry VIII. The king held Holbein in high regard, and even sent him to record the likenesses of some of his prospective wives before deciding whether to marry them.

Perhaps the greatest of the artists of the Northern Renaissance was Albrecht Dürer (1471–1528). The son of a goldsmith, he was apprenticed to a painter and woodcut illustrator, and it was in woodcuts, engravings, and drawings that Dürer would do his greatest work. He traveled throughout Europe, making two trips to Italy. Between 1512 and 1519 he worked for the Emperor Maximilian.

Dürer's remarkable attention to detail make his works nearly perfect representations of people, animals, and plants. Among his works is a treatise showing fortifications for cities, castles, and towns.

The prosperity of the cities of the Netherlands produced many patrons who wished to have both themselves and their possessions captured on canvas. In the works of Flemish and Dutch painters, interiors of homes are lovingly detailed. The human body is not idealized as much as is the case with Italian art. Though not all painters showed human beings "warts and all," as did Brueghel and Dürer, the people in the Northern Renaissance paintings are recognizably distinct individuals.

PRINTING

The introduction of paper from China and the invention of movable type contributed substantially to the explosion of knowledge associated with the Renaissance and the scientific revolution that followed it. Johann Gutenberg's "forty-two line" Bible, published in the city of Mainz in 1454, was the first book printed in Europe using the new process. Printing spread rapidly, for the intellectual climate of the time gave printers a ready market for their work. By the end of the 15th century, virtually every country in Europe but Russia had a printing press. It is estimated that over 10 million books came off the presses in the first 50 years after Gutenberg's Bible.

For instance, the Englishman William Caxton (c. 1422–1491), learned about printing while living in Cologne about 1470. He returned to England, where he set up his own press in 1476 and printed the first book in English. By the end of his life he had printed copies of most of the existing works of English literature, including Chaucer's *Canterbury Tales* and Sir Thomas Malory's *Morte d'Arthur*.

Although the press of Johann Gutenberg eventually went bankrupt, printing quickly became a viable business. By 1500, it is estimated, there were more than 200 printing presses in Germany alone, and more than 10 million copies of 35,000 different books had been printed.

The invention of printing provided a cheap and fast way of spreading sources of information. Printed books made knowledge available to the masses, and literacy increased with the availability of books.

Books also facilitated cross-fertilization of ideas among those with the most creative and inventive minds. The rapid spread of the humanists' ideas made their work that much more influential. Scholars and apprentices in the trades no longer had to rely solely on the teachings of their masters. They could acquire knowledge and even skills independently, through the printed word.

In the centuries that followed, printing was the most important single instrument that made possible Europe's advances in science, discovery, philosophy, and religious ideas.

SUMMARY

Around the year 1500, several historical currents began to take Europe into the early modern age. Monarchs in England, France, and Spain reduced the power of the nobility to create the beginnings of a strong central government. Growth in trade and manufacturing, combined with more efficient methods of agriculture, produced new wealth and helped Europe's population rise to what it had been before the Black Death.

The Renaissance, which had flowered in Italy, spread to the northern countries of Europe, where it took on distinctively northern characteristics. Northern humanists developed the idea that human life had value in and of itself and speculated on proper ethical values and political systems. Northern Renaissance artists developed their own styles, themes, and techniques. Finally, the first European books printed from movable type made possible the rapid spread of ideas and knowledge. As we shall see, these intellectual and technological developments produced a revolution first in religion and then in scientific knowledge in the two centuries following the year 1500.

QUESTIONS

1 The Renaissance is viewed as a transitional period. In what ways were the people of this time still attached to the past, and in what ways were they looking towards the future?

2 What factors encouraged the growth of unified nation-states in Spain, France, and England when at the same time the Holy Roman Empire and Italy seemed to be moving in the opposite direction?

3 Assess how the growth of trade and industry contributed to changes in medieval European society. In what ways were these changes beneficial and in what ways were they negative?

4 Briefly describe the humanistic Christian philosophy developed by Erasmus. In what ways did his emphasis differ from that of the medieval Church?

5 Contrast the philosophies of Thomas More and Niccolo Machiavelli. In what respects was each man the product of his native country?

BIBLIOGRAPHY

BARRACLOUGH, GEOFFREY. "A World Through European Eyes," Chapter 1 of *Turning Points in World History*. London: Thames and Hudson, 1979. *An essay with some surprising conclusions about the impact of Europe on the world and of the world on Europeans.*

CASTIGLIONE, BALDASSARE. *The Book of the Courtier*. New York: Penguin Books, 1978. *Through a series of fictional conversations, Castiglione defines the ideal courtier and portrays the manners and customs of an age. An outstanding primary source.*

CELLINI, BENVENUTO. *Autobiography*. Modern Library ed. *One man's highly personalized testament of the times in which he lived. This book teems with rogues and heroes; a real Renaissance thriller.*

KETCHUM, RICHARD M., ed. *The Horizon Book of the Renaissance*. New York: American Heritage, 1961. *A panorama in both word and picture of every facet of Renaissance society.*

MACHIAVELLI, NICCOLO. *The Prince and the Discourses*. Modern Library ed. *The famous— sometimes infamous—work by the patriarch of modern-day political science. The "Discourses" throw more light on what is written in "The Prince."*

PHILLIPS, MARGARET MANN. *Erasmus and the Northern Renaissance*, rev. ed. London and Totowa, N. J.: Boydell Press and Rowman & Littlefield, 1981. *A sympathetic portrayal of both the human and intellectual side of the "Prince of Humanists."*

2

> Unless I am convicted by scripture and plain reason—I do not accept the authority of popes and councils, for they have contradicted each other—my conscience is captive to the word of God. I cannot and I will not recant anything, for to go against conscience is neither right nor safe. God help me. Amen. Here I stand, I cannot do otherwise.
>
> MARTIN LUTHER

> I am descended from a long line of Christian emperors of this noble German nation, and of the Catholic Kings of Spain [and] . . . . Austria. They were all faithful to the death to the Church of Rome, and they defended the Catholic faith . . . . I have resolved to follow in their steps . . . [even at the risk of] . . . my lands, my friends, my body, my blood, my life, and my soul. A single friar who goes counter to all Christianity for a thousand years must be wrong.
>
> EMPEROR CHARLES

The Reformation

In 1517, an unknown Augustinian monk from Saxony prepared a list of propositions on the subject of reform in the Roman Catholic Church and, according to tradition, posted them on the door of the castle church in the city of Wittenberg. Martin Luther's *Ninety-five Theses* set in motion a movement—the **Reformation**—that spread across Europe, shaking the very foundations of the Church and creating a split in Christianity whose consequences are still with us today.

Even in today's society the topic of the Reformation can evoke strong emotions. *Reformation* implies a change from within for the better—clearly a Protestant term, while the words *revolt* and *revolution* suggest a forcible break with the Catholic Church. Even the phrase *Catholic Counter-Reformation* has partisan overtones, for it suggests that the Roman Catholic Church was forced to initiate reform to check or counter the inroads made by the Protestants. The word *Reformation* is used in this chapter only because it has become customary and traditional to do so when referring to the religious upheavals of the 16th century.

The analysis of the causes of the Reformation gives the student of history a rare opportunity to tread in the footsteps of historians as they search the past for relevant primary sources. Leopold von Ranke (1795–1886), the founder of the "scientific school" of historiography, helped to put the Reformation in perspective as an integral part of European history, rather than just a subject for debate among Protestant and Catholic historians. The historian Wilhelm Dilthey argued that both the Renaissance and Reformation are expressions of individual freedom and a rebellion against the ideas and traditions of the Middle Ages. Ernst Troeltsch, a Protestant theologian turned sociologist, contends that the Reformation is primarily an extension of the Middle Ages, particularly in the religious area. The disciples of Karl Marx tend to see the religious movements of the 16th and 17th centuries as class struggles motivated by economic gain. In a non-Marxist variation of the same theme, R. H. Tawney, in his book *Religion and the Rise of Capitalism*, tries to show a connection between the origins of the Reformation and the rise of cities and the growth of commercial and industrial activities.

ORIGINS OF THE REFORMATION

The questioning of papal authority and the widening cracks in the monolithic structure of the Roman Catholic Church did not begin with Luther. Since the 13th century, the temporal authority of the Church had been on the decline. The last serious effort to establish Church supremacy over kings in both spiritual and temporal affairs had occurred at the beginning of the 14th century, and by the end of that century, the Church, although still the center of religion in western Europe, was no longer a dominant political force.

JOHN WYCLIF AND JAN HUS

Early reformers such as John Wyclif (1320–1384) in England and Jan Hus (c. 1370–1415) in Bohemia denied the authority of the pope over all of Christendom and asserted the authority of the scriptures over Church teachings. Wyclif, a scholar-priest and teacher from Oxford, favored a literal rather than a traditional interpretation of the Bible. To ensure that more people could read the Bible for themselves, he wrote the first English translation of the New Testament. Wyclif denied that priests were endowed with any special authority from God and he railed against the luxury and pomp of the papacy. He advocated a return to the apostolic simplicity and poverty that existed in the early days of the Christian Church:

••• *The [churchmen of England] set more price by the rotten penny than by the precious blood of Christ . . . . they live in luxury, riding fat horses with harness of silver and gold . . . . they are robbers . . . malicious foxes . . . ravishing wolves . . . gluttons . . . devils . . . apes . . .*[1]

Wyclif was able to escape persecution for his views because of special geographical and political circumstances. The English Channel protected England's independence from continental influence. In addition, both the English kings and nobles coveted the land and wealth of the English Church. Efforts by Church authorities to arrest Wyclif and try him for **heresy**, or expression of a belief that deviates from established Church doctrines,[2] were frustrated by the nobles and by Wyclif's supporters.

In 1381, however, a violent and bloody Peasants' Revolt spread across England, and any support that Wyclif had from king and lords evaporated as it became clear that many of the rebels looked to the words and ideas of Wyclif as justification for their actions. However, before Wyclif could be apprehended and tried again for heresy, he died. Seventy-five years later Wyclif was put on trial *in absentia*, and found guilty. His bones were dug up and removed from consecrated ground, and his writings were consigned to the flames.

Wyclif's ideas did not die with him. His followers and students, known as *Lollards* (poor preachers), spread Wyclif's ideas throughout England and across the channel to the continent. Jan Hus, a priest of Bohemia who was influenced by Wyclif, attacked the abuses of the clergy. Although supported for a time by the Holy Roman emperor, Hus was seized by Church authorities in 1414 and burned at the stake as a heretic a year later.

IMPACT OF THE RENAISSANCE ON THE REFORMATION

Although Wyclif and Hus said many of the same things that reformers would repeat a century later, the climate of the times was not yet right for the ideas to take hold. It was

---

[1] Will Durant, *The Reformation. Story of Civilization* series (New York: Simon & Schuster, 1957), p. 34.

[2] "Public expression" is the significant point in defining a heresy. Only when an unorthodox doctrine is publicly expressed is it considered a threat to the spiritual well-being of the faithful.

the Renaissance that provided the passion and the intellectual atmosphere necessary for the success of the Reformation.

The Renaissance Church had corrupt and worldly popes such as Alexander VI (1492–1503), but it also had its share of saintly leaders such as Paul III (1534–1549). Even the best of the pontiffs were becoming increasingly secularized. The financial needs of Rome were never-ending if the popes were to compete with the courtly splendour and artistic elegance of such families as the Medici in Florence. **Simony** (the selling of Church offices), **nepotism** (the dispensing of Church positions and titles to relatives), **absenteeism** (the conferring of Church offices on individuals not physically present), and **pluralities** (the giving of multiple benefices to one person) all were questionable practices that did not redound to the greater honor and glory of the Church. Particularly abusive was the sale of **indulgences**, in effect, pardons for sins. It was believed that Jesus, the Virgin Mary, and the saints had accumulated an excess of "good deeds" while on earth and that these were stored in heaven to be distributed to the faithful at the pope's discretion. With the Church's growing demands for money and the worldliness of some popes, it is hardly surprising that the same kinds of abuses and secular corruption occasionally found their way into national churches and monastic religious orders.

Also contributing to the widening cracks in the Church's foundations were the assaults of humanists on Church authority. The Roman humanist Lorenzo Valla had shown that the so-called *Donation of Constantine*, upon which the papacy had based much of its claim to secular power, was a forgery. Other scholars had pointed out the errors and disparities in the several translations of Aristotle's scientific works, which the Church used to reconcile and unify all knowledge, both sacred and secular. Since the Church had tied its intellectual and the-ological fortunes to an error-ridden body of knowledge, some concluded that it could be wrong about other things. The faith of the Middle Ages was in danger of falling prey to the spreading influence of Renaissance humanism. The growing discontent with papal claims of absolute authority within the Church also gave rise to the *Conciliar movement* in the early and mid-15th century. Some Conciliarists were monarchs who simply wanted the right to appoint high Church officials (bishops or archbishops) in their domains, and prevent the flight of money to Rome. Others were theologians who believed that a council of the Church, acting as a kind of parliament, should restrict the power of the pope.

REFORMATION IN GERMANY

The emergence of centralized states such as England, France, and Spain meant that the Churches in these countries began to take on an increasingly national character. French, Spanish, and English religious leaders started to look to their kings rather than to the pope for guidance in both temporal and spiritual matters.

Circumstances were different in Germany, however. In 16th-century Europe there were no political boundaries or geographical barriers that people could point to and call Germany. What was German was more a state of mind, a culture, a bond of language, an awareness of being German. Germans were ruled by a number of local princes whose loyalties to the Holy Roman emperor or to the Church in Rome varied. What was needed was a leader who could unite these varied interests. Many Germans resented the growing financial burden that had been imposed by the pope and the Holy Roman emperor to subsidize the construction of St. Peter's Basilica in Rome and the cost of a proposed European crusade against the infidel Turks.

THE ROLE OF MARTIN LUTHER

Although the ideas of the Renaissance had not yet substantially changed the medieval character of German society, humanism was sufficiently established in Germany so that religious reformers could expect some intellectual and moral support from the academic community. A rising German nationalistic spirit, the spread of humanism northward from Italy, and growing political and economic opposition to emperor and pope came to a head in 1517 in the actions and words of the virtually unknown Augustinian friar named Martin Luther.

Early Life. Martin Luther (1483–1546) came from hardy Saxon peasant stock. By the standards of the day, however, the family was reasonably well off, for young Martin was sent to the cathedral school at Magdeburg to complete his elementary education. In 1501, Luther was sent to the University of Erfurt to study law. Up to this point in his life there was nothing to suggest the future direction of his career. In recent years it has been popular among some historians to attribute Luther's religious interests and obsessions to his childhood experiences.

Martin Luther himself, however, had an explanation for his religious conversion. While returning home from his studies in July 1505, a summer thunderstorm overtook him. With the jagged bolts of lightning slashing through the evening sky, and the din of thunder mixing with the sound of crashing trees, the young Luther fell to his knees in abject terror, crying out to St. Anne that if he survived, he would become a monk. In the Germany of the time, a solemn oath taken at a moment of extreme peril would not be discarded lightly after the danger had passed. Whatever the motivation, and against his father's wishes, Martin Luther at the age of 22 entered an Augustinian monastery.

Luther's stay at the monastery at Erfurt was not a tranquil one. He seemed unable to rid his conscience of a personal feeling of

---

A 15th-Century Classroom

The historian Roland Bainton describes for us what it must have been like to attend grammar school in Germany at the end of the 15th century:

The schools . . . were not tender, but neither were they brutal. The object was to impart a spoken knowledge of the Latin tongue [a practical necessity for anyone interested in pursuing a scholarly profession]. The teaching was by drill punctuated by the rod. One scholar, called a "lupus" or wolf, was appointed to spy on others and report lapses into German. The poorest scholar in the class every noon was given a donkey mask, hence called the "asinus," which he wore until he caught another talking German. Demerits were accumulated and accounted for by birching at the end of the week. . . . But despite all of the severities the boys did learn Latin. . . . One of [Luther's teachers] . . . Trebonius, on entering the classroom always bared his head in the presence of so many future burgomasters, chancellors, doctors, and regents.[3]

[3] Roland H. Bainton, *Here I Stand: A Life of Martin Luther* (New York: Abingdon-Cokesbury Press, 1950), pp. 24–5.

---

sinfulness and lack of worth. It was while studying St. Paul's Epistle to the Romans (chapter I, verse 17), "The just shall live by faith," that Luther began to find the answers to his theological concerns and his anxieties about personal salvation.

Luther continued with his academic studies and earned a doctorate in theology in 1512. In 1510, he had visited Rome as a pilgrim and was shocked at the worldliness of

A portrait of Martin Luther, the young monk whose words and deeds would shake the foundations of European society.

the Renaissance papacy. He was sent to Wittenberg in Saxony to preach in the local church and teach in the newly founded university there. Wittenberg was under the control of Prince Frederick the Wise, one of the Electors of the Holy Roman Empire.

The Ninety-five Theses. If it had not been for a singular incident that took place in 1517, Luther might have lived out his days practicing his unique brand of Christianity, and influencing only a small group of like-minded intellectuals at the university.

It happened that Pope Leo X was in need of money to complete the building of St. Peter's Cathedral in Rome. One way of acquiring the necessary funds was by selling indulgences, and one of the most blatant practitioners of this art was a Dominican monk by the name of John Tetzel. Although Tetzel failed to get permission to sell indulgences in Wittenberg, he was able to lure many of Martin Luther's parishioners across

a nearby border. Following an impressive parade, Tetzel would harangue the assembled crowd with a sermon filled with references to hellfire and damnation and the perpetual torment of the souls of the departed:

• • • *Listen to the voices of your dear dead relatives and friends, beseeching you and saying, "Pity us, pity us. We are in dire torment from which you can redeem us for a pittance. . . . Will (you) let us lie here in flames? Will you delay our promised glory?" Remember, you are able to release them, for as soon as the coin in the coffer rings, the soul from purgatory springs.*[4]

Luther was unable to shut his ears to such chicanery. His own family roots were the same as those of the simple peasants and townsfolk who were being defrauded of their life's savings.

The result of Luther's anger was a hastily written response to the abuse of selling indulgences. These *Ninety-five Theses* were reportedly nailed to the church door of Wittenberg on October 31, 1517. Luther's attack on the selling of indulgences was three-pronged. First, Luther questioned why Germans should have to pay for the building of St. Peter's Basilica.

• • • *The revenues of all Christendom are being sucked into this insatiable basilica. . . . We Germans cannot attend St. Peter's, which is not necessary for us. Before long all the churches, palaces, walls, and bridges of Rome will be built out of our money.*[5]

Second, Luther questioned papal authority in the remission of sins. Finally, he emphasized the idea of salvation through faith alone and not by good works or papal absolution.

The Protest Spreads. It is unlikely that Luther was aware of all the implications of his

---

[4] *Ibid.*, p. 78.

[5] *Ibid.*, p. 80.

Tetzel, the Dominican monk who provoked Martin Luther's first public protest, is ridiculed in this contemporary cartoon.

statements at the time they were written. At the beginning, he did not intend that his words would be used to ignite the spark of religious and political revolution throughout Germany and Europe. At the most, he expected that what he had to say would be the opening salvo in a scholarly debate among theologians. However, the growing number of printing presses in Germany, combined with a growth in literacy among the general population, led to widespread dissemination of Luther's words in a very short time. A printed German translation of the Latin original made it available to all those who could read. Copies multiplied by the thousands as the public demand grew.

Luther began pouring out pamphlets and tracts expounding his position. In his tracts of 1519 and 1520, he thundered against the tyranny of Rome and appealed to the German princes to reform the Church. He delivered his own views on the sacraments and doctrines of the Church and explained his ideas of individual liberty to the common people.

Both the pope and the Holy Roman emperor were slow in moving against the monk from Wittenberg. By the time he was finally summoned to the imperial Diet at Worms in 1521, Luther had won the sympathy and support of much of the German populace. For political as well as religious considerations, Luther also had the protection, if not the wholehearted approval, of his prince, Frederick the Wise of Saxony.

Diet of Worms. At the Diet of Worms, against a backdrop of a city overwhelmingly on his side, Luther confronted the papal ambassadors and the new emperor, Charles V. When shown some 20 of his books and told to recant his heresy, he replied with a stirring reaffirmation of his faith that concluded with the now-famous words: "Here I stand, I cannot do otherwise." Having already been excommunicated (1520), declared to be a heretic, and denied the sacraments or aid of the Church, Luther was now, by the *Edict of Worms*, declared to be an outlaw in the empire, with a price on his head.

Luther was spirited away by Frederick the Wise and remained in hiding for over a year. While at Wartburg castle near Erfurt, Luther translated the New Testament into German. For his efforts, he is honored as one of the creators of the modern German language.

The term "protestant" to describe the Lutheran forces and those other dissenters that eventually left the Roman Church did not come into use until 1529. In that year, Emperor Charles V turned his attention to the rebellious German states and informed a diet of German princes meeting at the city of Speyer that the Edict of Worms was to be enforced throughout the empire and Catholic worship was to be restored. Several of the princes, along with 14 cities, protested against the order, which drew upon them the name "Protesting Estates." Henceforth those who defied the Church were known as Protestants.

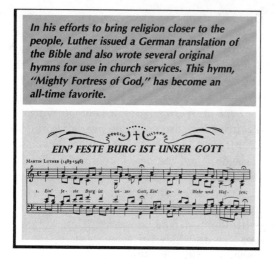

EIN' FESTE BURG IST UNSER GOTT

MARTIN LUTHER (1483-1546)

1. Ein' fe - ste Burg ist un - ser Gott, Ein' gu - te Wehr und Waf - fen;

LUTHERANISM

Luther wrote over 400 books and pamphlets during his lifetime, but the three so-called Reformation Tracts of 1520 became the basis for most of Lutheran theology from that time forward and contain the four basic elements of his teachings:

Justification by Faith Alone. Man's salvation is dependent solely on God's mercy and trust and belief in Jesus Christ. Good works, including indulgences, church attendance, and ritual are not essential for salvation. Nor are most of the sacraments: the only necessary sacraments are communion and baptism.

The Priesthood of All Believers. Faith is a personal experience and no intermediary is needed between a Christian and God. Priests have no divinely ordained powers. The clergy are a matter of convenience for the faithful, but not a necessity. Clerics in effect are providing direction and leadership for the faithful. (Nevertheless, Lutheranism kept much of the Catholic hierarchy except cardinals and the pope.)

Primacy of the Bible. Since the Bible is the sole source of divine revelation, religious dogma, as interpreted by the Church fathers, is not essential for salvation. Like faith, an understanding of the scriptures is a personal experience between the Christian and God. The Bible is not so much a book of knowledge or a code of ethics, but rather the revelation of God. All that is required to understand it is faith.

The Visible and the Invisible Church. The visible Church is the actual building of brick and mortar, and all the outward manifestations of faith such as church ceremonies and other good works. The invisible Church is the hearts and minds of the faithful—the personal relationship between the believer and God. The invisible Church is the only true Church, and membership in it is essential for salvation.

Every one of Luther's teachings challenged fundamental beliefs of the Roman Catholic Church. Other basic reforms advocated by Luther included elimination of monastic orders and permission for priests to marry. Luther himself took a wife when, in 1525, he married Katherine von Bora, a former nun. By all accounts the marriage was a good one, even though at times hectic with six children and a steady flow of invited and uninvited guests coming and going day and night. In putting food on the table, providing hospitality, and managing her husband's personal life, Katherine made no small contribution to Martin Luther's public career.

EFFECTS OF THE REFORMATION IN GERMANY

Recognition of the sovereignty of the state over the Church in temporal matters garnered support for Luther's cause among the German princes. His reduction of religious holidays was popular among the bourgeois of the towns. Not so popular with the same group was his opposition to even the mildest forms of usury—loaning money for profit. In both the political and economic spheres, Martin Luther's pronouncements are quite traditional. He stood with his peasant forebears in favoring an agrarian society. To Luther, civil authority must be upheld and rebellion extinguished no matter what the cost in human lives and property.

The proliferation of printing presses enabled Luther to publish his views on a wide variety of contemporary issues. Shown is the title page of a pamphlet on the Peasants' Revolt which he issued in 1525.

The Peasants' Revolt. The next few years found Luther and his movement embroiled in social unrest. Among those who had supported him at the Diet of Worms were the lesser knights. One of their leaders, Franz von Sickingen, claimed he had Luther's backing in his rebellion against the great landowners. However, Luther stayed loyal to the civil authority, thereby earning him the animosity of the lesser knights.

The major social challenge to Luther's cause erupted in 1524–1525, with the *Peasants' Revolt* in southern Germany. The Peasants' Revolt was a bloody rebellion in which some 100,000 people were killed and 50,000 left homeless. Villages were destroyed, and famine and disease took a terrible toll. Bandits, beggars, and the dispossessed roamed the countryside.

Although the primary sources of the peasants' discontent were economic and social, the rebels expected loyalty and help from Luther. They saw that his concept of the priesthood of all believers could be used to justify a more egalitarian society.

Initially, Luther was sympathetic to the peasants' demands for reform, but as the revolt turned increasingly violent, he supported law and order and the civil authorities. He wrote a tract entitled, "Against the Murdering Hordes of Peasants," and he encouraged the princes to be "both judge and executioner . . . to knock down, strangle and stab."[6] Luther's decision kept for him the support of some of the Protestant princes, but the price was high. Lutheranism ceased to be a mass movement, and many peasants returned to the fold of the Roman Catholic Church or took refuge in the numerous sects that began to separate from both Lutheranism and the Catholic Church.

Anabaptists. One such sect was the Anabaptists, so called because of their refusal to recognize infant baptism, which still remained a creed of the Lutheran Church. Freedom of conscience and sexual equality were among the beliefs of the Anabaptists, who refused obedience to any state church and looked to a pure and more simple Christianity. The Anabaptists allowed women to serve as pastors, and a few women, such as Ursula Jost of Strasbourg, were honored as prophets among the faithful. Wherever the Anabaptists took root, they were cruelly persecuted by both Catholics and Protestants alike. However, they endured, and such modern-day denominations as the Baptist, Moravian, and Mennonite churches grew out of the Anabaptist movement.

Religious Wars in Germany. By 1530, Charles V was ready to concentrate on the religious problems in Germany. One last at-

---

[6] Harold J. Grimm, *The Reformation Era: 1600–1650* (New York: Macmillan, 1954), p. 174.

33

tempt at reconciliation was made at a meeting in Augsburg in 1530. Since he had been declared an outlaw by the emperor and a heretic by the pope, Luther was not permitted to attend. The responsibility for stating the Lutheran case went to Philipp Melanchthon, one of Luther's loyal lieutenants. The *Augsburg Confession*, authored by Melanchthon, was an act of diplomacy aimed at appeasing the emperor and the Catholic leaders by highlighting the similarities rather than the differences between the two religions. Despite the concessions, no compromise was reached. It is the Augsburg Confession that became the basis for the fundamental creed of the Lutheran Church, even though at the time, Luther himself had objected to its conciliatory tone.

After 1531, opposition on both sides hardened. The Protestant princes joined in alliances, such as the *Schmalkaldic League* of 1531, while the Catholic princes formed their own leagues, dividing Germany into warring camps. The emperor's wars against the Turks prevented him from taking the initiative in Germany until 1546, when he was forced to intervene in the Schmalkaldic War. Although the emperor won a military victory over the Lutheran forces, it did not lead to a political or religious settlement in Germany.

By 1555, both sides, having fought to virtual exhaustion, were prepared to negotiate a peace. The resultant *Peace of Augsburg* recognized the realities of time and place. The principle of *cuius regio, eius religio* was established. This meant that each prince in the empire could choose the Lutheran or Catholic religion for his territory. However, it did not mean there would be religious freedom within each state—nor were any other religions recognized, such as the Calvinists or Anabaptists. In addition, there was a reservation declaring that any Catholic Church leader who became Lutheran after 1552 would have to do so as an individual and could not take his flock or his district with him into the new religion. While a victory for Protestantism, the Peace of Augsburg virtually assured the continued dismemberment of Germany into a mosaic of autonomous and semi-autonomous states.

SPREAD OF THE REFORMATION

Even though the ideas of Luther and his spirit of rebellion spread rapidly throughout Europe, Lutheranism as a formal religion was far more limited in its impact. Its major successes were confined to Germany—mostly in the north—and to parts of eastern Europe, and Scandinavia. Lutheranism did not have the evangelical appeal of the other Protestant sects that appeared.

SWITZERLAND

Luther's ideas gained ground in Switzerland, where the foundations already had been laid by such critics of the Church as Ulrich Zwingli (1484–1531). Luther and Zwingli agreed on most theological matters, although Zwingli, an admirer of Erasmus, was more philosophical and humanistic. As a young priest, Zwingli became noted for his oratory, and in 1519 was sent to the cathedral at Zurich. Zwingli's ideas of Church reform and his appeals to throw off Roman domination won over the people of Zurich. The reformers reshaped their religion with a vengeance in 1524. Responding to Zwingli's views that all ritual instruments of religion should be abolished, they went on a rampage, removing statuary, paintings, altars, and even the bones of local saints from their churches. By 1525, Zurich was a Protestant city.

Calvinism. Switzerland, and the city of Geneva in particular, became the focus of another Protestant sect—Calvinism. The founder of this new religious movement, John Calvin (1509–1564), spent his early years in France. He at first studied for the priesthood at the University of Paris, then transferred to the University of Orléans to study law. While at Orléans Calvin pursued a humanist education that included the study of Greek and

A portrait of John Calvin—on the one hand, an ardent "true believer," but also a legal scholar who used logic and reason to formulate his theology.

training, and his skillful use of compelling logical arguments combine to make the *Institutes of the Christian Religion* one of the most powerful and influential Protestant documents ever written.

Calvin's teachings on the scriptures and the question of **predestination** are the two cornerstones of his theology. The concept of predestination is predicated on the majesty of God and is based on the premise that God is omnipotent, omniscient, and omnipresent. If this is so, then God knows what the future holds for each individual. And if it is known who will be saved, even before they are born, then their salvation is preordained. According to Calvin, God has chosen an elected few. Calvin wrote,

• • • *Predestination we call the eternal decree of God by which He has determined*

Hebrew. These new interests brought him into contact with the ideas of Luther. In 1532, Calvin was threatened with arrest for helping to write an inflammatory attack on Catholic theologians in Paris. He spent the next few years in hiding, barely keeping one step ahead of the authorities. Eventually, he settled in Geneva, invited there by the municipal authorities who had just recently gotten rid of the local Catholic bishop. Except for three years of exile in the town of Strasbourg, Calvin spent the rest of his life in the service of his adopted city of Geneva, and in the service of his God.

Calvin's Basic Beliefs. During the first three years of his exile from France, Calvin wrote the *Institutes of the Christian Religion* (1536). He would spend the rest of his life revising and refining this mixture of theological treatise and personal declaration of faith. Calvin's talent with the pen, his legal

The dilemma of a 16th-century pope is depicted in this cartoon, in which the rifts between Luther and Calvin are as apparent as their common conflict with the Church.

CALVIN   LE PAPE   LUTHER

REFORMATION EUROPE

What political complications resulted from the mixture of Calvinist and Roman Catholics in Scotland, and of Anglicans and Roman Catholics in England?

Legend:
- Roman Catholic
- Lutheran
- Calvinist
- Anglican

ATLANTIC OCEAN

NORTH SEA

BALTIC SEA

MEDITERRANEAN SEA

IRELAND

SCOTLAND
Edinburgh

ENGLAND
London

NETHERLANDS
Amsterdam
Antwerp

FRANCE
Paris

SPAIN
Madrid

PORTUGAL
Lisbon

NORWAY

SWEDEN
Stockholm

DENMARK
Copenhagen

FINLAND

RUSSIA
Moscow

PRUSSIA

POLAND

HOLY ROMAN EMPIRE
Wittenberg
Magdeburg
Worms

PALATINATE

SWITZERLAND
Zürich
Geneva
Augsburg

BOHEMIA

DUCHY OF AUSTRIA
Vienna

HUNGARY
Budapest

ITALY
Rome
Venice

OTTOMAN EMPIRE
Constantinople

with Himself what He would have to become of every man. For . . . eternal life is foreordained for some and eternal damnation for others. Every man, therefore, being formed for one or the other of these ends, we say that he is predestined to life or to death.[7]

Clearly, one important step toward salvation required adherence to the precepts of Christianity as defined by Calvin in the *Institutes.* The implication was also that material success in this life could be further evidence that one is among the chosen.

Rule in Geneva. Calvin set about to apply his doctrine in the city of Geneva, which in the 1530s was a prosperous commercial center that had recently become an independent republic. It already had a zealous reformer in the person of William Farel, a Frenchman who had preached Church reform throughout Europe. Farel saw in Calvin a staunch partner who could help him organize and purify the Protestants of Geneva, whose beliefs were an amalgam of the tenets of Zwingli and Luther. Together, Farel and Calvin established an austere **theocracy**, or religious rule, in the city. Gambling, dancing, singing, and licentious behavior were condemned and transgressors punished. Although there was a secular council and a legislative code, the Bible and the clergy were the final authorities. The Calvinist clerical structure differed from that of Lutheranism. Bishops were eliminated. Above the minister was a council of ministers and elders of the Church known as the *consistory.* Calvin's rule, which lasted until his death in 1564, extended into every area of Genevan society, and dissenters had no place. From the Genevan Academy, which he founded, Calvin's followers spread over Europe and even to such far-flung places as Scotland.

---

[7] F. Roy Willis, *Western Civilization: An Urban Perspective,* Vol. 2 (Lexington, Mass.: D. C. Heath, 1973), pp. 380–1.

Calvinism and Capitalism

From the inception of the Calvinist movement, a disproportionate number of Calvinists have engaged in bourgeois occupations and commercial enterprises. Capitalism was most successful in those parts of Europe where the roots of Calvinism were the deepest, especially in England, Scotland, the Netherlands, and France. Some historians see a direct link between the "Puritan ethic" and the growth of commercialism and capitalistic enterprises. Others see the relationship as an incidental one: because of discrimination, according to this second school of thought, Calvinists found many occupational doors closed to them, and were thereby forced into various forms of private enterprise—particularly commercial activities.

SPREAD OF CALVINISM

Calvinist influence throughout Europe was more widespread than that of Lutheranism. Whereas Lutheranism seemed to flourish only where there was political protection, Calvinism seemed to thrive on adversity and persecution.

Outside of Geneva, Calvinism became the official state religion in only a few places. Examples are the Dutch Reformed Church of Holland and the Presbyterian Church in Scotland. Elsewhere, Calvinism prospered as a minority religion. In France, there was an initial flurry of interest in Calvin's ideas, for criticism of the Church and clergy had a long tradition there. At first, Francis I was tolerant of Protestantism—his sister Margaret of Navarre was an ardent Protestant. But Francis soon lost sympathy for some of

The austere principles of Protestant reformers were often manifested in violent actions. In this drawing, a group of Calvinist raiders destroy ornate objects which they consider symbolic of the corruption of the Church.

the more extreme Calvinists, known in France as *Huguenots*. His son, Henry II, became alarmed at the rapid growth of the sect within France, and eventually the Huguenots were persecuted nearly out of existence.

One reason that Francis I remained loyal to the Catholic Church was that he had already gained control of the Church within France. By the terms of the *Concordat of Bologna* (1516), the king gained almost complete power over the appointments of high church officials, including bishops and archbishops. Francis freely used this power to reward nobles and ministers who served him well. Francis' loyalty to the Church did not, however, stop him from making political alliances with Protestant German princes, when they proved useful to him.

REFORMATION IN ENGLAND AND SCOTLAND

In his early years, Henry VIII of England won a reputation as a champion of the Church. In 1521, he published a book attacking the Lutheran heresy, for which the pope awarded him the title Defender of the Faith. Henry's chief minister, Cardinal Wolsey, helped to direct the king's energies toward foreign policy. However, the failure of these policies weakened Wolsey's influence with the king.

Henry's 18-year marriage to Catherine of Aragon had failed to produce a male heir for the Tudor line. Henry developed the idea that the deaths of their infant sons reflected divine punishment for the fact that Catherine had earlier been married to his deceased elder brother.

Henry's eye fell on Anne Boleyn as a suitable wife. He instructed Wolsey to gain the pope's sanction for a divorce from Catherine. However, the pope refused because he needed the support of Catherine's nephew, Charles V. Wolsey's failure led Henry to call a Parliament in 1529 to declare the English Church independent of Rome. Wolsey was jailed on a charge of treason, and the Parliament passed numerous acts reducing the influence of the clergy.

In 1534, Parliament made a complete break with Rome, declaring by the *Act of Supremacy* that the king was the supreme head of the Church of England. In the years that followed, the king confiscated the extensive land holdings of the English monasteries. Henry overcame the opposition of English Catholics by distributing some of these lands to influential burghers and gentlemen. In 1539, severe laws of persecution further suppressed Catholic opposition. Among those severely dealt with was Sir Thomas More, Wolsey's successor as the king's lord chancellor, who was executed for his refusal to accept the king as head of the Church.

Except that it was headed by the king rather than the pope, the Anglican Church was orthodox in its doctrine and organization. Henry rejected the theology of Luther and other Protestant reformers and drew up his own "King's Book," which aside from its emphasis on salvation through faith and the authority of the Bible, was soundly traditional.

Henry's frail heir, Edward VI (1547–1553), and the Council of Regency, which governed at Henry's death, repealed many of

Henry VIII was both a monarch and the supreme prelate of the Church in England. In this portrait after Hans Holbein, Henry's secular role is more apparent.

the more repressive laws which had persecuted Protestant dissenters as well as Catholics. Although still a minority, Lutherans and Calvinists were influential, and during Edward's brief reign, the Anglican Church worked to bring about compromise with the extreme Protestants. These efforts included the creation of the first *Book of Common Prayer* and the promulgation of the official creed of the church in the *Forty-two Articles of Religion*. England was steadily drifting toward a uniform Protestantism.

John Knox, a Scottish peasant and priest turned reformer, began his work in England, where he helped write the Book of Common Prayer. Driven into exile when the Catholic Queen Mary Tudor ascended the throne of England in 1553, Knox took refuge in Geneva, where he absorbed the doctrines of Calvin. When Protestant nobles in Scotland rose in rebellion against their Catholic monarch, Knox returned to aid them.

Knox's form of Calvinism, called *Presbyterianism*, became a symbol of Scottish nationalism as the nobles overthrew the Catholic Queen Mary of Scotland and abolished the authority of the pope. The Scottish were aided in their rebellion by the English and their Protestant queen, Elizabeth I, who wanted to secure her kingdom against Catholic incursions. The rebellion in Scotland firmly established Presbyterianism and the rule of Protestant monarchs.

THE CATHOLIC REFORMATION

While Calvinism was the most vigorous Protestant movement in the second half of the 16th century, a resurgent Catholicism was making inroads into former bastions of Protestantism by luring back into the fold many of those who had fallen away from the Roman Church. In the first half of the 16th century, Catholic leaders had failed to take the Protestant threat seriously. By the 1540s, however, the seriousness of the Protestant challenge became evident, and by the 1560s, Roman Catholicism was on the offensive, seeking to regain what had been lost.

Reform from within, including the purging of corrupt practices, was not new to the Catholic Church. Beginning in the early centuries of the Christian era there had been major efforts at reform, culminating in the Cluniac movement of the 10th century and the founding of the Dominican and Franciscan religious orders in the 13th century.

REFORM IN THE SPANISH CHURCH

The crusading spirit was especially strong in Catholic Spain in the second half of the 15th century. In the struggle to drive the Moors out of Spain, religious unity and nationalistic fervor were interchangeable. In 1495, Queen Isabella entrusted the reform of the Spanish Church to Cardinal Ximenes (1436–1517), the Archbishop of Toledo. He first visited almost every monastery in Spain, where he found ignorance, lax discipline, and some corruption.

From the monasteries Ximenes went on to review the secular clergy, with the same results. He recommended and implemented stricter discipline for the monks and a higher level of literacy and educational requirements for all clerics. Passage of a civil-service exam was required before a priest was allowed to say Mass, or before a bishop was permitted to perform his episcopal duties. Ximenes founded three new universities at Alcala, Seville, and Toledo to promote free enquiry and raise academic standards. Within the confines of these universities, even the ideas of Martin Luther could be discussed openly and debated without fear of persecution. All of these spiritual and academic reforms were in place before Luther presented his Ninety-five Theses.

There was, however, a darker side to the Spanish reformation, and it was manifested through the advent of the Inquisition in 1480. The Holy Office, as it was known in Spain, was established by Ferdinand and Isabella under the direction of the Dominicans for the purpose of eliminating heresy and converting or driving out all Spanish Jews and the Moors. Its intent was as much political—as one way of unifying the country—as it was religious. The method used to achieve a confession from the accused could be brutal and harsh, and the end result often was death by burning at the stake. The Inquisition soon found its way to Italy and the rest of Europe. The execution of heretics, however, was not the sole province of the Catholic Church. Protestant reformers also severely punished those who deviated from orthodoxy.

CREATION OF NEW RELIGIOUS ORDERS

The inspiration for reform in the Catholic Church spread from Spain to Italy with the elevation to the papacy of several reform-minded popes, and the creation of new religious orders. The *Oratory of Divine Love*, founded in Rome in 1517, sought to revive spirituality in the Church through prayer and preaching, and by returning to the poverty and simplicity of the early apostolic Church.

The *Capuchins* ("small hooded men") were very similar to the Franciscan order. By taking a vow of poverty and preaching among the poor, they sought to counteract the argument that the Roman Church was too materialistic and neglectful of the less fortunate. The Capuchins also intended to blunt the charge that Protestant ministers were more effective preachers than their Roman Catholic counterparts.

The *Theatines*, established in 1524, set about reforming the secular clergy from the top down. They identified bright young men in the Church who had a chance of becoming future leaders. The Theatines would educate them, imbue them with reform ideals, and then wait for their disciples to become bishops, cardinals, or even pope.

A new order for women, the *Ursulines*, was established by Angela Merici in 1535. Merici had cared for the poor and the sick in Brescia and surrounding towns in northern Italy. In time, many helpers were drawn to her and soon an order was established to care for Christian girls. Over the years, the Ursulines developed a teaching role for women.

THE SOCIETY OF JESUS

By far the most effective of the new Roman Catholic religious orders in combatting Protestantism was the Society of Jesus. The *Jesuits*, as they are known, were founded by Ignatius Loyola (1491–1556), a Basque nobleman and soldier. After being seriously wounded in battle in 1521, Loyola took a vow that if he survived he would become a soldier of Christ. In 1523, Loyola made a pilgrimage to Jerusalem and later entered a grammar school to learn to read and write Latin. From there he went to the universities of Alcala and Paris to continue his studies.

In 1534, Loyola became the leader of a small group of students who, like himself,

In this painting by an unknown Renaissance artist, Pope Paul III gives his blessing to Ignatius Loyola, founder of the Jesuit order.

wanted to devote their lives to the service of the Church. They presented their ideas to Rome, and the order was officially sanctioned by the pope in 1540. Loyola provided direction for his followers by writing the *Spiritual Exercises* (1541), a handbook aimed at providing those who followed in his footsteps with the spiritual discipline necessary to be a soldier for Christ.

The "first principle and foundation" of the *Spiritual Exercises* states:

• • • *Man is created to praise, reverence, and serve God our Lord, and by this means to save his soul . . . . Therefore, we must make ourselves indifferent to all created things . . . we should not prefer health to sickness, riches to poverty, honor to dishonor, a long life to a short life . . . . Our desire and choice should be what is more conducive to the end for which we are created.*[8]

Members of the society took the usual vows of chastity and poverty to which was added a special pledge of obedience to the pope. The Jesuits hoped to be the first line of defense in the struggle with the infidel and the heretic.

In the struggle to turn back Protestant successes, the Jesuits' greatest victories came in central Europe against the Lutherans and in Poland and the southern half of the Netherlands against the Calvinists. Jesuit missionaries such as St. Francis Xavier and Matteo Ricci made their influence felt around the world in such places as China, India, the New World, and Africa.

PAPAL REFORM

The reform movement first reached into the papacy itself in the person of Adrian VI (1522–1523), a Dutch theologian and the last non-Italian to be elected pope until Pope John Paul II. Adrian was a friend of Erasmus and had been the tutor of Charles V. He came to the papacy with full knowledge of the task that lay before him, writing,

• • • *We know that for many years many abominable things have occurred in this Holy See, abuses in spiritual matters, transgressions of the commandments . . . . All of us . . . have strayed from our paths, nor for a long time has anyone done good; no, not even one.*[9]

However, during his reign of little over a year, he was barely able to begin the task of reform. The next pope, Clement VII, was a member of the Medici family, and fought a delaying action against the measures that seemed necessary to combat Protestantism.

Finally, Pope Paul III (1534–1549) began the task of reform by appointing a commission to investigate Church conditions and make recommendations for change. The commission's report was a compendium of

[8] Lewis W. Spitz, *The Protestant Reformation* (New York: Harper & Row, 1985), p. 305.

[9] *Ibid.*, pp. 295–6.

Church abuses, including the traffic in indulgences, simony, the appointment of corrupt church officials, and the excessive use of papal power. It ended with an exhortation to the new pope "to raise up again the name of Christ, obscured both by the heathen and by us clerics, and to restore it, and to heal the sickness in our hearts and works, to bring the little sheep of Christ into one single fold, and also to turn away from us the well-deserved wrath and vengeance of God, which we can see is ready to fall down upon our heads."[10]

In response, Paul III called for a general Church council to address problems in the Church, clarify dogma, and initiate appropriate reforms.

THE COUNCIL OF TRENT

The *Council of Trent*, begun in 1545 by Paul III, continued its work intermittently until 1563, when it ended under the papacy of Pius IV. The council was attended by high-ranking churchmen from Italy, Spain, France, and Germany who hoped to reunite Christendom under the banner of the Roman Church. However, Protestantism had gone too far and there was no real chance of reaching an accommodation. Since conciliation with Protestantism was out of the question, the council concentrated on determining the future direction of the Church and strengthening its opposition to the Protestant Reformation. By reaffirming the exclusive right of the Church to interpret the scriptures, by insisting that good works as well as faith and the seven sacraments were essential to man's salvation, and by confirming the efficacy of indulgences, the Council of Trent refuted the doctrines of Luther and reaffirmed the supremacy of the Church.

The Vulgate, a translation of the Bible into Latin by St. Jerome in the 4th century, was declared the only official version. Latin, as opposed to national languages, was enshrined as the language of the Church. The council upheld the idea of the priesthood as a special condition apart from that of the laity; the clergy was to remain celibate. Veneration of the saints and devotion to the Virgin were declared to be helpful to spirituality.

The Council also attended to practical matters by imposing educational reforms upon the clergy and prohibiting them from profiting from the sale of indulgences. Church leaders were warned against superstition and immorality and were enjoined to exercise and maintain strict discipline over the clergy. By subjecting Catholic dogma and practice to the most rigorous reforms in the history of the Church, the Council of Trent immeasurably strengthened Catholicism, and by clarifying its basic doctrines established the foundation of the modern Catholic Church.

---

[10] *Ibid.*, p. 297.

SUMMARY

The Protestant Reformation brought an end to the universal Church of the Middle Ages. Even in countries ruled by Catholic monarchs, the churches were becoming nationalized. Humanism and the Renaissance spirit, however, suffered a setback. With Protestants and Catholics holding firm to their beliefs, there was little room for compromise, and even less of an opportunity for the free and rational discussion of differing viewpoints. There seemed to be no middle ground upon which reasonable people could meet to resolve their differences. As will be seen in the next chapter, the future course of the Reformation would be determined more by political, military, and economic factors than by religious concerns.

QUESTIONS

1 What led Martin Luther to make his stand at the Diet of Worms? Was it solely a matter of conscience, or were other factors involved?

2 Was the Reformation a natural outgrowth of the Renaissance? Give reasons for your answer.

3 Explain the four basic beliefs of Martin Luther, and describe how each conflicted with the fundamental doctrines of the Catholic Church.

4 What aspects of Calvinism might account for the fact that it continued to grow in popularity, especially among city-dwellers, while Lutheranism did not?

5 What evidence is there that reform was an ongoing process in the Catholic Church, and not merely a response to Protestant successes?

6 Describe the Augsburg Confession, the Peace of Augsburg, and the Council of Trent. What was the intent behind each, and how successful were they?

BIBLIOGRAPHY

BAINTON, ROLAND H. *Here I Stand: A Life of Martin Luther*. New York: Abingdon-Cokesbury, 1950. *A sympathetic but balanced account of Martin Luther and his times, with an extensive discussion of theology.*

BOLT, ROBERT. *Man for All Seasons*. New York: Random House, 1962. *A modern play portraying Thomas More as an unwilling martyr; a man who searched for a way to obey his king and still live with his conscience.*

ERIKSON, ERIK H. *Young Man Luther*. New York: Norton, 1962. *An insightful application of psychoanalysis to the study of the past by one of the pioneers in this field.*

LABALME, PATRICIA A., ed. *Beyond Their Sex: Learned Women of the European Past*. New York University Press, 1980. *Two essays, by Roland Bainton and Natalie Zemon Davis, are particularly relevant to the Renaissance and Reformation eras.*

MOSSE, GEORGE L. *The Reformation*, rev. ed. New York: Holt, Rinehart and Winston, 1969. *A straightforward and concise overview of the Reformation era.*

PALMER, M. D. *Henry VIII*, 2d ed. New York: Longman, 1983. *An up-to-date introduction to the reign of Henry, with emphasis on the English Reformation. Primary source documents are included, and serve as a point of comparison with the text.*

TUCHMAN, BARBARA W. "The Renaissance Popes Provoke the Protestant Secession: 1470–1530," Chapter 3 of *The March of Folly*. New York: Ballantine Books, 1985. *A discussion of the failings of six Renaissance popes and how their actions contributed to the upheaval of the Reformation era.*

● *There must be some exquisite pleasure in governing, to judge from the numbers who are eager to be concerned in it. . . . it seems that with all our volumes on the subject, from Plato to Machiavelli, we are not well acquainted with the duties of the heads of state.*

VOLTAIRE

Politics, Religion, and International Relations: 1500 –1648

The early modern period in European history saw the death of the concept of a united Europe and the beginnings of the system of sovereign nation-states which has lasted down to the present day.

The rise of Protestantism was a chief factor in the breakdown of European unity. No longer could the Roman Catholic Church serve to unite the continent. For nearly 150 years, struggles between Protestant and Catholic divided the peoples of Europe and were a primary cause of bitter and devastating wars. One of these, the Thirty Years' War, helped to weaken another institution that had also been a source of European unity—the Holy Roman Empire.

But the politics of this era is not just the story of religious struggles. This is also the period that saw the rise to power of several of history's most colorful and best–loved kings and queens. To a large degree, the history of early modern Europe is also the story of the personal and family struggles of such great monarchs as the Holy Roman emperor Charles V, Philip II of Spain, Elizabeth I of England, and Henry IV of France. Like the religious rivalry of the time, the battles of these rulers to preserve or enlarge the territory under their sway contributed to fundamental changes in the European balance of power—to the decline of the Holy Roman Empire and of the German states, and to the rise of the nations of Spain, the Netherlands, France, and England.

The "New" Monarchs. By 1500, the monarchs of England, France, and Spain had already begun the process that would lead, ultimately, to the creation of the modern nation-state. Out of the civil strife and feudal violence that afflicted much of Europe from the mid-15th century on, there emerged a few rulers who were able to impose civil order and peace from above. An earlier generation of historians thought of these rulers as "new men," but, for the most part, they were just expanding upon and extending the policies of the most successful kings of the late Middle Ages. By providing law and order within their domains, they established the principle that the hereditary monarch was the only legitimate source of public authority.

The kings found a ready ally against the nobility and the church in the emerging middle class. The structure of government was reordered so that parliamentary bodies could be ignored or neutralized. With more productive tax-collecting techniques money was available for standing armies loyal only to the monarch. The invention of the longbow and the adaptation of gunpowder for military uses put the common foot soldier on a par with the caparisoned feudal knight. The king in his person was symbolic of the "common-weal," and he was expected to act always in the best interest of his subjects.

THE EMPIRE OF CHARLES V

When Charles I ascended to the throne of Spain in 1516, he united vast territories from both sides of his family. On his father's side, Charles inherited the Hapsburg family holdings in Austria in addition to Hungary, Bohemia, Silesia, and Moravia—as well as all of the Burgundian lands of his paternal grandmother, Mary, which included the Franche Comté, the Netherlands, Luxemburg, and Flanders. From his maternal grandparents Ferdinand and Isabella, Charles received Spain, Sardinia, the Kingdom of the Two Sicilies, and a growing overseas colonial empire. The precept by which the Hapsburgs appeared to multiply and prosper—"Where others have to fight wars, you, fortunate Austria, marry!"[1]—seems to have held true in the case of Charles.

In 1519, Charles was elected Holy Roman emperor. Thereafter he was known as Charles V, since, although he was the first Charles to rule Spain, he was the fifth Charles to serve as Holy Roman emperor. With his election, Charles could also lay claim to most of Germany and other related territories within the traditional boundaries of the Holy Roman Empire. Charles V ruled this empire of vast proportions until his retirement in 1556.

CHARLES AS EMPEROR: BROKEN DREAMS AND HARSH REALITY

At first glance it seems that Charles' resources would enable him to dominate the European scene—politically, economically, and militarily. Behind him he had the military strength of Spain, the commercial prosperity of the Netherlands, and a never-ending flow of gold and silver from the New World. It is no wonder that on becoming Holy Roman emperor, Charles was admonished that "God had placed him on the road to universal monarchy, raising him above all other kings and princes."[2]

Charles V did indeed dream of uniting all of Europe under the stewardship of a single ruler. He was a man of sophistication and urbanity who preferred the velvet glove to the mailed fist. But Charles also was a ruler who had to struggle constantly with a tangled web of serious problems. He was never able to resolve one problem in isolation from the others. This continual rush of overlapping obstacles ultimately prevented him from achieving his dream of a united Europe. First of all, the polyglot of languages, cultures, and religions found within the empire made unlikely the creation of a stable and uniform system of government. Then, the very size of the empire meant that Charles was required to spend a good proportion of his time holding on to what he already had. To the east, the Ottoman Turk was knocking at the door of Vienna, and the Lutheran heresy kept Germany divided and not readily susceptible to imperial jurisdiction. In addition, the French Valois continued to be a threat wherever French and Hapsburg lands or interests touched.

THE HAPSBURG-VALOIS RIVALRY

The European land holdings of Charles V excited the envy of the French king Francis I.

---

[1] R. R. Palmer and Joel Colton, *A History of the Modern World*, 4th ed. (New York: Knopf, 1971), p. 76.

[2] Lacey Baldwin Smith, *The Horizon Book of the Elizabethan World* (New York: American Heritage, 1967), p. 49.

The Valois king Francis I presided over the Renaissance in France. His admiration of Italian culture may have been one motive for his interventions in Italy.

The lands of the empire were twice the size of France and surrounded that country on three sides. Francis had tried to obtain the position of Holy Roman emperor himself, but had lost out to Charles in the imperial election of 1519.

In the first round of fighting in Italy (Chapter 1), the French had received Milan by the Treaty of Brussels in 1516. Charles V reasserted the traditional imperial claim to Milan and both sovereigns looked around for allies. Francis, in an attempt to get English support, invited Henry VIII to France in 1520. He hoped to win over the Tudor monarch by a lavish display at Calais known as the Field of the Cloth of Gold. Henry VIII enjoyed the tourneys and hospitality, but then returned home and agreed to back Charles.

Imperial troops took Milan in 1521, moving on to Genoa in the following year. Fran-

cis moved in 1525 to reclaim Milan, gambling all on one battle at Pavía. The French forces were decisively defeated and Francis was taken prisoner. He was released the following year on the condition that France would renounce its claims to any part of Italy as well as to the Netherlands and Burgundy. Francis had no intention of adhering to this agreement, and the pope agreed that it was not binding as it was signed under duress.

The pope was alarmed at the extent of imperial control within Italy. He joined with France, Venice, Florence, and Milan in the League of Cognac to oppose imperial ambitions in Italy. Charles V's reaction was to send imperial troops to take Rome. The resulting sack of Rome in May 1527 went on for several days. Some of the soldiers were Protestant, and they defaced churches and destroyed priceless religious objects. Thousands of people were massacred and shops were looted. The pope was captured and forced to give up additional territory to the imperial forces.

Francis made three more military attempts to engage the emperor and regain territory in Italy. He was unsuccessful.

After the deaths of both Francis and Charles V, the Treaty of Cateau Cambrésis was signed in 1559. Through it, the Valois king of France renounced all claims on Italy, but the rivalry between the Valois and the Hapsburgs was established as a permanent factor in European diplomacy. The two could be found on opposite sides in every major international conflict until the middle of the 18th century.

CHARLES V AND THE OTTOMAN TURKS

Charles V had to face a revivified Ottoman Empire under the sultan Suleiman the Magnificent (1520–1566). In 1521, Suleiman took advantage of the Hapsburg-Valois fighting in Italy to besiege and take Belgrade.

After Pavia, Francis negotiated an alliance with the Turks so that Suleiman could concentrate his attacks on the Hapsburgs to the advantage of France. In 1526, the Turks moved into Hungary, and at the Battle of Mohacs defeated the Hungarians and killed their king. Imperial troops led by Charles V's brother recaptured most of the country in 1527. But Suleiman's troops returned two years later, retook Hungary, and kept moving until they reached Vienna. During the month-long siege of Vienna, the fighting was desperate. The countryside and suburbs around the city were destroyed. Although the Turks managed to tunnel through and destroy some of the city's wall, the city held out until a relief force arrived.

GERMANY: A PROBLEM WITHOUT A SOLUTION

Constant Turkish and French pressure and the increasing drain on the imperial treasury conspired to block Charles' dream of a united Europe. In addition, he failed to unify Germany under the imperial banner and reverse the spread of Lutheranism. The best chance of eradicating Lutheranism had been in the first years after 1517. However, these were the years when Charles was getting himself elected Holy Roman emperor. In order to win the support of the Electors, Charles had to promise to respect what was "customary" in ruling the empire. And what was "customary" was interpreted by the Electors to mean local independence and autonomy from imperial edicts.

Later, Charles had to refrain from issuing such edicts to the German states where Lutheranism had taken root, in order to obtain the military support of those states in the escalating war with the Turks. The end result was that Lutheranism was not eradicated, and the German states were not united.

In October 1555, with his hair turned snow white and his hands so palsied that he could hardly hold a book, a weary Charles announced that he would abdicate his throne in favor of his brother, Ferdinand I, and his son Philip II. Ferdinand received the Austrian holdings and an opportunity to lay claim to the imperial throne, while Philip fell heir to the Spanish titles and lands. From this time forward the two branches of the Hapsburgs, the Spanish and the Austrian, would remain separate.

With the exception of his feat in stopping the Turks at the gates of Vienna, there is little that Charles could point to with pride in his tenure as emperor. For over 30 years he had struggled mightily only to keep the status quo. In the end he was forced to seek the seclusion of a monastery, old beyond his years and broken in both health and spirit.

PHILIP II AND SPAIN

Philip II of Spain (1556–1598) excites more debate among historians than almost any other European monarch. To some he will always be a religious fanatic whose name is inextricably linked to the Spanish Inquisition and the intolerant and barbarous treatment of heretics for which that institution is known. To others, he is known as Philip "the Prudent"— a man who never acted without carefully considering every possible alternative.

Philip's inheritance included Spain, the Netherlands, Burgundy, Milan, the Kingdom of the Two Sicilies, Sardinia, the Spanish colonial empire, certain holdings along the western coast of Africa, and after 1580, Portugal and the Portuguese empire in the eastern hemisphere. And yet, even though Spain was at the pinnacle of its strength, Philip's ambitions would stretch that power beyond the breaking point. Spain would never again approach the greatness it achieved for a brief time in the 16th century.

PHILIP'S DOMESTIC POLICY

Philip's interests were more parochial than cosmopolitan, more national than international. He was interested in seeing a united Europe only if it could be under the domination of Spain. To Philip there was only one true religion, and anyone or anything that challenged the authority of the Roman Catholic Church had to be dealt with firmly.

Philip II inherited half of the empire of his father, Charles V. Through his ruthless suppression of Protestantism in Spain and elsewhere, he established his monarchy as a center of the Counter-Reformation.

The Escorial (Spanish for "slag-heap"), Philip's palace on the outskirts of Madrid, reflected the personality of the king who erected it. It was sombre and massive, with only small windows, and was intended to serve both as a mausoleum for the kings of Spain and as a monument to medieval Spanish Catholicism.

One of the hallmarks of Philip's reign was the agonizing slowness with which he acted. Philip once said, "It is well to consider everything,"[3] and he practiced what he preached. No detail was too small for his scrutiny. No responsibility could ever be delegated. Even on his deathbed, Philip continued to plan for his own funeral, down to the last detail. He ordered his coffin brought to his bedside so that he could see for himself that his remains would fit comfortably in their last resting place.

[3] *Ibid.*, p. 196.

The Escorial palace, built by Philip II, served both as a royal residence and as a mausoleum.

THE FOREIGN POLICY OF PHILIP

Philip established his permanent capital in the city of Madrid, close to the geographical center of Spain. He involved more of his subjects in the process of government by expanding the number of Royal Councils, groups of civil servants to which he turned for advice. Most importantly, Philip threw all his support behind the Inquisition, out of a belief that by eradicating heresy he would provide unity for Spain in a united and purified church. The Inquisition, the court established for the prosecution of heretics, was at its most repressive during Philip's reign. Many books were banned. Spaniards were forbidden to study at foreign universities. There was a wave of burnings of men and women suspected of being Protestants.

Unlike his father, Philip II had no responsibility for central Europe—that obligation was now the concern of his uncle, Ferdinand I. Instead, the Mediterranean area became his principal focus of attention, since the Iberian peninsula, like southern Italy, jutted far out into the Mediterranean Sea, making Spain vulnerable to attack from Turkish forces based in North Africa.

Although Philip was wary of alliances with other states, the menace posed by the Turks of the Barbary Coast was such that he responded to the pope's plea for international cooperation in a new crusade to crush the Turks. In May 1571, Spain and Venice entered into an agreement to form the Holy League.

All that summer the forces of the Holy League prepared for a showdown at sea with the Turks. When the *Battle of Lepanto* finally took place, in October 1571, it was the largest sea battle ever fought up to that time. It was also one of the bloodiest. Hours of fierce hand-to-hand combat between Christian and Turkish sailors resulted in 50,000 dead and 125 galleys wrecked or sunk. Some of the ships' crews suffered a 90 percent casualty rate. Nevertheless, it was a stunning victory for the Christian forces. A participant in the

The battle of Lepanto reestablished Christian control of Venice and of the eastern Mediterranean. The Ottoman Turks soon continued their expansion in North Africa, however.

Battle of Lepanto, the great novelist Miguel de Cervantes, wrote later that it was "the most exalted event of the past, the present, or the future."[4]

To Philip, Lepanto was intended to isolate Turkish naval strength in the eastern Mediterranean area. Philip was successful in achieving this goal, but success was more elusive in the Netherlands.

REVOLT IN THE SPANISH NETHERLANDS

Philip had said at one point that he would rather die 100 deaths than be the ruler of heretics. Although not a majority, a large number of Protestants lived in the 17 provinces that made up the Netherlands. Antwerp became a haven for Huguenots who fled from France, as did other cities in the Netherlands. The major gulf created by the Spanish king's expression of religious intolerance was widened by his insistence on reestablishing absolute power over the Netherlands after they had enjoyed years of relative independence.

Philip also felt disdain for the occupations of banking and trade, which were the

[4] Marvin R. O'Connell, *The Counter Reformation: 1559–1610* (New York: Harper & Row, 1974), p. 364.

49

lifeblood of the Netherlands. Not long after his accession to the throne, he levied heavy new taxes on commercial activity, replaced local officials with his own appointees, established the Inquisition in the Netherlands, and sent in an army of Spanish troops. The outraged Netherlanders rose in revolt. Angry mobs sacked Catholic churches, smashing statues and stained glass windows.

Philip's response to the revolt was to send in the ruthless Duke of Alva to impose a military solution to the troubles. Alva established a dictatorship ruled by a small tribunal called the Council of Troubles, which became popularly known as the "Council of Blood." Under its rule, thousands were sentenced to death and taxes were increased.

The Netherlanders found a leader in William of Orange, a Catholic noble whose lands had been confiscated by the Spanish. In 1564, William of Orange gave a remarkable explanation of why the rebellion was at the beginning so widely popular: "However strongly I am attached to the Catholic religion, I cannot approve of princes attempting to rule the consciences of their subjects and wanting to rob them of the liberty of belief."[5] William organized Catholics and Protestants alike to fight Philip's tyranny. William's support increased when the Spanish garrison in Antwerp mutinied and sacked the city in 1576.

After Philip sent in the brilliant general Alexander Farnese, the Duke of Parma, in 1578, the cities of the ten southern provinces fell back into Spanish hands. But in the north, the Dutch used their sea power—they were nicknamed "the sea beggars" by the Spanish—and successfully harassed arriving Spanish fleets. Fighting dragged on for years. The truce of 1609 formally recognized that a standoff had occurred, although formal independence was not granted until the Peace of Westphalia in 1648.

In fact, before the end of the 16th century the seven northern provinces were sufficiently strong to unite into a new, independent nation. In the following century the Dutch Republic was to enter into its Golden Age, and became a major force in the commercial, cultural, and intellectual life of the European world.

Amsterdam became one of the great cities of Europe. Refugees with important skills flocked to the city from all over Europe. Although the Dutch Republic was Calvinist in religion, there was more tolerance there than in most other European countries. Refugees from Antwerp brought their banking and financial skills to Amsterdam, and the city replaced Antwerp as the financial center of Europe.

Amsterdam also had the finest merchant marine in Europe. It used this to become a great trading power. The city offered all commercial services. Its price list became the list for Europe as a whole. Credit, insurance, commercial legal talent, and brokerage were all available there. Dutch printing presses turned out some of the most important works of the period. The butter and cheese of Holland were exported all over Europe. The riches of the Dutch Republic supported a middle-class life-style that was the envy of the rest of Europe.

THE SPANISH ARMADA: 1588

The revolt in the Netherlands was not Philip's only concern in the 1580s. The English had also begun to pose a serious threat to Spain and, equally important to Philip, to the Catholic Church. English ships were beginning to prey on treasure-laden Spanish galleons coming from the New World. Elizabeth of England was openly aligning herself with the Dutch rebels, providing them with money and supplies. Then, in 1587, the Scottish Catholic queen Mary Stuart, whom many Spaniards had hoped would succeed Protestant Elizabeth, was put to death at English hands.

---

[5] *Ibid.*, p. 147.

Philip decided he had to act. His original plan was a grand one—to send an *armada*, or fleet, of ships up to the Netherlands, where they would pick up the Duke of Parma's army and then proceed with an invasion of England. But, short of a miracle, there was no hope that Parma's heavy troop barges could elude the fast Dutch flyboats that patrolled the coast of the Netherlands. Parma's army would never reach the shores of England.

The great *Spanish Armada* which was poised and ready to sail in 1587 was the greatest naval force the world had ever seen—130 ships, 30,000 men. But even before the ships weighed anchor, the English captain Sir Francis Drake raided the Spanish port of Cadiz, destroying 30 ships and plundering precious stores and equipment.

When the Armada finally reached the English coast, it encountered other serious difficulties. Many of the Spanish galleons were too cumbersome and slow-moving to maneuver easily, and could not compete with the lighter, faster English vessels. Also, the English had developed a new and more effective naval strategy. They darted in and out of the Spanish formations, firing broadsides. Empty English ships were set on fire and sent floating among the anchored Spanish ships at night.

Then, to make matters worse, the Spanish force encountered a great storm which blew its remaining ships north, toward the rocky coast of Ireland. Those Spaniards who were shipwrecked on the Irish coast had to contend with English soldiers who had been given orders to kill all Spanish soldiers and sailors on sight. An even worse fate awaited those who managed to avoid the Irish coast and head for home. A quarantine was imposed on them to prevent the spread of disease, and thousands died of hunger or illness on board ship, literally within sight of Spain.

The defeat of the Spanish Armada was a decisive one. It certainly marked a crucial turning point in the histories of both Spain and England.

The failure of the Armada proved to the rest of Europe that Spain was not invincible. The cost of the venture had stretched Spanish resources to the breaking point, at the same time as the rebellion in the Netherlands and the beginning of a war with France (see below). Like his father Charles V, Philip had taken on too many problems with too few resources—and failure was the result. Although it did not spell the immediate death of the Spanish Empire, the defeat of the Armada seriously undercut Philip's grand design for Spain, his religion, and Europe.

A GOLDEN AGE OF CULTURE; POLITICAL DECLINE
During the reigns of Philip II's successors, Philip III and Philip IV, Spain declined politically. It was never again a great power, as it had been during the reign of Philip II. But in spite of political decline, this period is known for its culture as Spain's Golden Age. The novelist Miguel de Cervantes (1547–1616) created one of the great figures in world literature in his *Don Quixote*. Cervantes parodied the traditional tales of knight errantry, but the book glows with humor and warmth. Cervantes' life was almost as exciting as his book. He served at Lepanto, where his left hand was maimed. During later fighting with the Turks, he was captured and spent five years as a slave in Algiers.

In painting, Philip II patronized El Greco (c. 1541–1614), seen by many as the most characteristically Spanish painter. Born in Crete, it was only after he arrived in Spain that his distinctive style emerged. The elongated figures on his canvases, many of which depict saints, reflect the religious fervor of Counter-Reformation Spain.

The Spanish theater reached a high point of achievement at this time. Lope de Vega (1562–1635), the most prolific dramatist of all time, is said to have written more than 1800 plays, as well as many works of poetry. Spanish drama was obsessed with the idea of honor. Later, Pedro Calderon de la Barca (1600–1681) would carry Spanish drama to its greatest heights. In *La Vida Es Sueno*, Calderon would return to Cervantes' theme of illusion and reality.

TUDOR ENGLAND

For the English, the defeat of the Spanish Armada was a great and significant victory. It launched England on the path to becoming a sea power of world rank. It also marked the zenith of one of England's greatest dynastic families, the Tudors, under Elizabeth I.

Every loyal citizen rejoiced over the victory. Elizabeth addressed her victorious soldiers and sailors on the field of Tilbury with the following words:

• • • *My loving people . . . I know I have the body of a weak and feeble woman, but I have the heart and stomach of a king. I myself will take up arms. I myself will be your general, judge, and rewarder of every one of your virtues in the field.*[6]

TUDOR GOVERNMENT

The English dynasty which ruled from 1485 to 1603, the Tudors, placed its stamp on the country's institutions. Although the Tudors wielded considerable power, they relied as well on their own popularity and the support of their subjects. Moreover, they were adept at controlling or manipulating the important institutions of early modern Europe, including the church, the aristocracy, and the military.

Unlike most other European systems, Tudor government relied on local authorities—unpaid justices of the peace and sheriffs—to interpret the royal will.

Of the two houses of the English parliament, the House of Lords, which included all Englishmen with titles, contained many who were granted their titles and their estates by King Henry VIII. Moreover, one-third of the seats in the House of Lords were held by bishops of the Anglican Church, also Henry's appointees and defenders.

The other branch of Parliament, the House of Commons, in Tudor times consisted primarily of the English middle class—landed gentry, lawyers, and merchants—who were provided freedom of speech and freedom from arrest in return for their adherence to the wishes of the throne.

The House of Lords and House of Commons usually cooperated with each other, for both had members from the same families. This situation arose essentially as a result of the English practice of *primogeniture*. By this practice, only the eldest son inherited the family's noble title, estate, and seat in the House of Lords. The younger sons were thus forced to find their own paths to fortune and political power—by entering middle-class professions, and often, by marrying the daughters of the middle class. Hence, many aristocratic English families were represented in both Houses of Parliament, and most of the members owed many of their privileges to the throne.

Although English monarchs had sources of revenue from personal wealth, they had to get Parliamentary approval to impose taxes for extraordinary expenses such as war. Parliament's power of the purse encouraged the Tudors to avoid extraordinary expenditures, including the maintenance of a standing army in peacetime. One of the effects of this policy was to eliminate one power base, the military, that might challenge the authority of the throne. At the same time, it limited the power of the monarch, who lacked a military force which he or she might use to intimidate potential rivals.

Another component of Tudor rule provided that the central government administration be a national institution supported by taxes, rather than part of the king's royal household. While this system relieved the king of the burden of paying for expenditures out of his own personal wealth, it also held potential for Parliamentary power, given that body's authority to approve taxes for the costs of government.

---

[6] Lacey Baldwin Smith, *Op. cit.*, p. 290.

Queen Elizabeth I reconciled the religious disputes that divided her subjects, and defeated the best efforts of Philip II to reinstate a Catholic monarchy in England.

THE ELIZABETHAN PERIOD

The last of the Tudors, Elizabeth I (1558–1603), was probably England's most popular monarch and one of its greatest. Elizabeth, "Good Queen Bess," had a commanding personality and presence, much like her father Henry VIII, and loved her royal position and the pageantry that accompanied it. She has been described as a child of the Renaissance, broadly educated in the Greek and Latin classics and fluent in six languages. She was skilled in archery and the hunt. Although she headed the Anglican Church in a religious era, she was skeptical and tolerant of differing religious opinions. Elizabeth's reign was a glorious period in English history, as is reflected in one of her nicknames, "Gloriana."

The Religious Settlement. Elizabeth's predecessor was her half sister, Mary, who unwisely married Philip II of Spain, joining England to Spain in a close alliance that threatened England's sovereignty. Mary's personal zeal for Catholicism led her to persecute Protestants. These moves aroused the resentment of many English people against the pope and Catholicism.

Mary's reign was short, and in 1558, Elizabeth I, daughter of Anne Boleyn and Henry VIII, became Queen of England. Elizabeth had been raised a Protestant, but her political skills prevented an outbreak of religious warfare.

Through an act of Parliament in 1559, the Church of England (Anglican Church) was reinstated. An Act of Uniformity prescribed the use of a Book of Common Prayer as the only legal form of worship. However, the later Thirty-Nine Articles that set forth the doctrine of the Church of England were flex-

During Elizabeth's reign, the monarchy maintained good relations with Parliament.

ible enough for many Catholics to accept—provided they accepted the queen as the head of the Church instead of the pope. The English liturgy remained close to that of Roman Catholicism. As a result, religion did not become a force for disunity in England during Elizabeth's reign.

Elizabeth and the Economy. Elizabeth did much to strengthen the country economically. Parliament took over the regulation of requirements for apprenticeships and the levels of wages—areas which had once been the province of local guilds. Flemish weavers and Turkish dyers were imported to assist in building a domestic cloth industry. A Poor Law was passed to insure that all who could work did so. Local tariffs that interfered with trade were abolished and the formation of overseas trading companies such as the East India Company was encouraged.

Elizabeth's power was not absolute. Parliament still had considerable authority. But Elizabeth, like many of her Tudor forebears, had a genius for working within the established institutions of English society while at the same time retaining great power. This she did largely by force of her strong personality, and a thorough understanding of how the English system worked.

An Age of Splendor. The reign of Elizabeth coincided with a great age of literature. Under such poets as Edmund Spenser (1552–1599) who sang the praises of Elizabeth in his *Faerie Queene*, and William Shakespeare (1564–1616), England rose to literary heights that have never been surpassed. William Byrd (1543–1623), the greatest English composer of the time, was a favorite of Elizabeth, who loved to sing and dance.

This was the period in which the great English theater was born. Shakespeare's plays and his use of language have affected the English language ever after. Shakespeare

The plays of Shakespeare and other dramatists reflected the many successes of Elizabeth's long reign. Shown at right is the Swan, one of the three London theaters in which Shakespeare's works were performed.

shared in the spirit of pride in country that was a hallmark of Elizabeth's time. He glorified both the country and the Tudor dynasty in his history plays. In his *Richard II*, Shakespeare puts in the mouth of John of Gaunt perhaps the most famous eulogy for a country in the English language:

This happy breed of men, this little world,
This precious stone set in the silver sea,
Which serves it in the office of a wall,
Or as a moat defensive to a house
Against the envy of less happier lands—
This blessed plot, this earth, this realm, this
England.[7]

Shakespeare was not the only dramatist of this period, although he is considered the greatest. His contemporaries Christopher Marlowe and Ben Jonson wrote plays that are still performed and give pleasure today.

CIVIL WAR IN FRANCE

The glorious reign of Elizabeth in England coincided with a time of strife in France. During the 30 years from 1559 to 1589, France was wracked with religious civil war.

Though the French Calvinists (Huguenots) were a minority, most were from the bourgeoisie or the nobility, and their influence was far out of proportion to their numbers. In addition, they were concentrated in cities and coastal areas where they dominated commercial and business activity.

RELIGIOUS WARS

When Henry II died in 1559, the situation in France was ripe for the rise of religious factions. Henry's three sons were all young— the eldest was 15—and weak, dominated by their mother, Catherine de Medici. With no strong ruler on the throne, France's great baronial families rose to fill the power vacuum.

Catherine de Medici ruled France on behalf of her young son, Charles IX, from 1560 to 1574. Although she advocated a policy of tolerance toward Protestants, she was widely blamed for the St. Bartholomew's Day massacre.

Two of these families soon became aligned with the religious factions of the day. The patriarchs of the Guise family represented the more conservative Catholic party. The Huguenots looked to the Bourbon family and to its able young leader, Henry of Navarre, for leadership. Catherine was not able to obtain the cooperation of either party, and her efforts to reach an accord with the Huguenots inspired violent countermeasures from the conservative Guise faction. Soon roving bands of armed men were terrorizing the countryside, fighting with each other and pillaging and plundering as they went.

St. Bartholomew's Day Massacre. Things came to a head on the feast of St. Bartholomew's Day in August 1572. Thousands of Calvinist nobles and their retinues, who were assembled in Paris for the marriage of the Huguenot leader Henry of Navarre to Margaret de Valois, were beset by armed Catholics. By evening, the Seine ran red with Protestant blood.

The *Saint Bartholomew's Day Massacre*, as it is called, soon spread from Paris into

---

[7] *Shakespeare: the Complete Works*, ed. G. B. Harrison (New York: Harcourt Brace Jovanovich, 1968), p. 443.

The bitter events of St. Bartholomew's Day, 1572, were depicted by an eyewitness to the scene. The massacre of Huguenots in Paris and in other towns throughout France precipitated a series of civil wars which were not resolved until 1598, when Henry IV issued the Edict of Nantes.

the provinces. Over 10,000 Huguenots were put to the sword within a matter of days—and within weeks French Catholics and French Protestants were at each other's throats in a renewal of the bloody civil war. This phase of the civil strife in France came to be known as the War of the Three Henrys, for it soon devolved into a struggle between King Henry III, the third of Henry II's sons to ascend the French throne; Henry of Guise, leader of the Catholic party; and Huguenot leader Henry of Navarre.

A turning point came in 1588. That year, Henry of Guise was assassinated on the order of Henry III. The compliment was returned the following year when Henry III was murdered by one of Guise's distraught followers. The dying Henry III recognized Henry of Navarre as his successor. Although Henry of Navarre had a legal claim to the French crown, the civil war continued.

Now Philip II, who had thrown Spanish prestige and money behind the Guise family, decided to press his own claims to the French throne. The choice seemed to be between a Spaniard and a Huguenot. Most Frenchmen preferred Henry of Navarre to a foreigner. However, Catholic sentiment was still strong in many parts of the country, particularly in Paris. The Catholic party refused to recognize a Huguenot king. Then, in 1594, Henry of Navarre embraced the Catholic faith. Newly anointed as Henry IV (1589–1610), he is reputed to have said, after accepting the crown, that "Paris is worth a Mass." The conversion and accession of Henry IV marked the end of France's religious civil war.

A Voice of Reason: Montaigne. Henry's decision to convert to Roman Catholicism was symptomatic of a new but growing spirit of moderation and reasonableness on matters of religion. A number of French political leaders and thinkers were coming to the conclusion that no creed was worth decades of civil war.

One of the leading thinkers and writers of the period was Michel de Montaigne (1533–1592), a man who viewed all human differences—of religion and of culture—with tolerance. One of Montaigne's favorite sayings was a quote from the Roman playwright Terence: "I am a man; I consider nothing human foreign to me."[8] Montaigne invented the essay as a literary form, and his essays reflected the new reasonable and dispassionate spirit that was beginning to take hold in France.

THE REIGN OF HENRY IV

With the accession of Henry IV, the star of France began to rise. Henry and his chief adviser, the Duke of Sully, reversed the downward trend in the French economy that had been brought on by years of religious strife. Canals were built, roads repaired, the tax burden on the peasants reduced, old industries revitalized, and new industries introduced, including the production of silk in southern France. Commerce and trade were enhanced with the outfitting of a royal navy and the subsidizing of a merchant marine. Exploration led to the founding of settlements and trading posts in India and Canada. At the same time that the central government's authority was increasing, the power of the nobility was being curbed.

Henry IV did not forget his former co-religionists. In the *Edict of Nantes* of 1598, Huguenots were granted complete freedom of conscience, the right to publicly practice their religion in specified places, and the right to hold public office. To guarantee that the Edict's rights would be enforced, the Huguenots were allowed to garrison specified

Cardinal Richelieu successfully promoted the authority of the French monarch both at home and abroad through the use of diplomacy and decisive military actions.

cities, primarily in southern and western France. The Edict of Nantes stands as a monument to religious toleration in an age of intolerance. It brought internal peace to France.

Henry's assassination in 1610 by a religious fanatic brought to an abrupt end one of the most successful and, in the opinion of the great majority of his subjects, one of the most popular reigns in the history of the French monarchy.

RISE TO POWER OF CARDINAL RICHELIEU

After Henry's death, the crown went to his nine-year-old son, Louis XIII, for whom his mother, Marie de Medici, served as regent. One of Marie de Medici's protégés, Cardinal Richelieu, became a chief royal adviser. From 1624 until 1642, Cardinal Richelieu

---

[8] Edith Simon, *The Reformation* (New York: Time-Life Books, 1966), p. 126.

dominated both the domestic and foreign policy of France. His two political goals were to make the king supreme in France and France supreme in Europe.

To achieve his first goal, Richelieu employed a variety of tactics. He ignored the Estates General, relying instead on a royal council headed by himself and composed largely of representatives of the middle class. The council came to be known as the "Thirty Tyrants." Richelieu saw to it that the wings of the nobility were clipped by strengthening the army, demolishing many of the feudal castles, and creating the role of the *intendant*. The intendants were representatives of the royal government who kept their eyes on the various districts of the country. They had the power, invested in them by the king, to regulate tax collection, administer justice, and recruit soldiers. The intendants seriously undermined the authority of the provincial nobility, who had once been the supreme power in their districts.

Richelieu also stripped the Huguenots of many of their military and political rights, although they retained a degree of religious freedom.

The second aim of Richelieu's policy, to make France supreme in Europe, required the humbling of the Spanish and Austrian Hapsburgs. The major vehicle for implementing that policy was to be the Thirty Years' War.

THE THIRTY YEARS' WAR The origins of the *Thirty Years' War* (1618–1648) can be traced to ongoing unrest in Germany. The Peace of Augsburg of 1555 had given princes the right to choose either Lutheranism or Catholicism for their domains. However, this policy failed to take into account the rising tide of Calvinism throughout Germany. As Calvinism spread, Protestant German states created a league to protect themselves, and Catholic German states organized a league of their own in response. Both leagues, poised for conflict, looked to the great powers of Europe for support. This religious tension was compounded by the ongoing efforts of the Holy Roman emperor to impose a central authority over Germany, and the lesser German states' struggle to resist imperial domination.

BOHEMIAN AND DANISH PHASES (1618–1629)
The first phase of the Thirty Years' War began in Bohemia, after several Calvinist churches were desecrated and Calvinist nobles began to fear the loss of their religious liberties. When two representatives of the emperor arrived in Prague to negotiate, they were thrown from a window, in keeping with an old Bohemian custom known as "defenestration." Soon afterward, the Bohemian nobles sought help from the Protestant Union, the league of German states that had been formed to protect Protestant interests. But Holy Roman emperor Ferdinand II, with assistance from Spain, easily defeated the Bohemians and their Protestant allies. Efforts to reinstitute Catholicism in Bohemia were quickly gotten under way.

The emperor's success in reinstituting Catholicism in Bohemia alarmed other nearby Protestant princes. In 1625 the Lutheran king of Denmark, Christian IV, moved his forces into Germany to oppose the threat of an imperial advance. The emperor retaliated by enlisting the services of the Czech soldier and adventurer Count Wallenstein and his army of 50,000 mercenaries. Wallenstein's army, fighting for plunder and booty more than for any religious or political cause, brutally ravaged the German countryside. Whole villages were destroyed. Villagers who did not manage to escape faced savage treatment—being dragged behind horses, having their thumbs crushed, or even being thrust into a hot baker's oven. By 1629 Wallenstein's forces had driven the Danes out of Germany.

That same year, Emperor Ferdinand issued the *Edict of Restitution*, which returned to Catholic hands much of the property acquired by the Lutherans since the Peace of Augsburg. Fear gripped German Protestants. It appeared that nothing could stop the Catholic and imperial juggernaut.

SWEDISH AND FRENCH PHASES (1630–1648)

At this point both the Swedes and the French began to worry about the increase in Hapsburg power. Cardinal Richelieu was not yet prepared to enter the fighting himself, but he readily granted the Swedes financial and diplomatic aid in mounting a campaign against the Hapsburgs.

In King Gustavus Adolphus of Sweden, the Protestants at last found a worthy champion for their cause. The Swedish king was a talented leader who earned his nickname "Lion of the North." The armies of the Holy Roman emperor were no match for the Swedes, who quickly scored several stunning victories.

A Swedish victory at the battle of Lutzen in 1634, however, cost Sweden dearly—Gustavus Adolphus was killed. A number of Protestant German princes, weary of fighting and increasingly fearful of Sweden's power, took the opportunity to make a separate peace with the emperor. It appeared as if peace were at hand. However, neither the French nor the Spanish were happy with the developing truce in Germany. The French feared that the Hapsburgs retained too much power, the Spaniards that they retained too little.

By 1635 the French army had begun to march on the Rhine. The French were joined by the Swedes and the Dutch. Spain responded with support for the Hapsburg empire. Soon Germany had become little more than a battleground for foreign troops. For almost ten more years, Germany was wracked by pillaging, plundering, and wanton killing and destruction.

The common people of Europe—especially the peasants—paid the highest price in suffering and ruin during the religious wars of the 16th and 17th centuries.

THE RESULTS OF THE THIRTY YEARS' WAR

The Thirty Years' War resulted in the devastation of Germany. Nearly one-third of the population was killed. In Hesse alone, 300 villages were destroyed. Some cities were reduced to as little as one-fifteenth of their former populations. The land was laid waste, and death by starvation became as common as death in battle.

The German poet Schiller was one of many to reflect on the particularly brutal and savage nature of this war:

● ● ● *The burnt castles, the ravaged countryside, the villages reduced to ashes presented the spectacle of an appalling devastation while their inhabitants, condemned to poverty, helped to swell the number of incendiary bands: and barbarously delivered to their compatriots*

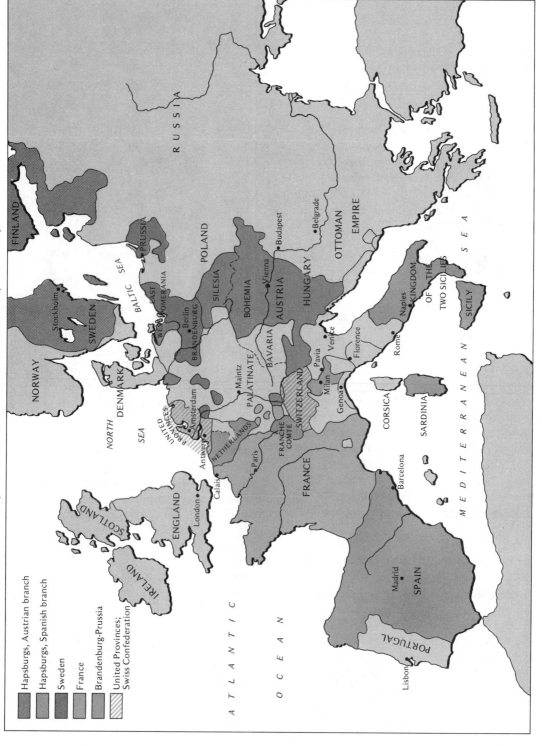

EUROPE AFTER THE PEACE OF WESTPHALIA, 1648
Which nations and newly independent countries profited most from the dissolution of the Holy Roman Empire?

Hapsburgs, Austrian branch
Hapsburgs, Spanish branch
Sweden
France
Brandenburg-Prussia
United Provinces;
Swiss Confederation

ATLANTIC

OCEAN

NORTH

SEA

BALTIC

SEA

MEDITERRANEAN

SEA

IRELAND

SCOTLAND

ENGLAND
London

NORWAY

SWEDEN
Stockholm

FINLAND

RUSSIA

DENMARK

Calais

Paris
FRANCE

UNITED
PROVINCES
Amsterdam
Antwerp
NETHERLANDS

PALATINATE
Maintz

Berlin
BRANDENBURG
WEST
POMERANIA
EAST
PRUSSIA

POLAND

SILESIA

BOHEMIA

BAVARIA

Vienna
AUSTRIA

HUNGARY
Budapest

Belgrade

OTTOMAN

EMPIRE

FRANCHE
COMTE
SWITZERLAND

Pavia
Milan
Genoa

Venice

Florence

Rome

KINGDOM
OF THE
TWO SICILIES
Naples

SICILY

CORSICA

SARDINIA

Barcelona

SPAIN
Madrid

PORTUGAL

Lisbon

the misery which they themselves had suffered . . . . All the vices flourished in the shadow of anarchy and impunity, men became as wild as the countryside . . . . The soldier was lord.[9]

So long did the war last that many grew accustomed to this violent, lawless way of life. On the eve of the peace treaty, one camp follower had this to say: "I was born in war, I have no home, no country and no friends, war is all my wealth and now whither shall I go?"[10]

The 30 years of warfare, and particularly the decline in population, had a devastating effect on the economy. Trade routes, commercial ties between cities in the Hanseatic League, and the embryonic middle class declined in number and effectiveness between 1618 and 1648. After 1648, Germany was even less of a political unit than it had been before the war.

The Peace of Westphalia. The two treaties that ended the Thirty Years' War and that together are known as the *Peace of Westphalia* were the product of the first general peace conference in European history. The conference was the first at which the participating states recognized no common or higher bond, such as subservience to pope or emperor. The concept of a united Europe had been replaced by the modern European system of independent sovereign states.

Under the terms of the peace, lands that had been given to the Catholics as a result of the Edict of Restitution were restored to their former status. The peace also renewed the concept of *cuius regio eius religio*, this time granting Calvinism legal status on a par with the Lutheran and Catholic religions. More importantly, the general tenor of the agreement encouraged rulers to be more tolerant toward the minority religious beliefs of their subjects as long as they were practiced in private. By statute, religious issues were no longer subject to deliberation in the Imperial German Diet unless both Protestants and Catholics agreed to consider them.

The Peace of Westphalia also put one more nail in the coffin of the Holy Roman Empire. The Dutch Republic and Switzerland were recognized as sovereign states, legally independent of any affiliations with the empire. Both France and Sweden were granted bits and pieces of territory on the edges of the imperial dominions.

Most importantly, over 300 German states and "free cities" achieved virtual independence from imperial taxes, military recruitment, and a foreign policy heretofore dominated by the Hapsburgs.

The Peace of Westphalia had happy consequences for several other European nations as well. Sweden acquired western Pomerania and much of the rest of the German coastal area bordering the Baltic Sea. Although Sweden did not have the population or the resources to remain a great power indefinitely, these acquisitions helped her to take her moment in the sun in the 17th and early 18th centuries, under the reigns of Gustavus Adolphus and Charles XII.

Another winner was the German state of Brandenburg, which acquired the eastern half of Pomerania and isolated parcels of land between Berlin and the Rhine River. This would lay the basis for the rise to power of Prussia (Chapter 7).

The differences between Spain and France were not resolved at Westphalia, and war between these two nations continued for another decade, until the Treaty of the Pyrenees was signed in 1659. France emerged from the Thirty Years' War as the big winner, for the twin threats of the Austrian and Spanish Hapsburgs had been neutralized. France's diplomatic and military successes would provide the foundation for the grand age of Louis XIV.

---

[9] Philippe Erlanger, *The Age of Courts and Kings* (New York: Anchor Books, 1970), p. 162.

[10] C.V. Wedgewood, *The Thirty Years War* (London: Jonathan Cape, Ltd., 1938). Anchor Books paperback ed., p. 485.

SUMMARY

Between 1500 and 1648, the religious and political disputes of Europe flared into several bitter and destructive wars. The idea of a united Europe was shattered, and in its place arose the system of competing nation-states. The Hapsburg domains were permanently divided between those in Spain and Portugal, and those in eastern Europe. The northern provinces of the Netherlands won their independence, and immediately became one of the most important centers of European business and trade.

The period also saw golden ages of culture in Spain and England. But in the century that followed, Spain went into political decline, while England would continue its rise to become one of the major political powers on the world stage.

QUESTIONS

1 Of the rulers discussed in this chapter, which are the best examples of "new monarchs"? Substantiate your answer.
2 Charles V and Philip II were among the most powerful European monarchs since the days of Charlemagne, and yet both failed to achieve their goals. What circumstances contributed to their failures?
3 Although Henry IV was a Protestant in a country that was overwhelmingly Catholic, he was the victor of the War of the Three Henrys. How can his success be explained?
4 Compare the domestic policies of Richelieu and Elizabeth I. What methods did each use to consolidate power in the hands of the monarch? How were these methods tailored to the institutions of their respective nations?
5 What impact did the religious wars of the 16th and 17th centuries have on the economy and social structure of Europe?

BIBLIOGRAPHY

BRANT, SEBASTIAN. The Ship of Fools, trans. Edwin H. Zeydel. New York: Dover, 1962. A graphic and at times humorous portrayal of 15th-century European middle-class society. Its poetic format is enhanced by a series of woodcuts, some of which may be the work of Albrecht Dürer.

BALDWIN SMITH, LACEY. Henry VIII: The Mask of Royalty. Boston: Houghton Mifflin, 1973. A scholarly work on the effective use of power in Tudor England during the time of the "new monarchies."

BRAUDEL, FERNAND. The Structures of Everyday Life, trans. Sian Reynolds. Vol. 1 of the series Civilization and Capitalism: 15th–18th Centuries. New York: Harper & Row, 1981. A leading practitioner of the interdisciplinary approach to history describes the daily existence of peoples throughout the world during the 15th to 18th centuries.

CHUTE, MARCHETTE. Shakespeare of London. New York: E. P. Dutton, 1957. A successful effort to separate Shakespeare the man from the literary deity that he has become in the last 350 years.

JENKINS, ELIZABETH. Elizabeth the Great. New York: Coward-McCann, 1958. The author's vivid portrayal of the queen has been one of the few biographies to stand the test of time.

MATTINGLY, GARRETT. The Armada. Boston: Houghton Mifflin, 1959. A classic work on the heroic confrontation between Spain and England, with special emphasis on the international crosscurrents of diplomacy.

WEDGWOOD, C. V. The Thirty Years' War. Anchor Books ed. New York: Doubleday, 1961. The author's scholarship is matched by her ability to make an era and its people come alive through the written word.

4

European Exploration and Expansion

Luis Vaz de Camoens [KAM-o-enz] wrote the *Lusiads* to celebrate the deeds of Vasco da Gama and other Portuguese explorers. Writing in the style of Virgil's *Aeneid*, Camoens portrayed the Portuguese explorers of the 15th and 16th centuries as heroes comparable to those of the classical world.

The *Lusiads* also reflect an **ethnocentrism**, or feeling of cultural superiority, that afflicted most Europeans when they thought of the world beyond their own borders. Camoens' belief that the Portuguese were the first people to sail the seas east of Africa is an example of this attitude.

The period of European exploration and discovery from the 15th through the 17th century was pivotal not only for European history but also for the history of the world. During this period Europeans explored almost every corner of the earth. The effects of this exploration on Europe were to invigorate its economy, stimulate the development of new ideas, and alter the relationships among European powers. This period also marks the first step leading to Europe's domination of the rest of the world, a condition that was to continue until the 20th century.

WHY EUROPE? It could be argued that Europeans were not the most likely candidates to achieve domination over much of the world. The subcontinent of Europe occupies only about six percent of the earth's land area. Yet, for all its lack of size, Europe had been fragmented politically since the end of the Roman Empire. For centuries, Europeans lived on the edge of political extinction; threatened in succession by the Huns, Moslems, Vikings, Mongols, and the Ottoman Turks.

By the mid-15th century, Europe was only one of several great civilizations throughout the world. It was not the largest, the most powerful, the richest, or even the most technologically advanced. The ancient and sophisticated civilizations of China and India were matched by the growing power of the Islamic civilizations of the Safavids in Persia and the Ottoman Turks. In addition, the peoples of Africa had produced the prosperous civilization of the Songhai empire, and the Aztec and Inca peoples of the Americas had demonstrated that the civilizing process was not limited to the continents of Asia, Africa, and Europe.

The voyage of Columbus inspired many speculations concerning the natives of the New World. Shown are two conjectures sketched by a Nuremberg artist in 1493.

Nevertheless, it was the Europeans who sought out the rest of the world. It was they who first circumnavigated the globe and in the process mapped most of the world's continents. Between the 15th and 18th centuries, Europeans would explore and establish colonies on every continent with the exception of Antarctica.

THE CASE OF CHINA

For centuries before the rise of European civilization, the Chinese empire had a highly developed system of government which made possible Chinese advances in science and art. The Chinese were at least as skilled in navigation and in the construction of large ocean-going vessels as the Europeans. Between 1405 and 1433, the Chinese government sponsored seven major expeditions into the Indian Ocean and to the coast of East Africa, led by Cheng Ho, a court eunuch. At about the same time that Prince Henry of Portugal was making his first tentative efforts to sail down the west coast of Africa, the Chinese were sending out expeditions consisting of as many as 60 ships and over 25,000 men.

These enterprises clearly showed China's technological, logistic, and economic superiority over Europe in outfitting and launching a major naval expedition. Nevertheless, the Chinese did not seek to establish commercial bases, nor did these voyages lead to a permanent Chinese presence in the Indian Ocean.

Why, with this head start, did the Chinese fail to follow up on their discoveries? The answer lies in China's view of itself in relation to the rest of the world. The Chinese referred to their land as the "Middle Kingdom," a name that reflected their ethnocentric view of the world. The Chinese felt that the world outside their own boundaries had little to offer them; also, the Chinese did not have the zeal of later European explorers. Chinese trade goods, such as silk and pottery, were in high demand in the rest of the world, but the Chinese did not want any European products except gold and silver. The high cost of outfitting ocean-going expeditions was, in the view of the Chinese, simply not justified by any gain.

Moreover, the Chinese empire was governed by a rigid hierarchy with the emperor at the top. The ancient Chinese philosophy of Confucianism taught that each person had obligations to others above and below himself in the social scale. As children must obey their parents, taught Confucius, so must the subjects obey the ruler. Thus, when the emperor decided that the voyages of

Cheng Ho were to stop, they stopped. There were no individual tradespeople, freebooting explorers, or rival rulers to strike out on their own. Cheng Ho's voyages were condemned and his logs and reports on the expeditions were destroyed.

Three-masted caravels with square-rigged sails and jib sails were more seaworthy than earlier ships, and also carried more cargo. Shown is an artist's rendering of the Santa Maria.

THE NATURE OF EUROPE

In contrast to China, Europe was divided into entities that ranged in size from the tiny principalities of the Holy Roman Empire to countries the size of France or Poland. Yet this unique social and political structure encouraged a consistent and protracted policy of exploration and colonization.

In Europe, someone with an idea or a new way of doing things could shop around until he found a place that would give him necessary freedom and opportunity. Columbus, for example, peddled his ideas throughout Europe until he found the sympathetic ear of Isabella of Spain. If taxes or restrictions were too high in one country, merchants and makers of capital could relocate in another state more receptive to their interests.

Empires tend to be more rigid in their policies than small nations operating in a competitive environment. The merchant class in China was subordinate to the emperor and his bureaucracy of scholar-officials. In Europe, by contrast, the merchants—the bourgeoisie—replaced the feudal nobility as advisers to the monarch. European kings now depended on merchants and bankers for money, and hence, for advice. This kind of relationship, based on a mutual advantage, did not exist in China nor to any significant degree in the other non-European empires of that period. Thus, the competition between states that existed in Europe, as well as the close relationship between the rulers and the commercial interests of Europe, were factors that encouraged active exploration for new sources of wealth, trade, and markets.

Europe in the mid-15th century was also rediscovering the knowledge of classical times, including geography. This stimulated a new interest in cartography, or map-making, and better maps were produced to show the shorelines of European countries.

Further technological developments of the time included ship design and navigation. The narrow-hulled *caravels* with square sails, usually hung on three masts, proved to be remarkably stable for ocean-going voyages. Columbus' flagship, the *Santa Maria*, was a ship of this type. Another advantage of sailing ships over those that depended on oars was that fewer crew members were needed—thereby creating more room for cargo.

Europeans were among the first to understand and use to their advantage the world wind system. Thus Columbus began his voyage at the Canary Islands, where the prevailing winds blew west. To return home, he followed a northeast course until he caught the ocean winds that blew east.

The Chinese were the first seafarers to discover the use of the compass for finding directions, and compasses were in use in the Mediterranean by the 12th century. The European contribution was the discovery, first recorded by a Portuguese in 1514, that the needle of the compass did not point to true north. The adjustments resulting from this discovery vastly increased the accuracy of

Navigational tools such as the astrolabe, an improved compass, and better maps contributed to Europeans' successes in charting new courses on the open seas.

maps. Astrolabes, used to measure the altitude of sun or star, had been invented by the ancient Greeks and developed by astronomers in India, Persia, and Arabia during the 7th century. European navigators of the 15th century used the device to determine the latitude of a ship at sea.

REASONS FOR EXPLORATION

From the time of the Roman Empire, Europe had been supplied with silks, spices, and other luxury materials from the East. In the 13th century, Marco Polo had traveled to China when it was part of the Mongol Empire, which stretched from eastern Europe to the Pacific. Marco Polo's book about his travels raised European consciousness about China and its fabled wealth, and was an incentive for European exploration.

The rise of the Ottoman Turks cut off the direct land route from Europe to the Orient, and the European supply of Chinese goods and spices was controlled by Venetian merchants who had a monopoly granted by the Ottomans. The Venetians received the merchandise at cities such as Cairo and Constantinople and then transported them to the major European cities. Thus, countries like Portugal and Spain were put at a trade disadvantage. It was partly to break this trade monopoly that these two countries led the way in seeking new routes to the East.

In addition, both Spain and Portugal had a strong crusading tradition, which stemmed from the fact that they had driven the Islamic Arabs out of their countries. From the *Reconquista* came a zeal to protect and spread Christianity.

PORTUGUESE EXPLORATION

By the mid-14th century, the Portuguese had driven the Moors out of their part of the Iberian peninsula, and they were ready to turn their attention elsewhere. Spain was still completing its part in the *Reconquista*, a fact that gave Portugal an advantage in the race to acquire a maritime empire.

Across the Strait of Gibraltar was the North African city of Ceuta, one of the major entry ports for gold into Europe. In 1415, the Portuguese attacked and conquered Ceuta with the intent of establishing a base against the Moslems and dominating the trade routes. The Portuguese also hoped to make contact with Prester John, a legendary Christian ruler of fabulous wealth who was said to live in central Africa. To Portugal's surprise and consternation, Ceuta soon dried up as a staging point for bringing gold into Europe, and efforts to follow the gold trade by land to its source met stout opposition from the Moslem kingdom of Morocco.

THE ROLE OF HENRY THE NAVIGATOR

No person played so large a role in the early explorations as Prince Henry (1394–1460), third son of John I of Portugal. Henry, a veteran of the Ceuta campaign, learned there about the trade routes that stretched across the Sahara and brought the gold from the interior of Africa, where it was mined. Henry established a school at Sagres, in southwest Portugal, to draw together the information available on maritime exploration.

To Henry's school came mariners and scientists from all over Europe. They brought with them knowledge of instrument-making, ship design, astronomical observation, and the making of maps and charts. Henry's captains thus benefited from the best Europe had to offer in maritime skills. It was Henry's shipbuilders who developed the caravel.

Henry's original plan was to sail along the African coast to outflank the Moslem power and reach the source of the gold. A contemporary biographer of Henry the Navigator described his motives in exploration. The first was "a wish to know the land that lay beyond the isles of Canary and that Cape called Bojador." The second was that "if there chanced to be in those [undiscovered] lands some population of Christians . . . many kinds of merchandise might . . . find a ready market."[1] A third reason was to discover the power of the Moslem enemy; a fourth to find Prester John and enlist his support against the Moslems; yet another was to spread Christianity.

The initial task in rounding Africa was to round Cape Bojador to the south of Morocco. Beyond lay what mariners of the time called the "green sea of darkness."[2] The first of Henry's ships passed Bojador in 1434. As the explorers pushed down the coast, they established way stations, but efforts to move inland were halted by Europeans' vulnerability to subtropical diseases and the opposition of native populations.

SLAVERY

In 1441, south of Cape Bojador, the Portuguese obtained gold and some slaves. The slaves, on being transported to Portugal, were baptized as Christians and sold. In the next five years, nearly a thousand slaves were captured or bought from African chiefs along the coast. Because the trade was lucrative, Prince Henry ordered the establishment of a fort on an island opposite Cape

As a result of Portuguese activities in Africa, slavery became a prominent feature of New World colonization. Here, the introduction of slaves to the English colony of Jamestown is depicted.

Blanco. This was the first European trading post overseas.

Soon the Spanish were also visiting the African coast and African slaves became a familiar sight in Seville. Then the British, Dutch, and French joined the slave trade. It expanded further when the European nations established empires in the New World. There, slave labor was extensively used in mining for gold and silver, and on sugar plantations. It has been estimated that over 9 million Africans were taken as slaves between 1441 and 1870, wreaking havoc in both human lives and conditions in Africa during this time.

Slavery became an integral part of European exploration and colonization. In Lisbon, household slaves became a part of upper-class Portuguese life. A permanent slave market was established on the waterfront. More than 150,000 slaves were sold here before 1500.

---

[1] F. Roy Willis, *Western Civilization: An Urban Perspective* (Lexington, Mass.: D.C. Heath, 1973), p. 415.

[2] John R. Hale, *Age of Exploration* (New York: Time-Life Books, 1966), p. 21.

ROUNDING THE CAPE

As the Portuguese moved down the coast of Africa, it soon became their goal to try to round the continent to reach the fabled land of India, the source of spices. Success was attained by the voyage of Bartholomew Dias in 1487. He was forced to turn back by his crew after rounding the Cape, although the way to India was open. On returning home, Dias called the cape he had navigated the Cape of Storms. But King John I, optimistic about finding a sea route to India, renamed it the Cape of Good Hope.

To follow up the achievement, John's successor, Manuel I, chose Vasco da Gama. Da Gama set out in 1497 and rounded the Cape. Instead of crossing the Indian ocean, however, he sailed up the east coast of Africa. At the port of Malindi, he was fortunate in finding an Indian pilot willing to guide him to India. He landed at the city of Calicut on the west coast of India, where the sultan of the city welcomed him. Da Gama believed that the Hindu temples in Calicut were Christian ones. He saw in the Hindu goddesses representations of the Madonna.

On da Gama's return to Lisbon, Manuel exulted at the success of the voyage, which returned in profits many times the cost. Manuel took for himself the grandiloquent title of "Lord of the Conquest, Navigation, and Commerce of Ethiopia, Arabia, Persia, and India." His fellow monarch, Francis I of France, sneeringly referred to Manuel as "the grocer king."[3]

THE PORTUGUESE EMPIRE

It became clear that through the ports on the Malabar coast of west India flowed not only Indian goods, but also the products of all east Asia, including silks, spices, and gems. The Portuguese took advantage of the local hostilities between the sultans who ruled the ports. Europeans, throughout the history of their exploration and colonization, frequently played off one local ruler against another. Gradually, the Portuguese overcame the trade monopoly previously held in these ports by Arab traders.

The Portuguese had the good fortune to move into the Indian Ocean at a time when India was disunited. The Mongol rulers did not establish their rule over all of India until later in the 16th century.

Alfonso Albuquerque, the Portuguese Governor General in India, understood the importance of Portuguese sea power in maintaining their position. He wrote to his king:

• • • if once Portugal should suffer a reverse at sea, your Indian possessions have not power to hold out a day longer than the kings of the land choose to suffer it.[4]

In fact, even with their firepower at sea, it is unlikely that the Portuguese could have survived long without the sufferance of local rulers. To the sultans of India, a few white faces were a novelty, and the presence of a handful of ships had no great significance. Besides, the Europeans were forced to pay for their purchases with gold and silver bullion, for they had little else to offer Eastern merchants. (It was not until the 19th century, with the introduction of opium into China from India, that the balance of trade began to favor the Europeans.)

In 1509, the Portuguese defeated the Arab fleet, and in 1510 established a post in the city of Goa. It was from here that they were to rule their commercial empire in the East. They also built fortified bases at Aden on the Red Sea, Ormuz on the Persian Gulf, and on the east coast of Africa.

---

[3] Philip D. Curtin, *Cross-Cultural Trade in World History* (Cambridge University Press, 1984), p. 139.

[4] Carlo M. Cipolla, *Guns, Sails, and Empires* (New York: Random House, 1965), p. 138.

The Portuguese went further east, establishing posts in Malaya and the Molucca Islands—then known as the Spice Islands—thus gaining control of some of the most valuable spices at their source. From the Spice Islands, Portuguese sailors and Jesuit missionaries made contact with both China and Japan.

In 1500, on a voyage to India, the Portuguese captain Pedro Cabral was blown off course and was carried by trade winds across the Atlantic. Through this fortuitous accident, Brazil was claimed for Portugal. Because of the more profitable nature of its Asian empire, the Portuguese initially ignored Brazil. It was 30 years before Portugal made an effort to colonize Brazil. As a result the colony grew slowly. But as it became clear that the land had resources for mining and sugar plantations, it attracted more immigrants. By the 16th century, it became the most important of the Portuguese colonies, and remains to this day a center of Portuguese culture.

SPANISH EXPLORATION AND COLONIZATION

The Spanish had followed the development of Portuguese exploration with interest. Even though the Portuguese had proceeded in as secretive a manner as possible, it did not take Spain long after the completion of the *Reconquista* to begin its own overseas explorations. The Spanish too were interested in reaching the riches of the East.

DISCOVERY OF THE NEW WORLD

The popular belief that Christopher Columbus' achievement was in proving that the world was round is a false one. The shape of the globe was known by all educated Europeans of the late medieval period. Columbus merely took this idea to its logical conclusion and decided to try to reach China by sailing west. He made the idea seem more plausible by his underestimation of the size of the world and an overestimation of the

The commercial ventures of the Portuguese were centered in Africa, India, and the Far East, but they also staked a claim in the New World. A map dating from 1556 shows the coastline of Portuguese Brazil.

size of the Asian continent. To Columbus, the trip across the Atlantic to China and India would be a relatively short one.

Columbus proposed his plan to several of Europe's rulers, including John II of Portugal, Henry VII of England, and Charles VIII of France. All turned him down, in part because his demands for the journey were too ambitious. In addition to three ships and crews, Columbus wanted a noble title, viceroyalty over any new lands, and a ten percent share of all trade.

Ferdinand and Isabella of Spain finally granted Columbus' demands. Setting out with three ships from the port of Palos on August 3, 1492, Columbus headed for the Canary Islands. Leaving there after repairs and supplying, he sailed into the unknown on September 6. Little more than a month later, his crews mutinied. Columbus consulted his charts confidently, and gave his word to turn back if land were not sighted within three days. Two days later, at around 2 A.M. on October 12, the lookouts sighted coral cliffs in the light of a nearly full moon. Columbus

Columbus and his crews landing in the Bahamas. To the end of his life, Columbus believed he had discovered a series of islands east of Asia.

landed in what is today an island in the Bahamas. However, he believed that he had reached the Indies.

Over a series of three more voyages, Columbus discovered some more islands in the Caribbean, and the coasts of South and Central America. He died in 1506, still without understanding that he had reached a continent that was until then virtually unknown to Europeans.

In 1493, Spanish entry into the race for overseas dominions was recognized by the pope. In an amazing display of ethnocentricity, even for those times, the pope settled the territorial dispute between Spain and Portugal by dividing the world between them. Drawing a *Line of Demarcation* on the map, the pope decreed that territory east of it was Portuguese; that to the west the province of Spain. The following year, the *Treaty of Tordesillas* reaffirmed the papal division, resulting in Portugal's claim to Brazil after Cabral's later voyage.

Commenting on the papal Line of Demarcation, Francis I observed, "I should very much like to see the passage in Adam's will that divides the New World between my brothers the Emperor Charles V [who ruled Spain] and the King of Portugal."[5] Indeed, the Treaty of Tordesillas did not seriously hamper any nation from pursuing its own self-interest.

Many doubted from the start that Columbus had reached the Orient. The people that he met did not fit previous descriptions of Japanese, Chinese, or Indians—although the name ''Indians'' was ever after applied to the native peoples of the Americas. All speculation ended, however, in 1513, when Vasco de Balboa discovered the Pacific Ocean. That vast body of water, which in fact occupies nearly half the world's circumference, had to be crossed before the size of the world was truly known.

The achievement of circumnavigating the globe belongs to Ferdinand Magellan, a Portuguese explorer who organized an expedition for the king of Spain. Sailing on September 20, 1519, with five ships and 265 men, Magellan himself was killed in a fracas with native people in the Philippines. On September 7, 1522, after nearly three years, one of Magellan's ships returned to Spain

[5] John R. Hale, *Op. cit.*, p. 57.

A map of the mid-16th century reflects the discovery of the Pacific, the presence of cannibals in Brazil, and the disposition of territories among the European powers.

under the command of Juan Sebastian del Cano. A second ship made port later. Through their efforts, Magellan's men had roughly determined the true extent of the world.

CONQUISTADORES

The Spanish lost little time in colonizing their territories. Rumors of a large gold supply drew a force of Spaniards led by Hernando Cortez to Mexico. "We Spaniards," said the explorer, "suffer from a disease that only gold can cure."[6] In 1519, Cortez started toward the capital of the Aztec empire. As the Spaniards approached the city of Tenochtitlan, they were awed by its splendor. Cortez was to describe it to Charles V as the most beautiful city in the world. Bernal Diaz, one of Cortez' companions, wrote of "things never before seen or dreamed about," and reported, "Some of our soldiers asked if what we had seen was not a dream."[7] Cortez' admiration, however, did not keep him from destroying the city.

At the time Cortez saw it, Tenochtitlan was a city of about 300,000 people, about five times the size of London. Built on an island in a lake, the city was connected to the mainland by three causeways. Cortez was guided through the city by the emperor Montezuma:

• • • *We saw a multitude of boats upon the great lake, some coming with provisions, some going off loaded with merchandise . . . And we saw the terraced houses, and along the causeways other towers and chapels that looked like fortresses . . . . We turned our eyes to the great market-place and the host of people down there who were buying and selling: the hum and the murmur of their voices could have been heard for more than a league. And among us were soldiers who*

An Aztec drawing shows Cortez accepting the surrender of the Aztec king while seated on the king's throne.

had been in many parts of the world, at Constantinople . . . and at Rome; and they all said they had never seen a market so well ordered, so large, and so crowded with people.[8]

Within three years, Mexico was conquered and Tenochtitlan destroyed. How could a relative handful of Spaniards destroy a powerful and sophisticated empire of more than a million people? The question has never been fully answered. We know that the Spanish were at the time the premier fighters of Europe, relentless and ferocious. By an amazing coincidence, the Aztec religious annals had predicted the arrival of white people who would conquer at just this time. The Aztecs had seen neither white men nor horses before, and their will to resist was sapped by the belief that the Spaniards were gods. Of course, the Spanish also had the advantage of their firearms, further strengthening the Aztec belief that they were some sort of divine beings.

There was initially a brief period of Aztec

[6] *Ibid.*, p. 105.

[7] Nigel Davies, *The Ancient Kingdoms of Mexico* (Hammondsworth, England: Penguin Books, 1983), p. 199.

[8] F. Roy Willis, *Op. cit.*, p. 426.

EUROPEAN COLONIZATION IN THE LATE 17TH CENTURY

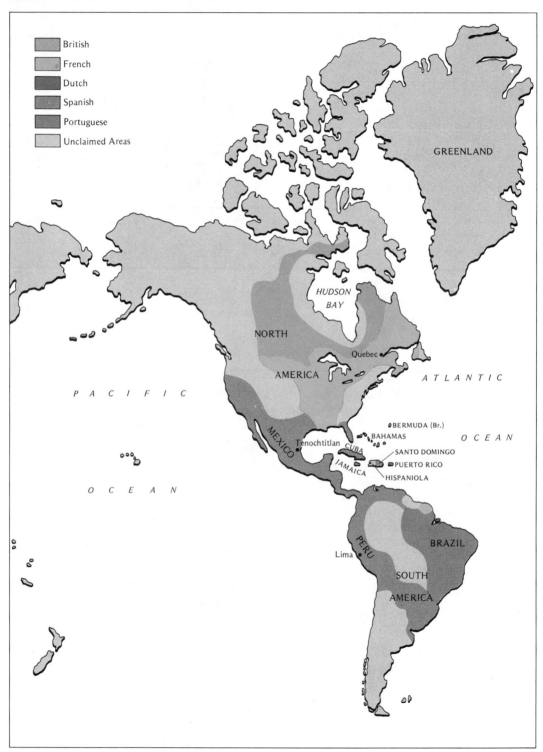

British
French
Dutch
Spanish
Portuguese
Unclaimed Areas

GREENLAND

HUDSON BAY

NORTH

AMERICA

Quebec

PACIFIC

ATLANTIC

BERMUDA (Br.)

BAHAMAS

MEXICO

Tenochtitlan   CUBA

JAMAICA

SANTO DOMINGO

PUERTO RICO

HISPANIOLA

OCEAN

OCEAN

BRAZIL

PERU

Lima

SOUTH

AMERICA

Why did European colonists penetrate to the interior of the American continent, but generally remain in the coastal areas of Africa and Asia?

ICELAND

BRITISH
ISLES

BALTIC SEA

NETHERLANDS

EUROPE

FRANCE

PORTUGAL

SPAIN

AZORES
(Port.)

MADEIRA
IS. (Port.)

CANARY
IS. (Spain)

CAPE
VERDE
IS.
(Port.)

• Cape Bojador

GAMBIA

Cape
Coast
Castle
(Br.)

ANGOLA

Mombasa

Mozambique •

MADAGASCAR

CAPE OF
GOOD HOPE

RUSSIA

A S I A

S I B E R I A

CHINA

JAPAN

PERSIA

• Ormuz

ARABIA

Aden •

INDIA

Bombay (Br.)
Goa (Port.)
Calicut
Cochin (Dutch)

BENGAL

• Calcutta

Madras
(Br.)
Pondicherry
(Fr.)

CEYLON
(Dutch)

Macao
(Port.)

SIAM

PHILIPPINE IS.
(Spain)

SUMATRA

JAVA

BORNEO

CELEBES

SPICE IS.

NEW GUINEA

I N D I A N

O C E A N

AUSTRALIA

TASMANIA

73

The conquistadore Francisco Pizarro, an illegimate son of a poor Spanish noble, explored the Andes, conquered Peru, and founded the city of Lima.

New World had never been exposed to most European diseases, and thus had no immunities to malaria, yellow fever, measles, influenza, and many other afflictions. The pre-Columbian population of 25 million in Mexico dropped to less than one million in the span of 75 years. There is some evidence to indicate that these epidemics spread to the North American Indians with just as devastating an effect, leading the first European colonists from Florida northward to believe they had discovered an almost empty land that was theirs for the taking.

SPANISH EMPIRE

Both Spain and Portugal depended on private enterprise in the early years of their empires. In the colonies of New Spain and Peru, for example, the government established the *encomienda* system of land tenure. The *conquistadores* acquired immense tracts of land and, in effect, became medieval lords of the manor. The Indians were forced to work the soil, and like the medieval serfs, they could not be removed from it. For two days a week they were permitted to work their own parcels of land. Cortez himself claimed 25,000 square miles of Mexico, and complete power over the services of 100,000 Indians.

With time, the king of Spain assumed control of this colonial empire. The Council of the Indies, established by Charles V in 1524, ran things from Spain, while in the colonies officials known variously as viceroys, governors, or captains general had the final say.

Spanish culture and religion not only thrived in the New World; they completely dominated what little remained of native culture. Both sword and plague, carried to the new land by the *conquistadores*, did their work well. By 1607 when the English founded their first successful colony at Jamestown, Virginia, the Spanish had already established universities in Mexico City and Lima, Peru. Cathedrals, churches, and missions sprouted everywhere, from Cape Horn to California. Not until the early

resistance when the Spanish destroyed several ancient temples. Cortez lost about one-third of his force during these hostilities. He returned to Tenochtitlan in 1521, lay siege to the city, and destroyed it block by block. Using the Aztecs as slave labor, he rebuilt the city as the center of the Spanish colony he had established. Today it is Mexico City.

In the 1530s, the Inca empire centered in Peru was conquered by Spanish *conquistadores* under the leadership of Francisco Pizarro. Pizarro had profited by Cortez' experience with the Aztecs, learning that in a society with a god-king at its head, the chopping off of that head leaves the people in a state of confusion, unable to take effective action. Pizarro captured and killed Atahualpa, the leader of the Incas.

The Spanish brought with them in their bodies, on their horses, livestock, and even the rats aboard ship, the most devastating weapon of all—disease. The peoples of the

19th century did Spanish colonial dominance of the Americas come to an end. And it was not until the end of the 19th century that Spain lost Cuba and the Philippines. One needs only to go as far as the southwestern United States to understand the pervasive influence of Spanish culture even today.

DUTCH EXPLORATION AND COLONIZATION When the Dutch Republic proclaimed its independence from Spain, its society entered a new dynamic phase. The Dutch began to assert their commercial and economic strength. Dutch traders were backed by a government that worked closely with its commercial interests.

The Netherlands had been an important shipbuilding power since the 15th century. The Dutch invented a new kind of ship known as the *flyboat* which had a shallow draft and a large cargo area. The flyboat was able to navigate shallow coastal waters as easily as it took to the high seas. Dutch flyboats took most of the Baltic Sea trade from the Hanseatic League, and soon commanded most of Europe's coastal trade as well. After the Portuguese brought their rich cargoes from the East to Lisbon, Dutch shippers picked up the goods and carried them to the rest of Europe.

Spain and Portugal were united under one rule in 1580. The Spanish king then closed the port of Lisbon to the Dutch. This was a serious blow to a country that depended heavily on trade. In the flush of independence and with the aim of protecting their trade, the Dutch went after the Portuguese overseas posts.

In 1595, the Dutch sent the first of their expeditions to the Spice Islands. In 1602, the Dutch East India Company was formed, merging the rival Dutch companies under government authority to control the spice trade in the East Indies.

The Dutch destroyed the Portuguese fleet

In his ship the Half Moon, Henry Hudson explored the river named after him and claimed its valley for the Dutch.

in the East Indies and drove the Portuguese from the area. They then set about trying to control the political and economic affairs of the archipelago of Malaya, thus establishing a territorial empire rather than just a commercial one. The Dutch Empire in the East Indies was to last until the middle of the 20th century.

In addition, the Dutch established themselves on the Indian coast and on the island of Ceylon. In the middle of the 17th century, they formed a colony at the southern tip of Africa, the Cape of Good Hope. The Cape Colony was the beginning of today's South Africa. Dutch explorers were the first Europeans to see Australia. Later, the British would supplant the Dutch in India, South Africa, and Australia.

The Dutch were also interested in the New World. In 1609, Henry Hudson, an English captain in the service of Holland, claimed the area around the Hudson River valley for the Dutch. Settlers arrived from Holland to colonize the area. However, in 1664, the English captured the Dutch holdings there, which included the city of New Amsterdam, renamed New York.

FRENCH EXPLORATION

France took little part in the early voyages of discovery. French exploration of the St. Lawrence River began in 1524 but did not result in permanent settlements in the New World until 1608, when Samuel de Champlain established the city of Quebec. Few colonists followed, partly because the French government barred religious dissenters from seeking a refuge there. After 1660, Louis XIV encouraged a policy of mercantilism that gave a boost to the French Canadian settlements (Chapter 5). However, the greater sea power and larger colonial population of the English eventually doomed France's foothold in Canada.

In the 17th century, French explorers charted and claimed the areas surrounding the Great Lakes and the Mississippi River. But the government made little attempt to colonize this vast area, known as Louisiana. In 1803, Napoleon I sold it cheaply to the fledgling government of the United States.

In 1664, France began to establish a network of trading posts in India. But during the Seven Years' War (Chapter 5), the French lost these possessions as well as Canada.

The French explorers Jolliet and Marquette discovered a route to the upper Mississippi in 1673. A decade later, La Salle reached the mouth of the river and claimed the surrounding territory for France.

THE ENGLISH COLONIES

The voyages of John Cabot and his son Sebastian along the North American coast in 1497–98 formed the basis for the British claim to North America. The English concentrated their efforts on colonization and exploitation, rather than on discovery.

Like the Dutch, English entrepreneurs were free of direct government control, for they raised their capital from private sources. English merchants, backed by royal charter, were the first to make extensive use of joint-stock companies to control trade in distant areas. The most important of these was the British East India Company, founded in 1600. At first, it concentrated its efforts on the Spice Islands, but soon established bases in India that would later form the foundation for Britain's empire there.

Joint stock companies similar to the East India Company backed the first successful English colony in the New World—at Jamestown, Virginia, in 1607—and colonies in the Caribbean islands of the West Indies, Bermuda, and the Bahamas. Before long, the English established additional colonies on the mainland. The English monarchy did not attempt to establish a uniform government over its New World colonies. Instead, they were encouraged to develop their own forms of self-government, a policy that would later help them to revolt against Britain.

Another reason for the notable success of the English colonies was the political and religious conflict that disturbed England in the 17th century. By fleeing to America, dissenters found refuge by forming their own settlements, or by settling in colonies that allowed a greater measure of religious toleration than the home country. Thus, the English colonies drew large numbers of immigrants who contributed their skills and industry to the economic success of their new homeland.

From their colonies in South America, the Spanish established regular trade routes across the Pacific, but it was not until the

NOVA BRITANNIA.

OFFERING MOST

Excellent fruites by Planting in
VIRGINIA.

Exciting all such as be well affected
to further the same.

LONDON
Printed for SAMVEL MACHAM, and are to be fold at
his Shop in Pauls Church-yard, at the
Signe of the Bul-head.
1 6 0 9.

SIGNIFICANCE OF THE EXPLORATIONS

The opening of new ocean trade routes marked a decisive shift in the center of European trade, from the Mediterranean to the Atlantic. With the economic growth of Spain, Portugal, England, Holland, and France came the decline of Italy. The countries of central Europe, with little or no access to the sea routes, were also at an economic disadvantage.

During its period of prosperity, Holland became Europe's largest importer of spices, sugar, porcelain, and decorative beads. The Dutch spent their profits on middle-class pleasures—fabrics, furniture, food, and household goods. In this atmosphere of economic prosperity, they could afford to be patrons of the arts as well (Chapter 8).

NEW PRODUCTS

The extension of trade also brought novel foods and luxury foods to Europe. Europeans had discovered the joys of consuming sugar instead of the traditional sweetener, honey, during the Crusader era. Much of the impetus behind the slave trade lay in the need for workers on the sugar plantations of the Spanish colonies in the New World.

Coffee, long known to the Arabs, who may have imported it from Africa, became a popular beverage in Europe during the 17th century. With its growing popularity, it was planted in the Dutch East Indies, the Caribbean, and South America. A French naval officer, Gabriel de Clieu, is said to have shared his ration of water on the Atlantic voyage with a coffee plant he had obtained from Louis XV's greenhouse in Paris. This plant then took root in the French colony of Martinique, and became the source of a majority of the coffee plants later grown in the Americas. Throughout Europe, coffeehouses, or "cafes," became immensely popular gathering places.

Similarly, the habit of smoking tobacco was introduced into Europe by Sir Walter Raleigh, who had learned it from the Indians

late 18th century that an English navigator, using new methods of measuring distance at sea, completed most of the mapping of the Pacific. Captain James Cook located many new Pacific islands, including Hawaii, and mapped New Zealand and the east coast of Australia. Cook's voyages proved that there was no large land mass in the southern hemisphere to "balance" the known continents in the northern hemisphere as many European geographers had theorized. His discoveries completed the task of determining the size of the world and mapping in a general way all of the inhabited continents.

of Virginia. At first, tobacco was believed to possess healing powers. Its popularity endured despite the condemnation of clergy and King James I. The economic importance of the tobacco crop to the English colonies of the New World was permanent.

THE COMMERCIAL REVOLUTION

During the period between 1500 and 1700, Europe saw a *commercial revolution* resulting from the overseas expansion of trade. With the exception of Spain and Portugal, most of the new powers gained long-term advantages from the commercial revolution.

The skill of the Dutch and English sailors, combined with the economic policies of their governments, led to the growth of *capitalism* as a means of organizing large business enterprises. Private capital, as we have seen, was the basis of the companies that exploited the wealth and trade of the lands that Europeans had discovered. Trading companies were formed by selling shares to a large number of investors, and these shares could be bought and sold on the open market. This form of business organization was later applied to other business enterprises, such as mining and factories. The commercial success of European exploration and colonization stimulated the development that made Europe the dominant force in the world until the 20th century.

In contrast, the lead in world exploration gained by Portugal and Spain can today be seen as beginning a long period of decline for those nations. The Portuguese had to rely on Asian merchants as middlemen, since they were never able to gain direct access to the source of the spices. The Portuguese empire also had other inherent weaknesses. The spice trade was a crown monopoly, and the kings of Portugal were unwilling to plow profits back into the enterprise so that it could be maintained and expanded. From 1580 to 1640, Spain and Portugal were united under one king. Since that king was Spanish, Portuguese interests tended to be ignored, thereby leaving their empire open to encroachment by the Dutch and eventually the English. The first English circumnavigator of the globe, Sir Francis Drake, coolly sailed through areas supposedly dominated by the Spanish and Portuguese from 1577 to 1580, picking up a rich cargo on his way back to England.

From 1530 until the early 17th century, Spain had a virtual monopoly on the steadily increasing supply of gold and silver coming from the New World, and yet gained little benefit from this great wealth. Spain lacked a viable middle class to manage its newfound wealth, nor did it have a strong agricultural base. As a consequence, Spain was unable to meet the needs of its colonists for food or industrial goods.

Both Charles V and Philip II overestimated the amount of bullion available from the New World. In order to finance foreign adventures such as the building of the Armada and the war in the Netherlands, Philip II had to borrow vast sums from foreign bankers which he was never able to fully repay. What gold and silver that did arrive in Spain did not stay there long enough to do any good. It moved on immediately to the banking centers of Europe, or to pay the Spanish army in the Netherlands.

There was an inflationary rise in prices in Europe in the 16th century due to the circulation of large amounts of gold and silver. The inflation rate went up 600 percent over the hundred-year period. This was especially damaging to the Spanish peasant, who found that the prices for his agricultural products did not rise at the same rate as the goods he needed to buy on the open market. When the treasure shipments fell off in the early 17th century, the Spanish economy was unable to adjust. The result was a lengthy depression from which Spain never fully recovered.

SUMMARY

The European voyages of discovery from the 15th to the 17th centuries gave Europe an advantage in trade that made it a dominant world force. Privately financed joint-stock companies in Holland and England reaped much of the benefit of the development in trade, giving rise to the capitalistic system. The profits gained from trade and colonization enterprises provided much of the capital for the Industrial Revolution that began in the 18th century.

The advantage that England, Holland, and other countries of Europe's Atlantic coast gained was matched by a decline in importance of the Mediterranean nations. Although Spain and Portugal established overseas empires, they squandered the wealth brought by trade and exploitation, and entered a long period of decline.

QUESTIONS

1 What role did technological advances play in the success of Europeans during the era of discovery and colonization? What historical forces and circumstances contributed to the Europeans' ascendancy?

2 What prevented the Chinese from expanding outward in the same manner as the Europeans?

3 Compare the colonial empire of Spain and the predominantly commercial empires of Portugal and the Netherlands.

4 How did the colonial policies of England and France differ? Why was England more successful than France in establishing and keeping her colonies in the New World?

5 Identify the following terms: reconquista, Ceuta, Treaty of Tordesillas, encomienda, flyboat, Commercial Revolution.

BIBLIOGRAPHY

DAVIS, DAVID BRIAN. *Slavery and Human Progress*. New York: Oxford University Press, 1984. *A scholarly work by one of the foremost historians of the institution of slavery. The title refers to the fact that slavery was once considered a crucial factor in the progress of Western civilization.*

DEL CASTILLO, BERNAL DIAZ. *The Discovery and Conquest of Mexico*, trans. A. P. Maudslay. New York: Farrar, Straus, 1956. *An eyewitness account of the activities of the conquistadores in the New World.*

ELLIOTT, J. H. *The Old World and the New: 1492–1650*. London: Cambridge University Press, 1970. *Mr. Elliott analyses the intellectual, social, political, and economic impact of the Americas upon Europe.*

MORISON, SAMUEL ELIOT. *Admiral of the Ocean Sea: A Life of Christopher Columbus*. Boston: Little, Brown, 1942. *Still the best biography of Christopher Columbus.*

PARRY, J. H. *The Age of Reconnaissance: Discovery, Exploration, and Settlement, 1450–1650*. Los Angeles: University of California Press, 1982. *A lively and scholarly chronicle of two crucial centuries in the history of Western civilization.*

POLO, MARCO. *The Travels of Marco Polo*. New York: Orion Press, 1958. *The single most important book in stimulating European curiosity about the world beyond Europe's borders.*

The Nation State: Contrasting Systems

● *To know how to dissimulate is the knowledge of kings.*

Not least among the qualities in a great King is a capacity to permit his ministers to serve him.
CARDINAL RICHELIEU

● *I have loved war too much; do not copy me in that nor in my extravagance. Relieve your people as soon as you can, and do what I have been too unlucky to do.*
LOUIS XIV

● *A wise Tory and a wise Whig, I believe, will agree. Their principles are the same, though their modes of thinking are different.*
SAMUEL JOHNSON

● *The sovereign is absolute; for, in a state whose expanse is so vast, there can be no other appropriate authority except that which is concentrated in him.*
CATHERINE THE GREAT

● *Kings are not only God's Lieutenants upon earth, and sit upon God's throne, but even by God himself they are called Gods.*
JAMES I

5

● *Princes thus act as ministers of God and his lieutenants on Earth. It is through them that he rules. . . . This is why we have seen that the royal throne is not the throne of a man, but the throne of God himself.*

JACQUES BOSSUET

The Age of Louis XIV

The political theory of the *divine right of kings* was epitomized by the reign of King Louis XIV, the third member of the Bourbon dynasty to succeed to the throne of France. This theory, expounded by such theorists as Bishop Jacques Bossuet, claimed that a king's power derived from God. Divine right gave a monarch complete authority over his subjects and was the prevalent justification for royal power in 17th-century Europe.

During the 72 years of Louis' rule (1643–1715) the power of the French throne became nearly absolute. The king and his ministers used the theory of the divine right of kings to justify the extension of royal power and authority—to the point where it was as nearly as possible total power over their 18 million subjects. Louis XIV is reported to have said, "*L'etat, c'est moi*" (I am the state), and indeed he was.

DIVISIONS OF FRENCH SOCIETY In early modern times, the powers that rivaled the king were essentially the other key institutions within the society—the nobility, the army, the church, and the rising merchant class, also known as the *bourgeoisie*.

THE NOBILITY

In France, the nobility's power derived partly from their authority as the landowners who ruled the vast peasantry. Over the peasants who lived on his land, the noble had nearly total authority: he determined their income, he served as judge in their disputes, and he held them to their numerous feudal obligations. These obligations included keeping the roads of the state in good repair, acting as servants to the noble family, paying taxes, giving 10 percent of their earnings to the church, and a variety of other duties.

French peasants had no way to resist their landlord's power, for they lacked the means to rebel. They were forbidden to keep arms of any kind. Also, since they lived in small villages, over scattered separate estates, it was next to impossible for them to meet and organize themselves. (When revolution eventually came to France a century later, it began with the urban population, and only later spread to the countryside.)

In the 17th century, the power of the nobility was beginning to decline. One factor in this decline was that noble estates had become smaller over the years, and the nobility relatively poorer. By Louis XIV's time, there

82

The peasants of France had few rights but many responsibilities. They bore the financial burden of the government, for the nobility and clergy were exempt from taxation.

were as many as 300,000 nobles in a total population of 18–20 million—but many of them had little income.

THE ARMY

Another factor that contributed to the decline of the nobility was the rise of the national army. One traditional source of the nobles' power in France had been their feudal military role. Since medieval times, nobles had had their own armies and could fight wars for—or against—the king. But the introduction in the late 15th century of a national army conscripted and paid by the king had begun to erode this source of noble power. The new national army was controlled by and loyal to the French king. The officers in the army were nobles, but they derived their power, glory, and income from the royal treasury.

Louis XIV did much to further tighten royal control of the army. His secretary of state for war, Michel le Tellier, and his son, the Marquis de Louvois, introduced for the first time a regular, pyramid-like chain of command. At the top was the secretary of war, a servant of the king. Louis and his ministers also introduced a regular system of troop inspection to insure that discipline was kept.

As the king harnessed the power of the army, he also worked to increase its size and strength. He raised the number of troops from 100,000 to 400,000, and enlisted the services of renowned experts in such fields as fortification and topography. The forts built during the reign of Louis XIV were not surpassed until the 20th century.

This newly reorganized and fortified army was to play a central role in the consolidation of power behind the French throne.

THE ROMAN CATHOLIC CHURCH

Another source of power that had long rivaled the king was the Roman Catholic Church. The Church controlled the spiritual allegiance of nearly all French subjects. But the authority of the Catholic Church had been weakened by the effects of the Protestant Reformation. The French Catholic Church became increasingly independent from Rome, and the Church relied on the power of the French monarchy to preserve Catholicism in France.

As a result, over the years prior to the accession of Louis XIV, the French court came to control the appointment of high Church officials in France. The careers of the two cardinals prominent in 17th-century French history—Richelieu and Mazarin—illustrate this power. Richelieu became a cardinal because his noble family had inherited the right to make the appointment; Mazarin had in turn acquired his cardinal's hat from the king through Richelieu's intercession. Although the Catholic Church retained power over the spiritual lives of the French people, its power was in part dependent on the throne.

THE BOURGEOISIE

The *bourgeoisie*, or merchant class, was another rival to royal power. The growth of trade and industry had made many bourgeois wealthy. This new wealth might have enabled them to form a rival base of power.

83

However, the bourgeoisie had been co-opted. Louis XIV had given many positions of power in his government to members of the middle class, the effect of which was to make them loyal to the throne.

All of these factors contributed to the nearly absolute authority which Louis XIV held over the state which he governed. Moreover, the claim of the authority of divine right clinched the monarch's rationale for his royal rule.

LOUIS THE KING During the same years in which Louis XIV extended royal power in France, England experienced a civil war and revolution (Chapter 7), which led to the development of constitutionalism and to the lessening of royal power in that country. The reasons for these contrasting developments are complex, and raise the question of "whether the times make the man or the man makes the times"—that is, the question of the role individuals play in history. Although different traditions, cultures, and political, economic, and social systems were involved, the determination, ability, and quest for glory of Louis XIV were certainly important factors in determining the course France would take in the 17th century.

ACCESSION OF LOUIS XIV

The way to Louis XIV's rise to power was cleared by two men dedicated to serving the French state, Cardinal Richelieu and Cardinal Mazarin. The extension of royal authority in France had already begun under the leadership of Cardinal Richelieu. Richelieu, as we have seen, had been the power behind the throne during the reign of the weak and indifferent Louis XIII. He remained the chief minister of France until his death in 1642, and his success at reducing the power of the French nobility contributed to the power of Louis XIII's successor. In addition, France's involvement in the Thirty Years' War made it the strongest power in Europe.

In 1643, Louis XIV succeeded his father, Louis XIII, to the throne. He was only five years old at the time, and during his youth, power was delegated to his mother, the Regent Queen Anne of Austria, a member of the Hapsburg family. Anne, in turn, gave authority to Cardinal Mazarin, whom it is said she loved. Mazarin, of Italian descent, was never a priest; he received his church appointment as cardinal from the French throne.

Mazarin not only served as chief minister to the young king, but also supervised his education. The schooling Louis received under Mazarin's direction emphasized the role and duties of monarchy. One of his schoolboy assignments was to write repeatedly the line, "Homage is due to kings. They do what they please."[1] Louis learned this lesson well.

THE FRONDES

Widespread discontent with the extension of royal power under Richelieu and Mazarin, and with the increase in taxes which had resulted from France's participation in the Thirty Years' War, led to two revolutions in France. These were known as the *Frondes*, named after a child's game of stone throwing. Nobles, bourgeoisie, and Paris workers joined in the protests. Both the first Fronde, which began in 1648 when Louis was just ten, and the second Fronde, which began in 1650, started when barricades were erected in the streets of Paris and fighting broke out.

The Frondes ended in failure, however, primarily because the various groups which had been united in their discontent could not agree about their goals. The nobles and the bourgeoisie each wanted more power—but each group wanted it at the expense of the other. The bourgeoisie and the city workers wanted the nobles to share the tax load

---

[1] Maurice Ashley, *Louis XIV and the Greatness of France* (New York: The Free Press, 1967), p. 11.

While still a youth, Louis XIV returned to Paris in triumph after the failure of the second Fronde.

and a few wanted to overthrow the monarchy altogether.

Aristocratic fears of the potential power of the Paris mob led to the collapse of the second Fronde and the restoration of royal authority. When Louis XIV reentered Paris at the end of the second Fronde, he struck a regal pose, although only 14, and was greeted by the assembled crowd with cheers of "*Vive le roi!*" (Long live the king!).

This failed attempt at revolution only intensified royal power, and served to convince the young king of the need to control the nobility. Throughout his reign, Louis XIV withheld from the nobles all positions of authority and by the end of his life had virtually eliminated their power. He relied instead on the bourgeoisie, and gave them most of the political appointments.

THE COURT OF LOUIS XIV

One of the strategies Louis XIV used in the campaign to consolidate his power was to move the royal residence from Paris to Versailles, a sleepy village a few miles outside the capital city. There the king was no longer vulnerable to the insurrections of the Paris mobs. To the new court, he invited thousands of nobles to live or visit. Under his watchful eye, they were distracted by the glory and the amusements of court life and kept from causing any real political trouble.

The Palace of Versailles. The palace at Versailles was the most fabulous of its era, and perhaps of any other. Designed and constructed under Louis XIV's guidance, the new royal palaces housed the entire court— the king and his family, the royal ministers, nobles, servants, entertainers, artists, and

85

As this portrait demonstrates, Louis XIV knew how to act the part of a divine-right monarch.

writers. Ten thousand people resided there at any given time.

The palace architecture, the work of Louis Le Vau and Jules Hardouin Mansart, became the model for all Europe. The architecture of Peter the Great's city of St. Petersburg and of Schönbrunn Palace in Vienna imitated that of Versailles. The formal gardens surrounding the palace included 1200 orange trees. The gardens' many fountains contained 1400 jets that spouted water from canals constructed to redirect the flow of the Eure River. It is said that thousands of French workers died from marsh fever to make possible the flowing fountains.

Throughout the terraces and gardens were marble statues from all of Europe. Within, the palace was decorated with the finest tapestries and priceless paintings and furniture; elegant wood carvings and ornate silver pieces were designed and acquired to fill the thousands of rooms.

Louis XIV's palace at Versailles symbolized the splendor of the French monarchy. It also had another purpose: by attracting French nobles to live at his court, Louis XIV prevented them from building rival power bases elsewhere.

The main palace, whose facade is over one-fourth of a mile long, contains the Hall of Mirrors—a room 200 feet long decorated on one side with 17 costly Venetian mirrors, each 30 feet high. It is estimated that the construction and furnishing of the Palace of Versailles cost the French people nearly half a billion dollars. Versailles illustrated dramatically the power and the glory of the French monarchy.

Life at the Court. Life at the court of Louis XIV was splendid and luxurious. The style of living that evolved there set standards of etiquette, taste, and protocol for all of Europe. Every aspect of life was governed by an intricate system of manners and every moment of the king's day was attended by elaborate ceremonial. Even Louis' arising from bed was an important public spectacle, at which it was considered a great privilege to participate in even so small a way as helping the king to put on his shirt.

Louis worked on the affairs of state for eight to ten hours a day, but in his free time joined his many guests at sumptuous feasts, elaborate balls, hunts, tournaments, operas, and theatrical performances. The other residents whiled away the days at various pursuits; among the most popular was gambling. On one occasion, one of the king's ministers lost and won four million francs (ten million dollars) in a single evening.

Patron of the Arts. During the reign of Louis XIV, the French became the cultural as well as the political leaders of Europe. Louis loved a good show, and his years on the throne marked the great era of classical French theatre. Pierre Corneille (1606–1684) and Jean Racine (1639–1699) wrote stark, intense tragedies that are still regarded as among the great challenges for aspiring French actors and actresses. Molière (pen name of Jean Baptiste Coquelin, 1622–1678) produced timeless comedies that satirize snobs and hypocrites of all sorts. Molière's plays—Louis's personal favorites—are still performed and enjoyed today.

Louis XIV's favorite playwright, Molière, in costume. The comedies of Molière were part of the entertainment offered at Louis' court at Versailles.

The court passion for theatrical productions also led to the first flowering of French opera, in the works of Jean Baptiste Lully (1632–1687) and Jean Philippe Rameau (1683–1764), and to the birth of ballet. The king was so fond of the ballet that he often danced in productions himself and established the first permanent ballet school.

Under Louis' guidance, the French language also reached new heights of refinement. The French Academy, a group of 40 specially selected men of letters, was directed to produce a national dictionary that established proper usage for all words and expressions in the language. French soon became the tongue spoken in cultured and diplomatic circles all over Europe.

Louis was the foremost patron of the arts in Europe, bringing to the court at Versailles painters, architects and inventors, musicians and poets, composers and playwrights—all of whom he subsidized at great cost.

"The Sun King." Louis' nickname was "the Sun King" and his emblem was the sun. Both were fitting choices. Just as the planets revolve around the sun, so did everything at Versailles center around Louis. All seemed calculated to add to his glory, and reflected his childhood lesson that kings do as they please.

Louis fathered at least eleven children. All of his sons he named Louis, after himself. Although seven of these were the sons and daughters of his first wife, the Spanish princess Maria Theresa, the rest were the offspring of his several mistresses. Louis forced his mistresses to pay calls on the queen in order to create the appearance of a happy family. Two of these women ended their days in convents after the king had tired of them. However, on the death of Maria Theresa, Louis secretly married the last of his mistresses, Madame de Maintenon. The two were close companions to the end of his life and, it is said, he remained faithful to her.

DOMESTIC POLICY OF LOUIS XIV

The luxurious life enjoyed by the king, his wives and mistresses, and the thousands at court cost untold millions of francs. To pay for it all, the crown depended on taxes collected from the peasantry and on the profits to the state which resulted from the economic policy of mercantilism.

TAX POLICY

The system of taxation in France, one of the sources of royal wealth, had three major flaws. The first was the inequitable distribution of the tax load. The primary taxes were the *taille* and the *gabelle*. The *taille* was a tax levied on either property or income, depending on the province. The *gabelle* was a tax on salt, a necessity not only to add taste, but essential to preservation of meat. There were indirect taxes as well, mostly associated with trade—import, export, and custom duties. But the nobility, the clergy, and many government officials were exempt from most taxes. The burden of taxation thus fell upon the peasantry, who represented as much as 90-95 percent of the population, but who were the least able to pay. Thus the tax system of France served as a burden to the peasantry and as a source of privilege to the upper classes.

The second flaw in the French tax system lay in the method by which taxes were collected. This was a procedure known as *tax farming*. After taxes were levied on a district, the would-be tax collectors, called tax farmers, bid on the right to collect the taxes from the district. The winner, the highest bidder, owed the government the amount of his bid; at the same time, he had royal authority, backed up by the powers of the French army, to extract from the peasantry as much as he could collect. He then pocketed the difference. This system of tax farming created private wealth, but impoverished the peasantry. It also deprived the royal treasury of considerable income. In 1661, 25 percent of the taxes collected went into private pockets rather than into the royal treasury.

A third flaw in the tax system in France at the time of Louis XIV was inconsistency. There were great regional variations in the taxes and in the extent to which tax collection was enforced. This type of regionalism was prevalent in France until the French Revolution of the 18th century, and did much to weaken the state.

Despite the defects of the system, neither Louis nor any of his ministers was willing to propose reform, for to do so would outrage both those who depended on the collection system as a source of private wealth and, more importantly, the nobles who enjoyed their privileged exempt status.

In order to attempt to keep pace with the numerous expenses that resulted from Louis' lavish life-style and numerous wars, taxes were simply raised. During the reign of Louis XIV they nearly doubled: in 1661 the government collected $212 million; in 1715, $380 million. Yet royal indebtedness continued to increase. One of the principal causes of the revolution that came to France in 1789 was the tax system. The failure to reform it eventually brought down the Bourbon dynasty.

MERCANTILISM

Instead of tax reform, Louis XIV's answer to France's economic problems was the policy of *mercantilism*.

In order to achieve a favorable balance of trade, the theory of mercantilism advocated state intervention to create a self-sufficient economy that exported more than it imported. Mercantilists promote such measures as state stimulation of industrial growth and state efforts to regulate foreign trade to achieve this goal. Thus, the mercantile system conformed to and extended to the economic realm the power of Louis XIV. Mercantilism was closely associated with the concept of *bullionism*, that is, the theory that the wealth of a state is measured by its supply of bullion—gold and silver. Lacking gold and silver mines, France's source of bullion was a favorable balance of trade, which is achieved by exporting more than one imports.

Colbert. The architect of French mercantilism was Jean Baptiste Colbert (1619–1683), a financial expert of bourgeois origins who had gained the attention of Mazarin and was appointed Louis's Controller-General of Finance. Although Colbert controlled royal finance, he did not acquire the power which had been held by Richelieu and Mazarin. Mazarin had once advised the young king Louis that he would do best to serve as his own chief minister. When the cardinal died in 1661, Louis took his mentor's advice. No longer would there be a first minister, such as Richelieu and Mazarin had been, to whom other ministers were answerable. Instead,

Jean Colbert, the influential finance minister of Louis XIV, promoted a policy of mercantilism.

Louis would retain all royal authority in his own hands. He would rely on Colbert and his other ministers for advice only.

Colbert used a variety of measures in his efforts to achieve the mercantilist goal of an economically strong and self-sufficient France. He attempted to reform the royal treasury by using the power of the state to prosecute those brokers and tax collectors guilty of corruption. He also reorganized and reduced expenses of the royal household. He encouraged scientific growth, and supervised the construction of Versailles.

To encourage new French industry to manufacture goods which France imported—goods such as woolens, tapestries, glass, and lace—he gave manufacturers subsidies, monopolies, tax incentives, loans without interest, and permission to establish monopolies. He established the renowned Gobelins tapestry workshop and school, which made France the world's leader at this demanding craft. He imported skilled foreign workers and forbade the emigration of

French artisans. He also introduced extensive government regulations, enforced by state inspectors. By ensuring the high quality and size uniformity of French products, Colbert hoped to increase foreign demand for these goods. To facilitate internal trade, he developed royal highways and a national canal system.

French Overseas Expansion. Colbert was also committed to the development of a French overseas empire, the purpose of which was to generate a supply of cheap raw materials and to serve as markets for manufactured goods. He increased the size of the French navy from 20 ships to 270, and built the docks and ports necessary for both military and commercial vessels. He established trading posts in India, ship fueling stations in the Indian Ocean, slaving stations in Africa, and trading posts in 14 Caribbean sugar islands.

Colbert also encouraged French exploration in the New World. During this period, Antoine de Cadillac founded a French colony at Detroit, and Louis Joliet and Jacques Marquette explored the Mississippi River in 1673. Soon after, René-Robert Cavelier, Sieur de La Salle, navigated the Mississippi to its delta, the site of today's New Orleans. He claimed the surrounding area, which was named Louisiana in honor of the king. Colbert organized and granted monopolies to trading companies, such as the West India Company and the East India Company. His colonial policy laid the foundations for the first French overseas empire. At the same time, it increased rivalry with the other imperialist nations, England and Holland. This rivalry, along with the increased tariffs on English and Dutch imports, contributed to a series of costly wars against those two states, as we shall see.

Although Colbert's reforms modernized the French economy, they did so at the expense of the peasants and the working classes. These two groups continued to bear the tax burden and, in addition, they now

On instructions from Colbert, Sieur de La Salle explored the Mississippi River valley. He reported the presence of lead, timber, and valuable pelts, and speculated that pearls might also be found.

had to endure the rigid regulation of working conditions and the low pay necessary to bring profits to French industry. These hardships came on top of four great famines that struck France during the reign of Louis XIV—in 1648–1651, 1660–1662, 1693–1694, and 1709–1710—and caused untold thousands to starve to death. Combined with these crop failures, the effect of Colbert's reforms was poverty for the masses. A traveler to France during this time commented, "One sees men, women, and children . . . scratching the earth with their nails, searching for roots which they devour when they find them. Others less industrious scrabble the grass along with their animals, others completely broken lie along the roads waiting for death."[2] It has been said that Louis did

[2] Geoffrey Treasure, *The Making of Modern Europe 1648–1780* (London and New York: Methuen, 1985), p. 45.

everything for France but nothing for the French. Certainly the economic policies of his reign exacted a terrible toll.

RELIGIOUS POLICY

Louis XIV equated national strength with national unity. His motto was "*un roi, une loi, une foi*" (one king, one law, one faith). Louis had done much to create a spirit of national unity among the French people. It irked him, therefore, to observe that the French were still not a people of "*une foi*"—one faith.

Although France was a Catholic country, since 1598 the Huguenots (French Protestants) had enjoyed freedom to worship as they chose. In that year the first Bourbon king, Henry IV, had converted from Protestantism to Roman Catholicism to attain the throne. Then, in order to mollify the French Protestants who had for years regarded him as their leader, he had issued the Edict of Nantes. The Edict safeguarded the religious freedom of the Huguenots.

Louis XIV, however, was bothered by the presence of the Huguenots. Unlike his grandfather, Henry IV, Louis dreamed of establishing religious uniformity in France. Cardinal Richelieu had stripped the Huguenots of rights to maintain separate armies and towns when he amended the Edict of Nantes in 1629. A series of edicts further reduced Huguenot freedom. But to Louis' mind these still did not go far enough, so, in 1685, he revoked the Edict of Nantes. As a result of the revocation, Huguenots were forbidden to worship or to maintain their church schools and were frequently harassed by Louis' troops. On some occasions tortures such as pouring boiling water down the throats of Protestants were used to gain converts. Huguenot ministers who attempted to hold services were executed.

Although the Huguenots were forbidden to leave the country, over 200,000—out of a total of one million—managed to escape. Many of these were skilled artisans who fled to the Protestant states of England, Holland,

and Brandenburg, taking with them their expertise in such skills as silk and tapestry manufacturing. Although Louis succeeded in establishing religious uniformity, his brutal treatment of the Huguenots not only cast a shadow on his new rule but also strengthened the economies of his enemies.

Another religious group that offended Louis XIV's devotion to religious unity was the *Jansenists*. The Jansenists derived their teachings and name from Cornelis Jansen, who preached a kind of Calvinist philosophy within the Catholic Church. The pope condemned Jansenism as a heresy in 1653.

The famous scientist and philosopher Blaise Pascal (1623–1662) defended Jansenism and stirred up a controversy that soon became important among French intellectuals. Louis decided to suppress the Jansenists, in part because he believed that some of their followers had revolted against him during the Frondes. The center of Jansenism was at Port Royal, a convent near Paris. In 1713, Louis had it leveled to the ground.

THE WARS OF LOUIS XIV

In 1667 Louis embarked on a policy of war in Europe which continued throughout his reign and, in fact, was also pursued by his heir and great-grandson, Louis XV. Ultimately these wars nearly destroyed France. The loss of life was staggering; perhaps as many as one-fifth of all French subjects died as a result of Louis' militarism. These wars depleted the royal treasury and devastated the French economy, with the monarchy spending annually three times the amount collected in royal revenues. In the year of Louis XIV's death, 1715, the national debt equalled over 3 billion livres, an astronomical sum.

There were four primary underlying causes for Louis' militarist policy, including 1) his desire for the glory which he believed accompanied military victories; 2) his hope of destroying England and Holland as trading rivals; 3) his aim to diminish the power

THE WARS OF LOUIS XIV

Did Louis succeed in extending the borders of France to her "natural frontiers"?

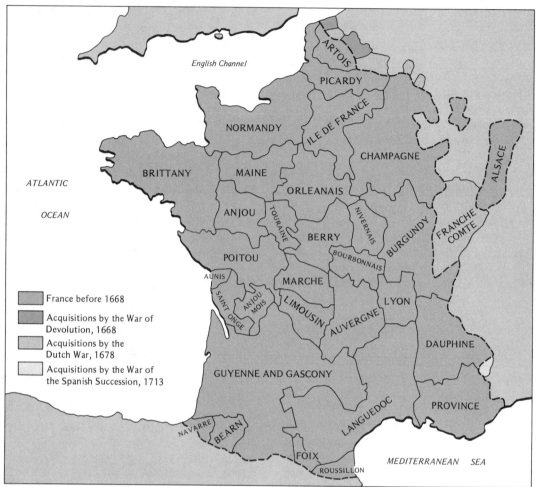

France before 1668

Acquisitions by the War of Devolution, 1668

Acquisitions by the Dutch War, 1678

Acquisitions by the War of the Spanish Succession, 1713

and prestige of the Hapsburgs, the dynasty that was the chief rival of the Bourbons; and 4) his intent to expand France to its natural frontiers—the Rhine River, the Pyrenees Mountains, and the Alps. Like most aggressors, Louis found excuses for his acts of aggression.

THE WAR OF DEVOLUTION, 1667–1668

His first war, fought against the Dutch, is known as the *War of Devolution. Devolution* means the passing on of rights and property. This war, like many of Louis' future wars, was fought over a question of inheritance.

Louis claimed that the Spanish Netherlands (Belgium) rightly belonged to his wife, who was the eldest child of Philip IV, the Spanish Hapsburg king. In fact, Maria Theresa had renounced all rights to Spanish territory at her marriage, but Louis claimed that the fact that her promised dowry had never been paid negated her renunciation.

The events of this war established a pattern that was repeated several times over the course of Louis' long military career: his initial military successes incited an alliance against him—on this occasion an alliance of the states of Holland, Sweden, and England—which ultimately forced him to back down and return much of the territory he had conquered.

THE DUTCH WAR, 1672–1678

As Louis was to do repeatedly, he waited several years then launched another war against his enemy. This second war, against the Dutch, was begun in 1672. Once again, a coalition formed against him—this one composed of the Austrian and Spanish Hapsburgs, the German state of Brandenburg, Denmark, and the Dutch. And again, Louis was forced to withdraw from the war.

However, the French had fought well—at times brilliantly. Two of the great military geniuses of the time, strategist Henri de Turenne and fortification expert Sebastien de Vauban had joined forces in the campaign against the Dutch. Military sieges of border towns were strategically alternated with deft diplomatic maneuverings. And although in the Treaty of Nimwegen (1678), Louis was again forced to return part of his conquest, he did retain Artois, the Franche-Comté, and parts of Alsace and Lorraine. These new territories, all on France's eastern frontier, gave life to Louis' dream of a French border on the Rhine.

In fact, the Treaty of Nimwegen marked the peak of Louis' military success. He had demonstrated French strength against an array of opponents, and he had acquired territory which strengthened his frontiers. But these victories, these gradual steps toward control of the lands between France and the Rhine, were not enough for the Sun King.

THE WAR OF THE LEAGUE OF AUGSBURG, 1688–1697

As Louis' aggressive acts intensified, his neighbors once again began to ally against him. In 1686, France's many enemies joined together in the League of Augsburg, a coalition which included Austrian Hapsburg Emperor Leopold; the Hapsburg king of Spain; the German states of Bavaria, Saxony,

The Dutch leader William of Orange, later king of England, devoted his career to battles against Louis XIV.

and the Palatinate; Sweden; and the Dutch Republic.

In 1689, when the Protestant William of Orange became king of England, replacing the pro-Catholic and pro-French James II, that country also joined the League. England under William had several reasons to oppose Louis, including the religious issue, William's Dutch connection, France's trade and naval rivalry, and English fear that Louis' military conquests would upset the balance of power in Europe. Maintaining the balance of power has always been a major component of English foreign policy, for the government feared that the dominance of the continent by any one power could threaten England's own independence through either economic boycott of English goods or by an invasion of the British Isles.

Despite the unity of his enemies, Louis launched a new series of attacks in 1688, this time against the German cities on the Rhine.

The French writer Voltaire (Chapter 8) described the French attacks:

• • • *It was the heart of winter. The French generals . . . announced to the citizens of those flourishing and well-ordered towns, to the inhabitants of the villages, and to the masters of more than fifty castles, that they would have to leave their homes which were to be destroyed by fire and sword. Men, women, old people, and children departed in haste. Some went wandering about the countryside; others sought refuge in neighboring territory, while the soldiery . . . burnt and sacked the country.*[3]

The *War of the League of Augsburg* dragged on until 1697. When peace was finally made, at Ryswick in the Netherlands, borders and the balance of power were left about as they had been when the war began.

THE WAR OF THE SPANISH SUCCESSION, 1701–1714

The last of Louis' wars, the *War of Spanish Succession*, again pitted the French king against the rest of Europe. The immediate cause of this conflict—or rather, Louis' excuse—was the impending death of the childless Hapsburg king of Spain, Charles II. Both Louis XIV and the Emperor Leopold claimed the throne. Each was a grandson of a former Spanish king, Philip III, although both of their claims were weakened by the fact that they were based on maternal, not paternal, lineage. Although the principle that succession could only be through male lineage had not yet been established in Spain, it had been established in France in the 14th century with the introduction of the Salic Law. However, both rulers also claimed the Spanish throne through their wives; both Louis and Leopold were married to granddaughters of Philip III.

There had been several attempts to settle the dispute through diplomacy, by dividing

up the holdings of Spain. But these efforts all proved futile. On the pope's advice, on October 2, 1700, Charles II signed his will. This document stipulated that the Spanish throne should go to Louis XIV's grandson, the 17-year-old Philip, with the provision that the thrones of Spain and France should never be united in any one person. Charles signed the will not a moment too soon; on November 1, 1700, he died.

Despite the promise not to unite the rule of Spain and France, it soon became apparent that Louis XIV controlled his young grandson and was in fact ruling Spain from Versailles. In September 1701, England and the Dutch joined Emperor Leopold to form the Grand Alliance, a coalition that also included Denmark, Sweden, Brandenburg, Savoy, and Portugal—in fact, most of Europe, for only Spain and Bavaria remained allies of France. In May 1702, the nations of the Grand Alliance declared war on France.

Underlying the conflict was far more than a dynastic dispute. Other causes included resentment of Louis for his prior acts of aggression, fear that the French threatened the balance of power in Europe, the English fear of the growing French fleet, and, not least, numerous colonial and trade rivalries. In fact, because of this involvement of lands overseas together with the nations of Europe, the War of the Spanish Succession is often said to be the first "world war."

The Battles of Blenheim and Gibraltar, 1704.

Although the war dragged on until 1713, two major battles that brought Grand Alliance victories and inevitable defeat to France were fought in 1704. One was the *Battle of Blenheim*. The leader of the English forces at Blenheim was John Churchill, the Duke of Marlborough. Churchill was Captain-General of all of Queen Anne's armies and the man responsible for the formation of the Grand Alliance and its Grand Army. When he learned of Leopold's losses at French hands in Germany, he led the British army on a long march from the North Sea to

---

[3] Will and Ariel Durant, *The Age of Louis XIV* (New York: Simon & Schuster, 1963), p. 692.

English troops under the leadership of the Duke of Marlborough storm the town of Blenheim, near Augsburg, in 1704. The English, whom Louis XIV had termed "a nation of shop-keepers," won this important battle.

the Danube in August 1704. At Blenheim plain, fighting alongside the great Italian general Eugene of Savoy, Marlborough led an English force of cavalry and infantry against the French army. His descendant, Winston Churchill, described Marlborough's victory:

• • • *At the head of eight squadrons he broke the center, routed the French cavalry, drove many thousands to death in the Danube, cut to pieces the remaining squares of French infantry, surrounded the great mass of French troops crowded into the village of Blenheim, and as dusk fell on this memorable day, was able to write his famous letter to his wife: "I have not time to say more, but to beg you to give my duty to the Queen, and let her know her army has had a glorious victory.[4]*

---

[4] Winston Churchill, *A History of the English Speaking Peoples,* Vol. 3, *The Age of Revolution* (New York: Bantam Books, 1963), p. 42.

At Blenheim the French suffered a disastrous defeat and great losses. This military defeat came on the heels of a naval disaster that had occurred a week earlier, when an Anglo-Dutch fleet had captured the strategic Rock of Gibraltar. From the Rock of Gibraltar, access to the entire Mediterranean could be controlled. For the next two centuries, England's control of Gibraltar enabled it to turn the Mediterranean into an "English lake."

Subsequent battles brought new defeats to Louis, whose offer of favorable peace terms was refused by the allies in 1706. In 1709 and in 1710, Louis was again rebuffed in his attempts to withdraw from the war. After each failure to end the fighting, Louis introduced new taxes to pay for newly recruited armies. In the process he nearly destroyed the French economy. At last, on April 17, 1713, all of Louis' enemies but Austria signed the *Treaty of Utrecht*. After another year of war, the Austrian government made a separate peace treaty with France, the *Treaty of Rastatt.*

The Peace of Utrecht. Underlying the terms of the treaties of Utrecht and Rastatt there were two guiding principles: first, that the balance of power should be restored in Europe, and second, that national sovereignty was more important than dynastic ties between royal families.

England was the major beneficiary of Louis' wars. By the terms of the Treaty of Utrecht, England retained the Rock of Gibraltar. Moreover, she received significant overseas concessions which added to her empire and provided the foundation for future conquests from France. England received Newfoundland, Nova Scotia, and the Hudson Bay area, which formed the core of British Canada. At least of equal importance were the commercial concessions granted to England. These included a preferential tariff with Spain, the right to send one ship a year to trade with the Spanish colonies, and a monopoly of the traffic in slaves to the New World. Fishing rights off Newfoundland were left vaguely defined, and would prove an ongoing source of conflict between France and England.

The Austrian Hapsburgs received the Spanish Netherlands, along with Milan, Naples, and Sardinia. The Dutch regained the "barrier fortresses" against France, and were given a trade monopoly of the river Scheldt.

For their roles in the war, the Elector of Brandenburg and the Duke of Savoy were awarded small grants of territory and titles. The Elector of Brandenburg was henceforth to hold the title "King of Prussia." The Duke of Savoy also assumed the title of king.

Philip V was allowed to retain the throne of Spain, but only on condition that the crowns of Spain and France were never to be united. From the time of the *Peace of Utrecht* until the Napoleonic era, Spain and France would remain separate.

The treaties that comprised the Peace of Utrecht set a European political order which, in general, lasted for the remainder of the 18th century. Moreover, the war strengthened England. It not only expanded her overseas empire, but also, in conferring on her control of Gibraltar, made England in effect the negotiator of Europe, that nation most able to preserve the balance of power.

The Legacy of Louis' Wars. The wars of Louis XIV had a devastating effect on France. They drained the French treasury and brought poverty and hardships to the French people. These things, along with Louis' perpetuation of the inequitable class and tax systems, led eventually to the French Revolution of 1789, as we shall see.

Moreover, Louis' wars established policies that were to affect Europe for the next half century. They intensified conflict between the European powers, conflict which would eventually erupt in two more lengthy and costly "world wars."

CONFLICTS IN EUROPE Louis XIV died in 1715. He had outlived both his son and grandson. His dying words to his five-year-old great-grandson, who would succeed him as Louis XV, were: "Do not imitate me in my taste for building, nor in my love of war. Strive, on the contrary, to live in peace with your neighbors. . . . Make it your endeavor to ease the burden of the people, which I, unhappily, have not been able to do."[5] Unfortunately for France, the boy did not take his great-grandfather's advice.

The wars that wracked Europe in the decades after Louis' death deserved to be called "world wars" perhaps even more than did the War of the Spanish Succession. They involved extensive fighting both in America and India, and the results of the conflicts

[5] Wallace K. Ferguson and Geoffrey Bruun, *A Survey of European Civilization*, 3rd ed. (Boston: Houghton Mifflin, 1958), p. 512.

were to prove decisive in the history of both these two bases of colonial empire.

THE WAR OF THE AUSTRIAN SUCCESSION, 1742–1748

The first major war to be fought after Louis' reign ended was the *War of the Austrian Succession*. This war had two components which eventually blended into one large struggle. One of these components was the overseas conflict between England and Spain that had erupted in 1739, and that is known as the *War of Jenkins' Ear*. The War of Jenkins' Ear began when an English seaman, Captain Jenkins, presented to the English Parliament his severed ear, which he claimed had been cut off by the Spanish coast guard. Rooted in colonial and commercial rivalries, this conflict between England and Spain soon blended into the war that had erupted on the European continent in 1742, the War of the Austrian Succession.

This second war was yet another to be fought over dynastic conflicts. It was brought about by the fact that Emperor Charles VI (1711–1740) of Austria had no male heir. Hoping to guarantee the succession of his daughter, Maria Theresa, Charles negotiated with the other members of the Hapsburg family and the diets of the territories of the empire, an agreement called the *Pragmatic Sanction*. Other European powers also agreed to it. The parties to this agreement guaranteed that at Charles' death his lands would devolve to his daughter undivided.

Despite this agreement, two months after Charles' death the Prussian ruler, Frederick the Great, invaded Austrian territory and took the Austrian province of Silesia. It is said that Frederick's motto was, "Take what you want; you're never wrong unless you have to give it back." France and Spain joined forces with Prussia and other German states against Hapsburg Austria. England and the Dutch supported Austria in its stand against the French.

Because issues of commercial and colonial rivalry again underlay the dynastic question that had been the initial cause of the war, fighting soon spread to the overseas empires of the nations involved.

In North America, fighting occurred between the French Canadians and New England colonists. The French launched a series of attacks on Nova Scotia and New England frontier areas. In addition, French privateers used Louisbourg as a base of operations against ships from New England. Louisbourg was strategic to French Canada because it guarded the St. Lawrence River, which ran through the heart of French Canada. In June 1745, the Governor of Massachusetts organized an expedition that blockaded the port, and after a short siege took it. A French attempt to recover it failed.

In India, the French fared better. Although the British harassed them by sea, the French governor Joseph Dupleix attacked the badly fortified British post at Madras. The French then occupied the city.

The Treaty of Aix-la-Chapelle (1748), which ended the war, guaranteed Maria Theresa's rule of the Hapsburg empire. However, it only partially restored the balance of power in Europe, for Frederick was allowed to keep Silesia, thereby doubling Prussia's population, adding rich mineral deposits to its economic resources and demonstrating that nation's military strength.

Outside of Europe, the Peace of Aix-la-Chapelle called for reciprocal restoration of territory on the part of Britain and France. Thus, Madras was returned to Britain and Louisbourg to France. This move was unpopular in the New England colonies, which had supplied the force that took Louisbourg.

THE SEVEN YEARS' WAR, 1756–1763

The growth of Prussia led to a dramatic reversal of the alliances of the great powers of Europe that is known as the *Diplomatic Revolution of 1756*. In order to counter Prussian

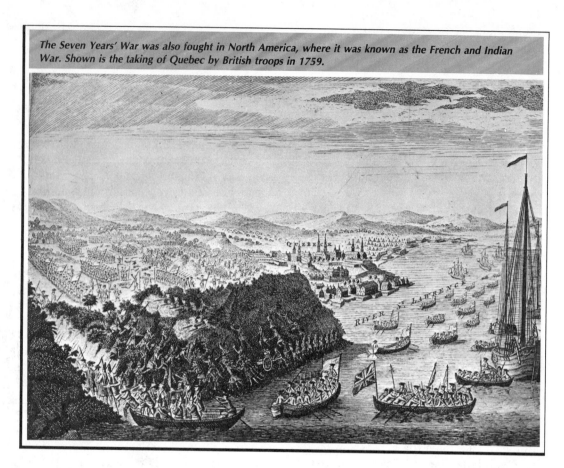

The Seven Years' War was also fought in North America, where it was known as the French and Indian War. Shown is the taking of Quebec by British troops in 1759.

strength, Austria joined her former enemy France, along with Russia, in a new alliance system. On the other hand, impressed by the new Prussian army, England abandoned her long-standing ally, Austria, and allied herself with Prussia instead.

War broke out in Europe in 1756. The initial causes of the conflict, which came to be known as the *Seven Years' War*, were again issues of dynastic rivalry—this time focused on the partitioning of Prussia—and of balance of power. However, the war became a world war as France and England continued their struggle for colonial and commercial supremacy in the West Indies, in India, and in North America, where the war is known as the French and Indian War.

Frederick the Great's Prussia fought alone to a stalemate in Europe while England won a series of victories overseas. England's colonial victories forced France and her allies to withdraw from the war in 1763.

The Effects of the Seven Years' War. Overseas, the war was a triumph for Britain. In the American colonies, British troops under James Wolfe captured strategic forts and sailed up the St. Lawrence River to Quebec. When he took Quebec, France was forced to give up most of her empire in Canada. Moreover, as a result of other British victories, France lost one of her islands in the West Indies, and her foothold in India. The war damaged France's prestige and depleted her treasury, contributing to the financial crisis which led to revolution in 1789. Britain, on the other hand, confirmed her position as the world's strongest colonial power and maintained her control of the seas.

SUMMARY

Louis XIV gave his name to an age in European history, and in the view of many historians he deserves to be called a great monarch. Certainly, during Louis' reign, France was a great military power. Moreover, his style and his court influenced all of Europe. The years of his rule coincided with and contributed to an era of cultural grandeur—especially in literature, architecture, and art—and the cultural achievements of his reign were such that French culture in fact dominated Europe for the next two centuries. Even today, the dominance of the French language in the world of diplomacy can be seen in such international terms as coup d'état, coup de grace, entente, *and* détente.*

Yet Louis' militaristic and expansionist policies brought nearly continuous warfare to the European continent. The cost of these wars bore heavily on the French people, and left a legacy of death, poverty, and deprivation which contributed to the French Revolution. If one measures greatness by power and influence, Louis XIV was indeed a great monarch. Alternatively, if greatness is judged by its effect on human well-being—on life, liberty, and equality—his greatness is in doubt.*

QUESTIONS

1 Define divine-right *monarchy* and absolute *monarchy*. What is the difference between them?
2 In what ways did Louis XIV increase his power? Which groups in French society lost power as a result?
3 In what ways did Louis XIV's court at Versailles serve to increase his power and prestige?
4 Define mercantilism and bullionism. What policies did these economic theories lead to?
5 What were the aims of Louis' foreign policy? What were the results?
6 What were the short-term and long-range effects of Louis' reign? Was he a great king?

BIBLIOGRAPHY

BELOFF, MAX. *The Age of Absolutism, 1660–1815*. New York: Harper & Row, 1962. *This brief study surveys the European scene and describes in some detail the nature of absolutism in specific countries.*

CAIRNS, JOHN C. *France*. Englewood Cliffs, N. J.: Prentice-Hall, 1965. *A brief survey of French history and culture, from the origins of the nation to the present.*

CHURCH, WILLIAM F. *Louis XIV in Historical Thought*. New York: Horton, 1976. *This work surveys the historiography of Louis XIV's reign, from the views of Voltaire to present historical interpretations.*

LEWIS, W. H. *The Splendid Century: Life in the France of Louis XIV*. Anchor Books ed. New York: Doubleday, 1957. *This is social history at its best. Lewis captures life in the 17th century with sketches of the king and his court, the Church and the army, and other facets of Louis XIV's society.*

PACKARD, LAWRENCE BRADFORD. *The Age of Louis XIV*. New York: Holt, Rinehart, 1957. *A survey of the age of Louis XIV, with major sections on political, international, and cultural history.*

6

● *That which concerns the mystery of the King's power is not lawful to be disputed; for that is to wade into the weakness of Princes, and to take away the mystical reverence that belongs unto them that sit in the throne of God.*

JAMES I

The Growth of Constitutionalism in England

One of the recurring themes of European history in the 17th and 18th centuries is the issue of the power of the monarchy versus the power of groups such as the church, the nobility, and the army. In France, as we have seen in Chapter 5, Louis XIV succeeded in establishing royal authority and the principle of divine-right monarchy by wresting power from contending groups within French society.

By contrast, in England a century-long struggle between the Stuart dynasty and its subjects produced an unwritten constitution which forced the monarchs to share power with some of their constituents and which guaranteed civil and political rights to many English subjects. As a result of these events, England evolved a constitutional system which would provide the framework and the institutions on which the 19th- and 20th-century English democracy could be built.

Historians continue to seek the evidence to explain the differences between England's history and that of other European powers, but some distinctions are apparent. As in most examinations of historical events, the keys to understanding England's unique experience lie in the history of its political, social, economic, and religious institutions; in the impact of individual personalities; and, on occasion, to quirks of fate.

THE STUARTS: JAMES I Unmarried and childless, Queen Elizabeth on her deathbed in 1603 named as her successor James VI of Scotland. James, who became James I of England (1603–1625), was the only child of the ill-fated Mary Stuart, who was executed by Elizabeth in 1587. (Mary had been implicated in a plot with the Catholic Philip II of Spain, allegedly against the Protestant English throne.) Taken from his mother when he was a baby, James was raised as a Protestant in Presbyterian Scotland and had inherited the Scottish throne as James VI.

James' critics have described him harshly: as nervous and excitable, fond of swearing and dirty jokes, slovenly in dress and in table manners. He loved to ride and hunt, and once, reportedly, after slaying a stag, smeared himself in its blood. He married Anne of Denmark whom, it was said, he never loved.

Throughout James' reign, scandals surrounded the court. One of his favorite friends was implicated in a poison murder but was nevertheless pardoned by the king. Another, the Duke of Buckingham, was the real power behind the throne in the last years of James' reign. Buckingham was so much disliked by Parliament and the public that when he was murdered in 1628, there was national rejoicing.

JAMES' PHILOSOPHY OF GOVERNMENT

Whatever his personal predilections, it was James' philosophy of government and his ignorance of the realities of England which created the problems he experienced as king. He inherited a political system which he did not know and did not try to understand. Instead, he attempted to enforce the divine-right theory of monarchy rather than continuing the Tudor system, where the ruler had

Puritans urged James I to simplify the Anglican Church, arguing that Luther and Calvin had seen no need for a hierarchy of bishops.

James I lacked the political skills of his predecessor, Elizabeth, but his reign was marked by two positive achievements: the King James edition of the Bible, and an absence of foreign wars.

shared power—"the king in Parliament"—or at least had pretended to. As James interpreted the divine right of kings, a doctrine which he took from French absolutist thinking, a subject should no more question a king than he should dispute the authority of God. A king ruled by divine authority and acted as God's agent in his designated sphere. James' answers to the fundamental political questions of power and authority can be summarized: the king receives his power from God; the king, not the church, interprets God's will; the king answers only to God; hence the king has absolute power.

JAMES I AND RELIGION

Even though he had been raised as a Scottish Protestant, James admired and supported the established Church of England that he headed. He resisted the demands of the Puritan movement in England. The Puritans' desire to "purify" the Anglican Church of any traces of Roman Catholicism in organization and practice disturbed him greatly be-

101

James I also faced dissent from Catholics, who resented the discriminatory measures taken against them. Shown are Guy Fawkes (third from right) and his fellow conspirators.

cause it represented a break in the unity of church and state in England. Among the other reasons for his opposition to the Puritans was his recognition that freedom to decide religious questions implied a similar opportunity to decide political ones, and he would brook no political dissent.

At the Hampton Court conference of church leaders convened by James in 1604, 1000 clergy with Puritan leanings presented him with the *Millenary Petition* which called for modest reforms in the Anglican Church, including the elimination of the hierarchy of church officials. James' notorious response—"no bishop, no king"—implying his insistence on a hierarchy of bishops and archbishops, only postponed the confrontation. Out of the same conference came the *King James Version*, or Authorized Version, of the Bible which did much to stabilize the English language and has been ranked with Shakespeare in terms of literary merit.

James was at first lenient toward the Catholics in England, in the hope of uniting them under his rule. He lifted the fines against those who did not attend the Anglican Church. However, when the number of those attending services dropped alarmingly, he reinstated the fines. Angry at James' action, a small group of extremist Catholics plotted

to blow up the Parliament building when the king, his council, and the members of Parliament were assembled. On November 5, 1605, the *Gunpowder Plot* of Guy Fawkes to blow up the king and Parliament was discovered before it could be carried out. James responded by severely persecuting the entire Roman Catholic community in England. The episode also originated an English national holiday, for November 5 is still celebrated as Guy Fawkes Day, complete with fireworks.

JAMES I AND PARLIAMENT

In addition to the religious dissent which plagued his reign, James encountered conflict with Parliament. This conflict stemmed from Parliament's differing interpretation of the power and authority of the king, for its members believed that they rightfully should share power with him. In their view, the authority for their power lay in tradition and custom, the English "constitution," including the Magna Carta and the liberties which it implied. Though not a single written document like the American Constitution, the English Constitution was, nevertheless, a set of rules, rights, and privileges, some written and some not, which had accumulated by firmly established precedents over the previous centuries. The 17th century's long quarrel between the Stuart kings and Parliament was indeed a classic clash between two political theories: monarchy based on the theory of divine right; and *constitutionalism*, predicated on a sharing of power between the king and his subjects.

The Apology of the House of Commons, 1611. James' first Parliamentary session, from 1604 to 1611, furnished the model for the quarrel between the monarchy and Parliament. Three key issues emerged: Parliamentary privileges; the fact that Parliament could not convene without a summons from the king and he could dismiss it at will; and the issue of whether ordinances issued by the king could override laws accepted by king and Parliament. On the first issue, Parliament won the confrontation, for James generally acknowledged its members' privileges. The second issue emerged when the Parliament refused to grant new taxes for the king. He responded by dismissing it.

In answer to James' action, in 1611 the House of Commons produced one of the key documents in the constitutional struggle, "Apology of the House of Commons," which asserted the privileges of Parliament and reiterated that the king could not make laws without the consent of Parliament.

Ignoring Parliament's protests, James attempted to rule without calling Parliament to request the money grants which it had the power to give him. However, the need for these funds forced James to reconvene Parliament in 1614.

The Great Protestation, 1621. After a stormy two-month session, James dismissed the Parliament again until 1621. At that time, the outbreak of the Thirty Years' War led James to seek funds from Parliament to support the efforts of his son-in-law, Frederick, the Elector of Palatine, in his quarrels with the Holy Roman Empire. In this, the third Parliamentary session of his reign, James was once more confronted with a Parliament determined to gain concessions. Again its members produced a petition, *The Great Protestation of 1621*, which demanded that Parliament receive the right to discuss foreign affairs. James' response was to tear up the petition and dismiss Parliament without receiving the money grants he sought.

In 1624, James was compelled by his need for money to fight the Spanish to summon Parliament once again. In exchange for funds, he permitted Parliament to debate foreign policy. When James died in 1625, his quarrels with Parliament were not resolved, but Parliament had gained from him several important concessions and had set precedents which the members assumed would be honored by his successor.

CHARLES I (1625–1649) Charles I succeeded his father at the age of 25. Not so intelligent as James, Charles shared his father's exalted view of the power of the monarchy. A religious family man, he was at the same time petty and indecisive. He loved to hunt and was an excellent shot with gun or crossbow. He may have suffered from polio as a child and he spoke with a stammer. One week after he ascended the throne he married Louis XIII's sister, Henrietta Maria, who influenced him greatly in later years. In the early years of his reign, he was under the influence of his father's favorite, the Duke of Buckingham.

CHARLES I AND PARLIAMENT

Unlike his father, who avoided wars to prevent Parliament from exercising leverage over him for extraordinary grants of money, Charles engaged in six military expeditions against Spain and France in the first four years of his reign. As a result of his need for revenues, he summoned Parliament in 1625; it granted him only one-seventh of his money requests. When his second Parliament in 1626 refused to grant any war monies, he dismissed it and resolved to raise funds without its approval. He pawned the crown jewels, mortgaged crown lands, and tried to collect free gifts from the people.

The Petition of Right, 1628. When his efforts to gain revenues by royal ordinance and an attempt at a forced loan failed in 1627, Charles was again desperate. In 1628 he summoned his third Parliament, which agreed to grant one-year subsidies to the king only if he accepted its *Petition of Right*. This document is another constitutional landmark which sought to restrict the king's power and protect the rights of his subjects. It contained four basic demands: recognition of the writ of *habeas corpus*, which forbade imprisonment without demonstrated cause; agreement that martial law could not be declared in peacetime; acknowledgment that forced loans were forbidden, and thus only Parliament could introduce new taxes; and the king's promise that billeting of soldiers in private homes would be forbidden unless the occupant's consent was obtained. In June 1628, Charles signed the petition and received in exchange the requested war subsidies.

War with Scotland. Further quarrels with Parliament led Charles to dismiss it in 1629. For the next 11 years he attempted to govern without it. He succeeded in doing so by making peace with France and Spain and through the support and advice of William Laud (1573–1645), whom he appointed in 1633 as Archbishop of Canterbury, the religious head of the Anglican Church. As president of St. John's College, Oxford, Laud had purged the university of Puritans. With Charles' encouragement, he sought as archbishop to rid all England of Puritan influence. Charles' persecutions against them led many Puritans to migrate to North America, where they settled the Massachusetts Colony. Others went into hiding.

As a result of Laud's policy, King Charles became increasingly unpopular. Under Laud's influence, Charles took his campaign against the Puritans to Scotland, where he tried to impose the Anglican Church's prayer book and hierarchical organization on the Scottish Presbyterians. The result was two *Bishop's Wars* against the Scots. In the second war, the Scottish army invaded England, requiring Charles to summon Parliament in 1640 to request new revenues.

THE ENGLISH CIVIL WAR

This new parliament, known as the *Long Parliament*, which convened in 1640, set the stage for a confrontation between king and Parliament which blended political and religious issues. A series of steps led to civil war. The first was an act of revenge against Thomas Wentworth, the Earl of Strafford, nicknamed ''Black Tom Tyrant,'' a former parliamentary leader who had joined the king in the 1630s. In 1640, the House of Commons arrested and tried Strafford; he was executed in 1641. At the same time, Archbishop Laud was imprisoned in the Tower of London, the notorious prison which had housed many famous English men and women over the centuries.

In the face of Parliament's rebellion, King Charles made peace with Scotland. Under the leadership of John Pym, the Long Parliament forced Charles to make several concessions. He agreed that 1) Parliament could not be dissolved without its own consent; 2) Parliament must be convened every three years; 3) there could be no taxation without Parliamentary approval; and 4) the concessions contained in the 1628 Petition of Right were to be confirmed.

Parliament itself soon became divided into royalists and radical Puritans who sought to reform the Anglican church. When these radicals gained passage of the *Grand Remonstrance* (1641), which demanded parliamentary approval of the king's advisers and army officers, the king made a serious error by marching into the House of Commons with armed guards to arrest five leading members, including John Pym. This defiant act was the last step before the civil war.

The First Stage, 1642–1646. The immediate cause of the first stage of the war was a parliamentary document, *Nineteen Propositions*, an ultimatum to the king which would have ceded nearly total power to Parliament. The king could not agree to this, and civil war ensued.

Besides the political issue, the religious question—Anglican vs. Puritan—was an important factor. Less important but nonetheless real were longstanding social alignments. In general, the old English aristocracy supported the king while the newer classes—merchants, manufacturers, small and tenant farmers—supported Parliament. The parliamentary faction, popularly known as the *Roundheads*, also received support from the navy and most of the towns. Within

Parliament, about 300 members of the House of Commons and about 30 members of the House of Lords were Roundheads.

The king's party, known as the *Cavaliers*, included 175 House of Commons members and 80 members of the House of Lords. Outside Parliament, most Roman Catholics, headed by the Catholic queen Henrietta Maria; the members of the Anglican Church; and most landed gentry (non-noble large landowners) were Cavaliers.

During the first two years of the war, 1642–1644, the king won most of the confrontations, but in 1644, at the *Battle of Marston Moor*, the Roundheads, supported by Scottish armies, won their first major battle. In 1645, a reorganized army, the "New Model Army," under the leadership of the Puritan leader Oliver Cromwell (1599–1658), defeated the king decisively at the Battle of Naseby, turning the tide of the conflict. In 1646, the king surrendered.

The early advantage which experienced men and a well-equipped cavalry gave the king had been overcome by a strictly disciplined, efficiently-run military machine whose leader believed that God was on his side. As Cromwell wrote later of Naseby, "God did it and it is wonderful in my eyes."[1]

The Second Stage, 1648–1649. The civil war, however, was not over. Parliament itself divided between the majority—who wanted a limited constitutional monarchy that permitted the existence of a king, but one who was limited by the dictates of Parliament—and the radical few Independents (Congregationalists) led by Cromwell, who wanted to abolish the monarchy altogether. Although in a minority, Cromwell's faction controlled the Parliamentary army which had defeated the king.

Oliver Cromwell had been a member of the gentry who championed the cause of the

Soldiers of Cromwell's Puritan army were known as Roundheads *because they scorned the elaborate coiffures of the day.*

lower classes, from whom most of the Independents were drawn. He was a religious zealot, as were they, who believed that God had inspired his victory. Cromwell hoped to establish a Congregational Church which would have no hierarchy of officials.

By 1648, when the civil war resumed, virtually all of England, including the Scottish army and most of Parliament, supported the king. Opposing them was Cromwell, leading the New Model Army and "rump Parliament," about 100 radical members.

The *Rump Parliament* was created on December 6, 1648, when all Presbyterians were forced out of the sitting parliament in what

---

[1] Goldwin Smith, *A History of England* (New York: Scribner's, 1966), p. 331.

became known as "Pride's Purge." Colonel Pride, under Cromwell's orders, carried out this exclusion of all but Independents from the parliamentary body. The second stage in the civil war lasted only a few months, with decisive victories won by Cromwell's army, concluding with the capture of the king.

THE EXECUTION OF THE KING

In January 1649, a court of commissioners appointed by the Rump Parliament tried King Charles I on the charge of treason. On January 30, 1649, he was found guilty and sentenced to death, with the execution to be carried out immediately. On a cold, snowy January afternoon, Charles was taken from St. James Palace to a scaffold at Whitehall, a half mile away.

Addressing the crowd, Charles said he died a good Christian who had forgiven those who caused his death. Helping the executioner put his hair under a small white satin cap, he laid his head upon the block and gave his own hand signal to the executioner. The severed head was then shown to the assembled crowd, and one of the crowd yelled, "This is the head of a traitor."[2]

Charles' death was a turning point, for most English subjects were appalled by his execution at the hands of the radical Cromwell and his followers. Few people felt his acts had warranted a death sentence, and as time passed, he was seen more as a martyr than as a villain.

The regicide had a profound effect upon England's subsequent history. Never again would England maintain a standing army in peace time, nor execute a monarch. As for the kings, never again would a monarch attempt to rule without the participation of the House of Commons.

---

[2] Winston Churchill, *A History of the English-Speaking Peoples*, Vol. 2, *The New World* (New York: Bantam, 1963), p. 216.

A sketch of Charles I being led to the executioner was made by an eyewitness to the scene. The king maintained his dignity to the end.

"Humpty Dumpty"

The execution of the king inspired the nursery rhyme "Humpty Dumpty."

Humpty Dumpty sat on a wall,
Humpty Dumpty had a great fall.
All the king's horses and all the
*   king's men*
Couldn't put Humpty together again.

THE INTERREGNUM 1649–1659

England was now transformed into a republic led by Cromwell and his army. This new government abolished both the monarchy and the House of Lords and established a Council of State, 41 members chosen annually by the House of Commons. The real power rested in Cromwell's hands.

The Diggers and Levellers. During this period a more radical group known as the *Diggers* emerged. They were led by Gerrard Winstanley, who opposed private ownership of property and believed in agrarian communism. The Diggers represented a further extension of the ideas of the *Levellers*, originally supporters of Cromwell who advocated an extension of the franchise (right to vote) on the basis of some small holding of property. Cromwell executed most of the leaders of this movement and broke the power of those Levellers who remained in the New Model Army. As the currently-established authority in England, he wanted no popular pressure to challenge his dominance.

IRELAND AND SCOTLAND

When Ireland and Scotland rose in arms in support of the claims of Charles I's son, the furture Charles II, Cromwell conquered Ireland in 1649 and 1650. He confiscated two-thirds of the land and transferred its ownership to the English landlords to pay off his soldiers and financial backers and as an attempt to eliminate Roman Catholicism. This transfer of Irish land, devastation of much of the countryside, and killing, directly or by starvation, of one-third of the Irish people, laid much of the foundation for future conflict between Ireland and England. The "curse of Cromwell" is still a phrase which conjures up fear and loathing in the Irish.

Cromwell did not act so harshly toward the Scottish when in the winter of 1650, Charles II was crowned king in Scotland, and in the spring of 1651 the Scottish army invaded England. Instead, Cromwell used his military victory over the Scottish at Worcester to temporarily unite Scotland, Ireland, and England under one government. Charles II escaped from Cromwell's soldiers, after hiding all day under an oak tree.

THE PROTECTORATE, 1653–1659

In 1653 Cromwell dissolved the Rump Parliament and wrote a new constitution for England. He created an executive branch composed of the Lord Protector (himself) and a Council of State of 15 members to advise him. Because the one-house Parliament which he introduced turned too quarrelsome, in 1655 Cromwell introduced a military dictatorship that divided England into 11 military districts, each under the control

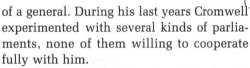

Oliver Cromwell as Lord Protector. The leader of the revolt against the Stuarts is presented as a stern and dedicated soldier.

of a general. During his last years Cromwell experimented with several kinds of parliaments, none of them willing to cooperate fully with him.

In 1658, Cromwell died, and his son Richard attempted to succeed him, but Richard lacked the prestige and ability necessary to retain control. It became apparent that the system of government which Oliver Cromwell had established depended on his personal leadership.

THE RESTORATION In 1659 General George Monck seized control of the military and recalled the Long Parliament of 1640, which then dissolved itself in favor of a new freely-elected "Convention" Parliament. In 1660 the Convention Parliament recalled Charles II from exile and crowned him. Cromwell's experiment with a form of republican government had proven too radical for most English subjects, who welcomed this return to monarchy. On the other hand, the civil war and the interregnum period had established the authority of Parliament once and for all. In fact, Charles II owed his crown to Parliament. However, the quarrels between the monarchy and the Parliament were far from ended.

CHARLES II (1660–1685)

The new king, Charles II, was a clever, charming, selfish man who cared little for politics and a great deal for women. He made a financially profitable marriage to Catherine of Braganza, sister of the King of Portugal, whose dowry included the ports of Tangiers in North Africa and Bombay in India. Her Catholicism seemed no threat; she and Charles were childless, although he sired at least five illegitimate children.

Charles' fondness for mistresses—by one count 13—led to one embarrassing occasion when he introduced his wife Catherine to his mistress Barbara. Catherine, it was said, suffered a nosebleed from the humiliation, fainted, and was carried from the room.

Charles II triumphantly entered London after being recalled from exile by the Parliament.

The Court of Charles II. Charles presided over a scandalous court, and eliminated all of the Puritan "blue laws" which Cromwell had introduced to restrict certain kinds of literature, all types of theatrical diversion and any other activities considered "ungodly." Charles' *Restoration* was accompanied by a resurgence of literature, especially drama staged in the London theaters which had been closed in 1642 by the Puritans. Restoration drama took most of its comedic style from abroad, in particular from the French playwright Molière. Restoration plays such as those by William Congreve (1670–1725) tended to mock decency and virtue, the very values which the Puritans prized.

Surely, John Milton's *Paradise Lost* (1665) was an epic out of tune with the times in its emphasis on the search for a "new Eden" through the coming of Christ. Milton (1608–1674), whose life spanned the years from the Stuart accession to the Restoration and beyond, was known as the greatest of the Puritan writers though he loved beauty and music as they never did.

In the early years of Charles II's reign, two disasters struck London. A plague, not unlike that which had devastated Europe in the 14th century, hit London in 1665, taking 70,000 lives. The following year, the Great Fire of London, which raged for five days, destroyed over 13,000 buildings.

Among those prominent buildings built to restore London after the Fire were many, including St. Paul's Cathedral and other churches, designed by the brilliant architect Sir Christopher Wren (1632–1723). In addition to being an architect, Wren was a professor of astronomy and a mathematician of considerable renown. He had only six months of architectural training in Paris in 1665 before he was called to the reconstruction task which made him famous.

The Parliamentary Settlement. Charles, raised in the France of Louis XIV, had little interest or understanding of English politics, and delegated most of his authority to Ed-

The Great Fire devastated London in 1666. The massive rebuilding which followed changed the face of the city.

ward Hyde, the Earl of Clarendon, who was responsible for the restoration settlement. The restored Stuart monarchy accepted all of the acts passed by the Long Parliament between 1640 and 1642 including the principle of *due process of law* which prevented the king from imprisoning a subject without arraignment and trial, and the law which required that Parliament be convened at least once every three years.

Also included in the settlement was a general pardon for those who had participated in the revolution, except for the judges who had condemned Charles I. Thirteen of these were executed for their act of regicide.

Frustrated that Oliver Cromwell was dead and hence could not be tried for his rebellion, members of the government disinterred his body from its honored place in Westminster Abbey. On the anniversary of Charles' execution, the corpse was hanged and beheaded.

The Religious Settlement. The religious settlement was contained in the *Clarendon Code*, a series of laws which restored the Anglican Church to its full authority and contained provisions against the discredited Puritans and against Roman Catholics. By the provisions of the Test Act of 1673, only Anglicans were allowed to participate in na-

tional or local government or hold military positions. This political requirement remained in force until 1828 for *dissenters*, those Protestants who would not conform to Anglican beliefs and practices, and until 1829 for Roman Catholics.

Beginning of Political Parties. In all, the Restoration gave Parliament, not the king, the upper hand. Two factions emerged among the powerful and influential men of Parliament. The "court" party under the leadership of the Earl of Danby supported the king, the concept of divine-right monarchy, and the established Anglican church. Their opponents called them *tories*, originally a name for Irish cattle thieves.

The rival faction, the "country" party, led by the Earl of Shaftesbury, advocated parliamentary supremacy and toleration of Protestant dissenters. Their opponents called this group *whigs*, a term for Scottish robbers who murdered their victims.

Neither of these factions could be considered a political party in the modern sense, for they lacked central organization and clear political platforms. Moreover, both were composed of a handful of aristocratic families who dominated 17th-century English politics; they were not popular movements. Nevertheless, each served as an embryo for the later emergence of the party system.

The Popish Plot, 1677. Charles' rule was dominated by continuing religious conflicts centered on Roman Catholicism. Charles himself was married to a Roman Catholic. More importantly, Charles had entered into the *Treaty of Dover* with the French king Louis XIV. This treaty contained a secret provision that at some opportune moment Charles would declare himself a Catholic and would receive a large subsidy from France.

In 1678, a Baptist preacher named Titus Oates fabricated a tale of a Jesuit plot to murder Charles, massacre Protestants, and establish a Catholic monarchy under Charles' brother, James, the Duke of York. Although none of the story was true, it inflamed the public and the Parliament, and soon the secret provisions of the Treaty of Dover leaked out. As a result, the Whig majority in the House of Commons attempted to prevent the succession of James to the throne, but failed to get support from the House of Lords. In 1681, Charles dismissed Parliament and for the next four years ruled without its advice, his expenses underwritten by subsidies from Louis XIV.

During those years, Charles launched a series of attacks on the Whigs; two were executed and their leader, the Earl of Shaftesbury, fled to the continent and died in Holland. With him into exile went John Locke, the political philosopher whose observation of the hectic political scene in England led him to evolve a new theory of government (Chapter 8).

THE REIGN OF JAMES II (1685–1688)

When Charles II died in 1685, his brother James succeeded him. James was serious, honest, and devout, but also arrogant, obstinate, and insensitive to the political and religious realities of England.

James' accession to the throne presented a religious problem, for he had recently married the Catholic Mary of Modena and had himself converted. He had fathered two daughters by his first wife, Anne Hyde, and both—Mary and Anne—were Protestants.

At James' succession, the Duke of Monmouth, the illegitimate son of Charles II, tried to win the throne. He had hoped that he could gain the support of Protestant dissenters against the Catholic-leaning James, but only a few thousand, mostly peasants, joined him. The veteran royal troops under the leadership of John Churchill, later the great Duke of Marlborough, easily crushed the rebels. The Duke of Monmouth was executed and his followers wiped out.

Once securely in power, James moved quickly to return Roman Catholicism, appointing Catholics to all the key national and local government positions, the military, and the universities. In 1687 and 1688 James issued two Declarations of Indulgence which would have permitted free worship of Protestant dissenters and Catholics. When seven Anglican bishops refused to read the *Act of Indulgence* to their congregations, they were arrested and charged with sedition, but a jury found them innocent.

The final blow to James' rule came in June 1688 when his wife, Mary of Modena, gave birth to a son, thus establishing Catholic succession to the throne. A rumor spread that the baby was not James and Mary's son, but had been smuggled into the Queen's bedroom in a warming pan. There is no evidence of the truth of this rumor, but the infant was widely known as the "warming pan baby."

THE GLORIOUS REVOLUTION

By autumn 1688, Whig and Tory leaders were united in their opposition to James, yet they were reluctant to resume the civil war. The leaders of the two parties jointly issued a discreet invitation to William of Orange, the ruler of the Netherlands and the husband of James' eldest daughter, Mary, to invade England.

WILLIAM (1689–1702) AND MARY (1689–1694)

In November, William sailed across the Channel and landed unopposed in southwestern England. With a small army, he moved slowly toward London, gaining supporters along the way. When James' soldiers, under the command of John Churchill, defected and turned against him, James fled without offering resistance.

None of the rebels wanted James to be captured, for they did not want another trial and execution of the reigning monarch, as had occurred with Charles I. Moreover, to maintain the appearance of legality, they preferred to pretend that James had abdicated. For these reasons, James II was allowed to escape to France. The *Glorious Revolution* had succeeded without a shot being fired.

John Churchill, later Duke of Marlborough, helped to engineer the "escape" of James II. He later became the primary adviser and chief military general of the Protestant Queen Anne.

Rock-a-bye-Baby

A contemporary nursery rhyme described the events of the Glorious Revolution:

Rock-a-bye baby [James' son] in a
    tree top,
When the wind blows [the wind
    blowing William's fleet across the
    Channel], the cradle will rock,
When the bough breaks, the cradle
    will fall,
And down will come baby, cradle
    and all.

The Bill of Rights. In January 1689, an assembled Convention Parliament proclaimed that James had abdicated, and invited William and Mary to take the throne as joint rulers of England. Along with the invitation was included a *Bill of Rights* (1689) with the following important provisions: 1) Parliament was to meet annually. 2) Parliament controlled the king's revenues. 3) Subjects were guaranteed the right to petition the king. 4) The monarch guaranteed freedom of election to and debate within Parliament. 5) Subjects were guaranteed reasonable bail and trial by jury. 6) The king could not suspend the laws. 7) A standing army in peacetime was illegal without Parliament's consent. 8) No Roman Catholic could hold or share the throne of England.

A subsequent *Toleration Act* (1689) gave dissenters freedom of worship, but not political rights; Roman Catholics did not have religious or political equality until the 19th century.

This political and religious inequality was extended from England into Ireland, which the Protestant Stuarts treated as an English colony. Governmental power and most property in largely Catholic Ireland was given to English and Scottish Protestants who usually lived in London as absentee landlords. Within Ireland, there was established a harsh religious code against Catholics. It outlawed Catholic priests and schools and excluded Catholics from public office, professions, and the holding of property. These disabilities encouraged Irish Catholics to ally themselves at any given time with England's enemies and to struggle for the next three centuries for political independence from England. The blood conflict today between Northern Irish Protestants and the rest of Ireland has its roots in 17th-century English history.

The Act of Settlement, 1701. On the positive side, the Glorious Revolution and its Bill of Rights, Toleration Act, and finally, the *Act of Settlement* (1701), represent very important milestones in English constitutional history. First of all, the Bill of Rights and the Act of Settlement marked a victory for Parliament, for no one could forget that William and Mary received their crowns from Parlia-

The fact that William and Mary were presented their crowns by the Parliament demonstrates the importance of the Glorious Revolution: they ruled by invitation, not by "divine right."

ment. Furthermore, all future monarchs would be required to receive parliamentary assent for any war, for only Parliament had authority to raise a standing army. The supremacy of the House of Commons over the House of Lords was firmly established, too, for it held the power to grant revenues to the king.

In addition, by its passage of the Act of Settlement, Parliament established and secured the Protestant succession to the English throne. It took this action in 1701 because James' son, James Edward (the Old Pretender), who was in exile in France, was recognized by Louis XIV as the rightful king of England. This fact, combined with the childlessness of William and Mary, meant that James' Catholic son might well succeed to the throne.

The Act of Settlement stipulated that the throne would go to Anne at William's and Mary's deaths. Should she die without direct heir, as it appeared she would, the throne would go to the Electress of Hanover—Sophia, the Protestant granddaughter of James I—and her descendants. The Act of Settlement also provided that all sovereigns of England should be Protestants and that they were forbidden to leave the country without parliamentary approval. As Parliament prescribed, the last Stuart monarch, Anne, succeeded to the throne in 1702 and ruled for 12 years. At her death without heir in 1714, the Hanover line was established with the accession of George I, son of Sophia.

THE REIGN OF ANNE (1702–1714)

During Anne's reign, English participation in the War of the Spanish Succession proved very beneficial to the country. England's victory in 1713 brought recognition of her military supremacy and greatly increased her commercial and colonial empire, at the expense of France and Spain. Also during Anne's reign, the *Act of Union of 1707* joined the kingdoms of England and Scotland, further strengthening England's position in Europe.

Changes were occurring within England even as she was establishing herself as a power to be contended with in foreign affairs. These changes were interconnected and had social, economic and political implications for the future of the country.

Socially, the gentry and country squires who owned large estates became the most influential class, serving as local administrators, as justices of the peace, and winning control of the House of Commons. During this period many of the great English country houses, such as the Duke of Marlborough's mansion, Blenheim, were built. Demand for wool and wheat brought high profits to the gentry, and they used this money to build elegant homes with vast grounds and sculptured gardens.

While the gentry class prospered, the rural wage earner sank into near poverty. The yeomen, or small independent landowners, also lost status, and many of them became tenant farmers. This agricultural development was partly caused by the continuing process of land enclosure and the elimination of common pastures.

In fact, the gap between rich and poor in the 17th and 18th centuries in both rural and urban England was considerable. In the cities, of which London with a population of 500,000 was the largest, the merchants and lawyers prospered enough so that many could purchase large rural estates which would enable their offspring to marry into the aristocracy. Below them were ordinary merchants and shopkeepers who earned a decent living.

Farther down the economic scale were the craftsmen and artisans who prospered in good times and starved in bad. At the bottom were the day laborers for whom employment was random. Lacking economic wherewithal and political power, they often resorted to thievery and rioting. In fact, mob violence in town and countryside was frequent and was harshly suppressed—with execution the usual penalty.

The death of Anne in 1714 marks a major turning point in English history, not only because it brought to an end the ill-fated Stuart dynasty, but for two other reasons. First, the religious issue which had divided England since Henry VIII's break with the Roman Catholic Church in the 16th century had been settled. The Church of England was firmly established, and intolerance of dissenters had become a key aspect of its policy. Secondly, constitutionalism was now a fact: the Glorious Revolution had conserved and sanctified the English parliamentary structure. The landed aristocracy dominated politics, while the monarchy remained the constitutional center of government.

THE HANOVERIANS For more than a century, the first three Hanoverian monarchs, George I (1714–1727), George II (1727–1760), and George III (1760–1820), ruled England. During the reign of the foreign Hanoverians the English cabinet system slowly emerged, in part because of the inabilities and incompetencies of George I and George II. German by birth and education, obstinate and domineering, neither fully grasped the intricacies of the English political system.

THE GROWTH OF A PARTY SYSTEM

Throughout this period, the monarchs sought the support of whichever faction— Whig or Tory—held a majority in the House of Commons. From that majority, they appointed the king's ministers and advisors. The royal inner advisory group met informally and indeed made most of the government's decisions. They, in turn, were forced to answer for their policies to the other members of their party in the House of Commons, which held the power to approve standing armies and to grant revenues to the king. This royal inner council became forerunner of the modern cabinet system. Developed from necessity and circumstances, it was informal, unwritten, and unofficial. Nevertheless, it was an important step in England's evolving political system.

Another precedent in the 18th century was the emergence of the *prime minister*. The first politician to receive this title was Sir Robert Walpole (1676–1745), a successful businessman and country squire who had earned a reputation as a financial genius through his handling of a disastrous speculation known as the South Sea Bubble. His financial policies were designed to benefit his own class of country gentlemen and to keep the poor working hard by paying them low wages. In 1722 he became the leader of the Whig party. Through his capacity to lead, his loyalty to the king, hard work, and perhaps a little bribery, he dominated politics until 1742. He established the principle of a prime minister as the leader of the inner council and developed further the cabinet and party system to the point where *Whig* and *Tory* became very partisan terms.

Because of the degree of partisanship which existed under the first three Georges,

The author Samuel Johnson with friends at his favorite club, the Cheshire Cheese.

and because these Hanoverian kings were relatively unpopular among the English, the 18th century was a time for political satire of all sorts. Most notable among those who commented in this way upon public affairs were Joseph Addison (1672–1719) and Richard Steele (1672–1729), who wrote and published the journals *The Tatler* and *The Spectator*; Jonathan Swift (1667–1745), author of *Gulliver's Travels*; and Samuel Johnson (1709–1784), the famed compiler of the *Dictionary of the English Language.*

Johnson was perhaps the most opinionated of all, a devout Tory and supporter of Anglicanism who reveled in conversation. He habitually attracted hosts of eager listeners at his favorite eating club, the Cheshire Cheese, where he pontificated on all subjects—particularly politics. His counterpart in the artistic world was William Hogarth (1697–1764), whose satirical paintings of

The artist William Hogarth often commented upon the social issues of his time. In this painting, a gentleman is about to be seized and imprisoned for debt.

18th-century social life are well known. Even music in England had a partisan flavor in that the foremost composer of the early 18th century, George Frederick Handel, began his career in England by writing for Queen Anne (*Te Deum*) and continued in service to the Hanoverian rulers.

In the arts, England remained much indebted to Continental models and leadership, though the paintings of Hogarth and the famed portraitists, Joshua Reynolds (1723–1792) and Thomas Gainsborough (1727–1788), were strictly English in content and inspiration. Only in literature did the English develop forms and substance with a distinctly national flavor, such as the satires of Johnson and his set and the novels of Daniel Defoe (1660–1731) and Samuel Richardson (1689–1761).

THE AGE OF GEORGE III (1760–1820)

Unlike his predecessors, George III was English-born. Succeeding his grandfather, he came to the throne as a young man, and reigned for 60 years. Pious, serious, and stubborn, he failed to adjust to the changing times and suffered from recurring episodes of apparent mental illness. Early in his reign he challenged the supremacy of the Whigs, who had dominated politics since 1715. In the first decade of his rule seven prime ministers followed each other in rapid succession, until Lord North succeeded in holding a majority for 12 years. During his reign, George III was able to manipulate Parliament through royal patronage. He believed that the monarchy should rule above parties, without the limitations of the cabinet system.

It was during the reign of George III that the American colonies revolted and won their independence. Part of the cause of the colonists' revolt was economic, for England, like France in this period, pursued a policy of mercantilism. This economic policy required government intervention to guarantee a supply of bullion (gold and silver), to be achieved by a favorable balance of trade; the colonies' providing cheap raw materials and guaranteed markets for manufactured goods; and all trade being carried on British ships. The American colonists sought to avoid these restrictions, often by smuggling, for they believed their economic development was stifled by British mercantile policy.

Intensifying the economic problem was parliamentary taxation, justified on the grounds that British defense of the colonies was expensive. Between 1763 and 1774, the Parliament passed 13 taxation acts which served to unite the colonists in protest against British policy. The colonists also resisted parliamentary attempts to legislate directly for them and refused to accept the supremacy of the British Parliament. Moreover, they were influenced by the ideas of John Locke and other thinkers of the Enlightenment whose theories of self-government they espoused. At the same time, the colonists believed that they were guaranteed all of the privileges which Parliament itself had gained at the expense of the English monarchy.

To make this point, the colonists were finally forced to declare their independence from England and go to war against their former protectors. In this struggle they were supported by the French, who were not so much pro-American as anti-British, and individual liberal idealists from other European countries, such as Poland and Prussia. After a series of initial defeats in the first year of the war (1776), the colonists slowly and painstakingly began to win a few important battles against the British until they had secured all but the southern colonies. With the defeat of General Cornwallis at Yorktown, Virginia, in the fall of 1781, the English were finally driven from all the colonies, and the *Treaty of Paris* in 1783 recognized the United States as an independent country. This victory by the colonists humiliated George III and his Parliament and set the stage for the sweeping reforms of the 19th and 20th centuries (Chapter 13).

SUMMARY

Despite the loss of its colonies in North America, England emerged from the period of Stuart kingship, the Cromwellian Protectorate, and the rule of the first three Georges, as a preeminent power. English naval superiority was unquestioned, and major changes in agriculture and manufacturing would lead the way to still greater economic advances.

Compared with the prevalent political systems on the European continent, the English system evolved in a unique fashion in the 17th and 18th centuries, as the British Parliament wrested power from the ruling monarchs. A constitutional system was firmly established, whereby the monarch's power was limited by the Parliament. At the same time, the hereditary branch of Parliament, the House of Lords, lost power to the elected branch, the House of Commons. Moreover, two political factions emerged, the Whigs and the Tories, which later evolved into the English two-party system. During the 18th century the practice of drawing a cabinet of the king's advisers from the majority party in Parliament was institutionalized.

England was not yet a democracy, for only about one in ten English subjects had the right to vote and the king and the hereditary House of Lords still held considerable power. However, the emergence of new political institutions formed the basis for the political reform movements of the 19th and 20th centuries (Chapter 13).

QUESTIONS

1 What was the political philosophy of King James I? How does it compare with that of Louis XIV of France?
2 Describe constitutionalism in the English tradition. What bearing did this tradition have upon the conflict between James I and the Parliament?
3 What were the causes of the English civil war? What were the results?
4 To what extent was religious controversy a factor in English politics in the 17th century?
5 What part did the personalities of the rulers of 17th-century England play in the events of the era? Would different kings have changed the course of modern English history?
6 Describe the settlement of England's political and religious conflicts at the end of the 17th century.

BIBLIOGRAPHY

FRASER, LADY ANTONIA. *Oliver Cromwell: The Lord Protector.* New York: Knopf, 1973. *This popular biography offers one of the best glimpses into the character of Oliver Cromwell.*
KRONENBERGER, LOUIS. *Kings and Desperate Men: Life in Eighteenth-Century England.* New York: Vintage Books, 1959. *A social history of both the aristocracy and the poor of 18th-century England, with commentary upon their cultural life, and sketches of leading political figures.*
PLUMB, J. H. *The First Four Georges.* New York: John Wiley, 1967. *An eminent British historian has written a brief, readable account of the period between 1714 and 1830—an era of confusing political history. At the same time, Plumb captures the personalities and foibles of the four Georges.*
SEAVER, PAUL S., ed. *Seventeenth-Century England: Society in an Age of Revolution.* New York: New Viewpoints, 1976. *This work reflects current interest in social history: it does not treat the civil war and Glorious Revolution, but instead issues such as social mobility, agriculture, labor, and the growth of the electorate.*
WEDGEWOOD, C. V. *A Coffin for King Charles: The Trial and Execution of Charles I.* New York: Time, Inc., 1964. *In describing the events surrounding the execution of the king, Ms. Wedgewood offers insight into Charles' character and the political issues of his rule.*

Eastern and Central Europe

Although one could question the accuracy of Frederick of Prussia's evaluation of Peter the Great (cited above), it does symbolize the emergence of Russia as a nation to be reckoned with in the 18th century. Prussia and Russia, along with Austria, came to dominate central and eastern Europe.

Beginning in the 17th century and extending into the 18th century, the growth of absolute monarchy added impetus to the emergence of the nation-state. The sovereign was absolute only when compared to the role of the monarch in earlier times. The so-called absolute monarchs did not have the technological capacity to intrude into the public and private lives of their subjects. Each ruler was limited by tradition as well as the immediate political and economic needs of the time.

THE HAPSBURGS   The Thirty Years' War left Germany prostrate and divided. The Treaty of Westphalia further weakened the Holy Roman Empire by giving to the different "states" almost complete independence. These states ranged in size from knights' individual domains to the Austrian realm. Soon, many of these states

were imitating the absolutism of the French monarchy, establishing miniature Versailles and courts and armies.

THE RECOVERY OF THE HAPSBURGS

Leopold I (1658–1704) attempted to deal with the changed circumstances of the Holy Roman Empire after the Thirty Years' War and the Peace of Westphalia. Instead of trying to breathe new life into the empire, he concentrated his energies on the Hapsburg family holdings in Central and Eastern Europe. These included Austria, part of Hungary, and Bohemia.

Leopold was faced with two direct threats to his power. To the west was a revivified France under Louis XIV, dedicated to the traditional anti-Hapsburg policy. Louis was concerned that no strong German state arise on his border. Thus he meddled in the affairs of the petty German states, and encouraged the Ottoman Turks in their struggle against the Hapsburgs to the east.

The revitalized Ottoman Empire held much of eastern Europe, including most of Hungary. The Ottoman goal was nothing less than the capture of Vienna itself. In 1682, an Ottoman army of 200,000 men, assembled by

The Hapsburg emperor Leopold I. His claim to the Spanish throne contributed to the outbreak of the War of the Spanish Succession in 1701.

the Grand Vizier Kara Mustafa, marched up the Danube valley. Leopold's forces, outnumbered, retreated and in July 1683, the Turks surrounded Vienna and lay siege to the city. For two months the Viennese held out—long enough for the army of the *Holy League* to arrive and relieve the city. The Holy League was an alliance of Austria, Poland, and Venice. Its forces, led by the Pole John Sobieski, included volunteers from many European countries, including France.

After the Turks were thrown back from Vienna, the Holy League rapidly moved onto the offensive against the Ottoman Empire. At the Battle of Zenta in Serbia in 1697, the Turks were forced to sue for peace. By the *Treaty of Karlowitz* of 1699, the Hapsburgs gained control over all of Hungary, Croatia, and Slavonia.

CREATION OF A POLYGLOT EMPIRE

The fight with the Turks gave the Hapsburgs control over a vast area composed of a patchwork of different languages and cultures. Be-sides the portion in central and eastern Europe, the Hapsburg lands also included Belgium and parts of Italy. The achievement of the Hapsburgs was to meld this conglomerate group into at least a partly coherent empire which they ruled from Vienna.

From the start, the army, court, and government were international. Czechs, Hungarians, and Italians played a large part in the administration. The landowners in this cosmopolitan society felt greater sympathy with each other than with the lower classes who worked their vast estates. The Hapsburg government dealt almost exclusively with the landowners, and left them to deal with the peasants.

No diet was established for the empire as a whole. Instead, the different systems of the component parts were left in place. In Bohemia, Hungary, and Austria, the diets were controlled by the landholding class. The peasants remained in a position of virtual serfdom. The Hapsburgs remained indifferent to local conditions as long as the different territories provided the requisite amount of troops and tax revenues.

The one unifying feature of the Hapsburg empire was Roman Catholicism. The Hapsburgs had been the protectors of Roman Catholicism from the time of the Reformation. During the Thirty Years' War, after the failure of a revolt in Bohemia, Catholic missionaries poured into the country. Bohemia, which had had a substantial number of Protestants, became a Catholic country. The Hapsburgs destroyed the traditional elective Bohemian monarchy, and Czechs were not to have an independent state again until after World War I.

The same treatment was meted out to Hungary, which also had a substantial Protestant population. The Hungarian nobles had the same power as the German nobles to pick the religion of their own estates. During their occupation of Hungary, the Turks had favored the Protestants, calculating that they would be less interested in a union with the Catholic Hapsburgs. This only increased the determination of the Hapsburgs to eliminate Protestantism in Hungary. Here too the elective monarchy was overthrown and the ruler of the Hapsburg lands was made the hereditary ruler of Hungary. A rebellion of Hungarians led by Prince Francis Rakoczy—with the aid of Louis XIV—raged from 1703 to 1711. It was put down with great ferocity.

THE PROBLEM OF SUCCESSION

Because the Hapsburg territories were tied together by their dynastic connection, it was crucial that the succession be secure. Soon after the reconquest of Hungary, Charles VI negotiated the Pragmatic Sanction (Chapter 5), ensuring that after his death, his empire would pass intact into the hands of his daughter, Maria Theresa. In this he was successful, although it was her husband, Francis of Lorraine, who was to get the title of Holy Roman Emperor.

Charles VI was also faced with a European conflict over Poland. *The War of the Polish Succession* (1733–1735) was precipitated by the internal weakness of Poland and the rapacity of her neighbors, each of whom sought dominance there. Fought between France, Spain, and Savoy on the one side, and Russia and Austria on the other, the war began when each side supported a different claimant to the Polish throne. The subsequent Russo-Austrian victory guaranteed the dominance of these two nations in Poland and paved the way for the eventual partition of that hapless state. England's neutrality prevented an escalation of this conflict into a general European war.

THE RULE OF MARIA THERESA (1740–1780)

From the time of her accession in 1740, Maria Theresa was confronted with a threat of war. In 1740, the Hapsburg possession of Silesia was invaded by Prussia (Chapter 5). The *War of the Austrian Succession* showed the lack of support for the Hapsburgs in their own domains. The townspeople of Breslau,

The empress Maria Theresa posed for a formal portrait with her husband and 13 children.

the capital of Silesia, refused to allow the Austrian troops to enter the city, claiming they were protecting the town's liberties. In Bohemia, about half of the magnates favored the French and their German supporters. Maria Theresa could gain support in Hungary only by confirming the ancient liberties of the Hungarian nobles.

Nevertheless, Maria Theresa, with some assistance from England, proved to be a resourceful leader. In 1748, when the war came to an end with the signing of the Treaty of Aix-la-Chapelle, she had beaten back her enemies. Her husband, Francis, was recognized as Holy Roman emperor, and Austria regained all lost territory except for Silesia, which remained in Prussian hands.

The shock of the War of the Austrian Succession forced Maria Theresa to consider a reorganization of her empire. Her consolidation of power was to set the course for the Austrian empire through the 19th century. In her efforts at reform she was assisted by ministers of varying nationalities, including the talented and astute Count Kaunitz, from

119

the province of Moravia in Czechoslovakia. The objectives of the reform were to ensure the flow of tax money and soldiers and to weld the empire more strongly together. To accomplish this, Maria Theresa had to break the power of the diets in the different areas. Because of the promises to Hungary during the war, its power was not challenged. But the diet of Bohemia was dissolved, and administrators controlled by the government in Vienna took over many of the functions of the former local governments, such as tax collection. A tariff union was established between Bohemia and Austria, making the area the largest free-trade zone in Europe.

In order to get greater manpower for her armies and also from humanitarian motives, Maria Theresa made an effort to improve the status of the peasants of central and eastern Europe, who still lived in a condition of serfdom. Laws were passed to curtail the abuses against peasants by their lords. For example, the labor obligations of the peasants were usually limited to three days a week. Although these regulations were often evaded, there was some improvement in the peasants' condition.

THE REIGN OF JOSEPH II (1780–1790)

Maria Theresa was succeeded by her son Joseph II, who had reigned jointly with her in the last years of her life. Joseph II was influenced by the ideas of his time—the Enlightenment (Chapter 8)—and was impatient for reform. His motto was that good government called for "the greatest good for the greatest number." During the ten years of his rule, decrees poured forth on many different matters. He decreed that taxation should be equal for all classes of the population. His mother had made steps toward that goal earlier, but he carried it forward. Punishments were also to be equal. Aristocrats found guilty of crimes were exhibited in the pillories. In addition, punishments were made less cruel. For his efforts, historians have termed him a *benevolent despot*.

The emperor Joseph II attempted to improve economic and social conditions for the lower classes within his empire. Here, he is shown visiting a peasant family.

To force through his reforms, Joseph further reduced the power of the local diets and magnates of different territories. In addition, he tried to extend his reforms to Hungary, something his mother had never attempted. He also allowed freedom of the press and gave equal civil rights to the Jews of the empire, even making them eligible to serve in the army and to obtain patents of nobility.

Joseph increased the size of the bureaucracy and made it more centralized. He tried to unify the administration through the universal use of German. Training schools were established for new bureaucrats. A special section was established to spy on government officials to see if they were doing an efficient job.

Joseph also attempted to develop the empire economically, even setting up an East India Company, but these measures came to little. Many of his other reforms likewise met with failure. They aroused the opposition of the Hungarians and the Belgians, who openly revolted at the time of Joseph's death in 1790. His failure was due in large part to the lack of adequate government machinery to carry out such basic reforms and the failure of his successors to continue his efforts.

THE RISE OF PRUSSIA The destiny of the state that was to become known as Prussia was linked to the Hohenzollern family. In medieval times, the land holdings of the Hohenzollerns were in a small area in the south of the Holy Roman Empire near Switzerland. But in the early 15th century, one branch of the Hohenzollern family was awarded the Margravate of Brandenburg by the emperor. Brandenburg, centered around the city of Berlin, was located in the northeastern border of the empire. The Hohenzollerns acquired, along with the title of Margrave, the status of Imperial Elector, one of those privileged to choose the Holy Roman Emperor.[1]

After accepting Lutheranism in the 16th century, the Margraves of Brandenburg assumed a position of leadership among the Protestant princes of Germany. Much of their wealth came from the confiscation of Church property. In the next century, the Hohenzollerns began adding to their territory.

Mark, Cleves, and Ravensburg, three small enclaves of land in the Rhine valley, became part of Brandenburg in 1614. None of these areas were contiguous with one another—nor did any of them border Brandenburg. Lands acquired later suffered from the same disadvantage of not having common boundaries. Thus, the foreign policy of the

Hohenzollerns was dictated by the need to unite the diverse parts of their holdings through conquest and diplomacy.

In 1618, the Margrave of Brandenburg acquired through inheritance East Prussia on the Baltic Sea. The origins of Prussian military tradition can be found in the medieval Order of Teutonic Knights. In the early 13th century, this quasi-religious military order was sent to the eastern borders of Germany to protect Christians and encourage the spread of Christianity. With the Reformation, the Knights' military code of behavior became the foundation for the Prussian officers' corps. The East Prussian landed nobility, known as *Junkers*, were the major source of officers for the army and bureaucrats for the government. The Junkers' religion, Lutheranism, strengthened those links by encouraging the faithful to serve loyally both king and state.

Brandenburg-Prussia suffered along with the rest of Germany during the Thirty Years' War. However, after 1640, Frederick William, The Great Elector (1640–1688), succeeded in following a policy of neutrality until the war ended in 1648.

THE GREAT ELECTOR

Frederick William fell heir to a state consisting of three semi-independent areas—Brandenburg, East Prussia, and bits of territory along the Rhine River. He soon added Pomerania, as a consequence of the Peace of Westphalia in 1648. Almost immediately, Frederick William set about creating a power base founded on the absolute authority of the ruler, a loyal and efficient bureaucracy, and a standing army.

In order to pay for his standing army, Frederick William introduced a land tax and adopted a system of excise taxes on all goods that entered towns. To facilitate commerce, a canal was built between the Oder and Elbe rivers. New industries were established, including cloth, paper, and iron.

Louis XIV's revocation of the Edict of

---

[1] The terms **margrave** and **margravate** are compounds of *mark* or *march*, the name given to a border kingdom in Charlemagne's time, and *graf*, meaning "count" or "earl." A *margrave* was thus a military governor of a border province.

A policy of welcoming refugees to Prussia was initiated during the reign of the Great Elector.

Nantes in 1685 gave Frederick William an opportunity to strengthen his country economically. Twenty thousand Huguenots believed Frederick William when he said: "We have never thought to arrogate to ourselves the dominion over consciences." Religious refugees throughout Europe voted with their feet and fled to Brandenburg-Prussia where they were welcomed by the Great Elector. Many of the refugees were skilled craftsmen and artisans who made a decisive contribution to Prussian industrial growth in the 18th century.

Unlike Louis XIV, who came to rely increasingly on the bourgeoisie, Frederick William cast his lot with the Junker class. He molded the Junkers into a "service nobility" of those who received their titles and positions based on loyalty and service to the ruler, rather than by birth. The aristocrats demanded a high price for their unquestioned loyalty and service to the king—and the price was paid by the Prussian peasant. Serfs lost their few remaining rights, and the feudal system continued as an essential part of German society.

FREDERICK WILLIAM I (1688–1713)

The Great Elector's successor, Frederick William I, benefited from his policies. The increased size of the army gave Brandenburg–Prussia a greater voice in international affairs. During the War of the Spanish Succession, Frederick joined with the Austrian Hapsburgs in opposing France. He used the crisis to gain the consent of the Hapsburg Holy Roman emperor to take the title "King of Prussia" in 1701. This new title increased the independence and prestige of the kingdom, for Prussia had never been ruled by the Holy Roman emperor. As the years passed, the name Kingdom of Prussia would be applied to all the holdings of the Hohenzollerns. Frederick I gathered artists and scientists at his court. The capital city of Berlin was beautified and its learned men organized the new Society of Science in 1700.

Frederick William despised everything French, even to the extent of dressing condemned criminals in French clothes at their hanging. He was penurious to a fault, forcing his family to wear hand-me-down clothes, dismissing many servants, and closing off most of the royal residence during the winter to save fuel.

He allowed himself one extravagance, the recruiting and maintenance of an elite military unit known as the *Potsdam Guard*. This 1200-man unit was recruited throughout Europe and around the world. The one basic requirement was size: all members had to be at least six feet tall, and one special unit was limited to those close to seven feet. In an effort to breed home-grown giants, Frederick William ordered that all tall Prussian men marry tall women. His precious giants were never risked in battle, but when the king was depressed or ill, all 1200 would march in close-order drill through his bedroom with trumpets blaring and cymbals crashing in an effort to relieve the royal gloom.

Frederick William I refined and built upon the system that he inherited. Although loathing all things French, he followed the

During the reign of Frederick William I, the size of the Prussian army more than doubled. Shown is the elite corps of tall soldiers known as the Potsdam Guard.

lead of Louis XIV in championing royal absolutism and the divine-right monarchy. He formed a bureaucracy based on the principle of decisions by committee, rather than strong department heads, such as existed in France. However, Frederick William never surrendered any of his autocratic authority to subordinates, as is evident in the following admonition made to all his subjects:

• • • *One must serve the King with life and limb, with goods and chattels, with honor and conscience, and surrender everything except salvation. The latter is reserved for God. But everything else must be mine.*[2]

The Prussian army became a finely honed military machine under Frederick William's tutelage and direction. Through conscription, the size of the army increased from 38,000 to 80,000 men. Promotions in the officer corps increasingly were based on merit rather than title or influence.

Frederick William's motto was, "It cannot be done with the pen if it is not supported by the power of the sword." Because the proportion of soldiers to population was so large, there were scarcely enough peasants to farm the land. In 1733, Frederick William established a system whereby officers recruited their own serfs for part-time army service. The enormous role that the army played in Prussian life is summed up by a minister of France who later wrote that Prussia was "not a country with an army, but an army with a country."[3]

Frederick William also strengthened the government bureaucracy by creating a civil service system in which advancement depended on proven ability and experience. He introduced compulsory elementary education, on the assumption that an educated citizenry was more valuable to the state. As this program was implemented, Frederick became known as the "schoolmaster of Prussia." Those with no fixed career were put to work in the army or in public service projects.

FREDERICK THE GREAT (1740–1786)

With the accession of Frederick II, better known to history as Frederick the Great, Prussia began to influence the balance of power in Germany and, ultimately, in the rest of Europe. Within a few months of assuming power, Frederick unleashed the army that had been so carefully built up by his father.

Early Life. Frederick the Great had a stormy relationship with his father. The son's penchant for French literature, playing the flute, and French clothes did not endear

---

[2] Stephen J. Lee, *Aspects of European History: 1494–1789*, 2d ed. (London & New York: Methuen, 1984), p. 185.

[3] Geoffrey Treasure, *The Making of Modern Europe, 1648–1780* (London & New York: Methuen, 1985), p. 446.

him to the father. Relations between Frederick William and his son deteriorated rapidly after the boy was brutally beaten in the presence of servants and army officers. In 1730, at the age of 18, Frederick ran away with a friend. Before they had gotten far, the young men were apprehended and tried as army deserters. Frederick was forced to watch while his friend was beheaded.

Frederick William imposed upon his son a strict regimen of training for kingship. Frederick served a tour of duty in the army as a private, after which he was thrown into the bureaucracy, beginning at the lowest rung on the civil service ladder. When Frederick's time came to rule Prussia in 1740, at the age of 28, he was eminently qualified to fulfill his kingly obligations. In later life, Frederick the Great freely acknowledged the debt he owed his father in training him to govern, and in leaving him a politically unified and militarily strong country.

The War of the Austrian Succession. Within a few months of coming to the throne, Frederick was at war with Austria and its

Frederick the Great resolutely guided his country through the devastating Seven Years' War. This portrait of the great general was made in the twilight of his career.

ruler Maria Theresa. With an obvious flair for diplomacy, Frederick negotiated an alliance with France and Bavaria aimed at stripping Austria and Maria Theresa of land and power. The Elector of Bavaria desired the imperial throne, France wanted the Austrian Netherlands, and Prussia was interested in the industrial district of Silesia—an Austrian possession rich in natural resources and strategically located along the Oder River. There is little question that Maria Theresa's femaleness as well as her newness to the Austrian throne were determining factors in Frederick's attitude toward Austria.

To the world, Frederick justified his invasion and occupation of Silesia with the public pronouncement that, "I have been compelled to send my troops into the Duchy [Silesia] in order to prevent others seizing it."[4] Privately, he saw Silesia as a buffer zone between Austria and Prussia, a commercially valuable trade center, and as a rich source of natural resources. Although Frederick gained Silesia, he now had an enemy in the empress of Austria. In addition, Prussia was vulnerable because it consisted of bits and pieces of territory all over the map of central Europe. Any determined and well coordinated attack by a coalition of resourceful enemies would most likely lead to the dismemberment of the patchwork quilt called Prussia.

The Seven Years' War. Frederick proved to be more skillful as a warrior than as a diplomat. By 1756, he found himself encircled and entrapped in a web of alliances woven by Maria Theresa. Aligned against Prussia were the four major military powers on the continent of Europe—Austria, France, Russia, and Sweden. Only England, out of concern for the fate of Hanover (the ancestral home of the English kings), and out of a desire to maintain a balance of power in Eu-

[4] Stephen J. Lee, *Aspects of European History,* p. 193.

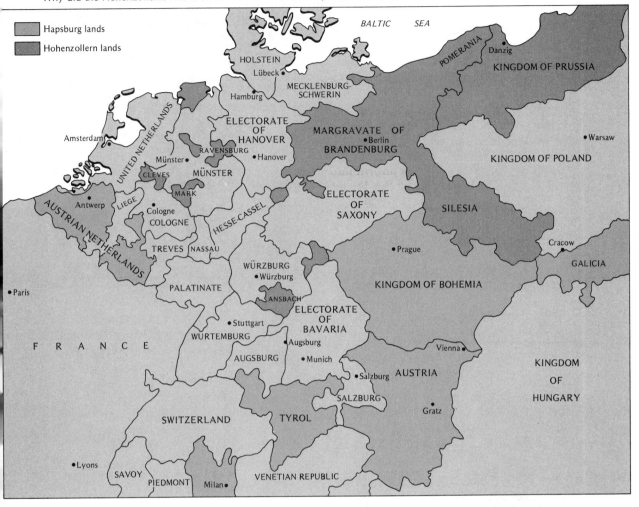

rope, sided with Prussia. Although England supplied financial assistance and was of some help militarily, on the world stage Frederick and his army stood virtually alone on the battlefields of Europe for the next seven years.

During the Seven Years' War (1756–1763), the martial ineptitude of Prussia's enemies, the military genius of Frederick, and luck combined to save Prussia from annihilation. Shorter lines of supply and communication, the inability of his enemies to coordinate their attacks, and Frederick's brilliant tactical use of his well-trained army enabled the king of Prussia to keep one step ahead of disaster. Virtually every part of Prussia was conquered and ravaged at least once, including the capital of Berlin. Each of his enemies had to be confronted in battle time and time again. In comparing his difficulties to a man being swarmed over by flies, Frederick observed that: "When one flies off my cheek, another comes and sits on my nose, and scarcely has it been brushed

125

off than another flies up and sits on my forehead, on my eyes and everywhere else."[5]

In 1762, with his own battalions demoralized and decimated, an empty treasury, and three foreign armies moving in for the kill, the situation appeared hopeless. Luckily, the Tsarina Elizabeth of Russia, one of Frederick's most implacable enemies, died suddenly. She was succeeded by her nephew, Peter III, who had intense admiration for Frederick and everything Prussian. Frederick immediately freed all Russian prisoners and sent them on their way home. With Russia now sitting on the sidelines, Frederick's remaining enemies lost any stomach for continuing what had become an exhausting and costly war.

In the Peace of Paris that ended the Seven Years' War, Frederick kept Silesia, and Prussia retained its major power status, but the cost had been high. Frederick himself described the war's effects:

• • • *It is necessary to imagine whole countries ravaged, towns ruined completely, others half burnt, 13,000 houses of which not even the vestiges remain, lands not sown, inhabitants destitute of food, farmers lacking 60,000 horses for labor and in the provinces a decrease of 500,000 people, which is considerable in a population of 4,500,000 souls.*[6]

Personally, Frederick emerged from the crucible prematurely gray and aged before his time. But he was wiser, and after 1763 he began to follow his own sage advice: ". . . the acquisitions which one makes by the pen are always preferable to those made by the sword."[7]

In the years left to him, Frederick kept occupied with intellectual pursuits, improving the economic health and prosperity of his

Frederick's castle at Potsdam was frequently the scene of musical and philosophical gatherings. On this occasion, Johann Sebastian Bach plays for the king.

nation and people, and attempting to fill in the geographical gaps separating the diverse parts of his country. A tireless worker, Frederick produced many writings on philosophy, politics, and government. He helped to design his famous rococo-style palace, Sans Souci, and composed music for his beloved flute. He encouraged education, carrying out an intensive drive to build schools and regulate what should be taught. He continued his father's work of creating an efficient bureaucracy by introducing a system of state examinations for government officials.

Prussia's economy thrived after the severe drain caused by the Seven Years' War. During Frederick's reign, hundreds of new factories opened, including plants for processing sugar, tobacco, and silk. The royal porcelain works in Berlin adopted the Meissen techniques that originated in Saxony. Berlin itself grew from 98,000 people to 150,000 by 1786. The population as a whole rose from 2 million to 5.8 million. Prussia grew in area by more than one-third; Frederick had not only acquired Silesia but East Friesland and West Prussia as well.

[5] *Ibid.*, p. 198.

[6] Geoffrey Treasure, *The Making of Modern Europe*, pp. 451–2.

[7] Stephen J. Lee, *Aspects of European History*, p. 201.

When Frederick died in 1786, he had rightfully earned the title of "Frederick the Great." Not only had he saved his country from destruction by his brilliant military tactics in the Seven Years' War, but he had elevated Prussia to great-power status in the European community of nations.

<h3>THE EMERGENCE OF RUSSIA</h3>

From the mid-13th century till the 15th century, the Mongols dominated Russia, separating the country from the rest of Europe. The Russian poet Alexander Pushkin, in comparing the Mongol influence with the Arab impact on the West, said of the Mongols that they were "Arabs without Aristotle and algebra and other cultural assets."[8] As a result, the Russians failed to experience until much later many of the elements in the mainstream of Western civilization, such as the Renaissance, the emergence of capitalism, and the age of exploration and discovery.

RISE OF THE PRINCES OF MUSCOVY

During the Mongol occupation of Russia, the princes of *Muscovy*, the grand duchy of Moscow, increased their domains even as conditions in the rest of Russia became more chaotic. From the beginning of the 14th century to the 15th century, the territory of Muscovy increased eight-fold. In 1380, the prince of Muscovy defeated the Mongols' Golden Horde at the Battle of Kulikovo. Although this battle did not end Mongol rule over Russia, it established the preeminence of Moscow among Russian cities. Of equal importance was the fact that Moscow became the residence of the Metropolitan, leader of the Eastern Orthodox Church.

IVAN III (1462–1505)

A new phase in Russian history began with the reign of Ivan III, the first prince of Muscovy to be independent from the Mongols. Ivan initiated a great building program for Moscow, importing architects and artisans from western Europe to beautify the city. He embarked on a program of expansion. By 1478, he had incorporated into his domains Novgorod and its surrounding territory, which reached the White Sea and Arctic Ocean. During his reign, Ivan quadrupled the size of Muscovy at the expense of the Poles, Lithuanians, and Mongols.

After the fall of Constantinople in 1453 to the Ottoman Turks, the Muscovites claimed that the center for Eastern Orthodoxy was now Moscow. Moscow was declared to be the "Third Rome," after the first Rome in Italy, and the "second Rome" at Constantinople. In 1477, when he married Sophia Palaeologus, niece of the last Byzantine Emperor, Ivan could lay claim to the Eastern Roman Empire, and the title of Caesar or Tsar.

IVAN IV (1533–1584)

Ivan IV, also known as "Ivan the Terrible," or "Ivan the Dread," reigned longer than any other tsar and was one of the most influential of Russian rulers in spite of the well-earned name given to him by his subjects. In a fit of uncontrollable anger, Ivan struck his own son and heir with the royal scepter, killing him instantly. It is, however, Ivan's policy of beginning Russia's expansion that is the hallmark of his reign.

Ivan destroyed the remnants of Mongol power, and added the entire basin of the Volga River to his domains. With the help of the Stroganov family, Ivan extended his authority eastward across the Ural mountains into Siberia. He was not as successful against the Ottoman Turks to the south or the Poles to the west. Although contact was made with England and western Europe, their impact on Russia during the reign of Ivan IV was minimal.

Domestically, Ivan convened the first national assembly representing a cross-section

---

[8] Nicholas V. Riasanovsky, *A History of Russia*, 2d ed. (London: Oxford University Press, 1969), p. 82.

of the Russian people, the *Zemski Sobor* ("Land Assembly"). Although it was only an advisory body, under weaker tsars its influence would be felt. Ivan IV also broke the power of the landed and hereditary aristocracy, known as the *Boyars*. Ivan IV accused the Boyars of treason, executing or exiling most of them and confiscating their lands. This property, known as the *Oprichnina*, became the personal domain of the tsar, and was outside of government control. To help him administer the land and ferret out traitors, Ivan appointed special guards called *Oprichniki*. The Oprichniki became a kind of secret police whose reward for reporting treasonous behavior was to administer the traitor's confiscated property.

An important achievement was Ivan's creation of a new kind of aristocracy, one based on service to the tsar rather than heredity. This group was expanded under later tsars.

THE TIME OF TROUBLES

Shortly after the death of Ivan IV in 1584, the new Russian state was confronted with a serious challenge. The period between 1598 and 1613 is known as the *Time of Troubles*. Dynastic struggles, foreign invasions, and natural disasters leading to widespread famine, contributed to a general malaise in Russian society. It was a period of turbulence and anarchy in which several pretenders to the throne appeared. One of them, Boris Godunov, a favorite of Ivan IV, ruled as regent for a time and was then proclaimed tsar in 1598 after Ivan's son Dimitri mysteriously died. It was widely believed that Boris had murdered Dimitri. Boris's Boyar enemies plotted against him, and in response he inaugurated a notorious secret police system. Boris, who had begun his reign determined to rule justly and wisely, died just as a rebellion in the name of a "false" Dimitri threatened to overtake his throne. The false Dimitri ruled only a short time before being overthrown by other pretenders, who inspired revolt throughout the country. A war with Poland plunged the country into further anarchy.

In 1613, the Zemski Sobor met to elect a new tsar. They chose 16-year-old Michael Romanov, a distant cousin of Ivan the Terrible's wife. He was too young to have made enemies or to have become involved in the political and fratricidal entanglements of the Time of Troubles. The Romanovs ruled Russia for the next 300 years, until 1917.

EXPANSION OF RUSSIA

In much the same frontier spirit as early Americans were impelled to move westward, the Russians moved inexorably east to reach the Pacific.

The process started in the 16th century during the reign of Ivan IV. In 1574, the region around Kazan was settled. In 1582, a Cossack leader, Yermak, invaded the Khanate of Siberia and destroyed it. Numerous Russian settlements were established there. In the beginning, the expansion was a product of individual enterprise rather than state initiative.

The primary economic benefit of this eastward expansion was the fur trade. Cossacks and raiders reached the Yeneisei River in 1619. By 1628 the Lena River was forded, and the Russians reached the Pacific in 1639.

The opening up of the lands of Siberia provided an area free from serfdom and an outlet for the energies of many Russians, just as the westward movement did in the United States. However, the state soon took some control of the great eastern territory. By 1700, the fur-bearing mammals were being depleted and the Siberian area became the site of penal colonies.

The eastward movement brought the Russians into contact with the Chinese. Toward the end of the 17th century, Russians expanded into territory that the Chinese considered part of their empire, leading to fighting between the two peoples. The dispute was settled by the *Treaty of Nerchinsk* (1689), which delimited the boundary of the two powers along the Amur and Ussuri rivers. This has remained the boundary with a few minor changes.

THE EARLY ROMANOVS

The first three Romanovs, Michael, Alexis, and Feodor, ruled from 1613 to 1689. During these years, a heavy burden fell upon the peasantry. The demands of military service and taxes forced many peasants to flee or choose voluntary slavery. The *Code of 1649* was put into effect in order to insure an adequate quota of recruits for the army, and to increase the tax base. By the code, peasants were bound to the land and considered as property. Runaway peasants and those who sheltered them were subject to severe penalties. The Code of 1649 firmly established serfdom in Russia at a time when it was disappearing in western Europe.

PEASANT REBELLIONS

Peasants continued to flee the land in large numbers, only to be hunted down by the nobles and severely punished. In desperation, some rebelled. The largest revolt was led by an illiterate Cossack named Stenka Razin, in 1670–71.

Razin began his career by leading pirate bands down the Volga River to the Caspian Sea. There, he raided the coasts of Persia. His exploits became legendary—ballads about him are still sung in Russia today—and he attracted a ragtag band of Cossacks and peasants, who followed him north, with the aim of capturing Moscow. During their advance, large numbers of serfs joined him.

Razin's political aims were vaguely defined, but drew on the intense well of resentment against property owners and government officials. When he reached the fortified city of Astrakhan, the working people revolted and turned it over to him. By 1670, it was estimated that he led a force of 200,000 people.

However, the tsar's forces were well trained and armed with Western weapons. They crushed Razin's troops, and captured Razin himself. The tsar's torturers were unable to wring a confession of guilt or remorse from Razin, and his silence under their torture became a part of Russian folklore.

CHANGES IN THE CHURCH

The 17th century also saw a split in the Russian Orthodox Church. The Patriarch Nikon wanted to vary such rituals as the way of giving the sign of the cross. He also wanted to change the spelling of the name of Jesus and correct mistranslations in Russian versions of the Bible.

A huge segment of the people, known as the *Old Believers*, resisted the changes. However, the government used the army to enforce them. The Old Believers had to either submit or be declared heretics. Most kept the old ways, believing that their persecution was a sign from God that the end of the world was near. Thousands committed suicide by self-immolation in their own churches, and countless others escaped to the northern forests. With the loss of its most

Russia and the Russians

The Soviet Union (Russia) today makes up one-sixth of the world's land mass. In length Russia covers the distance from San Francisco to London, almost half the circumference of the earth. Canada, the United States, and Mexico would fit comfortably within its borders. Geographically, Russia is more than a nation—it has the dimensions of a continent. But it was not always this large, and this chapter will tell the story of Muscovy's expansion.

For all its size, Russia historically has been a land-locked nation. The major navigable rivers have helped to reinforce Russia's isolation, especially from Europe. West of the Ural mountains, the Dnieper, Don, and Volga flow north-south into the Black or Caspian Seas. In Asiatic Russia, the three major river systems of the Ob, Lena, and the Yenesei run into the Arctic Ocean. The Arctic is frozen, the Caspian Sea is land-locked, and access to and from the Black Sea is controlled by whoever dominates the Bosporus and the Dardanelles.

The fact that Russia has few natural barriers within her borders has encouraged internal migration and favored political expansion. On the negative side, the lack of a natural barrier to the west has provided invaders with an unimpeded route into Russia since the Middle Ages. To the east, waves of nomadic tribes have for centuries invaded Russia from the heartland of Asia. The people of Russia are as diverse as the land they inhabit. The single largest ethnic group are the Slavs but there are also 150 other ethnic groupings.

Historical factors as well as geography and the forces of nature have influenced Russia and its people. The emergence of Russian civilization in the city of Kiev in the 6th and 7th centuries, the impact of Eastern Orthodox Christianity beginning in the 10th century, the Mongol invasions of the 13th century, and the rise of Muscovy all helped to mold the history and character of Russia.

devout adherents, the Church and its hierarchy became even more dependent on the tsar and the state.

THE AGE OF PETER THE GREAT With the deaths of Alexis Romanov in 1676, and of Feodor, his eldest son and successor, in 1682, a bloody palace struggle for control of the throne erupted between the families of Alexis' two wives. A truce finally was reached when Ivan V, the only remaining son from the first marriage, and Peter, the only male heir from the second marriage, were declared co-tsars. Since Ivan V was nearly blind, lame, and slow-witted, and Peter was only ten, a regent

had to be found. Peter's half-sister, Sophia, at the age of 26 became regent and the first woman ever to rule Russia.

SOPHIA: RUSSIA'S FIRST WOMAN RULER

For a woman to sit on the throne was noteworthy. Women in 17th-century Muscovy were treated little better than a man's chattel. Marriages were arranged, and before the ceremony the father of the bride would strike his daughter lightly on the back with a whip and say,

• • • this is the last time you shall be admonished by the authority of your father . . . but remember . . . should you not behave

RUSSIAN WESTWARD EXPANSION

What factors allowed for Russian expansion in each of the time periods shown?

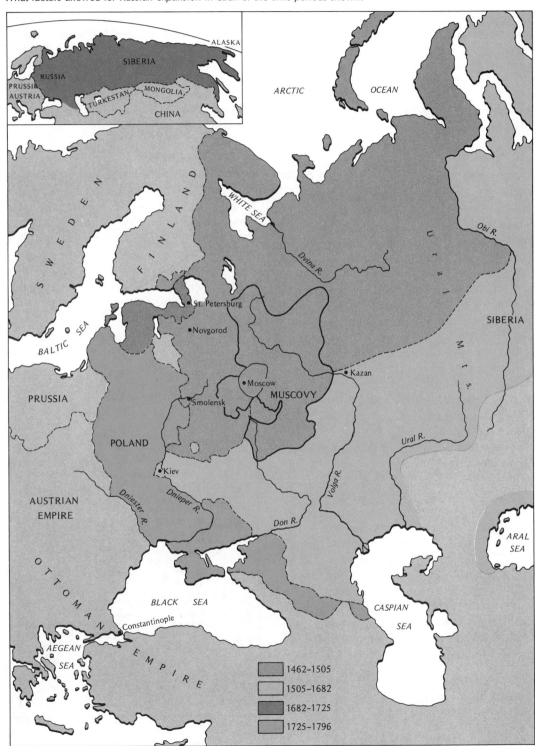

ALASKA

SIBERIA

RUSSIA

PRUSSIA
AUSTRIA

TURKESTAN

MONGOLIA

CHINA

ARCTIC   OCEAN

S W E D E N

F I N L A N D

WHITE SEA

Dvina R.

Obi R.

U r a l

BALTIC

SEA

• St. Petersburg

• Novgorod

SIBERIA

M t s.

PRUSSIA

• Smolensk

• Moscow

MUSCOVY

• Kazan

Ural R.

POLAND

• Kiev

Dniester R.

Dnieper R.

Volga R.

Don R.

ARAL
SEA

AUSTRIAN
EMPIRE

O T T O M A N

BLACK   SEA

Constantinople

CASPIAN

SEA

E M P I R E

AEGEAN

SEA

	1462–1505
	1505–1682
	1682–1725
	1725–1796

as you ought to toward your husband, he . . . will admonish you with this whip.[9]

At this point, the whip was given to the future husband who gallantly said that he would never have any need of a whip—as he attached it to his belt. Divorce was almost as simple as sending a wife to a convent. For some women the convent was a welcome refuge from their brutal husbands. Ironically, peasant women often had more equality than their counterparts in the noble class. Most serfs lived on the edge of survival, and the harshness of their existence meant that their wives, daughters, and sisters were called upon to share their responsibilities.

For the sisters and daughters of the tsar, marriage usually was out of the question. They were not permitted to marry foreigners for religious reasons, nor were they allowed to marry beneath their royal station, which eliminated every adult male in Muscovy. Theirs was a life of seclusion in a shadow world limited to the confines of the *terem,* or the women's quarters.

Sophia was able to escape the *terem* through a mixture of good fortune and exceptional talent. She persuaded her father to allow her to be educated, and her popularity with the *Streltsy,* or palace guard, enabled her to become regent after the death of Feodor in 1682.

Since the time of Ivan the Terrible, the Streltsy was the closest thing that the Princes of Muscovy had to a standing army. During peacetime, they were stationed in and around Moscow. Like the Praetorian Guard in the Roman Empire, the Streltsy were close to the centers of power—a position they used to influence royal successions.

Immediately after the death of Feodor, the Streltsy went on a rampage, believing that Feodor's death was due to poison. Hundreds, including members of Peter's family, were dragged from their hiding places in the Kremlin and brutally massacred. During the melee, Sophia—who, it was whispered, was not entirely innocent in the revolt—was able to parlay her popularity with the Streltsy into the appointment as regent. She served in this position until Peter turned 16 in 1689. Her competence as a ruler established a precedent that later enabled Catherine the Great to become tsarina of Russia.

PETER'S CHARACTER

Peter's impact on Russian history can best be understood by first taking a look at his personal life, both as a boy and man. Peter was of gargantuan physical proportions—around 6'9" in height and, in later life, tipping the scales at almost 300 pounds. Peter's physical strength also was legendary. Even under normal circumstances, he appeared as a man possessed, always on the move and expecting his energy to be matched by those around him. If the tsar could put in 20-hour days, so could his most exalted adviser and his humblest servant.

Throughout his life, Peter never lost his childlike interest in the things and people

Peter the Great studies shipbuilding in Holland. After making an extensive study of Western industries, Peter introduced industrialization to Russia.

---

[9] Robert K. Massie, *Peter the Great: His Life and World* (New York: Knopf, 1980), p. 32.

around him. When he visited Holland, he spent a brief period attending lectures on anatomy and studying surgery and dentistry. Back at the Russian court, Peter always kept nearby a small black bag of surgical instruments that he would put to use with little or no prodding if someone at court took ill or complained of a toothache. It is said that those in attendance at the Russian court were the healthiest in all of Europe.

WESTERNIZATION

Before Peter's two trips to the West in 1697–98, and again in 1716–17, Peter had been exposed to Western ideas while frequenting the "German Quarter," a suburb of Moscow built for foreigners. In Europe, Peter traveled "incognito," although no one doubted that the 6'9" Peter Mikhailov was in reality the tsar of Russia.

He learned of such things as the manufacture of cannon, the building of fortresses, the minting of coins, and above all the construction of ships. No tsar had ever visited western Europe before, and wherever Peter went he was the object of intense curiosity. In Europe, he recruited people whose skills and expertise were needed in Russia. In addition, he sent many Russians to be educated in the West.

Most of Peter's efforts at westernization had only superficial effects. His educational reforms were limited to technical schools, such as one for artillery. His attempts at providing a primary education for Russian children were doomed to failure because of the lack of trained teachers and the opposition of Church leaders. Economic reforms, especially in the area of heavy industry, had some initial success. By 1725, the year of Peter's death, Russia was producing more iron than any other country in Europe, including Great Britain.

For the most part, Peter's social reforms did not go beyond the Russian court, but one important exception was his decree on beards. Since beards were out of style in the

A cartoon showing a Russian noble being assaulted by a barber highlights one of Peter's more superficial efforts to westernize Russian society.

West, Peter decreed that all his subjects except for peasants and clergy must be clean-shaven. To the Orthodox Russian, the beard was a symbol of his belief and his manhood. But Peter, on seeing a bearded Boyar, would often grab the unfortunate by the beard and pull it out by the roots or shave him on the spot. Another decree ordered all but peasants to adopt Western-style clothes. Peter also liberated the rest of Russian court society by freeing women from the cloistered life of the terem and bringing the two sexes together in social gatherings. Parties in the new capital of St. Petersburg mimicked life at the Parisian court. Western-style gowns and ballroom dancing became the rage in St. Petersburg society. Peter's reforms at the apex of Russian society, however, did not filter down to the masses of Russian peasants. Instead, they increased the gap between the upper classes and the peasants.

GOVERNMENT REFORMS

Government reforms did result in some streamlining of the system, with more power accruing to the tsar and less to the Boyars. Peter established a collegial system of government administration. Each college, run by an 11-member board, was responsible for a specific function, such as the admiralty, the army, agriculture, and foreign affairs.

But Russia lacked trained personnel, and Peter brought in Germans, Swedes, and other foreign bureaucrats to make up this deficit. The use of foreigners in top-level government positions became a unique feature of Russian government. Peter replaced the old Boyar advisory body, the Duma, with a new group called the Senate, whose members were chosen directly by Peter. Provincial governors were also appointed directly by the tsar. It became their responsibility to collect taxes and to supply and maintain the army assigned to their provinces. The Senate became the fiscal watchdog to insure that the governors carried out their responsibilities.

Virtually all of Peter's reforms were motivated by military and financial needs. There was only one full year, and 13 other miscellaneous months, during Peter's 35-year reign that Russia was at peace. Approximately 75 percent of the budget was spent for military purposes. Reforms were based on expediency and the need to resolve immediate crises.

OPPOSITION TO WESTERNIZATION

Opposition grew to Peter's efforts at westernizing Russia. A revolt of the Streltsy in 1698, while Peter was still in the West, was quickly suppressed. On his return, Peter had 1200 executed, and eventually, all of the Streltsy regiments were disbanded. Thousands were forced into exile in Siberia.

Peter's domestic and governmental reforms weakened the authority of the hereditary nobility. His emphasis on merit and loyalty to the tsar and state as prerequisites for privilege and titles led to the creation of a new service nobility. The creation of a professional standing army eliminated the dependence of the tsar on feudal levies of peasant soldiers from the nobility.

In 1700, the Patriarch Adrian, an opponent of westernization, died. A new Patriarch was not chosen, and in the following year Church lands were secularized and their administration was taken over by the government. In the Church Statute of 1721, the office of Patriarch was replaced by the Holy Synod. Members of the Holy Synod included both lay persons and the clergy, and all had to swear allegiance to the tsar. The Church hierarchy became an integral part of the Russian bureaucracy.

BUILDING OF ST. PETERSBURG

Peter had never liked Moscow with its painful remembrances of his youth, and in 1703 he began the work of building St. Petersburg. Named after Peter's patron saint, the city was to be the glittering new capital of Russia as well as the tsar's window on the West. Located on the Baltic coast, where the Neva River flows into the Gulf of Finland, Peter's city took shape on a disease-ridden swamp where thousands of men were set to work draining the bogs and digging canals. Many died of disease and the furious pace of the work. Under the direction of French and Italian architects, a city of broad boulevards, Western-style villas, and winding canals rose from the swamps. By 1712, Peter's city, a symbol of the new Russia, a city that faced west, not east, was completed. Taking the title of "Emperor of all the Russias," Peter moved the government to St. Petersburg, forced his nobles to build their homes there, and encouraged foreign merchants and artisans to settle in the city. Soon, the city became the cultural and intellectual center of Russia and remained its capital until 1918, after the Bolshevik Revolution.

Peter inspects the plans for his capital city of St. Petersburg, on the Baltic Sea. The tsar referred to the city as his "window on the West."

PETER'S FOREIGN POLICY

In his quest for a warm-water port that could be used year-round, Peter turned first to the Ottoman Turks and the Black Sea region. Despite some limited success in and around the Sea of Azov at the beginning of his reign, Peter was denied access to the Mediterranean Sea by the Turks. The story was different in the north against Sweden.

Since the Thirty Years' War, Sweden's military power was virtually unchallenged in northern Europe. In 1697 an inexperienced boy of 15, Charles XII, came to the Swedish throne. Peter and his fellow monarchs in Poland, Saxony, and Denmark saw this transfer of royal power in Sweden as an opportunity for territorial acquisition. However, Charles XII, like Frederick the Great, had the advantage of inheriting a well-trained and well-equipped army, and he moved first. In August 1700, Charles inflicted a humiliating defeat on Denmark, and quickly wheeled eastward to meet a Russian army already in the Swedish territory of Livonia. At the *Battle of Narva* a Swedish army of 8,000 routed a Russian army of 40,000. The road was open to Moscow, but Charles decided instead to turn his legions in the direction of Poland.

Peter had nine years to prepare for the next confrontation with Charles. The church bells of Russia were melted down to make cannon, and new standards of discipline and training were imposed on the army.

By 1709, Charles was ready once again to attack Russia, and the Swedish army moved into the Ukraine, the breadbasket of Russia, in the hope of winning the support of the Cossacks. The Swedes' dwindling supplies and Peter's strategy of luring them into Russia's interior, where a terrible winter decimated their forces, gave the Russians the advantage. The *Battle of Poltava*, in South Russia, was a decisive victory for Peter. He then went on the offensive, conquering parts of Finland and the area of Livonia, reaching even into Sweden itself. With the consent of Prussia, which received parts of Swedish territory, Russia put an end to Swedish plans to seize northern European territory. The *Great Northern War* ended in 1721, and Peter had gained the Baltic shore for Russia.

What did Peter I of Russia accomplish during his reign as tsar that earned him the title of "the Great" almost in his own lifetime? His place in history rests on his success in implementing three goals: the opening of Russia to Western influences, his success in finding a warm-water port that would remain ice-free year round, and his elimination of opposition to the authority of the tsar.

CATHERINE THE GREAT (1762–1796) Catherine the Great of Russia is considered to have been one of the outstanding rulers of her age. Along with Frederick the Great of Prussia and Joseph II of Austria, she was among the best known of the *enlightened despots*. These three rulers took an active interest in the ideas of the Enlightenment (Chapter 8), even though they were rarely successful in applying them to their own territories.

Catherine, one of Russia's greatest rulers, was not Russian at all, but a minor German princess named Sophia, from the court of Anhalt Zerbst. At the age of 14, she was betrothed to Peter III, the heir to the Russian throne. In 1744, when she arrived at the St. Petersburg court, Elizabeth (1741–1762), the daughter of Peter the Great, ruled Russia. Sophia took the Russian name of Catherine, and in August 1745 she married Peter III. With a childish husband who ignored her, alone in alien surroundings, Catherine set about educating herself through books and by observation. She dedicated her energies to a study of the Russian language, land, and people. She soon acquired the mental and physical toughness necessary for survival.

On Christmas Day, 1761, Elizabeth died and Peter III came to the throne of Muscovy. From the beginning, Peter's policies were

Catherine the Great, the German princess who became tsarina of Russia. After an initial period of reform, Catherine reverted to a traditional, autocratic form of government.

unpopular. When Catherine learned that Peter intended to divorce her, she became a participant in a plot to overthrow him. With the help of the Guards' Regiments while Peter was away from the capital, Catherine was proclaimed empress. Peter was arrested, and within a month he was dead.

DOMESTIC POLICIES

Catherine began her reign with the intention of instituting internal reforms. She studied with interest the political philosophies developed during the European Age of Enlightenment, and in 1766 drew up a set of legislative reforms. These included restrictions on torture and serfdom, religious toleration, the extension of education, and limitations on large estates. She established hospitals and orphanages and encouraged artists and writers, even allowing the circulation of radical political works. She divided Russia into 50 provinces with the idea of giving autonomy to local officials.

In the end, however, Catherine's good intentions were not carried out. Without the support of the nobles, she could not hope to enforce her reforms, and her experience as empress convinced her that the nobles would never give up their privileges.

The bloody revolt by a Cossack named Emelian Pugachev in 1773 so alarmed Catherine that any ideas of freedom she had previously held were cast aside. Declaring himself to be Peter III—and claiming he had escaped from Catherine's plot to kill him—Pugachev roused hordes of disaffected people from among those who had been absorbed by Russian expansionism. His rebellion, like all uprisings in Russia prior to the 19th century, was brutal and spontaneous, lacking organization or a guiding ideology. In two years of burning, looting, and murder, Pugachev destroyed estates and monasteries and killed thousands of landowners, priests, and merchants. By the time he was caught and executed (1775), Catherine realized the absolute necessity for the support of the nobles. What few rights that remained to the peasants were taken from them and given to the nobility in return for their continued loyalty. The final blow to any liberal pretensions on the part of Catherine came in 1789 with the outbreak of the French Revolution. The execution of Louis XVI in 1793 completed her conversion to autocratic conservatism.

FOREIGN POLICY

Catherine's foreign policy was an extension of that begun by Peter the Great. Peter had solved the Swedish problem, and now it was Catherine's turn to deal with Poland and the Ottoman Turks. Included in Catherine's plans were a desire to control more of the Baltic coast, expansion westward into Poland, further pacification of the Ukraine, domination of the Don and Dnieper river basins, and command of the Black Sea. By the end of her reign in 1796, the Russian Empire had increased in extent by 200,000 square miles, and in population from 19 million to 36 million.

Catherine extended her empire to the borders of Austria and Prussia, and southward to the Black Sea. As a contemporary cartoon points out, her next goal might be Constantinople.

Partitions of Poland. Catherine desired a Poland friendly to Russian interests that would provide her with a buffer zone in the west. Poland was one of the largest states in Europe, both in territory and population. Politically and economically, however, it was one of the weakest. Within Poland's borders were a polyglot of languages and peoples, and only in a few areas were those of Polish extraction a majority. The Polish national diet was almost totally ineffective because any member could prevent the diet from taking action simply by voicing an objection. (This procedure was known as "exploding the diet.") The Polish nobility saw to it that the king, who was elected by them, was without any real authority. And the Polish peasants were among the most oppressed in all of Europe, making it difficult for the government to get mass support even when faced with a foreign threat.

With an eye to extending his own domains, Frederick the Great of Prussia encouraged Catherine to divide part of Poland with Prussia and Austria. In this *first partition of Poland* (1772), Poland lost one-third of its land and population.

Near the end of her reign, Catherine once again turned her attention to Poland. The Polish nobility, finally learning from their previous mistakes, reestablished a hereditary monarchy and strengthened the diet. Russia and Prussia were not prepared to accept the emergence between them of a new and more powerful Poland.

In 1793, Prussia and Russia took more Polish territory. After a final partition in 1795, between Austria, Prussia, and Russia, Poland ceased to exist as a separate political entity, and would not reappear on the map of Europe as an independent state until 1918.

The partitions of Poland gave Russia a common frontier with Austria and Prussia. In addition to the new territory, the Russian empire acquired new nationalities and ethnic minorities to absorb, including about one million Jews.

Conflict with the Turks. The Ottoman Turks, with French encouragement, attempted to consolidate their holdings along their border with Russia. But even with one eye on Poland, Catherine was more than a match for the sultan of Turkey. In the *Treaty of Kuchuk Kainarji* (1774), Russia was permitted a military presence in the Crimea. Russian merchant ships were allowed free passage through the Black Sea straits to the Mediterranean. Russia also gained the right to protect the religious interest of Greek Orthodox Christians within the Ottoman Empire. This last provision allowed Russia to interfere in the domestic and foreign affairs of the Ottoman Empire, a circumstance that would take on greater significance in the 19th century.

By the end of her reign in 1796, Catherine's Russia had achieved great-power status. Russia now had common frontiers with Austria and Prussia. The Baltic Sea was not yet a Russian lake, but it had ceased to be a Swedish pond, and there was a permanent Russian presence in the Black Sea. Catherine's policies also created a "Polish problem" for Russia and Europe that would linger throughout the 19th century and well into the 20th.

SUMMARY

The three states of Austria, Prussia, and Russia developed autocratic systems in the 17th and 18th centuries. All three countries cooperated in increasing their territory. By the end of the 18th century, they had common borders. During this time, a series of extraordinary rulers in all three countries organized effective government institutions and increased the power of the monarchy. By the end of the 18th century, the Austrian and Russian empires were expanding at the expense of the declining Ottoman Empire. The aims of these two powers would be more difficult to reconcile in the 19th century.

QUESTIONS

1 By the terms of the Peace of Westphalia (Chapter 3), Germany, the Dutch Netherlands, and Switzerland became independent of the Holy Roman Empire, and other lands—except direct possessions of the Hapsburgs—were permitted freedom of private worship. How was the character of the empire changed by these terms, and how well did the Hapsburgs adapt? Evaluate the reigns of Leopold, Maria Theresa, and Joseph II.

2 List the criteria that should be used to determine if a historical figure deserves to be called "great." Is Maria Theresa just as deserving of the title as Catherine the Great?

3 Over the years, the name "Prussian" has become synonomous with militarism. Briefly describe the history and the rulers of Brandenburg-Prussia, and explain how this reputation came about.

4 How did geography and climate influence the course of Russian history? Why did Muscovy and its princes became the nucleus of the emerging Russian state?

5 How successful was Peter the Great in achieving the following goals: 1) the westernization of Russia, 2) finding a "window to the West," and 3) firmly establishing the autocratic authority of the tsar?

6 Identify the significance of the following terms in Russian history: Zemski Sobor, Oprichniki, Time of Troubles, Code of 1649, terem, Pugachev, and partition of Poland.

BIBLIOGRAPHY

BLANNING, T. C. W. *Joseph II and Enlightened Despotism.* London and New York: Longman and Harper & Row, 1979. *A concise and lively account of Joseph II as "enlightened despot." Includes a section of helpful primary documents.*

CATHERINE THE GREAT. *The Memoirs of Catherine the Great.* New York: Bantam Books, 1957. *The young Catherine wrote this personal and frank recollection of life at the court of St. Petersburg before she became "empress of all the Russias."*

CRANKSHAW, EDWARD. *Maria Theresa.* New York: Viking Press, 1969. *A sensitive biography of the only woman to rule the ancestral realms of the Austrian Hapsburgs. Her attempts to modernize Austria are contrasted with generally successful efforts to preserve her kingdom against the other major powers of Europe.*

FAY, SIDNEY B. and KLAUS EPSTEIN. *The Rise of Brandenburg-Prussia to 1786,* rev. ed. Robert E. Krieger Publ. Co., 1981. *A comprehensive overview of the expansion of Prussia through the reign of Frederick the Great.*

MASSIE, ROBERT K. *Peter the Great: His Life and World.* New York: Knopf, 1980. *This book won the Pulitzer prize for its portrayal of the life and times of Peter the Great.*

THOMSON, GLADYS SCOTT. *Catherine the Great and the Expansion of Russia.* Westport, Conn.: Greenwood Press, 1985. *A straightforward introduction to the age of Catherine the Great—not limited, as the title implies, to foreign policy.*

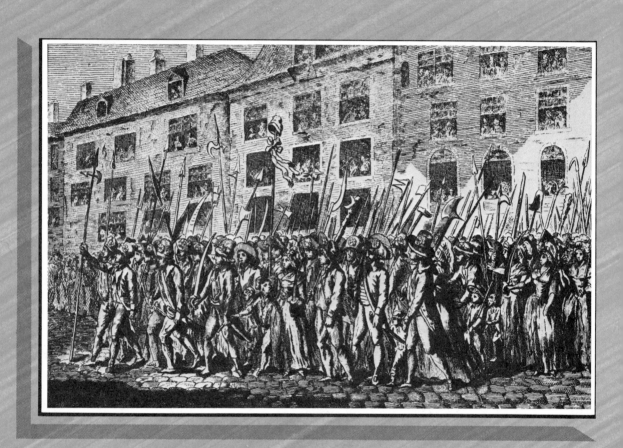

Revolutions in Thought and Life

● *Man is born free, and everywhere he is in chains.*

JEAN JACQUES ROUSSEAU

● *Power is my mistress. I have worked too hard in conquering her to allow anyone to take her from me or even to covet her.*

NAPOLEON I

● *He [Napoleon] is an ordinary human being after all! Now he will trample underfoot the Rights of Man, being a slave to his own ambition; now he will put himself above everyone else and become a tyrant.*

LUDWIG VON BEETHOVEN

● *If all mankind, minus one, were of one opinion, and only one person were of the contrary opinion, mankind would be no more justified in silencing that one person, than he, if he had the power, would be justified in silencing mankind.*

JOHN STUART MILL

Nature and Nature's Laws lay hid in Night:
God said, "Let Newton be!": and all was Light.
ALEXANDER POPE

The Scientific Revolution and the Enlightenment

One of the traits of the human mind is the need to see order and reason in the universe, and to find ways to explain natural events. Moreover, human thought progresses not at a steady pace but intermittently, and human history has been marked by periods in which new ideas emerged rapidly.

During a relatively brief period in early modern European history, from about 1540 to 1700, there occurred an intellectual revolution which dramatically changed the way in which people perceived the world about them. This change in the view of the universe was known as the *scientific revolution*. It represented a shift in focus of intellectual interest from the spiritual to the physical world. During the scientific revolution, thinkers sought natural laws to explain how the universe functions. The scientific revolution, in turn, laid the intellectual foundations for the *Enlightenment*, also known as "the Age of Reason." During the Enlightenment, the concept of natural law was applied to government and society. People sought to discover laws that governed human behavior. Enlightenment thinkers believed, in the words of the English poet Alexander Pope, that "the proper study of mankind is man."

THE SCIENTIFIC REVOLUTION

The basis for the scientific revolution lay in fundamental questions regarding the sources of human knowledge. To the medieval thinker, there were essentially three authoritative sources of knowledge. First, there was the Bible, which contains God's truth revealed to humanity; secondly, the scholarship of medieval Christian thinkers, especially Saint Augustine and Saint Thomas Aquinas, who sought to interpret the scriptures; and finally, the thought of ancient Greek and Roman philosophers. Reliance on these authorities left many gaps in human knowledge.

The dramatic change wrought by the scientific revolution was rooted in the acceptance of reason and experience as sources of knowledge, in addition to the authorities recognized during the medieval period. Out of the new approach to learning came the *scientific method*. The scientific method relies on the combination of three sources of knowledge: human reason and logic; experimentation, consisting of observation and measurement by instruments; and mathematics. These three sources of knowledge were in themselves not new. Each had been used prior to the scientific revolution. The ancient Greeks had applied logic and mathematics to their theories, and medieval scholars had used logic and observations to buttress their interpretations of Holy Scripture.

The genius of the scientific revolution lay in the way people used these new sources of knowledge. Logic, experimentation, and mathematics were used together to arrive at rational conclusions. Two different methods of reasoning were utilized. One was the **inductive method** first developed by Aristotle. When using the inductive method of reasoning, a scientist gathers facts about individual cases and uses them to reach a conclusion or general theory. The **deductive method,** on the other hand, involves first formulating a conclusion or theory in the form of a hypothesis, and then seeking evidence to support the theory. During the scientific revolution, as today, scientists used both kinds of reasoning, deductive and inductive.

Underlying the growth of the scientific method lay the assumption that there is unity and order in the universe, and that by application of reasoning, human beings can discover the "natural laws" which govern the world about us.

THE HELIOCENTRIC THEORY

The earliest medieval idea challenged by the new approach was the **geocentric** theory, according to which the heavenly bodies revolved around the earth. This theory had been formulated by the Greek philosopher Ptolemy in the 2nd century, and accorded with the Biblical interpretation of God's creation of the world. It was also supported by the observation that the earth does not appear to move, while the sun, moon, stars and planets do indeed appear to do so.

The first European to question the geo-

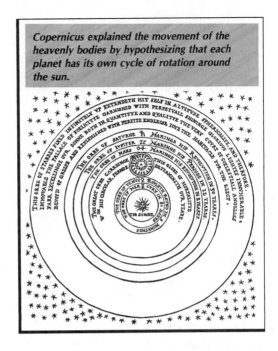

Copernicus explained the movement of the heavenly bodies by hypothesizing that each planet has its own cycle of rotation around the sun.

centric theory was the Polish-born professor of mathematics, Nicolaus Copernicus (1473–1543). Copernicus developed the **heliocentric** theory, which holds that the earth revolves around the sun. It was only a theory, for he lacked the scientific instrument—a telescope—by which he might seek proof. In 1543, Copernicus' theory was published in a book titled *Concerning the Revolution of the Heavenly Spheres.* Copernicus asserted that the earth rotates on its axis every 24 hours and makes an annual movement around the sun. The heliocentric theory ran counter to accepted religious thought and was ignored.

Several decades after the publication of Copernicus' work, a German mathematician, Johan Kepler (1571–1630), provided evidence for the heliocentric theory. A brilliant mathematician, Kepler used mathematics to formulate the laws of planetary motion. He demonstrated that the orbits of the planets are elliptical and that planets move more rapidly when they are nearest to the sun in their orbits.

A few years later, the Italian astronomer

Galileo Galilei (1564–1642) utilized a new invention, the telescope, to observe the heavens. Galileo discovered ridges on the moon, the moons around the planet Jupiter, and the rings around Saturn. From these and other observations, Galileo concluded that the heliocentric theory must be valid. In 1632 he published *Dialogue Concerning the Two World Systems* in which he compared the heliocentric and geocentric theories, and concluded that the former was a more reasonable hypothesis.

However, at the time of Galileo's studies, a conservative spirit dominated the Catholic Church. Thus, the year after Galileo made public his new ideas, Church authorities summoned him to Rome, where he was tried and convicted of heresy and required to sign a recantation of his theory. He was sentenced to life imprisonment and required to do penance by repeating the seven Penitential Psalms once a week for three years. The sentence proclaimed by the Church explained the reason for this action:

• • • *The proposition that the sun is the center of the world and does not move from its place is absurd and false philosophically and formally heretical, because it is expressly contrary to the Holy Scriptures.*[1]

In his recantation, Galileo swore to "abandon the false opinion that the sun is the center of the world and immovable, and that the earth is not the center of the world, and moves."[2] After the sentencing and the signing of his recantation, Galileo is reported to have muttered under his breath, "the earth does move, however."

These three early, seminal thinkers, then, developed the heliocentric theory; in the process, each utilized separately the rudiments of the scientific method. Copernicus provided the initial logic, Kepler the mathe-

Galileo used the telescope to confirm mathematical explanations of planetary movement. He then wrote a treatise on the world systems of Ptolemy and Copernicus.

matical proof, and Galileo the observations through his telescope.

REASONING AND MATHEMATICS

The scientific revolution was given impetus by the work of several philosophers and mathematicians. New roles for reason and mathematics in the pursuit of knowledge and truth were cornerstones of the scientific revolution.

One of those who did much to change the way in which people used their reasoning powers was an Englishman named Francis Bacon (1561–1626). Bacon's *Novum Organum* ("New Instrument"), published in 1620, developed the concept of inductive reasoning. To arrive at scientific laws, Bacon argued, it was necessary first to experiment, then to draw tentative conclusions, called hypotheses, and finally to experiment further to demonstrate the validity of the hypotheses.

---

[1] Raymond P. Stearns, *Pageant of Europe* (New York, 1965), p. 67.

[2] *Ibid.*, p. 68.

Bacon suggested that scientific advancement could best be pursued as a collaborative activity. In his *New Atlantis*, he gave a blueprint for a utopian society, one feature of which was an academy of scientists provided with sufficient funds. Scientific societies did spring up in the 17th century. In 1662, the Royal Society of London for the Improvement of Natural Knowledge was founded. This and other societies spread new scientific findings throughout the elite of society.

The work of the Frenchman René Descartes (1596–1650) was important in two respects. First, Descartes developed further the deductive method of reasoning. In his work he stressed the capacity of the human mind to reach knowledge through the use of reasoning and logic. He put forth the idea that the habit of doubting or questioning all preconceptions or assumptions was a necessary part of any investigation. In fact, he went so far as to question his own existence before proceeding to other problems. This proof was supplied in his famous statement, *Cogito ergo sum*. ("I think, therefore I am.").

Descartes was also one of the great mathematicians of his day. He developed analytic geometry, which enabled astronomers to translate relationships between bodies in space into algebraic equations.

This was just one of several important developments in mathematics at this time. In France, Blaise Pascal developed a theory of probabilities. Gottfried Leibniz (1646–1716) in Germany and Isaac Newton in England simultaneously developed the branch of mathematics called calculus.

In addition to all these developments in intellectual theory, there were many important breakthroughs of a more practical nature. These both helped advance further the scientific revolution and demonstrated the usefulness of scientific progress to other aspects of life.

A number of scientific instruments were invented: the telescope, the microscope, the

The French mathematician and philosopher René Descartes. Through his extreme skepticism, Descartes emphasized the difficulty of discovering the "truth" about any given subject.

slide rule, the first adding machine, the mercury barometer, and the air pump. An illustration of the application of scientific theory to practical inventions was the creation of the Dutchman Christian Huygens (1629–1695), who invented the pendulum clock by applying Galileo's theory that a pendulum of fixed length completes its swing in a fixed amount of time regardless of the extent of the pendulum swing.

PHYSICS

Some of the greatest advances of the scientific revolution were made in the field of physics. An Irishman, Robert Boyle (1627–1691), did ground-breaking work on the properties of gases. He studied the behavior of gases at various temperatures and pressures, and formulated the law that the volume of a gas at a constant temperature varies inversely with its pressure.

The greatest scientist of this period was

Isaac Newton (1642–1727). His synthesis of earlier discoveries and his own original ideas were combined into principles which define the physical-mathematical laws of the universe.

Especially significant were Newton's three fundamental laws of movement. These are: 1) A body at rest tends to stay at rest; a body in motion tends to remain in motion unless compelled to change by an impressed force. 2) The change in motion is proportional to the impressed force and takes place in the straight line by which that force is impressed. 3) For every action there is an equal and opposite reaction.

Most important of all was Newton's theory that gravity is a universal force affecting all matter. Legend has it that Newton recognized that an apple which he observed dropping off a tree fell to the earth because its mass is minute compared to the mass of the earth. This observation, or one similar, formed the basis for his laws of gravity. He reasoned that the law of gravity also applied to the universe—the moon is pulled to the earth by the force of gravity; the pull of the moon causes the oceans' tides.

In his *Mathematical Principles of Natural Philosophy* (1687), Newton provided the mathematical evidence for his law of universal gravitation: that every particle of matter attracts every other particle with a force proportional to the product of the two masses, and inversely proportional to the square of the distance between them.

Newton's laws served as the basis for physics until the 20th century and mark the culmination of the scientific revolution.

ADVANCES IN MEDICINE AND BIOLOGY

During this period of breakthroughs in astronomy, mathematics, and physics, other thinkers applied the scientific method to the study of the human body.

One of the earliest was Leonardo da Vinci (1457–1519), whose interest in the new approach of experimentation and observation

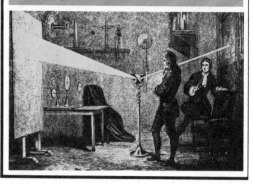

Isaac Newton studies the effect of refracting light. Newton's various experiments and theories provided a unified explanation of everyday phenomena.

compelled him to dissect corpses—illegally—to learn about the human body. From his observations he left us numerous notebooks. They are filled with remarkably accurate sketches, testimony to his other career as a great artist.

Andreas Vesalius of the Netherlands (1514–1564) can be considered to have founded the science of anatomy. After dissecting numerous dogs and humans, Vesalius visited cemeteries to collect human bones so that he could study the human skeleton. He published the first anatomy text, *Humani Corporis Fabrica*, in 1543.

One of his contemporaries, Paracelsus (1493–1541) of Switzerland, recognizing that the body is composed of chemical elements, studied chemistry. His introduction of drugs as medical treatment earned him the title of the "father of pharmacy."

A little later, the Englishman William Harvey (1578–1657), through dissection and observation became the first scientist to demonstrate the role of the heart as a pump to circulate the blood. Harvey was also the first to maintain that the blood circulates in the body in a single, continuous flow. Harvey's discoveries corrected the misconception of the Greek physician Galen who had theorized that the human body contains two different kinds of blood—one flowing through the blue veins of the body, the other flowing through the red arteries.

The work of da Vinci, Vesalius, Paracelsus, Harvey, and others significantly advanced human understanding of the body and laid the foundations for the great accomplishments in medicine of the 19th and 20th centuries.

The same impulse to careful observation that gave rise to the new breakthroughs in the study of human anatomy also led to advances in other branches of biology. Thousands of new plants and animals were observed and catalogued. This led to the problem of how to classify the different forms. A great advance in biology was made when the Swedish doctor Carl Linnaeus (1707–1778) devised an orderly system of classification. Linnaeus divided all living things into groups called *genuses*, based on common features. Each genus was then divided into *species*. Every plant or animal was assigned two Latin names—that of its genus and that of its species. Linnaeus' system of classification, with modifications, is still used to this day.

SUPERSTITIONS AND WITCHCRAFT

Like most intellectual movements, the scientific revolution had little immediate im-

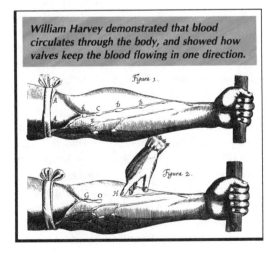

William Harvey demonstrated that blood circulates through the body, and showed how valves keep the blood flowing in one direction.

pact on the lives of ordinary people in modern Europe. For example, despite the advances in the field of medicine, serious misconceptions about human anatomy and physiology continued to be widely held.

The most dramatic instance is the notion of the four humors, a theory developed by the ancient Greeks. According to this theory, the body contains four fluids, or "humors"—black bile, yellow bile, blood, and phlegm—and human illness is the result of imbalances among the fluids. It was common practice for barbers to supply customers with leeches, which by taking blood were supposed to restore the balance of fluids. The practice of bloodletting continued into the 19th century. George Washington's death was no doubt hastened when he was bled in an attempt to cure his pneumonia.

Moreover, the discoveries of the scientific revolution spread only slowly from the intellectual elite to the rest of society. Most people held a variety of superstitious beliefs, including faith in astrology, ghosts, spirits, and magic. Superstitions were particularly popular in Germany, perhaps because of the insecurity engendered by the Thirty Years' War. German princes commonly relied on court astrologers for advice.

Belief in the existence and power of witches was common both in Europe and in America in the 17th century. In the English colony of Massachusetts in the town of Salem, 200 people were tried for being witches in the summer of 1692. These trials, the infamous *Salem witch trials*, resulted in the execution of 20 people.

The total number of women condemned and burned as witches during this time is unknown, but it is estimated that in the period from approximately 1550 to 1700, 5000 were executed in Switzerland, 700 in Germany, and 1000 in England.

The fact that it has almost always been women rather than men who have been accused of witchcraft has led historians to speculate as to the reason. The most obvious

Despite great advances in science, superstition—especially belief in witchcraft—persisted in the 17th century. In most cases, the condemned were women.

answer is that belief in witchcraft is one manifestation of the *misogyny* (hatred of women) prevalent in the culture. Among other explanations is the fact that these accused women were generally older, lower-class, and widowed—often outsiders in their own communities. Some churchmen preached that women were more vulnerable to the lure of the Devil. By the 18th century, however, witch hunts had ended, and, in general, superstition had declined.

THE ENLIGHTENMENT

The 18th–century Enlightenment is in many ways a continuation of the scientific revolution which preceded it. The thinkers of the Enlightenment hoped to apply the scientific method to human behavior and to society. Just as the scientists sought to discover the natural laws which govern the physical world, Enlightenment theorists sought to find laws which govern human institutions. Moreover, the Enlightenment was rooted in three new theories about human beings: **individualism**—the importance of the individual and his rights as a member of the society; **relativism**—the idea that different ideas, cultures, religions, values, and behavior have equal merit to one's own; and **rationalism**—the conviction of Enlightenment theorists that humans had the ability to arrive at the truth through the power of reasoning.

In large measure these new beliefs arose out of the work of the thinkers of the scientific revolution. The great advances made in the sciences encouraged a new respect for the powers of logic and of the human mind. The reliance of scientists on their ability to observe and weigh evidence, as opposed to traditional deference to authority, led to an increased estimation of the capabilities and worth of the individual.

Another factor in the development of the new attitudes of the Enlightenment was the growth of the European overseas empires. Many Europeans read about the cultures of American Indians, Africans, and Asians in the increasingly popular travel books that were published. Occasionally visitors from overseas appeared in Europe itself. After two delegations from Siam arrived in Paris in the 1680s, Siamese culture became the rage in fashionable Parisian circles. This increased exposure to foreign ways led to the growth of a more relativistic outlook.

There was also a weakening of belief in the traditional forms of religion. Baruch Spinoza (1632–1677), the son of a Jewish family in Amsterdam, made his living as a grinder of lenses for spectacles, telescopes, and microscopes. He developed a system of philosophy that emphasized the importance of ethical thought as a guide to conduct. His philosophy questioned the organized religions of his day, both Judaism and Christianity. Although he believed in God, he denied the divine inspiration of the Bible, and rejected miracles and all religious manifestations of the supernatural. To him, ethics determined by human reason were more important than the tenets of revealed religion.

Moreover, the theorists of the Enlightenment were optimists who believed that once they had detected the laws governing human society, these laws could be used to improve the human condition. Some of them saw human society as potentially perfect.

A sketch by Albrecht Dürer of a Tupinamba Indian from Brazil was commissioned by the emperor Maximilian I. Such contacts with other societies led to a concept of cultural relativism.

LAWS FOR WAR: COMENIUS AND GROTIUS

The Enlightenment not only had roots in the scientific revolution but was also a response to the political strife of the 17th century, especially the havoc wreaked by the Thirty Years' War. Writing during that bloody conflict, the German John Comenius (1592–1670) was a forerunner of modern political thinkers. He challenged traditional views of politics and war, and sought to reduce conflict by remaking society:

• • • *We are all citizens of one world, we are all of one blood. To hate a man because he was born in another country, because he speaks a different language, or because he takes a different view on this subject or that, is a great folly. . . . we are all equally human. . . . Let us have but one end in view, the welfare of humanity, and let us put aside all selfishness in considerations of language, nationality, or religion.*[3]

For Comenius, the reduction of conflict between humans depended on the spread of education.

The Dutchman Hugo Grotius (1583–1645) was another early theorist who attempted to apply the concept of natural law to human existence. Humans are rational beings, Grotius maintained, and as creatures of God they have natural duties and natural rights that transcend human–made laws. Those natural rights include the right to exist and to participate in society.

Grotius is best remembered for prescribing laws to govern international affairs. Although wars are sometimes inevitable, he said, the only just war is a war of self-defense. Preventive wars and wars waged for territory, conquest, or to spread an unwanted form of government, however beneficial, are unjust. Moreover, even in a just war, nations have the obligation to conform to civilized standards of behavior.

Most of the duties and rights outlined by Grotius have been recognized as the rules for conducting war throughout modern times, including the requirement of beginning the conflict with a declaration of war, and the obligations to honor treaties, to protect civilians, and to treat prisoners decently. Although both Comenius and Grotius wrote before the Enlightenment, they nonetheless laid the foundations for modern political thought.

[3] Will and Ariel Durant, *The Age of Reason Begins* (New York: Simon & Schuster, 1961), p. 582.

LAWS FOR SOCIETY: HOBBES AND LOCKE

The dominant form of government of the 17th and 18th centuries was divine-right monarchy. Proponents of divine-right theory maintained that the monarch rules by a God-given right and is God's representative on earth. As such, he should have absolute power over his subjects.

However, the rise of scientific theory and decline of orthodox religions challenged divine-right theory and raised anew the most basic political question—that of the justification for political power. What gives one human being or a group of human beings the right to rule over others?

The philosopher Thomas Hobbes (1588–1679) lived in England during the time of its civil war and witnessed the overthrow of the divine-right monarch Charles I and Oliver Cromwell's experiment with a republican form of government (Chapter 7).

Living in exile in Paris during Cromwell's rule, Hobbes published his treatise on political philosophy, *Leviathan* (1651). In it he used the idea of natural law to justify one-man, absolute rule. Hobbes replaced the divine-right justification of absolute monarchies with an argument based on the nature of human beings.

In Hobbes' pessimistic view, human life in a state of nature was "solitary, poor, nasty, brutish, and short." Without authority, human beings were selfish and egotistical, hence were frequently in conflict with each other, and required governments which would protect them. Unable to rule them-

Thomas Hobbes pictured the state as a Leviathan, or monster, for he believed that its sovereignty must be absolute.

selves, men and women voluntarily surrendered their own political authority to a ruler in a social contract. As a part of the contract, the ruler was obliged to use his absolute power to prevent conflict. For their part, the ruler's subjects were obligated to accept his authority. They surrendered their freedom in return for order. Although Hobbes provided a defense for absolute monarchy, he made a break with the past in applying the scientific method—philosophical, rational explanations—to government.

John Locke (1632–1704) can be considered the father of democratic theory. Educated at Oxford, Locke became the aide of an English politician who plotted against the restored English monarchy under Charles II and James II. He fled to Holland in 1683 when his mentor's schemes failed. With the overthrow of James II during the Glorious Revolution, Locke returned to England in 1689 and published three books he had written in exile, *Two Treatises on Civil Government*, *An Essay Concerning Human Understanding*, and *The Letter Concerning Toleration*.

In the *Two Treatises*, Locke rejected Hobbes' theories and presented a more optimistic view of the nature of humans. He contended that humans in their natural state are in fact rational beings—peaceful, not warlike. In a state of nature, Locke argued, humans lived in freedom and equality, and since this is true, government's only role in a civilized society is to protect and preserve the inalienable rights of humankind. These natural rights, to Locke, were *life*, *liberty*, and *property*. Like Hobbes, Locke believed that government is a social contract, but unlike Hobbes, Locke perceived the contract as one among the *governed*, the majority of whom delegate their authority to the ruler. Should the ruler fail to protect life, liberty, or property, the people have the right—even the duty—to overthrow him.

Locke's ideas manifest the political attitudes of the Enlightenment: optimism re-

John Locke posited the right of subjects to overthrow a ruler who had disappointed them. His writings provided a justification for the events of the Glorious Revolution.

garding the nature of human beings; reliance on rationalism, emphasis on the rights of the individual, and belief in natural laws for politics. For the 17th century, these were radical concepts which questioned the rationale of most established governments of the day, and advocated revolution. Locke's books were widely read, his theories often debated, and his principles adopted by many political leaders. These included Thomas Jefferson and the American revolutionaries of the 18th century. The American Declaration of Independence echoed Locke's words.

THE PHILOSOPHES

In the 18th century, France became the center of the Enlightenment. The price exacted by the wars of Louis XIV had left the nation discontent with absolute rule. Moreover, the weakness of King Louis XV had strengthened the position of both the aristocracy and the middle class.

These conditions made for a society ripe for the dissemination and discussion of new political ideas. The growth of a new, literate middle class created a large reading public who eagerly absorbed new ideas and concepts, such as those of the *philosophes*. The philosophes were a group of French philosophers who publicized and popularized the ideas of the Enlightenment. Middle-class people read and discussed their books and pamphlets in the many coffee-houses that became popular during this time. By 1720, there were over 300 of them in Paris alone.

In polite society, the center of intellectual life was a new institution called the *salon*. Salons were weekly meetings at private homes where women of wealth entertained writers, the clergy, bankers, patrons, and aristocrats. In the salons, people of different origins discussed the leading political and social theories of the day. The salon provided a unique opportunity for women to participate in intellectual and political activity. Although their role was primarily a social one, these hostesses usually joined the conversation. Seldom had women enjoyed such influence as they did during the Enlightenment in France. The philosopher Jean-Jacques Rousseau remarked of the woman of his time: "Everything depends on her; nothing is done except by her or for her."[4] The idea of female equality was not, however, part of Enlightenment theory; women were viewed primarily in their roles as wives, hostesses, mothers, and mistresses. Only a few enlightened thinkers like the Marquis de Condorcet advocated civil equality for women.

Voltaire (1694–1778). The leader of the French Enlightenment was the philosopher Voltaire (pen name of François-Marie Arouet). A brilliant writer, witty and polemical, Voltaire popularized the ideas of the Enlightenment and was widely read and quoted. To most of his writing he brought a humorous or satiric touch. This shows especially in his epigrams, a Voltarian specialty:

The philosophe Voltaire wrote poetry, history, and plays as well as polemical essays on the evils of the Old Regime.

• • • In general, the art of government consists in taking as much money as possible from one class of citizens to give it to the other.

If God did not exist, it would be necessary to invent him.[5]

Voltaire was especially critical of religious bigotry, and his phrase, "Ecrasez l'infame" ("Crush the infamous thing") became famous. Although he attacked orthodox religion, like many intellectuals of his time Voltaire was a *Deist*: that is, he believed that a good and powerful God exists, created life, and should be worshiped. Deists believe that the existence of God is revealed in reason and in the order of nature. They also believe in eternal life. However, they reject orthodox Christianity, which they view as based on

---

[4] Peter Gay and the editors of Time-Life Books, *Age of the Enlightenment* (New York: Time-Life Books, 1966), p. 41.

[5] *Ibid.*, p. 58.

superstition, not reason. Many Deists compared the universe to a precisely made machine, like a watch, with God serving the role of watchmaker who created the universe and set it in motion. As his creation, it ran perfectly and hence did not require his intervention.

Montesquieu (1689–1755). Another prominent philosophe was the influential political thinker, Baron de Montesquieu (Charles de Secondat). Montesquieu elaborated on the earlier ideas of Jean Bodin (1530–1596), and argued that climate, geography, history, and social and economic conditions affect the form of government a society should adopt. In *The Spirit of the Laws* (1748), Montesquieu argued that republics can flourish only in small countries or city-states; monarchies, in nations of moderate size and temperate climates; and *despotism* (absolute rule), in large empires in hot climates.

These ideas had little impact, but another of Montesquieu's theories, that of the *separation of powers*, had great influence and helped inspire the writers of the United States Constitution. According to this theory, the best guarantee of individual rights lay in the creation of separate and independent executive, legislative, and judicial branches of government, each of which would provide checks and balances to the powers of the others.

Diderot (1713–1794). Yet another important figure in the French Enlightenment was Denis Diderot. Diderot was the editor of the voluminous *Encyclopedia* whose purpose was to collect the writings and the technological discoveries of the Enlightenment thinkers. Over a 30-year period, Diderot published 35 volumes of essays, including many written by Voltaire.

Jean Jacques Rousseau (1712–1778). The most radical of the French political theorists was Jean Jacques Rousseau. Unlike the *philosophes*, Rousseau rejected civilized society, and glorified man in his natural state: "the noble savage." In *The Social Contract*, Rous-

Rousseau was the most radical of the French theorists. He reacted against the rationalism of the leading philosophes, arguing that emotion and instinct are equally important guides for human behavior.

seau envisioned a perfect society in which the people rule themselves.

Rousseau believed that the community depended on a contract, both social and political, among the people themselves. The contract was an understanding under which the individual will of members of the society combined into the *General Will*. This General Will should be the sovereign of the society. Rulers, be they kings or representatives, were only delegates of the people.

Rousseau's ideas serve as a bridge between the idea of the Enlightenment thinkers, with their emphasis on reason, and the emergence in the 19th century of a new intellectual movement, **romanticism,** which placed more emphasis on the emotional side of human beings, on the exotic and remote, on the virtues of nature, and on the perfectibility of society. The blend of Enlightenment political thought and Rousseau's romanticism was manifested in the tumultuous era of the French Revolution, as we shall see in the following chapter.

ENLIGHTENMENT THINKERS IN GERMANY

The Enlightenment also touched the states of Germany. The foremost representative of that movement in Germany was Gotthold Ephraim Lessing (1729–1781). Like so many of the leading figures of the age, Lessing was a man of diverse talents. He was a playwright, critic, and philosopher. In his plays, reviews, and occasional writings, Lessing showed devotion to the principles of truth and tolerance. He did much to free German writers from the shackles of narrow and dogmatic thinking. His seminal work, *Laokoon*, was an influential study of the relationship between poetry and painting.

Another 18th-century German who played a key role in the development of Western thought was the philosopher Immanuel Kant (1724–1804). In certain respects Kant was a product of the Enlightenment. Yet Kant's chief work, the *Critique of Pure Reason* (1781), has been called the work that marked the end of the Enlightenment. In this study Kant examined the limitations of human reason and of human capacity to understand the world. For much of the 18th century both of these had been the objects of boundless faith.

THE FINE ARTS

As in many other ages, the art of this period reflects the political, religious, social, and cultural currents of the time. The most important development in the arts in the late 16th and 17th centuries was the *baroque* style. The term was given to the movement later and comes from *barocco*, the name for an irregular pearl. Baroque art in contrast to Renaissance art stressed the dramatic and the

emotional. As the style evolved it became more ornate. Figures in sculpture twisted and turned, showing extreme emotions of religious ecstasy or pain. Colors were heightened and painters favored violent contrasts of light and dark. The artists' concern with the movement of light on figures reflected the growing scientific curiosity about the nature of light itself.

Baroque buildings, sculptures, and paintings were often large in scope. One of the aims of baroque artists was to have the viewer participate in the emotion of the theme of the art. Dramatic techniques, such as tricks of perspective that attempted to get the viewer into the picture, were favored.

The different arts drew upon each other. Architecture took on a sculptural effect. Many sculptures were indistinguishable from small architectural works. There was an attempt to get a total dramatic effect by blending all of the arts together, as in a church or palace.

Religious Baroque. There were basically three kinds of baroque. The first developed after the Council of Trent and was mainly a religious art of the Counter-Reformation and of Italy. It reflected the militant Catholicism asserted by the Council of Trent. While the Protestants had criticized the Church for being too lavish in art and ceremony—and indeed were destroying statues in Geneva— Rome responded with a new program of building in the lavish baroque style. Similarly, since Protestants stressed the importance of faith over good works, many Catholic works of art now took the portrayal of good works as a theme. Subject matter included images such as Christ helping the poor. The role of the Virgin Mary, downplayed by Protestants, was exalted in Catholic art.

The religious art of the Counter-Reformation strove to involve the viewers emotionally, to help them participate in a religious experience. The sufferings of saints and martyrs were portrayed in gory detail.

Bernini's Ecstasy of Saint Teresa. *The baroque style of art, with its emphasis on religious emotion and drama, became the emblem of the Counter-Reformation.*

The center of this art was in Rome, and most of it was sponsored by the Vatican. The prime genius in the Vatican's effort to beautify Rome, and the greatest sculptor of his time, was Gianlorenzo Bernini (1598–1680). Bernini was named chief architect for the great cathedral of Saint Peter's in Rome, and his elaborate fountains and statues dotted the city. In such sculptures as *The Ecstasy of Saint Teresa*, he showed a genius for capturing religious emotion.

In painting, Michelangelo da Caravaggio (1573–1610) was the prime exponent of the new style. Using both religious and secular scenes, he portrayed the turmoil of the times. Caravaggio developed the style of using light for dramatic effect.

Royal Baroque. Another strain of the baroque was art that glorified rulers and power. Kings and princes were patrons of the baroque style throughout Europe. Painters such as Peter Paul Rubens of the Netherlands (1577–1640) did work for such monarchs as Marie de Medici of France. Rubens' canvases were large swirling pictures of people in mythological or historical scenes. The figures twisted and turned in very dramatic compositions. His pupil Anthony Van Dyke did portraits for the Stuart kings.

Diego Velasquez (1599–1660), the painter at the court of the Spanish king Philip IV, created canvases that showed the full range of people from kings to paupers and court jesters. His careful composition and subtle rendering of light have inspired admiration for generations.

The royal baroque was seen also in the architecture of the time. The techniques of contrast and drama were used in palaces such as the grand and imposing Versailles (Chapter 5) to indicate the role of the ruler. There were also programs for the beautification of cities such as Paris and London. The widening of streets to give a grand vista is a baroque technique.

Dutch Baroque. Although the baroque style was originally tied to Catholicism, it spread into the northern Protestant countries as well. In Holland, a middle-class baroque developed. Here, religious themes were replaced by those of family, trade, and science. To these themes were applied the techniques of contrast of light and dark, and the strong sense of drama typical of the religious baroque. The Dutch baroque also drew on the tradition of painting that had developed during the Northern Renaissance. This tradition had placed great emphasis on detail, as exemplified in the work of Jan Van Eyck.

Holland in the 17th century was probably the most prosperous country in Europe. A middle-class civilization had arisen and the painters of the country glorified this. The interiors of homes, as well as landscapes of the city and surrounding countryside, were popular subjects. The prosperity of the middle class also created a large market for art, and a widespread consciousness of what made

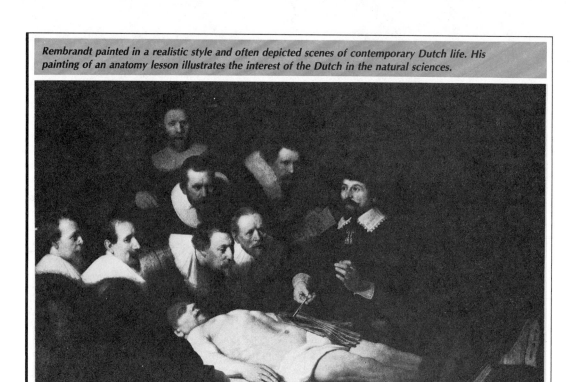

Rembrandt painted in a realistic style and often depicted scenes of contemporary Dutch life. His painting of an anatomy lesson illustrates the interest of the Dutch in the natural sciences.

good art. The size of the art market made specialization on the part of painters possible. Some became known for their still lifes, others for genre scenes, portraits, or landscapes.

The three premier painters of the Dutch baroque were Franz Hals (c. 1580–1666), Jan Vermeer (1632–1675), and Rembrandt van Rijn (1606–1669). Hals' portraits are dramatic and colorful. Vermeer painted both landscapes, such as his *View of Delft*, and interiors. The stillness of the moment captured in time is one of the hallmarks of Vermeer's work.

The greatest of the Dutch painters was Rembrandt. Over a long career, Rembrandt painted just about every kind of picture. His use of light to illuminate the faces of people in his portraits has never been surpassed. His painting *The Anatomy Lesson* shows the Dutch concern with medicine, a field in which the country excelled.

Music of the Baroque. Music which incorporated the baroque emphasis on the capturing of tension and emotions through the use of ornamentation and elaboration was first produced in Italy. Some of the music of the Italian baroque was religious, such as the masses of the great church composer Palestrina (1525–1594), but there was also a sizable body of secular music produced at this time. Palestrina and others composed numerous small secular works for voices called madrigals. Claudio Monteverdi (1567–1643) developed the musical genre of the opera. The opera, in its simultaneous use of different arts (music and drama) and in its general extravagance, was a typically baroque form.

Some of the greatest baroque composers came from the Protestant nations of northern Europe. There such men as Johann Sebastian Bach (1685–1750) built on the earlier achievements of the Italian baroque com-

The child protegy Amadeus Mozart, shown here with his father and older sister, gave concerts all over Europe. His music expressed the optimism and the humanistic orientation of the Enlightenment.

posers. Bach, who was the organist in a church in Germany, produced a huge body of work. His church music—including such sublime works as the *Mass in B Minor* and the *St. Matthew's Passion*—employs the baroque characteristics of drama and ornamentation. These works are suffused with deep religious feeling. Bach also produced a vast body of instrumental music and opera-like vocal works called cantatas.

Composing at the same time were the Germans George Philip Telemann (1681–1767) and George Frederick Handel (1685–1759). Handel achieved his greatest success after moving to Britain. His *Messiah* and operas are important parts of the musical repertory.

THE ROCOCO
As the 18th century began, art started to change. It became more informal. Colors became more muted and a more intimate style developed. This style is known as *rococo* (from the Italian word for "shell") because of the curves that are characteristic of it. Rococo art could be just as ornate as the baroque

but it was usually on a smaller scale. It was adjusted to the salon rather than the palace.

The rococo often depicted frivolous subject matter. Pastel colors were in vogue and charming scenes of cherubs were popular. The rococo style was popular for decoration. China had captured the imagination of Europe at this time, and its influence can be seen in Chinoiserie, a European attempt to copy the Chinese style.

Examples of rococo painting are most abundant in France, where the greatest of the rococo artists, Antoine Watteau (1684–1721) resided. Another important French rococo painter was François Boucher (1703–1770), who was a favorite of Madame Pompadour, the mistress of Louis XV. Rococo architecture also became important in the German states, where churches and public buildings were elaborately ornamented.

THE CLASSICAL STYLE
A reaction to the frivolity of rococo occurred in the middle of the 18th century. The new interest in classical studies in Enlightenment circles brought a neo-classical look to the arts. Painting, music, architecture and sculpture all acquired a new sense of balance, dignity, and human proportion.

Perhaps the greatest achievements in this period were found in music. A number of important developments had occurred in the musical world. Vienna had become the musical capital of Europe, bringing together musicians from both Italy and Germany. Here the great composers of the day came together and learned from each other.

The 18th century also saw a great expansion in the role of musical instruments. For centuries music had been primarily vocal. Now such stringed instruments as the violin and the cello were perfected by such master instrument-makers as Stradivari and Guarneri. A number of new wind instruments— the oboe, bassoon, clarinet, and flute—also came into regular use. Perhaps most important of all was the development of the piano.

The two most important composers of the classical era were Franz Joseph Haydn (1732–1809) and Wolfgang Amadeus Mozart (1756–1791). Haydn, drawing on the possibilities of the new orchestral instruments, developed the symphony into one of the great genres of Western music. Mozart composed for the newly developed piano. In his piano works, as well as in his operas, symphonies, and occasional music, he produced music that has never been surpassed for its blend of form and emotionality. His *Don Giovanni* and *The Marriage of Figaro* represent also the humane values of the Enlightenment.

In the visual arts, the French sculptor Jean Antoine Houdon (1741–1828) produced statues and busts of Enlightenment heroes on both sides of the Atlantic—Voltaire, Jefferson, Washington. The intelligence of Houdon's subjects shines forth in his work.

The French painter Jacques Louis David (1748–1825) exemplified the new classical style in painting. His works depict political scenes from the history of ancient Rome and project a sense of order and seriousness. His later paintings were to reflect the passions of the French Revolution and the glorification of Napoleon.

SOCIETY AND POPULAR CULTURE

During the 17th and 18th centuries, European life changed greatly. The growth of trade with the rest of the world meant greater wealth for European countries, particularly those on the Atlantic seaboard. Also contributing to the increase in wealth were new methods of industrial production and more productive agriculture.

Greater personal wealth brought about a rise in the standard of living. More people could afford the necessities of life. Many were freed from reliance on physical toil to provide a bare subsistence. Others could now afford luxuries that previously were enjoyed only by the nobility. Some altogether new luxuries became available.

In the 18th century there was a greater emphasis on a kind of civility that gave a more polite tone to society. All sorts of fripperies—wigs, ribbons, and jewels—became popular.

Yet another hallmark of upper- and middle-class life during the age of the Enlightenment was a marked gullibility among those who were supposedly well-educated and discerning. Openmindedness to new ideas often degenerated into susceptibility to the proposals and schemes of all manner of quacks. People called phrenologists, for example, convinced many people that a person's character could be analyzed by studying the bumps on his head. In many respects, the tendency to superstition of earlier ages had not died.

For the majority of people at the bottom of the social scale, the change in life style was slight. Much of life was still arduous. The average life span was 35 years. More than three-fourths of the people lived in poverty without any leisure time to improve their minds.

Punishments for lawbreakers were severe. Public executions were the penalty for even minor offenses. In contrast to medieval times, when poverty was regarded as one of life's misfortunes, it now became punishable as idleness. Whipping and forced labor were prescribed for those who did not appear industrious enough. It was a callous age, in which a typical amusement was to display inmates of asylums in cages. Bearbaiting and animal fights were popular sports.

The vast majority of Europe's 80 or 90 million people lived in the countryside. Cities were small. The two largest were London and Paris. There were few cities of more than 40,000 people. Because the transportation system was primitive, most people were isolated in the villages of their birth. Local affairs were all that occupied their interest. Hints of the wider world came only with news of soldiers marching through the countryside.

SUMMARY

During the scientific revolution, from about 1540 to 1700, many European thinkers developed a new way of looking at the natural world. Their discoveries were made possible by the use of scientific method. In the century that followed, an intellectual movement saw Europeans reexamine human institutions and the condition of humankind.

The currents of thought set in motion by the Enlightenment influenced the American Revolution and, shortly after, the French Revolution, as we shall see in Chapter 9.

QUESTIONS

1 What was revolutionary about the scientific revolution—i.e., how did it differ from the medieval approach to science?
2 What was the significance of Isaac Newton's theories?
3 Describe the relationship between the scientific revolution and the Enlightenment.
4 Compare and contrast the ideas of Thomas Hobbes and John Locke.
5 In what ways do the ideas of the Enlightenment influence the 20th-century world?

BIBLIOGRAPHY

ANTHONY, H. D. *Sir Isaac Newton.* New York: Collier, 1960. *This biography presents both personal details and an explanation of the scientific accomplishment of Newton.*
BIRN, RAYMOND. *Crisis, Absolutism, Revolution: Europe, 1648–1789/91.* Hinsdale, Ill.: Dryden Press, 1977. *The Enlightenment is placed within the framework of political and social history: in this way, the reader acquires a sense of the impact of intellectual history.*
GEYMONAT, LUDOVICO. *Galileo Galilei.* New York: McGraw Hill, 1965. *The author, an Italian philosopher of science, joins biographical material with an analysis of Galileo's scientific thought.*
KEARNEY, HUGH. *Science and Changes, 1500–1700.* New York: McGraw Hill, 1971. *This work surveys the scientific revolution, and includes many useful sketches and pictures to illustrate the ideas of the period.*
KRIEGER, LEONARD. *Kings and Philosophers, 1689–1789.* New York: Norton, 1970. *An extensive survey of the philosophers of the period and their impact on the kings who adopted the principles of enlightened absolutism.*
WOLF, ABRAHAM. *A History of Science, Technology, and Philosophy in the 16th and 17th Centuries.* Gloucester, Mass.: P. Smith, 1968. *This is the standard survey of intellectual developments in early modern Europe.*

The French Revolution

Charles Dickens' historical novel, *A Tale of Two Cities*, depicts the dramatic events of the first French Revolution. However, it has been said that truth is stranger and a thousand times more thrilling than fiction, and the turbulent and complicated episodes of France in the period from 1789–1815 are evidence of the truth of that adage.

During that brief revolutionary period, French society witnessed the establishment of a constitutional monarchy, the overthrow and execution of the king, the introduction of a liberal republic, a reign of terror when thousands were sent to the guillotine, an unsuccessful attempt at constitutional government, and the advent of an emperor, Napoleon I, whose rule mirrored in many respects the characteristics of the hated Bourbon dynasty. Throughout most of the period, France was at war with its neighbors. Napoleon's conquest of Europe extended France's empire to the outskirts of Moscow before it ended in the defeat of Waterloo. At the end of this turbulent era, the Bourbon dynasty was restored to limited power.

Beyond the excitement generated by the events themselves, the French Revolution remains important to historians for several reasons. Among them: The French Revolution was the first attempt in Europe to put into practice the dramatic ideals of the Enlightenment—liberty, equality, and fraternity (*Liberté, Egalité, Fraternité*—the rallying cry of many of the revolutionaries). Secondly, this revolution was successful: it ended the absolutism of the Old Regime (*l'ancien régime*) in France and, during the Napoleonic wars that followed, spread democratic ideals throughout Europe.

Thirdly, in their attempts to put their ideals into practice, the revolutionaries experimented with several constitutional models which serve as case studies of the strengths and weaknesses of various forms of constitutional government. Finally, the French Revolution heralded the advent of modern nationalism and patriotism, with all of the beneficial and negative effects of both.

CAUSES OF THE REVOLUTION

The French Revolution was in fact not a single event, but a series of occurrences. The first stage of the Revolution in 1789 brought political and social changes. The king, Louis XVI, was forced to accept a constitution limiting his authority. The privileges of the French aristocracy were swept away. The fact that such radical changes were wrought in a six-month period suggests a great depth and breadth of dissatisfaction with the Old Regime.

The underlying reasons for the first stage of the Revolution in 1789 include the following factors: 1) the inequities of the social system of the *ancien régime*, 2) the opposition of the intellectuals to the status quo, 3) the absolute power of the French monarchy, 4) the personal inadequacies of Kings Louis XV and XVI, and 5) the financial crisis which confronted the French government in the years immediately preceding the Revolution. We shall examine each of these factors in some detail.

THE INEQUITIES OF THE ANCIEN REGIME

The inequities of the French social system were the effect of a rigid class system in which the people were sharply divided between the privileged few and the unprivileged many. The privileged groups were the aristocracy and the clergy; the unprivileged were the peasantry, the middle class—or *bourgeoisie*—and the urban workers.

The French Aristocracy. The aristocracy consisted of nobles who had either inherited or purchased titles. This nobility enjoyed a vast range of advantages which had been theirs since medieval times. Only the nobility were eligible for high-ranking positions in two of the organizations—the military and the Church—that were the primary sources of political power, authority, and prestige in pre-revolutionary society.

Another important advantage enjoyed by the nobility was exemption from most major taxes. Also, the nobility, as landowners, received the income generated by their property, and had considerable power over the peasants who lived on their land and worked for them.

The French Clergy. The Roman Catholic clergy of France also enjoyed many privileges. First, they were exempt from the major taxes. Although the lower clergy, such as village priests, came from the middle and lower classes of the society, and identified with the interests and discontent of the non-privileged classes, the high clergy—bishops, abbots, archbishops, and cardinals—were, as we have seen, drawn from the members of the aristocracy. The Roman Catholic Church owned about one-fourth of the rural land; hence, the higher clergy, as landlords, also were targets of the disgruntled peasantry.

The Peasantry. One of the principal unprivileged groups in pre-revolutionary France was the peasantry. Legally, the peasants were no longer serfs, as they had been during the feudal period; that is, they were no longer legally obligated to live and work on the estates where they were born. However, they were economically tied to the lord for their survival and they owed a number

This 18th-century cartoon depicts the economic and social relationship between the three traditional classes of France—nobility, clergy, and peasantry.

of obligations to their landlords. These included unpaid labor to maintain the roads of the estate, known as *corvée*, and an annual cash or in-kind payment to their noble.

These remnants of the feudal system heavily disadvantaged the peasants who worked the soil. At the time of the Revolution, French peasants owned only one-fourth of the total land. Like peasants everywhere, then and now, their greatest desire was to own their own land.

Though landless, powerless, and disadvantaged, French peasants nevertheless bore the burden of the tax system and, in addition, were required to pay an annual tithe (10 percent of their earnings) to the Roman Catholic Church.

The Bourgeoisie. The rising middle class of France (the bourgeoisie)—the merchants, traders, industrialists, lawyers, and other professionals—were also included among the non-privileged groups. Like the peasants, they were responsible for paying numerous state taxes, and they were not eligible for prominent positions in the military, the Church, or the government.

Many members of this group strove to enter the ranks of the aristocracy, and some were successful, purchasing noble titles which the monarchy willingly sold as a source of state revenue. Those who were not elevated to the aristocracy deeply resented their lack of prestige and of social, economic, and political power, and chafed under the financial burdens that the inequitable tax system laid upon them. It is not surprising that many leaders of the revolution came from the educated, articulate middle class.

The Proletariat and the Petit Bourgeoisie. A final group, the urban workers (proletariat) and the small shopkeepers (the petit bourgeoisie), also were among the non-privileged. They were important disproportionately to their numbers, for living primarily in Paris, they could easily be recruited to create public disorder.

The Opposition of the Intellectuals. As we have seen in Chapter 8, France was the center of Enlightenment political thought, and French intellectuals in the 18th century—men like Voltaire and Diderot—not only theorized about new political ideas but actively encouraged reform of the French political, social, and economic systems. Moreover, these ideas were popularized among the upper and middle classes in the salons and coffee houses.

But the calls for reform evoked no response from the monarchy; instead the intellectuals were condemned—Voltaire, for one, was imprisoned occasionally, and even served a sentence in the Bastille, the notorious Paris prison. He and other intellectuals became alienated from their society, concluding that there was little chance to reform the regime, that only its overthrow could bring political equality and social justice to France. The success of the American Revolution in the 1770s and 1780s provided them with a model for a new order.

THE POWER OF THE THRONE

The French monarchs, members of the Bourbon dynasty, had for over a century been the most powerful in western Europe, excluding the Romanovs of Russia. Laws were simply pronounced by the king and his ministers—as edicts.

There had been in France two distinct bodies of citizens who had in earlier centuries served as rivals to the king's judicial and legislative power. The first, the 13 courts of law known as *parlements*, had historically viewed themselves as the supreme courts of the state, with the authority to abolish laws—the king's decrees—if they were judged to be beyond the scope of the king's authority. Louis XIV had successfully destroyed the power of the *parlements*, although they still existed. At the time of the Revolution, many members of the *parlements* were eager to reassert their authority.

The second group, the *Estates-General*, supposedly representing all of the French people, had also traditionally been consulted by the king. The Estates-General was divided into three Estates, or bodies. The First Estate was composed of the Catholic clergy, the Second Estate of the nobility, and the Third Estate of everyone else, or about 97 percent of the population. The inequality of the composition of the Estates-General mattered little, for it had not met for 174 years. In the years before the Revolution, nearly all power lay in the hands of the monarchy, and all dissent was forbidden.

THE WEAKNESS OF THE KINGS

The absolute power of the French throne unfortunately coincided with the reigns of two kings with many personal deficiencies—Louis XV and Louis XVI. Louis XV came to the throne at the age of five in 1715 and reigned for 59 years. He has been described as intelligent but lazy and bored, and until 1743 he delegated considerable power to his childhood tutor, Cardinal Fleury. When

Marie Antoinette, the Austrian-born queen of Louis XVI, was noted for her extravagances.

Louis XVI, a weak and indecisive king, did not heed his most able advisers.

Louis XV died in 1774, the throne went to his 20-year-old grandson, Louis XVI, who was dull-minded and indecisive. In the critical years before and during the revolution, Louis XVI was poorly equipped to cope with the myriad of problems confronting his people. His shallow wife, Marie Antoinette, the daughter of Maria Theresa, Empress of Austria, was equally insensitive to the plight of their subjects. One of their chief pastimes was hunting. Louis slew thousands of animals—by one estimate 190,525 animals in a 13-year period, each killing of which he carefully noted in his diary. Marie Antoinette collected riding costumes—31 outfits in November 1781 alone.

THE FINANCIAL CRISIS

The dire condition of the royal finances was yet another underlying cause of the revolution. The most serious problem the French government faced in the 18th century was inadequate revenues. It became increasingly apparent that some kind of tax reform was necessary if the government were to escape bankruptcy. On the eve of the revolution one finance minister after another attempted reform.

In 1783, Charles de Calonne, who believed that the only solution was to reform the tax laws and to tax the privileged classes, was named finance minister. But this proposal raised the important question of who had the power to approve new taxes. Calonne knew that the *parlements* would resist tax reform, for they maintained that equal taxation would threaten the traditional hierarchy of privileges which defined the social orders.

The Assembly of Notables, 1787. To get around the *parlements*, in 1787 Calonne encouraged the king to call a special *Assembly of Notables*, a handpicked group of the privileged who he hoped would approve the new tax laws and so give them legality. However, the Assembly of Notables was too clever for Calonne; its members agreed in principle to equal taxation, they said, but rejected the specific proposals contained in Calonne's tax package. Calonne's ploy had failed, and he was replaced by Lomenie Brienne.

Brienne took Calonne's proposal directly to the *parlements*, but they maintained that it was beyond their power to approve new taxes. Instead, they said, only the Estates-General, which had not met since 1615, could approve new taxes. Although the Revolution is usually dated from 1789, in a sense the rebellion had already begun. At stake were two issues: the king's power and the concept of privileges which characterized the old regime.

The Estates-General. King Louis XVI decided to eliminate the *parlements* and to call the Estates-General, which, he hoped, would accept the tax proposal. However, the first two Estates, the privileged clergy and the no-

bility, held two-thirds of the votes in the Estates-General, for each group voted as a body. Therefore, on the question of taxing themselves, the first two estates would surely band together and vote against the reform.

To combat the likelihood of this outcome and to force a compromise, the king suggested that the Estates-General should vote by head, with each delegate having one vote. The First Estate had 308 representatives, the Second Estate, 285, for a combined total of 593. If the king's proposal were adopted, they could therefore be outvoted by the Third Estate, which had 621 delegates.

THE REVOLUTION

With the historic meeting set for May 1, 1789, the king encouraged free debate and elections among potential delegates to the Third Estate. By so doing he unintentionally unleashed their power. Articulate candidates seized the opportunity to engage in earnest debate, and they began to issue pamphlets. One of the most effective pamphlets, *What Is the Third Estate?*, was written by the Abbé Sieyes, in January 1789. In response to the question of the title, the author retorted, "Everything."

In addition, Louis XVI encouraged his subjects to transmit to the government their lists of grievances, which were known as *cahiers*. The result was an avalanche. Although the king intended to use the *cahiers* to force the aristocracy to agree to his plan, many of his subjects believed him to be sincere and assumed that the Estates-General would consider and rectify their numerous grievances.

In the quarrel between the aristocracy and the king, each side had forgotten the great majority of the population. They had opened a Pandora's box of trouble and couldn't close the lid.

THE NATIONAL ASSEMBLY, MAY 1789

When the day came for the meeting of the Estates-General, the Third Estate refused to

The painter Jacques Louis David portrayed the excitement of the revolutionaries in June, 1789, as they pledged to stand together under the "Oath of the Tennis Court."

organize itself in its separate meeting hall. It demanded instead that the three estates meet jointly and vote by head. After a five-week deadlock, some of the lower clergy joined the members of the Third Estate, and on June 17 the members of this body declared themselves the National Assembly. When the delegates found themselves locked out of their meeting hall on June 20, they adjourned to a nearby tennis court and swore an oath of determination not to be disbanded. On June 24, more than half of the clergy joined the rebels in the National Assembly and on June 25, 47 nobles joined their ranks. The king then ordered the rest of the clergy and nobles to join the National Assembly.

THE FALL OF THE BASTILLE: JULY 14, 1789

The revolt thus far had been a moderate, bloodless middle-class rebellion. But on July

The storming of the Bastille, on July 14, 1789, is one of the most famous episodes of the Revolution.

14 the revolution spread to the working-class sections of Paris when a mob of men and women stormed the Bastille, the dreaded prison of the king. When soldiers defending the prison joined the rioters, the Bastille fell. July 14, *Bastille Day*, is today recognized as the French national day of independence.

Unsure of his next move, the king considered seeking foreign military help, but instead accepted the National Assembly, which by then was meeting at Versailles, attempting to develop a new government for France.

THE CONSTITUENT ASSEMBLY, 1789–1791

In July 1789, the National Assembly, now calling itself the Constituent Assembly, started to draft a constitution for France. The members of the Assembly produced a general statement, "The Declaration of Rights of Man and the Citizen," which closely resembled the American Bill of Rights. It began: "All men are born and remain free and equal in rights." The fact that this document excluded women led the female playwright Olympe de Gouges to write a pamphlet, "The Rights of Women," which outlined an equitable marriage contract giving women equal property rights. De Gouges was guillotined during the Reign of Terror. The issue of women's equality was ignored by the Constituent Assembly.

The Great Fear and the August Decrees.
During the summer months of 1789, 20,000 nobles left France. Among the peasants, the rumor circulated that the emigrés intended to return with foreign troops to put down the revolution. In response to this rumor, a panic called "The Great Fear" shook the countryside. Peasants went on a rampage of murder, arson, and looting. In this atmosphere of urgency, the moderates in the National Assembly acted quickly to legalize the social revolution which was taking place.

On the night of August 4, the nobles and clergy in the National Assembly renounced all of their privileges: hunting and fishing rights, church tithes, exemptions from taxes, the right to sell government and church offices, and the many other privileges they had enjoyed for centuries. In one evening, in what has been called an "orgy of renunciation," the *ancien régime* was swept away by the August Decrees.

The final revolutionary act of 1789 came on October 5, when the women of Paris began demonstrations for bread. These women represented the lower classes and their goals were mainly economic—more food—rather than political—participation in the new government. Yet, when 6000 women marched to Versailles, they also pressured the king to acknowledge the August Decrees and to move back to Paris where they might watch him more closely. At this point, the violent episodes of the Revolution temporarily ended.

Flight of the King and new Constitution, 1791.
For the next two years, the Constituent Assembly ruled France and wrote the constitution. Although a variety of views were represented in the Assembly, the moderates who won out favored a constitutional monarchy, which retained the king but limited his powers.

In June 1791, with the constitution nearly finished, the king attempted to flee the country. He and his family, disguised as servants, set off by coach for Varennes on the Belgian border. But a guard recognized the king from his profile on French paper money, and the royal family was returned to Paris. On September 14, 1791, under house arrest, the king took an oath to uphold the new constitution, which was to go into effect on October 1.

The new constitution created a one-house legislature, the Legislative Assembly, yet left considerable power in the hands of the king. But the king's attempt to leave the country doomed an excellent piece of work, for even the proponents of the constitutional monarchy were now skeptical about the wisdom of the decision to retain the monarchy. Nevertheless, the new constitution was put

in place, the Legislative Assembly was elected, and the king appointed his ministers, as the constitution provided.

THE RISE OF THE JACOBINS

The death blow to the new government was dealt when war broke out between France and Prussia and Austria in April 1792. The French had begun the war with an invasion of the Austrian territory of Belgium, where they hoped to spread the Revolution. However, the invasion of Belgium failed, and by August 1792 the Austrian and Prussian armies were at the French borders.

At this point, a nervous and high-strung man named Maximilian Robespierre (1758–1794) came to the fore. Robespierre was the leader of the *Jacobins*, a radical faction among those who supported the Revolution. Most were members of the bourgeoisie. Deriving their name from the Jacobin convent in which a radical group called the Paris

Club met, they had grown into a nationwide network of political clubs that used propaganda and occasionally terrorist tactics in their efforts to establish a republic in France. Robespierre and the journalist Jean-Paul Marat (1743–1793) urged the Paris working classes to join forces to depose the king, whom they blamed for the failure of the war.

On August 9 and 10, 1792, a Paris mob, mostly shopkeepers and craftsmen, forced the Legislative Assembly to suspend the king and to imprison him and his family. At that point, the Assembly moved the election of a new representative body, the National Convention. The Convention was to be responsible for judging the king and writing a new constitution for France.

A few days later, on September 2, 1792, the Paris mob began a massacre of prisoners, claiming that they were plotting the overthrow of the new regime. Actually, of the 1100–1400 prisoners executed, only a few were aristocrats. The September massacre demonstrated the effectiveness of the Paris rioters and the ease with which they could threaten the more moderate leaders.

The Death of the King, January 1793. In the election for the National Convention the largest number of seats was won by the Jacobin faction, which intended to establish a

An executioner showed the head of Louis XVI to an approving crowd in January of 1793.

This portrait of Marie Antoinette, sketched by David as she was led to the executioner, presents a sharp contrast to the life of ease and luxury that was hers as queen of France.

The guillotine was the recent invention of a French doctor named Joseph Guillotin who had sought a humane means of execution to replace the more torturous methods of the noose or the chopping block.

republic in France. In a trial held by the National Convention in January 1793, Louis XVI was found guilty of treason by a vote of 387 to 334, and sentenced to death. On January 21, the former king of France was taken through the streets of Paris to the Place de la Revolution where a guillotine and an excited crowd awaited him.

Before the blade of the new device fell, Louis tried to speak to those assembled:

● ● ● *Frenchmen, I die innocent; it is from the scaffold and near to appearing before God that I tell you so. I pardon my enemies. I desire that France. . . .*[1]

The drums interrupted a speech he never finished. The blade fell upon his neck and his head dropped into the waiting basket. To prove the deed was done, the executioner lifted the severed head by its hair and showed it to the crowd. On October 16, 1793, Louis' widow, Marie Antoinette, met the same fate. Many others were soon to follow.

The Reign of Terror, July 1793–July 1794. While the National Convention attempted to write a new constitution, the government in France was carried out by two committees, both dominated by Robespierre and his Jacobin followers. These were the Committee of Public Safety and the Committee of General Security.

Using as their excuse the crisis of the war, the committees declared they needed to stamp out any threat to their power. Claiming that they were surrounded by counter-revolutionaries, they ignored established judicial procedures, and in their place set up revolutionary tribunals which rapidly tried and executed about 16,500 "enemies" of the revolution. Another 10,000 to 15,000 were executed without benefit of trial. Most of the victims were ordinary people—farmers and workers. A few (12 percent) were nobles and priests who did oppose the Revolution; a few were political rivals to Robespierre's power. But during this bloody period, which has come to be known as the *Reign of Terror*, Robespierre and his followers used the watchwords "liberty, fraternity, and equality" to justify the systematic destruction of democratic ideals. One of their victims, Madame Roland, who along with her husband had taken an active role in the Revo-

---

[1] Quoted in Will and Ariel Durant, *The Age of Napoleon*, Vol. XI (New York: Simon & Schuster, 1975), p. 52.

lution, summarized it best on the day of her execution: "Oh Liberty, what crimes are committed in your name!"[2]

The Revolution Spreads. The political fervor of the Republic led to a reversal of fortunes on the battlefield. The Republican soldiers were fired by the dream of spreading the Revolution. It was not long before the struggle against Austria and Prussia began to turn. The French scored an important victory at Valmy in September 1792. The Republican army then went on the offensive.

The war that began in 1792 was to last with some pauses for the next quarter of a century, and would bring a fundamental change in warfare. In the 18th century, wars had been fought by professionals who practiced definite conventions of fighting. The French Revolution brought the idea that, as one leader declared in the Constituent Assembly in 1789, "Each citizen should be a soldier, and each soldier a citizen."[3]

Women were especially active during the revolution. They wrote pamphlets and in a few cases formed political clubs. The largest and best known such club was the Republican Revolutionary Women. This organization generally supported the aims of the Republic and fought primarily for economic rights. During the short reign of the Republic, women did acquire equal property rights and equal access to free primary schools. The reign of the clubs was brief, however, for Robespierre disliked politically active women.

[2] *Ibid.*, p. 67.

[3] Crane Brinton, *A Decade of Revolution* (New York: Harper & Row, 1963), p. 96.

Charlotte Corday murdered the Jacobin leader Marat, who had been responsible for the deaths of thousands of priests and royalists. The bloody days of the Reign of Terror followed.

In the first year of war, 300,000 men were drafted into the army. In 1793, the Convention decreed the *levée en masse*, under which all the resources of the nation were to be made available to win the war. The army raised about 750,000 men—the largest ever assembled by a European power. Thus was born the concept of the nation in arms, which has become a feature of modern war.

However, these military successes made the French people less tolerant of the dictatorial policies they were being subjected to at home.

The extremes to which Robespierre and Marat took the revolutionary ideals led to the deaths of both. Marat was assassinated in July 1793 by a young woman from Normandy, Charlotte Corday, who stabbed him as he sat in his bathtub. She later died on the guillotine.

Robespierre lived another year, until July 1794, when his excesses began to frighten even his supporters. As he rose to speak in the National Convention, many feared that he intended to name a new list of "traitors," perhaps even themselves, to be destroyed. A mob prevented him from speaking and in the ensuing confusion, Robespierre was shot in the jaw. His wounds were not fatal, but his politics were. The following day, his head in bandages, the architect of the Reign of Terror was himself decapitated by the guillotine.

THE THERMIDOREAN REACTION AND THE DIRECTORY, 1794–1798

Robespierre's death occurred in the month of Thermidor (according to the new revolutionary calendar), and the change in national mood it brought about is known as the *Thermidorean Reaction.* Previously, the Revolution had become progressively more radical; after Thermidor, much of its excesses were halted. Political prisoners were freed from the jails in some provinces and cities.

Newspapers, now enjoying greater freedom, attacked "tigers thirsting for human blood,"[4] and rejoiced in Robespierre's downfall. Theaters presented plays which ridiculed the Republicans. Fancy clothes became fashionable again, replacing the austere styles of the Terror.

Soon, the two great committees were stripped of their powers. The Jacobin Club in Paris was closed, and a "white terror" was carried out against suspected Jacobins at the end of 1794 and beginning of 1795.

The constitution which the National Convention had written had never been put into effect. Yet another Republican constitution was written with provisions to prevent the excesses of the Terror. A new government, called the *Directory,* established an executive of five men chosen by the new two-house legislature. The new constitution went into effect in September 1795. For the next four years, the various factions in French politics attempted to gain a majority in the Directory.

Many of the Directors were corrupt, and amassed fortunes at the expense of the public. Although economic conditions were bad and famine stalked part of the land, the Directors spent money on wasteful display.

In its war policies, the Directory was successful. The army won victories under the guidance of young republican generals. In 1795, Spain, Holland, and Prussia made peace with France, and two years later, the Austrians were forced to sign the Treaty of Campo Formi.

France had gained a paramount position on the Continent, similar to that it enjoyed under Louis XIV. France surrounded itself with "sister republics." The Austrian Netherlands were annexed, and the left bank of the Rhine was in French hands. Holland, called the Batavian Republic, and the northern portion of Italy, called the Ligurian Republic, were closely bound to France. They had to support the French army and paid an indemnity to the country that had "liberated" them.

Three *coups d'état* (sudden overthrows of government by a few) took place during the Directory period. In the final one in November (Brumaire) 1799 two directors—Sieyes, author of the famous pamphlet, and Charles Maurice de Talleyrand-Perigord—attempted to eliminate Republican influence permanently. In this coup, called the *Coup of Brumaire,* Sieyes and Talleyrand used a young general, Napoleon Bonaparte, whose troops drove the legislators from their meeting hall. The conspirators seized power and proclaimed a new form of republic, the Consulate.

NAPOLEON

The many changes of government in France, against the background of war, made possible the rise of

---

[4] *Ibid.,* p. 196.

a military dictator. The country was exhausted by the rapidly occurring changes that were taking place. Napoleon followed proper form by always linking himself to the revolution, promising to maintain its achievements.

EARLY LIFE

Napoleon Bonaparte (1769–1821) was born on the island of Corsica in August 1769. This Italian possession had been sold to France only 15 months before his birth; hence Napoleon's family had their roots in Italian culture rather than French. His parents claimed noble lineage. Napoleon was the fourth of 13 children; his siblings who lived to adulthood were to share in his later good fortune and power. At the age of 10 the young Napoleon was sent to a French military academy, and at the age of 15 he entered the advanced military school, the Ecole Militaire in Paris.

When the Revolution came in 1789, Napoleon supported it and became an officer in the Revolutionary army. Promoted to general when he was only 24, he was put in command of the Italian campaigns and soon won a reputation for daring, for military genius, for the loyalty of his troops, and for victories. The victories came one after another until he had conquered most of the Italian peninsula. These successes brought Napoleon the attraction and the support of the government, and precipitated the decision of Sieyes and Talleyrand to identify him as their strong man in the Coup of Brumaire.

NAPOLEON AND THE CONSULATE, 1799–1804

This young and daring general quickly turned the tables on Sieyes and Talleyrand and took command of the French domestic situation as eagerly as he had commanded his troops. Although he proclaimed his support for the ideals of the Republic, he nonetheless introduced a dictatorship to bring order to the chaos of France in 1799.

He instituted many reforms—for example, in the civil service and the treasury.

This romantic painting of Napoleon by David depicts the young general as he crossed the Alps into Italy.

Through these he guaranteed the French equality and fraternity. In exchange, he deprived them of their liberty. He succeeded in doing so in part because men such as Robespierre had so twisted and distorted the democratic ideal during the Reign of Terror that it had lost its importance to many French citizens.

Among Napoleon's reforms was the establishment of a national education system. Another was a new constitution, which he presented to the public in a *plebiscite*—a popular vote—that required them either to accept fully his version or to allow him to govern without the restrictions of a constitution. Napoleon's popularity, his support by the army, and the general exhaustion that had resulted from the dizzying events of the previous decade combined to bring the constitution public approval.

Modeling his constitution closely on the forms of the ancient Roman republic, Napoleon put the executive branch of the new government in the hands of three consuls, with Napoleon himself First Consul.

Relations with the Church. A number of the reforms Napoleon instituted under the Consulate did much to ensure his popularity with a populace that longed for the return of order and, to some degree, of the status quo.

He reconciled many to his new government by making peace with the Roman Catholic Church. Back in 1790, the Constituent Assembly, in the Civil Constitution of the Clergy, had claimed power over the Catholic clergy in France, had put priests on the government payroll, and claimed the right of the government to appoint bishops. The pope was to have no jurisdiction in France. In the later years of the Revolution, all religion had been declared counter-revolutionary and a movement of de-Christianization launched.

Both of these measures had aroused considerable antipathy among the French people. Thus, there was much rejoicing when, in 1801, Napoleon and the pope signed an agreement called the Concordat. This document restored the Vatican's authority over the French clergy and reestablished traditional Catholic practices in France.

The Concordat strengthened Napoleon's power over a largely Catholic France. In the catechism taught in French religious schools, children recited, "to honor and serve our Emperor is to honor and serve God himself."

The Napoleonic Code. Another of Napoleon's great achievements as First Consul was the codification of the over 300 overlapping and confusing legal systems of the *ancien régime* and the revolutionary assemblies. This massive job of collating and condensing resulted in five codes, each of which governed a different aspect of the nation's legal life, and which together assured all French citizens of legal equality.

While the *Napoleonic Code* grounded French society in the principle of equality, it also established a fairly traditional and middle-class framework for much of French life. Women were granted only very restricted property rights; fathers were given extensive authority over their children; labor unions were banned. The Napoleonic Code has remained the basis of the French legal system to the present day. In addition, the Code was spread throughout Europe through Napoleon's conquests. It influenced the legal systems of Belgium, Italy, Holland, and the colony of Louisiana.

THE FIRST EMPIRE, 1804–1815

The Consulate was a sham. The new government provided for universal male suffrage, but there were few real choices left to the electorate. They chose notables from a list presented to them; these notables were then available for government appointments. Some of the notables sat in the new legislative bodies, the Senate and the Tribunate, but neither of these bodies had any significant power. The main agency of government was the Council of State, which was under the control of the First Consul—Napoleon. For five years he preserved this phony system while he tested the waters of public opinion.

By 1804 Napoleon felt confident enough to propose that he be named consul for life, and the citizenry enthusiastically endorsed this action in another plebiscite. Thus emboldened, Napoleon wrote yet another constitution for France. In this latest document, he proclaimed that the government of the Republic resided in an emperor, himself, and declared the First Empire of the French. Because the new constitution had been ratified by plebiscite, Napoleon could claim that the power of the emperor derived from the French people.

In a symbolic act designed to solidify his authority, in December 1804, Napoleon reenacted an ancient ceremony of coronation in which the pope consecrated him. The crowning of Charlemagne in 800 A.D. had symbolized the founding of a successor empire to Rome—the Holy Roman Empire. Now, with papal sanction, a new empire was to take its place. However, Napoleon placed

In 1804, Napoleon crowned himself emperor of the French.

the imperial crown on his head himself. In so doing he made it clear that, while the pope might give the new emperor his blessing, the pope would not have power over him.

As Napoleon I, Emperor of the French, he made the office hereditary and established a court comparable to those of the Bourbon dynasty. He divorced his first wife, Josephine, and in 1810 wed Marie Louise, the niece of the Austrian Emperor and member of the royal Hapsburg family. Ironically, by his marriage, Napoleon became the nephew-in-law of the deceased King Louis XVI.

Napoleon also placed his relatives on various thrones. His brother Joseph was for four years king of Naples and later king of Spain. His brother Louis became the king of Holland, and his brother Jerome, king of Westphalia. His sister Caroline succeeded Joseph as monarch of Naples. His stepson became viceroy in the kingdom of Italy, and his uncle was elevated to cardinal in the Roman Catholic Church. Napoleon had restored absolute monarchy under a new form, and had established a new Bonaparte dynasty.

NAPOLEON AT WAR

It was his early military success that brought Napoleon to power. During his rule of France, he would use his military genius to conquer much of the continent of Europe, nearly succeeding in bringing all of it under the control of the French Empire. After disastrous defeat and exile, he would return, quickly assembling yet another army and nearly restoring his former power. Napoleon is justly regarded as one of the great generals of all time.

EARLY CAMPAIGNS

During the time of the republic, England had joined Austria and Prussia in their contest with the French, forming an alliance known as the *First Coalition*. After the peace treaty with Austria was signed, France and England remained at war.

In 1798 the Directory ordered Napoleon to turn the French army against the English. Rather than invade England directly, Napoleon decided instead to launch his Egyptian campaign, which had as its goal the conquest of England's prize possession, India.

Napoleon captured the island of Malta as a staging area, and took the Egyptian port of Alexandria in July 1798. Marching south, he took Cairo and won the battle of the Pyramids against Egyptian troops. His plan was to move eastward after securing Egypt, but on August 1, the French fleet in the Mediterranean was destroyed by an English fleet under the command of Admiral Horatio Nelson at the Battle of the Nile. Cut off from supplies, Napoleon's venture was doomed to failure.

Nevertheless, his daring but unsuccessful campaign threatened the Mediterranean and Middle East interests of Austria and Russia, and in 1798 a *Second Coalition*, this time between Austria, Russia, and England, was formed.

Under the leadership of Napoleon, French aggression echoed the expansionist policies of France during the previous century. This

THE NAPOLEONIC EMPIRE AT ITS HEIGHT
How did Napoleon acquire his allies in Europe?

The Empire

States controlled by France

Allied states

× **Battles**

RUSSIAN EMPIRE

Moscow

× Borodino

× Smolensk

BLACK SEA

SWEDEN

Oslo

BALTIC SEA

NORWAY-DENMARK

Copenhagen

× Tilsit

× Friedland

× Eylau

DUCHY OF WARSAW

P R U S S I A

Berlin

× Leipzig

× Lützen

× Jena

CONFEDERATION OF THE RHINE

Austerlitz ×

AUSTRIAN EMPIRE

Vienna

Buda × Pest

× Hohenlinden

ILLYRIAN PROVINCES

Ulm ×

SWITZERLAND

ITALIAN KINGDOM

Marengo ×

Genoa

Rome

KINGDOM OF NAPLES

ELBA

CORSICA

SARDINIA

SICILY

MALTA

MEDITERRANEAN SEA

Athens

NORTH SEA

ENGLAND

London

IRELAND

Brussels

× Waterloo

Paris

FRENCH EMPIRE

ATLANTIC OCEAN

Madrid

SPAIN

PORTUGAL

Lisbon

Cape Trafalgar

Napoleon's conquest of Egypt led to new fashions of dress known as the Empire style. Hot-air balloons such as the one in the background were used for military reconnaissance as well as pleasure trips.

added to the wariness the Revolution had already caused in the rest of Europe. The crowned heads of Europe had shuddered at the decapitation of King Louis XVI, and many monarchs feared the contagion of French revolutionary ideas.

Napoleon's desire to consolidate his political position at home led to a brief interval of peace between 1801 and 1803. But soon a *Third Coalition*—of England, Austria, and Russia—brought war once again.

The French navy could not match the British fleet, and in 1805 Nelson established British naval supremacy at the Battle of Trafalgar, destroying most of the French navy and that of their Spanish allies off the coast of Spain. The French managed to hold Spain, but lost many soldiers in the guerrilla war that developed.

On land, however, the French army was repeatedly victorious. In 1805 the Russian and Austrian armies were defeated in the famous Battle of Austerlitz, in which Napoleon's speed and a brilliant strategy enabled him to defeat a force twice the size of his own. In 1806, at the Battle of Jena, the French overwhelmed the Prussian army. The vic-

torious French cavalry galloped unopposed over northern Germany, and took the war to the Russian border where the Russian army was defeated. By the Treaty of Tilsit, signed in 1807, Russia was forced to accept an alliance with France.

Napoleon organized the German states into the Confederation of the Rhine. The princes of the states agreed to renounce all support for the Holy Roman Empire; Francis II took the title Emperor of Austria; and the Holy Roman Empire was formally ended. This series of victories brought France's enemies to their knees, and Napoleon's First Empire ruled all of western Europe. The French army seemed invincible.

THE CONTINENTAL SYSTEM, 1807–1812

To oppose Napoleon only Britain remained. Since Napoleon could not combat Britain's naval strength, he turned instead to economic war. He introduced the *continental system* which forbade the importation of British goods into Europe. This trade blockade of England, however, was unenforceable. Few Europeans were motivated to

In 1806, after defeating the Austrians and Prussians in two major battles, Napoleon triumphantly entered Berlin.

forego commodities like sugar or tobacco in order to accommodate their conqueror. The blockade failed.

When Russia withdrew from the continental system and resumed trade with Britain, Napoleon decided to retaliate. Forming a Grand Army of 700,000 men drawn from all over Europe, in June 1812 he invaded Russia.

The Invasion of Russia, 1812. The decision to invade Russia was a risky one, for the dry summer season in that country is short— three to four months—and the long cold and snows are numbing to both men and horses. The spring thaws turn Russia into a swamp. Napoleon's strategic plan was designed to take these climate problems into account, for he intended to reach the key city of Moscow by September 1. By his reckoning, the conquest of Moscow would force the Russian government to capitulate. Failing that, he intended to camp out the winter in the city and resume his conquest the following summer.

In June 1812, Napoleon set out with the Grand Army, and in September, defeated the Russians at the Battle of Borodino. But when the Grand Army entered Moscow on September 14, 1812, the city burst into flames— the Russians had set fire to its wooden structures before retreating. With the Russian army blocking the route south to a more temperate climate, Napoleon's options were either to camp out the winter in the ruined city or to retreat along the northern invasion route.

After five weeks of delay, during which Napoleon attempted fruitlessly to negotiate a settlement with the Russian tsar, he chose to pull out his huge army by the northern route. But the cold and snow had set in by mid-October and the retreat was a nightmare. Napoleon's soldiers froze and starved to death, wagons bogged down in the snow and could not be moved, military discipline collapsed, and the once magnificent Grand Army degenerated into a mass of pitiful men

With Moscow in flames, Napoleon retreated the same way he had come, and most of his army perished.

struggling to return home. The casualties were enormous: of the 611,000 troops who had entered Russia, 400,000 died of battle wounds, starvation or exposure, and 100,000 were taken prisoner.

THE WAR OF LIBERATION, 1813–1814

The calamity at Moscow united Napoleon's enemies. In the spring of 1813, England, Prussia, Russia, and Austria joined forces to launch the war of liberation. In October 1813, a newly-raised French army was smashed at Leipzig in the Battle of the Nations—the greatest battle in terms of the number of men engaged until the 20th century. The French were forced back within their own frontiers. When Napoleon ignored peace overtures, the allies invaded France from all directions. In March of 1814, France surrendered.

By the terms of the victory, Napoleon was forced to abdicate unconditionally. He was allowed to retain his title of emperor, but was to rule only the isle of Elba, 19 miles long and 6 miles wide, off the coast of Tuscany. On the same day, the Senate proclaimed Louis XVIII, the brother of Louis XVI, the King of France. (Louis XVII was the young son of Louis XVI, who died in a Paris prison in 1795.)

WATERLOO, JUNE 1815

The Bourbon dynasty was restored, but not to its full powers. The new king could not be an absolute monarch after the events of the French Revolution, and Louis XVIII wisely did not attempt to be. He allowed the formation of a legislature with certain guaranteed rights and powers. However, a number of the emigrés who had returned to France at the accession of the new king proved far less sensible than Louis. Many of these terrorized former adherents of the Revolution. In this atmosphere, a wistful sympathy for the exiled emperor grew.

In March of 1815, Napoleon escaped Elba and, calling his former troops to join him,

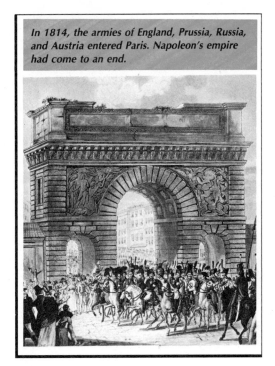

In 1814, the armies of England, Prussia, Russia, and Austria entered Paris. Napoleon's empire had come to an end.

entered Paris in triumph, soon after Louis XVIII had fled the city. But Napoleon's new reign lasted only 100 days. The allies once again banded together against him. Choosing to initiate the fighting, Napoleon picked as his battleground the lowlands of Belgium. There, he won a significant victory against the Prussian army under General Blucher at Ligny on June 16. Napoleon's Marshal Grouchy was assigned to pursue Blucher while Napoleon turned to engage the British and Dutch forces commanded by the Duke of Wellington. The decisive *Battle of Waterloo* was fought on June 18. The two sides fought savagely from early morning, and Napoleon had almost secured the victory when Blucher's forces unexpectedly arrived to support Wellington and turned the tide of the battle against the French.

In early evening Napoleon fled to Paris. After failing to escape on a ship, he threw himself on the mercy of the British, who imprisoned him on the island of Saint Helena. He died there six years later at the age of 52.

SUMMARY

France in 1815 was radically different from the France of 1789. The Revolution had destroyed the Old Regime and brought to France the principle of constitutional government. Since 1789, France has always had a legal document of one sort or another that defines and limits the powers of the executive, legislative, and judicial branches of the government. Ever since, France has had a popularly elected, representative legislature to shape the laws governing the society. French civil rights have been guaranteed, and equality has been the guiding principle of the society, if not always the practice. In addition, the wars of the period spread democratic ideals to the rest of Europe and inspired patriotism and nationalism both within France and within the states who fell victim to the conquering armies.

At the same time, the revolutionary era brought political instability to France. As we shall see in Chapter 11, during the 19th century France continued to experience revolution and to experiment with a variety of political systems. The reign of Napoleon ended French liberty, and negated all of the modest gains that women had achieved during the Republic, including property and marriage rights.

Despite these less happy consequences, the French revolutionary period from 1789 to 1815 is a watershed in the history of modern Europe and the world.

QUESTIONS

1 What is the significance of the French Revolution?
2 Compare the life of the privileged classes of the ancien régime to that of the unprivileged classes.
3 What were the causes of the revolution of 1789?
4 Evaluate Louis XVI and consider the extent to which he unintentionally contributed to the revolution. Compare him with Louis XIV.
5 Why did the first revolution and the first French constitution fail?
6 What was the Reign of Terror? In what ways did the policies of Robespierre distort the principles of the first revolution, i.e., liberty, equality, and fraternity?
7 Evaluate the policies and the impact of Napoleon Bonaparte. Was he a great leader?

BIBLIOGRAPHY

BRINTON, CRANE. *A Decade of Revolution: 1789–1799.* New York: Harper & Row, 1963. This classic study covers the period in detail, and provides useful conclusions about the long-term, positive effects of the Revolution.

DICKENS, CHARLES. *A Tale of Two Cities.* London: Dent, 1971. An exciting novel which describes the impact of the French Revolution upon fictional individuals. Dickens' characters—especially Madame Defarge—enliven and dramatize this turbulent period.

GERSHOY, LEO. *The French Revolution, 1789–1799.* New York: Holt, Rinehart, 1960. A general discussion of the causes, scope, and results of the first ten years of the Revolution.

GRAHAM, RUTH. "Loaves and Liberty: Women in the French Revolution," in *Becoming Visible: Women in European History,* ed. Bridenthal and Koonz. Boston: Houghton Mifflin, 1979. A discussion of the role of women in the Revolution, and the gains and losses they made.

LEFEBVRE, GEORGES. *The Coming of the French Revolution.* New York: Untage, 1947. LeFebvre's analysis of the Revolution in terms of class interests is widely used by historians, but oversimplifies the causes of some critical events.

LOOMIS, STANLEY. *Paris in the Terror.* New York: Lippincott, 1964. An account of the dramatic events of the Reign of Terror. Loomis' account of Charlotte Corday and her assassination of Marat provides a sense of participation in the event and an insight into the complexity of the Revolution.

10

I turn the jigger, and run molds. I come at 6. Sometimes I come at 4. I worked all last night, till 6 o'clock this morning. I have not been in bed since the night before last. There were eight or nine other boys working last night. All but one have come this morning. I get three shillings and sixpence. I do not get any more for working at night.

The Industrial Revolution

The small boy's account of his work in a 19th-century pottery mill cited above was given to a British government commission. It was not unique. The litany of horror stories was repeated throughout the country. For the Industrial Revolution was a force that brought both bad and good consequences.

The phrase *révolution industrielle* was used first in France in the 1820s, when the mechanization of the French cotton industry was compared to the French political revolution of 1789. However, Arnold Toynbee (1852–1883), an English economist and reformer, is credited with inventing the term in the sense that it describes a dynamic change in the course of Western civilization.

Since Toynbee, there has been a running debate over the nature and significance of the Industrial Revolution. Most historians associate its origins with England, after which it spread to the Continent and, eventually, around the world. The American economic historian Charles Beard (1874–1948) interpreted the Industrial Revolution as erupting on an almost medieval England "like a thunderbolt from a clear sky."[1] In stark contrast to Beard's cataclysmic interpretation is the view of later economic historians, who characterize this "revolution" as an evolutionary process that "has been going on for two centuries and had been in preparation for two centuries before that."[2] Despite efforts to expand and even contract the time span of the first Industrial Revolution, the traditional dates of approximately 1760–1830 have been generally accepted as the years when an "evolution" or "revolution" occurred in the way certain items were produced in England.

Although the Industrial Revolution is still taking place in some nations, and has yet to reach a few of the more distant corners of the globe, it can truly be said that it has touched and continues to touch the everyday lives of people all over the world. Yet it had its beginnings and its greatest initial impact in one country, Great Britain.

---

[1] M. W. Flinn, *Origins of the Industrial Revolution: Problems and Perspectives in History*, ed. Hugh F. Kearney (London: Longmans, Green & Co., 1967), p. 3.
[2] Rondo Cameron, "The Industrial Revolution," p. 378.

INDUSTRIALIZATION IN BRITAIN

Traditional interpretations credit the beginning of the Industrial Revolution in Britain to the existence of a government that encouraged economic freedoms, a population expansion, the enclosure movement, and a variety of inventions, all of which brought about the evolution of a factory system.

POPULATION GROWTH

The problem with many of these explanations is that it is difficult to distinguish between cause and effect. For example, the population increase in England between 1700 and 1800 was 61 percent, and in less than one-third of that time, between 1800 and 1831, the population increased again by 64 percent. However, it is not possible to conclude from these figures that population growth and the Industrial Revolution are inextricably linked. Although it is true that many historians view population growth as a major factor in precipitating the Industrial Revolution in England after 1780, it is not the only factor, and it is conceivable that the Industrial Revolution could have occurred without it. In the 18th and 19th centuries in Ireland, for example, there was rapid economic growth and no corresponding population increase, and in Russia, the converse was true: that is, a high birth rate did not precipitate an industrial revolution, at least not until the end of the 19th century.

The birth rate in England between 1760 and 1830 did not increase significantly, which leads to the conclusion that the primary reason for the population explosion was a marked decline in the rate of mortality. Many factors influenced this decline. The availability of greater quantities of vegetables and of more fresh meat during the winter months, due to the introduction of root crops as fodder for the livestock, had resulted in a more balanced and healthier diet for many Britons during this period. Personal cleanliness due to the availability of

---

POPULATION FIGURES

England and Wales:
Pop. 1700—5.75 million
  1750—6.1 million
  1800—9.25 million
  1850—18 million

France:
Pop. 1700—22 million
  1750—24 million
  1800—29 million
  1850—36 million

From: Penguin's ATLAS OF WORLD POPULATION HISTORY

---

inexpensive soap and the use of less costly cotton underwear helped to eliminate disease and many of the hygienic problems related to unsanitary living conditions. The use of brick and slate in housing instead of wood and thatch was a major deterrent to disease-carrying pests. Paved roads, adequate drainage and sewage disposal, laws against burials within town limits, and the elimination of open wells which often were contaminated resulted in a healthier urban population. Medical advances, especially in the field of surgery and rudimentary preventive medicine, also contributed substantially to a decline in the mortality rate.

The rapid rise in the population of England came at the very time when there was a greater demand for human resources to meet the needs of an increasingly industrialized and mechanized economy. The relationship between the population and industrialization was symbiotic in the sense that industrialization was, in large part, made possible by the population growth which occurred in England. At the same time, the jobs created by the Industrial Revolution ensured the livelihood of greater numbers, thus allowing population growth to continue.

In addition to such factors as hygiene, diet, and medical care, demographers—people who study populations—must consider many other aspects of a society. For example, the average age at which women marry also influences population size. The older the woman, the more say she will have in planning the size of her family, and the shorter the span of time for child-bearing. Other factors to be considered in the study of 18th-century Europe are the agrarian economy and the guild system. During much of the medieval period, the population of rural areas was limited by how many people the land could support—leading to use of birth control measures, or the sending of infants to foundling homes where many died within a year. In the medieval guild system, apprentices were not permitted to marry, and most other young men were also expected to demonstrate an ability to support a family before they married.

AGRICULTURAL REVOLUTION AND ENCLOSURES

The Glorious Revolution of 1688 firmly established the sovereignty of Parliament over the monarchy. And in Parliament, the landholding "squirearchy" and the London merchants dominated the government. Through purchase and a series of Parliamentary Enclosure Acts, more and more public and private acreage fell into the hands of a dwindling number of large landholders. The *Enclosure Movement* between 1760 and 1843 fenced off and consolidated seven million acres of previously open fields and communal land. The result was an increase in agricultural productivity, experimental innovation, and specialization. Unlike the "yeoman" farmer, whose landholding and available capital was sharply limited, the great landlords could afford to invest in new equipment and experiment with new agricultural techniques.

New artificial methods of livestock breeding, more effective use of fertilizers, and more advanced crop-rotation techniques greatly increased agricultural productivity. Charles ("Turnip") Townshend, through the use of crops such as clover and turnips, enhanced the nutrients in the soil, increased harvest yields, and provided fodder for livestock during the winter months. With the production and refinement of iron plows after 1800, Jethro Tull's invention of the seed drill, and the availability of the McCormick reaper after 1834, agriculture became more like an industry. It had a rational system of organization; it adopted scientific methods to study productivity; and it utilized the machinery produced by the inventors of the age.

These developments were advantageous to the large landowners, but the same Enclosure Movement which benefited the landed gentry helped to create a landless and mobile working class. The *Agricultural Revolution*, for so these changes were called, meant that fewer people were needed to produce food for those earning a living in nonagricultural occupations. Thus was created a ready source of labor for the new industries developing in the towns, and the advent of the Industrial Revolution would find an England rich in both human and natural resources.

The mobility of people from the country to the town in 18th-century England was made easier by both natural geography and man-made factors, such as a growing and diverse transportation system. The British Isles are relatively small and compact, with few natural barriers, several navigable rivers, a number of deep-water harbors, and an excellent system of coastal waterways. Be-

A successful industrial revolution is usually preceded by a revolution in agriculture. The steam-powered threshing machine shown here is characteristic of the marriage between the two revolutions.

ginning in the 18th century, these natural advantages in communication were supplemented by a well-placed network of canals and turnpikes.

THE IMPORTANCE OF CAPITALISM

A flexible and sophisticated monetary system supplemented by an adequate and relatively cheap supply of capital was another prerequisite for the Industrial Revolution. This money supply can be state-controlled, as was the case in pre-industrialized Russia in the late 19th century, or it can be essentially in private hands, as was the case in 18th-century England. The English subscribed almost without exception to the idea of economic individualism and private ownership of all economic assets, including the supply of money. But it was the effect of complex historical forces over a long period of time that made possible the degree of development needed to support the Industrial Revolution.

By the end of the Middle Ages, the rise of cities, the evolution of an economic order based on money as well as land, and the development of a commercial credit system had created a favorable climate for industrial growth. Renaissance individualism, the advances in science during the Age of Reason, and the expansion of markets during the era of discovery and exploration, also provided a foundation for industrialization. In addition, the Protestant Reformation encouraged rebellion against certain medieval values such as the "theory of usury," which, by its strictures against using money to make money, prohibited the use of capital for investment. Beginning in the late Middle Ages, the commercial revolution enlarged the scope of economic activity from the regional or local level to a world-wide scale, and provided another source of capital and a motivation for profit-making.

The growth of English colonies in North America in the 17th century contributed to the accumulation of large amounts of capital, much of it coming from profits made in the slave trade. For this reason London merchants were able to provide capital for the Industrial Revolution during its early years. Not only did they have the money to invest, but they were accustomed to trusting foreign agents and investing in new and risky ventures.

The Bank of England, founded in 1694, played a major role in the success of the Industrial Revolution during its initial phase. The existence of a national bank helped to stabilize and standardize financial matters throughout Britain. The availability of uniform bank notes, the arranging of short-term loans, and the ability to transfer capital quickly were some of the advantages of having a national bank. In the 19th century, "penny" savings banks made available capital accumulated from the more skilled and hence, better-paid, among the working classes. The most effective means of assembling capital from the middle classes was the

An English banker of the 17th century. The growth of a stable, regularized banking system enabled English capitalists to finance their first industrial ventures.

insurance business. Lloyd's of London, for example, began to sell marine insurance in the 1690s.

Stock exchanges were another important new feature of the European economic scene. The London Stock Exchange opened its doors for the first time in 1773, but it was Amsterdam which was the center for commercial and banking activities in Europe until the American Revolution. Prior to the Revolution, the Dutch had invested heavily in British industry, but when the government of the Netherlands provided assistance to the American colonists during the Revolutionary War, the British government confiscated all Dutch investments. Amsterdam never recovered from that financial setback, and London became the banking and financial center for international trade until World War I.

During the early years of the Industrial Revolution in England, the initial amount of capital needed to start a business enterprise was relatively small. Much of the money for a new business came from relatives, friends, and from the hard-working and thrifty early entrepreneurs themselves, who usually invested almost every penny of profit back into their ventures. Coincident with the earliest stages of the Industrial Revolution, there was a fortuitous lowering of interest rates in England. This situation encouraged business activity—and once the Industrial Revolution got started, it took on a momentum of its own. Profits began to skyrocket upward, and there was no shortage of people or institutions willing to invest in new projects.

By the mid-18th century, England exhibited a number of the preconditions necessary for a successful industrial revolution: a large and readily available source of labor, an improved and satisfactorily functioning agricultural system, and a largely centralized and well capitalized financial system. While most European countries did not have all these factors in place, as England did, several were quite advanced economically and so-

In France, the government licensed and protected certain labor-intensive industries such as tapestry-making. By this means, mercantilists hoped to create worldwide demand for high-quality, distinctively French products.

cially. France, in particular, had an economy which had expanded as fast as, if not faster than England's during this period. The obvious question then is: why did the Industrial Revolution develop first in England rather than in France or some other country?

WHY ENGLAND, NOT FRANCE?

France was the most likely challenger to England's claim as the birthplace of the Industrial Revolution. In 1700, the population of France was 20 million to England's 5.8 million. By 1780, the French population was 26 million for an increase of 35 percent, while England's was 7.5 million for a growth rate of 29 percent. England's smaller size was an advantage, however. Urban markets in England were never very distant from their sources of supply, while in France, trans-

portation lines were both costlier and longer. The French economy suffered from restrictive, mercantilistic policies well into the 18th century, while in England, mercantilism was discussed and debated more than it was practiced.

Other impediments to economic change in France were the regulations and institutions which governed commercial and industrial activity. An archaic legal system in France allowed medieval guilds to continue to regulate some segments of the economy, such as mining. Subsurface mining rights were less restrictive across the Channel. The early mines in England were controlled by individuals, the same men who owned the farm land above them. This obviously encouraged much greater individual initiative than the outdated French system.

An economic crisis in France in 1723, precipitated by the questionable financial practices of a Scot named John Law, resulted in the demise of the French equivalent of a central bank. For the rest of the century the French people's distrust of all banking institutions put France at a disadvantage when trying to compete for available capital.

Moreover, by 1780 England was far ahead of France in technological innovation. As early as 1624, Parliament had passed a Statute of Monopolies which ended most monopolistic practices, and at the same time established a patent system. Inventors prospered and inventions proliferated. Much was done on all levels to foster the development of innovative ideas. Private agencies, as well as Parliament, encouraged inventors by offering monetary prizes for the most useful and successful inventions.

Religion was another factor which played a role in the inventive genius of the English people. Over the years, Puritans and other religious dissenters had grown used to breaking with custom. They often found traditional professions and occupations closed to them, especially those in government. These non-conformists sought new outlets for their abilities by opening their own trade schools and universities with a curriculum more relevant to contemporary commercial and industrial needs than that of the Church-affiliated schools. Consequently, a disproportionate number of the early technological breakthroughs in the Industrial Revolution were achieved by Scottish Presbyterians associated with the universities of Edinburgh and Glasgow.

The French government, in contrast, adopted a different policy after the Edict of Nantes, which had permitted religious toleration, was revoked in 1685. Restrictions against French Protestants (Huguenots) were so harsh that many fled to England, Holland, and Prussia, taking their talents, skills, and as much of their wealth as they could carry with them. Since the Huguenots were an important force in French business and commercial life, their departure had serious repercussions on the future economic development of France.

It has been suggested that the proclivity of the English for technological innovation and industrial growth can be explained by the possibilities of social advancement that such activities opened up. The French aristocracy was more protective of their seignorial privileges and less willing to associate with the increasingly powerful and wealthy middle class than was the English nobility. In England, it was not uncommon for the son or daughter of the English gentry to marry a son or daughter of a London merchant. Indeed, the aristocracy were much involved in the changes which occurred in England during the late 18th and early 19th centuries. English aristocrats took the lead in experimentation and innovation during the Agricultural Revolution. Members of the English gentry, and even some of the titled nobility, could be found in virtually every phase of the Industrial Revolution, as investors in a variety of entrepreneurial enterprises, and as owners of mines or, occasionally, even cotton mills.

There was no parallel to this commingling of class on the continent of Europe. As one economic historian puts it: "The British nobility and gentry chose to meet the newcomers on middle ground: they reaffirmed their distinction of blood and breeding; but they buttressed it with an active and productive cultivation of gain."[3] Contemporary observers found English businessmen of whatever class more practical and acquisitive than their opposite numbers on the Continent.

There appear to have been some sound reasons for this difference in attitudes. For example, the French had an overabundance of labor, so they saw little need to challenge the authority of the guilds or to revamp the so-called "putting-out system," which was labor-intensive and not particularly efficient. In this type of rural cottage industry, a cloth merchant would buy the raw materials and distribute them to individuals, usually women, who would then produce the finished product at home. The merchant-owner had complete control over the process from start to finish, without any long-standing ob-

---

[3] David S. Landes, *The Unbound Prometheus: Technological Change and Industrial Development in Western Europe from 1750 to the Present* (London: Cambridge University Press, 1969), p. 70.

Early capitalists utilized the cottage industry, or "putting-out system," to acquire a supply of yarn and finished cloth. Shown is a typical hand loom of the preindustrial age.

A British coal mine. Coal provided the high temperatures needed to smelt iron and to fuel the steam engines of the Industrial Revolution.

ligations to those he employed. This system worked quite well as long as the largest machine used was a hand-loom and there was no shortage of labor.

Furthermore, France had an almost unlimited supply of wood to be used as fuel for the smelting of iron and other metals. The English were not so fortunate in their available fuel sources above ground. If British industry were to develop further, then the English needed an alternative fuel to wood, and this need could well have been a major cause of England's head start in the development of technology. Increasingly, they had to resort to the use of coal as an alternative to wood. When open-pit mining gave way to tunneling, ways had to be found of clearing the mines of water and gases. Thus the shortcomings of the British situation were, perhaps, as important as its advantages in determining that Britain would be the first country in western Europe to become industrialized.

JAMES WATT AND THE STEAM ENGINE

Power-driven machinery, independent of human or animal power, and separate from the natural forces of wind and water, is an essential factor in any successful industrial revolution. R. J. Forbes tells us, "The four basic technical achievements of the Industrial Revolution were: (1) Replacement of hand tools by machines, (2) The introduction of new prime movers, (3) The mobile prime mover, (4) The factory as a new form of organization and production."[4] Whether or not one agrees with Forbes' assessment, it is obvious that the steam engine was a crucial factor in each of the four categories.

The knowledge that provided the scientific base for the invention of the steam engine did not come from James Watt alone.

[4] Charles Singer, et al., eds., *A History of Technology*; Vol. 4, *The Industrial Revolution: c. 1750–1850* (New York and London: Oxford University Press, 1958), p. 150.

Discoveries in the first half of the 17th century, when the scientific revolution was in its early speculative and theoretical stages, paved the way. The first important finding was that atmosphere has weight. This led to the invention of the barometer and an awareness that air under the proper conditions could be used to move an object. Not too much later, these theories all came together and found their practical application because of the aforementioned need for a substitute fuel for wood.

By the early 18th century as the wood shortage grew more acute, the demand for coal increased. When the mine shafts were driven deeper into the bowels of the earth to get this coal, the problem of flooding became increasingly serious. Thomas Savery (1650–1715), a military engineer, was the first to attempt a solution to the problem of water in the mines by inventing the first practical steam pump. Independently, Thomas Newcomen (1663–1729), a tool salesman for copper mines, developed a one percent efficient engine that worked more on the principle of atmospheric pressure than steam. It remained for James Watt (1736–1819), the son of a Scottish shipwright and carpenter, to improve the efficiency and design of the earlier steam engines.

At the age of 19 James Watt traveled to London to learn the trade of making mathematical instruments. Upon his return to Scotland, he was employed as a maker of precision instruments for the University of Glasgow. In 1763 he started tinkering with a non-functioning Newcomen engine, and in the process of getting it to work, he improved its design. Joseph Black, a chemistry professor at the University of Glasgow, took an interest in Watt's activities to the extent of collaborating with him and lending him money. In addition, Watt took up surveying in order to get more money for his experiments. Not long after this, Watt met John Roebuck, an industrialist interested in new methods of draining coal mines, and at Roebuck's urg-

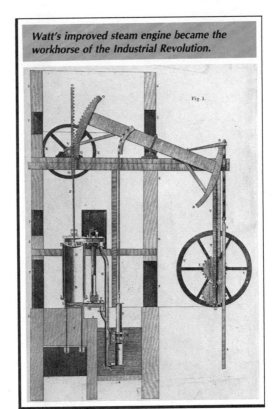

Watt's improved steam engine became the workhorse of the Industrial Revolution.

ing, in 1769 Watt applied for and received a patent with the title, "A New Method of Lessening the Consumption of Steam and Fuel in Fire Engines."

While on one of his visits to London, Watt met Matthew Boulton, a well-known industrialist who needed a more efficient way of operating his water-powered machinery. After John Roebuck went bankrupt, Matthew Boulton became Watt's benefactor and business partner for the next 25 years. Watt and Boulton joined the "Lunar Society," an association devoted to the advancement of science that included among its members Erasmus Darwin (the grandfather of Charles Darwin) and Joseph Priestley, the chemist who discovered oxygen.

In 1775, Watt had his patent renewed for an additional 25 years, until 1800. Watt still had not resolved the problem of getting the metal parts of his steam engine sufficiently

James Watt (top) and Matthew Boulton, the inventor and the entrepreneur, formed a partnership that lasted 25 years.

steam engine the next year, 1776. The relationship between the two partners was ideal since Watt hated the business side of the enterprise, and Boulton liked nothing better. Watt retired in 1800, handing over his lucrative business to his sons.

The career of James Watt reflects many of the essential elements and characteristics of the Industrial Revolution in Great Britain. It is unlikely that James Watt would have received the training and support at the more Establishment-oriented Oxford and Cambridge that he received at the University of Glasgow with its greater curricular emphasis on the physical sciences and the practical applications of math. As a result, James Watt and his business partners were among the first to apply the systematic experimentation of the pure sciences to industrial technology. There was little in the separate component parts of Watt's steam engine that was original. James Watt's genius was in his ability to synthesize the ideas of others.

For the first time there existed a flexible and reliable power source, independent of the vagaries of nature, man, or animal. Consequently the factory system gained a degree of geographical freedom. Factories could now be built closer to the sources of labor and raw materials rather than near the natural sources of power such as rivers. With the advent of the steam engine, the quality and quantity of most manufactured products went up, and prices went down. Some segments of the labor force, such as the hand-loom weavers, were hurt by steam power, but workers in most industries, such as metalworking, transportation, and textiles, benefited from these innovations.

TEXTILES AND RELATED INDUSTRIES

At the beginning of the 19th century, Britain's colonial empire was just one of several markets open to British business interests around the world. The traditional trade in woolens was limited only by the amount woven. In addition, British merchants were

precise to withstand the friction and pounding caused by the pistons in his rotating engine. This final technical obstacle was resolved when Boulton and Watt acquired the services of John Wilkinson, who had patented a more accurate boring machine for cannon which could be used to create the precision parts that Watt needed for his new engine. With the problem of precision boring solved, Watt and Boulton sold their first

The steam engine company founded by Watt and Boulton was located in Soho, near Birmingham.

excited by the future possibilities for the cotton trade if only more raw cotton could be produced and spun into finished products. Part of this problem was resolved in 1793 by an American, Eli Whitney. Whitney's invention, the cotton gin, was able to facilitate the process of separating the seeds from the fibres. The production of raw cotton rose astronomically and so too, unfortunately, did the need for slave labor to work the fields in those areas where slavery continued to survive as an institution. Now all that stood between the English merchant-entrepreneur and immense profits was a more efficient way of spinning thread and weaving cloth.

By 1793, many new inventions were already in place and ready to handle the increased flow of raw cotton. John Kay's flying shuttle (1733) doubled the amount of yarn which could be spun at one time. James Har-

greave's spinning jenny (1764) multiplied by 12 the amount of thread that could be spun simultaneously. Richard Arkwright's water frame (1769), originally intended to be operated by horse power rather than water power, wove a finer yet stronger thread than previous machines. Because of its cost and size, and the need for water power to operate it, Arkwright's invention had to be housed under one roof, which meant that Arkwright was one of the founders of the modern factory system. Arkwright also was among the first in the textile industry to use Watt's steam engine to power his machinery. The use of steam power in the textile industry spread rapidly, resulting in the concentration of cotton mills in towns and cities rather than in the countryside near the sources of water power.

Each industry had its own requirements

Eli Whitney devised a means to separate seeds from cotton fibers. His machine revolutionized the textile industry, but also breathed new life into the institution of slavery.

Hargreave's spinning jenny did the work of 12 hand looms.

mill owner had a place on his payroll for every member of the family. Often, iron foundries and other forms of heavy industry were encouraged to locate adjacent to textile mills in an effort to lure children and female employees by finding work for fathers and husbands. Some industries such as the chemical industry required the concentration of workers in a single location because of the need for close supervision. A few industries were almost completely dependent on other forms of manufacturing for their survival. The chemical industry, for example, had as its biggest customer the owners of textile mills. Most heavy industries, like those involving metals, had a symbiotic relationship with mining.

Because of a rising demand for iron plowshares and other metal agricultural implements—not guns, as is often assumed—heavy industry came into its own in the 18th century. Iron production was helped by the building of an intricate network of canals throughout England between 1750 and 1800.

TRANSPORTATION

By 1830, most of the principal streams in England were linked by a network of 2500 miles of canals. Transportation costs for bulky items such as coal or metal ores were

and needs, but in some cases the needs of one industry complemented those of another. For example, the textile industry did not require previously-trained labor or brute strength, a fact which led to a work force consisting largely of women and children. The

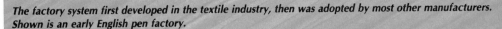
The factory system first developed in the textile industry, then was adopted by most other manufacturers. Shown is an early English pen factory.

cut by 75 percent. Canal construction also gave the civil engineering profession the impetus to design and build the bridges and railroads needed in the 19th century.

Canals were not the only form of transportation to be utilized by the Industrial Revolution. Entirely new means of getting goods from one place to another were developed as a result of some of the discoveries which were part of the industrialization process. The railroad was one such method, even though its antecedents pre-dated the Industrial Revolution. As early as the 1630s, a form of railroad without artificial power, known as a *tramline*, was being used in coal mines. Then in the 18th century, the advent of the steam engine for the first time raised the possibility of an artificially-powered mobile machine. Richard Trevithick (1771–1833) developed a less cumbersome high pressure steam engine that could build up safely to 50 pounds of pressure to the square inch. About the same time, Henry Cort's *puddling process* (a method used to burn off the impurities in molten iron ore by exposing the heated ore to oxygen while stirring it) led to the production of iron rails that were sturdy enough to withstand the considerable weight of multiple-wheeled steam engines. In 1825, the 12-mile-long Stockton and Darlington railroad, built by George and Robert Stephenson, opened for business. A few years later the Manchester and Liverpool Railway (1830) was ready for operation. By the 1850s, 8000 miles of track had been laid, so that all moderate-sized English towns were within relatively easy reach of a rail line.

The advent of railroads brought many significant changes in the British way of life. A national standardization of time was now required as a necessary safety measure to prevent train wrecks. Because of the railroads it was possible to have a newspaper that could be delivered all over the country in the same day, and commonality of information could

Bystanders observe the opening of the world's first commercial railroad—the Stockton-Darlington line—in 1825.

therefore be achieved. Railroads made the entire nation more mobile, which in turn contributed to uniformity in social customs, speech patterns, and generally, a greater sense of a national identity.

Not all new developments resulted in greater fellow-feeling and a breaking down of differences, however. Both railroad and passenger ship lines reinforced social and

A caricature of a British "railroad king." The men who built and operated railroads were some of the most conspicuously wealthy magnates of the age.

economic class distinctions by pricing accommodations according to one's social and economic standing. The Thomas Cook Travel Agency, for example, began as a business catering to poorer customers out for Sunday excursions. Inequities occurred when government regulations forced some property owners to sell land that was needed for the railroad right-of-way. It was not until 1878, with the establishment of a railroad commission, that regulations were rigidly and consistently enforced nationwide.

Another variation in transport resulting from the advances of the early phase of industrialization was the ocean-going steamship. In 1838, the first vessel of this type was constructed, and in 1845 the first steamship with an iron hull was built. Ocean voyages now became more reliable, and passengers and cargo could be transported more cheaply. Steam power, however, required a dependable source of fuel located at regular intervals along shipping lanes, and it became necessary for nations with worldwide maritime ambitions to acquire coaling stations around the globe.

All these changes led to still further developments, some of great magnitude and continuing importance. New and cheaper methods of transportation facilitated the expansion of both national and international markets. Meeting the increased demands of shipping and railroad construction in turn led to the expansion of iron and steel production and other related industries. Once the Industrial Revolution was firmly established, it developed a momentum of its own which was especially evident in terms of the competitive forces which it unleashed among nations vying for prestige and power.

EFFECTS OF INDUSTRIALIZATION

Britain experienced industrialization before any other nation in the 19th century. The British Isles became known as the "workshop of the world." Almost immediately other nations and other peoples sought to follow Britain's lead by emulating British technological advances.

Machine-produced goods from England's factories enabled English entrepreneurs and merchants to undersell the rest of the world. Robert Owen, the famous British capitalist and social reformer, noted in his autobiography that cotton cloth could be bought in the 1850s for 1/63 of what that same cloth would have cost in the 1790s. The British, and later, European, technological superiority that produced such inexpensive, high-quality products helps to explain European domination of world trade. It also was a factor in motivating the imperial expansion of some European nations in the second half of the 19th century.

SOCIAL COSTS OF INDUSTRIALIZATION

The social cost of industrialization, however, was often very high. New cities sprang from small country towns, while thousands of people flocked to already overcrowded cities looking for employment. Large-scale urbanization was the most dramatic effect of industrialization. The gap between rich and poor became increasingly noticeable as the cities multiplied and the countryside became depopulated. Working conditions in most factories were at best endurable, and at worst, barbaric. In Scottish mines, children would put in eight- to ten-hour days, and their elders worked even longer. Women carried wicker baskets filled with coal, weighing as much as 170 pounds, up multiple lad-

Young children strain to push a coal cart in a mine shaft. Abuses such as this led to laws that restricted the use of child labor.

ders with the only illumination coming from candles they held clenched in their teeth. Sometimes, in order to win one of these jobs, workers had to sign agreements to work in a mine for up to 25 years. The testimony of laborers as recorded in "blue books" on the occasion of the various government commissions investigating conditions in the workplace attests to the extreme exploitation by employers of many men, women, and children in mines and factories.

The story of factory apprentices is especially depressing, with children as young as seven working 16 hours a day, six days a week. Poor food, unventilated rooms made noxious by candle smoke, and an almost savage disciplinary policy were the order of the day. Documented accounts exist of brutish supervisors punishing children for the most minor of infractions with beatings, the filing down of teeth, or pinching until the fingernails met in the flesh. Although this degree of inhumane treatment was the exception, so too was the enlightened treatment of reformers like Robert Owen who gave his apprentices clean living quarters, decent food, shortened working hours, and even a modicum of education. Most employers fell somewhere between these two extremes, and working conditions for apprentices and, eventually, all employees, did improve.

In most cases, government action, rather than private initiative on the part of individual employers, was responsible for the improvement in the conditions of the working classes. In 1802, the Peel Act provided minimum standards of health and hygiene as well as limiting the number of hours a child could work each week. Over the course of the 19th century, as the right to vote was extended, the political power of those newly-enfranchised classes increased and brought about more legislative action on behalf of the workers. By the early 1870s, workers were using organized political agitation to press for better working conditions and higher wages (Chapter 13).

Even as the industrial workers fought for improvements in their situation, some observers of the English scene prior to industrialization—writers like George Eliot—pointed out that life in rural England had not been as idyllic as some poets and philosophers would lead us to believe. In her novel *Felix Holt*, Eliot suggests that beneath the charm of the country village was a society which might be characterized as self-satisfied, gullible, and sometimes vicious in its intolerance of differences. In Eliot's opinion, the industrial town or city, dirty and disagreeable as it might be, was at least a dynamic and responsive environment where attention was focused on the social problems of the day and attempts were made to solve these problems.

Furthermore, factory work with all its problems had a degree of permanence that seasonal farm labor would never have. Financially, most families were better off laboring in a milltown than they were trying to eke out a living on a few acres of overworked farm land. Prospects for the future were better, too, in the city than in the country. Generally, salaries did go up during the course of the Industrial Revolution, while prices went down. Those who suffered most by industrialization were the skilled artisans who had lost their livelihood and jobs to the unskilled workers. During the early years of the Industrial Revolution, the greatest demand was for unskilled labor because of the nature of the work and the fact that the less skilled could also be paid at a lower rate than those with more specialized training.

In considering the social effects of the Industrial Revolution, it could be argued that the economic well-being of most people improved. Employment was steadier, and, as noted, prices were generally going down while wages were going up. However, the impact of being uprooted from familiar and comfortable surroundings to move among strangers in an alien environment under crowded conditions cannot be measured solely in quantitative terms. Consideration should be given to the psychological effects on a person who has worked outside most of his life to suddenly being confined within the four walls of a factory, under the regimentation imposed by a time clock. Obviously, there are a variety of factors which need to be considered in order to assess the impact, in human terms, of English industrialization.

To further complicate the analysis is the question of whether the Industrial Revolution affected women, both quantitatively and qualitatively, in different ways from the way it affected men. Women were an important part of the work force before, during, and after the Industrial Revolution. Throughout, they were paid just half as much as men, and working conditions could be just as exploitative in the home as in the factory. In the long run, it would seem that women received many of the same benefits from the Industrial Revolution as men, including an improved standard of living and eventual political, if not economic, equality.

One benefit which women derived from the Industrial Revolution was awareness that as female factory workers they shared similar problems and concerns. This commonality of feeling bred by close association at the same sort of work contributed to the organization of a working-class feminist movement (Chapter 13). Ultimately, this movement brought women the same sort of political gains and leverage which laboring men had achieved through the reform bills of the 19th century.

A NEW BURST OF INDUSTRIALIZATION

In the second half of the 19th century, there was a new burst of industrialization. The leader in this phase of the Industrial Revolution was Germany. The unification of Germany in 1871 and the economic policies followed by Bismarck (Chapter 15) gave impetus to the growth of German industry. Chemistry became one of Germany's major industries, after German chemists discovered ways to make cheap dyes for the textile industry. Germany soon led all other nations in industrial production. France, Belgium, the United States, and Japan also underwent major growth in their industrial capacity after 1850.

A new source of power, which was to revolutionize transportation, was the result of work by two German inventors. In 1886, Gottlieb Daimler (1834–1900) perfected an *internal combustion engine* that used gasoline for fuel; he applied the engine to building one of the first automobiles. Not long after, another German engineer, Rudolf Diesel (1858–1913) produced an improved internal combustion engine. Using petroleum oil as fuel, the *diesel engine* could power larger vehicles such as trucks, ships, and locomotives. Though steam engines continued in service for a long time, the two types of internal-combustion engine eventually became the major sources of power for all major modes of transportation, and gave rise to the development of related industries, including petroleum-refining, steel, and rubber.

Steam as a source of power for factories was eventually replaced by electricity, due to the work of a number of inventors. The Englishman Michael Faraday (1791–1867) first constructed an electric generator in 1831. However, its efficiency was low, and

Alexander Graham Bell made a long distance call from New York to Chicago in 1892. Inventions such as the telephone, electrical generators, and the telegraph dramatically affected everyday life.

hence it had little commercial importance. Further discoveries, notably those of the American Thomas A. Edison (1847–1931), produced generators efficient enough to power large industrial machines. Edison's electric light bulb began to replace gas lighting in all major cities after he installed the first central power stations in London and New York in 1882. It was not long before most factories could draw upon municipal power sources as well.

The field of communications also saw significant discoveries. The American Samuel F. B. Morse (1791–1872) combined the work of earlier scientists to produce an efficient telegraph in 1837. Telegraph lines soon linked the major cities of the United States and Europe, and in 1866, the first successful underwater cable was laid across the Atlantic Ocean. Ten years later, the Scottish-born Alexander Graham Bell (1847–1922) invented the telephone, permitting direct voice communications over long distances. By the end of the 19th century, the Italian Guglielmo Marconi (1874–1937) had developed a way to send electric signals without wires, thus opening the way for the worldwide instant communications network we take for granted today.

SUMMARY

Undeniably, the Industrial Revolution is one of the most significant occurrences in all human history. Whether it is considered in terms of the vast changes it wrought or in terms of its continuing influence over 200 years after it first began, its effect on all areas—political, social, economic and cultural—has been profound. From agriculture to transportation, from mining to manufacturing; in every occupation and in every environmental setting throughout the world, there is no area which has remained untouched by the events of the end of the 18th century and the first half of the 19th century in Britain. To this day, historians continue to debate why industrialization happened when it did and where it did. There is no doubt that because of the Industrial Revolution our world has been inalterably transformed for all time.

QUESTIONS

1 Using population studies as one example, discuss some of the problems that historians face in analysing the nature and causes of the Industrial Revolution.

2 How did the Enclosure Movement contribute to conditions favoring an Industrial Revolution?

3 Define capitalism, and identify the sources of capital available to entrepreneurs during the early years of industrialization in England.

4 In the mid-18th century, France was richer, more powerful, and larger in area and population than England. How, therefore, can you account for the fact that the Industrial Revolution began in England?

5 "Overall, the Industrial Revolution improved the material well-being of most people. The same cannot be said about the quality of life." Evaluate the validity of this statement in regard to women, children, entrepreneurs, and skilled artisans.

6 How did the creation and expansion of railroads influence British society? Have there been any comparable kinds of influences on American society?

BIBLIOGRAPHY

ASHTON, T. S. *The Industrial Revolution: 1760–1830.* New York: Oxford University Press, 1964. *One of the most interpretive and concise introductions to the English Industrial Revolution.*

BRIGGS, ASA. *A Social History of England.* New York: Viking Press, 1983. *In a beautifully illustrated book, supplemented with lively narrative, the author takes the reader on a "grand tour" of English society from prehistoric times to the present.*

DICKENS, CHARLES. *Hard Times.* New York: Signet Classics. *One of the most powerful portraits of the effect of industrialization on the working poor. Coketown, a fictional locale in England, is a place of unrelieved gloom, and few of its inhabitants—be they mill owner or trade-unionist—are exemplary characters.*

FLINN, MICHAEL W. *Origins of the Industrial Revolution.* New York: Barnes & Noble, 1966. *An excellent summary of the various interpretations of the causes of the Industrial Revolution.*

LOUISE A. TILLY and JOAN W. SCOTT. *Women, Work, and Family.* New York: Holt, Rinehart and Winston, 1978. *A detailed study of working women in France and England from 1700 to the present. The emphasis is on how changing techniques of production have influenced women and their role in society, both in and outside of the home. One of the major strengths of this work is the inclusion of primary sources.*

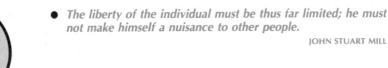

● *The liberty of the individual must be thus far limited; he must not make himself a nuisance to other people.*

JOHN STUART MILL

Society and Ideas in the 19th Century

The dominant ideas of each era are firmly rooted in the previous ones. In some cases, these ideas represent the further development or logical conclusions of earlier ideas, and they progress along a fairly straight line. Often, new ideas represent a synthesis of the past; a combination of two or more previous trends which form a new philosophic position. Occasionally, the new is a reaction to the old. Each of the dominant ideas of the 19th century—nationalism, liberalism, socialism, and romanticism—illustrates one or another of these patterns.

NATIONALISM   One of the most important characteristics of 19th-century Europe was the rise of *nationalism*. The various states of Europe were, and are, comprised of people of widely varying languages, cultures, religions, traditions, and history. Nevertheless, the concept of nationalism that arose in the 19th century incorporated intense feelings of loyalty for one's native soil, its history, and its destiny. It embodied a strong sense of identity with people who share one's land, religion, language, culture, and traditions.

Nationalism in the 19th century was influenced by the French Revolution. Among the French there was intense pride in their Revolution, enthusiasm for the principles of liberty, equality, and fraternity, and the determination to spread these ideas to the rest of Europe. These feelings and attitudes coalesced into a new French nationalism. As a result, the wars of the Revolution were waged with patriotic zeal.

The wars of the French Revolution engendered new waves of nationalism in the rest of Europe. The other European states rallied to their own flags in response to what they perceived as an attempt by France to force the entire continent into its mold. The yearning for national sovereignty grew, culminating in the political unification of Germany and of Italy in 1870.

The numerous national minorities within the Austrian, Ottoman, and Russian empires were also imbued with national fervor, and much of the political, military, and international history of these years was shaped by the hunger for national independence. Nor were the British Isles immune from nationalism. The "English race" was glorified and its achievements exported to much of the world under the guise of nationalism. Nationalism was indeed one of the driving forces of the 19th century.

LIBERALISM Liberalism was a political idea which represented a logical progression from earlier ideas. Viewed in relation to other political terms, a *liberal* wants to make changes in the status quo while a *radical* wants to make wholesale changes; a *revolutionary* wants to overthrow the system entirely and replace it with a totally different one; a *conservative* wants to preserve the system as it is; and a *reactionary* wants to return to an earlier system. Liberalism is a relative term, however, and only derives meaning when placed within the context of a given time and place. What is liberal in one period may be reactionary in another.

Political Liberalism. The primary tenet of classical 19th-century liberalism was freedom. The best example of a liberal political thinker was John Stuart Mill (1806–1873), who in his essay "On Liberty" advocated the full freedom of the individual to pursue his or her own self-development. Classical liberals like Mill sought ways to guarantee freedom of thought and expression, of political association, and of the press. They believed that governments should interfere as little as possible with the political lives of their citizens; the primary role of government was instead to protect individual liberty. The purpose of a constitution was to define individual liberties and to produce a set of rules which would deter governments from arbitrary exercise of power.

Liberals in this period did not generally advocate complete democracy or universal suffrage. There were a handful, however, including John Stuart Mill, who did support equal political rights for women.

The movement for rights for women had begun in the 18th century, at the time of the French Revolution. In 1792, Mary Woll-

The liberal ideology of John Stuart Mill influenced many educators and later reformers, both in England and in British colonial territories.

stonecraft (1759–1797) wrote *A Vindication of the Rights of Women*. In this book, Wollstonecraft argued that women should be considered as moral and intellectual equals to men and should receive equal education. However, she was primarily concerned with women's rights and needs in the context of their roles as wives and mothers, not as autonomous human beings.

• • • *Would men but generously snap our chains, and be content with rational fellowship instead of slavish obedience, they would find us more observant daughters, more affectionate sisters, more faithful wives, more reasonable mothers—in a word, better citizens.*[1]

Liberal principles had the greatest impact in those countries where there was already a political system in which reform could

---

[1] Mary Kinnear, *Daughters of Time: Women in the Western Tradition* (Ann Arbor: University of Michigan Press, 1982), p. 101.

Mary Wollstonecraft wrote an influential feminist tract in the late 18th century. Her daughter, Mary Shelley, created the character of Frankenstein.

published *The Wealth of Nations* in 1776. In this landmark work of economic thought, Smith rejected the economic principle of mercantilism, which advocated government intervention in economic affairs. Smith instead developed the theory of *laissez-faire*, which was based on the belief that economics was governed by natural laws. Hence, the government should avoid interference in economic affairs and allow these laws to function. Moreover, Smith believed that every individual is motivated to improve his or her own condition in life and therefore should be left free to do so.

Thomas Malthus (1766–1834), a clergyman in the Church of England, applied Smith's theories to the problem of popula-

occur, such as in the United States and England. Liberals in France advocated similar principles and repeatedly sought reform through constitutionalism, but they met with only limited success.

Liberalism also existed in the rest of Europe to some degree and was a factor in reform movements in the German and Italian states. More frequently, however, in 19th-century Europe, the principle of liberalism was associated with political freedom for national groups rather than for individuals, and most of the revolutionaries of 19th-century Europe were motivated more by nationalism than by liberalism.

CLASSICAL ECONOMIC LIBERALISM

Classical liberalism in economics had its origins in the economic theories of the Englishmen Adam Smith, Thomas Malthus, and David Ricardo. Each of these men applied the earlier scientific concept of natural law to the economic sphere.

Adam Smith (1723–1790), a graduate of Oxford University and professor of logic,

Adam Smith's influential book The Wealth of Nations *demonstrated such "natural laws" of the economy as that of supply and demand: i.e., when the supply of a product is lower than the demand for it, prices will rise.*

tion. He published his *Essay on the Principle of Population* in 1798. Malthus' thesis was that population growth tends to outstrip food supply; hence, misery, poverty, and starvation are inevitable for some. This depressing conclusion had a widespread influence, especially among England's upper classes, who blamed the poverty around them not on themselves or the problems of early industrialization, but on the poor—whom they faulted for bearing too many children. Like Smith, Malthus believed that he had discovered a natural law which could not be avoided.

David Ricardo (1772–1823) wrote the first definitive book on economics, *Principles of Political Economy and Taxation* (1817). Among the theories included in this book was "the iron law of wages," which stipulated that wages must be based on the supply of and demand for workers. When the market price exceeds the natural price, the worker is well off; when it does not, the worker's lot is miserable. Like Smith and Malthus, Ricardo advocated a governmental policy of *laissez-faire* regarding wages.

SOCIALISM Socialism evolved from an earlier concept of *collective* rather than *individual* well-being, and was also influenced by the economic patterns and working conditions that prevailed during the Industrial Revolution.

The Industrial Revolution had produced a radical change in the way many human beings earned their living—more and more people worked in factories rather than in fields, shops, or cottages. Moreover, the Industrial Revolution, beginning in England, occurred within the economic system of capitalism, where the new factories were owned by individual investors who employed industrial workers for wages. In privately owned factories, unfettered by government regulations or restrictions, the laboring classes were often exploited. Forced to work long hours at low wages, these industrial workers were forbidden to unionize, bargain collectively or to strike.

SOCIALIST THEORY

Inspired by compassion for the working classes, various theories of socialism arose as an alternate economic system to capitalism. All socialists agreed on four basic premises: 1) Capitalism as it existed was unfair to the industrial laborer, for the factory owner enjoyed profits that were earned at the expense of the worker. 2) In place of private ownership of the means of production (the factory), there should be some collective ownership. Collective ownership can take essentially only two forms: *communal ownership*—for example, all of the laborers in a factory might own and operate it together; or *state ownership*, in which the state owns the means of production in the interests of its citizens. 3) The wealth of the society should be distributed equally, based on some plan or formula. 4) A socialist economic system would transform human nature.

Although all socialists agreed on fundamental premises, they often differed in the ways they proposed for converting these premises into concrete plans for an economic system. Two of the principal groups of socialists were the *utopian* and the *scientific* socialists.

The Utopian Socialists. Utopian socialists dreamed of a perfect society. Often they proposed to reach this goal by creating model communities to which the members voluntarily belonged and shared their labor and its rewards. Most of the early utopian socialists were inspired by the egalitarian principles of the French Revolution.

One of the first of these was Henri de Saint-Simon (1760–1825). Saint-Simon had been a member of the French aristocracy who had fought in the American Revolution and returned to France dedicated to the revolutionary movement there. In his view socialism was the logical economic counterpart to Christianity.

The utopian Robert Owen built a model factory in New Lanark, Scotland.

Saint-Simon developed a formula to be applied to the distribution of wealth in the society: everyone should work, and rewards should go "to each according to his capacity [ability] . . . and according to his works."[2] That is, he proposed equality of economic opportunity based on ability. Saint-Simon did not provide a blueprint for applying his formula. In his book *The New Christianity* (1825), he appealed to Europe's rulers to eliminate poverty.

The utopian Robert Owen (1771–1858) was a Welsh factory owner who turned the Scottish town of New Lanark, where he owned a mill, into an experimental model community. Here the workers were provided decent housing and working conditions, and educational opportunities were provided their children. Later, Owen established a

similar community in New Harmony, Indiana. Neither experiment lasted.

Charles Fourier (1772–1837), another French socialist, also proposed model communities in which workers would pool their capital, live in communal buildings, and engage in both agriculture and manufacturing. A mathematician, Fourier proposed a formula for distributing the earnings of the community. Fourier's ideas contained a mystical element, including his belief in the magic of numbers. His utopian dream was never instituted.

Karl Marx and Scientific Socialism. The *scientific socialism* of Karl Marx, also known as *communism*, was the most radical type of 19th-century socialism. Although Marx agreed with the basic premises of the early socialists, he advocated a total socialist system, which could be brought about only by the overthrow of the capitalist society.

Karl Marx (1818–1883) was born in Germany to Jewish parents, but his father, Hein-

---

[2] Frederick B. Artz, *Reaction and Revolution 1814–1832* (New York: Harper & Row, 1963), p. 213.

Karl Marx, the most radical socialist, believed that capitalism would inevitably be overthrown in the advanced industrial democracies.

that is, he argued that the way in which goods are produced and the way in which the wealth of the society is distributed determine everything else in the society—its legal, political, and cultural institutions, its traditions and beliefs. For example, in the capitalist system, Marx maintained, theft is a crime because the capitalist believes in private ownership of property.

From the philosopher George Wilhelm Friedrich Hegel, Marx borrowed the idea of the **dialectic**; that is, the idea that in every system the conflict between something (the thesis) and its opposite (the antithesis) produces a new combination of the thesis and the antithesis. Connecting his materialistic interpretation (economic determinism) with Hegel's dialectic, Marx produced a theory of dialectical materialism.

Another basic element of Marxist thought emerges in the opening line of the *Communist Manifesto*: "The history of all hitherto existing society is the history of class struggle."[3] Marx believed that economic classes are the root of all human conflict and that conflict between those classes is inevitable. Conflict between the bourgeoisie and the proletariat, for example, is unavoidable, for each wants something at the expense of others; the bourgeoisie want profit, which they can only obtain by keeping workers' wages low and prices high. The proletariat wants high wages and low prices, at the expense of the bourgeoisie.

Marx also offered a prophecy for the future, what he viewed as an inevitable development in the history of class struggle. Capitalism would be overthrown in the struggle between bourgeoisie and proletariat, and the victor would be the proletariat.

When all the world had experienced the revolution, Marx went on to say, the state would no longer be needed and would

rich, adopted Lutheranism when Karl was six years old. Although Marx later rejected orthodox religion as "the opiate of the people"—a belief system that kept the poor from rebelling against the unjust conditions in which they lived—as a youth he was a practicing Christian. In 1843 Marx met his future collaborator, Friedrich Engels, the son of a wealthy German textile manufacturer who owned a factory in Manchester, England. Marx, exiled from Germany and then France for his radical ideas, in 1847 joined a secret society, the Communist League, and in 1848, he and Engels were commissioned by the German Democratic Workers Party to draw up a pamphlet, *The Communist Manifesto*, which outlined the basic beliefs of this small organization.

The first basic premise of Marx's thought is his **materialist** interpretation of history. Marx believed in *economic determinism*;

---

[3] Karl Marx, *The Communist Manifesto* (Peking: Foreign Language Press, 1968), p. 30.

Marx's theories encouraged a growing trend toward labor organization. The first international workers' union was formed in 1863, with Marx as its president.

"wither away." The end of all classes would bring an end to class conflict. At that point, all human beings would share equally in the wealth of the earth, in Marx's formula, "from each according to his ability, to each according to his need."[4]

Despite his confident predictions, Marx's theory is full of errors. No capitalist society has progressed the way Marx predicted it "inevitably" would, for none of the advanced industrial states of his time—France, England, Germany, the United States—have experienced the revolution he expected.

Instead, Marx's theories have been applied to the preindustrial states of the world where they have been used to justify dictatorship and to form the basis for economic systems aimed at producing growth in third-world countries.

Marxism was the most radical among the new ideas of the 19th century. It had a radical effect on the future of the world, although not in the way Marx predicted.

---

[4] *Ibid.*, p. 76.

LOOKING AT SOCIETY

The 19th century saw the professionalization of fields such as economics and history, and the creation of new branches in the social sciences. These developments were the result of the increase in knowledge—which made specialization necessary—and the application of scientific methods and of such concepts as natural law to the study of human behavior.

HISTORY

Formerly, history had been the work of amateurs. In the 19th century, the field became professionalized and specialized. Subdivisions within history, such as economic history, emerged as separate fields of study.

Nationalism was a great stimulus to the study of history. For example, French historians such as Jules Michelet (1798–1874) studied the development of France as a nation. They debated the role of the French Revolution, posing questions such as whether it was a positive or negative force, and what roles individuals and different classes played in the Revolution.

The spirit of nationalism stimulated historians to look to their countries' past to explain their present situation. Leopold von Ranke (1795–1886) was the foremost German historian of his day. Although he studied Germany, he was also proud of being a European, and he warned about the perils of too great an absorption in one's own country.

Von Ranke's work was also important because he stressed the use of primary sources to capture the past. He felt that commentaries on the past were not as useful as the observation or records of contemporaries. Impressed with the achievements of 19th-century science, he wanted to apply the scientific method to the study of history.

THE SOCIAL SCIENCES

The 19th century was the seedtime for the social sciences as a separate branch of history. Auguste Comte (1798–1857) gave the field of *sociology* its name and established much of its methodology. Comte divided sociology into two main branches: the study of social organization and the theory of social progress. He shared the optimism of many 19th-century thinkers. Influenced by Saint-Simon, he believed that society was constantly evolving into a higher state.

Another social science that developed during the 19th century was *anthropology*. Influenced by the theories of Charles Darwin, physical anthropologists studied the different human races. A chief aim of early studies was to determine which of the races was the superior, the "fittest," in Darwin's terms. The work of early anthropologists distorted Darwin's ideas. Their primary intent was to provide rationales for a growing number of racists among white Europeans, particularly those who espoused the supremacy of the Anglo-Saxon and Nordic races.

At the same time, cultural anthropologists began to study scientifically the societies of both complex and primitive cultures. They made an effort not to judge the many different customs and mores they investigated and observed, but simply to chronicle and explain them. The work of the cultural anthropologists led to a new relativism about previously unquestioned notions of right and wrong.

ADVANCES IN SCIENCE Science took gigantic strides in the 19th century. The increasing number of people involved in the scientific pursuits was one reason for this phenomenon. The desire to find practical applications was another. Discoveries in science not only built on existing knowledge but also opened whole new areas of study.

MEDICINE

One of the areas in which an immediate impact on human lives was felt was the advance in medical knowledge. Here three men were particularly important. The first was

Patients in Louis Pasteur's clinic receive a vaccination against rabies. Pasteur also solved another major health problem of his day: the bacterial contamination of milk, beer, and other products.

Louis Pasteur (1822–1895), a French chemist. Pasteur was the first to demonstrate that many diseases in plants and animals were caused by bacteria, and that these bacteria could be killed by raising the temperature of their environment. Milk could be purified by a process of heating, which came to be known as *pasteurization*. This discovery caused an enormous improvement in health.

Pasteur's work was built on by a Prussian, Robert Koch (1843–1910). Koch took Pasteur's findings and made them into a science. Using the microscope, he identified many of the bacteria that caused specific diseases. By the end of the century the bacteria that caused tuberculosis, typhoid, cholera, bubonic plague, and diphtheria had been identified. Humans now had the opportunity to free themselves from some of the scourges of the past.

Sir Joseph Lister (1827–1912) used Pasteur's work to develop the theory of infection. Realizing that germs were carried on a doctor's hands and surgical instruments, he instituted the practice of antiseptic surgery, thereby greatly reducing the risks of danger-

Surgeons who followed Lister's advice used carbolic acid to lessen the risk of transmitting germs in the operating room. Before Lister's time, it was thought that infections were generated spontaneously.

ous infections being transmitted during an operation.

Yet another important advance in surgery was the development of the first anesthetics. These made possible many kinds of surgery that had previously been out of the question. The use of anesthesia also made surgery a less fearsome prospect for patients.

CHEMISTRY AND BIOLOGY

The field of chemistry was stimulated by a growing interest in chemicals for both military and peacetime purposes. Perhaps the most important advance in chemistry was the formulation of the periodic table of elements by the Russian chemist Ivan Mendeleyev (1834–1907). This represented a first-rate piece of deduction, and its information on the properties of elements paved the way for the advances of the 20th century.

The field of biology saw developments that set off the greatest controversy of the 19th century. This controversy centered around the pioneering work of the English naturalist Charles Darwin (1809–1882) and his theory of **evolution.**

From his observations of nature, Darwin posited that a process known as natural selection took place. Over years of breeding, traits that enhanced a species' chance of survival tended to be reinforced. For example, speed was important to a deer to avoid predators, and the swiftest of the deer would be the ones who would live to reproduce—thus passing on their traits to their offspring. Over a period of time, Darwin argued, this "survival of the fittest" had brought about change in living organisms. The result was an enormous number of species of animals and plants each uniquely and ideally suited to play a particular role in the natural world. Darwin published his findings in 1859 in a book, *On the Origin of Species by Means of Natural Selection.*

The book created an uproar. Church leaders felt it destroyed the premise that God had created each type of life and that each was immutable. The implication that even man might have evolved from a lower species of animal made Darwin's theory especially controversial. Nevertheless, it was accepted by most biologists of the day.

The theory of evolution also had a wide-ranging impact on people's thinking in other areas. If the world of nature was an arena of

Darwin observes the movement of a tortoise on the Galápagos Islands. During his five-year voyage in the South Pacific, Darwin developed his theory that species develop traits which help them cope with specific environmental factors.

struggle for survival rather than of harmony, then perhaps it was inevitable that human society should be also. People used evolutionary thinking to justify the existence of poverty. They cited the doctrine of "survival of the fittest" to claim moral superiority for individuals who achieved wealth or for races who rose above other races.

A closer study of just how traits are transmitted from one generation to another was made by an Austrian monk, Gregor Mendel (1822–1884). In his monastery garden, Mendel crossed garden peas that had different traits, such as different colored flowers. From the results, he arrived at a mathematical formula for heredity. His findings, although they lay unnoticed for years, eventually became one of the foundations for the study of *genetics*.

PHYSICS

Developments in physics at the end of the 19th and the first years of the 20th century revolutionized both science and much thinking in other areas.

Electricity and Electromagnetism. Physicists from all over Europe turned to studying electricity. The Frenchman André Ampère (1775–1836) in 1820 discovered the mathematical equation for the flow of electrical current. In 1826, Georg Ohm (1787–1854) of Germany explored the resistance of different metals to electricity. He arrived at *Ohm's Law*, which describes the relationship of current, voltage, and resistance. The Scottish physicist James Clerk Maxwell (1831–1879) tied together much of the known information on electricity and formulated his theory of *electromagnetism*. He theorized that electromagnetic waves travel at the same speed as light and are different manifestations of the same phenomenon.

The Nature of Matter and Energy. Nineteenth-century physicists considered that the atom, whose existence had been posited early in the century, was indivisible. It was thought to be the smallest building block of

Albert Einstein was perhaps the most influential scientist of the 20th century. This photograph was taken in 1905, the year he published his theory about matter and energy.

matter. In addition, scientists of the time believed that there were just 92 kinds of atoms that in various combinations made up all the matter in the universe. The discovery of X-rays and their radioactive properties by W. K. Roentgen (1845–1923) and Henri Becquerel (1852–1908) in the 1890s changed that. The property of radioactivity—possession of which meant that a substance disintegrated spontaneously—showed that atoms could not be indivisible. Further research resulted in the discovery of smaller particles called protons, neutrons, and electrons within the atom.

From this discovery, the German scientist Albert Einstein (1879–1955) developed a new theory of matter and energy in 1905. Einstein's theory posited that matter and energy were different forms of the same thing, that one could be changed into the other in accordance with the famous formula $E = mc^2$. This idea was a complete break with the past. Formerly, matter had been regarded as indestructible: that is, people assumed it could only be changed into different forms. From Einstein's theory came the theoretical underpinning of many of the developments in physics of the 20th century.

LOOKING AT THE INDIVIDUAL

Theories of human behavior had been prevalent since classical times. As recently as the 17th and 18th centuries, John Locke and René Descartes had both put forth theories as to how individuals observe external objects and process information. Locke, for example, had believed that all human knowledge is based on sensations.

But psychology as a separate science did not develop until the late 19th century. In 1879, a German, Wilhelm Wundt (1832–1920), opened a psychological institute at the University of Leipzig. Here he tried to use the techniques of other sciences, such as physics and physiology, to find out how sensations, images, and human consciousness are interrelated.

The earliest psychological theories grew out of work with animals. Wundt did many laboratory experiments with animals. Another important theorist also based his theories about human behavior on work with animals. This was the Russian Ivan Pavlov (1849–1936). Pavlov's most famous experiments involved repeatedly feeding dogs immediately after ringing a bell. Pavlov demonstrated that eventually the ringing of the bell alone, whether or not it was followed by food, would cause the dogs to salivate. From these experiments he concluded that much of human behavior is conditioned response, the product of upbringing, and not the result of free choice or conscious reasoning.

Other evidence of the nature of human consciousness had come from the study of mental illness. The French physician Philippe Pinel had made an effort to study the causes of mental illness. But it was a Viennese physician, Sigmund Freud (1856–1939), whose theories most influenced the field of psychology.

Early psychological theories were based upon work with animals. From his experiments, Pavlov concluded that most human behavior is a matter of conditioned reflexes.

A clinic for patients suffering from hysteria. By probing the unconscious mind, Freud found ways to treat patients who had been considered incurable.

Freud speculated that the cause of much mental illness was to be found in the early experiences of the patient. He believed that early experiences shaped the individual in later life. In addition, he believed that the sexual urge was perhaps the strongest instinctual drive of the individual. From *repression*, or denial, of this drive came many of the abnormal thoughts and desires of the patient.

To treat his patients, Freud advocated the practice of *psychoanalysis*, in which the doctor tries to discover the significant experience of the patient's early life. To reach this information, Freud believed that it was important to look at the content of the patient's dreams, which he believed provided a clue to the unconscious mind. The unconscious, he believed, contained all the repressed urges of the individual and was a source of creativity as well as of problems.

ROMANTICISM A new intellectual trend of the late 18th and early 19th centuries, *romanticism* was primarily a literary, artistic movement, expressed in literature, music, and painting. But romanticism was also a frame of mind, a particular pair of glasses through which to view the world.

Romanticism was in part a reaction to the scientific revolution and the Enlightenment, which, as we have seen, stressed the powers of the human mind and its ability to reach objective truth through rational thought. Romanticism glorified the human heart and stressed emotions and feelings.

Romanticism was also a reaction to the Industrial Revolution and its products, such as iron machinery and scientific instruments of death—heavy artillery and the guillotine. Instead of such material progress, romantics glorified the medieval past, their own national history, the remote and exotic, the beauty of nature, and mystical events.

The turn from the rationalism and optimism of the Enlightenment to the romantic outlook began late in the 18th century in the work of such writers as Jean-Jacques Rousseau. Although he is often considered one of the philosophes, Rousseau went so far as to attack reason. In his novels, *Emile* and *La Nouvelle Héloïse*, he glorified natural human instincts and emotions.

ROMANTICISM IN LITERATURE

The romantic movement saw its greatest literary flowering in England. There, the first 25 years of the 19th century were a period of great poetic energy and innovation. The poets William Wordsworth (1770–1850) and Samuel Taylor Coleridge (1772–1834) both strove to show the supernatural in a natural context, although each approached this goal in a different fashion.

Wordsworth sought to find a sense of the mystical or mysterious in ordinary, natural settings. Many of his poems, such as "I Wandered Lonely as a Cloud" or "My Heart Leaps Up When I Behold a Rainbow in the Sky" are set out of doors.

Coleridge, on the other hand, attempted to make supernatural events seem real, or natural. His "Rime of the Ancient Mariner" is a tale of eerie events which result from an old seaman's failure to appreciate and love all of God's creatures. After slaying an albatross, the mariner finds himself aboard a phantom ship, becalmed at sea.

The Romantic poets often led colorful, tragic lives. George Noel Gordon, Lord Byron (1788–1824), was as famous for the romantic nature of his life as for his poetry. He left his wife and his home in England and threw himself into the tumultuous revolutionary politics of Italy. Although Byron scorned the "natural supernaturalism" of Wordsworth and Coleridge, and in one of his major works,

A reverence for nature inspired the work of many romantic poets and painters. In William Turner's painting of a shipwreck, sailors are overwhelmed by the power and violence of a storm at sea.

Don Juan, satirized the romantic movement, he nonetheless showed many of the hallmarks of romanticism in his poetry. Many of his poems, for example, are set in exotic places in Europe or the Middle East.

Romanticism in German literature flowered in the movement known as *Sturm und Drang* ("storm and stress"). Writers of the *Sturm und Drang* period exulted in the depiction of intense emotion. The towering giant of German literature, Wolfgang von Goethe (1749–1832), began his long career as poet and playwright during this period. One of his early works, a short novel called *The Sorrows of Young Werther*, is the story of un-

happy young love. It became a best-seller all over Europe.

ROMANTIC PAINTING

Romantic painters often chose nature for their subjects. They especially delighted in depicting the sky and the sea, both of which could evoke a wide array of feelings. In the work of English artist William Turner (1775–1851), landscapes and seascapes often have an aura of the mystical or the supernatural about them. More concerned to capture feelings than to accurately depict reality, the subject matter of Turner's later paintings, such as *The Slave Ship*, is sometimes

In his painting Liberty Leading the People, *the French romantic Eugene Delacroix portrayed the triumph of Parisian revolutionaries in 1830 (Chapter 12).*

scarcely recognizable. Turner especially liked to paint storms.

Other romantic painters focused on historical events. In their work they emphasized the dramatic, even the terrifying aspects of their subject matter, and often idealized the people involved. One of the best representatives of this school of romantic painters was the French artist Eugene Delacroix (1798–1863). Delacroix, like many romantics, was drawn to distant lands and he traveled to Greece and the Middle East. A number of his paintings, such as *The Massacre at Chios*, were inspired by events he witnessed during his travels. Delacroix also produced paintings that glorified revolutionary events in his native France. One of the best known of these is *Liberty Leading the People*, which depicts the men and women of the French revolution of 1830.

In Germany, romantic painters such as Caspar David Friedrich (1774–1840) were inspired by the work of medieval artists. Their efforts to capture the old sense of meticulous attention to detail became known as the *Gothic Revival*.

ROMANTIC MUSIC

The transition from the classical age to the romantic in music came in the work of the great German composer Ludwig van Beethoven (1770–1827). Beethoven was a man of rough ways and deep feelings. As a young man, he knew deep depression and loneliness. Although he began work in the tradition of Haydn and Mozart, he soon took the new forms they had developed, particularly the symphony, and transformed them into vehicles for the expression of the most profound and intense human emotions. To capture the depth of his feelings he greatly expanded the size and weight of the symphony. He added instruments to the orchestra, greatly lengthened movements, and, in his last symphony, the Ninth, even incorporated vocal music into his work. In his Third Symphony, the *Eroica*, he took as his

Beethoven's music expressed the emotion and energy of the romantic movement.

theme the nature of heroism. This symphony was originally dedicated to Napoleon, but Beethoven later removed the dedication on the grounds that Napoleon had proved himself a tyrant. The work is characterized by explosive energy.

The trend toward grandeur in music was continued after Beethoven by composers like the Frenchman Hector Berlioz, who scored some of his pieces for orchestras of hundreds of musicians.

Other romantic composers, such as Franz Schubert and Frederic Chopin, tried to capture a more intimate world of feelings in their music. They explored such genres as the song and short pieces for the piano such as preludes, etudes, and waltzes. Chopin's music, in addition, reflected his deep feelings for his native country, Poland. Other romantic composers who used nationalistic themes were Richard Wagner, whose cycle of operas, *The Ring of the Nibelung*, is based on a medieval German epic, and Anton Dvorak, who used native Czech themes in his music.

GROWING REALISM IN THE NOVEL

The 19th century saw the great flowering of the novel, a relatively new literary form that had become popular in the previous century. Throughout Europe, literacy had increased and the audience for the novel was the growing middle class.

After the first few decades of the century, when novels were often set in exotic places, novelists took to examining some of the problems in their increasingly industrialized societies.

In England, Charles Dickens (1812–1870), the best-loved and most widely-read novelist of the Victorian era, presented such a complete and accurate portrayal of his society that his books surpass the work of many historians in their ability to evoke the age. Dickens was born into extreme poverty and was keenly aware of the injustices of his society. His novels had a strong moral cast; they aimed to arouse indignation and compassion over these injustices.

Dickens' earlier works, such as *David Copperfield* and *Oliver Twist*, are known for the humorous and satirical light in which society is presented. In many of the later novels, such as *Bleak House* or *Great Expectations*, Dickens gives his readers a much more somber vision of the hypocrisy and greed he saw around him. Even these later works, however, are peopled with characters so well-drawn that they elicit from most readers a smile of recognition.

What Dickens did for Victorian England, the French novelists Honoré de Balzac (1799–1850) and Emile Zola (1840–1902) did for France. In Balzac's nearly 100 works, there is a conscious effort to give a complete and accurate picture of post-revolutionary French society. Balzac sought to incorporate in his works as many different occupations, professions, and levels of society as he could. His novels and stories together con-

Through his character Oliver Twist, Dickens portrayed the lives of destitute children in the work-houses of Victorian England.

tain over 2000 different characters. He referred to his works collectively as *The Human Comedy*.

Later in the century, Emile Zola tried consciously to unite the new social sciences with art in an approach to the novel called *naturalism*. Naturalism aimed to present a dispassionate look at society. Zola was especially fascinated with the new theory of heredity. In his cycle of 20 novels he explored the development of hereditary character traits in a family over five generations. Like Balzac, he also used his novels to probe into every phase of life—from the struggles of the lower classes to the corruption of government officials and the wealthy. The best known of Zola's works are *L'Assommoir*, *Germinal*, and *Nana*.

A BREAK WITH THE PAST

In the last 30 years of the 19th century, the plastic arts, particularly painting, took on a new look. There were changes in both the subject matter and the techniques used.

IMPRESSIONISM

In the 1890s, a group of artists rejected the standards of the French Academy that had heretofore been a major force in French art. They chose to paint outdoors, trying to capture the transient effects of light, rather than in the traditional artist's studio. Black was taken out of the palette and bright colors predominated. Some of the representatives of this group—known as the *Impressionists*—were Claude Monet, Auguste Renoir and Edouard Manet.

The Impressionists also scorned the classical and historical subjects of the painters of the past. Instead they tried to capture the fleeting moments of everyday life. Many viewers were shocked. Impressionist works did not look like the paintings of the past, and violated the common idea of what "art" should be.

POST-IMPRESSIONISM

Another group of painters went even farther than the Impressionists. Representatives of this group are Vincent Van Gogh, Paul Gauguin, and Paul Cezanne. They used colors that were farther divorced from the traditional ones. Perspective, which had been weakened by the Impressionists, was thrown out altogether. Cezanne tried to stress the geometric shapes of landscape, thus reducing the painting to its simplest essentials.

In the last years of the 19th century and the first years of the 20th, painting changed even more. The completely new look and break with tradition was the result of many factors. European artists had seen the art of other cultures that made no attempt to reproduce the Western idea of perspective. The influence of Japanese prints and African sculptures was important for several artists.

Einstein's idea of relativity and Freud's theory of the unconscious mind, both of which posited the existence of another reality apart from the classically perceived one, also influenced artists. Artists in small groups, particularly in Paris, inspired each other to new developments. A Spaniard, Pablo Picasso (1881–1973), and a Frenchman, Georges Braque (1882–1963), developed *cubism* in the early years of the new century. Cubism was an attempt to show several views of an object within the same picture. Picasso's painting *Les Demoiselles d'Avignon* caused a sensation. It combined

Zola's novel Germinal *concerns the life of coal miners during a strike. Zola sympathetically described the lives of ordinary laborers during the Industrial Age.*

cubism with some of the impressions that Picasso had gained from African art.

In the years just before World War I, all of the arts changed radically. The new forms of painting were taken to their logical conclusion by Wassily Kandinsky in the first non-representational painting.

In music, the traditional sound of Western music was also transformed. Arnold Schoenberg, his pupil Alban Berg, and Igor Stravinsky experimented with *atonal* music. In this type of music, the traditional keys, or chromatic scales, established by Johann Sebastian Bach are ignored. This development has strongly affected 20th-century music, although it has not gained favor with the general public. Even today, it does not command the popularity of the classical music of the 17th and 18th centuries.

POPULAR CULTURE AND AMUSEMENTS

The advances in science during the 19th century affected the lives of ordinary people in a variety of ways. A person born at the beginning of the century was living in a different world at the end of it.

Transportation and communications (Chapter 10) had made the world smaller than it had been in 1800. The continents were linked by cable telegraph. Telephone service had begun, making instant communications possible for the first time.

Among the most startling new inventions was that of photography. In 1839, the Frenchman Louis Daguerre (1789–1851) displayed the shiny, silver-coated "pictures from nature" that he called daguerreotypes. These delicate objects caused a sensation, and soon the daguerreotype process spread all over the world. Within 20 years, other photographic processes were discovered, making possible photographs on glass (ambrotypes), metal (tintypes), and paper. The making of various kinds of photographs became easier and less expensive, and it became possible for anyone to have his or her likeness recorded for preservation in family albums, or to send to loved ones from far away. Photographers soon moved from the studio into the outdoors, and families collected pictures of exotic sights in faraway places. From about the 1860s, stereo photographs were taken, and the stereoscope viewer became as common in the family parlor as the television is today.

The great improvements in transportation, beginning with railroads, made it possible for the average person to travel from his or her village or town. For the first time, vacations became a regular part of middle-class life. As railroads reached the sea, seaside resorts for all classes of society grew up. In Britain and France, special trains carried passengers from the cities to these resorts each Saturday after work.

Bicycles were first made in the early part of the 19th century, but did not gain wide public acceptance until the development of a "safety" bicycle, with two wheels of equal size, chain drive, and pneumatic tires around 1890. After that, bicyclists, both men and women, became a common sight in cities. The bicycling rage of the 1890s wrought a change in female fashions, for greater comfort and mobility.

Spectator sports also became popular in the 19th century. Soccer ("football" outside the United States) was the most popular, with teams of union or town members and, later, professional teams drawing crowds of avid fans.

Other entertainments were provided in the music halls that sprouted throughout Europe. In the music hall, ordinary people could enjoy the pleasures of music, comedy, and drama that had been founded at the theater and opera. Music-hall stars became well-known and lionized in the popular newspapers that soared in circulation. The admission charge was low, and many of the performers encouraged audience participation. Competition in this form of entertainment came after 1900 with the beginnings of the motion-picture industry.

SUMMARY

The dominant ideas of the 19th century—nationalism, liberalism, socialism, and romanticism—had a profound effect on people and events. The spirit of romanticism permeated the period and was interwoven in the other major ideas. It was an era of optimism and of faith in human progress, as humans appeared to be able to harness the natural forces of the universe. Wars were frequent, but limited; no major conflict occurred between 1815 and 1914. Many thought that they had learned the secrets of peace-keeping and a few believed that they had discovered the key to the creation of a perfect society. It was a century of great creativity in both the arts and sciences.

QUESTIONS

1 Why was nationalism especially intense in the 19th century? To what extent is nationalism an important feature of today's world?
2 Define 19th-century classical liberalism. Who were the classical economic liberals of that period? Why and how were they influential?
3 What key ideas do all socialists hold in common?
4 How is Marx's scientific socialism different from other forms of socialism? What is meant by "economic determinism"?
5 What were the important scientific advances of the 19th century?
6 Define romanticism. What does this movement have in common with other important concepts of the 19th century?

BIBLIOGRAPHY

COLERIDGE, SAMUEL TAYLOR. "The Rime of the Ancient Mariner." In Louis Untermeyer, ed., *A Treasury of Great Poems.* New York: Simon & Schuster, 1942. *Coleridge's poem epitomizes the romantic in literature: his subject, the old sailor, experiences supernatural events that appear real and believable.*

GEORGE, MARGARET. *One Woman's Situation: A Study of Mary Wollstonecraft.* Urbana: University of Illinois Press, 1970. *A biography of the writer and professional career woman who is often considered the founder of the women's movement.*

MARX, KARL. *The Communist Manifesto.* Peking: Foreign Language Press, 1968. *This short handbook outlines the basic theories of Karl Marx and Friedrich Engels, and is the primer for today's Marxist societies.*

MILL, JOHN STUART. *On Liberty.* Edited by Alburey Castell. Arlington Heights, Ill.: Harlan Davidson, 1947. *Mill's influential essay on the nature, extent, and limits of liberty is an example of 19th-century liberal thought.*

SNYDER, LOUIS L. *Varieties of Nationalism: A Comparative Study.* Hinsdale, Ill.: The Dryden Press, 1976. *This detailed monograph discusses the nature, history, and many worldwide varieties of nationalism.*

The Impact of New Ideas

● Error has never come into my mind.
  CLEMENS VON METTERNICH

● The cause of which my name is the symbol—that is to say, France regenerated by the Revolution and organized by the Emperor.
  NAPOLEON III

● A nation is the universality of citizens speaking the same tongue.
  GIUSEPPE MAZZINI

● We [the English] seem, as it were, to have conquered and peopled half the world in a fit of absence of mind.
  SIR JOHN SEELEY

● We are here to claim our rights as women not only to be free, but to fight for freedom.
  CHRISTABEL PANKHURST

● Population, when unchecked, increases in a geometrical ratio. Subsistence only increases in an arithmetical ratio.
  THOMAS MALTHUS

217

12

• *When France sneezes, Europe catches cold.*
CLEMENS VON METTERNICH

Reaction and Revolution (1815–1856)

The year 1815 was a watershed in European history. Napoleon Bonaparte's domination of France and most of Europe ended with his defeat at Waterloo. However, the ideas that had energized the French revolutionaries had been diffused throughout the continent. Although Napoleon denied his subjects liberty, he had institutionalized the principles of male equality and fraternity. Moreover, he had instilled nationalism in France and had evoked anti-French nationalism among the peoples whom his armies conquered.

Napoleon had also redrawn the map of Europe, and in the wake of his defeat had left to the victors the task of reestablishing states and the boundaries between them. Just as he, a single man, had engraved his ideals and enforced his vision upon the continent, another individual, Clemens von Metternich (1773–1859) of Austria, assumed the task of shaping the future of Europe and the world.

Each of these men contributed to the ferment and the unrest that characterized European politics in the first half of the 19th century. Underlying the conflict was the rise of the middle and working classes, who had found their voices in the tumult of the French Revolution and who demanded that they be heard again in the revolutions of the first half of the century. Europe's population explosion, already underway, added to the volume of their voices. Between 1700 and 1800, the population had nearly doubled; between 1815 and the eve of the world war in 1914, it would more than double.

The new breed of revolutionaries were motivated by three basic ideas—nationalism, liberalism, and *social reform*, the precept that governments should attend to the needs of their people and act in their interest. In contrast, reactionaries of the time strove to restore the old order of privilege and power for the few.

THE CONGRESS OF VIENNA The Congress of Vienna convened in the autumn of 1814 to ratify the Treaty of Paris of the preceding May, which had ended Napoleon's wars, and to negotiate a resettlement of the political structure of Europe. The representatives of the old order assembled in Vienna included the Austrian emperor, the kings of Prussia, Denmark, Bavaria, and Saxony, and the tsar of Russia. Thousands more attended as courtiers, ministers, and advisers. As Metternich himself

EUROPEAN POPULATION	
1700	118 million
1750	140 million
1800	200 million
1850	266 million
1914	460 million

put it: "When I got to Vienna . . . I found all Europe assembled in my antechamber."[1] The celebration of the old order's return to power included a conspicuous display of wealth and influence. As an aristocrat who attended the Congress described it:

• • • *Numberless magnificent carriages traversed the city in all directions [the imperial stables held 1400 horses at the disposal of the royal guests]. . . . The promenades and squares teemed with soldiers of all grades, dressed in the varied uniforms of all the European armies. When night came, the theatres, the cafes, the public resorts were filled with animated crowds, apparently bent on pleasure only. . . . Noise and bustle were everywhere.*[2]

THE "BIG FOUR"

The four nations that had secured the military victory—Great Britain, Prussia, Russia, and Austria—were represented respectively by Robert Stewart, 2nd Viscount Castlereagh (1769–1822), Britain's foreign secretary; the Prussian king, Frederick William III, and his ministers; the Russian tsar, Alexander I; and the foreign minister of Austria, Metternich. The loser, France, was represented by Charles Maurice de Talleyrand-Perigord (1754–1838), better known as Talleyrand.

---

[1] Dorothy Gies McGuigan, *Metternich and the Duchess* (New York: Doubleday, 1975), p. 325.

[2] Raymond P. Stearns, *Pageant of Europe* (New York: Harcourt Brace Jovanovich, 1961), p. 458.

Talleyrand. Talleyrand's agility at remaining on the winning side during the rapidly changing politics of the revolutionary era led one of his biographers, Crane Brinton, to entitle his book, *The Lives of Talleyrand.* Talleyrand came from an aristocratic family and had been a priest, in fact a bishop, before the revolution of 1789. He was a member of the Estates-General, and had voluntarily joined the National Assembly when it was founded in June 1789. Surviving the Reign of Terror by going into exile in England and America, he returned to France after the Directory was established, becoming the minister of foreign relations in 1797. When Napoleon overthrew the Directory and established the Consulate in 1799, Talleyrand was rewarded for his role in the coup by remaining as minister of foreign relations, a position he held until his break with Napoleon in 1807.

The emperor's defeat in 1814 brought Talleyrand another political opportunity. As a

Tallyrand could be an effective advocate for the new French government at the Congress of Vienna, for he had disassociated himself from Napoleon several years before.

219

member of the provisional government that paved the way for the return of the Bourbon dynasty, he was again rewarded, this time by the restored Louis XVIII, who named him minister of foreign affairs. It was in this capacity that he represented France at the Congress of Vienna and played a major role in gaining a reasonable settlement for France.

As Brinton has noted, Talleyrand's desire for power made it possible for him to change his principles with the ease with which one would change clothes. Nevertheless, this same propensity enabled him to capitalize on the conflicting ambitions of the four victors at Vienna and to secure for France a position of power in the settlement and in the ensuing years.

Alexander I. Tsar Alexander I of Russia also played an important role at Vienna. The grandson of Catherine the Great, Alexander was raised at court and educated by a Swiss tutor from whom he acquired some of the liberal ideas of Jean-Jacques Rousseau. By comparison with the other participants, he was probably the most reform-minded leader present, although still an autocrat. A man with a mystical bent, one of his major goals at Vienna was to preserve religious ideals; to establish not only political accord among the victors but also what he termed a "Holy Alliance" of Christian rulers. At the same time, Alexander was a politically astute ruler, who was determined to maintain the power and authority of the Romanov dynasty.

Lord Castlereagh. Lord Castlereagh, accompanied by the Duke of Wellington, who was both a soldier and a statesman, represented Britain's interests at the Congress. Castlereagh had been secretary of war during the Napoleonic Wars, ably organizing Britain's land and sea forces. Although he advocated a moderate peace settlement for France, his goal was to restore the balance of power in Europe and to make sure that neither France nor any other nation would ever overturn that balance.

Frederick William III. Although he may have been characterized as "the one who thinks for them all,"[3] the king of Prussia was a vacillating monarch who came under the sway of Tsar Alexander. Having persuaded Frederick William to support his bid for Polish lands, Alexander promised to back the king's wish to seize more territory for Prussia. Frederick William's excessive demands were moderated by the other powers, but he did manage to emerge as the proprietary leader of the other German states.

Clemens von Metternich. The man who most dominated the Congress of Vienna and indeed the next 33 years of European politics was Count Clemens von Metternich. Born into the Austrian nobility in 1773, Metternich, as a student at the University of Strasbourg in France, had seen first-hand the outbreaks of violence triggered by the events of the French Revolution. As a consequence, he hated and feared mob rule. Through his marriage into the family of a former chancellor of Austria, he acquired prestige, large estates, and an entrance into Viennese society. He served Austria as ambassador to Napoleonic France, and in 1809 became foreign minister, a position he held until 1848.

The extent to which Metternich was able to etch his world view on European politics between 1815 and 1848 has led many historians to dub the period "the Age of Metternich." Metternich once commented, "Few men have understood me; writers a hundred years hence will judge me very differently from those of today."[4] Historians differ on the question of whether he was a reactionary, seeking to restore Europe to an age gone by, or a conservative who established order and stability in the wake of mob rule. Whichever interpretation one adopts, historians generally agree that Metternich was instrumental in shaping events in Europe in the first half of the 19th century.

[3] *Ibid.*, p. 457.

[4] Arthur J. May, *The Age of Metternich, 1814–1848* (New York: Holt, Rinehart, 1963), p. 3.

Metternich was the main architect of the agreements reached at the Congress of Vienna.

RESTORATION AND COMPENSATION

The Congress carried on its discussions until June 1815, its conclusion a little delayed by the 100 days of Napoleon's return to power in March 1815. The final act of the Congress was signed on June 9, 1815.

The two underlying principles embodied in the peace settlement wrought by the Congress of Vienna were restoration and compensation. *Restoration* meant that the dynastic rulers of Europe were restored to their thrones: in the view of these royal peacemakers they were the legitimate rulers who had been unlawfully deprived of their domains by the French and the upstart Napoleon. The principle of restoration applied as well to political boundaries, which were to reflect the territorial divisions of 1792, before the French had embarked on their war of conquest.

One of the enthusiasts for the principle of restoration was Talleyrand, for the adoption of this settlement would restore the Bourbon dynasty and would preserve France's prewar territorial boundaries. Moreover, he effectively argued that a strong France was important to preserve the balance of power in Europe. In this way, Talleyrand saved France from dismemberment.

Accordingly, the final act of 1815 restored the Bourbon dynasty not only to France but also to Spain and the Kingdom of the Two Sicilies. The House of Orange was returned to Holland, and the House of Savoy to the Italian states of Sardinia and Piedmont. The pope retained his temporal possessions in central Italy, the Papal States, and the various German princes regained territories they had lost to Napoleon.

Drawing a New Map. Despite the adoption of the principle of restoration, the victors did not in fact restore the status quo of 1792. Their own national ambitions and the opportunity for gain motivated them to adopt as well the principle of *compensation*—a polite term for the centuries-old precept that "to the victor belong the spoils." Incorporating this principle, along with a determination to expand its trade and retain its naval supremacy, Britain compensated itself with some French and Spanish islands in the Americas; Heligoland from Denmark; and Malta and the Ionian Islands in the Mediterranean. Britain also acquired the colonies of Ceylon and the Cape of Good Hope (to become South Africa), both former colonies of its Dutch allies. To reward Dutch acquiescence, and to ensure a strong Holland as a bulwark against French expansionism, Belgium, formerly the Austrian Netherlands, was transferred to Dutch rule—to establish a united Kingdom of the Netherlands.

To compensate Austria for the loss of Belgium, the Austrians received the Italian states of Lombardy and Venetia. Moreover, Tuscany and several smaller Italian states were given to princes who were under the dominance of Austria—manifesting Metter-

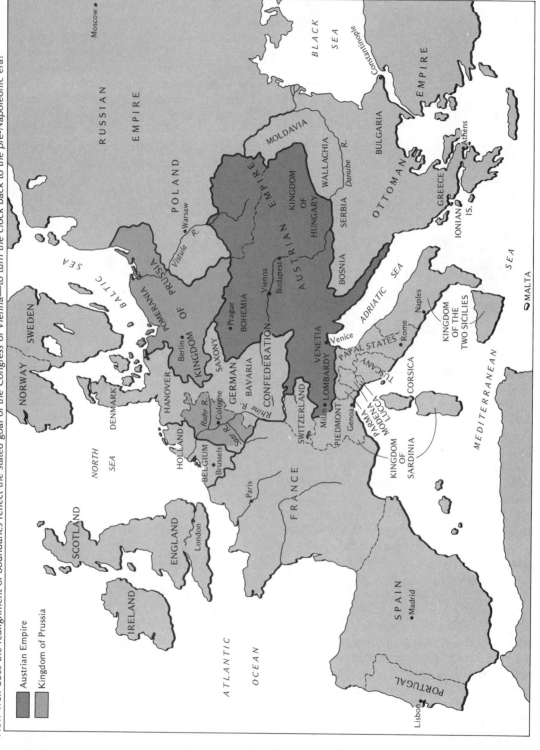

EUROPE IN 1815

How well does the realignment of boundaries reflect the stated goal of the Congress of Vienna—to turn the clock back to the pre-Napoleonic era?

Austrian Empire

Kingdom of Prussia

RUSSIAN EMPIRE

Moscow

BLACK SEA

OTTOMAN EMPIRE

Constantinople

POLAND

Warsaw

Vistula R.

MOLDAVIA

WALLACHIA

Danube R.

SERBIA

BULGARIA

BOSNIA

GREECE

Athens

IONIAN IS.

KINGDOM OF HUNGARY

Budapest

AUSTRIAN EMPIRE

Vienna

BOHEMIA

Prague

ADRIATIC SEA

MALTA

BALTIC SEA

POMERANIA

KINGDOM OF PRUSSIA

Berlin

SAXONY

GERMAN CONFEDERATION

BAVARIA

HANOVER

SWEDEN

NORWAY

DENMARK

NORTH SEA

HOLLAND

BELGIUM

Brussels

Cologne

Ruhr R.

Saar R.

Rhine R.

SWITZERLAND

VENETIA

Venice

LOMBARDY

Milan

PIEDMONT

Genoa

KINGDOM OF SARDINIA

PARMA

MODENA

TUSCANY

PAPAL STATES

Rome

Naples

KINGDOM OF THE TWO SICILIES

CORSICA

MEDITERRANEAN SEA

FRANCE

Paris

SCOTLAND

ENGLAND

London

IRELAND

ATLANTIC OCEAN

SPAIN

Madrid

PORTUGAL

Lisbon

Participants at the Congress of Vienna redrew the map of Europe to safeguard each nation's interests.

nich's disdain for the notion of a united Italy, which he declared was only a "geographical expression."

Austria's desire to dominate the German states of central Europe was made manifest in the creation of the German Confederation, a loose organization of 39 German states with a diet chaired by the Austrian Metternich. This realignment set the stage for the coming duel between Austria and Prussia for the domination of Germany.

Always adept at profiting from war, Prussia was also well compensated. Although forced to surrender part of its Polish possessions, Prussia acquired a strip of Swedish territory (Swedish Pomerania), a large piece of Saxony, and most of the Rhineland states, including Cologne and the Ruhr and Saar valleys. This arrangement enabled Prussia to maintain a "watch on the Rhine," thus protecting central Europe from any future French depredations.

Alexander's Russia too came in for its share of the spoils. Russia obtained part of Poland, including Warsaw, from Prussia. The tsar also retained territories which he had earlier seized from Turkey and Sweden. In exchange, Sweden received Norway from Denmark. These and other resettlements incorporated into the second Treaty of Paris in November 1815 refashioned the map of Europe, with Austria replacing France as the dominant power. Moreover, France was intentionally surrounded by strengthened states, constituting a *cordon sanitaire*, or chain of buffer states designed to prevent any renewal of French expansionism.

THE CONCERT OF EUROPE In an attempt to make this peace settlement permanent, Metternich sought to guarantee it in the creation of the *Concert of Europe* whereby the wartime coalition of Austria, Prussia, Russia, and Great Britain formed the Quadruple Alliance (joined by France in 1818). The members agreed to preserve the peace, when necessary, by convocating diplomatic congresses which would maintain the status quo in Europe.

In pursuit of his dream of a league of nations dedicated to rule by Christian ideals, Alexander I persuaded three of the other major powers to accept the concept of the *Holy Alliance*. This compact required its members to determine diplomatic policies within the concepts of Christian principles. Austria, Prussia, and Russia agreed in the Holy Alliance that:

● ● ● *the present Act has no other object than to publish, in the face of the whole world, their fixed resolution, both in the administration of their respective States, and in their political relations with every other government, to take for their sole guide the precepts of that Holy Religion, namely, the precepts of Justice, Christian Charity, and Peace.*[5]

All the princes of Europe, with the exception of the English monarch, the pope, and the sultan of Turkey endorsed the alliance. Britain's Lord Castlereagh characterized the Holy Alliance as "a sublime piece of mysticism and nonsense."[6] But there may

[5] Carre, Rene Albrecht, ed., *The Concert of Europe* (New York: Walker & Co., 1968), p. 33.

[6] Arthur May, *Age of Metternich*, p. 19.

223

have been a more pragmatic motive as well: Russia's policy of expansion southward to acquire territory in the Moslem Ottoman Empire was a possible factor in the tsar's determination to uphold Christianity.

REACTIONS AGAINST THE RESETTLEMENT

The forces of revolution swept Europe between 1815 and 1848, although the circumstances, the reasons, and the goals varied. In general, the revolutionaries were motivated by either liberal ideals or nationalism, or on occasion both. The victors' determination to preserve the settlement of the Vienna Congress led to several meetings of the European powers and to military interventions intended to stem the tide of revolution.

THE CARLSBAD DECREES

Within Germany, divided into separate states and loosely joined under Austrian leadership, there arose a strong desire for national unity, a movement especially prevalent among university students. This German nationalism was engendered by such patriots as Friedrich L. Jahn and Ernest M. Ardnt. As young men, both had been directly affected by Napoleon's conquest of their homeland, and each sought to revive German national spirit. A professor at the University of Bonn, Ardnt influenced the *Burschenschaften*, an organization of German students that spread to other universities. Its goals included German unity, increased participation in government, and German nationalism, embodied in its slogan, "Honor, Liberty, Fatherland." In October 1817, members convened at Wartburg to commemorate Napoleon's defeat at Leipzig in 1813 and to honor Martin Luther. During the celebration, which included many speeches, the singing of Protestant hymns, and the consumption of considerable quantities of beer, the students hurled books they considered offensive into a huge bonfire.

Their behavior horrified Metternich, for it

The first major protest against the resettlement agreements was the Wartburg Fest, organized by German students in 1817.

was the first public protest against the resettlement of Europe. His concern regarding their "subversive" behavior was exacerbated by the assassination of the German poet and playwright Auguste F. F. Kotzebue, who was also a Russian spy, by a member of the *Burschenschaften*. In response to the murder, Metternich convened a meeting of the nine German states at Carlsbad in 1819 and there issued a series of laws known as the *Carlsbad Decrees*. The decrees dissolved the *Burschenschaften*, introduced press censorship, and created watchdogs to spy on university professors and students. Using these decrees, Metternich was able to repress liberals and nationalists in the German states for several years.

UPRISINGS IN SPAIN AND PORTUGAL

The first major uprising against the European order established by the Congress of Vienna occurred in Spain in 1820. It was directed against the ruler of the restored Bourbon dynasty, Ferdinand VII. Popular uprisings forced the king to reinstate the constitution of 1812, which had been swept away at the time of Ferdinand's restoration. The victory was short-lived, for the French received the approval of the Quadruple Alliance to intervene, and Ferdinand was restored to full power. Although civil war raged in Spain until 1839, the major powers did not intervene again.

Portugal too experienced unrest when King John VI failed to abide by the constitution he had been forced to accept in 1820. Although another constitution was enforced in 1826, civil war raged in Portugal for several years. In both cases, constitutionalism had failed to resolve national problems in the Iberian Peninsula.

REVOLTS IN SICILY AND PIEDMONT

In Italy, nationalism was the driving force, for the desire for unity—*risorgimento*—led to the formation of several revolutionary groups, including a secret society called the *Carbonari* (charcoal burners), which met in the woods to plot resistance. In the Italian states, nationalism united with liberalism to attempt to overthrow the authoritarian regime restored by the Congress of Vienna. In 1820, the *Carbonari* revolted against the Bourbon King Ferdinand I of Naples, forcing the elderly monarch to grant a constitution that established an elected parliament.

In response, Metternich convened the Congress of Troppau, in Silesia, at which Austria, Prussia, and Russia denounced the Italian revolt as a subversive plot. Finally deciding to intervene, the Congress allowed the king of Naples to invite an Austrian army to Naples to abolish the constitution and restore the monarchy to its full powers. The Austrian army successfully intervened and remained in Naples until 1826. A student revolt in Piedmont against the restored House of Savoy was similarly put down by the Austrian army. The intervention of the powers of Europe had successfully stifled a national liberal revolution in the Italian states.

GREEK INDEPENDENCE

In 1821 a nationalist movement erupted among Greeks against their ruler, the Otto-

The Battle of Navarino, 1827. By defeating the Turkish fleet, Britain, Russia, and France helped Greece to win independence from Ottoman rule.

man Empire, and for the next six years the Greeks fought alone against the Turks. In 1827, however, Britain, Russia, and France intervened on behalf of Greek independence. In October 1827, the combined allied forces destroyed the Turkish fleet and, after another two years of fighting, the Turkish sultan yielded.

The Treaty of Adrianople gave Greece its independence and was guaranteed by the three intervening powers. Otto, the son of the king of Bavaria, became the first King of Greece. The three powers, especially Russia, had in fact intervened primarily to weaken the Ottoman Empire and to a lesser degree because of their cultural ties with Greece. Britain was also fearful that Russia would gain an advantage in the Mediterranean. The pattern of events between 1815 and 1830 demonstrated that acting in concert, the great powers were capable of inflicting their own political, ideological, and foreign policies on the lesser states of Europe.

THE REVOLUTIONS OF 1830

By restoring the Bourbon king Louis XVIII to the throne of France in 1815, the victorious powers demonstrated their desire to maintain a strong but conservative French state. Although Louis XVIII retained a parliament, it was dominated by the old aristocracy and the Roman Catholic Church. The latter was closely linked to the throne because of its dependence on the crown for its income.

Excluded from the franchise were most Frenchmen—middle class, urban workers, and peasants alike. A number of prominent Bonapartists were persecuted by the Bourbon regime. Marshal Michel Ney, Napoleon's brilliant general, whom the emperor once called "the bravest of the brave," and who had rejoined Napoleon for the 100 days, was tried for high treason and executed by a firing squad. Still, there remained many ardent Bonapartists among the French citizenry, and they would again have their day.

At the same time, the French economy recovered quickly after the war, and by the time of Louis' death in 1824, the country was stable and prosperous.

THE JULY REVOLT

Louis' brother and successor, Charles X (1824–1830), was a man of great will and determination and the leader of the extreme royalist faction. As the Count of Artois, he had led the emigration of nobles and clergy from France in 1789. He was determined to revive the political, social, economic, and religious institutions of the *ancien régime* and to restore divine-right monarchy to France.

Once in power, Charles paid an indemnity to the nobles to compensate for their confiscated estates and the loss of their privileges; in 1825 one billion francs were paid to the nobility. He also restored the privileges of the clergy, and restricted the freedom of the press. Charles quickly encountered opposition—from the middle class, which was excluded from government by heavy property qualifications; from the nonbelievers, who were angered by the Church's privileges; and from the city workers, whose wages declined during his reign.

When Charles appointed the reactionary Prince Jules de Polignac as the prime minister, the government was doomed. The lower house of the National Assembly, the Chamber of Deputies, was dissolved by Charles after it demanded Polignac's resignation, but the subsequent election in 1830 returned an even more liberal chamber.

In response, on July 25, 1830, Charles exercised his power to issue ordinances carrying the force of law. He placed further restrictions on the press, dissolved the newly-elected Chamber of Deputies, promulgated a new electoral law which disenfranchised three-fourths of the electors, and called for new elections. Paris was stirred to revolt. Liberal printers and journalists urged Parisians to armed insurrection, and barricades went up in the city streets. Three days of

Parisians staged a successful rebellion against the regime of Charles X in July of 1830. As a result, the Bourbon dynasty was unseated.

street fighting followed. Unable to control the situation, Charles abdicated in favor of his 10-year-old grandson and fled to England. He, in turn, was replaced by another member of the Bourbon family, Louis Philippe, the "Citizen King" (see below).

BELGIAN INDEPENDENCE

Inspired by the Paris uprising, Belgian revolutionaries revolted in Brussels in 1830. The Belgian union with Holland, enforced by the Vienna settlement, had been an unpopular one. The two states were different in many ways: the Belgians were Catholic, and spoke French or Flemish; the Dutch were Protestant, and spoke Dutch. The revolutionaries proclaimed their independence and easily defeated Dutch troops sent against them.

However, the future of Belgian independence lay in the hands of the great powers.

For several reasons the powers did not intervene. Russia and Austria faced their own difficulties; the French, themselves successful in revolt, supported the new state; and the British too were sympathetic toward the Belgian nationalists. To preserve the independence of the new state, in 1832 the European powers, led by Great Britain, sanctioned Belgium's sovereignty, and a German Prince, Leopold of Saxe-Coburg, was named king to head a constitutional monarchy. Leopold was the uncle of the future Queen Victoria of England and the son-in-law of the king of France, Louis Philippe. These royal connections clinched Leopold's power, and in 1839 the European powers guaranteed Belgian independence.

REVOLT IN POLAND, 1830

Poland had disappeared as an independent state after its third partition in 1795, when it was divided among Austria, Prussia, and Russia. Following the Congress of Vienna, Tsar Alexander I had created a new Polish kingdom in those territories under his control. Naming himself King of Poland as well as Emperor of Russia, Alexander had granted the Poles a very limited constitution and had restored the Polish language and the Roman Catholic religion.

Inspired by the successful French revolt in 1830, Polish liberals declared the overthrow of the Romanov dynasty and Polish independence. Although they hoped that the French would intervene on their behalf, no such assistance materialized. The French regime was unwilling to risk war with Russia.

Alexander's successor, Nicholas I, was devoted to absolutist principles and he had no intentions of allowing Polish independence. His army intervened to crush the revolt. Although the revolutionaries held out in Warsaw until September 1831, their cause was doomed. Their failure signaled the end of the separate Polish kingdom. Poland again became a Russian province, the constitution was suspended, and the Polish language outlawed. The rebels were severely punished—executed or sent to exile in Siberia.

REVOLUTION IN ITALY

The French revolt in 1830 also inspired the nationalist *Carbonari* in Italy. Having been suppressed in southern Italy, the revolutionaries continued the fight for Italian unity and independence through uprisings in 1831 against the Papal States and Bologna. However, Austrian intervention ended the revolts, and the *Carbonari* were eliminated as a major force.

In the wake of the failure of the liberal uprisings of 1830–31 and the dissolution of the *Carbonari*, a new association called Young Italy sprang up under the leadership of the Genoan patriot Guiseppe Mazzini. Inspired by the former glory of Italy and stirred by the spirit of independence and unity, Mazzini and his idealistic followers urged

The visionary patriot Mazzini hoped to achieve the unification and eventual independence of Italy.

the idea of *risorgimento* throughout Italy. Mazzini was a visionary whose idea of nationhood was "the totality of citizens speaking the same language, associated together with equal political and civil rights in the common aim of bringing the forces of society . . . progressively to greater perfection."[7] Mazzini's revolutionary activities were limited by his exile in London, but his ideas and goals were adopted by Guiseppe Garibaldi, the legendary soldier-patriot who became a leading figure in the *risorgimento*. He too spent years of exile—in South America—for urging revolution. However, the ideas of these republican leaders and the popular support they won helped keep alive the spirit of defiance in Italy and laid the foundations for further revolutions (Chapter 15).

REVOLUTIONS OF 1848

Across Europe the revolts of 1830–31 followed the pattern set in the previous

[7] S. C. Burchill and the editors of Time-Life Books, *Age of Progress* (New York: Time-Life Books, 1966), p. 98.

decade. Although the revolutionaries' goals varied, depending on local circumstances, a rising tide of liberalism was sweeping the continent. In Poland and Italy, the conservative principles of Metternich prevailed, and the revolutionaries foundered. However, the sheer force of the dual ideas of nationalism and liberalism could not be contained forever, and in 1848 nearly all of Europe was swept by revolution.

RULE OF THE "CITIZEN KING"

The successful July revolt in Paris in 1830 ended permanently the practice of divine-right monarchy in France. But with victory came the issue of its replacement. Two groups emerged: radical Parisian workers who supported the establishment of a republic; and middle-class liberals, represented by the journalist Adolphe Thiers,

The Paris rebellion of 1830 led to the accession of Louis Philippe, the "Citizen King."

who preferred constitutional monarchy. To prevent further conflict, the aging Marquis de Lafayette exerted his considerable influence to persuade the republicans to accept the accession to the throne of Louis Philippe, a cousin of Charles X. His reign became known as the *July Monarchy*.

Louis Philippe had good credentials. His father, Philippe of Orleans, had voted for the execution of Louis XVI in the National Convention, and Louis Philippe himself had taken an active part in the revolution. In August 1830, Louis Philippe accepted the title "King of the French." With his accession, the idea of popular sovereignty replaced divine-right monarchy. The "Citizen King" supervised a revision of the constitution which weakened the upper house of the National Assembly, abolished censorship, and ended state aid to the Church. The uneasy compromise between democracy and divine right was to be briefly successful.

Louis and his chief minister, François Guizot, followed a conservative policy of encouraging prosperity for the middle class, the government's chief support, and of disenfranchising the working classes by limiting the electorate to about 250,000 large property owners, although the population had reached around 35 million by 1848. Guizot advised those who demanded a greater share in government to "work harder, grow rich, and so gain the ballot."[8] In the France of the Citizen King, it was the men of property who ruled, and their official policy was peace and order.

Louis Philippe's regime remained in power partly because it was cautious and static and partly because its opponents were divided. Opposition ran the gamut from the reactionary "legitimists," who championed the return of the Bourbons, to the radical rev-

---

[8] Wallace K. Ferguson and Geoffrey Bruun, *A Survey of European Civilization*, 3rd ed. (Boston: Houghton Mifflin, 1958), p. 680.

The artist Honoré Daumier caricatured the bourgeois quality of the July Monarchy in this portrait of its legislators. François Guizot is seated at bottom left.

olutionaries, led by men like Louis Blanc, who denounced capitalism and called for collective ownership of property and government guarantees of full employment.

More radical still was the anarchist Pierre Proudhon, who had pronounced in his work *What Is Property?* that "property is theft." Fearing the power of the state, he called for its destruction. Karl Marx adopted some of Proudhon's ideas in *The Communist Manifesto*.

Among the other factions were Bonapartists who sought political power for Napoleon's descendants, one of whom, Louis Napoleon, had twice attempted to inspire revolt. Republicans, particularly artisans and peasants, looked to the France of 1792 as their model, demanding universal male suffrage and an end to property qualifications for the electorate.

The February Revolt. France in 1848 was a cauldron of dissent directed against the

Louis Blanc, a leader of leftist dissent during the July Monarchy, argued that the state should take control of industries and provide employment for all its citizens.

After the revolutions of 1848, Lamartine and Blanc declared the Second Republic and ran the government until a Constituent Assembly could be elected.

July Monarchy. Underprivileged and exploited, with no political power to change the laws and with no rights to organize to improve working conditions, the property-less workers, especially the urban masses, came to believe that revolution was the only way to obtain political and social justice. Heightening their unrest were the poor harvests and growing unemployment which plagued France and most of Europe in 1846–1847.

Through petitions, parades, and the staging of "political banquets," the revolutionaries of Paris made known their demands. When one such banquet of reformers was banned by an alarmed government in February 1848, barricades once more went up in the streets of Paris, especially in working-class neighborhoods. When troops who were called in to quell the rioters joined them instead, the government was doomed. Guizot resigned, and Louis Philippe fled to England. The revolution, however, was not yet over.

Revolutionary leaders, including Louis Blanc and the poet Alphonse de Lamartine, set up a provisional government and declared the *Second Republic*. Immediately they began to differ on the proper economic system for their new government. The more moderate Lamartine defended the capitalist concept of private ownership of property. For his part, Louis Blanc proposed the establishment of national workshops in which the government would finance factories owned and operated by the workers. The provisional government, which was to rule until national elections for a constituent assembly could be held, was dominated by the more radical republicans, including Blanc. Eventually, a modified version of his scheme of national workshops was instituted.

The June Days. In April the Constituent Assembly, elected by universal male suffrage, took its place in Paris. Its delegates, chosen from all over France and composed of moderates and conservatives as well as revolutionaries, were far less radical than the Parisians who had made the revolution. Fearful of losing the gains they had made, the workers of Paris revolted.

On May 15, some 100,000 people, mostly from the national workshops, attacked the Assembly, declared it dissolved, and established their own government. Troops quickly restored order, and the Constituent Assembly now began to root out the radical revolutionaries. The government proclaimed martial law and power was given over to the regular army. The result was the bloody *June Days* of the 24th through the 26th, during which class war raged in Paris. By June 26, the Assembly had won. Most of the revolutionaries were rounded up and executed or deported to French penal colonies.

LOUIS NAPOLEON (1848–1870)

With the insurrection crushed, and the radical revolutionaries along with it, the Constituent Assembly now turned to the issue at hand, the writing of a republican constitu-

After ruling three years as president, Louis Napoleon dissolved the Assembly and allocated its powers to himself. A year later, he declared himself emperor.

tion. To eliminate the power vacuum that was inevitable during the months it would take to complete its work, the Assembly agreed to create a strong executive in the hands of a president, to be elected by universal male suffrage before the constitution was completed. In the elections held in December 1848, four candidates emerged, including Lamartine and Louis Napoleon Bonaparte, nephew of the late emperor. Louis Napoleon gathered 5½ million of the 7½ million votes cast and was installed as president of the Second Republic.

The victory of Louis Napoleon can be explained in part by the fact that for millions of Frenchmen voting for the first time in their lives, Napoleon was the only political name they knew. He represented what was termed the Party of Order, in contrast to the radical city workers so feared and distrusted by the middle class.

However, Louis Napoleon was not content to serve only as president, limited to a four-year term and unable to succeed him-

self. Mindful of the power and greatness of France under Napoleon I, Louis was, as one historian has noted, "under a fatal impulsion to follow in his uncle's footsteps."[9] The results of the elections for the National Assembly in 1849 contributed to his plan to overthrow the republic. The 750 elected members were totally divided among monarchists, republicans, and a handful of Bonapartists. The monarchists were further divided into Legitimists and Orleanists, followers of the deposed Louis Philippe. Hence, no faction could mount a majority to oppose Louis Napoleon's rule. This reactionary Assembly enacted its political philosophy by prohibiting public meetings, censoring the press, restoring the supremacy of the Roman Catholic Church, and disenfranchising 30 percent of the voters.

In 1851, with only a year left to serve as president, and having built up his support within the army, Louis Napoleon engineered a military *coup d'etat*. When Parisians awoke on December 2, 1851, they discovered that the walls of the city had been plastered with placards calling for the people and the army to support the President, and decreeing the dissolution of the Assembly. Overnight, troops loyal to Louis had occupied the key points in the city and had arrested monarchist and republican leaders. Despite some resistance in Paris, the bloodless *coup* was successful.

On December 20, Louis asked the voters to approve his plan for a new constitution. Approval was overwhelming. In January 1852, Louis issued a constitution which gave him nearly unlimited powers, and extended his term of office for 10 years.

Louis, however, was not finished. In November 1852, he again asked the voters to endorse his plans—this time to transform the presidency into a hereditary empire. Nearly all Frenchmen concurred and on De-

[9] *Ibid.*, p. 683.

During the Second Empire, the French aristocracy once again enjoyed the pomp of a royal court.

cember 2, 1852, Louis Napoleon was proclaimed Napoleon III, ruler of the Second French Empire. A subsequent revised constitution consolidated his power. The dreams of French liberals and radicals were ended as the new Emperor ruled nearly as a dictator for the next 18 years.

The empire of Louis Napoleon was enthusiastically received by the majority of Frenchmen. For the middle class, it was a return to order and stability in which industry and business could and did flourish. Through a program of public works, Louis encouraged the growth of cheap transportation—railways, steamships, canals—which provided employment for workers and at the same time stimulated the growth of commerce. To make a capital city befitting an emperor, Louis embarked on an ambitious plan to modernize Paris. Under the direction of Baron Georges Eugène Haussmann, Paris was transformed into a spacious city of broad boulevards and open squares, replacing many of the narrow, crooked streets of earlier times. (The wide boulevards were also a

safety measure for the regime, as they made street fighting more difficult.)

Art and literature also flourished. Painters such as Jean Baptiste Corot (1796–1875), breaking with tradition, celebrated the French countryside with shimmering landscapes. Writers such as Gustave Flaubert (1821–1880) replaced the romantic literary tradition with a new school of realistic fiction.

Louis' foreign policy was marked by both successes and disasters. One adventure in the latter category was his ill-fated intervention in the Mexican Revolution: his candidate for the Mexican throne, the Hapsburg Maximilian, was executed by rebels. On the other hand, he successfully extended France's colonial empire in the Pacific, Algeria, and Indochina. Louis came to believe that he had the best army in Europe, a delusion which eventually brought about his downfall. During the Franco-Prussian War, in 1870, Napoleon was taken prisoner (Chapter 15). The French then proclaimed the end of his empire and the establishment of the Third Republic.

REVOLUTION IN THE AUSTRIAN EMPIRE

The revolution that began in France in early 1848 quickly spread to the rest of Europe. The French successes in February and June inspired the millions whose liberal principles had been stifled by Metternich. Economic changes wrought by the spread of industrialization had created new classes, new needs, and new ideologies. The ineptitude and the reactionary ideas of those in power also stimulated revolution.

For a brief period, middle-class liberals joined forces with the working classes of Europe in opposition to the reactionary regimes in power throughout the continent. But the radicalism of the extremist factions frightened many of the middle class, and the temporary unity dissolved. Ultimately, the failure of the two groups to present a united front contributed heavily to the failure of the revolutionary movements.

The Fall of Metternich. The 1848 revolt in Austria was inspired by the uprising in Paris. Liberal reformers, including middle-class business and professional men who resented the economic controls imposed by Metternich, joined the working classes—workers, peasants, and students—in the revolution in the streets of Vienna. These disorders during the first week in March forced Metternich into exile in England. Without him, the feeble Emperor Ferdinand I gave in to the major demands of the revolutionaries, which included the promise of a liberal constitution for the empire. Having no intention of keeping his promises, Ferdinand attempted to reassert his authority and the revolutionaries forced him to flee the capital in October.

Complicating the revolution in Vienna was the issue of the numerous national minorities who wanted *national autonomy*, or separation from the polyglot empire. In the Hungarian half of the empire, Louis Kossuth led the Hungarian diet to proclaim a constitution which would separate Hungary from German-speaking Austria. But within Hungary, the various other nationalists—Croats,

The 1848 revolution in Vienna led to the downfall of Metternich, who fled to England.

Slovaks, Serbs, Slovenes, Poles, Ruthenians, Italians—also clamored for national autonomy or independence. Many of them were Slavic in origin, and, led by the Czechs, a Pan-Slavic congress convened in Prague and demanded autonomy.

In June 1848, the wife of Prince Windischgratz, the military commander of Prague, was accidentally killed in a popular demonstration. In response, the prince bombarded the city of Prague, destroyed all resistance, and made himself the military dictator of the province of Bohemia.

In October 1848 Windischgratz and General Jellachich, the military commander of Vienna, bombarded that city until it surrendered. They executed scores of radical leaders in the wake of their victory.

The military victory in the Austrian capital led to the emergence of Windischgratz's brother-in-law, Prince Felix Schwarzenburg, as Austrian prime minister. He persuaded the emperor Ferdinand to abdicate in favor of the 18-year-old Franz Joseph, who ruled until his death in 1916. Schwarzenburg dissolved the newly elected Assembly in March 1849 and discarded its draft constitution.

In January 1849, mopping-up operations took place in Budapest, where Hungarians had also risen in revolt. The rebels of Budapest surrendered, and Russian troops called in by Austria ended the rebellion in the rest of Hungary in the summer of 1849. The Hungarian leaders of the revolt were also executed.

Uprisings in Italy. In the Austrian-held Italian provinces of Lombardy and Venetia, rebellion arose in 1848 as well. The aim of the middle- and working-class revolutionaries was a united, independent Italy. In Milan, the capital of Lombardy, popular uprisings in March spread throughout the city, and eventually the Austrian army was driven out of the province. Similarly, the Venetians proclaimed a republic on March 22. On that same day, King Charles Albert of Piedmont, under pressure from the revolutionaries, declared war on Austria in support of Milan. These nationalist yearnings were echoed in simultaneous revolts in other Italian states, including the Bourbon-ruled Kingdom of Two Sicilies, where revolts had broken out in January. Within weeks, contingents of soldiers from all over Italy engaged the Austrian army. But their success was short-lived. In May a successful counterrevolution restored power to the Bourbon dynasty in Naples. By July 1848, the Austrian army had launched a counteroffensive to restore the Hapsburg power.

REVOLT IN PRUSSIA AND THE TWO GERMANIES

Revolt came to the Germanies as well; on March 16, 1848, fighting broke out in the streets of Berlin, the capital of Prussia, forcing King Frederick William to make concessions. On March 18, he abolished censorship and announced a convention of the Prussian diet which would prepare a constitution. Simultaneously, liberals of the various German states called for a meeting in Frankfurt, held

The 1848 revolution in Berlin forced the Prussian king to make liberal reforms, and eventually led to the election of a national assembly.

on March 31, which would arrange for the election of delegates from all of the German states to develop a plan to create a united Germany.

The Frankfurt Assembly. The result was a German National Assembly composed of over 800 German representatives, which met for the first time in Frankfurt on May 18, 1848. The Frankfurt Assembly contained both liberals and conservatives. Some were bent on establishing a German republic; others, a constitutional monarchy. All agreed on the goal of a united Germany. Most agreed on the logical necessity of a federal union which would maintain some autonomy for the states.

The most critical issue was the question of including German-speaking Austria within a united Germany. Those who favored that alternative, the *Gross-Deutschland* faction, were outvoted by the *Klein-*

Deutschlanders, who agreed to offer the crown of a united Germany to the Prussian emperor, Frederick William. A dreamy, indecisive man who eventually went insane, the king denounced the offer of the Frankfurt Assembly, proclaiming that he did not want a throne which came from an elected assembly, or as he described it, "a crown from the gutter." He expressed his disdain in a letter to Baron von Bunsen:

• • • *But the crown you unfortunately wear dishonors one unimpressibly, stinking as it does of the Revolution of 1848, the silliest, most stupid, and the wickedest, if not, thank God, the most disastrous of the century. Such a fictitious coronet baked out of mud and clay is to be accepted by one who is the legitimate King by the grace of God, and that, too, by a King of Prussia who had the happiness of wearing, if not the most ancient, at all events, the noblest crown, and one that was not stolen by anybody.*[10]

Reaction in Germany. The plan for unity under Prussian leadership had failed. Moreover, the prestige of the Frankfurt Assembly was shattered by its support of the actions of the Prussian king regarding revolts in Schleswig and Holstein, two largely German-speaking provinces of Denmark. When the Danish army occupied Schleswig-Holstein, the Assembly of Frankfurt commissioned Frederick William to send Prussian troops to liberate them, but pressure from Britain and Russia forced him to conclude an armistice and withdraw his troops.

The German people, intoxicated with nationalism, regarded the withdrawal as a betrayal, and when the Frankfurt Assembly agreed to the armistice, the working classes of Frankfurt declared the liberal representatives traitors and invaded the meeting hall of the Assembly. When the middle-class members of the assembly relied on Prussian and Austrian soldiers to dispel the mob, they

The Frankfort Assembly was unable to unify the German people, and was replaced by a revitalized Hohenzollern monarchy.

were thus alienated from the working class and never recovered their prestige or authority.

The revolt, combined with Frederick William's refusal to accept the crown, ended the dream of a united, liberal Germany. The failure of the Frankfurt Assembly and the military power of the Prussian army restored the Prussian Hohenzollern monarchy. The king undertook a reactionary policy, with new restrictions on freedoms of the press and assembly. He preserved the power of the Prussian nobility—the Junker class—and the army. When unity came to Germany in 1870–71, it was through the military might—"blood and iron"—and the diplomatic genius of the conservative Otto von Bismarck (Chapter 15).

[10] Raymond Stearns, *Pageant of Europe*, pp. 599–600.

SUMMARY

In the first half of the 19th century, revolutions wracked Metternich's Europe, culminating in the revolutions of 1848. The revolutionaries were motivated by the ideals of nationalism and of limited democracy, and in many places, middle-class liberals and members of the working classes briefly acted in unison. Their inability to maintain unity was an important factor in the failure of the revolutions across Europe.

Instead, the forces of reaction were victorious in the aftermath of 1848. Although some reforms occurred, the regime of Napoleon III in France approximated dictatorship; the Hohenzollerns in Prussia reasserted their power; the Hapsburgs continued to rule Austria; and the unification of Italy created a constitutional monarchy under the leadership of the House of Savoy. Yet nationalism remained a driving force throughout the continent and democratic ideals were only stifled, not destroyed.

QUESTIONS

1 What were the underlying principles of the peace settlement achieved at the Congress of Vienna?
2 Who were the important people at the Congress of Vienna? What influences did they have on the settlement?
3 Evaluate the effectiveness of the Concert of Europe.
4 What caused the revolutions of 1848? What were the primary goals of the revolutionaries? Why did these revolutions fail?
5 Describe the philosophy of the reactionaries who came to power in Europe in the wake of the events of 1848.
6 What are the major factors contributing to the history of political instability in France?

BIBLIOGRAPHY

ARTZ, FREDERICK B. *Reaction and Revolution, 1814–1832.* New York: Harper & Row, 1966. *A survey of the Congress of Vienna and its aftermath.*

BRINTON, CRANE. *The Lives of Talleyrand.* New York: Norton, 1963. *Crane Brinton has captured the essence of this influential man and his long career in French politics.*

EYCK, FRANK, ed. *The Revolutions of 1848–49.* New York: Barnes & Noble, 1972. *This work provides an overview of the most complex series of events in modern European history—the revolutions of 1848–49—primarily through documents of the day.*

MAY, ARTHUR J. *The Age of Metternich, 1814–1848.* New York: Holt, Rinehart, 1963. *This slim volume provides an overview of the years of Metternich's dominance of Europe.*

NICOLSON, HAROLD. *The Congress of Vienna: A Study in Allied Unity, 1812–1822.* New York: Viking Press, 1967. *This is one of the standard studies in the diplomatic history of the period: the author is particularly effective in capturing the personalities of the leading figures.*

SCHWARZ, HENRY F., ed. *Metternich, the "Coachman of Europe": Statesman or Evil Genius.* Boston: D. C. Heath, 1962. *Eight essays reflecting the various historical interpretations of the controversial Metternich.*

13

● *My song is of that city which*
Has men too poor and men too rich;
Where some are sick, too richly fed,
While others take the sparrows' bread;
Where some have beds to warm their bones,
While others sleep on hard, cold stones,
That suck away their bodies' heat.

W. H. DAVIES

Victorian Britain: A Century of Reform

The leading ideas of the 19th century produced a sweeping reform movement which radically altered British society. These reforms occurred in part in response to the French Revolution, which had introduced the radical social concepts of equality, fraternity, and liberty. The reform movement also took place within the context of the Industrial Revolution that began in England in the 18th century. During the early years of the Industrial Revolution, industrialists could pay very low wages, require 80-hour work weeks, employ children as young as five years, and ignore the hazardous and unhealthy environment of the textile mills and coal mines they operated. Forbidden by law to unionize, bargain collectively, or to strike, the workers had no means whereby they might improve their standard of living or their conditions of work. Many resorted to drunkenness, prostitution, or crime in the face of unremitting poverty.

EARLY REFORM During the 19th century, the two leading political factions, Whig and Tory, evolved into full-blown political parties, *Liberal* and *Conservative*, each with its own political ideology.

Liberal political philosophy emphasized the concepts of individualism, humanitarianism, and the need for state intervention to achieve progress that would benefit the largest number of people. Conservatives took a slightly different stance in their espousal of "Tory paternalism," which suggested the need for the upper classes to protect the lower classes from exploitation but which did not propose any substantial change in the hierarchal order of society.

The reform movement in Britain was a slow, step-by-step process over more than a century during which the extension of the vote and many pieces of social legislation brought industrial democracy to Britain. The first instance of reform occurred under aristocratic Tory leadership.

REFORM FROM ABOVE
English participation in the wars against Napoleon brought depression, unemployment, and heavy taxation. This caused unrest and increasing violence, including riots by the *Luddites*, unemployed workers who sabotaged factory machinery because they blamed the Industrial Revolution for their hard times. In 1816, the rioting of a large

The Peterloo Massacre of 1816. Government cavalry soldiers charge into a crowd which had gathered to hear a call for parliamentary reform.

crowd required police action to quell the disturbance. Soon after, the March of the Blanketeers, unemployed Manchester workers who had initiated a march on London, was halted by government police forces.

The most serious riot, the Peterloo Massacres, occurred in 1819, when a large crowd of about 60,000 people gathered at St. Peter's Field in Manchester to hear the radical Henry Hunt speak on the need for parliamentary reform. When local magistrates ordered cavalry units to arrest Hunt, the cavalry charged into the crowd, killing 11 and wounding many more. The government response to this unrest was repressive: the Habeas Corpus Act was suspended, and limitations on freedom of assembly and the press were imposed.

The emergence in the 1820s of young, reform-minded Tories soon led to several important reforms. Sir Robert Peel (1788–1850), the Home Secretary, led revision of the harsh criminal code, abolishing the death penalty for over 100 offenses. He also organized the first professional police force in London, popularly known as the "bobbies." In 1828, Protestant Dissenters received full civil rights, and the next year, the Catholic Emancipation Act gave political rights to the nation's Roman Catholics. The fact that Tories initiated these reforms was important because it meant that there was a base for political change within both of Britain's major parties.

THE REFORM ACT OF 1832

The return to power of the Whigs brought still more reform legislation. The first was the *Reform Act of 1832*, which extended voting rights and redistributed seats in the

239

The king signs the Reform Act of 1832, which redistributed seats in the House of Commons according to census results.

House of Commons. Until 1832, voting for the House of Commons had been limited to landowners or leasers of land. Some of these eligible voters were tenants on the squires' estates, and since there was no secret ballot, the squires influenced the outcome by exerting pressure or distributing free beer. Moreover, the right to elect members bore no relationship to the population distribution. The coming of the Industrial Revolution had produced a population shift to the north and west of England, but growing cities like Manchester and Birmingham had no representatives in the House of Commons, while in rural areas, in so-called "rotten boroughs" where only a handful of people resided, there was full representation.

The 1832 Reform Act sought to remedy these problems. All boroughs with fewer than 2000 inhabitants were disenfranchised, and those with fewer than 4000 people lost one member. Sixty-five seats were added to give representation to the new boroughs.

Property qualifications were lowered, and a system of voter registration was introduced. This process led to the creation of county-level political party organizations.

The Reform Act of 1832 was not a democratic reform; only one in seven adult males were eligible to vote. Its primary significance was that popular pressure had forced its enactment, thereby opening a door to future democratization. The passage of this legislation was temporarily blocked by the House of Lords, but pressure from the House of Commons forced the king to take an active part in the issue. He threatened to "pack" the House of Lords with new members if the bill was not passed—thus establishing a precedent which was eventually utilized to destroy the power of the House of Lords.

SOCIAL AND INDUSTRIAL REFORMS

During the same period as the passage of the Reform Act, slavery was abolished. In 1772, slave-holding had been made illegal in Britain, and in 1807 the slave trade was abolished. Under the leadership of William Wilberforce and other abolitionists, legislation was enacted in 1834 which outlawed slavery everywhere in the British Empire.

In a similar humanitarian vein, the 1833 Factory Act addressed the problem of child labor. Employment of children under the age of nine was forbidden. For children 9–13 years old, the working day was limited to nine hours and each child was required to receive two hours of schooling per day. Those aged 13–18 were limited to 12 hours of labor, and inspectors were appointed to enforce the law. Subsequent factory legislation encompassed further limits on working hours for women and children and included safety provisions.

Some reforms enhanced local governments. The Municipal Corporations Act of 1835 reorganized city governments, providing for elections of councilmen, who in turn elected aldermen and a mayor. This reform

During the 19th century, Malthus' gloomy predictions seemed to be borne out by scenes such as this one, of grimy, crowded tenements in London's East End. But a series of reforms successfully dealt with many of the social and economic problems caused by industrialization and a population explosion.

increased efficiency and democracy at the local level, and provided the basis for the development of public works—water, sewers, police protection—sorely needed throughout the country.

These early reforms also were extended to education. Although there was no public educational system, there had long been in existence "voluntary" schools for the wealthy. In 1833, the government for the first time extended money grants to voluntary schools, a first small step in acknowledging that education was the state's responsibility. Nevertheless, children of the working classes received little real education except in the Sunday schools, where some were

taught reading, writing, and religion. On the national level, fewer than 50 percent of the population could sign their own names.

Not all legislation directly served the interests of the working class. In 1834, in the face of increased poverty, the nation's Poor Law was amended to restrict the number of people eligible for aid. Now under the control of commissioners in London, assistance to the poor living at home was limited to the sick, aged, and children. Unemployed able-bodied men were required to live in workhouses apart from their families, provided only with barest necessities. The idea was to make life in the workhouses so unpalatable that even the lowest-paid work outside would seem desirable. Eventually this new system did decrease the number of paupers in Britain (one of every nine people in England and Wales in 1840), but it was a very unpopular act nevetheless.

VICTORIA (1837–1901) In 1837, the 18-year-old niece of King William IV, Victoria, succeeded him to the throne. She became Britain's longest-ruling monarch, reigning until her death in 1901. A very capable woman, Victoria believed strongly in her obligation and her duty to her subjects. Her attitude was indicated by her statement, "I will be good," on learning that she would inherit the throne.

THE YOUNG QUEEN

The queen was a lively, energetic woman, fond of animals, determined and headstrong. In her youth, she had been dominated by her mother, the Duchess of Kent, and her chief advisor, John Conroy, who sought power for himself. Once Victoria came to power, she took an active personal interest in politics, though she was greatly influenced by her ministers, especially Benjamin Disraeli.

In 1840, she married her first cousin, Albert of Saxe-Coburg. Albert was an upright, conscientious man, and the royal couple's life together with their nine children was often used by contemporaries to exemplify happy family life. Victoria's children were raised with high moral standards in the middle-class English tradition.

Prince Albert's premature death in December 1861, at the age of 42, left Victoria bereft, for although this had been a politically-arranged marriage, it had been a love match as well. She outlived him by 40 years, but mourned his death until her own in 1901. She lived a more secluded life, rarely appearing in public, and then always dressed in mourning garb. This extended self-imposed seclusion contributed to the decline in the power of the throne during her long reign.

THE VICTORIAN AGE

The *Victorian Age* to which the queen gave her name was a period which emphasized religious values, the strict observance of the sabbath, Bible study, family devotions, and worldwide missionary work. It stressed propriety in dress, manners, and morals. It was an era of optimism, faith in progress, and the notion of self-help to reach success.

The Great Exhibition of 1851, sponsored by Albert, is often viewed as the symbol of the age. The Crystal Palace, a glass and iron structure erected in Hyde Park, housed 14,000 exhibits of industrial skills and crafts from all nations of the world. The Exhibition was intended to be a manifestation of society's progress. Six million visitors came to witness this spectacular phenomenon, to marvel at the accomplishments of their time and to be made aware of Britain's preeminence in industry, commerce, and finance. Prince Albert's personal triumph was also Britain's opportunity to demonstrate the superiority of its system over all others.

The Victorian Age saw a flowering of English literature. The novels of social protest of Charles Dickens (1812–1870) brought the

Queen Victoria posed for this family portrait in 1848, 11 years after her accession to the throne.

conditions of the poor to the attention of the reading public. William Thackeray (1811–1863) showed the not-so-innocent side of the era in his depiction of the amoral, scheming Becky Sharp in *Vanity Fair*.

Poets such as Alfred Lord Tennyson (1809–1892) invoked pride in England's achievements. Tennyson wrote a paean to the Crystal Palace Exhibition that ended:

Steel and gold, and cool and wine
Fabric rough on fairy fine . . .
And shapes and hues of Art divine!
All of beauty, all of use,
That one fair planet can produce.[1]

THE DECLINE OF ROYAL POWER

During Victoria's reign, the powers of the monarchy were gradually reduced. In part this was the result of the ineffectual rule of the first three Georges of the 18th century. It was also the effect of the increased power of the House of Commons. By the end of Victoria's reign, the primary role of the monarch was to advise and consult with the leaders of Parliament.

Both crown and Parliament had long recognized that no prime minister could perform his administrative duties without the support of the House of Commons. The precedent was established that the monarch must choose as prime minister one who could command a majority in the House. Hence, while the monarch continues today to make the official appointment of the prime minister, none but the leader of the majority party in the Commons can in practice be named or be able to function as the prime minister. By such an unwritten process was the royal authority diminished. Victoria and her successors held the crown and the symbols of authority, but not the power.

---

[1] Nikolaus Pevsmer, *High Victorian Design: A Study of the Exhibits of 1851* (London: Architectural Press, 1951), p. 12.

MID-CENTURY BRITAIN

The decline of the monarchy coincided with the increasing importance of public opinion. Two popular movements, the Anti-Corn Law League and the Chartist Movement, dominated public affairs around mid-century.

THE ANTI-CORN LAW LEAGUE

The Anti-Corn Law League was organized by two members of Parliament, Richard Cobden and John Bright. The league was supported by manufacturers who opposed the tariffs on wheat (known in England as corn) that were imposed by the Corn Law. This law protected landowners' interests by forbidding

A demonstration against the Corn Law. Repeal of the law, in 1846, benefited urban dwellers, who paid less for wheat, rye, and other grains imported from abroad.

the importation of lower-priced grain. In its place, the reformers wanted free trade in order to lower food prices and to increase profits for industry, which would now be able to increase its exports in exchange for the expected food imports.

The Anti-Corn Law League campaign, which included millions of pamphlets, numerous public meetings, and popular agitation, coincided with the Irish potato famine of 1845. The famine, along with a period of excessive rain which ruined English wheat crops, created food shortages which helped the League's cause. The prime minister, Robert Peel, responded with a temporary suspension of the Corn Law, but in so doing split his party, for many Tories were landowners who supported tariffs and opposed repeal of the Corn Laws. This division in the Tory ranks paved the way for 20 years of Whig political domination.

The repeal was a significant victory for the basic economic principle of Victorian Britain, the policy of *laissez-faire*. The repeal was also a triumph for the industrialists over the landowners. British farmers lost

their markets, and British agriculture rapidly declined. By the turn of the century, Britain was forced to rely on foreign food imports. The Anti-Corn Law League, as a successful coalition of the middle and working classes, demonstrated the effectiveness of popular agitation, which the working classes were learning to use, and organized political pressure, which was an increasingly effective tool of the middle class. This partnership was not to last, however, for the working classes soon learned that to middle-class industrialists, lower food prices meant the possibility of paying lower wages.

THE CHARTIST MOVEMENT

The *Chartist Movement* was a product of working-class agitation. In 1838 William Lovett and Francis Place drafted the *Peoples' Charter*, which contained six demands: 1) universal male suffrage, 2) the secret ballot, 3) equal electoral districts, 4) payment of salaries to members of Parliament, 5) no property qualifications for members of Parliament, and 6) annual general elections. These demands constitute a 19th-century "liberalism," a term which, as we have seen, has meaning only within the context of its own time and place.

After a Chartist convention in London in 1839, the leadership submitted three successive petitions to Parliament incorporating their demands. The third petition contained two million signatures, but the Parliament ignored all of the Chartists' pleas for reform. Without substantial middle-class support, Chartism never really had a chance and the movement gradually died out. Nevertheless, by 1918, all Chartist demands except annual elections had become law.

THE CRIMEAN WAR

The dominant political figure at mid-century was Henry Palmerston ("Pam") (1784–1865), a former Tory who led Whig governments as prime minister from 1855 to 1858 and again from 1859 till his death. Having served in earlier years as the foreign secretary, Palmerston's primary interest was foreign policy and his politics reflected the attitudes of Victorian Britain. His belligerent patriotism and policy of brinkmanship won him popularity from the masses, who saw him as a vigorous promoter of British interests abroad.

It was Palmerston who led Britain into the Crimean War of 1854–1856. This conflict had its roots in the decay of the Ottoman Empire and in the Russian desire to control the straits that linked the Black Sea with the Mediterranean. From the English perspective, 19th-century Russian expansionism posed a threat to Britain's empire in India.

The immediate cause of the war was a clash between Roman Catholics and Greek Orthodox priests over the question of control of the Church of the Nativity in Bethlehem,

A cartoon from the British magazine Punch *satirizes Russia's claim to protect Christians in Turkish-controlled territories. Palmerston's fear of Russia's intentions led to British involvement in the Crimean War.*

TURKEY IN DANGER.

Florence Nightingale organized the distribution of medical and food supplies for the soldiers fighting in the Crimea. Due to her determined efforts, the lives of many wounded men were saved, and standards of the modern nursing profession were established.

in Turkish territory. France claimed the right to protect Catholic interests; Russia, Orthodox ones. The tsar of Russia, Nicholas I, moved into the Turkish-controlled principalities of Wallachia and Moldavia (later Rumania). By the end of 1853, Russia and Turkey were at war. After the Russian navy sank the Turkish Black Sea fleet, France and England declared war on Russia, in 1854.

The war itself was fought mainly in the Crimea, with an allied siege of the Russian naval base at Sebastopol that lasted 12 months. The lack of military organization of the allied forces, and the lack of medicine and hospital care for wounded British soldiers, were reported by the London *Times*. They were further dramatized by the work of Florence Nightingale, who organized an army medical corps.

245

The war ended in 1856 after Austria entered the war and forced the Russians to evacuate the provinces of Wallachia and Moldavia. By the Treaty of Paris, the independence of the Ottoman Empire was maintained. In addition, Russian warships were prohibited from the Black Sea, and Russia gave up its claim to protect Christians in the Ottoman Empire. From the British point of view, the Russian threat to India had ended.

GLADSTONE AND DISRAELI

Palmerston's death in 1865 marked the end of an era and introduced a new wave of reforms. Many were the product of two rival politicians, William Gladstone (1809–1898) and Benjamin Disraeli (1804–1881). Both were men of outstanding ability.

EARLY CAREERS

William Gladstone came from a family of wealth and privilege and received a typical upper-class education at Eton and Oxford. As a young man, he had taken an intense interest in religion and briefly considered entering the Anglican priesthood. He entered Parliament as a Tory in 1832, the first Parliament elected after the Reform Act. When the party split over the Anti-Corn Law League in 1846, Gladstone followed the prime minister, Robert Peel, in joining a faction of Whigs, Peelites, Radicals, and Chartists, which became known as the Liberal Party. Gladstone was a strong opponent of British imperialism and became the primary leader of the Liberal party from 1865–1894.

Considered a great orator, Gladstone brought with him a strong sense of duty and the determination to have a religious impact on politics. In fact, he undertook a private campaign to rescue prostitutes from their profession, frequenting unsavory areas of London at least once a week to offer them charity and moral support should they reform themselves. His behavior was consonant with the Victorian Age's focus on respectability and public morals. For relax-

A cartoon from Punch *characterizes Disraeli and Gladstone as "Rival Stars." Although their foreign policies were very different, each sponsored important reform legislation.*

RIVAL STARS.

Mr. Bendizzy (Hamlet). "'TO BE, OR NOT TO BE, THAT IS THE QUESTION;'—AHEM!"
Mr. Gladstone (out of an engagement). [Aside]. "'LEADING BUSINESS,' FORSOOTH! HIS LINE IS 'GENE[R]LITY!' IS THE MANAGER MAD? BUT NO MATTER-RR—A TIME WILL COME—"

ation Gladstone felled trees, and in his strong Parliamentary speeches often utilized woodcutting metaphors to drive home his points.

Benjamin Disraeli represented a sharp contrast to Gladstone. A British Jew who never practiced the religion of his birth, Disraeli was a man of no personal wealth, no political connections, and no university education. Flamboyant in style and dress, he was a prolific writer who penned several romantic novels.

Disraeli became one of England's greatest prime ministers, especially effective in his solicitous treatment of the queen. "Dizzy" became, by her account, the queen's friend:

• • • *When one's beloved husband is gone, and one's children are married—one feels that a friend . . . who can devote him or*

*herself entirely to you is the one thing you
do require to help you on—and to
sympathize entirely with you.*[2]

Disraeli, like Gladstone, had changed his politics during the course of his years in public office. He began his career in 1832 as a radical. Unlike Gladstone, Disraeli believed strongly that Britain should add to its power by taking over lands and peoples outside Europe, and it was he who proclaimed Victoria "Empress of India" in 1876. Disraeli's initiatives, both at home and abroad, gave an impression of activism on the part of the Conservative party, and kept it and Disraeli in power for seven years between 1868 and 1880.

DOMESTIC AND FOREIGN POLICY

The Reform Bill of 1867 was initially prepared by Gladstone, but Disraeli coopted the bill and successfully steered it through Parliament, thus "dishing the Whigs." This major act extended the vote to most urban adult males, nearly doubling the number of subjects eligible to vote. But in the election of 1868, the voters rewarded the Liberals, with Gladstone serving his first term as prime minister from 1868–1874.

Gladstone undertook a series of reforms to meet the demands of Britain's discontented Irish subjects. His first step was to disestablish the Anglican Church in Ireland; that is, the Irish Roman Catholic population was no longer required to support what they considered to be an alien church. Another grievance of the Irish derived from their positions as tenants on land owned by absentee landlords. If the tenant improved the land or property, the landlord could evict or raise rents without compensation for the improvements. In response to this injustice, Gladstone pushed through an Irish Land Act which made such a practice illegal. This act

was a milestone in the gradual process of securing Irish rights.

Other important reforms were enacted during Gladstone's first ministry. The Education Act of 1870 established a public elementary school system supported by government grants. Attendance for children between ages 5 and 13 was made mandatory in 1880. Equally important was the 1872 Ballot Act, which had been one of the Chartists' demands. This legislation was an indispensable step in the process of instituting fair, democratic elections. It introduced the secret ballot, which made it much more difficult for employers to intimidate their workers at the polls. The next year, the Judicature Act simplified the national court system. Significant reforms in the army and in government made both institutions more open to merit. The army reforms under the leadership of Edward Cardwell led to the organization of an effective reserve army and ended the sale of military commissions, while the Civil Service Act of 1870 introduced competitive exams for candidates for the civil service. These and several other lesser reform measures contributed to Gladstone's reputation and popularity insofar as domestic affairs were concerned, but his pacifist foreign policy met with public disapproval in an age when many Britons supported military imperialism.

In the elections of 1874, a Conservative government under Disraeli was voted in. In 1875, the prime minister bought the majority shares of Suez Canal stock, which had been owned by Egypt's ruler. This widely popular purchase guaranteed British control of the Suez Canal, a vital short-cut to the British empire in India.

Disraeli's willingness to take a leadership role at the Congress of Berlin in 1878, to settle the war between Turkey and Russia over their eastern interests, was enthusiastically supported by the English. A new term for militaristic policy—*jingoism*—was taken from this popular rhyme:

---

[2] Elizabeth Longford, *Queen Victoria: Born to Succeed* (New York: Harper & Row, 1964), p. 354.

We don't want to fight but by Jingo if we do,
we've got the ships, we've got the men,
and we've got the money too.[3]

Disraeli also sponsored sweeping reform measures. The first, the Public Health Act of 1875, systematized sanitation laws. The Artisan's Dwelling Act paved the way for slum clearance and the erection of new dwellings. The River Pollutions Act took a step toward cleaning rivers that had been fouled by industrial waste. A Factory and Workshop Act of 1878 revised and improved regulations regarding working conditions. These reform measures were small but important pieces of social legislation which represented a recognition, even by Conservatives, that the state must concern itself with matters of public safety and health. People living and working together in large numbers in cities needed a new kind of protection which had not been necessary in the more personalized, less crowded rural setting.

The voters returned Gladstone as prime minister in 1880. Two domestic issues dominated his second term in office. The first, the Irish problem, led Gladstone to attempt passage of an Irish house rule act which would have created a nearly independent Ireland. The Irish question led to a splintering of the Liberal party to the extent that one group of Liberal-Unionists joined Lord Salisbury, a Conservative, in 1886 to defeat Gladstone in the general election. Because of this failure to resolve the Irish question, independence for most of Ireland was only achieved in the early 1920s—not through the peaceful means which Gladstone had envisioned, but through violence and rebellion against British rule. Even then, the largely Protestant northern portion, Ulster, remained under British rule and does so to this day, triggering acts of violence and terrorism that continue to concern the British government and the people who live there.

---

[3] *Ibid.*, p. 413.

A march in Belfast protests the exactions of English absentee landlords. The Liberal Party's commitment to Home Rule in Ireland brought about its defeat in 1886.

The second issue was a further extension of the franchise. Before Gladstone's second term ended, the Liberals passed the Reform Act of 1884. It extended the vote to two million more Englishmen, those agricultural laborers who had not been included when the industrial working class had attained suffrage in 1867.

THE CREATION OF DEMOCRACY The two major franchise acts, in 1867 and 1884, created a new electorate, primarily among the lower classes. Although numerous factory acts had gradually improved the conditions of labor, the disparity between the upper and lower classes continued to exist in the cities. This chasm between the classes was even more apparent in the countryside, where there were few who could be categorized as middle class to stand between the large landowners and those who worked their lands as tenants or small farmers. Only when these newly enfranchised voters acted collectively—through an organized labor movement and through a political party which spoke on their behalf—could their conditions be improved significantly.

The first small step in working class organization occurred in 1824 when the Combination Act was repealed, making the formation of labor unions legal. But unionization was slow to follow. The socialist Robert Owen attempted to form a national union, the Second National Consolidated Trades Union, in 1834. Owen's union was quickly joined by 500,000 laborers, but internal wrangling destroyed it.

Subsequently, unions were mostly organizations of skilled craftsmen whose expertise gave them leverage to use against their employers. The first important union, the Amalgamated Society of Engineers, formed in 1852, set the pattern. The union's power was impeded until 1875, when picketing during strikes was finally allowed. In 1876, under the government of the Conservative Disraeli, collective bargaining was legalized for the first time, paving the way for more effective unions.

Unionization of unskilled labor and the effectiveness of the strike as a weapon was demonstrated in an important test case in 1888, when young women working in London match factories struck successfully. Public moral and financial support made

A strike by London matchmakers in 1888 brought to light the abysmal conditions under which unskilled laborers worked. A dockers' strike the next year brought about a movement toward unionization and the formation of the Labor Party.

their victory possible, but during the same period attempts to unionize agricultural workers failed. Their plight was not so obvious to the many people who lived in cities, and there was, therefore, less sympathy for those who worked on the land than for their fellows employed in the factories. Strong leadership was also generally lacking among agricultural laborers themselves.

In the 1880s two intellectual movements attempted to bring leadership to the union movement and the newly enfranchised voters. The first, the Socialist Democratic Federation (SDF), founded in 1881 by H. M. Hyndman and William Morris, adopted a Marxist program but attracted few followers. The second, the Fabian Society, founded in 1884, was a movement of intellectuals such as the economists Sidney and Beatrice Webb, the novelist H. G. Wells, and the playwright George Bernard Shaw. This non-Marxist socialist group was named after the Roman general Fabius, who during the Punic wars avoided head-on battle with the Carthaginian general Hannibal, relying instead on a war of attrition. These socialists adopted Fa-

bius' tactic of avoiding direct confrontation with capitalism, instead advocating slow reform of the existing system. They proved influential beyond their small numbers, for they were articulate propagandizers of their cause in pamphlets and plays.

In an attempt to unify the labor movement representatives of four groups—the SDF, the Fabians, the Independent Labor Party (ILP), founded in 1893, and union leaders—met in London in 1900. They formed the Labor Representative Committee, which became the nucleus of the Labor Party. This new party was now prepared to compete with the two existing parties, Liberal and Conservative, for national political leadership. Although they won 29 seats (out of over 600) in the election of 1906, and 42 in 1910, the Laborites' hopes of passing legislation which would improve the lot of their constituents were blocked by the power of the House of Lords, whose approval was required for legislation to be enacted. The Liberal Party, likewise frustrated by the Lords' power, was itself hopeful of maintaining the electoral support of England's working classes.

THE POWER OF THE HOUSE OF LORDS

In 1911, under the leadership of Prime Minister Henry Herbert Asquith, the Liberals succeeded in passing the Parliament Act, which essentially removed the power of the Lords to block legislation. To be enacted, this bill required the approval of the Lords, who were, naturally enough, reluctant to vote away their own power. This obstacle was overcome by King George V, who threatened to name new members who would support the Parliament Act. The Lords complied and approved the legislation.

The breaking of the power of the House of Lords was the penultimate step in the evolution of English democracy. Political power now lay in the hands of the House of Commons, an elected body, and all adult males who owned any property whatsoever were eligible to vote. (Domestic servants,

Beatrice and Sidney Webb were among the founders of the Fabian Society. This group hoped to bring about improvements for the working class in a peaceful way, by convincing those in power of the need for reform.

bachelors living with their families, and those with no fixed abode were still excluded from the vote.) The remaining step was the extension of the vote to women.

The effort to secure the vote for women in Britain was only one element in a broader effort to acquire female equality. The early leaders of the feminist movement reacted against a society which deprived them of equal status and which perceived them not as individuals but only as members of their sex. By law, women had been deprived of equal property and civil rights; by custom, they had been denied equal educational opportunities and access to public office.

Early Feminists. Many of the pioneers in the world feminist movement were English, and the feminist movement may be said to have begun with the publication of *A Vindication of the Rights of Women* by Mary Wollstonecraft in the late 18th century (Chapter 12). In her writing and by her own life, she sought the opportunity for personal achievement regardless of sex, and within the context of her own time, she was successful. During an era when most middle- and upper-class British women were dependent on men for their livelihood, Mary Wollstonecraft was a self-supporting writer.

Another British woman who made important contributions to feminism was Caroline Norton (1808–1877). Her unfortunate marriage to a brutal man led her to challenge English laws that assigned all property, income, and child custody rights to husbands regardless of their fitness. As a result of her persistence over many years, Parliament in 1857 enacted the Reform of the Marriage and Divorce Laws which gave wives deserted by their husbands the right to keep their own earnings, to inherit and bequeath property, to sue, to be sued, and to enter into legal contracts. After Caroline Norton's death, the Married Women's Property Act gave married women the same property rights as unmarried ones. But not until 1973 did parliamentary legislation give mothers the same legal authority as fathers over their children.

Two women, English by birth, were instrumental in establishing women in the medical profession. Elizabeth Blackwell (1821–1910) emigrated to the United States, where she became the world's first trained and registered female doctor. She then established the Infirmary Medical School for women in New York in 1868, the first such institution. Her contemporary, Florence Nightingale (1820–1910), established the nursing profession and helped open the first school of nursing in 1860.

Another English woman, Emily Davies (1830–1921), founded a college for women at Cambridge University. Indicative of the prevailing attitude toward equal education for women was a satiric poem published in *Punch*, a British publication which frequently lampooned social woes:

Emily Davies founded Girton College, the first English college for women, in 1869.

Oh pendants of these later days, who go on
    undiscerning
to overload a woman's brain and cram our girls
    with learning,
you'll make such a woman half a man. The
    souls of parents vexing,
to find that all the gentle sex this process is
    unsexing.
Leave one or two nice girls before the sex your
    system smothers,
or what on earth will poor men do for sweet-
    hearts, wives, and mothers?[4]

But Emily Davies persisted until Cambridge University established Girton College in 1869, as a college (not a "girls" school) within the university system. Women were allowed to sit for the same examinations taken by male students, although they were given certificates instead of degrees when they graduated. Not until 1921 were graduates of Girton permitted to claim the B.A. degree and not until 1948 were they granted full equality within Cambridge University. By contrast, Oxford University granted full equal status to women in 1919.

Josephine Butler (1828–1906) fought against another manifestation of the double sexual standard of her time, the Contagious Diseases Acts of 1864, 1866, and 1869. These laws required women suspected of prostitution to undergo an examination for venereal disease. Ms. Butler fought for repeal of these Acts because they implied that only the woman, not her male partner, was unclean and criminal. She contended also that women suspected of prostitution were denied their civil rights by this mandatory physical examination. The Contagious Disease Acts were repealed in 1886.

These four women—and untold hundreds of others—were by their efforts and strong convictions able to bring about change in 19th-century English society. Not all of them dubbed themselves as feminists; never-theless, they were pioneers in the feminist movement.

The Suffrage Movement. The most broad-based feminist campaign was the effort to secure the vote for English women. The *suffrage movement* continued throughout the last half of the 19th century, with thousands of women actively involved in the campaign for the vote. An early supporter of the movement, John Stuart Mill, adopted the cause in 1865 and on his election to the House of Commons in that year proposed the substi-

The suffragettes were often arrested when they staged public protests and demonstrations. Police interventions made the events newsworthy, and helped to focus attention upon their cause.

---

[4] Jill Liddington and Jill Norris, *One Hand Tied Behind Our Backs* (London: Virago, 1978), p. 65.

tution of the word "person" for "man" in a voting franchise bill. Few in the House supported him.

Subsequently, many local suffrage societies appeared throughout the country. In 1897, they formed a national organization, the National Union of Women's Suffrage Societies, under the leadership of Millicent Fawcett (1847–1929). Within this umbrella organization, women sought support by addressing meetings and collecting signatures on endless petitions—to no avail.

The suffrage movement was divided in 1903 when Emmeline Pankhurst (1858–1928) formed the Women's Social and Political Union, and, with the support of her daughters Sylvia and Christabel, adopted militant tactics. These women, called *suffragettes*, attracted newspaper coverage for their sensational activities. These included chaining themselves to a fence outside 10 Downing Street, the prime minister's residence.

One of the suffragettes' most effective tactics was to interrupt political meetings, especially during the election campaign of Liberal candidates in 1906, with the pointed question, "Will the Liberal government give the vote to women?" These disruptions usually led to arrest and imprisonment. When the suffragettes engaged in hunger strikes in jail, they were force-fed by prison authorities. The negative image of starving women led the Liberal government to introduce a measure that the suffragettes called "the Cat and Mouse Act" in 1913. This law permitted women close to starvation to be released from prison until they regained their health, only to be rearrested and jailed again.

One of the unfortunate victims of the militant movement was Emily Davison, killed when she threw herself in front of the king's race horse at the Derby in 1913. Such tactics did not bring the vote. The first vote for women over 30 was granted in 1918, primarily because of women's contributions to the war effort during World War I.

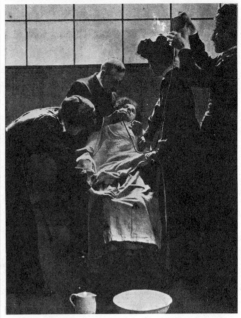

When suffragettes who had been jailed for their political activities went on hunger strikes, they were force-fed by prison authorities.

The extension of democracy in Great Britain could not be considered complete until women were given equal rights with men—at age 21. The Conservative government enacted this legislation in 1928, although some within the party continued to oppose it. As one of the cabinet members asserted:

• • • *I venture to say that the total sum of human happiness, knowledge and achievement would remain unaffected . . . If Sappho had never sung, Joan of Arc had never fought, Giddons had never played, and if George Eliot had never written.*[5]

On such an ambivalent note were women given the right to the franchise on the same terms as men, some 44 years after the Third Reform Bill.

---

[5] Second Earl of Birkenhead, F. G., *The Life of F. G. Smith, First Earl of Birkenhead* (London: Eyroe and Spothswoode, 1960), p. 159.

SUMMARY

The century of reform in Britain incorporated legislation that counterbalanced many of the negative effects of the Industrial Revolution. Moreover, the power of the throne was drastically limited, so that by the 20th century, the ruling monarch had become little more than an expensive figurehead. The limitation of the power of the aristocratic House of Lords, the extension of the vote to all adults, and the emergence of the Labor party were important political reforms which created the modern English democracy. These reforms were, in most cases, enacted as the result of public protest, mass movements, and occasional violence initiated by the more radical elements of society. The heritage of reform, with its roots in the 17th and 18th centuries, had provided both the precedent for reform and the political machinery which made peaceful change possible.

QUESTIONS

1 What were some of the problems that led to reform in 19th-century Britain?
2 What were the key characteristics of the Victorian age?
3 Trace the steps toward the establishment of a democratic system of government in England from 1832 to 1918.
4 Contrast the personalities and political policies of Gladstone and Disraeli.
5 Which reforms contributed to the improvement of the lot of the working classes in the 19th century? Why did the English take the lead in instituting reforms?
6 What gains did women make in 19th-century Britain? What obstacles did they face?

BIBLIOGRAPHY

FORSTER, MARGARET. *Significant Sisters: The Grassroots of Active Feminism.* New York: Knopf, 1985. The author's extensive research has unearthed much new material about eight British and American women who laid the foundations for the feminist movement.

HIMMELFARB, GERTRUDE. *The Idea of Poverty: England in the Early Industrial Age.* New York: Vintage Books, 1983. This lengthy monograph incorporates a discussion of the classical economists, the dissenters and reformers, and an analysis of the culture of poverty in the 19th century.

MAGNUS, PHILIP. *Gladstone: A Biography.* New York: E. P. Dutton, 1964. This biography includes an excellent, detailed discussion of British politics and of the character of the "great Gladstone."

MAUROIS, ANDRE. *Disraeli: A Picture of the Victorian Age.* New York: Time, Inc., 1965. This classic biography is unsurpassed by more recent studies in providing a sense of the flamboyant and unique personality of Disraeli and his role in 19th-century British history.

STRACHEY, LYTTON. *Eminent Victorians.* New York: Capricorn Books, 1963. Strachey provides devastatingly critical but very witty sketches of four prominent Victorians: Cardinal Manning, Florence Nightingale, Dr. Arnold, and General Gordon. As in his book on Victoria (listed below), Strachey reveals as much about the age in which he wrote—the 1920s—as about the Victorian era.

STRACHEY, LYTTON. *Queen Victoria.* New York: Harcourt Brace Jovanovich, 1921. Strachey's account of Queen Victoria remains among the best in conveying the flavor of the age and its prominent personalities. It also reflects Strachey's own age, the 1920s, with its cynicism toward the society's old institutions.

WOODHAM-SMITH, CECIL. *Queen Victoria.* New York: Knopf, 1972. This study is replete with details and pictures; a good counterbalance to Strachey's shorter and more negative portrait of the queen.

Nineteenth Century Russia: Reaction and Reform 1801–1894

The French statesman and author Alexis de Tocqueville, author of the text cited above, visited the United States for nine months in 1831–32. His *Democracy in America* is the classic account of the American way of life in the early years of the Republic. He never visited Russia, yet his comparison of Russia and America is both brilliant and prophetic.

Russia in the 19th century remained dedicated to the preservation of the status quo at a time when reform prevailed elsewhere in Europe. With some notable exceptions, domestic politics became fixed during the reign of Alexander I (1801–1825), and would not change appreciably until World War I. The emancipation of the serfs in 1861 failed to radically change Russia's social structure. Efforts to liberalize Russia's autocratic political system also met with little success, and the limited reforms that did take effect were rescinded during the last two decades of the century.

The Russian nobility had achieved a position of dominance during the reign of Catherine the Great, and this remained basically unchallenged throughout the 19th century. The main source of power, however, was still the tsar.

Despite the conservatism that prevailed, the 19th century would see the golden age of Russian literature, and a radicalizing of the Russian intelligentsia. In addition, the Industrial Revolution came to the Russian Empire in the last decade of the century.

19TH-CENTURY RUSSIA
At the beginning of the 19th century, 90 percent of the Russian people lived in rural areas. Approximately one percent of Russians were nobles, one percent were clergy, and four percent were the bourgeoisie who lived in towns of over 5000 population. Many of the professionals, including most bureaucrats, were non-Russians. Nearly all of the rest of the population consisted of serfs who worked either on state lands or lands belonging to the nobility.

Economically, Russia was still a nation dependent on agriculture. When the other nations of Europe began to industrialize, Russia fell significantly behind them in industrial output. It would continue to lag in this area for most of the 19th century.

ALEXANDER I (1801–1825)
Alexander I came to the throne after his fa-

ther, Paul, son of Catherine the Great, was murdered in a palace revolt. Paul was murdered by a group of conspirators that included the military governor of St. Petersburg and Alexander himself. Alexander claimed that murder was never part of the plan, and that his father was killed without his knowledge.

Alexander had been raised by his grandmother, Catherine, of whom he was a special favorite. Catherine the Great indoctrinated the boy in the ideas of the Enlightenment, choosing as his tutor a Swiss republican and revolutionary named Frederic La Harpe. Alexander was filled with the ideas of the philosophes; in his early years he was an enemy of serfdom and the aristocracy. But he learned almost nothing about the realities of Russian society. He was more comfortable speaking French and English than Russian. This gulf between Alexander and those he ruled created many problems for him.

The Napoleonic Wars and Their Effect. In 1812, Napoleon launched his invasion of Russia (Chapter 9). This invasion soured many Russian intellectuals and liberals on the ideals of the Enlightenment and the French Revolution. After 1812, Russian liberals lost their credibility with the tsar as the forces of reaction set in.

Russia emerged from the Napoleonic wars in a much strengthened position relative to the other major European powers. The crucial role played by Russia's 900,000-man standing army in Napoleon's defeat earned Alexander I a deference at the Congress of Vienna that had never before been accorded a Russian monarch. Alexander I saw himself as the protector of the status quo in Europe, and Metternich's helpmate in preserving the new peace.

Russia's borders with the rest of Europe were secure. Finland had become part of the Russian Empire in 1809. The Baltic states of Estonia, Latvia, and Lithuania, dominated by the German descendants of the Teutonic Knights, were firmly in the Russian camp.

Poland and the Polish people continued to serve as a buffer, although unwillingly, against any military threats from the west. To the south and east, the Ottoman Empire and China were too weak to pose any serious danger to Russian power.

A good deal of autonomy and freedom of expression were allowed in the recently conquered parts of the Russian Empire. Alexander made good on a promise to the Poles and permitted them to determine internal policy through a constitution and a national diet. Finland was also governed by its own diet. The Baltic region of the empire was made self-governing.

Autonomy of the outlying regions was due to a lack of trained government personnel rather than the ideals of 19th-century liberalism. Nevertheless, Russian peasants—imbued with a new sense of their worth after playing a leading role in the victory over France—began to be dissatisfied. All the new freedom seemed to be going to the non-Russians in the empire. Sentiments in favor of improving the lot of the Russian people began to grow.

Young Russian noblemen educated on the ideas of Voltaire, Rousseau, and Locke supplemented their book learning by traveling abroad to England, France, and the rest of Europe. After the defeat of Napoleon in 1815, allied armies occupied France for three years. Included in these occupation forces were 50,000 Russian troops, many of whom were noblemen who spoke French and were stationed in Paris. They discovered that the French had more freedoms and rights than they knew in Russia as members of the privileged aristocracy. In almost every respect, French civilization seemed superior.

Many army officers, on returning home, talked about a "new Russia" modeled on what they had seen and read about in the West. Secret societies were formed, with membership generally limited to a handful of young noblemen. After the secret handshakes and transfer of cryptic signs, they

The burning of Moscow during Napoleon's invasion of 1812. The Napoleonic campaign in Russia dramatically altered Russian views of Western society.

worked on a blueprint for reform in Russia. The Russian poet Alexander Pushkin expressed this desire for freedom:

We wait, our yearning hearts are beating
With hope of sacred liberty
As a youthful lover waits to see
The lagging hour of sweetheart-greeting.[1]

The more moderate elements favored a constitutional monarchy, while others supported a republic. All agreed that serfdom

---

[1] Nicolas Berdyaev, *The Origin of Russian Communism* (Ann Arbor: University of Michigan Press, 1962), p. 79.

had to be eliminated and that greater freedom was needed.

The Role of the Intelligentsia. Many of those interested in reform were part of a growing group in Russian society that came to be known as the *intelligentsia*. Unfortunately, the term *intelligentsia* defies exact definition. Its meaning within Russian society has changed over time. In the early 19th century, the intelligentsia were people who were educated and who usually came from the upper class. But more important than their social status was their attitude toward society. As defined by Richard Pipes, an American historian of 19th-century Russia:

. . . A member of the intelligentsia . . . is someone . . . more concerned with society at large, and willing, to the best of his ability, to work on society's behalf. . . . One's level of education and class status are of secondary importance. Although a well-educated and affluent person naturally is in a better position to understand what is wrong with his country and to act accordingly, it does not follow that he cares to do so. At the same time, a simple, semi-literate working man who makes an effort to grasp how his society functions and to work on its behalf does qualify.[2]

As the 19th century progressed, the intelligentsia increased in numbers and broadened its base by expanding into the lower classes. At the same time that the level of education among the intelligentsia declined, its members developed a heightened sense of social responsibility. By the 1870s, the intelligentsia had become more radicalized, providing much of the leadership for revolutionary movements in Russia.

Decembrist Revolt. The Decembrist revolt of 1825 provided the impetus for the growth of the Russian intelligentsia. The plotters, members of the secret societies, aimed to revolutionize the Russian system—the moderates wanting a constitutional monarchy, and the radicals favoring a republic. The death of Alexander in 1825 provided the plotters with their opportunity. The tsar had died without a legitimate heir and his brother Constantine had privately renounced his right to the throne in favor of a younger brother, Nicholas. In the days of confusion following Alexander's death, revolutionaries tried to install Constantine as tsar, believing that he would be amenable to their plans for reform. The conspirators were able to rally only a few troops from the St. Petersburg garrison. It is said that these muti-nous troops, hearing the slogan "Constantine and Constitution" believed that Constitution was the name of Constantine's wife. Most of the troops remained loyal to Nicholas, and the revolt quickly collapsed.

For all of its failings, the Decembrist revolt is the progenitor of all future Russian revolutions. The Decembrist movement gave rise to an ideal of *noblesse oblige*, that is, the duty of the upper classes and intelligentsia to sacrifice their lives, if need be, for the general good. All Russian revolutionaries from 1825 forward looked to the Decembrists for spiritual inspiration and justification.

NICHOLAS I (1825–1855)

Nicholas I was 30 years of age when he came to the throne in 1825. His childhood and adolescence coincided with the Napoleonic era, and his experiences convinced Nicholas that the philosophical principles of the Enlightenment and the French Revolution were to be avoided.

Domestic Policy. Nicholas believed that the mission of government and the tsar was to preserve the status quo. His policies reflected his belief that order and stability were the essential ingredients of a successful society. Nicholas' conservatism, in addition to blocking movements for reform, manifested itself in renewed support for religious orthodoxy, in his autocratic rule, and in glorification of Russian national culture. The reign of Nicholas I is epitomized by the slogan, "Orthodoxy, Autocracy, Nationality."

To Nicholas, the Church and state were coexistent and synonymous. Subjects who did not belong to the Russian Orthodox Church were suspected of disloyalty to "Mother Russia" and the tsar. Persecution of Russian Roman Catholics, Russian Jews, and all other nonorthodox groups became an official policy. All those living within the Russian Empire were expected to adopt Russian ways and to shed their separate ethnic identities.

---

[2] Richard Pipes, *Russia Under the Old Regime* (New York: Scribner's, 1974), p. 253.

Nicholas believed that he ruled Russia by divine right, and that therefore any criticism of the tsar or his government was the equivalent of a sin against God. To surrender any of the authority delegated to him by initiating reform, Nicholas believed, would be a crime against God's law.

The Decembrist revolt had a major impact on Nicholas I, and fueled his drive to rule Russia single-handedly. From 1825 on, Nicholas I kept a copy of the transcript of the confessions of the Decembrists at his bedside. It is said that he read from it every night. He was convinced that no one could be trusted, especially the nobles and the military, and he came to rely more heavily on the help of the middle class in ruling the country. Most of Nicholas' advisers, many highly capable, served him throughout his reign, providing Russia with a continuity of policy unparalleled in its history.

Changes did occur during Nicholas' reign, but these changes were intended to make the system more efficient rather than liberalize it. In the area of education, for example, Nicholas wanted all of his subjects to read and write so that they would be of more use to the state, and better able to obey written imperial edicts. However, as Sergei Uvarov, the minister of public instruction, so aptly phrased it, Nicholas was hoping to start a fire that would not burn. In other words, teaching the people to read and write might have the undesired effect of helping them to think on their own.

The most able of Nicholas' administrators was Michael Speransky. Former tsars had promised to bring the legal code up to date, but had failed to do so. Nicholas entrusted Speransky with this task. With the help of able assistants, in 1833 Speransky completed the tabulation of all Russian laws in 45 volumes.

Foreign Policy. Nicholas I was Metternich's willing pupil, eager to use the Russian army to help preserve legitimate regimes

The reign of Nicholas I began during the crisis of the Decembrist revolt in 1825, and ended under the cloud of the Crimean War in 1855. Here, he is shown quelling a riot inspired by a cholera epidemic.

anywhere in Europe. On occasion, Nicholas' enthusiasm had to be contained even by the conservative Metternich. When rebellion broke out in Belgium in 1830, Nicholas planned to send a Russian army across Europe to put down the revolt. The English, among others, were alarmed at the prospect of a Russian army massed just across the English Channel. Fortunately, Metternich talked Nicholas out of this rash plan.

Russia became involved in two conflicts with the Ottoman Turks during the reign of Nicholas I. The first instance was the Greek war for independence which began in 1821. Nicholas vacillated in his policy toward the war. He sympathized with the rebels because of their Orthodox Christian beliefs. On the other hand, his foreign policy was predicated on support for legitimate regimes. In the end, a third factor—Russian territorial ambitions in the Ottoman Empire—caused Nicholas to enter the war on the side of the Greeks. By the Treaty of Adrianople (1829), Russia received the right to maintain troops in the two Balkan principalities of Wallachia and Moldavia. Russia also gained control of the mouth of the Danube River, and control over the eastern shore of the Black Sea.

In 1853, Nicholas began to press for new concessions from the Ottoman Turks. These centered around a request for the right to protect Orthodox Christians who lived in the Ottoman Empire. Underlying this surface aim was Nicholas' dream of dividing the Ottoman Empire among the major European powers. After Nicholas moved large numbers of troops into Wallachia and Moldavia, the Ottomans declared war. They were joined soon after by Britain and France, both of whom felt threatened by Russia's designs in the Middle East.

The Crimean War laid bare serious flaws in the Russian social system. Russian armies, consisting mostly of poorly trained illiterate Russian peasants, were no match for the advanced technology and modern armies of western Europe. Within two years, Russia was suing for peace.

The Crimean War seriously weakened Russia and had major consequences for that nation's future foreign policy. At the Treaty of Paris of 1856, which ended the war, Russia lost the western shore of the Black Sea, its influence in the principalities of Wallachia and Moldavia, and the right to maintain a Black Sea war fleet.

After 1856, while their domestic policies remained conservative, Russian leaders followed a revisionist foreign policy. They pursued any course of action that promised to reverse the provisions of the Treaty of Paris. Russia, for example, supported the efforts of Bismarck to unify Germany under Prussian domination, because Bismarck promised to lend diplomatic support to Russia's efforts to regain her lost territory. Russian leaders of the 20th century were to regret this policy, for it placed a powerful and united Germany on Russia's western border.

Westernizers and Slavophiles. In the

1840s, the intelligentsia split over the question of what should be the future direction of Russia. A group who were known as the *Slavophiles* believed that the Russian people should look inward and emphasize those institutions that were uniquely Russian, such as the tsar and the Russian Orthodox Church. The *Westernizers* argued that Russia was a part of Europe, and that it was time for Russia to catch up with the West by adopting western institutions. Both Slavophiles and Westernizers had left and right wings, and on some issues, such as the abolition of serfdom, there was common agreement.

Alexander Herzen (1812–1870), the father of Russian socialism, attempted to reconcile the divergent views of the Slavophiles and the Westernizers. Herzen had been inspired in his youth by the revolt of the Decembrists. He spent most of his life in exile in Paris and London, where he issued radical publications intended for circulation in Russia.

Alexander Herzen, the father of Russian socialism, was one of the many Russian intellectuals who spent their most productive years in exile. Others were banished to Siberia.

After the failure of the revolutions of 1848, Herzen decided that socialism had a better chance of prospering in Russia than in the capitalist West. By stressing native Russian collective institutions such as the *Artel* (producer's cooperatives), and the *Mir* (peasant communes), Herzen won the admiration of the Slavophiles. And by continuing to advance basic individual rights such as freedom of speech, and remaining hostile to the autocratic authority of the tsar and the Russian Orthodox Church, Herzen retained the support of the Westernizers.

REFORM AND REACTION

Westerners and Slavophiles shared a common interest in reforming Russia. Also, Russia's crushing defeat in the Crimean War made all patriotic Russians enthusiastic reformers, if reform would regain for Russia its status as a major European power.

ALEXANDER II (1855–1881), "THE TSAR LIBERATOR"

Alexander II came to the throne in 1855, during the Crimean War. At the time of his accession people thought the new tsar would do little more than continue the reign that Nicholas had begun. Alexander had been extremely loyal to his father, and had actively participated in carrying out a number of Nicholas' repressive measures. However, he soon earned a reputation as a liberal reformer. The basis of that reputation was the liberation of the serfs.

The Emancipation of the Serfs. By the time Alexander II became tsar, the abolition of serfdom was an idea whose time clearly had come. Economically, serf labor, especially in industry, was inefficient when compared to the free work force of the West. Even Nicholas I, one of the most autocratic tsars, had started freeing serfs on state-owned lands. He formed committees to study the effects of gradual emancipation, and he appointed his son Alexander as a working member of several of these study groups.

Alexander II was hailed as the "tsar-liberator" in the early years of his reign, but later adopted a more reactionary policy in response to the growing militancy of radical groups.

There was no mistaking the sense of urgency in Alexander's voice when he said to the assembled nobles in an address in 1856, "It is better to abolish serfdom from above than to wait until the serfs begin to liberate themselves from below."[3]

By an imperial ukase in 1861, serfdom in the Russian empire was abolished. This decree emancipated 20 million peasants; they were now subjects of the empire rather than chattels of their landlords. No longer could they be forced to do unpaid labor for their former masters.

To think of Alexander II simply as a liberal reformer is to miss the point. All his life Alexander remained a conservative. He was not trying to destroy the autocratic system that he headed—rather, he was trying to preserve that system by making it more efficient, modern, and rational through the elimination of an outdated and unworkable institution. Alexander was able to accomplish what his predecessors failed to achieve because the time was right.

Although the landlords had to surrender some property to their former serfs, they kept about one-half, often the choicest parcels. The confiscated land did not go directly to the peasants, but rather to the peasant commune, or *Mir*. Landlords were compensated for their loss of property through the issuance of government bonds. Through their Mir, peasants were given 49 years to redeem the government bonds.

The emancipation of 1861 produced mixed results. Serfdom was gone, but the economic burden on the peasants was as heavy or heavier than before 1861. Peasants continued to be taxed, while they now had the additional obligation of collectively repaying the government bonds.

Also, for the first time, the Russian nobility's wealth was measured in paper rather than land. Boyars traded their government bonds for gold in London, Amsterdam, and the other commercial markets of Europe. They spent much of their accumulated wealth in the cities of the West, or squandered it on frivolities back in Russia. The Russian autocratic state could no longer depend on the effective support of a vital and stable aristocracy.

Other Reforms of the 1860s. The law abolishing serfdom spawned a series of related reforms that had far-ranging significance for Russian society. Now that nobles no longer held or exercised direct responsibility in local matters, a new administrative system had to be devised. In 1864 a series of edicts established a new type of local government, known as the *Zemstvo*. The Zemstvo assembly had limited powers to tax or make laws, and it was dominated by the property-owning classes. It provided for local welfare and

---

[3] *Ibid.*, p. 411.

education; most importantly, it was a training ground for democracy and self-government. On a national level, Zemstvo congresses were a sounding board for more radical ideas, and a preparatory school for future revolutionaries.

Also, overhaul of the legal system was needed now that the nobility no longer served both as judge and jury in local disputes. For the first time in Russian jurisprudence, everyone was equal before the law, there was trial by jury, and a distinction was made between civil and criminal cases.

The introduction of a court system created a need for lawyers, virtually a new profession in Russia. Since there was no censorship in the courts, and newspapers were allowed to print court proceedings in their entirety, court trials became a popular forum for criticizing the government. Unlike the legal profession in most countries, Russian lawyers often were the most articulate and radical opponents of government policy. The law schools served as a breeding ground for future revolutionaries.

The army also underwent reform—so much so that by 1877 when Russia once again went to war with the Ottoman Turks, the newly organized and trained Muscovite batallions made short work of their Turkish counterparts.

CONSERVATIVE REACTION The reforms of the early 1860s seemed to open a new chapter in Russian history. It was hoped that the abolition of serfdom would transform the peasant and Russian society. One landlord exclaimed that the emancipation had given peasants an entirely new outlook on life: "The people are erect and transformed: the look, the walk, the speech, everything is changed."[4]

---

[4] R. R. Palmer and Joel Colton, *A History of the Modern World*, 5th ed. (New York: Knopf, 1978), p. 526.

Alexander II's reforms spread beyond the borders of Russia proper into outlying parts of the empire, including Poland. However, the relaxation of the Draconian policies of Nicholas I towards Poland led to a demand for more rights and, ultimately, to open rebellion in 1863. With encouragement from Prussia, Alexander quickly extinguished the rebellion, but the shock waves lasted considerably longer. The belief that reform leads to violence, anarchy, and possibly revolution became widespread throughout the higher echelons of Russian society.

ALEXANDER III (1881–1894)

The conservatism engendered by the Polish rebellion was intensified after the accession of Alexander III. His reign set in motion a counterrevolutionary reaction which guided government policy until the revolution of 1917.

Reforms Overturned. On March 1, 1881, while Alexander II was returning to the palace from a parade, a bomb was thrown at his sleigh. Several members of Alexander's escort were wounded, and Alexander jumped out to attend them. Then another bomb exploded and mortally wounded him.

Although Alexander II had been following a policy of retrenchment rather than reform since the 1860s, many conservatives were still hostile towards him. They were convinced that his liberal policies had weakened the government. Alexander III was dedicated to eradicating the remains of his father's reforms, except for emancipation. Universities were purged of liberal professors, matriculation was limited to the wealthy and those of noble birth, and there was a tightening of censorship. Government funds for the Zemstvos were all but eliminated, and the "Third Section" (the government's secret police, established by Nicholas I) was revitalized and expanded.

Persecution of Minorities. Religious persecution returned to Russia with a vengeance under Alexander III. In the 1860s, the re-

were also pacifists, devised unusual methods of protesting religious persecution: they would burn down barns and, on occasion, walk naked down the main street of the nearest town.

Finland had been an uncomplaining member of the Russian Empire since 1809. Alexander III's plans for Russifying the empire cost Finland much of her autonomy, including the use of the Finnish language in the schools and courts. As a result, the Finns seized every opportunity to put some distance between themselves and their Russian masters.

GROWTH OF REVOLUTIONARY MOVEMENTS
Many among the Russian intelligentsia grew more committed to the ideals of reform. Alongside the conservative movement, in

forms of Alexander II had been a moderating influence on the anti-Semitism that had been a problem in Russia for centuries. Some Russian Jews had begun to hope that for the first time they would be allowed to enter into the mainstream of Russian society.

But in the 1880s, anti-Semitism became official government policy. A series of violent *pogroms*—government-sponsored attacks on those of the Jewish faith and their property—took place in the Ukraine. The May Laws of 1882 restricted Jewish settlement to southwestern Russia, established a quota system for Jews at the universities and high schools, and confiscated property, especially that of Jews living in the urban centers. These policies forced many Russians of the Jewish faith to flee their homeland, taking their talents and skills with them. Many others who stayed in Russia took up the cause of revolution.

Other religious groups also felt the wrath of Alexander III's policies. In Poland, it became illegal to convert people to Roman Catholicism, or for the Church to buy land. A group called the *Dukhbors*, farmers who

One manifestation of Alexander III's Russification policy was persecution of the Jews within the empire. As a result, thousands emigrated during the 1880s, and others became involved in revolutionary movements. This view of the pograms is by the American cartoonist Thomas Nast.

LIVE AND LET LIVE IN RUSSIA.
"Your money, Jew, or your life!"—*The cry for ages.*

part in response to it, a number of radical revolutionary movements sprang up.

Nihilism. One of the earliest of these mid-century revolutionary movements was **nihilism**. The definition of a nihilist is "one who destroys all in order to rebuild." Indeed, nihilists did call for an overturn of most of the values of earlier generations. They espoused free love, equality of the sexes, liberated styles of dress, and communal living. In his novel *Fathers and Sons*, Ivan Turgenev (1818–1883) painted a picture of a typical nihilist—his hero, Bazarov, who takes as his credo "two plus two is four and everything else is rubbish."

However, some nihilists believed in the use of reason and the scientific method to solve social problems. They wanted to know the facts, how something works, and what needs to be changed in order to make it work better. Some preferred to see change come from the top down in an orderly and peaceful manner. Nikolai Chernyshevski, a nihilist leader of the 1860s, viewed Turgenev's portrait of Bazarov as a caricature. Still, nihilists were, by and large, extremists.

Anarchism. Closely related to the nihilists in their beliefs were the **anarchists**. Michael Bakunin (1814–1876), one of the best known anarchists of the 1860s, called on the Russian people to free themselves from the shackles of the Church, family, property, and the state. He urged them to take up arms and destroy the government. Bakunin was typical of most Russian anarchists in his espousal of violence.

Since anarchists were opposed to all but the most minimal societal structure and organization, they had difficulty organizing opposition to the government. Also, they had only sketchy plans for what to do after the government was overthrown. Bakunin, for example, advocated the establishment of local free communities.

Populism. Of all the socialist movements of the late 19th century, **populism** had the greatest mass appeal. Thousands of well-intentioned young aristocrats, in addition to some of the daughters and sons of the urban bourgeoisie, went to live and work among the Russian peasants in the hope of bringing the light of knowledge and an awareness of the need for reform to their less fortunate countrymen. This movement to go and live among the peasants was known as the *Narodniki* ("Going to the People") *movement*. It was a noble enterprise, and those involved had the highest expectations for success. As one activist woman wrote:

• • • [*Our goal is*] *to elevate the people's psychology by our own example, and give them the idea of a purer life by making them acquainted with better morals and higher ideals; to call out their best feelings and strongest principles. We ought to tell the truth, not fearing to displease our hearers; and be always ready to confirm our words by our deeds.*[5]

But their high expectations were not realized. Most Russian peasants were respecters of tradition, and suspicious of those from the outside. The peasants did not know what to make of these young people with new clothes, soft, uncalloused hands, and sallow complexions which belied their claim to be fellow toilers of the earth. It did not take the peasants long to make up their minds, and those strangers who were not driven out of the village were handed over to the police. Large numbers of Narodniks went to jail. There they made friends and contacts that resulted in the formation of more militant revolutionary groups.

Originally the populists had believed that the Russian peasant, who lived simply and close to the earth, possessed an intrinsic goodness and humble wisdom. They believed that the salvation of the nation lay in

---

[5] Catherine Breshkovsky, *The Little Grandmother of the Russian Revolution: Reminiscences and Letters*, ed. Alice Stone Blackwell (Boston: Little, Brown, 1918), pp. 329–30.

tapping that vast wellspring of simple virtue. However, those who participated in the "Going to the People" movement learned that the peasants were not the "noble savages" previously imagined. Most activists became convinced that the government would have to be captured by violent means.

Although the winds of conservatism were blowing strong by the end of the 1860s, the views of activist populists were shared by many Russians. It should also be noted that by the 1870s, radical, revolutionary sentiment was growing stronger among those committed to the populist cause. Several revolutionary groups formed. One of these was the extremist group known as People's Will, which was organized in the summer of 1879. The People's Will advocated the use of terrorist tactics to overthrow the tsar, and its members were responsible for the assassination of Alexander II.

The Revolutionary Women. The appeal of the populist movement was such that for the first time in Russian history, large numbers of women became political activists.

Emancipation of the serfs helped to break down the Russian patriarchal social system and awaken in Russian women a demand for social equality. Denied access to universities at home, middle- and upper-class Russian women traveled to western Europe in search of a formal education. Most returned to Russia in the hope of advancing the cause of feminism. By the mid-1860s, women were playing an increasingly prominent role in many of the radical movements. Approximately 15 percent of all individuals arrested for political crimes in Russia between 1873 and 1879 were women. Sofia Perovskaia, for example, the first woman to be executed for a political crime in Russia, had played a leadership role in the successful plot to assassinate Tsar Alexander II in 1881. It was in the less violent but still militant Narodniki movement, however, that Russian women had their greatest impact.

THE RUSSIAN CULTURAL RENAISSANCE

In the 19th century, Russia experienced a cultural renaissance. The years between 1820 and 1880 are known as the golden age of Russian literature. The success of Russian writers was mirrored, although to a lesser degree, in art, history, philosophy, and music.

At first glance, it is incongruous that such a burst of creative energy would begin during the reign of Nicholas I, one of the most autocratic tsars. During the first half of the 19th century, in particular, the intelligentsia found the traditional avenues of creative expression in Russia closed to them. But ineffective methods of censorship allowed for a steady, although illegal, supply of books and ideas from the West. This, in turn, encouraged the growth of an underground literature and clandestine discussion groups; a tradition which continues in Russia up to the present day with a subterranean genre of literature known as "Samizdat."

Two of Russia's most acclaimed writers

Vera Figner was one of a growing number of Russian women who became involved in revolutionary groups. Her leadership role in the People's Will earned her a 20-year sentence in solitary confinement.

in the first half of the 19th century were the poet Alexander Pushkin (1799–1837), and the satirist and social critic Nicholai Gogol (1809–1852). Pushkin's father was a Boyar aristocrat, and his mother was the granddaughter of an Abyssinian prince. Pushkin received a French classical education in the tradition of the Enlightenment. His poetry was known for its classical elegance, yet also for the breadth of its sympathies. Pushkin wrote about life in provincial Russian society, and is considered to be the originator of realism in Russian literature. Pushkin's greatest work, the verse-novel *Eugene Onegin*, established one of the principal themes in Russian fiction—that of the unfulfillment of aristocratic provincial life. He has often been called the Russian Shakespeare.

Nicholai Gogol's father was a small land-owner in the Ukraine, and Gogol drew his inspiration from the Cossacks and peasants that he knew so well in his youth. In the play *Inspector General*, Gogol satirizes the provincial bureaucracy. His greatest work is *Dead Souls*, a devastating condemnation of the institution of serfdom and of the land-holding nobility. The hero of the story, Chichikov, travels throughout the Russian countryside buying for a pittance from local lords the useless contracts of their dead serfs. Since serfs are property and could be put up as collateral for a loan, Chichikov uses his bogus contracts to borrow money, which he then invests wisely, becoming a millionaire.

Populism in the Arts. The decades of reform and reaction were also a fertile period in the arts. Writers and musicians were deeply influenced by the political developments of the times, and populist themes are prominent in their works.

In the 1860s a school of music developed that sought to create a new popular style of music, one that drew its inspiration from the sounds and rhythms of human speech and the folk music of the Russian people. Those who involved themselves in the group included Alexander Borodin (1833–1887), Ni-

Nicholai Gogol's surrealistic novels portrayed the nightmarish inefficiency and corruption of the Russian bureaucracy. His "inspector general" was widely recognized as a parody of real-life bureaucrats in the tzar's service.

kolai Rimsky-Korsakov (1844–1908), and Modest Mussorgsky (1839–1881). In true populist spirit, a number of musicians prided themselves on their lack of formal training and lived together in a commune.

Foremost among the new school of composers was Mussorgsky, who made a significant contribution to the growing body of native Russian operas. His most famous opera, *Boris Gudonov*, took a story from Pushkin in which the focus had been on the Tsar Boris and made it into a tale depicting the plight of the Russian people.

The most popular Russian composer of this time was Peter Tchaikovsky (1840–1893). He also used Russian themes and the works of Russian authors such as Pushkin for his inspiration. His operas *Eugene Onegin* and *The Queen of Spades* are based on Pushkin's stories. Tchaikovsky mastered all the forms of music, and his pieces have become part of the standard musical repertory of Western orchestras. In addition, he composed music for the ballet, which the Russians were bringing to a peak of perfection during this period. His scores for *Swan Lake* and *The Nutcracker* are among the best-loved of all ballet music.

Another artist whose work reflected populist concerns was the great Russian nov-

elist Fyodor Dostoyevsky (1821–1881). Many populists were convinced that there was something of unique value deep in the soul of the Russian peasant, and much of Dostoyevsky's work reflects this concept. Early in his career, Dostoyevsky was fascinated by the splits and contradictions he saw in people's souls—the simultaneous existence of good and evil, the struggle between feeling and intellect. In such works as *Notes from the Underground* and *Crime and Punishment* he explores these themes.

In his later works, Dostoyevsky searched Russian society to find a source of redemption for its troubles. The main characters in his last novel, *The Brothers Karamazov*, all represent possible answers. The Grand Inquisitor represents that of political authority; Alyosha Karamazov represents that of traditional Christian faith; his brother Ivan, ra-

tionality. It is in the third Karamazov brother, however, that Dostoyevsky finds his answer. Dmitry Karamazov is a sensual, kindly, exuberant person. It is his spirit of loving life "more than the meaning of life" that the author sees as a source of renewal for Russia.

Another giant of Russian literature was Leo Tolstoy (1828–1910). After producing such masterpieces as *War and Peace*, an epic tale of Russian history, and *Anna Karenina*, a timeless exploration of the problem of family relationships, Tolstoy exchanged his aristocratic clothes for a simple peasant's shirt and confined his writing to simple moral tracts. It was only in such an existence, he thought, that a man could achieve real goodness and real happiness. For 30 years he

Russian agriculture did not benefit from the technology introduced in Europe during the 19th-century. As one consequence, peasants could not produce enough grain to feed a growing urban population.

preached a nonviolent moral revolution, a return en masse to the natural, simple farming life.

RUSSIA ENTERS THE 20TH CENTURY

In the late 19th century, Russian farmers were faced with a deepening agricultural crisis. Ukranian wheat, which was the only product that Russia had in sufficient quantity to help offset its unfavorable balance of trade with the rest of Europe, could not compete with cheaper grain from Canada and the United States. Sufficient capital was not available to mechanize Russian farming. Even on the rare occasion when a tractor was available, Russian peasants, suspicious of anything new, would let it sit idle, admiring its color rather than its utility.

In the second half of the 19th century, a population explosion intensified the problems in the countryside. As land was subdivided to meet increased family needs, the farms became smaller and less efficient. Many peasants were thus forced to leave the family plots and migrate to the cities. There they sought work in the factories.

WITTE AND THE RUSSIAN INDUSTRIAL REVOLUTION

By the 1890s, the Industrial Revolution finally caught up with Russia. The development of industry in Russia between 1880 and 1910 was due primarily to the efforts of one man—Count Sergei Witte (1849–1915). Witte was a political conservative with a pragmatic economic philosophy. Singlemindedly, he pursued the goal of having Russia catch up with the West.

Witte needed trained personnel and capital. Before 1860, banks, in the Western sense, did not exist in Russia. Even after the introduction of banks, their interest rates were so high that they were of little help in providing capital for Russia's industrial revolution. In order to gain the confidence of foreign investors, Witte had to prove that their investments would be secure.

By putting Russia on the gold standard in 1897, Witte stabilized Russian currency, and made investment in Russia more appealing on the international bond market. He encouraged industrialists to exploit Russian natural resources, and his imposition of a protective tariff also helped Russian industry. Between 1893 and 1898, under Witte's tutelage, Russia's industrial output doubled—and it doubled again by 1914. However, even as late as 1914, at least 75 percent of all Russians still lived in rural areas.

Witte was unable to foresee some of the social and political consequences of Russian industrialization. The middle class prospered, adding to its ranks engineers and government bureaucrats. But in Russia, there were no small entrepreneurs as in England or the United States. The typical Russian businessman was a millionaire who ran a large enterprise and usually depended on government subsidies.

Living and working conditions were abysmal in the urban industrial centers. Many workers lived apart from their families, in massive barracks near the factories. Moreover, the government banned any means by

One part of Witte's crash program of industrialization was the building of a Trans-Siberian railroad. Unfortunately, other sectors of the Russian economy—notably agriculture—could not yet support or benefit from such giant undertakings.

which they might improve their lot in life, such as unionization, collective bargaining, or strikes.

Since the government was the biggest employer in Russia, worker dissatisfaction with wages and working conditions had political overtones. Government workers became a fertile source for recruitment by revolutionaries. Although the Russian proletariat was small in number, about 1.5 percent of the population, its concentration in the two major cities—St. Petersburg and Moscow—gave it an influence far beyond its numbers.

THE REVOLUTION OF 1905

Revolutionary movements proliferated in Russia in the last years of the 19th century. Some of these sought to enlist the peasants. Others tried to bring their philosophies to fruition by organizing the Russian proletariat. One such group which came to the fore in the late 19th century was the *Social Democrats*—the Russian Marxists.

In the last decade of the century, yet another conservative, Nicholas II (1894–1917), ascended the throne of Russia. Like his father before him, Nicholas II insisted that autocracy was the only possible form for Russian government. Unrest began to grow. It was made worse by a poor showing in the Russo-Japanese War (1904–05). Patriotic Russians were embarrassed and outraged by the defeat, which they believed was brought about by their government's incompetence.

In order to defuse some of the power of the revolutionaries, the government allowed a priest, Father Gapon, to organize the proletariat in St. Petersburg. Under Father Gapon's leadership, the factory workers in the national capital drew up a petition in which they spelled out the conditions they wanted changed. One Sunday in January 1905, they assembled in front of the tsar's Winter Palace in order to present the petition to Nicholas.

But tsarist police shot into the crowd and killed several hundred of the demonstrators.

The events of "Bloody Sunday" snapped all remaining sympathy for or loyalty to the tsar. Strikes broke out. The peasants revolted. In Moscow and St. Petersburg, Marxists organized the workers into councils called *soviets*. In October 1905, the St. Petersburg soviet declared a general strike. Soon the strike spread to other cities and to the countryside.

In order to placate the revolutionaries the tsar issued the *October Manifesto*, in which he granted some of the reforms that had long been demanded. The Manifesto litical parties and allowed for legislature, the *Duma*. But th Russians eligible to vote was li tsar was able to nullify the e whenever they were not to his important result of the 1905 R that it gave the revolutionaries dom and whetted their appeti served as a training ground for revolution of 1917.

SUMMARY

·y of 19th-century Russia is a story of a gradually growing sentiment for
·r the creation of a place in society for the nation's common people. It is also
of repeated frustration of efforts to bring about such change. From the failure
·embrist revolt, through the wave of reaction that followed Alexander II's
of the serfs, to the inadequacy of the semi-constitutional government that
·om the Revolution of 1905, the frustration of reformers and revolutionaries
It was to come to a head in the Bolshevik Revolution of 1917, when at last the
·hange would meet with success.

QUESTIONS

1 the origins of the Decembrist revolt. Who participated in the revolt, and what
·ted them? What were the immediate and long range effects of the revolt?
·vas the meaning of the slogan, "Orthodoxy, Autocracy, Nationality"? How was
·ilosophy translated into action by Nicholas I?
·id defeat in the Crimean War affect Russian foreign and domestic policy in the
·1 half of the 19th century?
·id Alexander Herzen attempt to reconcile the views of the Westernizers and
·hiles?
·nore things change, the more they remain the same." How accurate is this quote
·ied to the emancipation of the serfs?
·actors contributed to the cultural renaissance in Russia between 1820 and 1880?

BIBLIOGRAPHY

·. Russian Thinkers. New York: Viking Press, 1978. The author, an independent
·is own right, has written a series of thought-provoking essays on some of the most
·19th-century Russian intellectuals, including Dostoyevsky, Tolstoy, Bakunin, and

·, FYODOR. Notes from the Underground. New York: Bantam Books, 1981. A short
·ul novel which reflects the author's philosophy, especially his distrust of reason and
·of radicalism.
·NEY. First Blood: The Russian Revolution of 1905. New York: Macmillan, 1964. This
·the causes and results of the Revolution of 1905 is written in such a way that the
·vents is not lost in scholarly detail.
·NEY. Years of the Golden Cockerel: The Last Romanov Tsars. 1814–1917. New
·millan, 1968. A tale of high drama and tragedy revolving around the last five Russian

·. Alexander II and the Modernization of Russia, rev. ed. New York: Collier, 1965.
·ntroduction to the life of the "Tsar Liberator," describing his attempt to modernize
·nding serfdom.
·N, HUGH. The Russian Empire: 1801–1917. London: Oxford University Press, 1967.
·ive work of scholarship—the most thorough single-volume survey of the period.
·MITH, C. B. The Reason Why. New York: E. P. Dutton, 1960. The story of the heroic
·is charge of the Light Brigade in the Crimean War, made famous by Alfred Lord
·poem of the same name. In this well-told tale by Ms. Woodham-Smith, the folly of
·nd of warfare in general—becomes apparent.

A portrait of the Holy Roman emperor Charles V by his court artist, Titian. Charles drew upon the resources of Spain and the New World to defend his vast territories against the Turks, the French, and the spread of Protestantism.

In the Battle of Lepanto (1571), the three powers of the Holy League united to challenge Turkish control of the eastern Mediterranean.

European visitors to Russia were fascinated with the open-air winter bazaars where peasants sold naturally frozen foods—including beef, lamb, and fish.

Gatherings in the salons of French aristocrats were one of the main vehicles for the spread of Enlightenment ideas. On this occasion, in 1755, a new work by Voltaire was introduced.

A fireworks display in Green Park, London, celebrated the end of the Seven Years' War in 1763. As a result of the war, Britain gained control of French colonial possessions in North America and India.

William Turner's Slave Ship was inspired by an actual incident in which slaves suffering from an epidemic illness were thrown overboard in mid-sea. Like other Romantics, Turner addressed the issues of his time in an allegorical or symbolic manner.

In a study of the entertainers and customers of the celebrated Moulin Rouge (1892), Toulouse Lautrec depicted the underside—the despondency and cynicism—of Parisian society in the prewar years.

In his painting **The Twittering Machine,** *Paul Klee* offered an ironic commentary about industrial-age man—in particular, his apparent desire to refashion the natural world.

While some artists glorified the Machine Age and others portrayed the alienation of modern man, the Dadaists took still another approach. Marcel Duchamp's painting **The Bride,** with its diagram of the subject's interior workings, expresses the humor and nihilism of this short-lived movement.

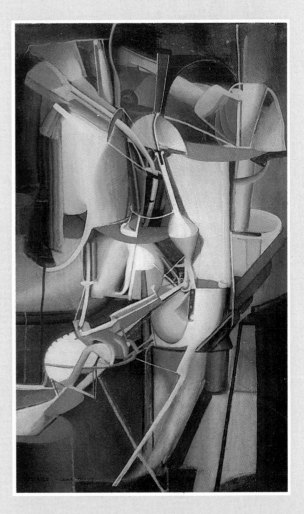

In 1919, Fernand Leger, an artist of the Futurist school, presented an admiring view of a Machine Age landscape in his painting entitled The City.

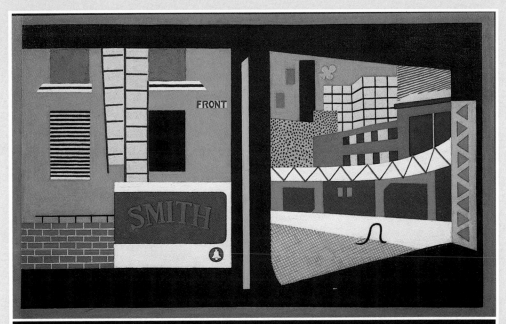

As the 20th century unfolded, three American artists recorded their impressions of New York, the most populous urban center of the United States. Paradoxically, each of these cityscapes is—like Leger's Futurist vision—devoid of people. Edward Hopper's Early Sunday Morning (below left) and Stuart Davis' House and Street (above) date from the Depression era, while Richard Estes' Ansonia (below) details with photographic precision the landscape of a present-day street.

Despite their long contact with European imperialists, most developing countries lack an industrial base and depend instead upon traditional agricultural techniques for their subsistence. Shown are (clockwise from top right): a floating market in Thailand; an oasis in North Cameroon, Africa; a Nile landscape near the pyramids in Egypt; a camel market in Morocco; harvesting of hemp in Kenya; and rice cultivation in Sri Lanka.

15

● *Politics, in the course of becoming History, is the story of a handful of men reaching for the levers of power.*

THEODORE WHITE

Triumph of Nationalism: The Unification of Italy and Germany

Seemingly, the forces of reaction in Europe had triumphed in the wake of the upheavals of 1848. Few of the social and political reforms envisioned by the revolutionaries, which had so alarmed the propertied and merchant classes, had been enacted. But the old dreams of nationhood were by no means dead or forgotten. A renewed spirit of nationalism marked the second half of the 19th century. In a little more than 20 years following the failed revolutionary movements of 1848, nationalism triumphed in Italy and Germany.

UNIFICATION OF ITALY By 1849 in Italy, the revolts that had briefly swept republicans into power had ended in failure. Austrian armies had routed the rebellious forces in the north, defeating the armies of Piedmont-Sardinia and driving out republican governments in Milan and Venice. The self-proclaimed emperor of France, Napoleon III, had dispatched an expeditionary force to topple a republic installed in Rome and to restore the Papal States to the pope. The Kingdom of the Two Sicilies was returned to its reactionary Bour-

bon rulers, and Piedmont-Sardinia was restored to the ruling House of Savoy.

It was not just the strength of Austrian and French armies that defeated the revolution, but also internal strife among Italians themselves. The conservative and moderate elements of Italian society, allied with the Church and the middle class, were alarmed at what they viewed as the excesses of the republicans. Seeing government by the people as a form of mob rule, moderates supported a constitutional monarchy. A conservative and pro-clerical faction favored an Italian state administered by the papacy. These antagonisms and divided loyalties did as much to defeat the *Risorgimento*—the Italian liberation and unification movement—as the armies of Austria and France.

THE ROLE OF PIEDMONT AND CAVOUR
In spite of its defeat at the hands of the Austrians, the kingdom of Piedmont-Sardinia was the only truly independent state in Italy, ruled by an Italian dynasty, the House of Savoy. Although conservative in his views, King Victor Emmanuel II retained the constitution that had been granted by his father

Camilo di Cavour, the architect of Italian unification, did not live to see the end-result of his handiwork.

and allowed some progressive reforms. In addition, Piedmont-Sardinia still had a well-trained army and above all, an ambitious, shrewd political leader in the person of its prime minister, Count Camilo di Cavour (1810–1861), who was determined to unite Italy under the rule of the House of Savoy.

A son of an aristocratic Piedmontese family, Cavour had taken part in the early revolutionary movements and had been briefly imprisoned. He was denied a role in political affairs until 1848, when he was elected to the newly installed Piedmont parliament. In the meantime, Cavour had managed his family's estates and amassed a fortune.

In 1850, Cavour was appointed minister of agriculture and commerce, and he set about to modernize the kingdom. He promoted improvements in farming and transportation, concluded commercial treaties with other nations, and pushed through a series of reforms designed to lessen the influence of the clergy. Cavour's reforms were directed toward his goal of creating a prosperous, stable Piedmont to which other Italian states could look for leadership. Unlike Giuseppe Mazzini, a nationalist leader who had been exiled from Italy because of his republican beliefs, Cavour was no idealist. He was a pragmatic realist, whose skill lay in his ability to direct political events to his own grand scheme—the unification of Italy under his king, Victor Emmanuel.

Cavour also realized that the divided and disparate states of Italy could never expel the Austrians and achieve unity without the help of outside forces. In order to ally Piedmont with France, he committed troops to intervene in the Crimean War in 1855, on the side of France and Britain. In part because of this intervention, Cavour obtained Louis Napoleon's agreement that France would wage war on Austria, a war which Napoleon reasoned would replace Austrian influence in Italy with that of France. Part of the agreement was an exchange of territories in which France would receive Savoy and Nice, and Piedmont would receive provinces in northern and central Italy.

In the spring of 1859, Cavour provoked Austria into declaring war on Piedmont, and true to his agreement, Louis Napoleon, with an army of 200,000 men, crossed into Italy. The combined Piedmont-French forces defeated the Austrians in two great battles at Magenta and Solferino, driving the Austrians once and for all out of Lombardy in the north. However, before a final victory could be achieved, Louis Napoleon, threatened by a hostile Prussia along his border and becoming aware that a united, strengthened Italy was not to the advantage of France, withdrew his forces and concluded a separate peace treaty with Austria. Between them, the Austrian emperor and Louis Napoleon forced King Victor Emmanuel to accept French annexation of Savoy and Nice, while allowing Piedmont to acquire only Lombardy.

THE UNIFICATION OF ITALY, 1859–1870

Why was the participation of the papal states essential to the unification movement?

Top left map:

SWITZERLAND
AUSTRIA-HUNGARY
SAVOY
FRANCE
NICE
PIEDMONT
LOMBARDY
VENETIA
ISTRIA
PARMA
• Milan
• Venice
MODENA
ROMAGNA
KINGDOM OF SARDINIA
LUCCA
TUSCANY
UMBRIA
PAPAL STATES
CORSICA (Fr.)
OTTOMAN EMPIRE
ADRIATIC SEA
• Rome
SARDINIA
• Naples
KINGDOM OF THE TWO SICILIES
Palermo •
SICILY

Top right map:

SAVOY (To France, 1860)
SWITZERLAND
AUSTRIA-HUNGARY
FRANCE
• Milan
VENETIA (Aus.)
ISTRIA
• Venice
NICE (To France, 1860)
TUSCANY
PAPAL STATES
OTTOMAN EMPIRE
ADRIATIC SEA
• Rome
• Naples
KINGDOM OF THE TWO SICILIES
Palermo •

Bottom left map:

SWITZERLAND
AUSTRIA-HUNGARY
VENETIA
ISTRIA
FRANCE
OTTOMAN EMPIRE
ADRIATIC SEA
• Rome
• Naples
Palermo •

Bottom right map:

SWITZERLAND
AUSTRIA-HUNGARY
ISTRIA
FRANCE
OTTOMAN EMPIRE
ADRIATIC SEA
★ Rome
• Naples
Palermo •

Embittered over Louis Napoleon's betrayal, Cavour resigned as prime minister, and his goal of achieving a united Italy seemed doomed. However, the defeat of the Austrian army incited uprisings throughout Italy, including the north-central region where followers of Cavour seized control of provincial governments. Unable to remain aloof from these events, Cavour returned as prime minister and masterminded the Treaty of Turin, in 1860, by which Piedmont annexed all the northern provinces except Venetia.

THE LIBERATION OF SICILY

Cavour had achieved his objective of Piedmontese supremacy in Italy, yet the Italian peninsula was still not united. Rome and the remaining Papal States were in the hands of the pope; Austria controlled Venetia; and the

Giuseppe Garibaldi was transformed overnight into a world-renowned folk hero after his unexpected conquest of Sicily.

Bourbons still ruled the Kingdom of the Two Sicilies. Reluctant to attack Rome and the Papal States for fear of French intervention on behalf of the pope, and unable to attack the Two Sicilies without provoking Austria, Cavour was content for the time being to strengthen Piedmont's position. However, he was forced into action by uprisings in Sicily and the insistence of the soldier-patriot Giuseppe Garibaldi (1807–1882) that all Italy must be free and united.

As a young seaman, Garibaldi had taken up arms to fight for an independent Italy. Forced into exile twice for leading insurrections, he returned to Italy in 1859 at the head of a band of volunteers ready to confront the Austrians. A militant republican who distrusted the compromises and maneuverings of Cavour, Garibaldi won widespread popular support. He became a symbol for the nationalist aspirations of all Italians.

Cavour returned Garibaldi's distrust. He was wary of Garibaldi's republicanism and was concerned lest the bold and impetuous leader disrupt stability through military adventures. Nevertheless, with Cavour's secret approval, Garibaldi and a contingent of volunteers, called The Thousand, set sail from Genoa in May of 1860 to invade Sicily. Joined by an aroused populace, Garibaldi's "Red Shirts" seized the city of Palermo, and within six months had conquered Sicily in the name of King Victor Emmanuel of Piedmont. From there, Garibaldi and his triumphant forces moved to Naples where, following the flight of its king, they entered the city. Flushed with his victories, Garibaldi prepared to march on Rome. But this was a move Cavour could not allow, for it would certainly bring a French army to protect the pope. In addition, Cavour was determined that no republicans would preside over the final unification of Italy.

Led by Victor Emmanuel, a Piedmontese army, with Louis Napoleon's consent, crossed through the Papal States in the fall of 1860 and met with Garibaldi's forces

Garibaldi and his victorious Red Shirts encounter Victor Emmanuel near Rome. At this meeting, Garibaldi agreed to support a constitutional monarchy in Italy.

south of Rome. The republican leader surrendered his command and agreed to accept a constitutional monarchy for Italy. By the end of 1860, the citizens of Naples, Sicily, and the Papal States had voted to join Piedmont. Only Rome and Venetia remained outside Piedmontese rule.

UNIFICATION

Cavour did not live to see an Italian kingdom, for he died in 1861, nine years before his life's work was finally completed by his successors. Through diplomacy, military incursions, and the mediation of Louis Napoleon, Venetia was turned over to Italy in 1866. The so-called Roman Question was solved when Napoleon withdrew his soldiers from that ancient capital during the Franco-Prussian War, and Italian troops marched in at the close of 1870. When Rome's citizens voted overwhelmingly to join the Italian kingdom, the unification of Italy was completed.

UNIFICATION OF GERMANY

By 1860, the German states, dominated by Prussia and Austria, formed a loose confederation of 39 states ruled by princes, dukes, and petty kings, largely unencumbered by democratic institutions. Discouraged and disillusioned by their failures in 1848, German liberals had emigrated by the thousands—many seeking refuge in the United States—and liberalism as a major force in Germany suffered a major setback. But in 1860, nationalist forces, impressed by the success of Cavour in welding together an Italian kingdom under the hegemony of Piedmont, arose again and began looking to the leadership of Prussia.

The Hohenzollern kingdom of Prussia seemed the logical leader of a united Germany. Although Prussia had emerged from the Napoleonic wars in a weakened condition, it had acquired additional lands, most of them in the Rhineland and most not contiguous with Prussia itself. More urbanized and industrialized than Prussia, these new territories and their peoples were incorporated into the framework of the Prussian system in varying degrees.

To strengthen its economy, Prussia in 1819 had abolished all internal tariff bars and established uniform trade barriers against foreign competition. Initially, this trade association, known as the *Zollverein*, was aimed at stopping the influx of English goods which posed a threat to Prussian industrial growth. It was so successful that by 1844 most of the states of Germany—except for Austria—had joined the customs union. Not only did the Zollverein encourage trade and industry within northern Germany, but it helped to establish an interlocking railroad and communications network throughout the German states.

The stimulation of a community of economic interests had political benefits as well. It encouraged the growth of German nationalism under Prussian hegemony. The Zollverein, directed by Prussia, bargained with foreign states, including England, France, and the United States. A common coinage system and a unified code of commercial law were created.

By the mid-19th century, Prussia had established itself as the economic leader of Germany, and political unification now was more than just a dream of philosophers and poets. First, however, Austria would have to be expelled from the German confederation and Prussia would have to become the dominant power.

THE ROLE OF OTTO VON BISMARCK

Slightly more than 50 years after the Congress of Vienna, nationalist hopes were fulfilled when Germany was united under Prussian domination and replaced France as the major force on the continent of Europe. That such a significant shift in European political relationships could take place during such a brief time is in no small part due to the efforts of a statesman who was born in that fateful

Otto von Bismarck would guide the destiny of Germany for nearly three decades. Until the end of the Franco-Prussian War in 1871, he pursued a militaristic foreign policy which earned him the title of the "Iron Chancellor."

year of 1815, when Prussian fortunes were at a low ebb.

Historians often disagree over the question of the role of individual genius in shaping the course of history. The modern social sciences have provided new dimensions to the study of the past, and many historians do not subscribe to the interpretation of larger-than-life personalities as the determining factors in the flow of past events. These historians argue that history is shaped by great impersonal forces—social, economic, cultural, technological—and that individuals are little more than puppets in this process.

Otto von Bismarck (1815–1898) and his role in the unification of Germany seem to provide an argument for the "great man" theory of historical causation. That Germany would have been unified with or without

278

Bismarck is likely, but that unification occurred when and how it did, and with the resulting consequences, was clearly due to Bismarck's personality and influence.

Bismarck was the most effective practitioner of *Realpolitik*—or the reality of politics as opposed to idealistic politics—in the second half of the 19th century. The forces of history did not shape Bismarck and his policies as much as the "Iron Chancellor" reworked those forces to shape his and Germany's destiny for years to come.

Heinrich Heine, the German poet turned journalist, describes the frustrations inherent in German history in the first half of the 19th century in the following quatrain.

Russia and France control the land,
Great Britain rules the sea.
Ours is the misty realm of dreams
Where there's no rivalry.[1]

It is from that kind of historical background and cultural experience that Bismarck would emerge to lead first Prussia and then all of Germany to a position of international prominence.

The Early Years. Otto von Bismarck was born in 1815 into the Prussian landed aristocracy—the Junker class. Because of his mother's wishes, young Otto did not receive the military training typical of most Junker sons; instead he had a more academic, civil-service-oriented education. At the universities of Göttingen and Berlin, Bismarck was better remembered for his dueling skills and his ability to consume large quantities of beer than for his devotion to studies. Göttingen was a center of liberal thought in Germany, and while there the young Bismarck briefly toyed with the ideas of republicanism. However, he quickly learned that discussing liberal philosophy and practicing it were two different things. He soon lost interest in rubbing elbows with the sons of middle-class merchants and lawyers, and he gravitated toward his own kind, the Prussian landed gentry.

Although not a scholar in a formal sense, Bismarck had an insatiable but poorly disciplined appetite for knowledge. It was said of him that he had a mind like a steel trap, and once a bit of information was lodged there, it would be subject to immediate recall when needed. He had a special interest in history, was well-read in a number of related disciplines, and could read and converse fluently in six languages, including English, French, and Russian. As a young man, Bismarck traveled extensively in Europe, which allowed him to put his considerable linguistic skills to use in observing and understanding other peoples and cultures.

In 1835, after dropping out of school under questionable circumstances, Bismarck embarked on a brief career in the civil service and also fulfilled his required one-year service in the Prussian army—a duty he did not find to his liking. However, while in the army, he did make the acquaintance of the Crown Prince and soon-to-be king of Prussia, Frederick William IV. In 1839, his career as a bureaucrat came to an end, and he returned home to manage his ancestral estates. Bismarck said of the Prussian bureaucrat and of himself that " . . . he is only a member of the orchestra. But I will play music the way I like or play none at all."[2]

However, a man of such physical energy and driving ambition could not be content for long as a country squire. In the late 1840s, Bismarck entered the diplomatic service, where he represented Prussia at the Diet of the German Confederation in Frankfurt. It was while ambassador to the diet that Bis-

[1] Gordon A. Craig, *From Bismarck to Adenauer: Aspects of German Statecraft* (New York: Harper & Row, 1965), p. ix.

[2] A. J. P. Taylor, *Bismarck: The Man and the Statesman* (New York: Random House, 1955), p. 19.

marck, hitherto an outspoken admirer of Austrian absolutism, received a rude awakening when he was able to observe Austrian diplomacy first-hand. Bismarck concluded that Austria would never accept Prussia as an equal partner in German affairs. If Prussia were ever to win recognition as a great power, it would have to do so over the lifeless form of Austria, and Germany would be the battleground. The conclusions reached and the lessons learned by Bismarck as a diplomat in the 1850s would remain fresh in his mind as premier of Prussia in the 1860s.

The Accession of Bismarck.
In 1861, King Wilhelm I officially ascended the throne of Prussia. Although somewhat more open-minded and rational than his predecessor, he was nevertheless a staunch autocrat. He had a soldier's training and a firm belief in a powerful army, which he reasoned was necessary if Prussia were to become the leader of a united Germany. Within four years, Wilhelm had precipitated a constitutional crisis over his plan to reorganize the army. Opposed by liberal members of parliament, he at first threatened to abdicate, a move which surely would have plunged Prussia into civil war.

Into this crisis stepped Otto von Bismarck. Having been sent as ambassador to Russia, he had been working to strengthen ties between the tsar and Prussia. He was recalled to Berlin in the fall of 1862, and met Wilhelm at the king's summer palace on the outskirts of the city. It is not entirely clear what transpired at that meeting, but Bismarck emerged as prime minister of Prussia. Ten days later he added to his titles and responsibilities that of foreign minister. Personal relations between the king and his first minister were never close and rarely smooth. But for the next 27 years it was obvious that Bismarck, not the king, held the reins of power in Prussia.

Bismarck's goals were two-fold: to make the monarch supreme in Prussia, and to make Prussia dominant in Germany. To achieve these ends he had to preempt the issue of nationalism from the liberals without conceding any other political reforms. In Bismarck's mind, domestic policy was subordinate to foreign policy. He believed that if the basic economic needs of the masses were provided for, they would not demand more political rights. Liberals, since they supported German nationalism, could hardly question Bismarck if his policy succeeded in expelling the Austrians and unifying Germany under Prussian leadership.

Bismarck felt that a successful foreign policy would resolve Prussia's difficulties. He expressed this view in his first speech in the lower house as prime minister. He stated forcefully that "Germany does not look to Prussia's liberalism but to her strength." And he went on to say in his most-often-quoted statement, "The great issues of the day will not be decided by speeches and the resolutions of majorities—that was the mistake made from 1848 to 1849—but by iron and blood."[3]

Bismarck needed time to prove the success of his foreign policy. For the next few years he ignored the parliament and spent the Treasury's money on building up the Prussian army. He censored the press when necessary, and ruthlessly overrode all opposition.

In his memoirs, written long after the fact, Bismarck claimed that from the moment he became prime minister he pursued and plotted in great detail an anti-Austrian foreign policy that would lead to Prussian domination of Germany. It takes time to make a new foreign policy, and Bismarck's contemporary remark, "Events are stronger than the plans of men,"[4] is probably a more accurate appraisal of his method of operation.

UNIFICATION THROUGH WAR
It must be said that Bismarck manipulated

---

[3] *Ibid.*, p. 20.

[4] *Ibid.*, p. 60.

Bismarck's goal of unifying Germany would have remained just a dream if it had not been for the military supremacy of the Prussian army. Here, Prussian troops parade in the capital city of Berlin.

events and took advantage of opportunities more skillfully than any other European statesman of the time. Furthermore, he was willing to use the power of the Prussian army to attain his goals. In the seven years before the establishment of the German Empire, three wars were fought: the Danish War of 1864 over the issue of Schleswig-Holstein, the Austro-Prussian War of 1866, and the Franco-Prussian War of 1871. Each war laid the foundation for the next, and the three combined were important factors leading to the outbreak of general war in Europe in 1914.

Schleswig-Holstein. To appreciate the sequence of events that led to the wars, one must first understand the Schleswig-Hol-

stein question. Lord Palmerston, the British politician-diplomat, said of this complicated territorial dispute that " . . . only three men understood the complexities of the problem. One of them has died, another has gone crazy, and I myself have forgotten it all."[5]

The two largely German-speaking provinces of Schleswig and Holstein on the Danish peninsula had been a source of humiliation for Prussia since 1852. In that year, King Frederick William, after occupying the provinces, had ignominiously withdrawn and acquiesced to the London Protocol con-

---

[5] Koppel S. Pinson, *Modern Germany: Its History and Civilization* (New York: Macmillan, 1954), pp. 132–3.

firming Denmark's hegemony over the territories. To the Prussians, Schleswig and Holstein remained an extension of their nation, and when King Christian IX of Denmark declared his intention to annex the provinces outright, Bismarck saw an opportunity to wrest them from Danish control. Reasoning that if Prussia acted alone, the other powers, especially England and France, would look upon it as military adventurism, Bismarck enlisted the aid of Austria.

In spite of a courageous defense by the Danes, the two provinces were overcome by Austro-Prussian forces in 1864, and Denmark relinquished its claim to the territories. Almost immediately, Austria and Prussia quarreled over the disposition of the spoils. Their conflicting claims were settled when it was decided that Prussia would administer Schleswig, and Austria would control Holstein.

The Austro-Prussian War. Border incidents between the two territories erupted almost immediately. It was apparent that the arrangement could only be temporary, and Bismarck began his preparations for war. He received assurances from Helmuth von Moltke, the army commander and the most brilliant military strategist of his time, that the Prussian army was prepared. On the diplomatic front, Bismarck had ensured the tsar's neutrality by supporting Russia's efforts to reverse its losses following the Crimean War. Through talks with Louis Napoleon, who envisioned himself as the champion of nationalist aspirations and who was willing to see Austrian power diminished, Bismarck secured the neutrality of France. As added insurance, he concluded an alliance with Italy. Having skillfully laid the diplomatic groundwork, Bismarck made sure that Prussian success in a war with the Hapsburgs would depend solely on the proficiency of its military machine.

Austria, with the wealth of its empire and superiority in size and population, con-

This cartoon by the French artist Daumier was made in 1867, after Austria's swift defeat in the Austro-Prussian War. Suddenly, the balance of power in Europe seemed very precarious.

trolled the German Confederation and had the support of the majority of the German states. Nevertheless, when war broke out in the summer of 1866, the mobility and speed of the Prussian forces and the tactics of von Moltke gave Prussia a stunning victory. Within seven weeks, the majority of the German states had collapsed before the Prussian armies, and in July the Austrian army was soundly defeated at the battle of Sadowa in Bohemia.

All of Europe was shocked at the speed with which Prussia defeated Austria. What was not recognized at the time was how the criteria used to determine the strength of a nation had been redefined by the Industrial Revolution. No longer would it be realistic to expect a primarily agrarian nation, such as Austria, to undertake a war against an industrialized and technologically superior state such as Prussia.

By the terms of the Treaty of Prague, which ended the conflict, Austria recognized the final dissolution of the German Confederation. Although leaving independent the southern German states of Bavaria, Wurtemberg, Baden, and Hesse-Darmstadt, Prussia annexed Schleswig-Holstein and Hanover along with other northern German states, forming the *North German Confederation*. Prussia's territory now stretched from the Rhine to the Russian border, and it comprised most of Germany.

Austria's defeat ended its dominance over Germany and reduced its empire. Within Austria, the emperor Franz Joseph began to initiate some reforms, including a parliamentary government. In 1867, ministers also worked out an arrangement, called the *Ausgleich*, with the restive Hungarian leaders. Under this agreement, Hungary became a semi-independent kingdom with its own constitution and parliament. The emperor remained king of Hungary as well as emperor of Austria. This so-called *Dual Monarchy*, which did not take into account the minority Czechs, Poles, Slavs, and other subject groups, was to last for 50 years, until after World War I.

Maneuvering Toward War. Traditionally, many historians have viewed the Franco-Prussian War of 1871 as the crucial military action in determining the course of European events in the second half of the 19th century. What happened in 1871 was almost predestined by the results of the Austro-Prussian War of 1866. The Prussian victory at Sadowa permanently changed the balance of power on the continent of Europe. As long as Austria and Prussia competed for control of Germany, France had been free to dominate western Europe. After 1866, these circumstances no longer existed, but Napoleon III was slow to recognize this *fait accompli*. Napoleon III mistakenly thought of Germany as being divided into three equal parts: the North German Confederation, the independent South German states, and the Austro-Hungarian Empire. In fact, there was only one power left in Germany, and that was Prussia.

As the crowds gathered in Berlin to cheer the first victorious military units returning from Sadowa, it was apparent that Bismarck had gained more than a justification of his foreign policy. With Bismarck's victory and his assumption of the leadership role in the German unification movement, domestic liberal opposition to his policies evaporated.

Bismarck devoted the next four years to consolidating Prussian hegemony in northern Germany. This he accomplished by persuading the rest of the 21 North German states to join the North German Confederation, with a new constitution and a two-chambered parliament. Although it seemed as if the states retained their independence, in reality they were controlled by Prussia, which directed military and foreign-policy matters and whose king had a veto over all legislation. Furthermore, there was no cabinet; only a chancellor who was by law required to be the prime minister of Prussia. It was a federal system in which Prussia was obviously the first among equals.

The South German states proved more reluctant, distrusting Prussian power and ambitions. These southern states were largely Catholic, and felt less affinity with the Protestant north. They did, however, increase their commercial and business ties with the northern states, and Bismarck was successful in convincing them that Napoleon III had designs on their territory.

THE FRANCO-PRUSSIAN WAR

France remained the only other major obstacle to Bismarck's dream of a united Germany. Napoleon III had suffered a series of reverses in foreign policy. The French had sympathized with liberation movements in Poland, putting them at odds with the Russians. Bismarck, on the other hand, backed

THE UNIFICATION OF GERMANY

To what extent did Prussia have the qualities usually considered essential to a successful nation-building movement? Consider factors such as commonality of language, heritage and culture; shared sense of purpose; and natural boundaries.

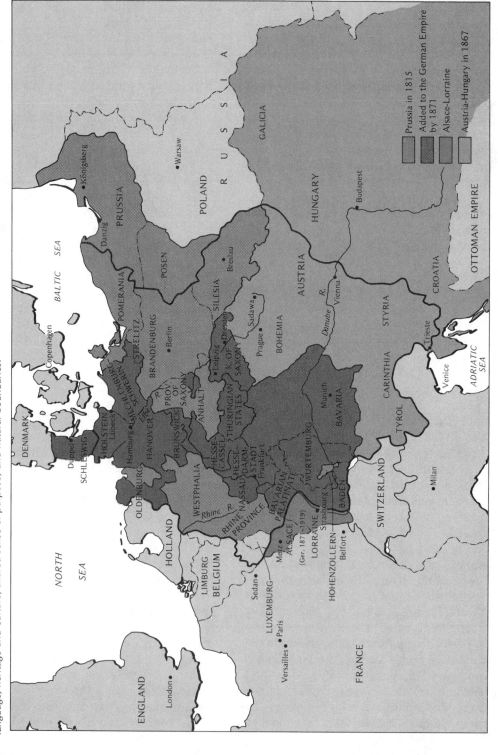

Legend:
- Prussia in 1815
- Added to the German Empire by 1871
- Alsace-Lorraine
- Austria-Hungary in 1867

Russia in suppressing the Poles. Then France began a disastrous attempt to install a French empire in Mexico with Maximilian, the brother of the Austrian emperor, as its head. When the United States protested, Napoleon withdrew his troops, leaving the hapless Maximilian to be seized and executed by Mexican revolutionaries.

In an attempt to reverse his diplomatic losses and revive his prestige, Napoleon intervened when the Spanish throne was offered to a Hohenzollern prince, a distant relation of Wilhelm's. The offer of the throne was, in fact, refused. However, under orders from Paris, the French ambassador in Berlin asked Wilhelm to agree that no Hohenzollern would ever in the future sit on the Spanish throne.

Wilhelm properly and politely refused this demand. The matter might have ended there, but Wilhelm, then in residence at the German spa at Ems, telegraphed an account of the meeting to Bismarck. Bismarck "edited" the *Ems dispatch*, and released it to the press. His version made it seem that Wilhelm had insulted the French ambassador. Public opinion in France demanded retaliation for this affront to national honor, and on July 19, 1870, France declared war on Prussia.

Metz and Sedan. Napoleon expected an easy victory. However, inept leadership produced a disaster for the French. The French army of the Rhine became trapped in the fortress of Metz, surrounded by Prussian troops in trenches. The other major part of the French forces, commanded by Marshal Maurice de MacMahon and accompanied by the emperor himself, moved to relieve the siege of Metz.

The main body of Prussian forces pinned down MacMahon's army against the Meuse River at the city of Sedan. Seeing that his forces were surrounded, with Prussian artillery pouring fire upon them from the heights around the city, the French emperor surrendered himself and his army on September 1.

In this informal portrait, Bismarck (left) meets with the defeated emperor Napoleon III of France. The battle of Sedan brought an end to Napoleon's career.

His letter to the king of Prussia stated, "Nothing remains for me but to give my sword into your hands,"[6] and the Second Empire was ended.

The Siege of Paris. When news of the humiliating defeat reached Paris, the enraged citizens formed a Government of National Defense. The new minister for foreign affairs met Bismarck in the middle of September, but could not accept Bismarck's demand that France give up the provinces of Alsace and Lorraine.

The Government of National Defense sent delegations into the countryside to raise a new army, but meanwhile, the Prussians moved up to surround Paris. Over a siege of

[6] Robert C. Binkley, *Realism and Nationalism* (New York: Harper & Row, 1935), p. 296.

Bismarck's terms for ending the Franco-Prussian War included the cession of Alsace-Lorraine to Germany. This demand was to become a major cause of tensions between the two nations.

CARICATURE OF THE "KLADDERADATSCH."

would keep alive the desire for revenge until 1914.

Whether Bismarck realized at the time that he was making a permanent enemy out of France by taking Alsace-Lorraine still is a subject of debate for historians. Perhaps he saw France as an implacable enemy regardless of the peace terms; or possibly he was trying to appease the Prussian generals who had been denied their pound of flesh in the Austro-Prussian War. Whatever the reason, it is generally accepted that the taking of Alsace-Lorraine was a major policy error, one that would return to haunt not only Germany and France but the entire world in the 20th century.

four months, the situation within the city became desperate. Without supplies of food, the proud Parisians were forced to eat horses and dogs, hunt sewer rats, and finally butcher the animals in the city zoo. At last, on January 28, 1871, the leaders of the government signed an armistice.

THE TREATY OF FRANKFURT

With the signing of the Treaty of Frankfurt in May of 1871, the Franco-Prussian War officially ended. France had to pay an indemnity of five billion francs, and a German army of occupation would remain in northern France until it was paid. In addition, the territories of Alsace and Lorraine were ceded to Germany. The indemnity was paid by the end of 1873, and the occupation troops were removed the same year. Unfortunately, the question of Alsace-Lorraine would remain a burning one for future relations.

Every time a Frenchman stood on the new border after 1871 and looked across at what had been part of France and now was part of Germany, he would be reminded instantly of the loss of French honor and prestige. This continual and tangible reminder of the decline of French dominance on the continent

BISMARCKIAN GERMANY

As the seige of Paris drew to a close, the leading German princes met at Versailles and proclaimed Wilhelm I the Emperor of Germany. The date January 18, 1871, marked Germany's birth as a nation. Berlin became the political center of the continent, as Paris and Vienna had been earlier.

A NEW CONSTITUTION

Several months later, the constitution of the new confederation was issued. The former states of the North German Confederation were joined by the four South German states. The new German *Bund* consisted of 25 political entities, ranging in size from the four kingdoms of Prussia, Bavaria, Saxony and Wurtemberg, to the three free cities of Hamburg, Bremen, and Lübeck. Each of these was to send delegates to a federal council or *Bundesrat*. A lower chamber, the *Reichstag*, was made up of 382 deputies elected by all male Germans over 24 years old.

This bicameral legislature held the potential of bringing Germany a truly representative government. However, the constitution vested all ministerial power in the president of the *Bundesrat*. The power to appoint the president, or imperial chancellor,

On January 18th, 1871, Wilhelm I was proclaimed kaiser, or emperor, of a united Germany at Versailles. Bismarck, the architect of this event, stands at the base of the dais.

was reserved for the emperor. Thus, the popularly elected *Reichstag* had in reality little power. Bismarck held the post of president of the *Bundesrat* for nearly 20 years.

RELIGIOUS PROBLEMS

The German Catholics, now a minority within the new German empire, took steps to strengthen their position. They formed the Center Party, which drew most of its support from the South German states. The Center Party's aims ran contrary to Bismarck's intention to centralize government power.

In his efforts to reduce the influence of the Catholics, Bismarck took advantage of the doubts created by the First Vatican Council's 1870 declaration that the pope was infallible in matters of faith and morals. A sizable group of Germans, known as the "Old Catholics," did not accept papal infallibility. Bis-

marck played them off against the papal supporters.

Members of the Jesuit order were expelled from Germany, and the German Empire broke off diplomatic relations with the Vatican. In 1873 and 1874, the German government issued decrees requiring anyone holding a clerical office to be a native German who had attended a German school. All clerical appointments were subject to state approval. Catholic bishops who opposed these decrees were arrested or expelled.

Bismarck called his policy by the grandiose name of *Kulturkampf*, or "struggle for civilization," and found support for it among German liberals. The anticlerical campaign included the secularization of education, a limitation of ecclesiastical authority, and dispossession of religious orders. Liberals agreed to an extension of police power to act against recalcitrant clergy. A critic noted that German liberals had rejected their previous ideals in the struggle: "Now their watchword is the police—police to the right, police to the left, police in the rear, police in front—ministerial decrees and arbitrary courts without appeal."[7] The rule of law guaranteed by the new German constitution had little meaning.

Even so, persecution only strengthened Catholic resistance. The Center Party increased its representation in the *Reichstag*. After 1878, Bismarck halted the *Kulturkampf* and turned his attention to countering the growth in power of the Social Democratic Party.

CREATING A WELFARE STATE

The Social Democratic Party was formed in 1875, combining followers of Karl Marx with members of the former Socialist party founded by Ferdinand Lassalle. The party attracted growing numbers of discontented workers to its ranks. Bismarck, no friend of socialism, sought to weaken the party's influence by a combination of repressive measures and legislation designed to ease the grievances of the workers.

To some degree, the socialists accomplished their aims by forcing the government to pass a comprehensive code of social measures. The Sickness Insurance Law (1883) ensured workers half-pay and medical attention for six months in case of illness. The Accident Insurance Law (1884) compelled employers to compensate workers disabled in work-related accidents. A pension of 20 percent of a worker's annual salary was to be paid to dependents of workers killed on the job. Finally, an Old Age Pension Act (1889) provided an annual income to workers retiring at 70 or who became incapacitated before that age.

---

[7] Carleton Hayes, *A Generation of Imperialism* (New York: Harper & Row, 1941), p. 86.

Germany's social legislation was far in advance of similar legislation by other European countries. It was not until more than 20 years later that France and England passed such legislation. The United States did not establish its Social Security program, similar to the Old Age Pension Act, until 1935.

Germany's social legislation had the effect of alleviating the discontent of workers, and gave Bismarck the public support he needed to continue his conservative policies. Socialist leaders denounced the moves as a means of insuring the continued health and expansion of the capitalist system. This was largely true; there was little opposition from Germany's industrial leaders, who were compelled by law to contribute to the funds established to pay social benefits.

INDUSTRIAL STRENGTH OF GERMANY

Both Bismarck's social policy and his military victories were made possible by the growth and prosperity of German industry. It was not until the mid-19th century that the Industrial Revolution had its full effect in Germany. However, it was accelerated by the scientific progress made after 1870, and German industry quickly made up for the head start gained by England, France, and other earlier-industrialized nations. Machinery, mining, textiles, chemistry, and the new electrical industry led the way in industrial growth. By the end of the 1870s, Germany was the foremost industrial power on the continent.

After 1878, Bismarck encouraged the growth of German industry by placing high protective tariffs on imports. The rapid growth of German industry can be seen in the fact that in 1871, only one-third of the population lived in towns and cities; by 1910, two-thirds of the German population lived in the industrial-based urban areas. By the time of World War I, Germany would surpass Britain itself in industrial output.

SUMMARY

The forces of nationalism succeeded in both Italy and Germany in the latter half of the 19th century. However, the achievement of nationhood came about not primarily as the result of liberal and republican efforts, but through the manipulations of politicians who served monarchs. Piedmont's King Victor Emmanuel became ruler of a united Italy through the efforts of Count Camilo de Cavour. In Germany, Otto von Bismarck made Wilhelm I of Prussia the unchallenged ruler of Germany, and Germany the preeminent power on the continent of Europe.

QUESTIONS

1 Cavour and Garibaldi each made unique and essential contributions to the cause of Italian unification. How successful was each man in achieving his particular goals?

2 Assess the role played by Napoleon III in the Italian Risorgimento, or unification movement.

3 To what extent did Bismarck shape the political and social forces of his time, and to what extent was he shaped by them?

4 Trace the background of the Schleswig-Holstein controversy, and explain how it precipitated a war between Austria and Prussia.

5 Defend or refute the following statement: "Bismarck preempted German liberals by embracing the traditionally liberal philosophy of nationalism and making it a basic tenet of German conservatism."

6 Explain the significance of the following terms: Risorgimento, Red Shirts, Ems dispatch, Alsace-Lorraine, Kulturkampf.

BIBLIOGRAPHY

HERDER, HARRY. *Italy in the Age of the Risorgimento: 1790–1870.* London: Longman, 1983. A study of the unification of Italy from a wide perspective, including consideration of Italian culture and coverage of the smaller states.

HIBBERT, CHRISTOPHER. *Garibaldi and his Enemies.* Boston: Little, Brown, 1966. An exceptional human interest story about the most colorful hero of the movement for Italian unification.

MAY, A. J. *The Habsburg Monarchy, 1867–1914.* Ann Arbor: UMI Research Press, 1951. A solid and thorough account of the decline of the monarchy after the battle of Sadowa.

MEDLICOTT, W. N. and D. COVENEY. *Bismarck and Modern Germany.* New York: St. Martin's Press, 1972. With economy and style, the authors set the stage for the emergence of a powerful Germany in the 20th century. This evaluation of Bismarck strikes a balance between the "great man" approach and the "great forces of history" approach.

SNYDER, L. L. *A Comparative History of Nationalism.* New York: Holt, Rinehart, 1976. A useful introduction to the varieties of nationalism.

TAYLOR, A. J. P. *Bismarck: the Man and the Statesman.* New York: Random House, 1955. A provocative and controversial study of the man of "blood and iron."

16

Take up the White Man's burden—
Send out the best ye breed—
Go bind your sons to exile,
To serve your captive's need;
To wait in heavy harness,
On fluttered folk and wild—
Your new-caught sullen peoples,
Half devil and half child.
RUDYARD KIPLING, 1899

European Imperialism in Asia

In the 19th century many European states carved out empires for themselves in Asia and Africa. This *imperialism*, or domination of one country by another, had three basic forms. The first form of imperial control was the *colony*. A colony was directly ruled by the European power that controlled it, and was regarded as an extension of the European state. It was run for the benefit of the mother country, and other European nations were blocked out of its trade.

Another form of imperial control was the *protectorate*. This was characterized by less direct rule by the mother country. The protectorate had its own government, but aspects of its policy were controlled by the European country. The imperialist power usually controlled both the foreign relations of its protectorate and its trading relationship with other countries.

The third form of imperial domination was the *sphere of influence*. Here the form of imperialism was indirect. The European power would exercise economic control over another state, while maintaining at least a pretense of respecting its political independence. Often the imperial power would have exclusive investment rights or trading privileges in its sphere of influence.

Great Britain led the way in imperialism, by 1900 controlling one-fourth of the population of the world and one-fifth of its land mass. France, Germany, Italy, and Belgium also acquired new overseas possessions in the 19th century. Two non-European powers entered the imperialist ranks: the United States obtained the Philippines, Puerto Rico, and Hawaii; and Japan acquired Korea and influence within China.

CAUSES OF IMPERIALISM There were many causes for the surge of imperialism in the late 19th century. The most important were economic motives, population pressure, and nationalism. Christian missionary activity, intellectual curiosity, and the force of public opinion also contributed to the imperialist drive.

ECONOMIC MOTIVES

The Industrial Revolution had intensified the need for cheap and plentiful new materials; at the same time, the industrialized powers sought new markets and new profits for their manufactured goods. For example, the textile mills of England required guaranteed, ample supplies of cheap India cotton. The finished product, cotton cloth, was then sold in India for considerable profit. But economic gain was by no means the only motive for imperialism. In many cases, especially in Africa, the cost of acquiring colonies far exceeded the profits to be gained. At least five other factors weighed heavily.

POPULATION PRESSURES

The phenomenal increase in European population in the 19th century was in part a by-product of the Industrial Revolution, with the resulting increase of both agricultural and manufactured products, and in part the result of some medical breakthroughs which extended life expectancy. In fact, the increase in population was the effect of a decreased death rate, not an increased birth rate as was widely believed at the time. This exploding population in turn intensified the demands for products, and also led to increased emigration. Between 1840 and 1940, about 60 million people emigrated from Europe to the rest of the world.

NATIONALISM

National pride, glory, and power were crucial factors in 19th-century imperialism. Nationalism was, as we have seen, one of the driving forces of the era, and, carried to excess, national prestige was elevated by overseas conquest. The British were proud of the fact that "the sun never set on the British empire," and the German emperor, eager to join the dash for colonies, asserted that "Germany deserved her place in the sun." Japan sought dominance in Asia to reflect the glory of "the land of the rising sun." Connected to the desire for glory for one's own nation was the quest for power, often for its own sake, and as part of the historic competition for power between the European states. During the age of imperialism, these contests for

power were waged throughout the world, in turn intensifying the animosities between the European states. Part of the motivation for the search for overseas influence was to deny it to a rival, or to prevent a rival from consolidating areas.

Another nationalistic factor that led to imperialism was the effect of social Darwinism on nations' actions. The idea of the survival of the fittest was extended into the international realm. European countries felt that their greater economic and military power entitled them to rule over weaker nations. European nations tended to judge non-Western cultures only by European standards, and thus saw them as inferior.

SCIENTIFIC AND INTELLECTUAL CURIOSITY

Scientific and intellectual curiosity also enticed European explorers to the African continent and to the Orient. Before 1800, the interior of Africa was unknown to Europeans, although they had conducted slave-trading activities in the coastal areas for several centuries. The interior of Asia, too, was largely uncharted. But the 19th-century movement of romanticism and the development of scientific inquiry encouraged Europeans' interest in finding out about these exotic cultures, climates, and landscapes.

MISSIONARY ACTIVITY

Another motivation for the imperialists of the 19th century was the desire to obtain converts to Christianity. In fact, in many cases, the missionaries were the first Europeans to land in the unknown parts of the world. The desire for converts originated from an altruistic desire to spread the Christian religion.

Secondly, Europeans' elevated notion of the "superiority" of their culture and civilization created a misguided sense that Europe was obliged to "rescue" the less fortunate of the world. In an unconscious expression of what today would be viewed as racism, the English poet Rudyard Kipling wrote of the "white man's burden" to transmit the values of Western civilization to the less fortunate of the world.

This altruistic motive was indeed sincere. Most missionaries not only sought converts but also established schools and hospitals in Africa and Asia. As a result of the dedication of many missionaries, European medical advances were spread worldwide, and the quality of life improved.

At the same time, the Europeans' chauvinist (superior) attitude led them to disregard, see as valueless, or often destroy native cultures. In many cases this attitude of disrespect sowed the seeds of native resentment and anger. This resentment blossomed into anti-Westernism, and the native populations rejected their conquerors in the 20th century.

PUBLIC OPINION

A final factor in explaining the imperialist march of the 19th century was public opinion and the press. Imperialism was popular. The citizens of the European states and the United States enthusiastically supported overseas expansion. The popular penny press which served a newly literate reading public glorified the accomplishments of the explorers and supported the frequent wars of conquest. For example, the slogan "Remember the Maine," coined by the Hearst newspapers, inflamed American public opinion in support of the Spanish-American war. The British reading public devoured accounts of the worldwide battles between British armies and the natives. In Germany in the 1870s and 1880s, public opinion pressured the government to pursue a more aggressive imperialism than the chancellor, Otto von Bismarck, desired.

IMPERIALISM IN INDIA

Imperialism in Asia took essentially two forms: 1) the outright acquisition of colonies in such places as India, Indochina, and Burma, and 2) the division of China into spheres of influence. The largest and most valuable colony controlled by any European power was India. As such it became known to the British as "the jewel in the crown."

CONSOLIDATION OF BRITISH RULE

Initial British inroads in India began with the East India Company, which received its charter and a monopoly on Asian trade in 1600. In 1603, John Middenhall, representing the company, landed in India and subsequently acquired trade concessions. In 1661, the company acquired Bombay, an Indian port city, and in 1715 the company gained numerous trade concessions. The French too were interested in the India trade, and the two powers competed for influence in India until the English victory in the Seven Years' War (Chapter 6).

The British gained a toehold in India during the time of the Mogul Empire.[1] In the 18th century, the Moguls steadily lost control over parts of India until its rulers became primarily figureheads. During this period, the British East India Company expanded its control over the Indian mainland, under the direction of the British governor-general. By the beginning of the 19th century, the East India Company controlled substantial parts of the interior as well as coastal trading areas.

Culture Clash. The East India Company pressed for reforms in government and acted to stamp out abuses which were deeply tied to the culture of India.

The Charter of 1813 allowed missionaries to proselytize (seek converts) throughout the country. Later, the practice of *suttee*, in which Hindu widows threw themselves on the funeral pyres of their husbands, was abolished by decree. Another custom that was forbidden was the *thuggee*, whereby people were killed as offerings to the god-

---

[1] The Mongol conquerors of India are often referred to as *Moguls*, or *Moghuls*.

An episode from the Sepoy Mutiny of 1857–58: Scottish troops engage a determined group of rebels. After the rebellion was put down, the British began to utilize native princes for local government.

dess Kali. These reforms aroused opposition among Indians, who feared that the British were trying to westernize them. Indeed this was what some company officials planned. Thomas Macaulay, then an official of the company government, told the House of Commons in 1833: "We must do our best to form a class of persons Indian in blood and color, but English in taste, in opinions, in morals, and in intellect."[2]

The Sepoy Mutiny. These cultural differences and the centuries of British military conquest and economic exploitation of India provoked an Indian uprising, the *Sepoy Rebellion*, in 1857–58. This rebellion occurred among the native enlisted men, the Sepoys,

in the British army in India, and was caused by the introduction of a new cartridge for the army's rifles. It was rumored among the Sepoys that the cartridge had been greased, either with beef or pork fat. Since the soldier had to bite off the end of the bullet before placing it into the rifle, this rumor caused anger in the ranks. For Moslem Sepoys, eating pork was forbidden; to Hindu Sepoys, the cow was sacred. Neither wished to bite the bullet, for religious reasons. The rebellion spread and British women and children were killed. However, the rebels had no coordinated plan of action—garrisons rebelled at different times. Delhi was captured by the mutineers and held for more than four months. Portions of the native army remained loyal to the British, however, and the company put down the mutiny with great loss of life before the end of the year.

---

[2] Alan Palmer, ed., *Nations and Empires* (New York: Newsweek Books, 1974), p. 34.

This Indian engraving depicts one of the legacies of British rule in India: a railroad system. Following Indian custom, the last car of the train is reserved for women and children.

THE BRITISH CROWN ASSUMES POWER

There were direct consequences of the Sepoy Mutiny. The following year, the East India Company was disbanded. In the future, India would be ruled by the Crown.

When the British monarch became the ruler of India, fundamental changes were made in the way Britain governed India. One lesson of the Sepoy Mutiny was that attempts at reforms often had consequences that could not be foreseen. Therefore, under the crown, no new reforms were undertaken. The British government consulted with the various Indian princes and often used them to administer local government.

British rule brought great changes to India. Roads and railroads were built to connect the different areas of the country; as a result of British rule, India had a larger railway network than any other Asian country. The modern communications that were a hallmark of 19th-century Europe also linked the urban centers of India.

The Industrial Revolution was brought to India, sometimes with devastating results. The cottage industries of the villages were hurt, and crafts and techniques that were part of the Indian culture from time immemorial were lost.

Some upper-caste Indians received the opportunity for a Western education. These Indians began to demand greater independence for their country. The formal beginning of the Indian independence movement dates from 1884, with the establishment of the Indian National Congress. Originally, the Congress called for greater self-rule within India. As time passed, demands for self-rule escalated to demands for full independence.

WESTERN EUROPE, CHINA AND JAPAN

European imperialism in China began in 1839, with the outbreak of the First Opium War between China and Great Britain. The underlying conflict between the two powers originated in the British desire for trade with China. For their part, the Chinese preferred to avoid contact with the rest of the world. China, the world's oldest continuous civilization, had been isolated from the West during most of its history, and wished to remain so.

THE OPIUM WARS

By the beginning of the 19th century, Europeans, especially the British, sought Chinese products—silk, spices, porcelain, and tea. Tea comprised over 50 percent of Chinese exports. But Chinese indifference to British goods in exchange created a problem for the British traders. Opium was the British solution.

In the 18th century, the British began a three-cornered trade system. British finished goods, like cotton cloth, were traded to India. In India, the traders took raw cotton and opium in exchange. Sailing on to China, they sold the opium for Chinese commodities like tea and silk. Returning home, the traders found eager buyers for the Chinese commodities, and the raw cotton was sold to the British textile manufacturers, who turned it into cotton cloth to be sold in India, beginning the cycle again. Although Chinese law forbade the importation of opium, the law was evaded, and by 1839 opium smoking had become an insidious habit of many Chinese. In this period the Chinese were buying about 200 tons of opium annually.

The First Opium War, 1839–1842. In 1839, the Chinese emperor decided to end the importing of opium. Acting on his orders, gov-ernment officials seized and destroyed the supply of opium stored in the southern city of Canton, the only port in China where foreign ships were allowed to land. Relations between China and Britain deteriorated, and war broke out between the two countries.

Fighting in the first Opium War began in the Canton area. British forces took the city and imposed a fine equal to the value of the destroyed opium. British naval forces then moved up the Yangtze to Nanking, and the Chinese sued for peace in 1842.

Prior to the war, the Chinese government had enforced numerous restrictions on foreign trade: only Canton was open to traders and only for a few months each year; foreign sailors could bring no women with them, and could carry no weapons; they could not travel in most of the city; and they were required to deal only with a guild of mer-

The First Opium War, which opened the door to foreign imperialists, was fought mainly on China's rivers and ports. Shown is the capture of Ting-hai by the British navy.

chants, known as the *co-hong*. By the terms of the Treaty of Nanking (1842), the Chinese were forced to open five trading ports, cede the island of Hong Kong to the British, pay an indemnity, and agree to the abolishment of the *co-hong*.

Subsequent treaties were signed with the United States and France, who also desired trade with China. These treaties granted the principle of *extraterritoriality*, or foreign sovereignty on parts of Chinese soil. For example, foreigners charged with crimes in China were not tried by Chinese laws in Chinese law courts, but in their own national courts in China, presided over by their fellow countrymen. This principle meant a loss of Chinese sovereignty. A *most favored nation clause*, which meant that any privileges extended to any foreign country by China would be extended to Britain, was agreed to by the two countries in the following year.

The Second Opium War, 1856–60. In 1856, a second Opium War occurred, between China and the British and the French. Although remaining technically neutral, the Russians and Americans shared in the treaty settlement at the end of the war in 1860.

The immediate causes of the conflict were the murder of a French missionary and the British claim that their flag had been insulted. Underlying these excuses was the emperor's reluctance to grant more concessions in China to the foreigners. After allied forces marched on China's capital at Peking and burned to the ground the emperor's Summer Palace, the Chinese once again came to terms.

The Second Treaty Settlement included eight different treaties with foreign powers between 1858 and 1860. These provided for 1) the opening of ten new treaty ports, 2) the foreigners' right to send ambassadors to China—in other words, full diplomatic relations, 3) a low tariff on imported goods, and 4) a strip of Chinese territory to be ceded to Russia. With the Second Treaty Settle-

General Gordon led the Chinese "Ever Victorious Army" which ended the Taiping rebellion.

ment, China lost full sovereignty over its territory. The treaty settlements ended the Chinese policy of isolation from the rest of the world.

THE TAIPING REBELLION, 1850–1864

While the foreign powers consolidated and exploited the gains the first Opium War had brought them, China was wracked by a long and destructive civil war, the *Taiping Rebellion*, which lasted from 1850 to 1864.

The rebellion was the result of the ambitions of Hung Hsiu-ch'üan, a Chinese mystic and religious fanatic who claimed to be the second son of God. He attempted to spread his particular brand of Christianity through military conquests of China.

Hung gained widespread support for the

Taiping program advocating brotherhood, shared property, and equality of the sexes. Fighting raged sporadically for a 14-year period, interrupted by bandit raids and the second Opium War. These internal disorders were eventually suppressed by the Ever Victorious Army, a Chinese army under the leadership, first, of an American from Salem, Massachusetts—Frederick Ward—and later by the British general Charles George Gordon, known as "Chinese" Gordon.

The effects of the rebellion were two-fold: the loss of 10 to 20 million Chinese lives and the further weakening of the Chinese government. During this same period, the Chinese customs service, responsible for the collection of tariffs on imported goods, was put under the direction of Sir Robert Hart, an Englishman who modernized it and made it efficient. Although the new customs service was considered the best in the world, foreign control of it further diminished Chinese independence.

THE RISE OF MODERN JAPAN

Japan emerged as a powerful nation only after centuries of isolation comparable to that of China. Before the 19th century, Japan had also refused to trade with Europeans— except for the Dutch, whom they allowed to land on a tiny island off of the coast, quarantined behind a high fence.

An End to Isolation. In 1853, the American Commodore Matthew Perry opened Japan to the West when he negotiated an agreement allowing American ships to land at two Japanese ports. Perry lured the Japanese into compliance by presenting them with enticing gifts, including a miniature railroad engine, cars, and track. Unlike the Chinese, who shunned the devices produced by Western technology, the Japanese were enchanted. Soon afterward, Japan extended trading privileges to the other powers.

The end of Japan's isolation brought internal disorder between the feudal leader of Japan, the *shogun*, and the Japanese nobility. But in 1867, the emperor began a new era for Japan, known as the *Meiji*, or enlightened government. The emperor, who had previously left the governing of the country to the shogun, became the leader of the country and the shogunate was abolished.

Rapidly, the Japanese introduced a dazzling array of reforms to modernize their country as they adopted Western technology, bringing about their own industrial revolution. They introduced a textile industry, a modern banking system, and a merchant fleet to facilitate trade with the West. The motto for the age was supplied by the emperor in poetic form:

This Japanese portrait of an American naval officer and his wife dates from about 1860. The Japanese were, in general, more receptive to foreign influences than the Chinese.

May our country,
Taking what is good,
And rejecting what is bad,
Be not inferior
To any other.[3]

In 1889, Japan adopted Western law codes and a constitution which included an elected two-house legislature. However, most power was theoretically retained by the emperor. A system of public education was established. Japan also laid the foundations for a modern army and navy and adopted a policy of imperialism.

These two Pacific nations, then, China and Japan, reacted in opposite ways to Western intrusion. The Chinese responded weakly and fell victim to the foreign powers. The Japanese rapidly imitated and joined them. Among the reasons for their different responses include China's long indigenous cultural tradition and sense of superiority, which contrasted with Japan's history of borrowing from other cultures. However, the Japanese adapted the borrowings, making them distinctly Japanese. Moreover, Japan's geographic situation, as a series of islands in the Pacific, made it more vulnerable to foreign influence than China.

The Sino-Japanese War, 1894–1895. A confrontation between Japan and China arose over the status of Korea. As a peninsula on the Pacific coast of Asia, Korea had for centuries been under the cultural and political dominance of China. When Japan became a modern imperialist power, it sought raw materials and markets for its industrial goods, and Korea, with its ample timber and mining resources, was an inviting target.

Internal disorders between progressive and conservative Korean factions provided the opportunity for Japanese intervention.

---

[3] N. Taylor Bregg, "Hagi: When Japan's Revolution Began," in *National Geographic*, Vol. 165, No. 6, June 1984, p. 772.

When both China and Japan sent troops to Korea to assist the Korean government, the two powers went to war in August 1894. Although the Chinese troops outnumbered those of Japan, the Japanese army was well equipped and trained and quickly won a decisive victory in February 1895.

The *Treaty of Shimonoseki* which followed demonstrated Japan's strength and China's helplessness; by the terms of this treaty China recognized the independence of Korea—which subsequently came under Japanese influence—and Japan was ceded the former Chinese possessions of the island of Formosa and the Liaotung Peninsula on the Chinese mainland. China was also required to pay a large indemnity and to open more ports to foreign trade.

NEW EUROPEAN INTERVENTION

The European powers were unwilling to allow Japan all the fruits of its victory. Russia, Germany, and France intervened and forced Japan to return the Liaotung Peninsula in exchange for an added indemnity payment. In return for their intervention, which they asserted had been on China's behalf, these powers demanded Chinese territory and concessions, triggering yet another round of claims by the other European powers. What ensued was a scramble for territory, ports, and economic concessions, including foreign loans and railroad and mining rights. France acquired the colony of Annam, in northern Indochina, and Kwangchow Bay. Russia received a lease on the Liaotung peninsula along with Port Arthur, and the right to extend the trans-Siberian railroad through Chinese territory. The Germans acquired Kiaochow Bay and railroad and mining rights. The British obtained a lease on the port of Weihaiwei. In a matter of months, the rapacious imperialists had forced the Chinese government to grant extensive territory and concessions, even though they had not participated in the war.

The Boxer Rebellion, 1900–1901. By 1900, the tide of China's fortunes was at a low ebb. In the minds of many Chinese, the essential question was how to restore their nation's sovereignty, dignity, and self-respect. To the members of a secret society called the Fists of Righteous Harmony (commonly known as the Boxers), the answer lay in an attempt to turn back the clock. Acting in defense of the old dowager empress Tzu-hsi, who secretly supported them, the Boxers in 1900 began a year-long attack on Westerners—burning bridges, destroying railway track, and killing missionaries. So ignorant that they thought their magic could protect them against bullets, the Boxers nevertheless drew widespread support from their fellow Chinese, and briefly controlled the countryside.

This French cartoon suggests that the Japanese would be overpowered by the Russian bear in the Russo-Japanese War. In fact, however, the Japanese were victorious.

Tzu-hsi, the empress dowager of China, secretly supported the Boxer Rebellion against the Western imperialist powers. She is shown with two of her retainers.

Attempting to drive the hated foreigners out of their country, the Boxers entered the capital of Peking, besieged the foreign diplomats in their section of the city, and killed the German ambassador. At that point, an international army of soldiers and marines from all the treaty powers marched on the city, freed the foreign representatives there, and subsequently forced the Chinese government to pay a large indemnity. Moreover, the foreign powers acquired the right to station guards permanently in the capital. Far from succeeding at their goal, the Boxers only contributed further to foreign influence and to China's weakness. In 1911, a revolution broke out in China, and the following year the Manchu dynasty ended. A republic was established in China (Chapter 23).

The Russo-Japanese War, 1904–05. China's weakness gave Russia an excuse to place troops in northern China and Manchuria to protect the Russian port facilities and railway system. These Russian actions and their success in acquiring mining and timber concessions in Korea alarmed the Japanese, who viewed Korea as their own special sphere of influence.

In February 1904, without a declaration of war, the Japanese launched a surprise attack on the Russian fleet and land installations, and began a siege of the Russian naval

EUROPEAN SPHERES OF INFLUENCE IN ASIA

What was the effect upon China of the European powers' "spheres of influence"? How did this form of imperialism differ from colonization?

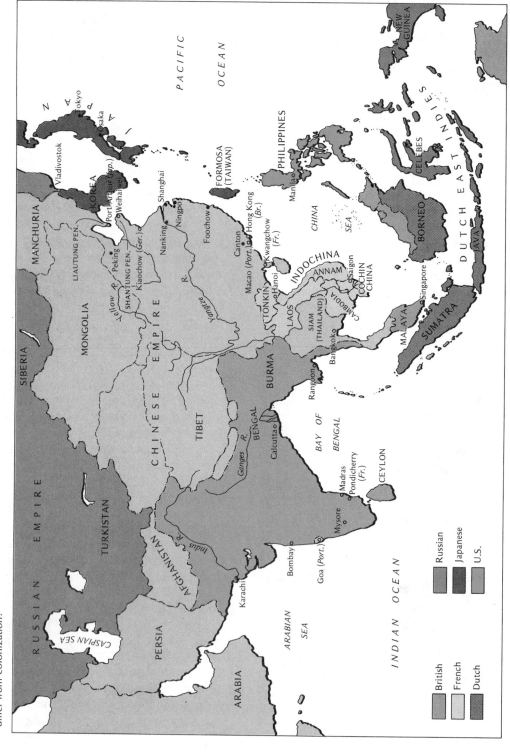

base at Port Arthur. The Japanese won a decisive victory at the Battle of Tsushima, destroying the Russian fleet.

The poor performance of the Russian forces contributed to a popular revolution in Russia (Chapter 14), and in 1905 Russia accepted U.S. President Theodore Roosevelt's offer to act as mediator between the two sides. In 1906, the *Treaty of Portsmouth* (New Hampshire) was signed between Japan and Russia. President Roosevelt subsequently was awarded a Nobel Peace Prize for his role in resolving the dispute.

The treaty gave Japan Russia's treaty rights in China and Manchuria, the southern half of Sakhalin Island, and recognized Japan's paramount interest in Korea. Japan had attained first-class rank as a world power. The Japanese victory over a European power stimulated nationalistic pride throughout Asia and contributed to the growth of independence movements.

IMPERIALISM IN SOUTHEAST ASIA AND THE PACIFIC

The European powers also took over most of Southeast Asia in the 19th century. Of all the countries there, only Thailand managed to retain its independence by playing off one colonial power against the others and by acting as a buffer between the colony of Burma, which Britain acquired in 1885, and the French colonial empire in Indochina.

THE FRENCH IN INDOCHINA

The French had a missionary presence in Indochina—the peninsula now divided between Vietnam, Cambodia, Thailand, and Laos—in the early part of the 17th century. French Jesuit missionaries helped to open parts of Indochina to French commercial enterprises. It was, however, only in the late 19th century that the French established a permanent presence there—an empire that was to last until after World War II.

As a result of the French participation in the second Opium War, French missionaries came under attack. The French sent in military forces, who captured Saigon and occupied other portions in Cochin China. In 1862, France was ceded this area, and in the 1880s, the French occupied Hanoi and moved into Tonkin and Annam. There, they skirmished with the Chinese, who had long claimed Indochina as part of their own sphere of influence. In 1885, China gave up its special claims and recognized the area as a French protectorate. The French in later years also gained control over Cambodia and Laos.

French colonial administrators took over the government of the area. Cochin China was ruled as a colony, and the rest of the area as protectorates. The French followed their usual principle of trying to instill French culture into their colonies. They established a school system in which subjects were taught in French, and French missionaries played an important part in the administration of the colonies.

THE ISLAND EMPIRES

The far-flung islands of the Dutch East Indies—present-day Indonesia—made up the largest and richest of the colonies of Holland. The Dutch government took over rule of the area from the Dutch East India Company in 1796. Under Dutch rule, the indigenous population was treated harshly, used almost as slave labor. The colony's greatest resource was the giant rubber plantations, whose profits enriched the Netherlands until the 20th century.

Spain ruled the Philippines until the end of the 19th century. During the latter half of the century, an independence movement arose. The Philippine nationalists' demands originally called for governmental reforms and were not anti-Spanish. Some of the leaders of the movement were of Spanish or part-Spanish descent. It was only when they saw that their hopes would not be fulfilled that they called for full independence. This goal was to continue even after the United States took over the Philippines after the Spanish-American War of 1898. In the same year, the United States annexed Hawaii.

The British hold on Malaya was primarily the work of one man—Sir Thomas Raffles. He bought Singapore from the local ruler, and under his direction, the settlement grew to become the most important city in Southeast Asia. As a colony, Malay was important for its resources of tin and its plantations. At first, Malay plantations were an important source of the staple food of the area, rice, but later rubber-tree plantations provided one of the important raw materials of the Industrial Revolution.

In addition, Britain enlarged its holdings in Australia and New Zealand during the 19th century. A gold rush in Australia in 1851 attracted many British settlers to the area. Australia was organized as a colony, but because it became largely peopled by Europeans, it was treated differently from other British colonies. By the outbreak of World War I, both Australia and New Zealand had acquired a great deal of home rule—similarly to South Africa and Canada.

BRITISH AND FRENCH COLONIAL POLICY

In general British policy toward its colonies in Asia and throughout the world was a pragmatic one. That is, the British did not have a consistent policy on colonial administration. The government responded to whatever conditions existed, loosening the ties of the empire whenever the indigenous population required it. Rebellion brought a delayed response adapted to the specific circumstances of the colony. As a result, Britain treated each colony differently.

Moreover, Great Britain in the late 19th century was itself an increasingly democratic nation whose government maintained that it was preparing the colonies for eventual independence. In practice, those British possessions with a white majority were given more self-government more quickly, in the somewhat racist assumption that they were more prepared for self-rule.

France, by contrast, followed a philosophy of empire, attempting to treat all its colonies the same. The essence of French policy was *assimilation*, that is, an attempt to form all colonial peoples into French men and women. In practice, this policy meant mandatory use of the French language; the teaching of French history, culture, and religion in the schools; and, in general, attempts to incorporate colonies as part of France, rather than preparing them for eventual independence.

SUMMARY

Western imperialism in Asia reached its peak by 1900, at which time nearly all of Asia was under the direct control or influence of the European powers, the United States, and Japan. This period of imperialism was motivated by several factors, including both economic and non-economic reasons, and was brought about primarily by military conquest. During the imperialist period, exploitation induced native nationalist movements, which eventually brought independence to these countries, but in the aftermath, most areas remained backward and nonindustrial. Their attempts to modernize and their difficulties in doing so are part of our contemporary world and will be discussed in Chapter 27.

QUESTIONS

1 What is the relationship between 19th-century imperialism, nationalism, and romanticism? To what extent are these ideas connected?
2 What were the underlying causes of 19th-century imperialism?
3 What different kinds of imperialism were practiced in the 19th century in Asia?
4 Contrast the histories of China and of Japan in the 19th century. Why was China more vulnerable and more victimized?
5 What advantages did the European imperialistic powers reap from their policies?

BIBLIOGRAPHY

BUCK, PEARL. *The Good Earth.* New York: Pocket Books, 1949. This is the classic novel of China's peasant people and their lives before the communist takeover.

COUPLAND, R. *Britain and India, 1600–1941.* London: Longmans, Green and Co., 1941. This brief study surveys the long and complex relationship between Britain and her colony of India over four centuries.

HOBSON, J. A. *Imperialism: A Study.* Ann Arbor: The University of Michigan Press, 1967. This study, written in 1902, presents a scathing indictment of imperialism, which Hobson believed was motivated primarily by economic forces. Hobson's importance lies chiefly in his impact on later writers, including Lenin.

LANGER, WILLIAM L. *Europe: The Diplomacy of Imperialism.* New York: Knopf, 1951. A classic study of imperialism from the perspective of European states during the most intense period of European imperialism.

PELISSIER, ROGER, ed. *The Awakening of China: 1793–1949.* New York: Capricorn Books, 1970. A useful survey of China from the imperialist period to the Chinese communist victory in 1949.

WINKS, ROBIN W., ed. *The Age of Imperialism.* Englewood Cliffs, N. J.: Prentice-Hall, 1969. This volume traces the history of imperialism through essays and primary sources.

17

During the time I was engaged in the slave trade, I never had the least scruples as to its lawfulness.

THE REVEREND JOHN NEWTON

Imperialism in Africa and Latin America

In 1800, Africa was known as the "Dark Continent," most of its terrain unknown to the West. By 1914, a few European states—Britain, France, Belgium, Germany, and Italy—had carved up most of Africa during the same period that they extended their influence in Asia. Their ability to conquer Africa came in part from their superior military technology. At the same time, African tribes offered little resistance, and in many cases, signed over their land through treaties.

For older colonies in the Western Hemisphere, the 19th century was a time when independence was gained from Spain and Portugal. The newly independent Latin American nations, however, had to face a strong, emergent United States to their north and contend with the economic power of the European nations. During this period, the new South American nations set patterns of dealing with their problems that would endure to the present day.

IMPERIALISM IN AFRICA The scramble for colonies in Africa occurred primarily in the last two decades of the 19th century. By the start of World War I, only Liberia and the ancient kingdom of Ethiopia were independent countries. Liberia had been established as a homeland for free American blacks in the 1820s.

Another haven for Africans fleeing slavery was established in the late 18th century by the British around the town of Freetown, today's capital of Sierra Leone. It was originally for slaves who had been given their freedom in exchange for fighting on the British side in the Revolutionary War.

AFRICAN VULNERABILITY

Several factors contributed to Africa's vulnerability in the 19th century. They included natural conditions in the continent that led to disunity, and the slave trade.

Natural Features. Africa's geographical features are important in understanding the continent's past and present. Africa encompasses 11.5 million square miles, more than three times the area of the United States. Yet its extensive coastline contains few natural harbors. The lack of harbors protects the interior from the outside world, but at the same time makes it difficult for Africans to sail to other parts of the world. Two great deserts, the Sahara in the north and the Kalahari in the south, serve as barriers to the territories

A slave market in North Africa. Africans were brought from the interior of the continent to coastal towns such as this to be traded.

beyond them. Although there are several major river systems, including the Congo, the Niger, the Nile, and the Zambezi, each has at least one feature which limits its usefulness for interior transportation. For example, most have steep rapids or falls which make travel hazardous.

The climate of Africa poses other problems which have deterred development. Average yearly temperatures are high, and areas like the tropical rain forests in the Congo region and along the west coast experience both excessive heat and high humidity. Rainfall presents a major problem, for it is not consistent, fluctuating between torrential amounts and drought. The rains are often so heavy that little of the water actually penetrates the soil, and causes serious erosion of the topsoil.

Africa is also plagued by insect pests which transmit several serious diseases. Mosquitoes carry malaria and yellow fever; the tsetse fly transmits sleeping sickness; and hookworms, lice, ticks, and fleas also contribute to a high death rate. It has only been in the 20th century that the population has grown rapidly. The total population of Africa today is 500 million.

These features of the African continent contributed to disunity, although during several periods centralized and sophisticated states did emerge, notably Ghana, Mali, and Songhai in the western Sudan, and Monomotopo in the southeast. In most periods of

African history, the peoples were politically organized on a local, tribal basis. Evidence of that localism is the fact that there are over 800 languages in Africa, some spoken only by a few thousand people. In turn, the multiplicity of languages served as one of the barriers to unification or the development of nation-states.

The Slave Trade. In addition to natural factors, Africa's inability to resist the Western imperialists was the result of the insidious European slave trade which began in the 15th century and continued into the early part of the 19th century. The European slave trade in Africa was begun by the Portuguese in the 15th century. The Dutch also engaged in slave trading in the 15th century. By the mid-16th century, the French began acquiring African slaves for its colonies in the West Indies, and England soon followed. At the peak of the African slave trade, the English imported more than half of the slaves. At least 15 million African slaves were transported to America.

The countries involved in slave trading usually did not go into the interior; instead they bought their slaves from Africans on the coast. The slaves were either prisoners of war or were nabbed by bounty hunters. Taken to the coastal area, the captives were placed in holding camps until a sufficient number had been collected to fill the holds of the foreign ships.

Among the slave trading ships captains there were the "tight packers" who chose to crowd their captives into very close quarters below deck with each slave given only enough space to lie in a fetal position. As a result, many died during the voyage. Enough survived, so the captains argued, to compensate for their losses. The "loose packers" provided each slave with several feet of space. Although fewer could be placed on board, these captains believed that the higher survival rate guaranteed higher profits when the slaves were sold—for example, the slaves were healthier and were more attractive to their potential buyers.

The slave trade was outlawed in Europe in the early 19th century, primarily as the result of protests by numerous abolition groups who successfully appealed to the consciences of Europeans.

The slave trade had a devastating effect on Africa in several ways. It depleted the population: in addition to the millions actually transported, untold millions of others were killed during the internal conflicts which the slavers instigated. The continent

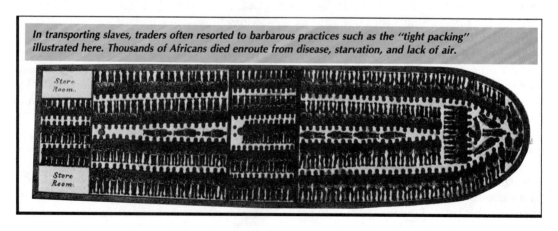

In transporting slaves, traders often resorted to barbarous practices such as the "tight packing" illustrated here. Thousands of Africans died enroute from disease, starvation, and lack of air.

was thus deprived of its healthiest, most robust young adults, including those who would have been the leaders of the future. The slave trade also invited internal disorder in what had been a very stable society. The slavers often traded alcohol and guns in exchange for the slaves, for instance, which further contributed to the political and social breakdown of African societies. A less tangible factor was the destruction of native culture under Western influence. Contrary to the firm beliefs of most 19th-century Europeans, African tribal groups had viable cultures which were closely adapted to the physical environment. For example, many tribes had developed effective political systems, often communal and democratic, in which the tribal members made political decisions by consensus.

THE EXPLORERS

In many areas south of the Sahara, the first Europeans in the interior were explorers. Many of these early explorers were British adventurers who were motivated by curiosity. North Africa had been known to Europeans since ancient times, but the vast areas of rain forest and grassland south of the Sahara remained a mystery.

Early Explorers. Among the first explorers in sub-Saharan Africa was James Bruce (1730–1794), a Scot who wanted to discover the sources of the Nile River. Although he did discover the source of one tributary, the Blue Nile, he afterwards learned that it had already been discovered 150 years earlier by a Portuguese Jesuit. But Bruce's book, *Travels to Discover the Source of the Nile*, sparked Europeans' interest in the vast interior of the continent.

The African Association, founded in England in 1788, sponsored expeditions to discover the source of the Niger River. In 1795–97, Mungo Park, also a Scot, discovered the upper reaches of the river and learned that it flowed east. In his diary he described his discovery:

• • • *looking forward, I saw with infinite pleasures the great object of my mission; the long sought for, majestic Niger, glittering in the morning sun, as broad as the Thames at Westminster, and flowing slowly to the eastward. I hastened to the brink, and having drank of the water, lifted up my fervent thanks in prayer.*[1]

Richard Lander, in 1830, traveled the Niger to its mouth. Lander was one of the few explorers killed by the natives, after several previous close encounters.

By mid-century, many expeditions were sponsored by the Africa Society, now renamed the Royal Geographical Society, which was often subsidized by the British government. A series of expeditions sponsored by the Society brought at last the discovery of the sources of the Nile. Richard Burton and John Speke discovered Lake Tanganyika and Lake Nyaza in 1858; in 1862, James A. Grant and John Speke proved the latter lake was the source of the Nile.

David Livingstone. Among the many explorers of Africa, one name is widely known: David Livingstone (1813–1873). In the career of Dr. Livingstone, one finds examples of three motives for imperialism: intellectual curiosity, the missionary spirit, and trade. Livingstone was a medical doctor whose first trip to Africa was sponsored by the London Missionary Society, an organization dedicated to the religious salvation of the "heathen" Africans. He also hoped to open Africa to trade. Livingstone outlined his views in a lecture at Cambridge University in 1857 when he said:

• • • *my object is to open up traffic along the banks of the Zambezi, and also to preach the Gospel. . . . Those two pioneers of*

---

[1] Margery Perham and J. Simmons, *African Discovery: An Anthology of Exploration* (Evanston, Ill.: Northwestern University Press, 1963), p. 80.

civilization—Christianity and commerce—should ever be inseparable.[2]

Dr. Livingstone first arrived in Africa in 1841. After spending eight years as a missionary, he began a series of expeditions in central Africa. He explored the area of the Niger, as so many others had done. He followed the Zambezi River, discovering Victoria Falls; crossed from the east coast to the west; and spent the last years of his life in the area of the Congo River.

Henry Stanley. These African expeditions excited the interest of Europeans and Americans and coincided with the growth of the reading public. The penny press, cheap newspapers, increased sales with sensational headlines and articles, often about African expeditions.

One of these papers, the *New York Herald*, owned by James Gordon Bennett, sent its intrepid reporter Henry Stanley (1841–1904) to the Congo in 1871 to find Dr. Livingstone, who hadn't been heard from in six years. The *New York Herald* published breathless accounts of Stanley's exploits. When Stanley at last happened upon the British explorer, he is reported to have greeted him with the famous line, "Dr. Livingstone, I presume?"—a conclusion which certainly didn't require unusual perceptiveness on Stanley's part. Stanley later returned to Africa to further explore the Congo, obtaining a sponsor, King Leopold of Belgium. On Leopold's behalf, Stanley made numerous treaties with local chieftains, who signed over the Congo to the Belgian king.

By mid-century, economics began to be a factor in African exploration, with the creation of several companies which received a charter to seek economic concessions. The Industrial Revolution increased European manufacturers' need both for raw materials,

such as cotton and rubber, and for markets for their industrial goods. Many hoped that African colonization would also provide an outlet for the population pressures felt by many European states. In fact, few Europeans migrated to Africa, for the climate, the prevalence of disease, the poor soil, and unfriendly natives discouraged most would-be colonists.

THE AFRICAN SCRAMBLE

As we have seen, nationalism and the desire for power, prestige, and glory for one's native land were compelling forces in this era. Nationalistic competition triggered the scramble for African colonies between 1879 and 1914. Leopold's activities in the Congo precipitated the scramble, when the other nations became alarmed at his success.

THE FRENCH AND BRITISH IN NORTH AFRICA

The Ottoman Turks had conquered most of North Africa, but during the 18th century, as Ottoman power declined, this area slipped away from Ottoman control, becoming virtually independent states. The French invaded Algiers in 1830, and after eight years of fighting, gained control of the area. To solidify their hold on the colony, the French encouraged emigration from France to Algeria. Other Europeans also emigrated there. It is estimated that by the end of the 19th century, there were almost one million Europeans in Algeria.

Napoleon's invasion of Egypt in 1798 led to change in Egypt. One of the leaders of the resistance to the French was Mohammed Ali. The invasion weakened the hold of the Ottoman Empire on Egypt, and Mohammed Ali assumed control of the country. He moved to westernize Egypt, building roads, encouraging Egyptians to study in Europe, and bringing European advisers to help the modernization efforts. Mohammed Ali also extended Egypt's borders to the Red Sea and into portions of the Sudan. To pay for these

---

[2] Phyllis M. Martin and Patrick O'Meara, eds., *Africa* (Bloomington, Ind.: Indiana University Press, 1977), p. 126.

EUROPEAN SPHERES OF INFLUENCE IN AFRICA, 1914

How did British-French rivalries in Africa affect their relations before World War I?

Legend:
- British
- French
- German
- Belgian
- Portuguese
- Spanish
- Italian
- Union of South Africa

GREAT BRITAIN
GERMANY
BELGIUM
FRANCE
ITALY
PORTUGAL SPAIN

Algiers Tunis
Tangiers
Casablanca
FRENCH MOROCCO
SPANISH MOROCCO
ALGERIA TUNISIA
Tripoli
MEDITERRANEAN SEA
Alexandria
El Alamein
Cairo Suez Canal
CANARY IS. (Sp.)
RIO DE ORO
SAHARA DESERT
LIBYA
BRITISH PROTECTORATE OF EGYPT
Aswan
MAURITANIA
Timbuktu
CHAD
RED SEA
Nile R.
SENEGAL
Dakar
GAMBIA
PORT. GUINEA
SIERRA LEONE
LIBERIA
IVORY COAST
GOLD COAST
TOGO
DAHOMEY
Niger R.
NIGERIA
Khartoum
ANGLO-EGYPTIAN SEDAN
Fashoda
ERITREA
Adowa
FRENCH SOMALILAND
GULF OF ADEN
BRITISH SOMALILAND
Addis Ababa
ETHIOPIA
UBANGI-CHARI
CAMEROONS
RIO MUNI
GABON
Congo R.
FRENCH CONGO
Leopoldville
CABINDA
BELGIAN CONGO
UGANDA KENYA
BRITISH EAST AFRICA
Lake Victoria
Lake Tanganyika
TANGANYIKA
GERMAN EAST AFRICA
ITALIAN SOMALILAND
ZANZIBAR
INDIAN OCEAN
ATLANTIC
OCEAN
ANGOLA
Lake Nyasa
NORTHERN RHODESIA
Victoria Falls
Zambezi R.
MOZAMBIQUE
SOUTHERN RHODESIA
MADAGASCAR
GERMAN SOUTHWEST AFRICA
BECHUANALAND
TRANSVAAL
SWAZILAND
ORANGE FREE STATE
NATAL
BASUTOLAND
CAPE COLONY
Cape Town

309

projects, Ali and his successors borrowed money from Europe.

Between 1859 and 1869, a French company built the Suez Canal, thus shortening the sea route to Asia by half. The building of the canal provided a link from the Mediterranean to British colonies in Asia, and came to be regarded as the "lifeline of the British Empire." During the 1870s, British prime minister Benjamin Disraeli took advantage of the perpetual need of the Egyptian rulers for money by purchasing Egypt's controlling interest of shares in the canal. The purchase of the canal shares propelled the British into a closer relationship with Egypt.

In 1882, the British declared a protectorate over the country. The French opposed this claim.

It was not surprising that France and Britain should come into conflict over their imperialist claims in Africa. The French dreamed of a French Africa stretching from east to west, while the British aim was a British Africa, north to south, "from Cairo to the Cape." When the British declared a further protectorate, over the Sudan, in 1898, the two nations nearly came to war. British troops entering the Sudan from Egypt encountered French forces at Fashoda. War was only averted when the French com-

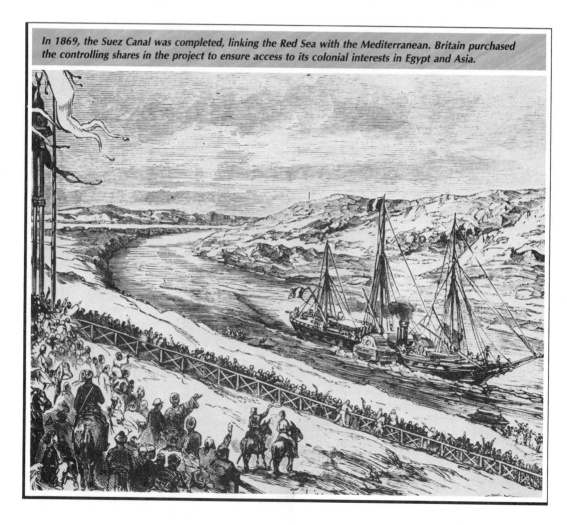

In 1869, the Suez Canal was completed, linking the Red Sea with the Mediterranean. Britain purchased the controlling shares in the project to ensure access to its colonial interests in Egypt and Asia.

mander withdrew on orders from his government, leaving open the way for British troops to control the Sudan for Her Majesty's government.

In 1904, the British and French came to an agreement on Africa. The French recognized the legality of the British position in Egypt in return for a British agreement that the French had a paramount interest in Morocco. This agreement was to have an important effect on the relations between the two countries (Chapter 18).

EUROPEANS IN WEST AND CENTRAL AFRICA

Although small European outposts had been established on the West African coast since the 15th century, the interior of this region was only colonized in the 19th century. In West Africa, the lion's share of the colonies were French. The French colonized Chad and the area known as Senegal. As in all their other colonies, the French attempted to carry out what was called the "French civilizing mission." They attempted to assimilate the indigenous people into the French culture and encouraged the use of French. A local, French-speaking elite was created, and schools used French as the primary language.

The French activity aroused opposition by the indigenous people. Samori Toure, the ruler of the Senegal Empire, opposed French advances, fighting them for several years. But the superiority of European armaments meant that the conclusion could never be in doubt.

The successes of the French in West Africa stimulated the British to seek colonies there. They added to the Freetown area the colonies of the Gold Coast (today's Ghana) and Nigeria.

THE BELGIAN CONGO

As we have seen, Henry Stanley had obtained the Congo for the Belgian king Leopold as his personal possession. The Belgian Congo was the most extreme example of ex-

Leopold II of Belgium at first ruled the Congo as a private possession. Scandals concerning slavery, however, led to government administration of the area.

ploitation by a European power. Under Leopold's International Congo Association (ICA), the first exploitable resources discovered were rubber and ivory. To develop those resources, natives were forced to work for the company; moreover the company assessed taxes on the native population in the form of rubber and ivory. By 1900, persistent rumors that natives were being mistreated in the Congo set off an international furor. In 1904, a British consul in Africa, Roger Casement, reported to the British parliament tales of terror tactics used by the ICA, including the charge that cannibals were allowed to devour natives who were unwilling to work or were delinquent in their taxes. As a result of stories such as these, Leopold was forced to create an international commission to investigate conditions in the Congo. The commission's findings concurred with Casement's allegations, and in 1908, the Belgian legislature forced Leopold to turn the Congo over to the Belgian government, which then ruled the colony directly.

The German victory over France in the Franco-Prussian War stimulated Germany's desire to become a great power. Part of the great-power role in the 19th Century was a colonizing effort. However, the German chancellor, Otto von Bismarck, was reluctant to become involved in the scramble for colonies. He did not want to risk alienating any European power that might support France's desire to avenge its losses in the Franco-Prussian War. Nevertheless German merchants and traders exerted pressure on the German government to provide them the power and influence necessary to stake their claims on African soil.

When Germany entered the scramble, the only part of the continent still uncolonized was East Africa. However, the British, after extending their control through Egypt and the Sudan, wanted to continue their southward march. The Belgians and Portuguese were also eyeing this region, seeking to extend their territories from the Atlantic eastward across Africa.

Thus, Bismarck called the *Berlin Conference* of colonial powers in 1884. The purpose of the conference was to establish rules for the scramble and thereby reduce the likelihood of a European war over rival colonial claims. The conferees were able to agree on specific rules, such as requiring the power that claimed an area to occupy it. A power could not land on an African beach and claim the territory inland to an unspecified distance.

As a result of the Berlin Conference, Germany was given territory on the west coast of Africa (today called Tanzania), on the southeast coast (today's Namibia), as well as the Cameroons and Togo. Britain received an east-coast territory north of the German holdings (today's Kenya). Farther down the east coast, Mozambique became a Portuguese colony, and in the interior Belgium extended the borders of the Congo.

The situation in southern Africa was complex. The Dutch had been the original settlers in the area, establishing a settlement at the Cape of Good Hope in 1652. This little Cape Colony grew over the years, attracting a sprinkling of Germans and French Huguenots. It was originally a way station for ships that needed supplies and repairs on their way to and from Asia.

Seeing the strategic potential of the territory, the British seized the outpost during the Napoleonic Wars and the area was formally ceded to them in 1814. When the British declared an end to slavery throughout the British Empire in 1834, the Dutch inhabitants, called *Boers*, moved north into the interior of the country on what they called the *Great Trek*.

In the early 1850s the British recognized the independence of the two Boer states in the interior, the Transvaal and the Orange Free State. But in the 1870s and 1880s, diamonds and gold were discovered in the interior of southern Africa, attracting people from all over Europe to develop the resources. British capitalists were in the vanguard of those hoping to make fortunes from the mineral discoveries. This time, tension between the Boers and the British exploded into war.

The *Boer War* (1899–1902) resulted in a British victory, but it caused enduring bitterness between the Dutch and the English settlers. During the war, the Boer farmers had adopted guerrilla tactics to fight British troops. In response, the British burned the Boers' farms, taking their wives and children as captives. The civilians were interned in camps, where sanitary conditions were horrible. Many died of disease and maltreatment; in fact, these were the first prisoner facilities known as concentration camps.

The British united all the colonies in southern Africa into the Union of South Africa in 1910. South Africa received a great

As governor of the British colony in South Africa, Cecil Rhodes played a central part in the conflicts which led to the Boer War. This French cartoon suggests that British interests in the area were maintained through wholesale devastation and bloodshed.

deal of self-government, although it recognized the British sovereign as its titular ruler, much as Canada and Australia did. However, the more numerous Dutch descendants ultimately won control of the country. Their racial policies toward the native black population of the area would bring them worldwide condemnation in the 20th century.

ITALY AND ETHIOPIA

With its unification, Italy too looked for colonies in Africa. It took control of Libya in 1912, but was ambitious for further conquest. It turned to Ethiopia, which had been Christianized during the early part of the Christian era. Isolated for many centuries, its rulers dated their line back to the Biblical King Solomon.

When the Ethiopian king, Menelik II, became aware of Italian designs, he procured Western arms for his troops. When the Ital-

ians met the Ethiopians at the *Battle of Adowa* in 1896, the Italians were routed. This was the only significant defeat suffered by a European power at the hands of native people during the imperialist period. Ethiopia's independence under African rulers was secured until Italy attempted to avenge its ignominious defeat in the 1930s.

AFRICAN IMPERIALISM

For the native African, European conquest had mostly negative ramifications. European powers sought to exploit their gains at the expense of the native population. In the early years, control over colonial areas was most often assigned to chartered companies. These companies exerted economic, political, and judicial power over the native population. Germany maintained such a system until 1890, when the government established its Colonial Office.

The fragmentary head at left, dating sometime between the 9th to 13th centuries, is an example of the sophisticated culture of West Africa in this era. The salt cellar (right) dates from the 16th century, and reflects Portuguese influence. The indigenous culture reflected by these artifacts was largely destroyed by the slave trade.

The French ruled their colonies directly with a colonial office which supervised the governor-general in each colony. But the French economic exploitation was often carried out by concessionaires, private companies who had nearly a free rein within their monopoly. Some of the worst excesses were the result of this policy. The native became an employee of the company, and forced labor was often used. On at least one occasion, the concessionaries kidnapped the women and children of surrounding villages and held them hostage to guarantee the cooperation of the native men. In another incident, natives who refused to work were maimed physically. A malingerer had his right hand cut off to serve as an example to his fellow workers.

The British adapted colonial policy to existing conditions, although most areas came under the jurisdiction of the British Colonial Office. Britain, too, granted charters to private companies for economic development. These companies operated agricultural concessions, and built railroads, warehouses, and similar facilities.

A second direct effect of European colonialism on native Africans was the disruption of the native cultures. Within the continent before European invasion lived a wide variety of people who can be categorized into three general types. The most numerous, the Negroes, accounted for a majority of the population; they in turn can be divided into several sub-types. In addition, there were Caucasoid people living in the area north of the Sahara, and a third group, the Bushmen, or Khoi, whose origins are unclear.

Within these three major types a wide range of cultures and languages existed, and thousands of political units functioned. Before the advent of the Europeans, the prevalent political organization was tribal, with the tribes ranging in size from a few hundred to thousands of people. Most relied on subsistence farming for their livelihood. During the colonial period, these native cultures were disrupted and in many cases were irrevocably lost.

The arrogant Europeans assumed that since most of the native cultures lacked written language, they were pre-civilized; and that lacking written records, they had no history. Today, as the result of developments in archaeology and anthropology, those assumptions are no longer valid. For example, it is now apparent that oral tradition—that is, the stories which are passed from one generation to the next—contain valid evidence from which a culture's history can be constructed.

The most disruptive effect of imperialism was the partition of Africa into separate states whose boundaries were based not on tribal divisions, but on arbitrary agreements between the European powers. In other words, the colonies created by the Europeans did not replicate any native cultural or tribal boundaries. As a result, one of the most critical problems confronting the independent African states today is the need to forge national unity, and a national sense of identity.

19TH-CENTURY LATIN AMERICA

Most of Latin America was conquered by Spanish *conquistadores* in the first wave of European imperialism in the 16th century. The lure of gold and silver, a sense of adventure, national pride, and the missionary spirit were motives here as well.

In the 19th century, Latin American countries gained their independence from Spain and Portugal. Independence did not, however, mean an absence of problems.

Native drawings of a priest and a conquistadore depict the two facets of Spanish rule in South America.

COLONIAL LATIN AMERICA

The colonial system of the Spanish and Portuguese had been set in the 16th and 17th centuries. The result was a vast empire ruled by the Spanish crown which directly administered these colonial possessions and mined their gold and silver ores. The Spanish crown worked with the Roman Catholic Church, which wished to convert the native population. In Brazil, the Portuguese crown and the Church similarly worked in conjunction. The Church was given complete control of the ecclesiastical affairs of the Spanish and Portuguese colonies. Both the state and the Church sought to infuse Spanish or Portuguese language and culture into Latin America.

In order to accomplish political, economic, religious, and cultural dominance, thousands of Spaniards and Portuguese emigrated to the New World, where they ruled a vast indigenous Indian and African slave population. They constructed a minority white rule and exploited the native populations—which remained ignorant, landless, and impoverished.

Spanish colonial society was rigidly stratified, with the European population holding the highest status. To have been born in Spain itself was the best of all. Those of European descent who were born in the colonies were called *Creoles* and had lesser status. It was from this portion of society that many of the leaders for independence would come. Beneath the Creole in status was the *mestizo*, or person of mixed Indian and European birth. At the bottom of society were Indians and African slaves. The mix of these peoples varied from region to region.

LATIN AMERICAN INDEPENDENCE

The Enlightenment and the French and American Revolutions had a great impact on Latin America. The ideas of the French Revolution excited intellectuals and stimulated them to call for independence. An Argentinian recalled:

• • • *Since I was in Spain in 1789, and the French Revolution was then causing a change in ideas, especially among the men of letters with whom I associated, the ideals of liberty, equality, security, and property took a firm hold on me, and I saw only tyrants in those who would restrain a man, wherever he might be, from enjoying the rights with which God and Nature had endowed him.*[3]

In 1791, Toussaint L'Ouverture (1743–1803) led a successful rebellion of slaves in Haiti. When Napoleon came to power, he sent troops to the island to regain French control, but a combination of Haitian resistance and the ravages of yellow fever defeated his efforts. Haiti became the second republic in the Western Hemisphere.

When Napoleon placed his brother Joseph on the Spanish throne in 1808, revolutions

broke out in parts of Latin America. Paraguay and Venezuela, for example, proclaimed their independence and attempted to establish republics. The defeat of Napoleon and the subsequent restoration of the Bourbon dynasty temporarily interrupted the independence movements.

Independence of Mexico. In Mexico, a Creole priest, Miguel Hidalgo (1753–1811), organized the Indians to achieve reforms. In 1810, Hidalgo openly declared Mexico's independence from Spain. His forces captured several provinces. But in 1811, Hidalgo was captured and killed by the Spanish. His work was carried on by another Creole priest, Jose Morales. Morales tried to extend further economic reforms. He too was captured and killed, in 1815.

Independence came to Mexico when both the reformers and conservatives united to bring it about. In 1820, a revolution broke out in Spain, and the Spanish king, Ferdinand VII, was forced to accept a constitution. Taking advantage of this disturbance in the mother country, the conservative leader Agustin de Iturbide (1753–1825) declared Mexico independent in 1821. Spain recognized the independence. Iturbide soon declared himself emperor of Mexico, but he was forced to abdicate in 1823, and a constitution established a Mexican republic.

Independence of Central America. The same year Mexico gained independence, the countries of Central America also declared their independence. In 1823, the countries formed the United Provinces of Central America. However, the union did not last. Its members today are the countries of Guatemala, Honduras, El Salvador, Nicaragua, and Costa Rica.

Independence of Spanish South America. With the restoration of Ferdinand VII in 1815, the Spanish monarchy tried to regain its former control over the South American colonies. But Spain was no longer a great power, and its empire was overthrown

---

[3] Benjamin Keen and Mark Wasserman, *A Short History of Latin America* (Boston: Houghton Mifflin, 1980), p. 146.

The revolutionary hero Simon Bolivar liberated the northern part of Spanish South America, paving the way for the creation of independent states.

through the efforts of three Latin American leaders.

The first of the Latin American rebels was Simon Bolivar (1783–1830), known as "the Liberator." Bolivar, a Creole, was born in Caracas, Venezuela. As a young man, he traveled in Europe and the United States, and saw for himself the effects of the American and French Revolutions. He became devoted to the cause of independence for South America. Bolivar mocked the power of Spain: "Can that nation carry on the exclusive commerce of one-half the world when it lacks manufactures, agricultural products, crafts and sciences, and even a policy?"[4]

---

[4] *Ibid.*, p. 152.

After participating in the earlier unsuccessful attempts at independence, Bolivar attained success in 1819. In that year, he led troops from Venezuela into Colombia, where he defeated the Spanish army. Bolivar became the President of the Republic of Great Colombia, which included today's Venezuela, Colombia, and parts of Ecuador and Panama.

The second great Latin American leader was the Creole rebel José de San Martin of Argentina. San Martin led troops that obtained the independence of Argentina in 1816. The Chilean Bernardo O'Higgins was the third rebel leader. With the help of San Martin, he forced the Spanish out of Chile in 1818.

In the early 1820s, the Spanish were expelled from Peru. The last major battle between Spanish and Latin American forces occurred in 1824. South America was now comprised of independent states.

Independence of Brazil. The independence of Brazil was the least difficult of all to achieve. When Napoleon invaded Portugal in 1808, the Portuguese royal family fled to Rio de Janeiro. After Napoleon's defeat, the royal family returned to Portugal, leaving their son Pedro in Brazil. During the turbulence in the rest of South America, the Brazilians asked Pedro to become their ruler. Brazil, therefore, peacefully proclaimed its independence of Portugal, and Pedro became its monarch.

PROBLEMS OF THE NEW REPUBLICS

The new republics of South America faced a wide variety of social and political problems, many of which were a direct legacy of Spain's colonial policies.

Social Differences. After independence, the racial separations instituted by the Spanish remained, with the white minority dominant and convinced of its own superiority. Spanish colonial policy had provided education and political representation to the

LATIN AMERICAN NATIONS—DATES OF INDEPENDENCE

How were Latin American independence movements affected by the Napoleonic era and the peace settlements of 1815?

GULF OF MEXICO

BAHAMA IS.

HAITI (*Fr.*) 1804

SAN DOMINGO 1843

CUBA 1902

MEXICO 1823

BR. HONDURAS (BELIZE)

JAMAICA

GUATEMALA

HONDURAS

NICARAGUA

EL SALVADOR

COSTA RICA

PANAMA

CENTRAL AMERICA: 1823

Panama Canal (1914)

PUERTO RICO

CARIBBEAN SEA

VIRGIN IS. (*U.S. and Br.*)

ANGUILLA (*Br.*)

GUADALOUPE (*Fr.*)

DOMINICA (*Br.*)

MARTINIQUE (*Fr.*)

WEST INDIES

BARBADOS (*Br.*)

GRENADA (*Br.*)

DUTCH ANTILLES

TRINIDAD (*Br.*)

Caracas

VENEZUELA 1830

BR. GUIANA 1966

DUTCH GUIANA (SURINAM)

FR. GUIANA

Bogotá

COLOMBIA 1819

Quito

ECUADOR 1830

Amazon R.

A n d e s M t s.

PERU 1821

Lima

BRAZIL 1822

BOLIVIA 1825

La Paz

PACIFIC OCEAN

PARAGUAY 1811

Rio de Janeiro

Sao Paulo

A n d e s M t s.

ARGENTINA 1816

URUGUAY 1828

Santiago

Buenos Aires

ATLANTIC OCEAN

Spanish colonial area

Portuguese colonial area

FALKLAND IS. (*Br.*)

318

white upper class, while the native population remained illiterate. This illiteracy compounded the problems of reformers who hoped to institute democratic governments, for much of the population was unprepared to exercise its political and civil rights.

Dependence on the Military. It had required military power to conquer and maintain the colonial possessions, and military force to gain independence. As a result, the new leaders tended to rely on military power not only to protect their new states from foreign threats, but also to subdue the native population. Since independence, military dictatorships have been most frequently the Latin American form of government.

Artificial Borders. The territorial divisions of the Latin American states were arbitrarily imposed by the conquerors; with independence there was often no unifying force of community of interest to hold together the new nation and its citizens.

Inequitable Distribution of Land. Colonial economic exploitations drained these colonies of their most important natural resources, gold and silver. What remained was agricultural potential, but Spanish policy had placed ownership of land in the hands of the Spanish nobility. The native population found themselves forced to work land they did not own. Like peasants everywhere they have sought land ownership, but the equitable redistribution of land has even today not occurred, resisted by the vested interests. The vast contrast between landed gentry and peasants, between the very rich and the abject poor, remains a critical problem and the source of widespread discontent in Latin America.

LATIN AMERICA AND EUROPE

Although the countries of Latin America gained political independence, they were closely tied economically to Europe. Latin America produced raw materials such as agricultural products, particularly beef and minerals—in return becoming a market for the manufactured goods of Europe. In their search for exports, many Latin American countries became dependent on single crops or a few limited resources. For example, Haiti exported sugar, Chile exported silver and copper, and Brazil exported coffee.

The European powers, led by Britain and France, invested heavily in the South American economies. They provided money for the building of railroads and financed mining operations. In return, they gained leverage over the Latin American countries. Often European investors would loan money to Latin American governments to restore or build ports or bridges. When the government showed signs that it would not repay the debt, investors would try to get their governments to force the Latin American government to pay. The French government, for example, used the pretext of the Mexican government's indebtedness when it sent troops to back Maximilian's claim to be emperor of Mexico in 1862 (Chapter 12). Europe thus exercised a form of economic imperialism over Latin America.

Yet this investment led to economic growth in the continent. In addition, many Europeans emigrated to South America in the 19th century—particularly to Argentina, Chile, and Brazil—bringing skills and economic expertise. In the 1880s, around three million Europeans came to South America.

The European influence was also seen in the culture of South America. European intellectual influence as well as styles could be found in the South American cities. A contemporary visitor described Peru in mid-century:

• • • *In the past four or five years great changes have taken place in Peruvian customs and practices; Parisian fashions now hold sway there. . . . The clothes of the upper classes do not differ at all from those of Europe; women and men dress exactly as in Paris; women scrupulously follow the dictates of the new styles, save that they do not cover their heads and that custom requires that they attend church dressed in black, with the mantilla, in all the severity of the Spanish costume. French dances are replacing the fandango, the bolero, and the native dances, which decency frowns upon. Scores from our operas are sung in the salons and even our novels are read there.*[5]

LATIN AMERICA AND THE UNITED STATES

During the 19th century, the United States expanded westward across North America and became a rich and powerful country. At the beginning of the century, it played a helpful role in supporting the independence of the new countries. In 1823, the United States issued the Monroe Doctrine, which announced that the United States regarded the hemisphere as closed to future colonization by any European powers.

Relations between the United States and the nations to the south soured as the 19th century progressed. In 1846–48, a war was fought with Mexico over Texas. After its victory, the United States gained about one-third of Mexico's territory.

But it was in the final years of the century that relations became less friendly. The United States had industrialized in the last half of the century, and it too was looking for markets and colonies. Spain had at this time only two American colonies left—Cuba and Puerto Rico. The Cubans revolted and the United States recognized their independence. In 1898, the United States went to war with Spain.

The Spanish-American War was a complete success for the United States. It demonstrated how powerful a nation it had become. It won victories both in the Pacific, where it took the Philippines from Spain (Chapter 16), and in the Caribbean. Puerto Rico became a territory of the United States, and Cuba was granted independence, with qualifications. The United States was

granted bases in Cuba and control over the foreign policy of the island.

The United States also interfered in the affairs of Latin America to build the Panama Canal. When Colombia—which ruled what is today Panama—stalled in its negotiations over the prospective canal, the United States backed a revolt by Panamanians against the Colombian government. The United States immediately recognized the new state of Panama in 1903, and the next year construction of the canal began. It was opened in 1914, with a long-term lease.

THE MEXICAN REVOLUTION

In the 1860s, Mexico was ruled by Benito Juarez, of Indian descent. During his reign, many reforms were made in the country. The power of the Church was weakened by the forced sale of its lands, the responsibility for education shifted to the state, and early attempts at ameliorating the plight of the poor were made.

Under Juarez' successor, Porfirio Diaz, these reforms stopped. Diaz ruled for 35 years. During his tenure, foreign powers were granted concessions in the country. Although Mexico experienced economic growth, very little of it affected the poorer peasants. At the turn of the century, Mexico was a country in which 77 percent of its 15 million people lived on the land.

In 1910, a revolution broke out in Mexico. It was to go on for seven years and keep the country in chaos during that time. The loss of life was enormous—some estimates put the death rate at about 12 percent of the population. In 1917, a new government ended the strife and a new constitution was written. The large estates were broken up and peasants received land. More power was granted to the *mestizos* who formed a large part of the population. Reforms were made in labor practices and the separation of church and state was established. This is the constitution under which Mexico lives today.

---

[5] *Ibid.*, p. 239.

SUMMARY

Imperialism in Africa and Latin America, perpetrated by the western European states, had a lasting effect on the indigenous populations by exploiting their resources and disrupting native societies and cultures. It also worsened relations between the Western states themselves and served as one of the major causes of World War I.

QUESTIONS

1 Why was Africa especially vulnerable to European imperialists?
2 What was the effect of the centuries-long slave trade on the subsequent history of the African continent?
3 What was the "African scramble"?
4 Compare French and British colonial policies.
5 What problems were faced by the new republics of Latin America?

BIBLIOGRAPHY

DAVIDSON, BASIL. *Which Way Africa?* Harmondsworth, England: Penguin, 1973. *One of the foremost historians of Africa analyses the impact of imperialism and assesses Africa's future.*
HALEY, ALEX. *Roots.* Garden City, N.Y.: Doubleday, 1976. *This popular novel effectively portrays the slave trade and its deleterious effects in Africa and in America. The novel also illustrates the use of oral tradition in reconstructing the past.*
KEEN, BENJAMIN and MARK WASSERMAN. *A Short History of Latin America.* Boston: Houghton Mifflin, 1980. *A survey of the complex and tumultuous history of Latin America.*
MANNIX, DANIEL. *Black Cargoes: A History of the Atlantic Slave Trade, 1518–1865.* New York: Viking Press, 1962. *This book is one of the most important studies of the African slave trade, its nature and its impact.*
OLIVER, ROLAND and J. D. FAGE. *A Short History of Africa.* Baltimore: Penguin Books, 1963. *This book traces the history of the continent from earliest times to the present, and includes useful chapters on archaeology and anthropology.*

Ideological Confrontations and International Conflict

● I look upon the People and the Nation handed on to me as a responsibility conferred upon me by God, and I believe, as it is written in the Bible, that it is my duty to increase this heritage for which one day I shall be called upon to give an account. Whoever tries to interfere with my task I shall crush. [1914]

WILHELM II

● This is not peace, it is an armistice for twenty years. [May 28, 1919]

FERDINAND FOCH

● I think there is a certain basis of truth in the fear which the Russian government is beginning to have of communism; for communism is Tsarist autocracy turned upside down.

ALEXANDER HERZEN

● This is the second time in our history that there has come back from Germany to Downing Street Peace with Honour; I believe it is peace for our time.

NEVILLE CHAMBERLAIN

● We shall not flag or fail. . . . We shall fight on the beaches, we shall fight on the landing grounds, we shall fight in the fields and in the streets, we shall fight in the hills; we shall never surrender.

WINSTON CHURCHILL

● War alone brings to its highest tension all human energy and puts the stamp of nobility upon those nations who have the courage to make it.

BENITO MUSSOLINI

323

The Underlying Causes of World War I

By 1914, the continent of Europe had spread its civilization throughout the world. The countries of Europe had assumed a political, economic, and intellectual dominance that was unchallenged. This dominance was to be undermined by World War I, however.

Although the actual precipitating event of the war was a terrorist action in the Balkans, the approximately 40 years before the war had seen developments that helped bring it on. It is these underlying causes that are the topic of this chapter. They include the forces of nationalism, which had an important influence upon the domestic politics and foreign policies of European nations; the splitting of Europe into two camps through a secret system of alliances; the growth of militarism; and tensions engendered by imperialism.

NATIONALISM AND DOMESTIC POLITICS Nationalism was the primary force of the 19th century. It brought about the unification of Germany and Italy, and caused other upheavals throughout Europe. It had been the primary force behind the revolutions of 1848, and continued to influence the domestic politics

of France, Germany, Italy, and Austria. In the final decades of the century, nationalism became of overriding concern in the Austro-Hungarian and Ottoman empires, as subject peoples struggled to create national borders that would reflect ethnic and cultural alignments rather than the political settlements reached at the Congress of Vienna.

THE CASE OF FRANCE
After the humiliating defeat of France in the Franco-Prussian War (Chapter 15), the government of Napoleon III was toppled, and the empire was replaced by a republic. Early in 1871, a new National Assembly was elected through universal male suffrage, officially establishing the republic. However, the transition from empire to republic was not to be an easy one. The peace terms imposed by Bismarck included the cession of Alsace-Lorraine, an indemnity of five billion francs, and the quartering of German troops on French soil until the indemnity was paid. The first task facing the new Assembly was to ratify this treaty.

The Paris Commune. The new National Assembly was dominated by royalist and bourgeois elements who hoped to bring

some 20,000 revolutionaries and deported another 7,500 to French penal colonies. The suppression of the radical republicans in Paris signaled the end of the radical socialist movement for the time being and put the propertied classes firmly in power in France. The savagery and the fratricidal nature of the Commune period also left a legacy of division and hatred between the classes.

Uncertain as to whether it wanted a monarchy or a republic, the National Assembly stumbled along, electing first a republican president, Adolphe Thiers, then a staunch monarchist, Marshal Maurice MacMahon. Finally, in 1875, led by Leon Gambetta, the republicans triumphed and several constitutional laws were passed which established the Third Republic. By 1879, moderate republicans controlled the government.

about a speedy resolution to the hostilities with Germany. However, the republicans of Paris, who had suffered the siege of their capital city and were bitterly anti-German, refused to recognize the authority of the Assembly or to accept the peace terms.

Instead, Parisians set up a revolutionary municipal council, known as the *Paris Commune*. Led by radicals known as *communards*, Paris organized for a civil war. For three months, from March to May, 1871, Paris was the scene of bloody fighting as the troops mustered by the Assembly ruthlessly suppressed the communards. On their part, the communards burned public buildings and executed the archbishop of Paris.

Finally victorious, the National Assembly, in its determination to eliminate all radical republican activity in Paris, executed

BETWEEN TWO TERRORS.
("WHITE" AND "RED.")

Revanchism. Although the Third Republic had established stability and restored order, the republican government was beset by crises during the 1880s and 1890s. Often divided among themselves, the republicans were prey to the hostility of the royalist and clerical forces, who were not yet reconciled to democratic institutions. In addition, corruption and inefficiency often plagued the government. The military, still smarting from its defeat in the Franco-Prussian war, was—along with many French civilians—imbued with the spirit of *revanche* (revenge) against Germany over the loss of Alsace-Lorraine and the continued presence of German troops on French soil.

The Boulanger Affair. Discontent with the government and the refusal of many Frenchmen to accept the surrender of Alsace-Lorraine as final led to the Boulanger affair of 1886–1889. As minister of war, General Georges Boulanger embodied the spirit of *revanche*. Through his fiery chauvinist speeches and writings and his expansion and strengthening of the military, he gained widespread popularity. The military, the clerical forces, and the monarchists rallied around Boulanger, and it seemed as if France was ready once again for the rule of a strong man. However, the Boulanger movement collapsed in 1889 when Boulanger failed to take advantage of his popular support to seize the government. Shortly thereafter, he was accused of treason and fled into exile.

The Dreyfus Affair. A further crisis in 1894 pitted the forces of reaction against the republican government when Alfred Dreyfus, a Jewish officer in the army, was accused and found guilty of betraying secrets to the Germans. Dreyfus' case was not helped by the strong anti-Semitic feeling that permeated much of European society. Although the evidence implicated a Major C. F. Esterhazy, a royalist and a Catholic, Dreyfus was condemned to life imprisonment in a penal colony. The Dreyfus case divided France, as monarchists, the military, and clerical forces

Captain Dreyfus is stripped of all insignia of military rank in the presence of his peers. The case became a national controversy after it was shown that the documents incriminating him had been forged.

condemned Dreyfus, while liberals and intellectuals, among them the novelist Emile Zola, demanded his exoneration. The hostility of the courts prevented Dreyfus from being acquitted, but he was pardoned by the president of the republic in 1899 and finally exonerated of all guilt in 1906.

The Dreyfus case discredited the royalists and their allies, and gave the republicans a chance to weaken the power of the military and of the clerical forces. By the beginning of the 20th century, the Third Republic was solidly under the control of the middle class. Although a rising tide of socialism and a labor-union movement would threaten the government, the Third Republic weathered the storms and remained in power until after World War II.

THE CASE OF GERMANY

By 1871, with the successful conclusion of the Franco-Prussian War, the balance of power in Europe had tilted in favor of Germany. Bismarck's policy aimed to preserve Germany's gains. The man of "blood and iron" before 1871 was transformed into a man of peace and moderation after 1871.

German policy changed, however, under Kaiser Wilhelm II (1888–1918). Wilhelm wanted Germany to play a greater role on the world stage. As he expressed it: "The waves beat powerfully at our national gates, and call us as a great nation to maintain our place in the world, in other words, to follow a world policy."[1]

The structure of the German state was not as monolithic as might be expected, given that its emperor was the final source of authority and power. Germany still was characterized by a degree of particularism in the individual states that made up the empire. Many of the emperor's advisers believed that this highly visible worldwide foreign policy, called *Weltpolitik*,[2] was the ideological and emotional cement needed to develop a sense of national unity and purpose.

However, the pursuit of *Weltpolitik* led Germany to challenge Great Britain on the high seas and around the world. This set the two powers on a collision course that made war possible in 1914. To what extent the inauguration of *Weltpolitik* was a decision determined by domestic politics or an arbitrary and highly personal decision by Wilhelm II is still a subject of much debate.

THE CASE OF AUSTRIA-HUNGARY

In the years preceding the outbreak of war, the Dual Monarchy of Austria-Hungary viewed with alarm the rising tide of nationalism that was sweeping through the peoples

---

[1] J. Salwyn Schapiro, *Modern and Contemporary European History (1815–1945)* (Boston: Houghton Mifflin, 1946), pp. 408–9.

[2] The term *Weltpolitik* ("world politics") described the Kaiser's policy of transforming Germany into a major global power through naval expansion and the acquisition of colonies.

The headstrong Kaiser Wilhelm II and his dreams of Weltpolitik *were a major force in international diplomacy during the prewar years.*

of its empire, which included Bohemians, Rumanians, Croats, Serbs, Slovaks, and Poles. The Slavs, united by language and culture, wanted to break away from the Dual Monarchy and form an independent state of their own.

To further complicate the problems of nationalism in the Austro-Hungarian Empire, the subject nationalities could find support from members of their ethnic groups outside the borders of the empire. Slavic nationalists looked to the independent state of Serbia for support. In turn, Serbia hoped—with Russian support—to expand its territory to include peoples of Serbo-Croatian heritage. Similarly, people of Italian descent in the empire looked to the newly unified Italy for their inspiration. Thus, the aspirations of its subject peoples often complicated the Dual Monarchy's relations with other nations.

In Austria, industrialization had increased the power of the urban middle class, which used its political influence to establish such liberal policies as the legalization of unions, insurance for workers, the regulation of factories, and universal male suffrage. A more liberal climate in Austria encouraged the aspirations of other peoples in the empire, and added to the existing conflicts.

One technique of appeasing nationalist pressures at home was to encourage anti-Semitic attitudes. Many Austrian parties that were otherwise liberal, such as the Christian Socialists, promoted anti-Semitism to get the support of the lower middle classes. The scapegoating of those of the Jewish faith was an ancient problem in Europe. In Austria-Hungary, the problem was complicated by the high number of successful Jewish businessmen and professionals in the arts and sciences.

THE PROBLEM OF THE OTTOMAN EMPIRE

Beginning with the war for Greek independence in the 1820s, the Ottoman Empire had been losing territory in the Balkans. As Turkey came to be known as "the sick man of Europe," the disposition of the Sultan's territory became a cause of dispute among the European powers.

The Russians encouraged unrest in the Balkans by appealing to *Pan-Slavism*, the idea that Slavs were united by common interests and ties that transcended political borders. The Pan-Slavic movement complemented a second, more practical motive for intervening in Balkan affairs: Russia's long-standing goal of controlling Constantinople and the Bosporus-Dardanelles Straits.[3]

---

[3] The Dardanelles and Bosporus straits, along with the Sea of Marmara between them, made up the waterway between the Black Sea and the Mediterranean (see map on page 260). Control of this passageway had frequently been a source of conflict between Russia and Turkey, because it was Russia's only access to the Mediterranean.

Austria feared that any breakdown of political stability in the Ottoman Empire might upset the precarious balance within its own empire. Additionally, Austria was fearful that its common border with Russia would be extended farther southward.

Britain was concerned about losing its virtual monopoly over trade in the eastern Mediterranean. Russian domination of the Straits or other parts of the Ottoman Empire would be a potential threat to the Suez Canal—Britain's "lifeline" to India.

France saw in the Balkan unrest an opportunity to "make mischief" in the hope that it might lead to a realignment of powers more favorable to the French goal of regaining Alsace-Lorraine.

Germany's interest in the Balkans can be summed up in Bismarck's statement that the area was not worth "the bones of a Pomeranian grenadier."[4] His involvement was aimed at ensuring that the Balkans would not serve as a tinderbox for a war that might engulf all the nations of Europe.

Conflict in the Balkans. The same spirit of nationalism that inspired the Slavs to seek independence also created upheaval in the Ottoman Empire. In 1908, a group of *Young Turks*, led by Mustafa Kemal, rebelled against the reactionary sultan and demanded a constitution. The revolution in Turkey provided Austria with the opportunity to annex outright the provinces of Bosnia and Herzegovina, which it had administered since 1878. Such a move was a challenge to the interests of Serbia, which was determined to incorporate the provinces into an expanded Serbian nation.

Counting on Russian backing, the Serbs began to arm. Germany proclaimed its support for Austria, while England and France remained aloof. Russia, not yet recovered from the Russo-Japanese War and the Rev-

---

[4] J. Salwyn Schapiro, *op. cit.*, p. 472.

olution of 1905, protested Austria's action but did not intervene.

The crisis passed, but in 1912, a more serious conflict threatened the peace, when the Balkan League of Serbia, Bulgaria, and Greece rose against the Ottoman Empire. The League was victorious, but Serbia and Bulgaria quarreled over territorial claims, and a second Balkan war erupted in 1913 over the spoils of the first. This time Bulgaria stood alone against Serbia, Greece, and Romania, and was defeated. Again, the victors raised conflicting claims. Serbia, determined to gain access to the Adriatic Sea through Albania, was thwarted by Austria, which demanded that Albania become an independent state. Russia supported Serbia's claims, but did not back up its support with arms. An agreement was finally reached by which Albania became an independent kingdom. By 1914, the Balkans had become known as the "powder keg" of Europe.

THE SYSTEMS OF ALLIANCES
In the years before World War I, Europe divided into two warring camps. The alliance system poisoned relations between countries largely because the secrecy of the specific terms of the alliances kept rival powers uninformed and tense. Most importantly, the alliance system ensured that a war between any of the great powers of Europe would include them all.

BISMARCK'S POLICIES

As Bismarck saw it, there were three threats to European peace and stability: economic recession leading to the rise of radical movements, the French desire to regain Alsace-Lorraine, and a possible war in the Balkans that could involve all the major powers of Europe. Bismarck counted on a healthy economy, a successful foreign policy, and his personal popularity to solve the first problem. The solution to the second problem was diplomatic isolation: a France without allies was no threat to Germany. The final

danger to European peace, the outbreak of war in the Balkans, was preventable as long as Austria and Russia did not pursue a collision course.

The Three Emperors' League. Bismarck's first step toward dampening the powder keg of the Balkans was through his creation of the Three Emperors' League between Germany, Austria, and Russia in 1873. This league, although informal, prevented Germany from being isolated, and kept the two potential protagonists in the Balkans, Austria and Russia, on talking terms.

The effectiveness of the league was tested when a series of insurrections erupted in the Balkans between 1875 and 1877. The Russians came to the aid of their fellow Slavs, and waged war with Turkey. Russia's success in this war alarmed both Britain and Austria, who feared that their own interests in the area would be threatened by a Russian victory. Bismarck quickly offered his services as an "honest broker" to mediate the conflict. The resultant Peace of Berlin, concluded in 1878, had something in it of substance for virtually every participant except Russia—the victor in the war. Tsar Alexander II blamed Bismarck for this diplomatic defeat.

The Triple Alliance. Bismarck looked elsewhere for an ally, and the logical choice was Austria. In 1879, the two empires forged a secret dual alliance in which each side agreed to come to the other's aid if attacked by Russia. Bismarck made it clear to his Austrian counterpart that Germany needed some control over Austrian activities in the Balkans in return for this commitment. As long as this unwritten proviso was observed, the danger of a European war beginning in the Balkans was minimal.

The treaty between Germany and Austria was the first of a series of secret treaties which eventually split Europe into two camps. Italy, fearing French designs on its interests in North Africa, joined the Austria-Germany alliance in 1882, making it the Tri-

"THE SISTERS THREE:" OR, THE TRIPLE ALLIANCE.

Then, in 1904, France and Britain formed the *Entente Cordiale*, an informal "gentleman's agreement," as opposed to a formal written alliance. Britain's entry into the system of alliances was the result of its increased concern over German commercial and colonial expansionism. When the French approached London with a way to strengthen both nations' positions in North Africa, the British expressed an interest. In return for Britain allowing the French to colonize Morocco, France would not stand in the way of Britain's plans for consolidating its position in Egypt.

ple Alliance. In 1887, when Russia refused to renew the Three Emperors' League, Bismarck signed a secret Reinsurance Treaty with the tsar, hoping that this would keep Russia from allying itself with France.

THE FALL OF BISMARCK AND THE TRIPLE ENTENTE

In the Reichstag elections of 1890, Bismarck's party lost. The new kaiser, Wilhelm II, with feigned reluctance, asked the man who had guided the destinies of Prussia and Germany for nearly 30 years to step down. To the young and headstrong Wilhelm II, Bismarck was an anachronism of a bygone era—someone who was standing in the way of Germany's glorious future.

With the bellicose and inexperienced Wilhelm II now guiding Germany's destiny, it was not surprising that the Reinsurance Treaty with Russia was not renewed. Russia was thus left free to form closer ties with France, and the result was a Russian-French alliance, signed in 1894. Bismarck's recurring nightmare that France and Russia would become allies—thereby creating for Germany the specter of a two-front war—was now a reality.

DROPPING THE PILOT.

By 1907, Britain had been drawn into the alliance between Russia and France. As a result of the Russo-Japanese War, Britain began to realize that Russia was no longer a major threat, and Nicholas II's promises of liberal reform in Russia made Britain more amenable to an alliance. The two nations resolved most of their colonial differences in Persia and Afghanistan, and the *Entente Cordiale* between England and France now became the *Triple Entente* between England, France, and Russia.

In April, 1911, a crisis was precipitated in Morocco when Germany sent a gunboat to the Moroccan port of Agadir and delivered an ultimatum to France. Germany's demand for compensation was based on France's violation of a 1906 treaty, the Treaty of Algeciras, which nominally guaranteed Morocco's independence. For a few days it appeared that hostilities were imminent, but since none of the nations involved were prepared for war, the crisis quickly blew over. One significant result to come out of the *Agadir incident* was a strengthening of the military ties between England and France.

MILITARISM The atmosphere of mutual suspicion and distrust that preceded the outbreak of war in 1914 precipitated a massive buildup of weapons among the nations of Europe. With the exception of Britain, all the powers inaugurated a military conscription system, drawing nearly every able-bodied male into their armed forces. Warfare, when and if it came, would no longer be waged by small professional armies, but would involve millions of combatants.

To equip such huge armies required the making of weapons, and not merely the old guns and cannons of earlier warfare, but new and more efficient arms. Machine guns, torpedoes and mines, high-explosive shells, and the new inventions of the airplane and submarine assured that war would be waged with a new and more deadly effectiveness.

THE NAVAL RACE

The armaments buildup included naval competition between Britain and Germany. The British invention in the late 19th century of the dreadnought, a battleship with increased speed and firepower, made all conventional warships obsolete overnight. For Britain, an island nation, control of the sea was viewed as a necessity. A two-to-one margin in ships over an enemy—or any two potential enemies—was seen as a minimum requirement by the British admiralty.

In 1897, Germany inaugurated a greatly expanded shipbuilding program, at the same time it was proclaiming the new foreign policy of *Weltpolitik*. This policy sent warning signals reverberating through the halls of the British admiralty and Parliament. In 1909, although the danger was not immediate, projected estimates for 1912 had Germany with anywhere from 13 to 21 dreadnoughts to Britain's 18—far from Britain's required two-to-one advantage.

The naval arms race alarmed the British public and government, and resulted in closer cooperation between England and France. As early as 1906, French and English representatives met to coordinate military plans in the event of war with Germany. These plans were firmed up in the succeeding years, and by 1914, French military strategy against Germany was dependent on immediate armed support from England.

SECRET MILITARY PLANS

One of the elements of the militarism that preceded World War I was that the plans drawn up by military leaders were prepared in secrecy, to the extent that they were often not known to the political leaders, the parliaments, and certainly not to the people. Sir Edward Grey, the British foreign minister, declared that between 1906 and 1911, he knew nothing of the details worked out by the British and French military leaders for projected operations in northern France in the event of war. Yet these plans virtually obligated Britain to come to the aid of the French in the event of a war between Germany and France.

The Schlieffen Plan. In Germany, Kaiser Wilhelm's chief military adviser, General Schlieffen (1891–1906), had developed a top-secret plan based on the likelihood of a two-front war. The Schlieffen Plan assumed that war would be waged against France in the west and Russia in the east. Since Russia would be slower to mobilize, most German forces would be concentrated in the west, where they would drive through Belgium and into France for a quick victory. The Schlieffen Plan necessitated the violation of Belgian neutrality, which Germany, as well as France and Britain, was by treaty obliged to uphold. But thanks to Bismarck's long and effective service to Wilhelm I, the authority of the kaiser had become preeminent: no one within the government—including the new German chancellor—had the authority to challenge the Schlieffen Plan or any other aspect of the kaiser's *Weltpolitik*.

IMPERIALISM In 1906, a little-known Russian Marxist by the name of Lenin wrote a pamphlet entitled, "Imperialism—the Highest Stage of Capitalism." In this work, *imperialism* is defined as the competition between capitalist states for colonies where they can safely invest their excess profits. Lenin's argument begins with the assumption that imperialism is the last stage of capitalism. He went on to say that these economically motivated rivalries inevitably lead to armed conflicts such as World War I. A corollary to this theme is reflected in the "merchants of death" theory—that the great armaments firms such as Krupp in Germany, Vickers in Britain, and Skoda in Austria-Hungary all had a vested interest in encouraging the outbreak of war.

Most historians consider Lenin's analysis to be too simplistic a view of the world situation. For example, while it is true that imperialist rivalries contributed to international tensions in the prewar years (see next page), they were certainly not the most important cause. Indeed, imperialist rivals such as France, England, and Russia fought on the same side during the war. Moreover, there is no evidence that the armaments companies influenced the political course of events, although they did provide their respective governments with the tools of war. In fact, businessmen in both Germany and England were among the foremost proponents of peace, for their interests depended upon a stable national economy and free economic interactions—conditions that certainly would not prevail in wartime.

ECONOMIC RIVALRIES

By 1900, nearly all European states, with the major exception of Britain, had adopted protectionist trade policies. However, commercial and industrial rivalries did not seem to excite public opinion or bring countries to the flashpoint of war, as did issues of national honor and prestige. Sir Edward Grey put it best when he said:

> The economic rivalry [with Germany does] not give much offense to our people, and they admire her steady industry and genius for organization. But they do resent mischief making. They suspect the Emperor of aggressive plans of Weltpolitik, and they see that Germany is forcing the pace in armaments in order to dominate Europe.[5]

The best example of an alliance in which financial concerns were paramount is that of Russia and France. French investment in Russia was widespread and pervasive in the years immediately preceding World War I. By 1914, one-fourth of all French investments outside the borders of France were with Russia. Germany had similar economic

---

[5] *Ibid.*, p. 186.

ties to Austria-Hungary, but its investments in Austria-Hungary were never profitable. Although economic considerations are a factor in the events leading up to World War I, there is no evidence to indicate that they were crucial to those making the final decisions about war or peace.

COLONIAL RIVALRIES

The European nations' quest for colonies in Africa and Asia precipitated rivalries on those continents that led to conflicts and tension, adding to the animosities that were developing in Europe. In Africa, as we have seen, France and England narrowly averted war in the Upper Nile Valley in 1898, when French interests clashed with those of Britain over the Sudan.

French and German rivalry in Africa reached a crisis point on the question of Morocco, as we have seen. The question was finally settled when France agreed to give Germany part of the French Congo in return for a French protectorate over most of Morocco. Tensions also mounted between Germany and Britain over their African possessions. German expansionism in Southwest Africa triggered Britain's fears of a threat to its South African territories. However, the two nations did agree in 1890 on their spheres of influence in Africa, with Britain recognizing Germany's claims.

In Asia, Britain and Russia were the chief rivals, with Britain retaining its control of India while the Russians extended their influence into Manchuria and Mongolia. In 1904, Tibet came under British control, and in 1907, Persia was divided between Russia and Britain. Since Russia had suffered a severe defeat in the Russo-Japanese War, and as Britain became more fearful of the growing German power, the two nations found it to their advantage to settle their colonial problems peacefully.

In 1914, there were no unresolvable imperial rivalries that required drastic measures such as war. However, as long as empire-building was seen as a vital national interest by the competing great powers, armed struggle was an acceptable risk and part of the climate of the times.

FIVE CITIES ON THE EVE OF WAR Europe in the years before World War I had about it a sunset glow. Looking back on this period, writer Stefan Zweig called it the "Age of Golden Security" and "a sweet time to be alive."[6] Winston Churchill recalled the "Old World in its sunset was fair to see."[7] Nowhere was this fair life experienced more fully than in the great capital cities of London, Paris, Vienna, Berlin, and St. Petersburg.

LONDON

London at the beginning of the 20th century was the largest city in the world both in area and population, a fitting capital for a world empire on which the sun never set. London's population had grown fivefold during the 19th century, and the city had absorbed the outlying areas. In 1900, around four million people lived in the city.

The reason for this expansion had been the Industrial Revolution and the growth of trade. London was the trade center of Britain and its main port. Along the Thames were miles of docks where ships unloaded the raw materials from Britain's colonies, and loaded finished goods made in Britain.

At the heart of London, in one square mile of buildings, was the power center of Britain's trade empire—"the City." In the City were the banks, commercial exchanges, and other institutions that controlled the economic destiny of Britain and its colonies.

London was a city of contrasts. At the top

---

[6] Orron J. Hale, *The Great Illusion* (New York: Harper & Row, 1971), p. 1.

[7] *Ibid.*

were the court and the aristocracy. Buckingham Palace and St. James' Palace were the focal points for their activities. For the wealthy financial classes, there were rounds of parties and the socializing in the exclusive private clubs that served as a home away from home. Life was not as glittering for the poor, although living conditions for the working class had improved by the end of the century.

PARIS

Prewar Paris was the Mecca of many Europeans who wanted to experience its manifold charms. The physical beauty of the city on the Seine had long attracted people, and the rebuilding of the city under the direction of Baron Haussman during the Napoleon's Second Empire had given it grand vistas and views, as well as parks and a sewer and water system that created healthy conditions for its people.

Paris had hosted several international exhibitions in the 19th century; for one in 1889, Gustave Eiffel had built the tower that bears his name. Dominating the city's skyline, it remained the highest building in the world until the 1930s. Parisians had first opposed its construction, but then had taken pride in it as a symbol of confidence in the new age.

At the end of the 19th century, Paris was the art capital of the world. Artists from Europe and America flocked there to study and to view the great works of art in museums such as the Louvre, but most of all to enjoy the spirit of sophistication and culture that permeated the city. Before World War I, Pablo Picasso, Georges Braque, and Gustave Rodin were among the artists working in the city. Many artists settled on the Left Bank,

The Seine River and the wide boulevards designed during the Second Empire are still among the central attractions of Paris.

French impressionist painters celebrated the charm of Parisian café society in the prewar era. This painting is by Auguste Renoir.

close to the university, because a room could be rented there for next to nothing.

Parisian night life was part of its legendary charm. For the wealthy, there were expensive restaurants where the finest *haute cuisine* could be found. Nightclubs offered daring entertainment that became a special attraction. The artists and writers gathered in small clubs where food was free as long as one had the price of a drink, and their conversations went on until the early hours of the morning. For many, the greatest entertainment was the experience of the city itself. One could linger at a table in an outdoor cafe, watching the crowds pass by. Paris street life, according to the Irish poet William Butler Yeats, was, "the blood and mire of humanity."[8]

VIENNA

Vienna hardly seemed to be the capital of a dying empire as World War I drew near. Franz Joseph had ruled since 1848, enduring both personal tragedy and political setbacks. Many Viennese had never known any other

[8] Rudolph Chelminski and editors of Time-Life Books, *Paris* (Amsterdam: Time-Life Books International, 1977), p. 66.

A glimpse of Viennese society in the prewar years—Hungarian musicians serenading customers at a coffee house.

ruler, and it seemed as if the empire of which Vienna was the capital would go on forever.

The oldest part of the city was the Inner City, surrounded by the *Ringstrasse*, which was two and one-half miles in circumference, 200 feet wide, and lined with rows of linden and plane trees. Since 1898, a giant iron ferris wheel had stood in Prater Park, an amusement park for the aristocrats and wealthy of the city.

Vienna, like Paris, had seen a period of municipal rebuilding, during the reign of Franz Joseph. Among the new structures were the Burgtheater, where the plays of dramatists like Hugo Von Hoffmansthal were presented, and the Opera.

More than anything else, Vienna was known for its music and dance. The waltzes of Johann Strauss provided the anthems of the city. Gustav Mahler had spent ten stormy

years, beginning in 1897, as director of the Vienna opera, and his brooding symphonies reveal a darker side of Vienna's life. At the same time, Arnold Schoenberg was creating a new kind of atonal music that would influence the postwar generation.

The life of the capital was dominated by a wealthy commercial class. Lavish restaurants specialized in elaborate Viennese pastries and cakes, each in itself a little culinary work of art. Lawyers, doctors, and university professors in their stiff collars and black coats lent a touch of dignity to the city. Among these was the physician Sigmund Freud, who was formulating his theories about unconscious or repressed thoughts by analyzing dreams.

BERLIN
The newest of Europe's great capitals, Berlin,

was an amalgam of several towns along the Spree River. Its growth paralleled that of Prussia and the German Empire. In 1816, its population was less than 200,000; in 1905, it was more than two million.

A system of canals, constructed by Frederick William the Great Elector, ran through the city. The grand boulevard *Unter den Linden*, with a mile-long strip of linden trees in the middle, ran from the royal palace to the Brandenburg Gate, completed in 1791. South of Unter den Linden was the great Tiergarten, a park where a statue of Bismarck and a pillar topped by a golden "winged victory" figure faced each other, commemorations of the architect of Germany's unification.

The life of Berlin reflected the vitality of a young, confident nation that had rapidly become one of Europe's greatest military and industrial powers. Soldiers from the Berlin garrison paraded proudly through the streets in their elaborate dress uniforms and silver *pickelhaubes*, or spiked helmets.

Berlin was also a booming business city, with crowds of bicyclists, pedestrians, and tramway passengers making their way to and from work. With its importance as the capital of a newly industrialized nation, Berlin drew people from all over the German states. One observer wrote: "Berlin has become the drainage canal for the provinces. All that is best and worst in the provinces comes pouring into this place—only the mediocre stay at home."[9]

ST. PETERSBURG

It was sometimes said that one of the mistakes of the Romanov dynasty was to rule from the least Russian city in Russia. St. Petersburg was built to be Russia's "window on the West," but it became more like a mirror of what was popular in western Europe. Foreign architects had designed many of the

A scene from the ballet "Firebird," created by Diaghilev with music by Igor Stravinsky. The Imperial Ballet School successfully merged Western and native Russian traditions to create its unique form of art.

city's great buildings in the baroque and classical styles. The language of the court and upper classes was French, and the Paris fashions of one year became the St. Petersburg style of the next.

Built on a swamp on the Neva River, St. Petersburg regularly suffered from floods. Its fog and rains, mixed with the smoke of factories, were as frequent and depressing as those of London. The imperial command that all of Russia's overseas trade pass through the city made it a bustling shipbuilding and commercial center. A canal system linked the city to the Volga River. The great avenue of the city was the *Nevsky Prospekt*, whose two and one-half mile length was lined with palaces, churches, government offices, and shops.

Numerous islands in the Neva held such imposing structures as the St. Peter and Paul

[9] Frederick V. Grunfeld and editors of Time-Life Books, *Berlin* (Amsterdam: Time-Life Books International, 1977), p. 99.

Fortress, now a prison where dissidents and revolutionaries, such as the young Feodor Dostoyevski, had been held before exile to Siberia. Many of the university's buildings were also on these islands, and uniformed students roamed the gloomy dormitories built for them there. In the brief summers, the city's population flocked to those islands that contained public parks; brass bands and restaurants opened for the season. This far north, there were some summer nights—the "white nights"—when the sun set only an hour or so before rising again.

The emancipation of the serfs in 1861 had drawn newly free laborers to the city; it grew from half a million population in 1864 to nearly one and one-half million in 1900. In 1910 less than one-third of its inhabitants had been born in the city. The poor working conditions led to unrest among the laborers, and the abortive revolution of 1905.

For the aristocracy, the capital was a city of culture and pleasure. They enjoyed luxuries such as the fabulous Easter eggs with intricate jeweled scenes inside created by Carl Fabergé.

The imperial theater and ballet presented lavish entertainments and conducted schools that produced some of Europe's greatest performing artists. Sergei Diaghilev, a former law student, became assistant director of the imperial theaters late in the century. He became famous for presenting to the rest of the world Russian ballets, dancers, and composers. Among his dance troupe were Anna Pavlova and Vaslav Nijinsky, both of whom were trained in the Imperial Ballet School in St. Petersburg. Igor Stravinsky, who was born near St. Petersburg and produced his first works there, composed ballets for Diaghilev and became one of the great musical influences of the 20th century.

THE MOOD IN EUROPE IN THE PREWAR DECADES

Shortly before the outbreak of World War I, sentiment about the impending conflict ranged from the German crown prince's prediction that it would be "a bright and jolly war," to the somber warning of Sir Edward Grey, the British foreign minister, that "the lights will soon be going out all over Europe." Yet even those who opposed the war were blissfully unaware of the drastic changes the next four years would bring.

Many factors and new currents of thought had combined to create an atmosphere in which war was seen as a desirable goal rather than a failure of diplomacy. In a school of thought known as *social Darwinism*, Darwin's theories had been taken from their rightful context in the natural world and applied to human society. In this new context, war could actually be viewed as a "survival technique"—a way to improve the human race through "natural selection" and "survival of the fittest."

In Germany, Friedrich Nietsche and other philosophers expressed a profoundly negative view of modern society, implying that technology and mass civilization had robbed human beings of their spirituality. In *Thus Spake Zarathustra* (1885) and other works, Nietsche's pessimistic view of the common man was offset by his vision of a race of "supermen" who would triumph over the mediocrity of their society. His emphasis upon individual initiative, action, and violence had a powerful influence on the young; not just in Germany but throughout Europe.

The idealization of war as the instrument of nationalism was even expressed by the French novelist and social reformer Emile Zola. In 1891, Zola proclaimed:

• • • *War is life itself. Nothing exists in nature, is born, grows or multiplies except by combat. We must eat and be eaten so that the world may live. It is only warlike nations which have prospered: a nation dies as soon as it disarms. War is the school of discipline, sacrifice, and courage.*[10]

---

[10] James Joll, *The Origins of the First World War* (New York: Longman, 1984), p. 186.

SUMMARY

Few of the citizens of Europe's great capitals sensed that the forces of nationalism, secret alliances, and imperialism would lead to a war that ultimately destroyed Europe's economic domination of the world. In the self-satisfied, luxurious life of the prewar period, the feeling was that Europe's prosperity could continue indefinitely. Indeed, it might have, were it not for the fact that many forces combined to bring the nations of Europe into a war that would annihilate millions of its young men, devastate large areas of the continent, and bring down three of the ruling families that reigned over empires in 1914.

QUESTIONS

1 To what extent might the spirit of revanche in France have contributed to the Boulanger affair and the trial of Captain Dreyfus? What was the impact of both events?
2 Discuss the philosophy of Weltpolitik and the dismissal of Bismarck. To what extent did the policies and decisions of Wilhelm II contribute to a climate favoring war in Europe?
3 The Balkans are known to students of recent history as the "powder keg of Europe." To what extent is this name justified?
4 Explain the circumstances that led to the Triple Alliance and the Triple Entente.
5 How did the alliance system created in the last decades of the 19th century and the early years of the 20th century contribute to an atmosphere that made war more than just a possibility?
6 Identify and indicate the significance of the following terms: Paris Commune of 1871, "honest broker," Three Emperors' League, and Schlieffen Plan.

BIBLIOGRAPHY

BRIDGE, F. R. and ROGER BULLEN. *The Great Powers and the European States System: 1815–1914.* New York: Longman, 1980. *An interpretive analysis of the international relationships and diplomatic entanglements that afflicted the "European states system" in the 19th century.*

HOFFMAN, ROBERT L. *More Than a Trial: The Struggle Over Captain Dreyfus.* New York: Macmillan, 1980. *This study goes beyond the tragic story of a man unjustly accused of treason to analyze the repercussions of the trial in France and throughout Europe, particularly as they relate to anti-Semitic prejudices.*

HOLBORN, HAJO. "Moltke and Schlieffen: The Prussian-German School," in *Makers of Modern Strategy,* ed. Edward Mead Earle. Princeton: Princeton University Press, 1971. *An exceptional, incisive explanation of the evolution of Prussian strategic military thinking.*

JOLL, JAMES. *The Origins of the First World War.* New York: Longman, 1984. *One of the best and most readable of the many volumes on World War I and its causes.*

STAVRIANOS, LEFTEN S. *The Balkans: 1815–1914.* New York: Holt, Rinehart and Winston, 1963. *Mr. Stavrianos assesses more than just the role of the Balkans in hastening World War I: the Balkans are used as an example of the virulent growth of nationalism in the 19th century.*

TUCHMAN, BARBARA. *The Proud Tower.* New York: Macmillan, 1966. *The author vididly conveys a sense of the pre-war era; Europe in the 15 years before World War I.*

WEST, REBECCA. *Black Lamb and Grey Falcon,* 2 vols. New York: Viking Press, 1940. *This is a travelogue of a visit made by the author and her husband to the Balkans in the 1930s. It is also a perceptive description of small nations and their peoples, closely related in time and place, yet often separated by long-standing traditions.*

19

The War to end all Wars.
WORLD WAR I ALLIED SLOGAN

World War I

World War I began on July 28, 1914, when the government of Austria-Hungary declared war on Serbia. Other declarations of war followed in rapid succession. Germany declared war on Russia on August 1, after Russia refused to stop general mobilization along the German and Austrian frontiers. On August 3, Germany declared war on France and invaded neutral Belgium. On August 4, Great Britain declared war on Germany. In less than one week, a series of events had catapulted Europe, and much of the rest of the world, into the most devastating and widespread war yet known to man.

THE ASSASSINATION AT SARAJEVO

In fact, the first shots of the war were fired a month earlier, on June 28, in the town of Sarajevo in the Balkans. On that day, Gavrilo Princip, a Serbian nationalist, stepped from a crowd and gunned down the heir to the Austrian throne, Franz Ferdinand. It was a tragic beginning to a tragic war, yet the events surrounding the assassination itself had a touch of the absurd.

Franz Ferdinand had traveled to Sarajevo to review Austrian troops which had been stationed there since the Austrian annexation of Bosnia in 1908. The Austrian annexation had angered Serbia, which viewed itself as the rightful leader of the Balkan states. As a consequence of this national sentiment, a group of extremist Serbians had formed a secret society known as the Black Hand. The mission of this group was to carry out assassinations of high Austrian officials. Although not directly sponsored by the Serbian government, the Black Hand had received training from Serbian army officers.

On June 28, a morning newspaper published a map of the route Ferdinand and his entourage would follow, from the center of the city to the barracks where the Austrian troops were quartered. As the procession passed through the streets of Sarajevo, a first assassination attempt failed. Returning to his hotel, the Archduke insisted that a new route be devised, and set off once more in his open touring car. Unfortunately, no one informed his driver of the new plans. A few blocks from the hotel, when the driver failed to turn as the new route required, aides shouted for him to halt. Just as the car came to a full stop,

This photo of Franz Ferdinand and his wife, Sophie, was taken just an hour before the assassinations that precipitated world war.

Princip arrived at the intersection. He stepped from the crowd and fired the fatal shots. Within seconds, the Archduke and his wife, Sophie, were dead.

This assassination precipitated World War I, and is viewed by historians as the immediate cause. All of the European powers condemned the assassination. The Austrian government resolved to take action against Serbia, because it believed that Slav nationalism inspired by Serbia could destroy its empire.

The July Diplomacy. Austria-Hungary turned to its ally, Germany, for support in an action against Serbia. At a fateful luncheon between the Kaiser and the Austro-Hungarian ambassador to Germany, Germany's consent was given. The so-called "blank check" of July 5 gave Germany's "full support . . . even if matters went to the length of a war between Austria-Hungary and Russia."[1]

With the assurance of German support, on

---

[1] Frank P. Chambers, *This Age of Conflict* (New York: Harcourt, Brace, and World, 1962), p. 14.

July 23 Austria presented Serbia an ultimatum with terms that compromised Serbia's independence. A reply was demanded within 48 hours. The Serbian reply came five minutes before the deadline and included acceptance of most of the terms, but this was not enough for the Austrians. On July 26, Austria began a partial mobilization, and two days later declared war on Serbia.

Declarations of War. Now the alliance system came into play. When the Russians, deciding to assist their fellow Slavs, began to mobilize on July 30, Germany demanded that Russia halt its preparation for war. When Russia refused, Germany declared war against Russia on August 1. France, an alliance partner of Russia, mobilized the same day—leading to a second declaration of war by Germany on August 3.

Mobilization was an important step. Because of the size of the armies and the plans that had been devised to fight the war, once mobilization had begun it was hard to stop. It required the use of national train systems, and all moves had been precisely scheduled in advance. By the Schlieffen Plan (Chapter 18), the Germans had planned for a quick victory in the west by marching through Belgium to France, leaving a minimum number of troops protecting their eastern frontier.

As a result, on August 2, Germany presented Belgium with a 12-hour ultimatum to allow free passage of troops through that country. Belgium refused and appealed to Britain, France and Russia. The British government demanded an answer from the Germans as to whether they would respect the neutrality of Belgium. The Germans responded by asking whether the British government was willing to go to war over "just a scrap of paper." When the Germans invaded Belgium, on August 3, Britain declared war on Germany. The only power in the alliance system that did not become involved was Italy. That country chose neutrality on the grounds that it had not been consulted about the moves of the Triple Alliance and that the war was not a defensive one.

Responsibility for the War. German responsibility for the war is apparent, but responsibility was shared by other powers. Austria was determined to smash Serbia, whatever the cost, and used Franz Ferdinand's assassination as an excuse to do so. Russia, too, was responsible, not only for its willingness to support Serbia, but for mobilizing along the German as well as the Austrian borders. France shared some of the blame as well. The French leader, Raymond Poincaré, was in Russia during the July crisis and did not attempt to restrain the tsar's government. Instead, the French desire for revenge led it to support Russia unequivocally. England, too, shared some of the blame. Although the foreign minister, Edward Grey, did attempt to mediate the quarrel in July, the British government failed to warn Germany that Britain might side with France and Russia.

THE WAR IN THE WEST

Crossing the Belgian border on August 3, lines of gray-uniformed German soldiers moved through the country. They overcame their first major obstacle on August 7th by taking Liege. Although Belgian fighters resisted, the Germans moved inexorably on, taking Brussels on August 20th. French attacks on the German army were repulsed.

The Battle of the Marne. By the end of August, German troops were in France. Meanwhile, a British Expeditionary Force (BEF) had landed on the continent. However, nei-

German infantrymen depart for the front in 1914, accompanied by friends and relatives. Many thought the war would be over in a few short weeks.

342

ther British nor French troops were able to halt the well-planned German advance, which now drew near to Paris itself. On September 2, the French government fled to Bordeaux, leaving General Joseph Gallieni to organize the city for the expected siege.

But the German armies had failed to coordinate closely in their long march from Germany. A gap had opened up between the first and second armies in the west, and to close it, the first army had turned east, presenting its flank, or side, to attack. This was spotted by a French reconnaissance plane. The British and French armies attacked on a front along the Marne River. To reinforce them, about 1200 taxicabs from Paris were used to rush French troops to the front. In what became known as the "Miracle of the Marne," the Germans were stopped.

The *Battle of the Marne* (September 5–12) marked the end of the German advance and Germany's hope for early victory. The casualties were high and foreshadowed the horrors of the war: 234,000 had been killed and another 1,400,000 wounded.

The Race to the Sea. The Germans fell back to the Aisne River, where they built trenches protected by barbed wire and machine gun posts. The Allies[2] quickly built a parallel system of trenches. In order to win a decisive victory, one of the opposing armies would have to outflank the other. Each side moved to the northwest in order to get around the opposing flank, but neither was successful in turning the flank. The process stopped when both sides reached the Atlantic. By the end of the year, a line of trenches stretched from the French coast to the border of Switzerland.

The difficulty of piercing this line was seen by the German attack at Ypres, around which lay a salient, or bulge, in the Allied line. The Germans attacked on three sides, but they could not take the city. The 475-mile-long trench line would form the battle line in western Europe for most of the duration of the war.

THE WAR IN THE EAST

Germany's dread of a two-front war had materialized. Unable to strike a decisive blow in the west, Germany found that it could not rely on its ally in the east.

The military shortcomings of the Austrians reflected their political dilemma at home. Most of the officers of their army were German-speaking and many of the recruits were from non-German-speaking parts of the empire. They did not have the same loyalty to the army that a united nation-state could expect.

On August 16, the Austrian army attacked Serbia but was thrown back. After reorganizing, the Austrians tried again in December, but were once more driven out. The Serbian commander was able to report on Christmas Day of 1914 that not a single Austrian soldier was on Serbian soil except as a prisoner of war. This was the inglorious end of the show of force that plunged Europe into war. It was only with the assistance of the Germans that Belgrade was taken and Serbia defeated in 1915.

The Austrian army was equally ineffective against the Russians. However, with the transfer of some troops from the western front, the Germans scored a great success against the Russians at the Battle of Tannenberg (August 26–30). The victorious commander was Paul von Hindenberg; he and his chief-of-staff Erich Ludendorff were to play prominent roles in the war.

The action on the eastern front established a pattern which prevailed until Russian withdrawal from the war. Whenever Russian armies were victorious over the Austrians, Germany transferred troops from the western front and won decisive battles. Germany's relationship to its Austrian ally

---

[2] In World War I, those who fought on the side of the Triple Entente powers were known as the *Allies*. Germany, Austria, and states allied to them were the *Central Powers*.

was summed up by a German officer: "We are chained to a corpse."[3]

THE WAR WIDENS

The war spread to become a worldwide conflict. Most of the European participants recruited troops from their overseas empires, and soon Canadians, Australians, New Zealanders, Indians, and Africans were involved in the fighting. The scope of the war was also expanded when, on August 23, 1914, Japan declared war on Germany and occupied German-held islands in the Pacific and German concessions in China. By this action, Japan was honoring its 1902 treaty with England, but was also eager to extend its influence on the Asian mainland. The Ottoman Empire, which controlled most of the Middle East, joined the war on the side of the *Central Powers.* In October, 1914, the Ottoman forces bombarded Russian ports. As a result, there was fighting around the Suez Canal—and throughout the Middle East, as the Allies lent support to Arabs rebelling against Turk-

---

[3] Dorothy and Thomas Hoobler, *The Trenches* (New York: Putnam's, 1978), p. 33.

ish rule. In 1915, Britain began to invade Germany's African colonies. Within a year, Italy, Romania, and Bulgaria were also to enter the war.

STALEMATE

Though some of the bloodiest fighting of the war took place along the trench line in the west, the line established by the end of 1914 was not to shift more than 11 miles until the last year of the war. The defensive strength of the trench system, however, enabled the generals to pull men out of sections of the trenches to go on the offensive elsewhere.

THE GALLIPOLI CAMPAIGN

Faced with stalemate in the west, the Allies planned to open a second front in the Middle East. The Turkish entry into the war had isolated Russia from its allies and from supply of war materials critical to the Russian war effort. Winston Churchill, then first lord of the British admiralty, produced a plan for a naval attack on the Dardanelles, the straits controlled by the Turks that provided access to the Black Sea and Russian ports. The two

British and Commonwealth troops near Gallipoli advance overland in an attempt to seize the Dardanelles from the Turks. The campaign failed, and Allied troops were withdrawn.

French artillery soldiers operate their weapon while wearing gas masks. Poison gas was one of the most deadly products of modern technology.

goals of the campaign were to take Constantinople, driving the Ottomans out of the war, and to link up with the Russian forces.

The naval attack, begun in February 1915, was initially successful, but when four allied ships struck mines, the Allies withdrew. They now launched an amphibious landing at Gallipoli in April. Ottoman troops were quickly reinforced with German troops and advisers, and the Allies failed to win the decisive victory that was hoped for. In December 1915, the Allies withdrew from Gallipoli. The failure of the Dardanelles campaign was a decisive blow to Russia's ability to carry on the war.

CONDITIONS OF WAR

The conditions for the average fighting man in World War I were abysmal. The new weapons of war and the drawn-out battle in the trenches produced a new kind of warfare, more deadly than any before.

Weapons of the War. Both sides in the war searched for new weapons that could produce a decisive advantage. Each side designed and built bigger guns for the days-long artillery barrages that preceded most attacks. The Germans first developed poison

The largest artillery weapon of the war was a German cannon known as the Paris Gun. It could fire a shell 82 miles. When the Germans brought it up by train and fired shells into Paris from 75 miles away, Parisians could not understand what was causing random explosions within the city. But the gun was inaccurate, and Parisians did not panic as the Germans hoped. Eventually, the Paris Gun was taken back to Germany. It was never found after the war.

With the advent of machine guns, trench warfare, and poison gas, the low-flying airplanes of the era became one of the few glamorous arenas of warfare. Shown at left is the German pilot Von Richthofen, known as the "Red Baron." At right, the American ace Eddie Rickenbacker.

gas, and the Allies soon followed suit. The problem with the use of gas was that there was no way to aim it toward enemy troops unless the wind was blowing in the right direction. Different types of gas masks were developed, but even so many were blinded, killed, or suffered permanent lung damage from gas warfare.

Both zeppelins and airplanes were used in World War I. At the beginning of the war, they were primarily used for reconnaisance of enemy positions. Later, bombs were dropped from airplanes onto enemy positions, but the low-flying aircraft were easily shot down. If there was any gallantry left in warfare, it was in the aerial battles fought between pilots of opposing sides—sometimes with pistols and rifles fired from open cockpits. The war produced a number of famous *aces*, pilots who had shot down at least five enemy planes.

The most effective weapon of the war was the machine gun. The hand-cranked machine gun had been developed in the 19th century, and newer technology had produced gas-fired guns that could shoot more rounds of ammunition more rapidly than the

old type. Aerial warfare became more deadly when machine guns synchronized with the propellers of planes enabled pilots to fire bursts directly ahead of them. In the trench fighting, defensive machine guns cut down attacking troops with withering fire. They also made charges by cavalry obsolete.

The superweapon that could break the defense's advantage was the tank, first used in 1917. Tanks could cross the "no man's land" between trenches and break through. They were not produced in great enough quantity to be a decisive factor until the final months of World War I, however.

Life in the Trenches. The trenches along the western front were at first merely shallow ditches. But they were reinforced and extended into a complex system as the war dragged on. They were dug deep enough so that a man could walk in them without his head showing. Tunnels and dugout rooms were hollowed out to make space for eating and sleeping.

It became apparent that just to exist in the trenches for a few weeks was a danger to health. After a rain, men walked in mud up to their knees. An American soldier recalled,

Allied soldiers in a trench. The unique conditions of war developed on the western front required men to eat, sleep, and fight in trenches for months on end.

"The men slept in mud, washed in mud, ate mud, and dreamed mud."[4] The dampness and winter weather brought pneumonia, influenza, and fungus infections. In addition, the men were continually bothered by rats and body lice. From the constant noise of artillery fire, many became "shell shocked," a condition of nervous breakdown that could be permanent.

The order to go "over the top" was the most terrible of all, for it became virtually a death sentence. Even after a preparatory artillery barrage, soldiers in the opposing trench would rake the attackers with machine gun fire. One observer described the aftermath of a battle in the mud:

• • • a khaki-clad leg, three heads in a row, the rest of the bodies submerged, giving one the idea that they had used their last ounce of strength to keep their heads above the rising water. In another miniature pond, a hand still gripping a rifle is all that is visible, while its next-door neighbor is occupied by a steel helmet and half a head, the staring eyes glaring icily at the green slime which floats on the surface almost at their level.[5]

ATTEMPTS TO BREAK THE STALEMATE

In 1915, on the western front, four million men were locked in struggle. Each side tried and failed to break the stalemate through massive attacks: at Ypres, at Neuve Chapelle, and at other points. During the year, each side gained an ally. Italy entered the war on the Allied side against their former partners in the Triple Alliance. In return, the Allies promised to give Italy two parcels of territory controlled by Austria-Hungary. The Central Powers gained Bulgaria as an ally through other territorial promises—yet the war remained a draw.

The Battle of Verdun. Early in 1916, the Germans turned their efforts to the line of forts on the French-German border—particularly Verdun, which was heavily fortified and defended by 175,000 troops. By attacking Verdun, the Germans hoped to bleed France and demoralize its forces.

The Germans began their attack with the heaviest artillery bombardment of the war on February 21, 1916. Over a million shells were fired against a 15-mile front on that day alone. A French survivor described the experience:

• • • Shells of all calibers kept raining on our sector. The trenches had disappeared, filled with earth. . . . The air was unbreathable. Our blinded, wounded,

---

[4] *Ibid.*, p. 80.

[5] Leon Wolf, *In Flanders Field* (New York: Viking Press, 1958), p. 230.

What happened to the "race to the sea"? What advantages would the Germans have gained by controlling France's western coast?

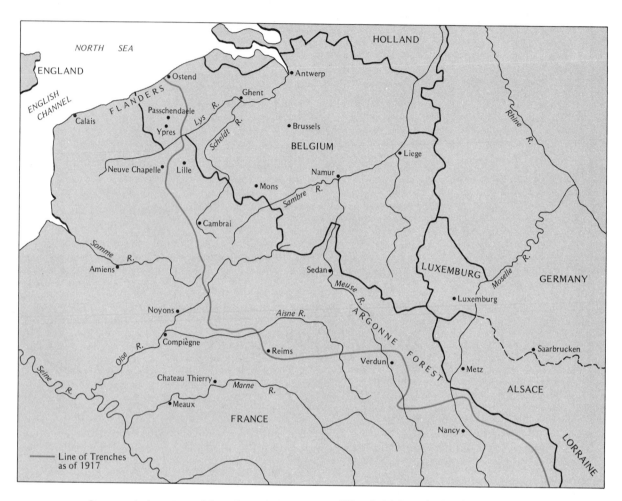

Line of Trenches as of 1917

crawling, and shouting soldiers kept falling on top of us and died splashing us with their blood. It was living hell.[6]

French General Henri Petain was sent to organize the defense of Verdun. The slogan of the French became, *They shall not pass!* as Petain moved to protect the one road that carried his supplies. Convoys of trucks rushed food, ammunition, and medical supplies along the road known as the "Sacred

Way." Although the forts adjoining Verdun fell, Verdun held. The French were aided by a Russian offensive that caused the Germans to divert troops to the east and by the British action on the Somme.

The Germans had bled the French but they themselves had taken stupendous casualties. The cost for the French was 315,000 men, and for the Germans, 281,000.

During the fighting at Verdun, Petain instituted a system of rotation of troops in order to reduce the time served by each soldier. As a result, 70 percent of the French

---

[6] Dorothy and Thomas Hoobler, *op. cit.,* pp. 111–12.

348

The battle for the French fort at Verdun was one of the most fiercely contested engagements of the war. This informal portrait of a group of French defenders conveys an idea of the grim struggle they have survived.

army served at Verdun. It seared the souls of all who were there, and would be a memory that contributed to later French policy.

The Battle of the Somme. The British responded to the French appeal for help with their major offensive of 1916, the Battle of the Somme. It began on June 24 with a seven-day artillery barrage. On July 1 came the order to go over the top. The German defenders reached for their machine guns. One German remembered:

● ● ● *We were very surprised to see them walking, we had never seen that before. . . . The officers went in front. I noticed one of them walking calmly, carrying a walking stick. When we started firing . . . they went down in their hundreds. You didn't have to aim. We just fired into them.[7]*

The British line crumpled but survivors regrouped and kept going. A few reached the

German trenches. The first day of the Somme was the worst day in the history of the British army. Sixty thousand casualties were suffered. The attack had been nearly a complete failure, yet the British commander, Douglas Haig, ordered the offensive to continue.

Three techniques worked in the later phase of the Battle of the Somme: the creeping barrage, in which the artillery fire was coordinated with the advance of soldiers; night attacks that had the element of surprise; and the introduction of the tank. The tank was used to make a gap in the German line, through which galloped British cavalry in one of the last effective uses of cavalry in warfare. But the artillery and the infantry could not keep up with the cavalrymen, and the Germans managed to send up reinforcements to close the gap.

The German commander ordered that all losses in the trench lines had to be retaken, a strategy nearly as wasteful as Haig's. By the time of the last major attack at the Somme, on November 13, British casualties numbered 420,000 men and the Germans lost at least that many.

THE WAR AT SEA

During the early stages of the war, the British navy had thrown a blockade around Germany, keeping ships from leaving or entering German ports. At the beginning, only ships that carried war materials were stopped, but later the blockade was extended to all ships bound for Germany, including those of neutral nations. To break the British blockade, the Germans turned to the submarines known as *U-boats*, from the German word *Unterseeboot*. They were effective at sinking British warships.

The only major sea battle between the British and Germans was the Battle of Jutland. On May 31, 1916, the German High Seas Fleet, under the command of Admiral Reinhard Scheer, met the British Grand Fleet, commanded by Admiral John Jellicoe, shortly before 6 P.M. The battle raged until

---

[7] *Ibid.*, p. 73.

nightfall, when the German fleet cut off the engagement and retreated to the safety of their mined area. Both sides claimed victory, but British losses were significantly higher: the British lost three battle cruisers, three armored cruisers, eight destroyers, and 6097 men. In contrast, the Germans lost one battle cruiser, five destroyers, and 2545 men. But the Germans had failed to gain access to the Atlantic for their fleet, and thus lost the opportunity to break the British blockade.

THE ALLIED DRIVE TO VICTORY

The fighting on the western front in 1917 produced two failed Allied offensives. The Nivelle offensive, led by French General Robert Nivelle in April and May, almost caused the collapse of the French army when a mutiny broke out among the troops. The extent of the mutiny is still a French military secret, but the efforts taken to suppress it caused great damage to French morale.

The second major offensive of 1917 was the Battle of Passchendaele, in which the British tried to use a larger number of tanks to attain their objective. Heavy rains in the area created conditions in which the tanks could not operate, however, and the Germans retaliated with mustard gas. Once again, the Allied offensive ground to a halt with only additional casualties to show for the effort.

However, two events of 1917 were to shape the final result of the war. A revolution in Russia ultimately led to that nation's withdrawal from the war (Chapter 20), and the United States entered the war.

THE UNITED STATES ENTERS THE WAR

The American decision to enter the war had its origins in the war at sea. In response to the British blockade, the German government declared all the waters around Britain a war zone in February, 1915. German U-boats were ordered to sink all enemy ships on sight.

Traditionally, international law stipulated that in the event of sinking, the crew and passengers be rescued. But submarines could not accommodate survivors. In addition, the German government would not guarantee the safety of neutral ships that sailed into the war zone (nor did Britain). German submarine warfare was interpreted as a violation of international law and naval practice.

Initial American Reaction to the War. At the beginning of the war, President Woodrow Wilson proclaimed the United States' neutrality. But his sympathies and those of many other Americans lay with the Allied side. America's cultural links to Britain, its historic ties to France, and outrage about the German attack on Belgium were important reasons. There were also extensive commercial ties to be protected. The need for war materials had created a lucrative market for American industry, and Allied governments had obtained extensive loans and credits from the U.S.

Steps to a U.S. Declaration of War. On May 7, 1915, the *Lusitania*, a British merchant liner carrying a cargo of ammunition as well as many civilian passengers, was sunk by a U-boat; 139 Americans drowned. Wilson sent a note of protest to Germany asserting American neutral rights under international law and calling for Germany to halt its policy of submarine warfare.

Although Germany halted unrestricted submarine warfare in March 1916, the success of the British blockade compelled Germany to reverse the policy in January 1917. The Germans were gambling that they could win the war before the power of the United States could be brought to bear. On February 1, 1917, the German navy's order went into effect: all ships within a wide ocean zone around Britain, France, and Italy were to be regarded as fair game. The United States severed diplomatic relations with Germany on February 3. Nevertheless, Wilson still tried to avoid war, since he had been reelected in

The sinking of the Lusitania by a U-boat aroused public opinion in the U.S., and was a major factor in the American decision to enter the war two years later.

1916 on the slogan, "He kept us out of war."

The final straw was the *Zimmerman telegram*. This secret message from the German ambassador to the Mexican government promised German support for Mexico in regaining its former territories of Arizona, Texas, and New Mexico if the Mexicans declared war. When the text of the telegram came to light, American opinion was galvanized.

On April 6, 1917, the United States Congress declared war on Germany. President Wilson outlined the country's war aims: "to fight for the ultimate peace of the world and for the liberation of its peoples, the German peoples included. . . . The world must be made safe for democracy."[8]

---

[8] Chambers, *op. cit.*, p. 66.

The entry of the United States into the war brought hope to the Allies. On the seas, the German submarine campaign had been effective in the early months of 1917, sinking 875,000 tons of Allied shipping in April. Britain would reach the end of its food supplies within two months. The United States navy sent destroyers to counter the submarines, and then introduced the convoy system (in which merchant ships traveled in groups with destroyer escorts) and the depth bomb to counter the effectiveness of the submarine. However, the most effective contribution of the United States was its economic and industrial resources.

THE HOME FRONTS

All the belligerent governments had to take steps to organize their industrial facilities to

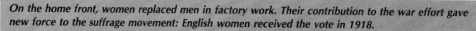
On the home front, women replaced men in factory work. Their contribution to the war effort gave new force to the suffrage movement: English women received the vote in 1918.

fight what was then the most expensive war in history.

But at the same time that industries were being geared up to supply materials for the war, large numbers of men employed in factories and on farms were being drafted into the armed services. Many of the jobs that had been reserved exclusively for men were taken by women, who thereby made an invaluable contribution to the war effort. Many of these women were never again content to be restricted to their traditional roles in the home. Their new attitudes would bring social changes after the war.

Germany was particularly affected by the shortage of war materials because of the British blockade. Both civilians and troops suffered from food shortages. In an effort to coordinate production, Walter Rathenau was placed in charge of all the factories of Germany, and his staff told factory managers what and how much to produce. German workers were told where they would work, and laborers were brought in from occupied territory.

When the war ended, governments did not relinquish all the economic powers they had assumed during the war. Government planning and some intervention in the economy continued afterward.

None of the European governments were able to pay for the cost of the war, and thus had to borrow a staggering amount. The United States was the principal lender, leading to its postwar position as the strongest nation of the world in economic power. By contrast, the nations of Europe, formerly *creditor nations*—who on balance lent more money than they borrowed or bought from others—became *debtor nations*.

THE DEFEAT OF THE CENTRAL POWERS
The takeover by the Bolsheviks in Russia in November 1917 (Chapter 20) gave the Ger-

man government an opportunity to gamble for victory. The new Soviet regime signed the Treaty of Brest-Litovsk with Germany in March 1918, in which Russia ceded most of the territory it had acquired since the time of Peter the Great. The treaty allowed the Germans to move substantial numbers of troops from the eastern front to the west and to launch a final, all-out offensive.

Ludendorff's Offensive. Hoping to win victory in the west, Germany began what they intended to be a decisive thrust unto France on March, 21, 1918. Devised by General Ludendorff, the offensive found initial success. Driving a wedge in the trench line 40 miles deep, the German army reached the Marne and was within 37 miles of Paris by mid-May, 1918.

In June, the American Expeditionary Force (AEF) made its first significant contribution, combining with the French to stop the German advance at Chateau-Thierry. By July, the Allies had gone on the offensive, aided by more fresh American troops. A series of Allied victories between August and November nearly drove the German army out of France and Belgium.

The Fourteen Points. In a speech to Congress in January, 1918, President Wilson laid down the principles on which he hoped a peace settlement would be based. The 14 points he enunciated did much to encourage

THE GERMAN EMPIRE AT ITS GREATEST EXTENT, MARCH 1918
How did German conquests affect Russia's ability to carry on the war?

Wilson's Fourteen Points

1. open covenants of peace
2. freedom of the seas
3. removal of all economic barriers
4. reduced armaments among all nations
5. an impartial treatment of colonial questions, having in mind the best interests of native peoples
6. the evacuation of troops from Russia and an invitation to its government to join the League of Nations
7. the restoration of Belgium
8. the return of Alsace-Lorraine to France
9. Italian frontiers to be drawn along clearly recognizable lines of nationality
10. the various nationalities of Austria-Hungary to have autonomous development
11. troops evacuated from the allied Balkan states and Serbia given access to the sea
12. the Turkish parts of the Ottoman Empire to be independent, but with a chance for autonomous development for nationalities other than Turkish
13. an independent Poland with access to the sea
14. a general association of nations to preserve peace—the League of Nations.

people within the Central Powers to think that a peace settlement would be a just one, and thus they shortened the war.

In subsequent speeches throughout 1918, Wilson embellished these points. He called for no *indemnities*, that is, no punitive financial demands on the loser-nations. Territorial settlements should be made for the benefit of the populations concerned, and not as spoils for the victors. From the German perspective, these points promised a moderate settlement.

The End of the War. During September and October of 1918, Germany's allies capitulated. Bulgaria and Turkey signed an armistice on September 30. As the Austro-Hungarian empire faced defeat, the various nationalities within it clamored for self-determination. On October 21, Czechoslovakia declared its independence, followed by Yugoslavia on October 29. An independent Hungary was established on November 1. On November 3, the Austrian government concluded an armistice with the Allies.

On that same day, German sailors at the naval base at Kiel mutinied, raising the red flag of revolutionary socialism. The revolution quickly spread through several key German cities, with councils of soldiers and workers declaring themselves to be the government in power. In these deteriorating circumstances, the abdication of Kaiser Wilhelm was announced on November 9, and a German republic proclaimed.

On November 8, a German armistice commission met with Allied representatives and asked for peace. The basis of the peace was to be the Fourteen Points with three modifications: the second point, freedom of the seas, was deleted at British insistence; the demand for autonomy for the peoples of the Austro-Hungarian empire was changed to independence, and the losers were to pay reparations, for the destruction of civilian property as a result of military action.

The Allies put forth terms that included the surrender of enough war materials to make it impossible for Germany to continue the war. The Germans were to evacuate their forces from the invaded countries, including Alsace-Lorraine, and withdraw beyond the Rhine River. The Treaty of Brest-Litovsk was to be cancelled. Meanwhile, the naval blockade of Germany was to continue.

The Germans had no choice. At 5 A.M. on

November 11, 1918, the German delegates signed the armistice in a railway car at Compiegne. At 11 A.M., hostilities ceased.

Effects of the War. The effects of this titanic struggle were profound. The dead numbered 10 million, with 20 million wounded. All of the wars of the previous century, from Napoleon's through the Second Balkan War of 1913, had cost less than four and one-half million casualties. Between August 1914 and February 1917, French deaths averaged one every minute. In Britain, too, a generation of young men had been destroyed. Many of the survivors were physically or psychologically maimed and would never lead normal lives.

The monetary cost of the war can only be estimated; direct costs probably were $180 billion, with the indirect costs nearly the same amount. Both losers and winners (except the United States) were saddled with national debts that would cause international monetary crises in the years ahead.

The land itself was devastated in a wide area of France and in many parts of eastern Europe. Three great empires—Germany, Austria-Hungary, and the Ottoman—lay in ruins, and during the course of the war, three great dynasties—Hohenzollern, Hapsburg, and Romanov—had been toppled. In many nations, both old and new, winners and losers, internal political conflict and social instability were the legacy of war.

THE POSTWAR SETTLEMENTS

The postwar settlements were responsible for much of the cynicism and disillusionment that pervaded the years that followed. By and large the treaties did not incorporate the principles of the Fourteen Points.

THE PEACE CONFERENCE

The peace conference convened in Paris on January 18, 1919. The losers were not invited to attend, and Russia was absent as well. Though 32 other nations sent delegates, the conference was dominated by the *Big Three*, the leaders of the United States, France, and Great Britain. President Wilson, the idealist, took the view that the United States was the only disinterested party at the conference, with no territorial or financial ambitions. Wilson believed his purpose was to guarantee the peace and make the world safe for democracy. Georges Clemenceau, the French premier, by contrast, was out for revenge. Known as "the tiger" for his ferocious defense of French interests, Clemenceau was usually at odds with Wilson during the conference sessions. Above all else, Clemenceau wanted security; the assurance that Germany would never again be able to threaten France. The third major participant, David Lloyd George, the prime minister of Britain, was often the mediator between the idealist and the tiger. But Lloyd George, too, sought a harsh settlement for Germany and security for Britain.

Two major tasks confronted the Paris peacemakers: to make an adequate settlement with Germany and to redraw the boundaries of east-central Europe. The first task was made difficult by the French and British war aims; the second, by the secret treaties that the Allies had signed during the war. For example, Italy had been promised Austrian territory, Romania was to be given Transylvania, and Serbia was to get Bosnia.

In addition, the peacemakers were to decide the fate of the German colonies and the non-Turkish areas of the Ottoman Empire. During the British campaigns in the Middle East, they had been helped by Arabs within the Ottoman Empire. For the Arabs, the goal was independence; for Britain and France, the objective was control of parts of Asiatic Turkey, including Palestine, Lebanon, Syria, and Jordan, which they had divided among themselves in a series of secret agreements in 1916 (the Sykes-Picot Agreement). In

The participants in the peace conference at Versailles: Vittorio Orlando of Italy, Lloyd George, Georges Clemenceau, and Woodrow Wilson.

1917, by the *Balfour Declaration*, the British government promised a homeland for Jews in Palestine.

The Versailles Treaty. By April of 1919, the statesmen had completed five treaties with the Central Powers. The treaty with Germany, the *Treaty of Versailles*, included several territorial concessions. Alsace-Lorraine was returned to France, and there were minor changes on the Belgian-German border. The territory of the Saar, which had valuable coal fields, was to be placed under international administration for 15 years. At the end of that time, a plebiscite was to be held there, giving the residents the choice of annexation by France or return to Germany. Some German territory was also given to the recreated state of Poland, with the port city of Danzig made a free city under international jurisdiction. (See map on page 373).

The German army was reduced to 100,000 men with an officer corps of 4000. The German fleet was limited to six battleships, six cruisers, six destroyers, and 12 torpedo boats; submarines were prohibited.

Germany and its allies were required to

relinquish their colonial possessions, which were to become *mandates* controlled by victor nations, primarily Britain and France. According to the terms of the mandates, the colonies were to be prepared for ultimate independence.

Article 231 of the treaty, the *war guilt clause*, required Germany to accept sole responsibility for having caused the war. The Allies argued that the chief German leaders, including the Kaiser, should be tried as war criminals. A few were subsequently tried, but the Kaiser was not among them, for he had fled to Holland, and the Dutch government refused to extradite him.

Article 231 was also used to justify the financial settlement. The total would not be calculated until 1921, but meanwhile Germany was to make a down payment of $5 billion. It was to turn over to the victors all of its large merchant ships, half of its medium-sized ships, one-fourth of its fishing fleet, and build 200,000 tons of shipping annually for five years, to be delivered to the victor nations. In addition, it was to make annual coal deliveries for 10 years to France, Belgium, and Italy; to deliver chemicals to France, and the industrial secrets of its dye industry to the Allies.

The German government saw the treaty for the first time in early May, 1919, and despite strong protests from press and public, approved it. On June 28, 1919, the fifth anniversary of the assassination at Sarajevo, German representatives signed the treaty amid impressive ceremonies in the Hall of Mirrors at the Palace of Versailles.

Treaties with the Other Central Powers. The Paris Peace Conference also drafted treaties with the other defeated nations. The Treaty of St. Germain with Austria marked the end of the Hapsburg dynasty. Austria gave up territory to Czechoslovakia, Poland, and Italy. At the beginning of the war, the Austro-Hungarian Empire had contained about 135,000 square miles and more than 30 million people; with this treaty, Austria consisted of 32,377 square miles and 6.5 million people. Without access to the sea, Austria surrendered its navy. Union with Germany was prohibited.

The settlement with Hungary, the Treaty of Trianon, deprived that state of nearly three-fourths of its land and 64 percent of its population, with territorial concessions to Czechoslovakia, Yugoslavia, and Romania. The Treaty of Neuilly with Bulgaria reduced it to the smallest of the Balkan states, with territory ceded to Yugoslavia, Greece, and Romania.

The treaty with the Ottoman Empire, the Treaty of Sevres, reduced it to the nation of Turkey. Iraq and Palestine were given as mandates to Britain; Syria (including today's Lebanon) was to be a French mandate. The Turkish people resented the treaty, and it increased support for the nationalist leader, Mustapha Kamal (1881–1938), known as Ataturk. Ataturk succeeded in overthrowing the sultan's regime and established the Turkish Republic in 1922. At a subsequent Allied conference, Turkey was given a more lenient settlement in the Treaty of Lausanne.

The League of Nations. The establishment of the League of Nations was Wilson's great hope, the embodiment of his dream that this should be the war to end all wars. The Covenant of the League was developed by a committee during the Paris Peace Conference. The Covenant of the League called for the organization to carry out the provisions of the peace treaties, to prevent aggression and war, to promote disarmament, and to carry out a number of social and humanitarian functions. The Covenant of the League became an integral part of the Treaty of Versailles. With the ratification of that treaty by the major powers, the League of Nations officially began in January, 1920. Ironically, the United States never joined—an ominous beginning for the League and for the hopes of permanent peace.

SUMMARY

World War I had permanent effects. Besides the physical losses, victors and vanquished alike were damaged economically and psychologically. The postwar settlements, far from resolving conflicts, only intensified them, as both camps nursed real and imagined wounds. Woodrow Wilson's dream that this would be the war to make the world safe for democracy died with the emergence of totalitarian regimes in the 1920s and 1930s. Wilson's other hope, that World War I would be the war to end all wars, is sadly ironic in the light of subsequent events. Instead, the terms of the peace settlements served as one of the causes of World War II, a conflagration so intense that civilian casualties alone amounted to many more millions than the total number of deaths in World War I.

QUESTIONS

1 What were the underlying and immediate causes of World War I?
2 Was a world war inevitable? Why?
3 What was the significance of the Schlieffen Plan? Why did it fail?
4 Why did the United States enter the war? What difference did American participation make?
5 Why did the European conflict turn into world war?
6 What were the primary terms of the Treaty of Versailles?
7 Who were the leading representatives at the Paris peace talks, and what did each want? To what extent did the settlement reflect their goals?

BIBLIOGRAPHY

REMARQUE, ERICH MARIA. *All Quiet on the Western Front.* This classic novel of the first World War views that conflict from the perspective of ordinary German soldiers, and captures the horror of the struggle that destroyed a generation of men on both sides.

TAYLOR, EDMOND. *The Fall of the Dynasties: The Collapse of the Old Order, 1905–1922.* This very well-written monograph traces the failures of the European dynasties—the Romanovs, Hapsburgs, and Hohenzollerns—before the war. Few writers have so well captured the personalities and the weakness of these leaders—Kaiser Wilhelm, Emperor Franz Joseph, and Tsar Nicholas II.

TUCHMAN, BARBARA. *The Guns of August.* New York: Macmillan, 1962. The best book about the summer of 1914 and the events that precipitated the "Great War." Tuchman combines excellent research and a fine writing style to explain the diplomacy and the events.

20

● *Citizens of Russia: A great event has taken place. By the mighty assault of the Russian people, the old order has been overthrown, a new, free Russia is born. The great revolution crowns long years of struggle. . . . The Provisional Government is animated by the belief that it will thus execute the will of the people, and that the whole nation will support it in its honest efforts to insure the happiness of Russia.*

THE PROVISIONAL GOVERNMENT

Russia: From Autocracy to Dictatorship

With the words quoted above, a hopeful Provisional Government enunciated its ideals for the future of Russia. The Romanov dynasty had lost the support of the Russian people because of its authoritarianism and its disastrous involvement in World War I. The liberal ideals of the Provisional Government, in contrast, provided hope that Russia would become a democratic state.

However, there were other forces at work in Russia. Mistakes by the liberals, and the determined leadership of a minority party, brought about a second Russian revolution in 1917. This revolution's guiding force was Marxism. The success of the Bolsheviks in creating a communist state was to have far-reaching effects on both Russia and the rest of the world.

THE RUSSIAN REVOLUTION The Russian Revolution of 1917 was really two revolutions. The first was a liberal revolution that promised a constitutional democracy. A second revolution later in the same year would establish a communist state in Russia.

THE CAUSES OF THE REVOLUTION

In the years since these tumultuous events occurred, historians have closely analyzed their causes. The immediate cause was the shortage of food in St. Petersburg after a long, hard winter. There were, however, deep-seated underlying reasons as well. They included widespread dissatisfaction with Russia's participation in World War I; loss of confidence in Tsar Nicholas II's leadership; numerous grievances among the peasantry and the industrial working class; the alienation of Russia's intellectual class; and the existence in Russia of revolutionary groups that hoped to seize power and then to apply their particular social and political philosophies to the Russian realities. In fact, nearly all segments of Russian society preferred some change in the regime which governed them.

Russia and World War I. The precipitating event of the revolution was Russian participation in World War I. Russia was ill-equipped to fight a modern war: in fact, it has been estimated that only one of every three Russian soldiers at the front was

Russian soldiers surrender en masse to German troops. The inadequacy of the tsar's military leadership was one of the issues that precipitated revolution.

equipped with a rifle. Military defeat and mass desertions followed.

Contributing to the military debacle was inept government leadership. At the outbreak of war, 15 million men were drafted into the army, despite the shortage of supplies to equip them. These young adult males had been of critical importance to the civilian war effort—in factories and fields. Their removal from the civilian work force placed an impossible burden of labor on women, old men, and children. As a result, Russia's war effort was severely crippled rather than helped by the massive draft.

At the same time, morale in the army suffered. The soldiers at the front, inadequately fed and armed, were prime targets of political agitators who sought to convert them to one cause or another. Many opponents of the Russian participation in the war successfully characterized it as the "tsar's war," which they viewed as unrelated to the concerns or needs of the common people.

Loss of Confidence in the Tsar. The Russian monarchy in 1917 was the most backward and autocratic of all of the governments in Europe. Moreover, in the leadership of Tsar Nicholas II, it was the most poorly led.

Nicholas II (1894–1917), the last of the Romanov dynasty to rule Russia, ascended the throne in 1894 at the death of his father Alexander III. Within five weeks, the young Nicholas, now 26 years of age, married Princess Alexandra of Hesse, a granddaughter of Queen Victoria. It was a love match. On the day of their engagement Nicholas wrote to his mother, "The whole world is changed for me; nature, mankind, everything; all seem to be good and loveable and happy."[1] His bride, "Alex," was equally enamored, writing in her husband's diary, "Never did I believe that there could be such utter happiness in this world, such a feeling of unity between two mortal human beings. I love you—those three words have my life in them."[2]

Although he was a model husband and father, Nicholas did not possess the personal characteristics necessary to make a good leader—physically, he was not the massive man his father had been, nor was he as determined or self-confident. Handsome, quiet, unsure of himself and indecisive, he was a weak man unequipped to deal with

[1] Alan Moorehead, *The Russian Revolution* (New York: Bantam Books, 1959), p. 19.

[2] *Ibid.*, p. 20.

the turbulent events of his time. He and his wife were nonetheless determined to preserve undiminished the power of the throne.

After the birth of four daughters, the royal family had rejoiced at the birth of their only son, Alexis, in 1904. However, it soon became apparent that the royal prince suffered from hemophilia. Thus afflicted, the child's life was always in imminent danger from the slightest cut or bruise, and his chances for survival to adulthood appeared negligible. Alexis' illness seemed to confirm Nicholas' judgment: "Whatever I try, nothing succeeds. I am out of luck."[3]

---

[3] *Ibid.*, p. 13.

The royal couple believed their luck had changed when they met Gregory Rasputin in 1905. Rasputin claimed to be a *starets* (a self-ordained religious man) who had traveled to the Holy Land. In fact, he was a scoundrel, an illiterate Russian peasant who had been driven from his native village as a horse thief. His moral beliefs included the principle that only those who had truly sinned could be forgiven, a philosophy which he practiced as well as preached. Nonetheless, he succeeded in treating the royal child's hemophilia. He convinced Nicholas and Alexandra that he was truly their "man of God." One of Alexandra's letters to Rasputin reveals the extent to which she was captivated by him:

Tsar Nicholas II, Alexandra, and their children. Lacking the qualities of a successful ruler, Nicholas nevertheless refused to permit any reform that might diminish his authority.

• • • My beloved unforgettable teacher, redeemer, and mentor! How tiresome it is without you! My soul is quiet and I relax only when you, my teacher, are sitting beside me. I kiss your hands and lean my head on your blessed shoulders.[4]

Rasputin's behavior—his drunken brawls, obscene language, and many love affairs—soon became the scandal of the royal court, and Russian Orthodox Church officials were horrified at the religious pretensions of this very unholy man. Thus, the tsar lost the support of two groups that had traditionally supported the monarchy—the aristocracy and the church.

---

[4] *Ibid.*, p. 73.

In December 1916 a member of the royal family, Prince Yusupov, and several other conspirators murdered Rasputin. The novice assassins lured Rasputin to Yusupov's home with the hint that Yusupov's pretty wife would be present. Arriving near midnight, Rasputin was served ample quantities of cyanide-laced wine and cakes—apparently with no ill effects. After two and one-half hours had elapsed, Yusupov in desperation shot Rasputin several times. Although Rasputin appeared dead, he later rose from the floor and chased Yusupov from the room. Two more shots and a kick in the head seemed to have slain the "holy man."

The conspirators tied the body with ropes and tossed it into the Neva River. Three days later the corpse surfaced, freed from the ropes and with water in the lungs—the actual cause of death was drowning! But the murder of Rasputin came far too late to salvage the reputation of Nicholas and Alexandra.

The mysterious self-proclaimed monk, Rasputin. His close friendship with Nicholas and Alexandra was widely seen as an embarrassment to the monarchy.

Peasant and Working Class Grievances. Another underlying cause of the Russian Revolution was widespread discontent among the lower classes. The Russian peasants, at least 75 percent of the population in 1917, were land-hungry. The end of serfdom in 1861 and the subsequent redistribution of land failed to provide them enough land to live beyond mere subsistence. Traditionally loyal to the tsarist system—indicated by a peasant saying, "we are yours, but the land is ours"—the peasants bore the economic burden of Russia's attempts to industrialize. The wheat they grew was exported to pay for machine tools and other materials needed for industrialization.

The Russian working class (the proletariat) were small in number (about 2.5 million people), equalling about two percent of the population. However, their concentration in the major cities of Petrograd (as St. Petersburg became known in 1914) and Moscow gave them influence far beyond their numbers. They were dissatisfied with their low wages, long working hours, undesirable working conditions, and the governmental ban on unionization, collective bargaining, and strikes.

Revolutionary Movements. Both peasants and the proletariat were potential recruits for the various revolutionary movements endemic in Russia since the last years of the 19th century. Several groups which eventually coalesced into the Social Revolutionary party, founded in 1901, hoped to establish socialism and industrialization in Russia by organizing the peasants.

Other revolutionaries sought to bring their philosophies to fruition by means of the Russian proletariat. The first such group were the anarchists, who believed that the primary source of human misery was government. Their solution was political assassination. Europe and America were witness to several successful anarchist assassinations by the turn of the century—those of King Humbert of Italy, U.S. President William McKinley, Empress Elizabeth of Austria, Sadi Carnot, the President of France, and Tsar Alexander II of Russia. Although the anarchists were successful in carrying out assassinations, they could not by that means destroy governments, and they were superseded in Russia in the late 19th century by the Social Democrats—the Russian Marxists.

As we have seen, Marxist theory argued that capitalism is unfair to the industrial working class, or proletariat, for the capitalist's profit deprives the worker of the rightful fruits of his labor. To Marx, the solution for this injustice was the seizure of power by the working class. The workers, led by the intelligentsia, would establish a temporary dictatorship and a socialist economic system in which the means of production, the factories, would be owned by the state. According to Marxist theory, states would ultimately "wither away." The peoples of the world would themselves collectively own the means of production and would share equally in the results of their labor. This final stage, communism, would represent the ideal society—a heaven on earth.

At the time of the Russian Revolution, Marxism was only a theory that had not yet been applied to any society. Moreover, it was a theory intended to apply only to industrialized societies where the working class comprised the majority of the population.

This gap between Marxist theory and the realities of Russia created difficulties for the Russian Marxists. Discussion among its leaders on how to proceed split the Russian Marxist movement (the Social Democratic Party) in 1903 into *Mensheviks* (minority) and *Bolsheviks* (majority). The Bolsheviks believed that the way to communist victory in Russia was by means of a small, tightly knit political party. Moreover, the Bolsheviks believed in "democratic centralism" within the party; that is, party decisions would be arrived at by democratic vote, but once the decision was made every member must support it. This introduction of dictatorship within the Bolshevik party foreshadowed the type of government it would eventually establish to rule the state.

Although the potential adherents to Russian Bolshevism were at the most 1 million people out of about 130 million Russians, the movement gained strength in the early years of the 20th century. In the 1905 Revolution (Chapter 14), the Russian Marxists played an important role.

THE MARCH REVOLUTION

On March 8, 1917, in the midst of the long Russian winter, many of the tsar's subjects in working-class sections of the capital city of Petrograd began demonstrations for more bread. The next day, March 9, the demonstrations spread when the demonstrators visited factories and convinced the workers to stop work and join them. On March 10, these disturbances had spread into a city-wide riot. The riots turned to revolution on March 11, when government troops sent in to put down the rioters joined them instead. The American ambassador, an observer of these disorders, reported:

• • • *About ten A.M. today a regiment of 1000 to 1200 men stationed in barracks about two blocks from the Embassy mutinied and according to reports killed their commanding officer because he would not join them. At 11:30 A.M. Mr. Miles phoned me . . . that some of the mutineers accompanied by many revolutionists had visited the munition factory adjoining the Austrian Embassy; had killed the officer in command there, and had ordered the men to quit work.*[5]

On March 14, just six days after the start of public disorders, Tsar Nicholas II abdicated in favor of his brother, Grand Duke Michael Alexandrovich. But the grand duke refused to take the throne. Instead, on that same day, March 14, the Provisional Government (P.G.) was formed, composed of members of the Russian legislature, the Duma. These events comprise the Russian Revolution of March 1917. It was spontaneous, nearly bloodless, and successful.

The Provisional Government. The revolution of March 1917 seemed briefly to establish a democracy for Russia. The new P.G. was dominated by the Constitutional Democratic Party (the *Cadets*), whose leaders were liberal democrats in the 19th-century tradition. The leaders announced that they intended to serve temporarily, pending the election of a constituent assembly, elected by universal suffrage, which would then determine the form of government which should rule Russia. This assembly would also write the constitution that incorporated that system. In its manifesto to the people in March 1917, the P.G. proclaimed its intentions and declared its commitment to the freedoms traditional in democratic governments—of speech, the press, assembly, and political action.

The Rise of the Soviets. The abdication of the tsar left a power vacuum in Russia. At the local level, tsarist officials were usually replaced by a **soviet**, a council composed of local leaders. In most cases, these local soviets had no connection or commitment to the P.G. centered in Petrograd.

Even in the capital, a *soviet* of workers and soldiers was established by radical leaders on March 12, the same day the P.G. took power. It soon rivaled the P.G. in authority among the masses. One of the soviet's first actions was to issue an order to the Russian army—Army Order #1—which democratized the army, calling on all army units to elect their own soviets which would be subordinate to the Petrograd soviet. Although the Petrograd soviet had no legal authority, many army units obeyed. Thus, from the very beginning, the P.G. lacked control over many local governments and army units. To make matters worse, the P.G. launched a major military offensive on July 1 which failed.

In those chaotic circumstances, the P.G. was nearly overthrown twice, the first time by violent demonstrations in Petrograd on July 3–7, 1917, which were led by various radical groups including the Bolsheviks. The commander-in-chief of the Russian army, General Lavr Kornilov, then attempted a military coup with an army march on the capital. His movement failed too. But although the P.G., now under the leadership of Alexander Kerensky, the leader of the Social Revolutionary Party, survived, it was severely weakened.

Without doubt, the P.G.'s decision to remain in the war was a fatal error. The P.G. had three reasons for this decision. Its leaders believed that they were honor-bound by agreements—to withdraw might bring military defeat to their allies. Also, the leaders believed that the decision to withdraw

[5] "Bulletin of the Provisional Government," March 7, 1917, in Robert V. Daniels, ed., *The Russian Revolution* (Englewood Cliffs, N. J.: Prentice-Hall, 1972), pp. 16–18.

Bolshevik street demonstrators run for their lives after being fired upon by soldiers of the Provisional Government, July 1917.

should be made by the democratically elected government that they intended to replace them. Finally, they believed that the army would be inspired to fight on in the spirit of "lofty patriotism." They misjudged the extent of disillusionment with the war effort and the effect of anti-war propaganda within the army rank and file.

THE NOVEMBER REVOLUTION

Throughout the summer months of 1917, as the Provisional Government floundered, the Bolsheviks spread their political philosophy and gradually acquired leadership of the Petrograd and Moscow soviets. On November 7, 1917, the Bolshevik faction of the Marxist social Democratic party seized power in a *coup d'état.*

Lenin's Role. The success of the Bolsheviks is due primarily to the leadership of one man, Vladimir Ulyanov (1879–1924), who used the pseudonym *Lenin,* after the river Lena which flows through Siberian Russia. Born on April 22, 1879, the second of six children, Lenin was the son of a provincial school inspector for the tsarist government. As a result, Lenin's father was a member of

the minor nobility of Russia. Little in Lenin's conservative origins hinted at his future political role. Nor, it seems, did he have an extraordinary childhood.

The turning point of Lenin's youth came when he was 17. In that year, his brother Alexander was hanged for his role in an unsuccessful plot to assassinate Tsar Alexander III. An outstanding college zoology student, Alexander Ulyanov had joined the People's Will, an anarchist group dedicated to political assassination.

After his brother's execution, the young Lenin began to study the writings of Karl Marx, and in 1879 organized a Marxist study group. Although he also studied law and passed his law examinations in 1891, he was more interested in revolutionary theory than in the practice of law. He soon became a leading member of the Marxist Social Democratic Party.

In December 1895, Lenin was arrested by the tsarist secret police, the Okhrana, and sentenced to 14 months in prison and then to three years of exile in Siberia. During his exile, Lenin had ample opportunity to study, to write to others dedicated to his cause, and

Lenin addressing a crowd on May 1, 1918. His devotion to the Bolshevik party during his years in exile enabled him to take control of the revolution after his return.

to plan the future. When he completed his sentence in Siberia, he went into voluntary exile in western Europe—Germany, England, Finland, Switzerland—where he remained until the 1917 revolution.

Lenin's years in the West provided him the time and freedom to develop his theories and to strengthen his leadership role in the party. One of his activities was to edit the party newspaper *Iskra* ("The Spark"), which was smuggled into Russia. In 1903, as we have seen, the Social Democratic Party split into the Mensheviks and the Bolsheviks, and Lenin took leadership of the Bolshevik faction. From 1903 to 1917, he developed his organization.

Although Lenin did not expect revolution to come to Russia in his lifetime, the March revolution inspired him to action. Returning to Russia, he outlined the Bolshevik position in his *April theses*: the Provisional Govern-

ment should be replaced by a soviet government; the new soviet state should nationalize (take over) the banks and all industrial production; all land should be nationalized; and Russia should withdraw from the war. Out of the April theses, Lenin created two slogans, *Peace, Land, and Bread* and *All Power to the Soviets*. Lenin's emissaries found widespread support for these ideas—especially among Russian troops stationed at the front—although most Russians did not know or understand Lenin's Marxist theories.

The Coup d'Etat. Although the Bolsheviks controlled the Petrograd and Moscow soviets, they did not control the All-Russian Congress of Soviets, which was preparing to meet in Petrograd on November 7. The All-Russian Congress was composed of over 600 leaders of the local governments from all over Russia; only about one-third of them were Bolsheviks.

Before the congress could begin, the Bolsheviks seized military control of Petrograd. During the night of November 6, their private military unit, the Red Guard, numbering about 20,000 armed men, occupied the railway stations, the state bank, the telephone exchange, the power stations, and the bridges. At 10 A.M. on November 7, the Bolsheviks announced the end of the Provisional Government. Prime Minister Kerensky could find no military units willing to defend the P.G. On that evening, the Red Guard besieged the Winter Palace, where the remaining ministers of the P.G. continued to meet. The battleship *Aurora*, under Bolshevik control, shelled the palace from the Neva River and by dawn on the morning of November 8, the *coup d'état* had succeeded.

Like the March revolution, the November coup had been nearly bloodless.

Lenin and his Bolsheviks were now in control of the city and, as well, the All-Russian Congress of Soviets. On the evening of November 8, Lenin addressed the assembly and proceeded to extract from the captive delegates approval for the Bolshevik platform—the end of private ownership of land and the establishment of the Council of People's Commissars under the presidency of Lenin. By this device, Lenin acquired power over all of Russia and the appearance, if not the reality, of a "people's democracy."

The regime which came to power in the November coup established a dictatorship which closely mirrored the hated authoritarian regime of the deposed tsar. The dream

On November 7, 1917, soldiers of Lenin's private army, the Red Guards, stormed the Winter Palace and deposed Kerensky's Provisional Government.

of liberal democracy for Russia died along with its defenders on that November day.

THE BOLSHEVIKS IN POWER

That a relatively small group of Bolsheviks could seize control of Russia astonished many—contemporary observers and historians alike. The Bolsheviks succeeded primarily for two reasons: the failures of the P.G., and the political shrewdness and fanaticism of Lenin.

CONSOLIDATION OF POWER

Having seized political power, Lenin was now faced with two primary tasks. He had to develop a blueprint for rule, and enforce that blueprint on the country. Lenin's genius lay in his ability to do both. Lenin telescoped two stages of Marxist theory—the democratic revolution to be followed by a proletarian one—into one stage, even though Russia had not yet experienced the industrial revolution and did not have a sizable proletariat. Lenin was a man of absolute convictions, he was intolerant of all opposition, and he was willing to use political terror.

Russian Withdrawal from the War. Quickly entering into peace negotiations with Germany, Russia formally withdrew from the war by signing the Treaty of Brest-Litovsk in March 1918. It was a disastrous settlement for Russia, which lost the Ukraine, Poland, Finland, Latvia, Lithuania, and Estonia.

RUSSIAN LOSSES FROM THE TREATY OF BREST-LITOVSK

26% of the population
27% of available land
32% of average crop yield
26% of railway system
33% of manufacturing industries
73% of iron industries
75% of coal fields

Lenin acceded to the German demands for several reasons. First, he had promised to do so and he realized that the Russian army was demoralized. Secondly, Lenin believed that the example of revolution in Russia would spark revolution in Germany. Lastly, Lenin was chiefly concerned with consolidating his power within Russia.

The Red Terror. One of the means whereby Lenin consolidated his power was through the creation of a terrorist police force, the *Cheka* (the Extraordinary Commission for the Suppression of Counterrevolution). Under the leadership of the ruthless Felix Dzerzhinsky, the *Red Terror* was proclaimed against all "enemies of the state." Thousands of "counterrevolutionar-

A revolutionary poster depicts the triumph of the Bolsheviks in November 1917. By the calendar in use at the time, the coup d'état occurred on October 25 and is still known as the October Revolution.

ies," mostly nobility, tsarist government officials, and leading capitalists were "liquidated," a euphemism for "shot on the spot." Ironically, the Cheka and the activities of the Red Terror closely resembled the police state maintained by the deposed and detested tsarist regime. It also resembled and foreshadowed the police state erected by Lenin's successors. In *The State and Revolution*, Lenin justified his policies: "Capitalism cannot be defeated and eradicated without the ruthless suppression of the resistance of exploiters."[6]

As part of his policy of rapidly applying Marxist theory to Russia, the Bolshevik government *nationalized* all industry and established food battalions—teams of Cheka men who went into the countryside and expropriated food from the peasants. By these policies, Lenin established himself as the dictator of "democratic" Russia. As he rationalized it:

• • • *The Soviet Socialist Democracy is in no way inconsistent with the rule and dictatorship of one person . . . the will of a class is at times best realized by a dictator.*[7]

The Civil War. Lenin's radical measures triggered a civil war in March 1918. The opposition, known as the Whites, consisted of various diverse groups—tsarist supporters, some of the peasantry, the fiercely independent Don Cossacks, the liberal democrats, and, for a period, the military forces of several foreign powers. Although they outnumbered the Reds—the name given to Lenin's forces because of the color of their flag—the Whites were poorly organized, widely dispersed, and had diverse political views and aspirations. The Red Army organized by Leon Trotsky had greater cohesion. By 1920,

the Red Army had attained control of most of the countryside.

War Communism, 1918–1921. Lenin used the demands of the civil war to intensify his dictatorship under the economic policy known as *war communism*. This economic policy created a *command economy* in which every facet of the economy—industry, trade, agriculture, and finance—was controlled by the government. The effect was disastrous—productivity declined, wartime food rationing continued, and the rate of inflation soared. In 1918, one dollar equalled 9 rubles; by 1920, one dollar equalled 1,200 rubles. In 1918, prices were 23 times higher than in 1913; by 1921, prices were 17,000 times higher than in 1913. In 1920–1921, five million Russians died of famine.

Lenin renamed the Bolshevik party the Communist party, moved the capital to Moscow, and established the *Comintern* (Communist International), a Moscow-based and directed international association whose purpose was to spread the revolution to the rest of the world through propaganda and subversion.

The New Economic Policy, 1921–1928. In 1921, Lenin moderated the policy of war communism by introducing the New Economic Policy (NEP), which reintroduced a degree of capitalism. In the subsequent reforms, Lenin restored a limited degree of free market competition, even while the government retained control of the "commanding heights" of the economy—banks, railroads, utilities, and heavy industry. The NEP succeeded in restoring the economy, at least to the pre-war level.

Many observers interpreted the NEP as the end of Lenin's experiment with Marxism. In fact, it serves as evidence of Lenin's pragmatism, his willingness—temporarily—to suspend economic theory to meet the realities of the Russian economy. As Lenin intended, the NEP was an interim measure to bring about economic recovery from World War I and the civil war.

---

[6] David Shub, *Lenin* (New York: Doubleday, 1950), Appendix.

[7] *Ibid.*

The Soviet Constitution. In 1919, a constitution for the new Union of Soviet Socialist Republics was written. Although the constitution (revised in 1936) created elected legislative assemblies at the local, district, provincial, and national levels, there was and is only one legal political party in Russia—the Communist party. The voter, therefore, merely rubber-stamps the candidates chosen by the party. Moreover, no provision was made for secret ballots—at the local level, elections take place by a show of hands. In effect, the constitution created a sham democracy.

LENIN'S DEATH

Lenin's health began to deteriorate in early 1922, when he suffered a stroke which left him temporarily paralyzed. For nearly two years, he continued to head the regime, although his ability to act decisively was seriously affected. He suffered a second stroke in December 1922, a third in March 1923, and a final, fatal stroke in January 1924, at the age of 54.

At his death Lenin was the father of the Soviet Union and the leading symbol of modern Marxism. One sympathetic account describes the public reaction of the hundreds of thousands of men and women who, in the bitter cold of January, stood beside the railway all the way from Gorky to Moscow—a distance of 30 miles—when his body was taken to the capital. Thousands of others came to Moscow to walk sorrowfully past his open coffin. His widow, a plain, stoutish woman, stooped from much work for the revolution, said afterward to representatives of his party: "I want to say to you that . . . Lenin's heart beat with ardent love for his workingmen and for all the oppressed. He never spoke of this himself, and I would not speak of it at any other, less solemn moment."[8]

The funeral was an affair of state with a proletarian touch. Lenin's body lay in state in the House of the Trade Unions while processions of workers and Red Army soldiers came to pay their last respects. The soldiers of the guard fired traditional cannon salutes. At the funeral, the pallbearers were ranking members of the party. When Lenin was buried at 4 P.M. on January 23, 1924, all of the factory whistles in Moscow blew. His body was embalmed and placed in a mausoleum in Red Square, next to the Kremlin wall. Ever since, tourists from Russia and the rest of the world have filed by his crypt to observe the remains.

---

[8] Elizabeth Seeger, *The Pageant of Russian History* (London: Longmans, Green, 1956), pp. 342–3.

SUMMARY

Conditions were ripe for revolution in Russia in 1917. Support for the autocratic government of the tsar was declining even among such groups as the aristocracy and the Russian Orthodox Church, formerly its two staunchest supporters. In March of 1917, demonstrations for bread started a process that led to the overthrow of the Romanovs. The Provisional Government that took power attempted to rule democratically, but mistakes by its leaders, such as the failure to withdraw from the war, left the government with inadequate popular support. A dedicated group of revolutionaries, the Bolsheviks, overthrew the Provisional Government and established the first Communist state, under the leadership of Lenin. His policies shifted according to need, but effectively laid the foundations for the harsh dictatorship of his successor, Joseph Stalin, as we will see in Chapter 22.

QUESTIONS

1 What were the underlying causes of the Russian Revolution? To what extent were the tsar's weaknesses a factor?
2 What were the aims of the Provisonal Government?
3 How did Lenin seize power? How can the success of his small minority be explained?
4 How did Russia in 1917 differ from Karl Marx's description of a society ready for communism?
5 Describe war communism and the NEP. Why and when did Lenin adopt these policies?
6 In what ways did Lenin's rule foreshadow the dictatorship of Joseph Stalin?

BIBLIOGRAPHY

CROSSMAN, RICHARD, ed. *The God that Failed.* New York: Bantam Books, 1959. *Accounts by six writers who flirted with communism and subsequently rejected it, primarily because of Stalin's rule.*

MASSIE, ROBERT. *Nicholas and Alexandra.* New York: Atheneum, 1967. *A fascinating account of the last tsar and his family relies on extensive research into their lives and deaths. Massie presents a sympathetic account of human beings who were destined but not equipped to rule.*

MOOREHEAD, ALAN. *The Russian Revolution.* New York: Bantam Books, 1959. *Although several more recent studies also trace the dramatic events of the Russian Revolution, none does it better than Moorehead. This paperback is a must for anyone who wants to understand the fall of the Provisional Government and the Bolshevik coup d'état.*

SHUB, DAVID. *Lenin.* New York: Mentor Books, 1948. *This standard brief biography of Lenin captures his personality and ideology, and supplements Moorehead's political history.*

TUCKER, ROBERT C. *Stalin as Revolutionary, 1879–1929: A Study in History and Personality.* New York: Horton, 1974. *Good biographies of Stalin are hard to find, for the dictator obscured many of the unsavory details of his life. But Tucker has produced a detailed account of Stalin's early life and of the hunger for power that led to his totalitarian dictatorship.*

VON LAVE, THEODORE. *Why Lenin? Why Stalin?* Philadelphia: Lippincott, 1971. *This influential work attempts to explain the riddle of the Bolsheviks' success within the context of Russian and European History.*

21

● *Adequate guarantees given and taken that national armaments will be reduced to the lowest points consistent with domestic safety.*

WOODROW WILSON

The Truce Between the Wars

World War I affected all facets of life in Europe. Destruction wrought by the war—particularly in France, where most of the fighting on the western front took place—was extensive. The troops of both the winning and losing sides returned home to find an economic situation that had changed for the worse. In many cases, they had no jobs waiting for them at home, because the factories that had been operating at full capacity now faced declining markets.

The new states that were drawn on the map of Europe by the Paris Peace Conference were in many cases not economically viable. In particular, the former states of the Austro-Hungarian Empire found that independence deprived them of the economic advantages that they had enjoyed as part of a united empire. Unused to democracy, these countries had to contend with a full spectrum of political groups, from monarchists to leftists inspired by the Russian Revolution.

Germany, which before the war had been a strong industrial power, found itself deprived of much of its resources of coal and iron. Fear of German aggression had led the Paris peacemakers to cripple Germany's economic base. The Allies had made matters worse by continuing the blockade on Germany until its representatives signed the peace treaty in 1919. There was suffering and even starvation in Germany during the postwar period. Not surprisingly, most Germans reacted bitterly toward those who had enforced such harsh terms on their nation.

Germany also faced political turmoil. The government that took power was controlled by the Social Democrats. In January 1919, German communists known as the *Spartacists*, led by Karl Liebknecht and Rosa Luxemburg, led an uprising to establish a soviet government. The Social Democrats used voluntary forces raised from demobilized soldiers to put down the rebellion; Liebknecht and Luxemburg were killed.

After elections, a National Constituent Assembly met at the city of Weimar to write a new constitution. The government that was established is known as the Weimar Republic. It continued to face threats and attempts at takeover from both the left and right.

Finally, the League of Nations, which had been the hope of President Wilson to ensure a permanent peace, proved to be too weak to accomplish its primary task. Part of its failure stemmed from the refusal of the United States to join the League, but it faced numerous other problems as well.

THE POST-WORLD WAR I PEACE SETTLEMENTS

To what extent did the boundaries of the new Central European states conform to Wilson's principle of national self-determination? What new problems arose?

Territory lost by Germany

Territory lost by Austria-Hungary

Territory lost by Russia

Rhineland—demilitarized zone

"NEW DIPLOMACY" VERSUS THE OLD

The "old diplomacy" had been practiced in Europe since the Treaty of Westphalia in 1648 by the leaders of the major European states. These few men had often determined in secret the fate not only of Europe but of the world. But the war had shattered the old system of diplomacy, with Germany the outcast, Austria-Hungary dismantled, and Russia under the control of the radical Marxists. American participation in the victory and the world scope of the war brought about a shift in the balance of power in the world, and the beginning of the end of European dominance.

President Woodrow Wilson intended the League of Nations to incorporate a new system of world diplomacy in which all nations would take part in a collaborative effort. The League was headquartered in Geneva, Switzerland, a neutral state symbolizing impartiality, justice, and the abandonment of narrow self-interest. Moreover, small nations as well as large were invited to join, based on their acceptance of the covenant of the League. That covenant, however, had been drafted by a small committee, in private, contrary to the principle of "open covenants openly arrived at." This violation of the spirit of the League foreshadowed the numerous inadequacies of the organization.

When the first session of the League Assembly met in November 1920, 42 nations were represented. Germany, Russia, and the United States, however, were not among them. Germany was excluded as the aggressor in World War I, and was not admitted until 1926. The Soviet Union was not invited to join because of the radical policies of the Bolshevik regime (Chapter 20); it became a member in 1935. The United States never joined.

The League operated through three agencies: the Assembly, the Council, and the Secretariat. In the Assembly, which met annually, each member had one vote. The Council, composed of four permanent members and four nonpermanent members (eventually expanded to 11), served as a cabinet with limited executive powers. The chief duties of the Council were to prevent war by restricting armaments and by resolving international disputes, and to control and supervise the mandates of the League. The third agency of the League, the Secretariat, was the civil service; it prepared the agenda for Council and Assembly sessions, performed clerical duties, and prepared documents for publication. A respected British Foreign Officer, Sir Eric Drummond, served as the first Secretary-General. In addition to the agencies that were part of the League, several international organizations worked closely with it, such as the World Court, sitting at The Hague, Holland, which handled international disputes, and the International Labor Office, whose purpose was to promote industrial justice.

THE UNITED STATES AND THE LEAGUE

The failure of the United States to join the League can be attributed in part to Wilson's desire to connect the League and its peace-keeping functions to the peace treaties. Because the League of Nations was tied to the Treaty of Versailles, it required the approval of two-thirds of the U.S. Senate.

On the issue of the League, the Senate was divided into three groups: those who were willing to accept the treaty with no reservations, those who wanted mild reservations, and those, led by Henry Cabot Lodge, who were unalterably opposed to the treaty and the League. To achieve a two-thirds vote, it was necessary for the first two groups to compromise. Wilson opposed any reservations on the League, and took his case directly to the voters. In September of 1919, he began a tour of the country to raise support for the League. On this tour he collapsed and returned to Washington paralyzed from a stroke. A broken man for the remainder of his term, Wilson remained bedridden and his wife acted as president in his name.

The new "peace palace" of the League of Nations in Geneva, Switzerland provided separate working areas for the Council, the Secretariat, and the Assembly.

In November, 1919, the Senate rejected the Treaty by a vote of 39–55. In August of 1921, the Congress approved a separate peace with Germany. The failure of the United States to join the League of Nations was the first of several blows to the hopes of the League and the new diplomacy. It also marked the beginning of the period of American isolation from world affairs that ended only with the Japanese bombing of Pearl Harbor in December, 1941.

THE FAILURES OF THE LEAGUE

Despite its inauspicious beginning the League succeeded in several constructive accomplishments: assistance to bankrupt countries, supervision of the mandates, and the resolution of disputes which did not involve the great powers, such as a Swedish-Finnish controversy in 1921 and a Hungarian-Yugoslavian crisis in 1934.

The League's great failure lay in its inability to stop war and to bring about disarmament. The League made two attempts in the early 1920s to develop a mechanism whereby international disputes could be pre-

vented from triggering a major confrontation. In each instance, the intent was to identify the aggressor and to pledge the member nations to support the victim.

The first attempt, the *Treaty of Mutual Assistance*, drafted in 1923, proposed that if hostilities broke out, the Council of the League should decide which party was the aggressor within four days. Then the members of the League would automatically be required to give military assistance to the other side.

This proposal was flawed because determining the aggressor in a dispute can be difficult. Moreover, it requires agreement on the issue of what action constitutes aggression. Is it starting the quarrel? Ordering general mobilization? Firing the first shot? Furthermore, to make this determination within four days, as the Treaty of Mutual Assistance proposed, was unrealistic. In the case of Japanese aggression in Manchuria in 1931, it took a League commission one and one-half years to make a decision (Chapter 23).

The Treaty of Mutual Assistance also mandated military participation by all members of the League. Few nations were willing to make such a *carte blanche* commitment to war. And in the unlikely event they were so willing, the result would not be to end the war, but to widen its scope, unless the would-be aggressor was deterred by the threat the League represented. In the face of these weaknesses, Great Britain, the Netherlands, and the Scandinavian states rejected the Treaty of Mutual Assistance in the League Assembly in September, 1923.

Another attempt was made in 1924 to draft a treaty to prevent war. The *Geneva Protocol*, a compromise brought forward by the British Labor prime minister, Ramsay MacDonald, provided for compulsory arbitration of international disputes. In this proposal, a nation unwilling to submit its disputes to arbitration was to be branded the aggressor. But the British overseas dominions opposed the Geneva Protocol, fearing it would drag them into Europe's quarrels. Under these circumstances, the British Conservative government, newly in office in March of 1925, rejected the proposal.

Thus, two attempts by the League to develop machinery to prevent war failed. Within the League's powers remained only the ability to invoke economic sanctions (boycott) against a country if it could be defined as the aggressor.

THE LOCARNO PACTS

What the new diplomacy had failed to accomplish was achieved by the old diplomacy with the signing of the Locarno Pacts on December 1, 1925. The Locarno Pacts represented reconciliation between the former Allies and Germany, and were intended to allay French apprehensions regarding potential German aggression. The product of the diplomacy of Gustav Stresemann, German foreign minister, and Austin Chamberlain, British foreign secretary, the pacts also paved the way for Germany to join the League of Nations in 1926.

The Locarno Pacts included a mutual guarantee of the French-German and Belgian-German borders, signed by France, Germany, and Belgium with Great Britain and Italy signing as guarantors. In other words, Britain and Italy would provide military assistance to the victim in the event of aggression by one of the signatories. This treaty provided security for France against potential German aggression. The Locarno Pacts also included arbitration treaties between Germany and Poland, Czechoslovakia, Belgium, and France, to allow for negotiations of any territorial disputes. Finally, a French-Polish and French-Czechoslovakian treaty provided for mutual assistance in case of attack by Germany.

These treaties were part of France's efforts to surround Germany with French allies, but the overall effect of the Locarno Pacts was to usher in a period of good relations between Germany and its neighbors. The "spirit of Locarno" with its promise of peace had a positive psychological effect on the war-weary world. Nevertheless, it was achieved by the old style of diplomacy—negotiated not in Geneva under the aegis of the League, but in the capitals of the major powers in secret. Although historians traditionally view the Japanese aggression in Manchuria in 1931 as the death knell of the League (Chapter 23), the Locarno Pacts also represented a revival of the old power politics.

ATTEMPTS AT DISARMAMENT

The League fared no better in its attempts to bring about mutual reduction of arms, one of Wilson's Fourteen Points. Disarmament of the loser nations at Paris was understood in 1919 to be a first step. Article three of the Covenant of the League called for "reduction of armaments to the lowest point consistent with national safety."

Yet the first arms agreement was negotiated outside the League in November 1921 when the United States convened the *Washington Conference* to discuss limitations on naval armaments. Attended by Great Britain,

In December 1925, representatives of Britain, France, and Germany met in London to sign the Locarno Treaty. The treaty represented a revival of the "old diplomacy," for the League of Nations was not involved in its preparation.

France, Italy, Belgium, the Netherlands, China, Japan, and Portugal, the Washington Conference produced the *Nine-Power Treaty*, which guaranteed the territorial integrity and independence of China, and a *Sino-Japanese Treaty* that removed Japanese troops from China's Shantung province and restored the former German concessions to China.

The conference also resulted in a naval armaments treaty which established a ratio for tonnage of capital ships (ships over 10,000 tons with guns larger than eight inches). The agreement established tonnage in a ratio of 5:5:3:1.67:1.67 for, in that order, Great Britain, the United States, Japan, France, and Italy.

This conference, and the subsequent *London Naval Conference of 1930*, were the only successful armaments agreements of the inter-war years. Although they were important steps toward arms reductions, they also contributed to Japan's sense of frustration and antagonism toward Britain and the United States. The agreements were repudiated by the Japanese as they prepared for conquest of Asia at the start of World War II.

Not until 1925 did the League act to fulfill its obligations under article three, by appointing a preparatory commission for a disarmament conference. This commission first met in 1926, and several times subsequently, without success. One of the keys to the failure to reduce arms was national self-interest. For example, Britain was willing to support the reduction of land forces to a very minimal level. France, on the other hand, feared a German invasion of its borders and refused to agree to any reduction in land forces. And while France was willing to support drastic reductions in naval strength, Britain, as an island state, refused to reduce the navy upon which its security depended. No arms agreements could be reached when the two major powers would not compromise.

In these circumstances, a Russian proposal in 1927 calling for immediate and complete disarmament was rebuffed by Western powers who feared Russian intentions. These armaments arguments demonstrate the atmosphere of fear and distrust in the 1920s.

The League's inability to negotiate arms limitations led the American secretary of state, Frank Kellogg, to put forth a plan renouncing war. This proposal was echoed by Aristide Briand, the French foreign minister, who produced a draft treaty outlawing war. Out of these proposals came the 1928 *Kellogg-Briand Pact* which stated that the contracting parties "condemn recourse to war for the solution of international controversies and renounce it as an instrument of national policy."[1] This pact was eventually ratified by 65 nations, many of whom did so with reservations. Britain, for example, claimed the right to go to war to defend the British Empire. The pact contained no machinery and no enforcement powers. The Soviet Union, not to be outdone, promptly produced its own version, the Litvinov Protocol, an Eastern pact for the renunciation of war, signed by the Soviet Union and four other

states. The concept of rival peace pacts characterizes the absurdity of world politics in the 1920s.

The last major League-sponsored disarmament conference met from February to July of 1932 at Geneva with 60 nations represented, including the United States. Like the rest, this conference failed to secure an international agreement. Article three of the covenant of the League would never be implemented.

REPARATIONS

The League was also responsible for carrying out the terms for collecting the reparation payments from the losing nations of World War I. The reparations issue proved to be the thorniest problem of the 1920s.

Historically, the loser nation was forced to pay an indemnity, usually punitive—that is, usually more than the cost of the war to the victor. This practice had the effect of creating a cause for the next war, and as such was denounced by Wilson. As a result, the original draft of the Fourteen Points did not include a provision for monetary exchange. Nevertheless, the victor nations, faced with large debts, convinced Wilson that the losers should pay "reparations," that is, the cost of all civilian damages caused by the war. The fact that the victors owed the U.S. $10 billion in wartime credits may have helped persuade Wilson to accept a reparations clause.

It was, however, impossible to determine quickly what the total "reparations" bill should be. Consequently, when Germany signed the Treaty of Versailles in June, 1919, it was given only the amount of the "down payment"—$5 billion, to be subtracted from a final bill to be tallied by May, 1921. Moreover, in the meantime, Germany would lose the coal of Silesia and the Saar, amounting to about one-third of its total coal production. From its remaining coal supply, Germany was to deliver to France, Italy, and Belgium 40 million tons a year for the next ten years. In addition, Germany surrendered

---

[1] Jules Davids, *America and the World of Our Time* (New York: Random House, 1960), p. 125.

most of its merchant and fishing fleets and its railway cars. These economic provisions served to cripple the German economy and made it more difficult for Germany to pay the eventual reparations bill. They also aroused resentment.

Before the final bill was assessed, the winners resolved the question of their share: 52 percent was to go to France, 22 percent to the British Empire, 10 percent to Italy, 8 percent to Belgium, and the remaining 8 percent to be divided among the other victorious participants. In 1921, Germany was presented with the final tabulation of its reparations bill: $56 billion. The total was arrived at by compromise between Britain and France. British and French bankers had calculated that Germany *could* probably pay $100 billion, but the British government preferred a lower figure, in hopes that German economic recovery would enhance international trade.

In response to the $56 billion bill, Germany made a counter-offer of $12.5 billion, contingent on the subtraction of the $5 billion already paid. The counter-offer was met with French occupation of three German cities, including Düsseldorf, in 1921. Germany responded with another proposal: $12.5 billion *without* deducting the $5 billion it had already paid. The reparations committee in turn lowered the $56 billion to $32 billion, and Germany reluctantly accepted this figure in April, 1921.

In reality, Germany could probably have paid $10 billion, or perhaps even $32 billion if there had been a revival of international trade, a reduction of tariff barriers, and a German desire to pay. None of these circumstances prevailed in the 1920s. Yet Germany made its scheduled payment for 1921, $250 million, but did so by borrowing money from London bankers. The immediate effect of this borrowing was a decline in the value of German currency, the mark. At that point, Germany asked for and received a partial moratorium on its 1922 payment, and the British prime minister, David Lloyd George,

proposed that an international conference on economic and other issues be convened in Genoa, Italy, in April, 1922.

The *Genoa Conference* was a colossal failure. Both the Soviet Union and Germany were invited, in view of the fact that their cooperation was important to the outcome. It was hoped that the Soviet Union would be willing to reconsider its decision to cancel old tsarist debts. The Germans, it was hoped, would cooperate in meeting reparations payments. Neither participant complied. Instead, the two outcasts made their own side agreement, the *Treaty of Rapallo*. In it, both renounced reparations, but the secret clauses were even more ominous. They provided Germany with an opportunity to violate the disarmament provisions of the Versailles Treaty. Forbidden to manufacture weapons on German soil, the Rapallo agreement allowed German ammunition-makers to build their factories in the Soviet Union.

Two other British hopes were dashed at Genoa. The first was that the United States would acknowledge the connection between German reparation payments to the Allies and Allied ability to make war debt payments to the United States. This, the United States steadfastly refused to do, demanding war debt payments even if Germany were to default on reparations. France, Lloyd George hoped, would reconsider its decision to refuse to discuss reductions in reparations at all. From the French perspective, nothing should prevent Germany from making its payments; moreover, France maintained that the Soviet Union must be made responsible for prewar tsarist debts. At that point, the Genoa Conference collapsed.

THE INVASION OF THE RUHR, 1923
Relations between the wartime allies were at a low ebb, and they sank even lower in the summer of 1922, when the reparations commission granted Germany a moratorium on its payments for the remainder of 1922. France refused to accept the moratorium,

In 1923, relations between France and Germany broke down over the question of reparations, and French troops moved into the Ruhr valley.

even though the German economy was experiencing runaway inflation and the collapse in the value of the mark. In 1914, four German marks had equalled one U.S. dollar; in November, 1918, the ratio was 56 marks to the dollar; in November, 1922, it was 7000 marks to the dollar. This devaluation of the mark was the result of issuing paper money without backing. In the context of German refusal to continue to make reparations payments, on January 11, 1923, French and Belgian troops invaded and occupied the Ruhr district in the Rhineland, the heart of industrial Germany. The French intent was to confiscate materials, primarily coal, to collect its reparations payment.

The Germans responded with a general strike. During the occupation, the govern-ment continued the printing of unbacked paper money. By November there were 2.5 *trillion* marks to the dollar. It took a wheelbarrow to transport enough paper money to the shop to buy a loaf of bread and quart of milk. German employers paid their workers hourly to escape the effect of inflation over an eight-hour day. Germany was on the brink of financial collapse. The French were affected as well. The German passive resistance had made the occupation fruitless; the occupation itself was costly, and it had provoked Britain, which did not support the use of military force against Germany.

By the end of 1923, the outlook for Europe appeared grim, but the Allies agreed to the formation of a committee under the chairmanship of Charles Dawes to develop a rescue plan. The *Dawes Plan*, put into effect in mid-1924, brought a temporary solution to the financial crisis. By this plan, Germany would receive foreign loans, of which 55 percent ($110 million) would be contributed by the United States. With the loan, Germany would resume reparations payments to the Allies. They, in turn, would make regular war-debt payments to the United States. The Dawes Plan, then, provided for the funneling of American funds through the European financial system, with fewer dollars returning to the United States than had been sent abroad. The solution, temporary though it turned out to be, succeeded in revitalizing

Germany's problem in meeting its reparation payments stemmed from the runaway inflation it experienced during the years 1919–1923. This stack of 100,000 German marks was worth only one U.S. dollar in 1922: a year later, the situation was even worse.

the economies of the European powers and in reducing tensions.

For Germany, the years from 1924 to 1929 are referred to as the *Era of Fulfillment*, given the economic recovery and the improved relations with Germany's former enemies. At the same time, the crisis left many scars. The period of runaway inflation had wiped out the German middle class, especially affecting those who lived on pensions. The economic crisis of 1923 foreshadowed the even more devastating depression of the late 1920s and early 1930s.

THE GREAT DEPRESSION

One of the problems facing postwar economic life was *economic nationalism*, a policy of high tariffs adopted by France, Italy, Czechoslovakia, Austria, Hungary, Germany, Great Britain, and the United States. In the third of his Fourteen Points, Wilson had called for free trade: "The removal, so far as possible, of all economic barriers and the establishment of an equality of trade conditions among all nations consenting to the peace. . . ."[2] But high tariffs were adopted for one or a combination of the following reasons: as a new source of revenues for the government, to defend the nation's trade against depreciated foreign currencies, to use as bargaining points with other nations, to protect weak industries from foreign competition, and as the economic component of nationalism. The policy of high tariffs increased the difficulty nations had in paying reparations or war debts. Transfer of funds between countries is usually one of two kinds: favorable balance of trade (exporting more than one imports), or exchange of gold. Half of the world's gold was in the hands of the United States and France. The French were hoarding gold for their "war chest," for what they

---

[2] *Annals of America*, vol. 14 (Chicago: Encyclopedia Britannica Co., 1968), p. 152.

feared would be yet another round of fighting with Germany.

Another problem in the 1920s was the interwoven finances of the powers. Twenty-eight states were involved as either creditors or debtors or both. By 1928, Germany owed 11 creditors. Britain and France were lending money to other states—Britain had 17 debtor nations, France 10—but both were borrowing from the United States, as was Germany as part of the Dawes Plan. The United States had 16 debtors. These debtors found it nearly impossible to pay their debts through trade. The American Fordney-McCumber Bill of 1922 and the Smoot-Hawley Act of 1929–30 forced debtors to pay with gold.

Partially as a result of the tangled web of international finance, the United States stock market collapsed. "Black Thursday," October 24, 1929, was the peak of the panic when a record number of stocks were sold. The crash in the United States did not create a correspondingly large crash in Europe. Instead, the economic decline was more gradual until 1931, when a large Austrian banking firm, Credit-Anstalt, proved to be insolvent, triggering a series of bank failures. Recognizing the effect on the economies of the European states, President Herbert Hoover issued in June 1931 a one-year moratorium, or postponement, of all intergovernmental debt payments.

The *Young Plan*, which had been created

A busy day on Wall Street, New York, in 1929. The headline above announced the stock exchange results on the day that would come to be known as "Black Thursday."

COMPLETE FINAL
★ ★ ★ ★ ★

The Sun

COMPLETE FINAL
★ ★ ★ ★ ★

VOL. XCVII—NO 49—DAILY.   NEW YORK, TUESDAY, OCTOBER 29, 1929.   PRICE THREE CENTS.

STOCKS OFF IN 16 MILLION SHARE DAY

in 1928 and ratified in 1930, was the final attempt to reach a reparations settlement. This plan placed on Germany the responsibility of collecting reparations payments and transferring them to the recipients, and the final figure for German reparations had been placed at $8 billion to be payable over the next 59 years. The world economic crisis of 1931, however, rendered the Young Plan defunct. At the *World Economic Conference* of that year, representatives of Germany, France, Belgium, Great Britain, Italy, and Japan agreed to end reparations, contingent upon American willingness to cancel their debts. The United States Congress passed a resolution that "it is against the policy of Congress that any of the indebtedness of foreign powers to the United States should in any manner be cancelled or reduced." Nevertheless, in 1932, most European states defaulted on their debts to the United States; in 1933, although several made token payments, most again defaulted. In 1934, all debtor nations except Finland defaulted, and none except Finland completed their war debt payments. Seventy percent of the total World War I debt was never repaid.

By 1934, the world was in the midst of economic depression. The effects of this monetary debacle were wide-ranging. The depression contributed to American *isolationism*; to many Americans in the 1930s, the events served to prove the folly of the United States' intervention in World War I. Moreover, the world depression seriously damaged the economies of the world's democratic states and contributed to their weakness in dealing with rising dictatorships (Chapter 22). The depression had a devastating effect on Germany and was a major factor in the rise to power of Adolf Hitler. It also contributed to Japanese aggressiveness in the 1930s, as the Japanese attempted to protect and stimulate their economy by means of a policy of imperialism on the Asian mainland.

POST-WAR CULTURE The dramatic effect of the Great War (as World War I was then known) on the inter-war years is evident not only in economic, political, and diplomatic developments, but on European society and culture as well.

SOCIETAL CHANGES

Women's contribution to the war effort was significant; yet when the war ended, women who had worked in factories during the war were replaced by returning veterans. As a kind of compensation for their part in the war effort—and for their new unemployment—women got the vote in several countries. In the United States, where the suffrage movement dated from the mid-19th century, women received the vote on a parity with men in the passage of the 19th Amendment in August 1920. In Great Britain, where the suffrage movement was a century old, women over 30 were given the vote in 1918, although men were eligible to vote at age 21. Not until 1928, with the passage of the so-called "Flapper Act," did British women get the vote at age 21.

Other opportunities appeared for British women in the 1920s. The Sex Disqualification Act of 1919 made possible the entry of English women into many professions. The first woman to hold high public office was Lady Mary Astor, who entered the British Parliament in 1919. Women were admitted to Oxford University at the end of the war. The emancipation of women from floor-length skirts and long hair also occurred in the 1920s—as did smoking in public, lipstick and rouge, slang, jazz, and the shimmy. Sunbathing and dieting were fads introduced in the 1920s.

The period between the wars introduced new sexual standards, in part because of new contraceptives, the popularization of Freudian psychiatry, the introduction of the concept of relativity to apply to ethics as well as physics, and the increase in divorce rates.

In the 1920s, women's hemlines were raised, a symbol of their liberation from prewar conventions. The era was also characterized by a revival of nightlife and a lively new form of music—jazz.

INTELLECTUAL AND ARTISTIC DEVELOPMENTS

The optimism of the 19th century, in what was regarded as an age of progress, was shattered by World War I. The nations of Europe, which regarded themselves as the most advanced in the world, proved capable of destroying each other's young men in a war whose causes were unclear at best. In reaction, artists and intellectuals questioned the basis of Western civilization. The intellectual world of the 1920s and 1930s is characterized by the dissonance of the music of Igor Stravinsky and other composers, who rejected the traditional standards of Western music. Many of these developments originated before the war, but their widespread acceptance came afterward.

T.S. Eliot (1888–1965), an American who became a naturalized British subject, expressed the despair and anguish of the postwar period in such poems as "The Waste Land" and "The Hollow Men." "The Hollow Men" begins:

We are the hollow men
We are the stuffed men
Learning together
Headpiece filled with straw.[3]

Art was greatly affected by the theories of Sigmund Freud. Attention was focused on the mind not as an orderly rational mechanism, but rather as one of flowing consciousness, with the subconscious—Freud's discovery—heavily influencing human actions. The stream-of-consciousness novel rejected the old standards of plot and character. Its practitioners, notably the Irishman James Joyce (1882–1941), tried to capture the stream of impressions that flow through the mind. Although not so revolutionary as Joyce, the French novelist Marcel Proust (1871–1922) tried to structure a new reality

[3] T. S. Eliot, *Complete Poems and Plays* (New York: Harcourt, Brace, 1952), pp. 56–7.

Picasso's painting The Three Musicians, *from his cubist period, established a new way of representing three-dimensional objects on canvas.*

in his series of novels known as *Remembrance of Things Past*.

In painting, Picasso continued his enormous output, switching styles in a ceaseless life-long effort to capture a different reality on canvas. Salvador Dali and other surrealists took inspiration from Freud's theory of dreams and depicted landscapes that could only exist within the mind.

By the 1930s, an *international style* of architecture had arisen. Originating in Germany, the Bauhaus school emphasized the unity of form and function, dispensing with decorative elements. The new architects attempted to make architecture as clean and functional as possible. The leader of this school was Walter Gropius (1883–1969). The style influenced not only public buildings, but offices, homes, and even furniture.

A typical Bauhaus structure. This style of architecture originated in Germany and is now common in cities throughout the world. It is characterized by clean, simple lines and an absence of ornamentation.

SUMMARY

The victors in the Great War hoped that the peace could be kept by international co-operation in the League of Nations. The League, however, was probably doomed at the outset by the failure of the United States to join and by the renewal of "old diplomacy," that is, private agreements among the major powers. Ultimately, the League failed to end the arms race and to prevent war. Moreover, the financial settlement the victors forced on Germany created serious economic problems for that nation and threatened to bring about a renewal of the fighting. The Dawes Plan provided a temporary solution to Europe's financial problems. But after a brief period of economic renewal between 1924–1929, the economic collapse known as the great depression engulfed the United States, Europe, and eventually the world. This economic crisis set the stage for the dramatic events of the 1930s, as the world plunged headlong toward a second world war.

QUESTIONS

1 What was the "old diplomacy"? How did Wilson hope to change that system?
2 Why did the United States fail to join the League of Nations?
3 Why did attempts at disarmament between the wars fail?
4 Why did the Allies demand high reparations from Germany? What was the long-term effect?
5 Evaluate the extent to which the Fourteen Points were enacted.
6 How did postwar society differ from that of the prewar period?

BIBLIOGRAPHY

GRAVES, ROBERT. *Goodbye to All That*. Garden City, N.Y.: Anchor Books, 1957. *The autobiography of an upper-class Englishman who fought in World War I. This book is one of the best in describing the effects of the war on a generation of young people, and illustrates the disillusionment of the postwar years.*

GRAVES, ROBERT and ALAN HODGE. *The Long Weekend: A Social History of Great Britain, 1918–1939.* New York: Norton Library, 1963. *This social history captures the spirit of Britain between the wars, from the popular amusements of the 1920s to the chaos of the 1930s.*

SMITH, GENE. *When the Cheering Stopped: The Last Years of Woodrow Wilson.* New York: Time, 1966. *This biography depicts Wilson's last years, after the stroke which may have been brought on, in part, by the controversy surrounding the League of Nations. Wilson served out the last two years of his presidency as an invalid, while his wife served as the surrogate president.*

TAYLOR, A. J. P. *From Sarajevo to Potsdam*. London: Thames and Hudson, 1965. *A very readable brief sketch of the important events in Europe from 1914 to 1945, with 165 photographs and maps. Taylor discusses political, cultural, and social history, and captures the spirit of those tempestuous years.*

22

● *Long live the new world of the twentieth century!*
Long live Fascist Italy!
Long live Soviet Russia!
Long live Hitler's Germany!
Long live the Spain one will make!
Down with the bourgeois parliamentary democracies!
FASCIST SLOGANS

Totalitarianism and the Democracies Between The Wars

Totalitarianism is a political phenomenon of the 20th century. Rooted in the broken dreams of the 1920s, it came to fruition in the 1930s, appearing throughout Europe in a variety of guises. Totalitarianism came to full bloom in the Soviet Union, Italy, and Germany. Although these states developed differing political systems, the totalitarian form of each government had major similarities.

As the term implies, totalitarianism is an attempt by government to totally control society. Each totalitarian state relied on the machinery and the symbols of a modern democracy, but was, in actuality, a single-party dictatorship. Each state claimed to rule on behalf of the people, and used some form of elections to demonstrate popular support.

The totalitarian dictators constructed authoritarian political systems in which all decisions were made at the top, and in which individuals were deprived of all the political rights on which democracies are based. There was no guarantee of freedom of speech, of assembly, of association, of religion, or of physical safety. The totalitarian regimes depicted themselves as saving the people from an enemy of the state: in Russia

the enemy was the capitalist class; in Fascist Italy, it was the communist movement; and in Nazi Germany, the Jews. Each used this threat to create a permanent state of crisis in which freedoms were withheld, and constitutions suspended.

Each of the totalitarian regimes incorporated a political philosophy that glorified the state over the individual. To gather support for this philosophy, they evoked nationalism, and sponsored mass rallies where citizens could demonstrate their patriotism and support of the regime.

Finally, each of these states followed a policy of aggression which left the democracies of Europe weak, divided, and unable to respond.

At the time, the three prominent examples of totalitarianism—Germany, Italy, and the Soviet Union—were viewed as very different regimes. The governments of Germany and Italy belonged on the "far right" of the conventional political spectrum, because Hitler and Mussolini openly glorified the power of the state. In the Soviet Union, on the other hand, Lenin and Stalin proclaimed the dictatorship of the proletariat, and stated that their ultimate goal was communism, a

Mass rallies, with crowds often numbering in the hundreds of thousands, were a hallmark of fascist regimes. Such rallies inspired a sense of solidarity and national purpose among those who attended.

stateless society. The soviet regime was accordingly viewed as leftist. In reality, however, the government of Joseph Stalin was a one-man dictatorship. For this reason, modern historians view these different totalitarian regimes as very similar in practice, however different they were in theory.

TOTALITARIANISM: Of the three exam-
THE SOVIET UNION ples of totalitarian-
ism, the first to establish itself was the Soviet Union. Historians have debated whether totalitarianism is inherent in Marxist-Leninist theory, or whether Joseph Stalin deviated from the theory when he constructed his dictatorship. It seems apparent, however, that the Marxist

principle of "dictatorship of the proletariat," even though it was viewed as temporary, made possible the construction of a modern totalitarian state.

THE LEGACY OF LENIN

After seizing power in November, 1917, Lenin began to consolidate his power and that of the state. Lenin and his Bolshevik party established a single-party dictatorship in which the state's interests superseded those of the individual. For example, in early 1918, Lenin instituted the Red Terror, using CHEKA to solidify his power. CHEKA was responsible for the deaths of thousands of the enemies of the new regime.

Although Lenin proclaimed a *soviet* government, that is, government by local councils, true power in the Soviet Union has always been in the hands of the leadership of the Communist Party. In turn, the party under Lenin, and later Stalin, controlled the army, the police, and the bureaucracy, the three critical levers of power. Lenin had justified this dictatorship:

• • • *The Soviet Socialist Democracy is in no way inconsistent with the rule and dictatorship of one person; that the will of a class is at times best realized by a dictator who sometimes will accomplish more by himself and is frequently more needed.*[1]

Lenin introduced war communism, coinciding with the outbreak of civil war, which created a command economy (Chapter 20). This policy was later abandoned for pragmatic reasons. But the precedents that Lenin established would be used by Joseph Stalin in a far more extensive manner.

STALIN'S SOVIET UNION

Lenin's illness and impending death raised the crucial question of who would inherit his power. In a way, the most logical successor was Leon Trotsky (1879–1940). Chairman of the Petrograd soviet at the time of the November revolution, Trotsky headed the Military Revolutionary Committee that actually carried out the November *coup d'état*. He had been commissar for foreign affairs, and as commissar for war (1918–1925) he was the chief organizer of the Red Army. Throughout the period he was a high-ranking member of the inner circle of the Communist Party. He was, as well, the most sophisticated Marxist theorist. On the other hand, he had disagreed with Lenin at the time of the party split in 1903, and he was viewed by his colleagues as aloof and cold.

The other candidate to succeed Lenin was Joseph Stalin (1879–1953). Born Joseph Dju-

Trotsky, the man who had organized the Red Army, was Lenin's chosen successor. He was soon outmaneuvered by Stalin, however.

gashvili in the northern province of Georgia he adopted the name Stalin, the Russian word for "steel." The son of a cobbler, young Joseph had higher ambitions for himself. He entered a Russian Orthodox seminary at the age of 15, but at 20, already a convert to Marxism, he was expelled from the seminary for secret revolutionary activities. Party work dominated the rest of his life. Before the revolution, using the alias Koba, he had been involved in organizing activities and even acted as highway robber to fill the coffers of the Bolshevik party. In the first communist government, he served as commissar for nationalities and then, in 1923, became the general secretary of the Communist Party.

Stalin's Rise to Power. Both Trotsky and Stalin had impressive credentials for the position of leadership of the Soviet Union. Before his death, Lenin wrote his "Political Testament," evaluating his successors. He was highly critical of Stalin:

• • • *Comrade Stalin has concentrated enormous power in his hands, and I am not sure that he always knows how to use that power with sufficient caution.*[2]

---

[1] David Shub, *Lenin* (New York: Doubleday, 1950), p. 188.

[2] *Ibid.*, pp. 184–5.

This photo of Lenin (right) and Stalin dates from 1919. At this early date, they had established the Bolshevik faction in power and prevailed in a civil war against the majority "Whites," who had hoped to establish a more liberal regime.

Praising Trotsky, Lenin noted that he had certain flaws as well:

• • • *On the other hand, Comrade Trotsky . . . is distinguished not only by his exceptional quality, personally; he is, to be sure, the most able man in the present Central Committee, but also by his too far reaching self-confidence and a disposition to be far too much attracted by the purely administrative side of affairs. These two qualities of the two most able leaders of the present Central Committee might, quite innocently, lead to a split.*[3]

After completing his political testament, Lenin added a postscript which indicated his displeasure with Stalin:

• • • *Stalin is too rude, and this fault . . . becomes insupportable in the office of General Secretary. Therefore, I propose to the comrades to find a way to remove Stalin from that position . . . [and find someone] more patient, more loyal, more polite, and more attentive to comrades.*[4]

Somewhat hesitantly, Lenin endorsed Trotsky to succeed him. But Stalin's post as general secretary of the party assured his ultimate victory, for as the party administrator he was able to place his supporters in key positions throughout the party structure.

Stalin and Trotsky were also engaged in an ideological struggle. Trotsky advocated "permanent world revolution," in which Russian communists should concentrate their energies on provoking proletarian revolutions in the rest of the world. By contrast, Stalin advocated "socialism in one country," a policy of consolidating the communist regime within the Soviet Union. Stalin's position, ultimately the victorious one, meant the introduction of nationalism into communist international theory and shaped the future of the Soviet Union.

By 1927, Trotsky had lost his position on the Central Committee, and was expelled from the party. In 1929, he was exiled from Russia. Emigrating first to Turkey and then to Mexico, in 1940 he was murdered by a Stalinist agent.

Stalin's Consolidation of Power. Stalin began to consolidate his power and introduce his interpretation of Marxist theory. In 1928, he abandoned Lenin's New Economic Policy, replacing it with central planning. In so doing, Stalin initiated an industrial revolution by allocating national resources to the development of heavy industry, at the expense of consumer goods. At the same time, Stalin introduced *collectivization* in agriculture. From this collectivization movement came "Soviet farms," government-owned and -operated, and collective farms in which the peasants pooled their land. The more prosperous peasant class, the *kulaks*, rebelled and were eliminated through a reign of terror in 1929–30. As many as 3 million peasants died.

The industrial revolution that Stalin introduced, although never adhering to the pre-established planning goals, did succeed in industrializing the Soviet Union. But the collectivization of agriculture has never attained its goal of self-sufficiency. A command economy and a form of state capital-

---

[3] *Ibid.*

[4] *Ibid.*

ism were the consequences of Stalin's economic policy.

The Purges of the 1930s. Stalin eliminated all possible opposition by means of a series of purges, beginning in 1933 with the creation of the Central Purge Commission. This commission subjected the entire party membership to a public purge process. In 1933–34, 1,140,000 members were expelled from the party. As the purges continued between 1933–38, thousands were arrested and many executed. Twenty-five percent of the army officer corps were arrested. Of the 1966 delegates who attended the 1934 Communist Party Congress, 1108 were arrested and charged with "antirevolutionary crimes." Of the 139 members of the Central Committee at the 1934 party congress, 98 were shot.

In the midst of this orgy of revenge, 54 of the most prominent party leaders were tried in three public "show" trials. These men were "old Bolsheviks," who had been party leaders since before the revolution. They were now charged with various crimes—conspiracy with Trotsky, acts of sabotage, espionage, counter-revolution, treason.

The first of the show trials, in 1936, featured 16 defendants, including Grigori Zinoviev and Lev Kamenev, both high-ranking associates of Lenin and former members of the *Politboro* (a five-man council within the Communist Party that formulated party policy). In the second trial in 1937, the 17 defendants included the country's leading political writer, Karl Radek. In the third trial in 1938, the 21 defendants included Nikolai Bukharin, editor of the state paper *Izvestia*, other important party leaders, and the head of the secret police. In all cases the defendants confessed publicly and were shot.

In his summation at the first trial, the prosecutor, Andrei Vishinsky, castigated these men:

● ● ● *A contemptible, insignificant, impotent group of traitors and murderers tried to trample with their bloodstained feet upon*

the most fragrant flowers of our socialist garden. These mad dogs of capitalism tried to tear limb from limb the best of the best of our Soviet land.[5]

That these prominent leaders of the Communist Party confessed to betraying the cause to which they had devoted their lives has puzzled many. Arthur Koestler, in his novel *Darkness at Noon*, proffers a scenario in which the protaganist suffers physical and psychological torture and confesses as a last, misguided act of loyalty to the ideology.

Stalin's purges eliminated any rivals for power in the Soviet Union and consolidated his dictatorship over the party, which in turn exercised nearly total power over Russian subjects. The regime that he erected contained all of the characteristics that would define future totalitarian states: an omnipotent state apparatus which controlled thought and eliminated dissent, a slave labor camp for enemies of the state, an impersonal bureaucracy, a demand for uniformity, destruction of individualism, and a command economy.

FASCIST ITALY The second country to adopt totalitarianism was Italy under the leadership of Benito Mussolini (1883–1945). The circumstances in which Mussolini seized power were caused in large degree by the effects of World War I.

DISCONTENT IN ITALY

When war began in 1914, Italy remained neutral. However, in 1915, the British, French, and Russians, seeking to break the military stalemate, offered Italy territory after the war in exchange for its participation on the Allied side. But at war's end, the principle of national self-determination thwarted the Italian effort to collect on the wartime promises, since most of the territory

---

[5] Elizabeth Seeger, *The Pageant of Russian History* (London: Longmans, Green, 1956), p. 376.

it sought was populated by a majority of non-Italians. The Italian prime minister Vittorio Orlando left the peace conference empty-handed. The Italian people felt betrayed by their allies and vented their anger not only at Orlando's government but also at the veterans, who were physically and verbally abused if they appeared in public in uniform. Many veterans returned home to public disapproval, joblessness, poverty, and chaos.

The cost of the war contributed to Italy's postwar economic problems. Like the other participants, Italy had borrowed heavily, and in 1919 the national debt was six times what it had been on the eve of war; the currency had depreciated to one-third its prewar value.

Italy's political system was not prepared to cope with the storms which these problems created. The democratically elected Chamber of Deputies was a hotbed of corruption, and its members—who were unpaid—often resorted to bribery and graft as a source of income. The democracy was new and unstable; universal male suffrage had only been granted in 1912. Two popular political parties arose after the war and the propertied classes feared that the emergence of these mass movements would threaten their wealth.

THE RISE TO POWER OF MUSSOLINI

In this chaotic setting, Mussolini founded the *Fascist Party*, the Fascio di Combattimento, in March, 1919. Its name was taken from the *fasces* (a bundle of rods with projecting axe blade), an ancient Roman symbol of imperial authority. Composed primarily of veterans, the Fascist Party was vehemently anticommunist and preached the glorification of war. War, the fascists believed, revealed the nobility of the Italian soul. The fascists depicted Italy as a dynamic, creative nation, destined to recreate the glories of the ancient Roman Empire.

Benito Mussolini was a likely founder for

By intimidating his political opponents—the socialists, communists, and others—Mussolini rendered it impossible for any but his own party to govern Italy.

such a movement. Of a lower-middle-class family, his father had been a socialist mayor of his village. As a boy, Benito was a bully, frequently engaging in back-alley fist fights. At the age of ten, he wounded a classmate at boarding school and was expelled. At a second school, his stay was also punctuated by brawling and bullying and another stabbing incident. Later, as the leader of his party, he led a group of thugs who beat up on political opponents. As dictator of Italy, he institutionalized brutality and violence to frighten his opponents—and in at least one case, resorted to murder.

Seizure of Power. The circumstances were ripe·for Mussolini's seizure of power. In the elections of May, 1921, 35 fascists, including Mussolini, were elected to the Chamber of Deputies. They represented around 250,000 party members recruited primarily from the lower middle class. During 1921, Italy experienced near civil war as the various political factions, including the fas-

392

cist *black shirts* and the communist red shirts, fought in the streets.

By the summer of 1922, the fascists had a private army of 300,000 men. On October 27, 1922, the fascist army began its march on Rome from Naples, having declared its unswerving loyalty to both the king, Victor Emmanuel, and to the Roman Catholic Church. The fascists' stated purpose was to rescue Italy from the radical left. The king feared the outbreak of open civil war between the radical left—communists and socialists— and the radical right—the fascists. All groups possessed private armies prepared to do battle in the streets.

Mussolini in Power. In these circumstances, the king named Mussolini premier on October 30, 1922. Mussolini had achieved political power legally—but by using threat and physical intimidation. Mussolini received from the legislature emergency powers for one year, which in effect made him the dictator of Italy. With his private army now organized into a militia, Mussolini purged local governments of all opposition and consolidated his power, erecting a police state under the motto, "All in the state, nothing outside the state, nothing against the state." The fascist regime which Mussolini created and the "legal" way in which he seized power are characteristic of 20th-century totalitarianism.

Fascist political movements later appeared in Belgium—the Rexists led by Leon Deyrelle; in the Romanian Iron Guard; in the British Union of Fascists led by Oswald Mosley; in the Spanish Fascist movement of Francisco Franco; and in the French Faisceau, led by Georges Valois.

NAZI GERMANY The regime which most closely epitomizes the phenomenon of totalitarianism was Nazi Germany. The *Third Reich* of Adolf Hitler (1889–1945) was, he believed, destined to endure "for a thousand years." (Instead, it was destroyed after only 12.)

Why did Hitler come to power? There are many explanations. Among them is the evil genius of Hitler himself. He was a master demagogue who told the German people what they wanted to hear. He promised to restore their national pride. He told them they were not to blame for their recent military defeat; that it was the Jews and socialists who had betrayed Germany—the "stab in the back" legend.

The German past contributed to Hitler's success. With a long history of authoritarianism, Germans yearned not for freedom but for security. They wanted a strong man to solve their problems, and Hitler was willing to be that man. Hitler restored Germans' confidence in themselves.

Hitler's political program was a catalogue of promises in which each group was led to think that it would be a special beneficiary of the policies of the new regime. Hitler promised jobs for the unemployed, protection of property against the communist threat, profits for large corporations, and survival for small business. Of all the reasons for Hitler's accession to power, the most important was the economic depression. The economic woes of Germany had wiped out the middle class, and the promises of national socialism seemed to offer solutions to those who had been dispossessed.

ADOLF HITLER'S RISE TO POWER
Adolf Hitler was born in a small town in Austria on April 20, 1889. His father was a customs official in the Austrian civil service. As a child, Adolf was an inattentive student who wanted to be an artist. When he was 14, his father died; five years later his mother died of cancer, and Adolf was left on his own.

The most formative and traumatic years of Hitler's life were spent in Vienna. Denied entry to the art academy for lack of sufficient talent, he did odd jobs, painted and sold picture post cards, attended the opera, read newspapers, and talked politics. His only friend in those years, August Kubizek, remembered him as sly, excitable, moody, despondent, and awkward.

In 1913, Hitler moved to Munich to escape military service in the Austrian army. The transplanted Austrian felt more patriotic toward Germany, and in 1914 he volunteered for the German army. The war years for Adolf were a time of fulfillment. He won the Iron Cross for bravery as a message-bearer and, late in the war, was gassed and temporarily blinded. Germany's defeat in 1918 was for him a terrible experience. Rather than accept it, he found scapegoats: the "November criminals"—socialists and Jews—who had betrayed the Fatherland by surrendering.

The Emergence of the Nazi Party. Hitler joined the German Worker's Party, one of several radical groups which sprang up after the war. Soon he was assigned the responsibility of building the party's propaganda unit. He quickly seized leadership of the movement, and in 1920 changed its name to the National Socialist German Workers Party. The term *Nazi* originated from the initial letters of the first two German words in the title.

In 1923, Hitler attempted an overthrow of the Weimar government, using the hero of World War I, General Ludendorff, as a front man. This attempt is often referred to as the *Beer Hall putsch*, for it began when Hitler leaped on a Munich beer hall table, fired his pistol into the ceiling, and declared the overthrow of the Weimar Republic. Moving into the streets, Ludendorff, Hitler, and their "Brown Shirt" supporters were quickly dispersed by the city police. Arrested and tried for treason, Hitler received a light sentence of five years. In Landberg prison, he was allowed frequent visits. Rudolph Hess, who had been imprisoned with him, served as his secretary. To Hess, Hitler dictated his autobiography, *Mein Kampf* ("my struggle"). A rambling, repetitive, ungrammatical work, *Mein Kampf* outlines Hitler's future policies

and the doctrine of Aryan superiority. The notion of a pure Aryan race is a fiction, but it was the basic premise on which he developed his racist ideology.

The Years of Preparation. Released from prison in 1925 after serving less than two years of his sentence, Hitler now determined to seize power through legal means. In the following months he developed his skills as an orator, spending hours in front of a mirror rehearsing his facial expressions and gestures. But the years from 1925 to 1929 were lean ones for the Nazi party, for Germany was at peace with its former enemies and was experiencing economic rebirth.

As a legal political party, the Nazi party made little headway. In 1924, the Nazis held 14 seats in the Reichstag, polling under a million votes. By 1928, its Reichstag seats numbered 11. The world depression provided Hitler his opportunity. As unemployment rose in Germany so did Nazi-party membership. In the elections of 1930, the Nazis polled 6.5 million votes, 18.3 percent of all votes cast, and won 107 seats. In 1932, in the depths of the depression, the Nazis won nearly 14 million votes (37.3 percent of the total) and 230 seats. These gains were directly related to German unemployment; by 1932 unemployment affected one of every two families.

In that economic crisis, the multitude of German political parties could not agree on a course of action. No single party could poll a majority of votes and form a stable government. Instead, cabinets could be created only by negotiating coalitions between two or

GERMAN UNEMPLOYMENT	
1929	1,300,000
1930	3,000,000
1931	4,350,000
1932	5,100,000
1933	6,000,000

A Nazi parade in Nuremberg, 1933. Like Mussolini, Hitler took advantage of the weakness of other political parties to seize power.

more parties. Once in office, the leaders of these parties inevitably came to disagree, and the coalition would then collapse, necessitating another election and the formation of yet another unstable coalition.

Hitler's Accession to Power. Such were the political circumstances in which Adolf Hitler found his opportunity. The president, Paul von Hindenburg, had authority granted him by the German constitution to appoint a chancellor who did not have a parliamentary majority. After numerous unsuccessful coalitions, Hindenburg turned to Hitler. On Jaunary 30, 1933, Hitler was appointed chancellor of Germany.

Once in office, Hitler consolidated his power by dissolving the Reichstag and calling for new elections to be held on March 5, 1933. At the same time, he persuaded President Hindenburg to issue a decree "For the Protection of the German People," which,

under the guise of preserving law and order, gave Hitler the right to prohibit public meetings and the wearing of political uniforms. All political meetings could be forbidden if, in the opinion of the authorities, public security would be endangered. Newspapers could be suppressed for the same reasons. By such "legal" means, Hitler was able to deny his political opposition freedom of speech, assembly, and the press.

On February 27, 1933, the Reichstag building burned to the ground. The police arrested a 17-year-old retarded Dutch boy who confessed that he had acted on behalf of the German Communist Party. There is some evidence that the Nazis themselves torched the building. Whatever the case, Hitler used the Reichstag fire to convince President Hindenburg to issue yet another decree on February 28 that suspended all individual rights guaranteed under the Weimar constitution. It also provided that if any German state government failed to take adequate measures to preserve order and public security, the central government had the right to intervene and establish its own authority. By these measures, Hitler took control of all state governments in Germany.

Hitler's private army, the Brown Shirts (the S.A), roamed the streets, terrorizing the opposition. Even so, the Nazis won only 43.9 percent of the vote in the election of 1933. In order to get a majority in the Reichstag, Hitler formed a coalition with the right-wing Nationalist party. This alliance gave him 52 percent of the seats. To get a two-thirds majority, he declared the Communist Party illegal, and the 81 communists who had been elected to the Reichstag were not allowed to take their seats.

Der Fuhrer. On March 23, 1933, the Reichstag passed the Enabling Act, which gave Hitler the power to issue decrees carrying the force of law. This act also prohibited any change in president or legislature; that is, it ended elections. When President Hindenburg died in March, 1934, Hitler fused the positions of president and chancellor and assumed the title of leader—*der Fuhrer*. He had also banned all other political parties and all trade unions. There was in fact no organized opposition to his power. He had overthrown the Weimar democracy by manipulating its constitution and the machinery of government. He had done so through terror and intimidation, and he had gotten away with it.

The Nazi Dictatorship. Between his accession to power in 1933 and the outbreak of World War II in 1939, Adolf Hitler consolidated his power and erected the dictatorship of the Third Reich. The secret police, the Gestapo, stifled all dissent. They opened letters, tapped phones, spied on citizens, arrested, condemned, and executed suspects without warrant or trial. During Hitler's Third Reich there was one police officer for every 155 people.

As part of the somewhat ambiguous ideology of "national socialism," Hitler introduced a planned economy. The unemployed were forced to work on farms and in factories under conditions selected by the government. Working hours were shortened to create more jobs. Women in industry were forced out of their jobs to make way for men. Laborers were forbidden to organize, bargain collectively, or strike. The government fixed wages, settled disputes, and dismissed employers and employees. In these ways, the Nazi regime resolved the unemployment crisis that had paved their way to power.

The Nazi system controlled all education, speech, and thought. In 1938, the government acquired control of the entire educational system. The Nazis altered the curriculum and rewrote textbooks to reflect their ideology. All newspapers, movies, theaters, radio programs, music, and painting exhibitions were incorporated into the Reich Chamber of Culture.

Persecution of Jews. The minister of propaganda, responsible for the big lies, was Dr. Joseph Paul Goebbels, whose venomous attacks on Jews echoed Hitler's warped ideology. In fact, the anti-Semitism of Nazi Germany was its most corrupt characteristic. Nazi persecution of Jews began with Hitler's seizure of power in 1933 and intensified in stages, to culminate in the *Holocaust*, the policy of genocide which resulted in the murder of six million Jews by 1945.

The Enabling Act of March 1933 authorized Hitler to set aside the concept of equal protection under the law. Two weeks later, he issued a decree which excluded all non-Aryans from holding public office in Germany. The passage of the Nuremburg Laws in 1935 excluded Jews from all professions: they could not be lawyers, judges, teachers, professors, doctors, or nurses.

Crystal Night, in November, 1938, was another step toward the eventual disaster. Jewish shops, homes, and synagogues throughout Germany were destroyed by mobs in the

This poster expressing anti-Jewish propaganda appeared in Vienna in 1938, the year Hitler took control of the Austrian government.

... We National Socialists must hold unflinchingly to our aim in foreign policy, namely, to secure for the German people the land and soil to which they are entitled on this earth. ... The soil on which some day German generations of peasants can beget powerful sons will sanction the investment of the sons of today.[6]

The living space was to be obtained in eastern Europe; the mostly Slavic peoples living there were to be enslaved to serve the German fatherland.

GERMAN REARMAMENT

Hitler began to implement his two-pronged foreign policy immediately upon attaining power in January 1933. In February, he secretly announced to high-ranking German military officers a massive program of unilateral rearmament.

---

[6] Adolf Hitler, *Mein Kampf* (Boston: Houghton Mifflin, 1971), p. 652.

streets, as the police stood by. It marked the beginning of forced exile and then, by 1939, the erection of ghettos and concentration camps. By 1941, the outright murder of Jews began with Hitler's adoption of "the final solution to the Jewish problem," or genocide (Chapter 24).

THE ROAD TO WAR IN EUROPE

World War II in Europe resulted from the two foreign policy goals of the Nazi regime. First, the Nazis aimed to reverse the Versailles Treaty that, in the eyes of most Germans, had brought ignominy to Germany at the end of World War I. Its second goal was to acquire *lebensraum* (living space) for the German people.

Inherent in the search for *lebensraum* was the Nazi ideology of the superiority of the Aryan race. In *Mein Kampf*, Hitler outlined this goal:

Nazi policemen arrest a Jewish man in Berlin. Beginning in 1939, the policy of deportation was replaced by more violent persecutions.

	1933	1939
NAVY	1 cruiser 6 light cruisers	2 battle cruisers, 3 battleships, 8 light cruisers, 22 destroyers, 60 submarines
AIR FORCE	none	2600 first line planes
ARMY	10 divisions 7 infantry 3 cavalry	39 divisions (5 armored, 4 fully motorized), trucks, motorcycles

In October 1933, Hitler withdrew Germany from the International Disarmament Conference, which was meeting under the auspices of the League of Nations. He claimed that while Germany was ready to meet its obligations, the other powers had failed to enact the clause which required all nations to reduce their armaments, not just the losers of the war.

In March of 1935, Hitler openly announced German rearmament, including the formation of the German air force, the *Luftwaffe*, and compulsory military service. Two months later, he instigated the Law for the Defense of the Reich which sanctioned economic mobilization for war, naming Dr. Hjalmar Schacht, a Nazi banker, the plenipotentiary for war economy.

In the face of Hitler's open defiance of the Versailles Treaty, the League formally condemned German rearmament in April 1935, but took no further steps.

THE POLICY OF COLLECTIVE SECURITY

The French relied on a system of collective security to contain Germany, negotiating treaties with Germany's neighbors, including Poland, Czechoslovakia, Belgium, and Romania. But Germany had already dented this system by a 10-year non-aggression pact with Poland, signed in January, 1934. In the face of German rearmament, Britain and France turned once more to the notion of collective security, meeting with the Italian dictator Mussolini at the Italian resort town of Stresa in April 1935. The result was what is

called the *Stresa Front*. The powers issued a joint communique that condemned German rearmament. A secret agreement between France and Italy provided for military action to prevent German violation of the demilitarized Rhineland or union with Austria.

In May of 1935, France signed a pact of mutual assistance with Russia. Russia and Czechoslovakia signed a similar pact. As it turned out, none of these measures would deter Germany. In June 1935, the Anglo-German Naval Agreement was signed, in which Britain permitted Germany to exceed the naval limitations of Versailles up to 35 percent of the British Commonwealth's surface fleet and 100 percent of its submarine fleet, merely legalizing what Germany had already done. This agreement torpedoed the Stresa Front's attempt to prevent further German violations of the Treaty of Versailles.

Four months later, Italy invaded Ethiopia in an attempt to connect its colonies of Eritrea and the Italian Somaliland. The League of Nations invoked economic sanctions against Italy. The sanctions did not, however, include an embargo on the oil that was vital to Italy's military economy, and Germany, no longer a member of the League, continued to supply Italy with critical materials such as steel and iron. The policy of sanctions proved to be a colossal failure.

THE REMILITARIZATION OF THE RHINELAND

On March 7, 1936, Germany sent troops into the Rhineland, in direct defiance of a clause in the Versailles Treaty. The intent of the clause had been to create a demilitarized buffer zone between Germany and France. The German action also violated the Locarno Pacts that Germany had signed in 1925.

Prior to this act, Hitler's generals had tried to deter him by warning that Germany was not yet ready for war. Hitler was prepared to withdraw his troops should France threaten war. But France failed to respond. This failure was in marked contrast to that nation's determination at the end of World War I never again to allow Germany to threaten it.

The explanation for French inactivity includes several factors. French military strategy relied on defensive action, including the construction of the Maginot Line, a massive cement barrier on the German frontier. Relying on this defensive position, the French army was unprepared to take military action in the Rhineland. Moreover, at the time of the remilitarization of the Rhineland, the French government, plagued by political factionalism, was experiencing a cabinet crisis. Another factor was *revisionism*, that is, the belief that the provisions of the Versailles Treaty had been unfair to Germany, as Hitler claimed, and should be revised. In this view, Hitler was a reasonable man with justifiable goals that should not be opposed.

Appeasement. Combined with these other factors was the still-fresh memory of the horrors and destruction of World War I. Many Europeans were determined to avoid another war at all costs, and this sentiment led to a policy of *appeasement*, or willingness to give in to Hitler's demands.

Appeasement was particularly strong in Great Britain. For example, the Oxford Union in 1933 debated the topic, "That this House will under no circumstances fight for its king and country." The members of the society, who would be the future officers and leaders in Britain's military, supported the topic by a vote of 275 to 153. Public opinion in Britain in 1936 would not have supported a joint effort with France to prevent Hitler's aggression.

In the view of many historians the remilitarization of the Rhineland is the pivotal event of the decade, for it made apparent the weakness of the League—and of Britain and France, in particular—and emboldened Hitler to proceed on his aggressive path.

TENSIONS INCREASE

In 1936, civil war erupted in Spain between the republican government and the fascist rebels led by Francisco Franco. In what was to be described as the "proving grounds" for World War II, both Germany and Italy intervened on behalf of the fascist rebels. At the peak of the intervention, Italy supplied 50,000 troops and 750 planes, while Germany supplied around 16,000 troops, planes, and tanks. The Soviet Union responded with aid to the republican government, including arms, planes, oil, food, and technicians. France, Great Britain, and the United States remained neutral.

Most ominous was the formation of the Rome-Berlin Axis in October, 1936. This German-Italian Pact was followed a month later by the Anti-Comintern Pact between Germany and Japan, ostensibly directed against the Soviet Union and communism. The formation of these alliances bound together the three future wartime allies known as the *Axis Powers.*

The Anschluss, 1938. Hitler's next act of aggression was directed at Austria. Since coming to power Hitler had sought such a union, or *Anschluss*, and viewed the Nazi party in Austria as a branch of his own organization.

In 1933, the Austrian government had dissolved the Austrian Nazi party, but in July, 1934, party members engineered a plot to overthrow the Austrian government. A group of Nazis dressed in Austrian police and regular-army uniforms shot and killed the chancellor, Dr. Engelbert Dollfuss. Another band of Nazis seized the radio station and announced a takeover of the government, but the scheme failed for lack of pop-

During the Spanish civil war, civilian targets were deliberately bombed from the air for the first time. Picasso's painting Guernica *commemorates the tragedy of civilians caught up in this new type of mechanized, impersonal warfare.*

ular support. Nazi behavior incensed world public opinion and Hitler temporarily abandoned his plan of union with Austria.

When another attempted Austrian Nazi *putsch* failed in January, 1938, Hitler adopted a new tactic. Inviting Austrian Chancellor Kurt von Schuschnigg to meet with him at his retreat at Berchtesgarden on February 12, Hitler subjected the Austrian chancellor to a long harangue regarding the Austrian government's treatment of Austrian Nazis. Schuschnigg was presented with an ultimatum demanding that the Austrian Nazi Arthur Seyss-Inquart be appointed head of the Austrian police, that the Austrian Nazi party be legalized, and that 100 German army officers be assigned as advisers to the Austrian army. Military invasion was threatened if the ultimatum were not accepted within three days.

Schuschnigg capitulated, but announced a plebiscite to be held on March 13 on the issue of Austrian independence, hoping to demonstrate to the world his people's distaste for Nazism. This announcement provoked phone calls from Hitler, again threatening German invasion. Schuschnigg gave in, naming Seyss-Inquart chancellor. Immediately, the German army crossed the frontier and occupied Vienna on March 12. Two days later Hitler rode through the streets of Vienna in triumph. After the Nazis occupied the country, a plebiscite ratifying Austrian annexation by Germany received 99.75 percent approval. Hitler had accomplished his goal virtually without opposition, and the Western powers again demonstrated their weakness.

The Czechoslovakian Crisis. Within the borders of the nation of Czechoslovakia, created at the end of World War I, was the *Sudetenland*, in which three million Germans lived. German nationalism in the Sudetenland was manipulated by Konrad Heinlein, who founded the pro-Nazi Sudeten German Party in 1935. Claiming that the Czech government persecuted Germans living in Czechoslovakia, Heinlein demanded autonomy for the Sudetenland, reparations for injustices, and freedom for Sudeten Germans to adopt Nazism. To the outside world the problem appeared to be an internal one, but

400

subsequent events make it apparent that Heinlein was working hand in glove with Hitler.

In May of 1938, Hitler issued a secret directive which announced his "unalterable" decision to smash Czechoslovakia. In response, Czechoslovakia partially mobilized its army. England, France, and the Soviet Union pressured Germany to mediate the Sudeten problem, and Neville Chamberlain volunteered to serve as negotiator.

After a series of meetings with Hitler, Chamberlain proposed a four-power conference to be held in Munich on September 28, 1938. Attending were Hitler, Chamberlain, the French premier Edward Daladier, and Mussolini, now acting as mediator. Conspicuously absent were any representatives of Czechoslovakia or of the Soviet Union.

On September 30, the infamous Munich Pact was signed. By the terms of this agreement, Germany acquired one-third of Czech territory, four million people, including one million Czechs, the Skoda armament works, and the defensible frontier. Having no allies or alternatives, the Czechs acceded. Neville Chamberlain returned to England triumphantly waving the sheet of paper containing the pact and declared, "There will be peace in our time." This sellout of the Czechs marked the peak of attempts to appease Hitler and to revise the Versailles Treaty.

In March, 1939, German troops occupied the rest of Czechoslovakia. Although the allies once again failed to come to the Czechs' defense, it was now apparent to even the blindest that Hitler was an aggressor, not merely following a pan-German plan, but determined to acquire *lebensraum* in eastern Europe. The policy of appeasement was demonstrated as a failure, for it only whetted the aggressors' appetites. The tragedy of Munich and of the 1930s is that it took so long for the Western powers to stop the aggressor. By delaying, they allowed him to consolidate his power.

The signers of the Munich Pact were, from left to right: Neville Chamberlain, Edward Daladier, Hitler, and Mussolini. Within six months, Hitler had violated the pact and completed his takeover of Czechoslavakia.

Picture Post, December 2, 193

SUMMARY

The 1930s witnessed the emergence of three powerful totalitarian states committed to brutality and violence against anyone who opposed them. These three states were dictatorships whose leaders—Stalin, Mussolini, and Hitler—appeared to be decisive, popular among the masses, and even invincible. By contrast, the democracies in the 1930s, especially France and Great Britain, seemed vacillating and weak.

The dictatorships seemed to have resolved the economic crisis which characterized the early 1930s. Russia did so through the application of Marxist theory, which in practice was a form of state capitalism (state ownership of all resources); Germany and Italy relied on private enterprise (capitalism), which was closely regulated by the state. France and Britain continued to face economic woes—unemployment, weak trade, limited industrial productivity. Politically, France was wracked by conflict and instability, with political extremes of left and right often in conflict. In fact, France seemed to be in the midst of a cabinet crisis each time Hitler made an aggressive move.

British politics in the 1930s brought coalition government to confront the economic problems. While the French people always feared potential German aggression on their frontiers, Britain's mood supported appeasement of the dictators. To many observers of the 1930s, it seemed that the humanistic values which had dominated Western civilization since Greco-Roman times were doomed by the dictators—the forces of darkness. On the eve of war, civilization itself was on the brink of disaster.

QUESTIONS

1. Define totalitarianism. How does it differ from authoritarian regimes of previous centuries—for example, that of Napoleon III?
2 What is a command economy? How does it differ from a market economy?
3 Why did Stalin win the power struggle after Lenin's death?
4 Define fascism as implemented by Mussolini.
5 How did Hitler achieve power? Was his seizure of power legal?
6 Why did England and France fail to stop Hitler's aggressions?
7 Was World War II inevitable?

BIBLIOGRAPHY

BULLOCK, ALAN. *Hitler: A Study in Tyranny.* New York: Bantam Books, 1961. *This is among the best accounts of Hitler and his Third Reich.*

DAWIDOWICZ, LUCY. *The War Against the Jews, 1933–1945.* New York: Holt, Rinehart, and Winston, 1975. *An account of Hitler's "final solution," not only in Germany but also throughout occupied Europe. Dawidowicz has amassed extensive details of the nightmare of the holocaust.*

KOESTLER, ARTHUR. *Darkness at Noon.* New York: Bantam Books, 1968. *This novel depicts the trial and execution of Rubashov, a thinly veiled example of the victims of Stalin's purges in the 1930s.*

MACK SMITH, DENIS. *Mussolini.* New York: Knopf, 1982. *An excellent biography of the back-street bully with confused fascist theories whose dictatorship influenced that of Adolf Hitler.*

ORWELL, GEORGE. *1984.* New York: Signet Books, 1981. *Orwell wrote this novel in 1949, in reaction to the repressive regime of Joseph Stalin. In it, he projects the ultimate totalitarian society where thought-control and doublespeak take the place of communication.*

SOLZHENITSYN, ALEKSANDR I. *The Gulag Archipelago.* New York: Harper & Row, 1975. *This lengthy account of the slave labor camps of Russia, written by one of Stalin's victims, is a stunning portrait of life under the dictatorship. The author estimates that Stalin's victims number 60 million.*

23

● *Dekansho [Descartes, Kant, and Schopenhauer]*
Dekansho
Half the year we live with them
The other half we sleep.

JAPANESE SAYING

The New Nationalism in Asia: China and Japan (1919–1939)

The seeds of nationalism sowed by the 19th-century imperialists in Asia came to flower in the 20th century. The two major independent states in Asia, China and Japan, had both been the targets of imperialists from America and Europe, but they had responded differently. China was forced to grant numerous economic and political concessions to the "barbarian" foreigners. In the 20th century, China experienced civil war as it strove to find a government that could deal with its internal and external problems.

Japan had avoided humiliation by imitating the West in the 19th century, borrowing a vast array of political, economic, and military institutions. In the 20th century Japan turned outward. In a display of extreme nationalism, Japan expanded at the expense of her neighbors, including China. The history of Asia between the world wars was in large part the conflict between these two powers. Their struggle led to the outbreak of World War II in Asia in 1937.

CIVIL WAR IN CHINA In the centuries-old Chinese political tradition, the emperor was in a sense a divine-right monarch, for he was perceived as having the *mandate from heaven.* If he failed to rule effectively, however, opponents to his power—warlords—would arise and vie with the emperor and each other for the right to rule. Should the emperor emerge victorious, it was perceived that he had retained the mandate from heaven. Defeat at the hands of a warlord would be interpreted as the sign that the emperor had lost the mandate, and the people would transfer their allegiance to the new emperor. This system provided for a change of rulers without an overthrow of the entire system of government. As such, it allowed for both revolution and stability.

Continuity in this society was preserved by the civil-service system, of Confucian origin, whereby the civil servants, the scholar-officials, perpetuated the governmental bureaucracy throughout the period of civil war and the accession of a new emperor. These civil servants earned their position by passing the civil service examination, a rigorous exercise which tested the candidate's grasp of the Chinese classics. Hence, the civil service system rewarded those who understood and retained the past. As such, the system

403

could be viewed as conservative; that is, it was designed to perpetuate the status quo.

THE GROWTH OF REVOLUTIONARY MOVEMENTS

In the beginning of the 20th century, the Manchu dynasty made some attempts at reform. The army was modernized under the leadership of Yuan Shih-kai, and schools were established that taught such Western subjects as science and foreign languages. In 1905, the traditional civil service examination for officials was abolished, ending the Confucian monopoly on education. But the reforms came too late to save the dynasty.

Stung by the humiliation at the hands of Westerners and even more by the defeats inflicted by the Japanese, many Chinese blamed the Manchu dynasty. In Chinese terms, the dynasty had lost the mandate of heaven. Secret societies sprang up dedicated to overthrowing the Manchus. But although most Chinese were dissatisfied with Manchu rule, they did not agree on what was to take its place.

The Role of Sun Yat-sen. In the late 19th and early 20th centuries, revolutionary movements appeared. One of the most important was led by Sun Yat-sen (1866–1925), a liberal whose political principles were based on the Western ideas of nationalism, socialism, and democracy. Sun is known as the Father of the Chinese Republic.

Sun Yat-sen was born in a small peasant village in South China. An older brother went to Hawaii where he prospered and sent for Sun to join him. While there, Sun studied in an English mission school and was taught Western ideas including Christianity and the English language. After three years he returned to China. Denounced in his native village when he flaunted his Christianity, he settled in Hong Kong and entered the study of medicine. He received his medical degree in 1892, but practiced only briefly before turning his full attention to Chinese politics. In 1907, he enunciated the *three people's principles*: the people's livelihood, the peo-

Sun Yat-sen sought to establish a democratic republic in China, and was the recognized leader of the early revolutionary movement. His Kuomintang government never controlled more than a small area, however, for traditional warlords retained their hold over most of the countryside.

ple's democracy, and the people's nationalism.

The Revolution of 1911. On October 10, 1911, students, revolutionaries and some soldiers rebelled against the government garrison in Wuhan, China. Many government troops came over to their side. The revolt spread throughout central China, and the plotters declared a republic. At the time, Sun was in the United States, but he hurried back to China, where he was named the provisional president of China.

The government turned to Yuan Shih-kai to put down the rebels. However, he was more interested in his own future than that of the Manchus, and negotiated a deal with the rebels. In return for receiving the presidency of China, Yuan agreed to obtain the abdication of the boy emperor, Pu Yi. In January 1912, Pu Yi abdicated and China officially became a republic.

Yuan Shih-kai was not interested in the

republican ideals of Sun and his associates. The elections that were carried out were a sham, and Yuan ruled as a dictator. Sun, who had been so important in the revolutionary movement, was shunted aside. In 1912, he formed the *Kuomintang (KMT)*, a party devoted to his ideals. He established himself in Canton, where he worked to build a government.

China had dissolved into anarchy. In the absence of a strong central government, warlords had taken over large chunks of the country and ruled them for their own benefit. Conditions were worse than they had been under the Manchus, and China lacked the unity that the dynasty had given it.

Modernization in China. Many Chinese in the late 19th and early 20th centuries recognized the impossibility of restoring traditional China. Foreign influences during the previous century had been pervasive. The alternative was to modernize China— copying the West, as Japan had done so successfully. Many Chinese advocated adopting a Western democracy and political institutions. It was felt that China would then lose its backwardness in the eyes of the West, and be able to assert its independence. Many Chinese went to Europe, the United States, or Japan to study.

One symbol of China's backwardness was the practice of binding women's feet, done since before 1000 A.D. This practice involved tightly binding the feet of girls at the age of two or three. With no space for normal growth, the bones broke and the flesh peeled away. The result was that adult women's feet were only three to four inches long. Walking on these bound and broken feet meant excruciating pain for women throughout their lives. Although a frequent explanation for this practice is that small feet were considered erotic, in reality it produced subservient, dependent cripples and reflected a culture which disparaged women. By 1900, many Chinese men and women sought to end the backwardness which foot-binding

represented by joining revolutionary societies.

> One young woman who had left the husband her family had forced her to marry, and abandoned her children, sailed to Japan to study. She summarized her despair in this poem entitled, "Regrets: Lines Written En Route to Japan."
>
> Sun and moon have no light left; Our women's world is sunk so deep, who can help us? Jewelry sold to pay this trip across the seas. Cut off from my family, I leave my native land. Unbinding my feet I clean out a thousand years of poison, with heated heart arouse all women's spirits. Alas, this delicate kerchief here is half stained with blood and half with tears.[1]

WORLD WAR I

While China was in turmoil, World War I broke out in Europe. On August 23, 1914, Japan declared war on Germany, and in September landed 25,000 troops on the Chinese mainland. The ostensible purpose of this invasion was to rid China of the German imperialists, who had stationed 4,000 embassy guards in their concessions. By November the Japanese army had captured the former German concession at Tsingtao.

In 1915, Japan presented the Chinese government under Yuan with the *Twenty-one Demands*. If granted, they would have given Japan dominant economic control of the German concessions in the Shantung province, as well as leases in Southern Manchuria. In addition, they would give the Japanese a right to intervene in China's internal affairs. China acceded to many of these demands,

---

[1] Jonathan D. Spence, *The Gate of Heavenly Peace: The Chinese and Their Revolution, 1895–1960* (New York: Viking Press, 1981), p. 52.

having little alternative. This led to a weakening of Yuan's government.

In August 1917, China joined the Allies and thus emerged from the war as one of the victors. But the presence of its delegates at the Paris Peace Conference was to no avail, for China failed to regain its concessions in the Shantung province.

The May Fourth Incident. When news reached China that the Allies had agreed to Japanese demands for Chinese territory, there was a great protest. In Peking, students staged a passive demonstration on May 4th at the Gate of Heavenly Peace. Violence erupted, as students ransacked the house of a pro-Japanese official and burned the house of a cabinet official.

The protest spread throughout the country. Strikes closed schools in more than 200 cities. Workers went on protest strikes in the factories of Shanghai. When the government tried to suppress the movement, more protested. The government in Peking—the government recognized by foreign governments—yielded to the protestors' demands. Some cabinet officials were fired, and the Chinese delegation at the Paris Peace Conference refused to sign the treaty.

Part of the spirit behind the *May 4th Movement* was a desire for fundamental change in the culture of China. Modernism was finally coming to China in the second decade of the 20th century. In 1915, the newspaper *New Youth*, edited by Ch'en Tuhsiu, called for Chinese youth to "be independent, not servile . . . progressive, not conservative . . . dynamic, not passive . . . cosmopolitan, not isolationist."[2] Ch'en and the other new reformers blamed many of China's problems on the role of Confucianism and China's devotion to tradition. They called for a greater emphasis on youth, equality of the sexes, and individuality.

CIVIL WAR IN CHINA

The intellectual ferment of the May 4th Movement led Chinese to study the political philosophies and systems of the West. Liberalism, nationalism, and Marxism were among those Western ideas that drew Chinese adherents. Followers of these ideologies competed for control of China and caused a civil war that was waged intermittently until 1949, when communist forces finally triumphed.

Formation of the Chinese Communist Party. The Chinese Communist Party (CCP) was rooted in the May 4th Movement. Disillusioned with their nation's leadership and with the West, some Chinese turned to Marx, Lenin, and Trotsky. In 1920, Marxist study groups appeared, organized with the assistance of a Russian agent, Gregory Voitinsky. Voitinsky represented the *Comintern*, the newly-formed Russian Communist state's mechanism for exporting communism.

Two early Chinese Marxists were Li Tachao, professor and chief librarian, and Ch'en Tu-hsui, professor of literature, both at Peking University. They influenced, among others, the young Mao Tse-tung (1893–1976). Mao, the son of a peasant who prospered from the red soil of the Hunan Province, was an eager student in his native village of Music Mountain, but his desire for an education conflicted with his father's zeal for exploiting his labor. His father's beatings provoked Mao to say later, "I learned to hate him."[3] At the age of 16, Mao left home to further his education. He was already a rebel, but one who loved to read the Chinese classics. As an adult, he would combine those contradictory qualities by molding revolutionary Marxism to fit classical China.

---

[2] John K. Fairbank, Edwin O. Reischauer, and Albert M. Craig, *East Asia: Tradition and Transformation* (Boston: Houghton Mifflin, 1978), p. 767.

[3] Ross Terrill, *Mao* (New York: Harper & Row, 1981), p. 14.

In July 1921, 12 delegates met at a private girls' school in the French section of Shanghai to form the Chinese Communist Party. The chairman of the four-day session was Ch'en; one of the delegates was Mao. The total membership of the party was about 50. Their notions of Marxism were not well-developed; nor did traditional Marxist theory fit the realities of China in the 1920s. China was a nation of poor peasants whose condition had been worsened through Western interference.

There were different reasons for the interest held by some Chinese in this new ideology. First, the Marxist revolution had succeeded in Russia. Moreover, although often considered a Western power, Russia is as well an Asian state. To many Chinese, Russia and China were both backward Asian states at odds with the European powers.

Kuomintang-Communist Coalition. Sun Yat-sen had established his power base in Canton at the sufferance of the local warlord. Sun was impressed by the discipline of the CCP members and by the success of the revolution in Russia. He was also favorably influenced by the Soviet government's offer to give up Russia's special concessions in China. (This promise was not carried out, however.)

When the Comintern sent negotiators to Sun, he agreed to a united front with the Chinese Communist Party. Communists could join the Kuomintang. In exchange, Russian advisers would help Sun train an army and organize the Kuomintang along more disciplined lines. Sun's wish was to use this coalition to move north and unify China. In Sun's view, his Nationalists could reject Marxist ideology and at the same time learn from the Russians how to carry out a successful revolution.

In fact, in the 1920s, the Soviet Union supported all three of the factions in China for a multiplicity of reasons. The U.S.S.R. supported the warlords with arms and ammunition, in order to continue the chaos within China and increase Russian influence; it supported the new CCP as part of the world communist movement; and it provided the Kuomintang with arms, ammunition, and advisers as a way of attempting to infiltrate and gain favor with the Nationalist movement.

Chiang Kai-shek. Sun Yat-sen's death in 1925 brought a new leader of the Kuomintang, Sun's brother-in-law, Chiang Kai-shek (1887–1975). Chiang, like Sun and Mao Tsetung, was born into a peasant family and became a revolutionary in his youth, during the turbulent years at the end of the Manchu dynasty. As a young man he expressed an interest in a military career and studied at a Japanese military academy. After joining the KMT he went to Russia in 1923 to study the Red Army. On his return to China he was made head of the Whampoa Military Academy, which was intended to develop a Nationalist army preparatory to the conquest of China.

Chiang Kai-shek became leader of the Kuomintang in 1925. Under his direction, the KMT took a more conservative path, expelling all Communist Party members from its ranks.

By 1926, Chiang began his Northern Expedition, a march of the KMT army against the various warlords entrenched in the rest of China. The Northern Expedition was very successful, and Chiang was able to set up a new government at Nanking in 1927, a provisional government for all of China in 1928, and to complete a constitution in 1931.

The Northern Expedition had been planned with the help of the communists within the KMT. Communist units had been assigned to infiltrate factories within major cities and organize the workers into uprisings. However, Chiang abruptly abandoned his communist allies in a bold attempt to eliminate any potential rivalry for control of the KMT.

In March 1927, the young Chinese communist Chou Enlai (1898–1976) led an uprising in Shanghai, expecting that Chiang would shortly arrive with military forces to consolidate control of the city. On April 12, Chiang did arrive, but immediately began a slaughter of the communists within the city. Chou escaped, but an estimated 5000 communists were beheaded by Chiang's forces. Another communist uprising in the city of Canton failed as well.

Split in the CCP. The purge of the communists from the KMT left them in disarray and divided as to how they should proceed. The party split into two factions. One group, led by Liu Shao-chi, Li Li-san and others, was willing to take its orders from the Moscow-directed Comintern. This segment of the CCP believed that the way to successful revolution in China was the Russian model; that is, through takeover of the major cities in cooperation with the proletariat—the industrial working class.

In the opinion of Mao Tse-tung, the way to communist revolution in China was not through the proletariat, but through the peasantry in the countryside. His philosophy was difficult to reconcile with traditional Marxism, but Mao succeeded in doing so, just as Lenin had done before him. Lenin had modified Marxism to apply it to Russia, an industrializing, but still economically backward society. Mao went a step further, describing China as being at a semicolonial stage. He adapted Marxism to the nonindustrial, peasant society of China.

The Long March. In 1927, Mao attempted a communist revolution in the countryside, the Autumn Harvest uprising. It, too, failed, and Mao barely escaped with his life. Combined with Chiang's purge of the KMT and the failures of the city uprisings, 1927 was a disastrous year for the CCP in China. Beginning with 50,000 party members, only a few thousand survived the year.

In October 1927, Mao and 1000 survivors withdrew to the hills of the Hunan province, in hiding from the KMT army. By 1934, Mao had collected a Red army of 100,000 men and a few hundred women. However, Chiang, having consolidated his power, was now conducting "extermination campaigns" against communists in the countryside. Mao set off on a long retreat from the Hunan province in the southeast of China toward the northwestern Shaanxi province, following a zigzag route thousands of miles long. On the arduous journey, Mao, who wrote poetry throughout his life, compared his struggles to the mountains through which they passed:

Mountains!
Like great waves merging in a crashing sea,
Like a thousand stallions
In full gallop in the heat of battle.

Mountains
Piercing the blue of heaven, your banks unblunted
The skies would fall
But for your strength supporting.[4]

The Long March ended in Shaanxi in October 1935. Many of the marchers had fallen along the way to the terrible hardships of the journey. However, it had several important effects. At a council of the party leadership

[4] *Ibid.*, p. 129.

After completing his 6000-mile Long March, Mao Tse-tung met with a Western journalist, Earl Leaf (second from left), in Yenan. At right is Mao's wife, Yang Kai-hui.

early in 1935, Mao was accepted as head of the party, a position he was never to lose. Chou Enlai's support had been crucial in Mao's winning the intra-party struggle, and he would remain a key aide of Mao's through the turbulent years that followed.

The survivors of the Long March formed a hardened core group around which a larger force could be built. The march became one of the central events of the Chinese communist struggle; those who endured its hardships felt they would ultimately triumph, as they did. From his base, Mao would build his forces and later conduct guerrilla warfare against the Japanese, who once again began to encroach on Chinese territory in the early 1930s.

JAPAN BETWEEN THE WARS

By contrast to the Chinese peasant society, Japan was highly in-dustrialized in the period between the wars. Its response to Western imperialism in the 19th century, as we have seen, was to rid itself of Western dominance by imitating the West. As such, it had adopted Western institutions, including a constitutional monarchy modeled after Germany's. Japan had modernized its military, erecting army and navy academies similar to those at West Point and Annapolis. It had further industrialized, developing transportation and communication systems, and in its own sphere had become an imperialistic power, seeking raw materials, markets, and outlets for its excess population on the Asian mainland. Japan's successes evoked ambivalent feelings among its neighbors. On one hand, it was admired as a symbol of Asian resistance to Western exploitation and domination. But at the same time, it was feared as an aggressor.

CHINA AND JAPAN, 1919–1939
What factors motivated Japanese expansionism in the Asian mainland?

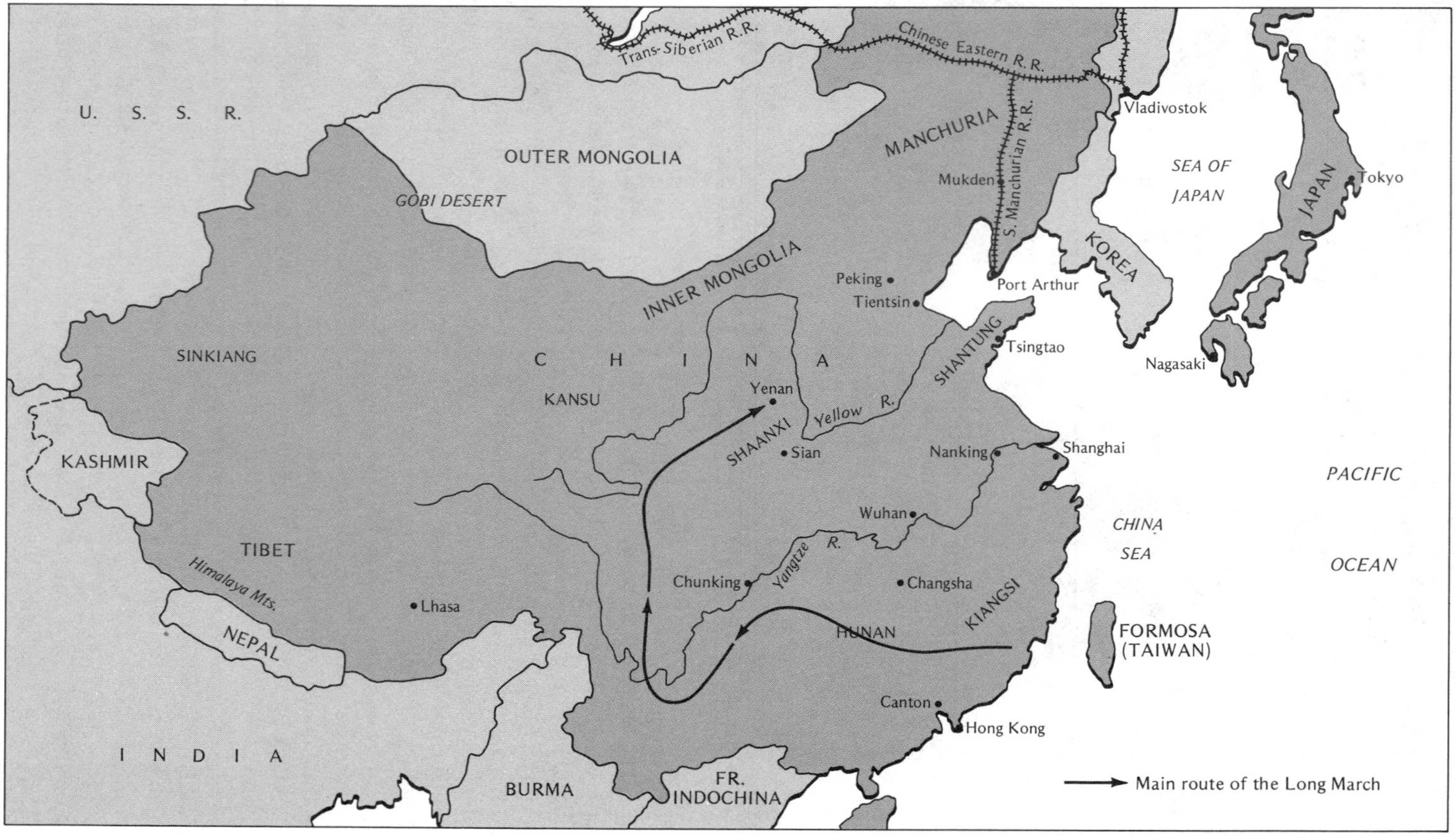

Main route of the Long March

PACIFIC OCEAN

Tokyo

JAPAN

SEA OF JAPAN

Vladivostok

Nagasaki

KOREA

CHINA SEA

FORMOSA (TAIWAN)

Chinese Eastern R. R.

S. Manchurian R.R.

Port Arthur

Tsingtao

Shanghai

Hong Kong

MANCHURIA

Mukden

SHANTUNG

Nanking

KIANGSI

Trans-Siberian R. R.

Peking

Tientsin

Yellow R.

Sian

Wuhan

Changsha

Canton

INNER MONGOLIA

C H I N A

Yenan

SHAANXI

Chunking

HUNAN

Yangtze R.

FR. INDOCHINA

OUTER MONGOLIA

KANSU

U. S. S. R.

GOBI DESERT

BURMA

SINKIANG

TIBET

Lhasa

Himalaya Mts.

NEPAL

I N D I A

KASHMIR

The 1920s in Japan have been viewed as the liberal period in its history, during which the vote was extended to all adult males (in 1925) and in which the parliamentary system of government began to work effectively. Leadership of the government alternated between the two major political parties. The 1920s also marked a period of peaceful international trade and of modest economic growth. Culturally, Japan was becoming more and more westernized. The Japanese version of the flapper, the *moga* (modern girl) characterized the growing interest in Western culture, from movies to jazz to baseball. The great Tokyo earthquake and fire of 1923, which claimed 130,000 lives, led to the modernization of the city.

Japanese Economic Problems. At the same time that democracy appeared to be flourishing in Japan, there were, in retrospect, more ominous signs. For one, the Japanese economy was dominated by giant corporations which controlled most of Japan's economy. *Zaibatsus* (literally, "wealth-cliques"), cartels of giant family corporations, controlled three-fourths of the capital in Japan. They also controlled one-third of all deposits in Japanese private banks, three-fourths of all trust deposits, and one-fifth of all life insurance policies.

Moreover, while the economy had continued to grow, its rate of growth in the 1920s was only 33 percent, a considerably lower rate than in the previous decades. Inflation after the prosperous wartime economy led to riots over the price of rice in 1918. The price of rice and of silk continued to decline in the 1920s, and the economic difficulties thus created were compounded by the world

After the devastating earthquake and fire of 1923, the modern capital city of Tokyo was constructed from the ruins.

depression which began in 1929. A new banking crisis in 1927 resulted in the closing of 20 banks and foreshadowed the hard times of the 1930s. Industrial conflicts followed in which the government was forced to use troops to suppress violence.

These economic disorders led to political conflict and the assassination of three prominent figures in 1921. In September, Yasuda Zenjiro, a prominent financier, was killed; in November, an unbalanced youth murdered the premier, Hara Takashi; and in the same month, a right-wing fanatic shot the socialist leader, Takao Heibei.

Japan's growing population created additional pressures on the government and demands on the economy.

JAPAN'S POPULATION GROWTH	
1600	18 million
1725	26 million
1873	30 million
1925	60 million
1930	65 million
1940	72 million
1950	83 million
1960	93 million
1975	112 million

Japanese Militarism. Other ominous signs in the 1920s included the continued independence of the military from political control. "Rich country, strong military" had been a slogan of the leadership which had modernized Japan in the late 19th century. Moreover, the constitution specified that the armed forces were under the direct control of the emperor, who in most other ways was a figurehead. Traditionally, too, the posts of military ministers in the cabinet (the minister for war, for example) could only be held by military officers on active duty.

More threatening in 1928 was the Chang-Tso-lin episode in which young officers of the Japanese army stationed in Manchuria killed Chang Tso-lin, the Chinese puppet ruler of Manchuria, by placing a bomb on the South Manchurian railroad. Although the evidence strongly implicated the Japanese army in the killing, the Japanese government did nothing. The prime minister, Giichi Tanaka, was forced to resign.

Tanaka's successor, Osachi Hamaguchi, attempted a more conciliatory foreign policy, but was hampered by the effects of the world depression that forced the Japanese to import rice to feed its growing population. Hamaguchi's attempts at modernization ended when a right-wing nationalist fanatic shot him in September 1930. For the next six years, until the military faction was finally in command of the Japanese government, political assassination was the order of the day.

Added to a militaristic tradition was an extremely nationalistic and anti-Western one. These sentiments were intensified by a new United States immigration law in 1924. Previously, the high rate of Japanese immigration into the U.S. had led to voluntary Japanese immigration restrictions. But the new law of 1924 excluded Japanese from immigration quotas altogether. The Japanese were insulted. They interpreted the law as a form of racial discrimination, a conclusion enhanced by the Australian "whites only" immigration policy and by the Western slogan "yellow peril," which had prompted the alternate slogans within Asia of "Asia for the Asiatics" and "white peril."

THE MUKDEN INCIDENT

The stage was set for one of the most important international events of the decade, the *Mukden Incident* of September 1931, which paved the way for the start of World War II in Asia.

This incident had its origins in the Japanese desire to gain control of Manchuria. This territory, while not part of China proper, had been an integral part of the Chinese empire since 1644, the year the

Chinese soldiers defend the Great Wall in northern China against Japanese invaders. By the end of 1931, the Japanese controlled Manchuria.

Manchus established their dynasty. For Japan, control of Manchuria was tempting, given the great resources of timber and minerals to be found there. Moreover, Japanese nationalists believed that the Soviet Union wanted to extend its influence in Asia by conquering Manchuria, and perhaps ultimately invading Japan itself.

The Japanese Kwangtung Army was stationed in Manchuria to protect Japanese railroad interests there. On the night of September 18, 1931, Japanese officers planted a bomb on the tracks of the Japanese-owned South Manchurian Railway near the city of Mukden. Blaming Chinese "bandits" for the incident, the Japanese launched a full-scale invasion of Manchuria. The incident was characterized in the Japanese press:

● ● ● *at 10:30 P.M. a group of lawless Chinese bandits northwest of the northern barracks bombed the South Manchurian Railway. Since they attacked our guards, a battalion lost no time to fight back.*[5]

The Japanese military put into effect the already formulated plans for the conquest of Manchuria, and by September 1932, the victory over Manchuria was complete. The Japanese created a puppet state, the state of Manchukuo, under the puppet emperor, Henry Pu-yi, the last of the Manchus, who had abdicated the Chinese throne in 1912.

The League. The Mukden Incident tested the prestige and authority of the League of Nations and revealed its fatal weaknesses. On September 19, 1931, the day after the Japanese invasion of Manchuria, the Chinese government appealed to the League of Na-

---

[5] Hugh Barton, *Japan's Modern Century*, 2nd ed. (New York: Ronald Press, 1970), p. 373.

tions and to the United States. The appeal to the U.S. was based on American participation in the Kellogg-Briand Pact (Chapter 21), which outlawed war as an instrument of national policy. One of the major Pacific powers by virtue of its possession of the Hawaiian and Philippine Islands, the United States declined to act on China's appeal.

In the Council of the League, Japan declared that it had no territorial designs on Manchuria, and on September 30, the Council unanimously adopted a resolution accepting Japan's assurances. When the Japanese army continued to advance in Manchuria, the League Council reconvened, and on October 24 resolved that Japan should pull its troops back to the legitimate railroad zone. The Japanese delegate stalled, asking for time to consult his government, and in the meantime, the League Council again adjourned.

On November 16, the Council again reconvened and began to imply that it might adopt economic sanctions against Japan, in light of the continued Japanese army advances. Finally, on December 10, 1931, the Council adopted the Chinese proposal for a commission of inquiry into Manchurian events. By that time, the Japanese military campaign to conquer Manchuria had essentially succeeded.

The Stimson Doctrine. A few weeks later, in January 1932, the American government sent a diplomatic note to the governments of Japan and China. The U.S. Secretary of State, Henry Stimson, outlined the position which China had put forth the previous September. The Stimson Doctrine declared that the United States would not recognize any agreement which infringed on the sovereignty of China or on the Open Door policy, nor any settlement brought about by military means. Whatever psychological effect such a doctrine might have had, it was apparent that the United States, in the throes of the depression, was not prepared to back its policy with military force.

The other major Asian power, Great Britain, was also in no position to conduct military operations in the Pacific. With its naval base at Singapore not yet complete, the British navy would have had to conduct operations from Malta in the Mediterranean. The British government regarded this option as too impractical for serious consideration.

The Lytton Commission. In early 1932, the Assembly of the League adopted a resolution that endorsed the Stimson Doctrine, and the Council created the Lytton Commission, named for the British chairman, the Earl of Lytton. For six months, the Lytton Commission toured Japan, China, and Manchuria, trying to investigate the Mukden Incident, the subsequent Japanese invasion, and the charges and counter-charges. The *Lytton Report*, published in October 1932, was unequivocal in its condemnation of Japanese actions in Manchuria. It concluded that the military operations by the Japanese troops could not have been regarded as self-defense, and that the new state of Manchuria could not have been formed without the presence of Japanese troops. For this reason, the report concluded, the Manchu regime could not have been the result of a genuine and spontaneous independence movement, as the Japanese had claimed. It had taken the Council and the Lytton Commission 13 months to arrive at conclusions apparent to the unbiased observer.

Japan Withdraws from the League. The Lytton Report also contained a series of recommendations to the League. These were debated at length, first by the Council, then by the Assembly, and finally by a special "Committee of Nineteen." At last in February 1933, the Assembly approved the Lytton report and passed a five-point resolution:

1) that the Manchurian dispute should be settled in accordance with the Covenant of the League, the Kellogg-Briand Pact, and the Nine-Power Treaty, all three international agreements that recognized Chinese sovereignty and independence.

2) that members of the League should not recognize any situation, treaty, or agreement not brought about this way.

3) that Japanese military pressure on China should cease.

4) that the eventual settlement should follow the recommendations of the Lytton Report.

5) that Sino-Japanese negotiations should be conducted under the supervision of the League Assembly.

When this resolution passed, the Japanese delegation walked out of the League, and soon after the Japanese government in Tokyo formally notified the League of its decision to withdraw. Peace in Asia, Japan declared, could only be assured by the recognition of Japanese hegemony in eastern Asia.

The Failure of the League. Thus, the Mukden Incident revealed the impotence of the League of Nations. In the face of blatant Japanese aggression, the League spent one and one-half years in deliberation of the initial incident. By the time its deliberations were complete, Japanese had conquered all of Manchuria and the Japanese army had entered China proper. Moreover, when the League finally reached its conclusions, in March 1933, it proved incapable of taking effective action. Having branded Japan the aggressor, the League could neither reverse Japanese conquests nor prevent Japan from further aggression.

The lesson of the League's impotence was not lost on Mussolini and Hitler. As we have seen, both dictators tested the democracies and the League in 1935—Mussolini by his invasion of Ethiopia, and Hitler by his announcement of German rearmament. For all practical purposes, the League of Nations was dead.

MILITARY GOVERNMENT IN JAPAN

The Mukden Incident was also a turning point in modern Japanese history. This military victory was greeted enthusiastically within Japan and marked the beginning of several atempts at military takeover of the Japanese government. In one unsuccessful attempt in May 1932, the prime minister was assassinated. In another attempt on February 2, 1936, 1400 men of the Imperial Guard began a systematic assassination of political leaders. The finance minister, who had cut military budget estimates, was shot in bed. The prime minister was saved by his alarm system; he hid in his steel-vaulted earthquake shelter.

After four days of violence, the emperor intervened and stopped the bloodshed. Although 15 ringleaders were shot, the rank and file were pardoned on the grounds that they had only been acting under orders.

The military emerged from this episode in a strong position, since units loyal to the government had been used to suppress the rebellion. Although never a totalitarian regime like those in Soviet Russia, Italy, or Germany, the Japanese militaristic regime, led by General Tojo Hideki (1884–1948), relied on purges of the liberal opposition, and control of the mass media and the educational system. Determined to dominate what they characterized as the *Greater East Asia Co-Prosperity Sphere,* the Japanese militarists embarked on World War II with their invasion of China proper in 1937.

WORLD WAR II IN ASIA The Japanese attack on Peking in 1937 was in fact the opening battle of World War II. The war lasted in China for eight years, further ravaging a country that had already seen revolution and civil war.

THE JAPANESE INVASION OF CHINA

After consolidating their hold on Manchuria, the Japanese made further moves in north China. They seized an area just south of the Great Wall and made it a demilitarized zone ruled by a puppet government.

In 1936, Japan signed the Anti-Comintern Pact with Germany. By this agreement, each of the two aggressors agreed to keep the other informed on the activities of the Comintern in their respective spheres. In a secret protocol, each agreed to come to the assistance of the other in the event of an attack by the Soviet Union.

The Marco Polo Bridge Incident. The Japanese garrison in north China held field activities outside Peking near the Marco Polo Bridge in July 1937. On the pretext that one of their soldiers was missing, they requested permission to search a neighboring city. When the permission was refused, the Japanese attacked the city by land and air and occupied it on July 8.

The Chinese government under Chiang Kai-shek at Nanking decided that it was time to fight. Chiang announced that China would "throw the last ounce of energy" into a "struggle for survival." The Japanese had never formally declared war on China and referred to the event as "the China incident."

China's forces were no match for the Japanese in modernization and armament. In ad-

dition, the main force of Chinese troops was located in central China to protect Shanghai and the capital city of Nanking. The Japanese attacked Peking at the end of July, and easily took the city on July 28th. Two days later, the Japanese took Tientsin.

The Fall of Shanghai and Nanking. The Japanese opened a second front against Shanghai, the financial center of China, and were surprised by the extent of Chinese resistance. Chiang threw some of his best troops against the Japanese, and—with an alarming cost in casualties—managed to hold them back for three months. With the fall of Shanghai, the road to Nanking was open.

As the Japanese troops approached Nanking, the government fled. It first established itself in Wuhan in central China and then moved to Chunking. To the new capital in the interior of China were relocated schools and factories. Many Chinese were on the move to the center of the country.

Japanese marines engage Chiang Kai-shek's forces on the streets of Shanghai. With its sizable business community, Shanghai had remained a stronghold of the Kuomintang as communist forces increased their control over northern China.

416

After the fall of Shanghai and Nanking, Chiang Kai-shek made a temporary pact with communist forces and relocated his government to Chunking. Here, he receives two American visitors, the journalist Lowell Thomas and General Wedemeyer.

The fall of Nanking was accompanied by widespread atrocities. After the Japanese took the city, they massacred about 100,000 civilians in what was known as the *rape of Nanking*. The world was shocked, but did nothing. The Japanese kept the facts of their brutal tactics from civilians at home in Japan.

OCCUPATION OF CHINA

Although the Chinese resisted, they could not stop the Japanese troops. As the Japanese moved inland, dikes in the Yellow River were broken to slow the enemy advance. In October 1938, Canton fell and on Christmas Day, Wuhan as well. With the fall of Wuhan the first phase of the war ended in the Far East. The Chinese had traded space for time. Although the Japanese were deep in the hinterland of China, they had not managed to defeat the nation.

Japan realized that a stalemate had been reached. It adopted the policy of having its troops live off the land and ruled conquered areas through puppet governors. In October 1938, the Japanese announced the *New Order in East Asia*. This was based on Japanese hegemony of the area in order to promote a joint defense against international communism.

The Japanese found two Chinese to rule a North and South China. However, Chiang's government survived at Chunking. With the outbreak of the war, the Kuomintang government had formed a *United Front* with the communists, now based in Yenan in the northwest of the country. Both parties agreed to cooperate in a joint effort against the Japanese. However, Chinese resistance after the initial phase of the war was limited to guerilla maneuvers, for Chiang Kai-shek was not willing to spend his army in attacks against the Japanese. The situation in the Far East would not change significantly until the Asian war was connected to the war in Europe. This occurred when the Japanese attacked the U.S. fleet in Pearl Harbor, Hawaii, in December of 1941.

SUMMARY

The new nationalism in China and Japan in the 20th century led China to turn upon itself, seeking a viable political system to replace the Manchu government which had fallen victim to Western imperialists. Japan, in imitation of the West, initiated a policy of aggressive imperialism. The history of these two Asiatic states converged in the late 1930s, when Japan began to expand into the mainland of Asia. These events in Asia assumed even greater proportions when Japan became one of the Axis powers by signing the Anti-Comintern Pact with Nazi Germany in November 1936. When the Axis was joined by Fascist Italy one year later, the three powers set off the tragic conflagration of World War II.

QUESTIONS

1 Compare the responses of China and Japan to Western imperialism. Why were they different?
2 What was the role of Dr. Sun Yat-sen in modern Chinese history?
3 What effect did World War I have on China? On Japan?
4 Describe the Soviet Union's policy toward China in the 1920s.
5 What were the effects of the Mukden Incident?
6 What were the causes of World War II in Asia?

BIBLIOGRAPHY

MATTHEW, HELEN G. *Asia in the Modern World.* New York: Mentor, 1963. *A collection of essays concerning the history, culture, and contemporary problems of modern Asia. This book is a good introduction to Asian civilization.*

SEAGRAVE, STERLING. *The Song Dynasty.* New York: Harper & Row, 1985. *A scathing indictment of Chiang Kai-shek and his family, who are characterized as both power-hungry and corrupt.*

SPENCE, JONATHAN. *The Gate of Heavenly Peace: The Chinese and Their Revolution, 1895–1980.* New York: Viking Press, 1981. *This political history introduces the reader to many of the leading figures in the revolution, most of whom until now have been unfamiliar to Westerners. It is a readable scholarly monograph.*

STORRY, RICHARD. *A History of Modern Japan.* Harmondsworth, England: Penguin Books, 1968. *A useful brief survey of the span of Japanese history, with special emphasis upon 19th-century modernization and 20th-century developments.*

TERRILL, ROSS. *Mao: A Biography.* New York: Harper & Row, 1981. *A study of Mao's life, thought, and impact upon China.*

VON DER MEHDEN, FRED R. *South East Asia, 1930–1970.* New York: Norton, 1974. *A brief survey of the culture and history of the area.*

● *Cry Havoc, and let slip the dogs of war.*
WILLIAM SHAKESPEARE

World War II

Three nations, Germany, Italy, and Japan, unleashed their military power to bring on World War II. World War II was truly a global war—fought in Europe, Asia, Africa, and the islands of the Pacific. In reality it was two wars, one starting in 1937 in Asia, the second beginning in Europe with the German invasion of Poland in 1939. In terms of the scale of operations and numbers of troops thrown into the conflict, this war was unprecedented.

OPENING PHASES OF THE WAR Hitler's series of aggressive actions in the 1930s culminated in March 1939, when he moved to occupy the rest of Czechoslovakia. On April 7, 1939, the Italians invaded Albania, overrunning the country in a few days. These actions demonstrated the ineffectiveness of the policy of appeasement pursued by the democratic countries of Europe.

THE OUTBREAK OF THE WAR
Britain ended its policy of appeasement by giving guarantees of support to France, Poland, Rumania, and Greece, and by introducing national conscription (a draft) to build its armed forces. Both Britain and France made overtures to the Soviet Union in an effort to contain the Germans, but the negotiations went badly. As a condition of its alliance, the Soviet Union insisted upon the right to send its army into Poland and the eastern Baltic states. But the Poles, who were allied to both Britain and France, would not agree to this term, fearing that the Red Army might proceed to occupy their country.

The Nazi-Soviet Pact. Instead, the Soviet Union turned to Germany with an offer. Although Hitler's dream of *lebensraum* in the east seemed to aim toward conflict with Poland and Russia, he was willing to accept a pact to avoid a two-front war. Thus, in what had seemed an unthinkable action, Germany and the U.S.S.R. signed the *Nazi-Soviet Nonaggression Pact* on August 23, 1939.

By the terms of the ten-year pact, each side agreed to remain neutral in the event of the other's going to war. In a secret clause, Germany acknowledged the Soviet Union's sphere of influence in the Baltic area, including Finland, Estonia, Latvia, and Lithuania. By another secret clause, the two powers divided Poland: the eastern portion would go to the Soviet Union, and the western portion to Germany.

It was an insidious agreement, for each power received a green light from the other to expand at the expense of the countries that lay between them. It was a cynical pact as well, for each nation in the past had depicted the other as the primary enemy. Hitler had destroyed the German Communist Party, and had allied with Japan in the Anti-Comintern Pact, whose purpose was ostensibly to check the expansion of communism. Stalin, on his part, had often characterized Nazism as the implacable enemy of his Marxist state.

Although the clauses of the agreement regarding Poland were secret, the Western powers knew the pact was a prelude to Hitler's invasion of Poland. Hitler had frequently denounced the gains that Poland had made by the post-World War I settlement.

The Invasion of Poland. At 5 A.M. on September 1, 1939, Germany invaded Poland. To justify his action, Hitler claimed that the Polish army had attacked a German border installation. The invasion of about 1,700,000 men incorporated for the first time the strategy of *blitzkrieg*, or "lightning war." A coordinated attack of motorized infantry, tanks, artillery vehicles, and airplanes swept across the Polish border. Within days, the Polish army and its many cavalry units were destroyed, although the city of Warsaw held out for nearly four weeks. The speed, power, and success of the German invasion shocked the world.

Although Britain and France declared war on Germany on September 3, neither took advantage of a brief opportunity to assist Poland. On September 17th, Soviet troops entered Poland and occupied the eastern half of the country, as outlined in the secret pact with Germany made on September 1. On September 27, Warsaw surrendered to the Germans and fighting ceased.

In November 1939, the Soviet army invaded Finland. Expecting a pushover, they were at first thrown back by the Finns. It was not until March 1940 that Soviet troops controlled the country. In June, the Soviets took over the Baltic states of Estonia, Latvia, and Lithuania.

THE FIGHTING FOR FRANCE

The end of hostilities in Poland brought a six-month lull in the German attacks, a period known as the "phony war," or *sitzkrieg*. Some Europeans hoped that Hitler's appetite for conquest had been satisfied.

Invasion of Norway and Denmark. In fact, Hitler was only waiting for spring. On April 9, 1940, German naval and air forces attacked Norway. Although the Norwegians fiercely resisted, and some fighting continued into June, most German objectives had been reached by the end of April. The conquest of Norway provided German submarines with a staging area for attacks on British shipping, and key airfields from which the Luftwaffe could raid British cities.

On April 9, the German army had also invaded Denmark, which surrendered almost immediately. This conquest guaranteed ample supplies of food products, enabling the Germans to withstand a naval blockade imposed by the British.

Invasion of the Low Countries. Hitler next turned to the Low Countries—Belgium, Holland, and Luxemburg. On May 9, 1940, Hitler assured the governments that Germany had no designs on their territory. The next day the Nazi *blitzkrieg* struck. In an act of terror, the Luftwaffe demolished the city of Rotterdam, and Holland surrendered on May 14. Fighting in Belgium lasted longer because British and French troops were rushed to that country to try to stem the attack. Nonetheless, on May 26, the Belgian government was forced to capitulate.

The Fall of France. French military strategists, looking at German actions of World War I, had based the defense of France upon the Maginot Line, a string of elaborate fortifications along the eastern border. They believed that the Ardennes forest north of the fortifications was too densely wooded for

After dictating armistice terms to France at Compiègne, Hitler expressed his elation in a dance-step for the benefit of visiting journalists.

speedy movement of tanks and troops. They were proved wrong when German troops smashed through the Ardennes and rushed to the sea.

Over 350,000 British, French, and Belgian troops were pinned down on the beaches of Dunkirk. It was only by a heroic British effort, in which anything that floated was sent across the English Channel, that these troops were ferried to safety in Britain. The so-called "Miracle of Dunkirk" took place between May 26 and June 3.

On June 10, Hitler's ally, Italy, declared war on France and Britain and invaded southern France. On June 14, Paris fell and three days later, the newly elected French premier Henri Petain requested armistice terms. The French general Charles de Gaulle went to Britain, where he established a *Free French* government in exile and organized military forces to resist the Nazis.

On June 22, France signed an armistice with Germany. At Hitler's insistence, this signing took place in the same railroad car in which Germany had surrendered at the end of World War I. By the terms of the armistice, the German army occupied the northern three-fifths of France, including all coastal areas. In the southern portion of the country, a puppet state called *Vichy France* was established under the leadership of Henry Petain and Pierre Laval. This area was occupied by German troops in November 1942.

Petain, who had led French forces during the battle of Verdun in World War I, rationalized that by collaborating with the Nazis he could prevent harsh treatment of French citizens. But both he and Laval carried out Nazi policy. French civilians were conscripted to labor in German factories, and French Jews were rounded up and sent to concentration camps. At the end of the war, both leaders were labeled traitors.

The fall of France shocked the world. The ease of the German victory, the devastating effectiveness of the blitzkrieg, and the rapid collapse of French resistance were staggering. Still in alliance with the Soviet Union and Italy, Germany occupied most of western Europe. Britain stood alone.

THE BATTLE OF BRITAIN

In July 1940, Hitler issued the directive for the invasion of Britain, dubbed Operation Sea Lion, scheduled to be implemented in August. Although his admirals protested that they lacked adequate naval vessels, Hitler was determined to deal with Britain before turning eastward. For a brief period, Hitler hoped he could reach an accommodation with Britain, but he underestimated the tenacity of the new British prime minister, Winston Churchill (1874–1965), who had replaced Neville Chamberlain in May 1940. In the face of the Nazi threat, Churchill had said, "I have nothing to offer but blood, toil, tears, and sweat."[1] He spoke for the British people, who prepared themselves for the Nazi onslaught.

---

[1] Frank P. Chambers, *This Age of Conflict* (New York: Harcourt, Brace, 1962), p. 509.

On August 8, the commander of the Luftwaffe, Hermann Goering, launched the German air attack on Britain. With 2670 first-line planes the Luftwaffe outmatched the British Royal Air Force (RAF), which had only 1475 first-line aircraft. But Britain had the advantage of the recent development of radar, which could track incoming planes.

The Luftwaffe's bombing targets were southeast harbors, channel shipping, airfields, factories, and radar stations. When this tactic failed, Goering added daily raids on London in the hope of breaking British morale. In response, the RAF counterattacked with bombing missions against key German targets, including invasion barges, canals, aircraft, and armaments factories.

Despite Goering's boasts that the Luftwaffe would gain air supremacy, it never did. Because of the Luftwaffe's failure, Hitler postponed the invasion of Britain indefinitely. Of the few hundred British pilots, Churchill remarked, "Never in the field of human conflict was so much owed by so many to so few."[2]

THE INVASION OF THE SOVIET UNION

In the spring of 1941, Hitler's planned invasion of Russia was delayed by his desire to control the Balkans prior to the attack. The Germans invaded Yugoslavia on April 6, 1941, and won victory in 11 days. Simultaneously, Hitler invaded Greece, defeating that country by the end of April. However, the delay in the Balkans would prove fatal to the campaign to conquer the Soviet Union.

At 4 A.M. on June 22, 1941, 165 divisions of the German army—about three million men—poured into the Soviet Union along a 2000-mile front. One Russian described the effect of the blitzkrieg as follows:

• • • An endless stream of troop trains moved eastward, evacuating workers and equipment, stocks of grain, cattle, farm machinery, etc. The roads and railway junctions were crowded with refugees. Towns and villages, and factories, too, stood in flames behind the enemy lines.[3]

By September 1941, the German armies seemed within reach of their goal: they had reached the outskirts of the key cities of Leningrad and Moscow. But with the onset of winter, the invasion stalled, and in December, the Soviet army launched a counteroffensive. Hitler had failed to learn the lesson that the Russians had taught Napoleon in 1812: like Napoleon, he had failed to achieve a victory before the snows came.

Hitler's plan for 1942 was to take the city of Stalingrad on the Volga river. The campaign was launched in June, but as the Germans approached the city, their pace was slowed: Stalin was determined that the city named after him should not fall. On September 13, German forces broke into the city and fought their way to control of it. Through October and November, the fighting was fierce, and much of the city was reduced to rubble. In the middle of November, Russian General Georgi Zhukov brought up Russian reserves and surrounded the city. Hitler refused the request of his commanding general to try to attempt a breakout and retreat. After huge losses, the remainder of the German army surrendered at the end of January 1943.

Stalingrad was a colossal defeat for the Germans, both in loss of men and resources, and in psychological terms: it was the first time that Hitler had failed to attain his objective. Moreover, the German invasion of Russia triggered Allied assistance to the Russian war effort. In July 1941, Great Britain and the Soviet Union concluded a mutual aid treaty, and in October, a second document provided that Great Britain and the United States would provide war materials and financial credit to the U.S.S.R.

---

[2] Ibid., p. 518.

[3] Academy of Services of the U.S.S.R., Institute of History, A Short History of the U.S.S.R. (Moscow: Progress Publishers, 1965), pp. 213–14.

Inhabitants of Leningrad gather water from a broken main during the Germans' siege of the city. One of every three Leningraders died of starvation, while Stalingrad suffered even heavier casualties.

AMERICA ENTERS THE WAR

As the Nazi armies overran Europe in 1940 and 1941, the American government, led by President Roosevelt, modified its policy of neutrality. In September 1940, the draft was introduced. And in August of 1941, Roosevelt met secretly with Churchill aboard a naval vessel off the coast of Newfoundland. The two leaders issued the *Atlantic Charter* to enunciate their peace aims, including the principle that they sought no territorial conquests and intended to work for the freedom of all peoples after the war's end. This meeting marked the beginning of a close Anglo-American alliance which would continue throughout the war. Eventually, 26 governments accepted the aims of the Atlantic Charter in joining the *Grand Alliance*.

Pearl Harbor. America's support for Britain and Russia stopped short of military involvement until its hand was forced by Japanese aggression in Asia. There, the Japanese militarist government continued to strengthen its hold in China in an undeclared war that had been fought since 1937 (Chapter 23). In September 1940, Japan occupied French Indochina, triggering an American embargo on the sale of scrap iron and steel to Japan. That same month, Japan concluded a wartime alliance with Germany and Italy.

The Japanese viewed the United States Pacific fleet as the major obstacle in its goal of Asiatic dominance. Without warning, on December 7, 1941, the Japanese air force launched a simultaneous attack on the

HITLER'S EMPIRE AT ITS GREATEST EXTENT, NOVEMBER 1942
Based on the pattern of conquests shown here, was Hitler's policy based on the principle of lebensraum or world domination?

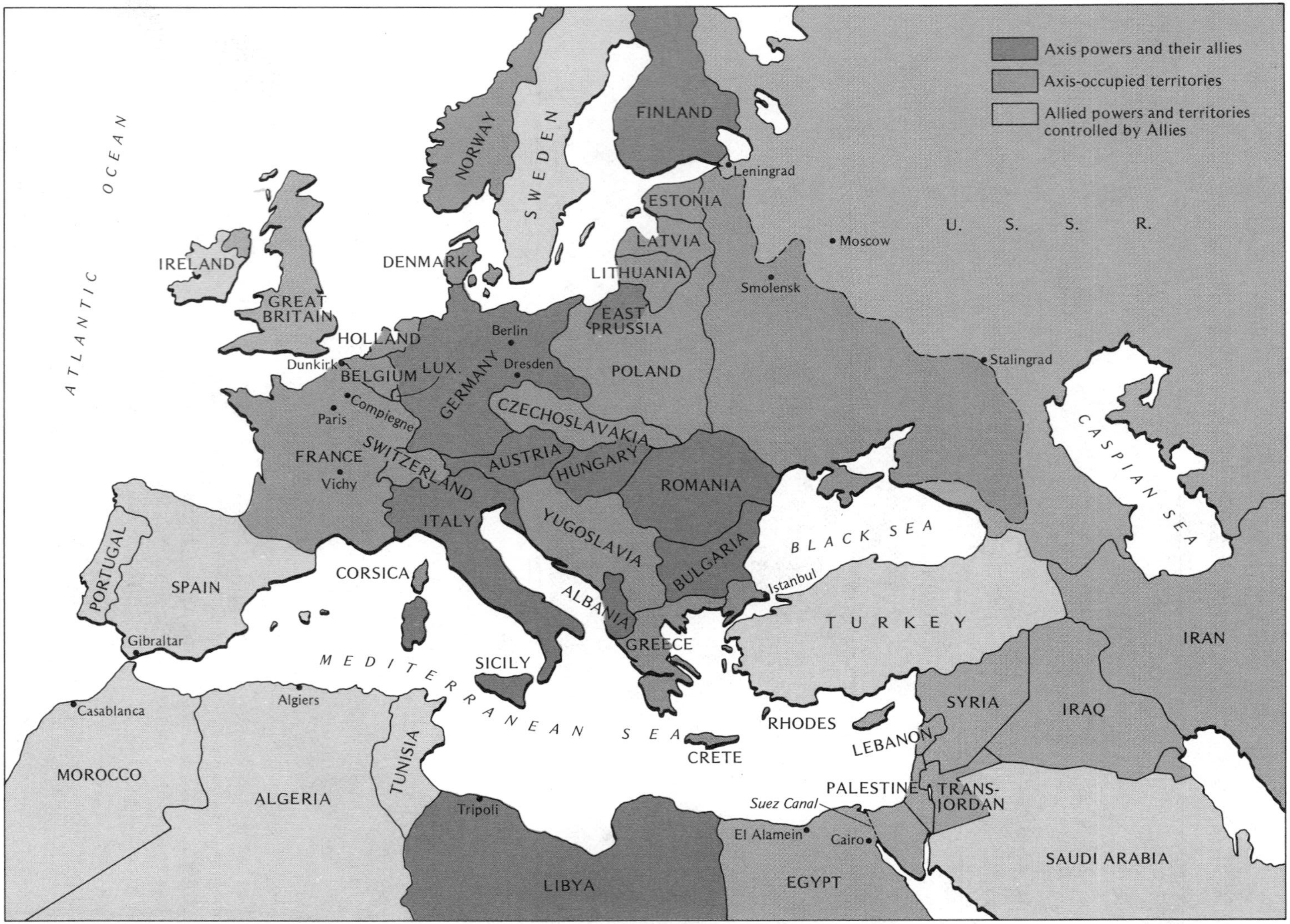

Legend:
- Axis powers and their allies
- Axis-occupied territories
- Allied powers and territories controlled by Allies

U. S. S. R.

CASPIAN SEA

IRAN

IRAQ

SAUDI ARABIA

SYRIA

TRANS-JORDAN

LEBANON

PALESTINE

RHODES

Cairo

EGYPT

Suez Canal

El Alamein

TURKEY

BLACK SEA

Istanbul

CRETE

Stalingrad

Moscow

Smolensk

Leningrad

FINLAND

ESTONIA

LATVIA

LITHUANIA

EAST PRUSSIA

POLAND

ROMANIA

BULGARIA

GREECE

ALBANIA

YUGOSLAVIA

HUNGARY

CZECHOSLOVAKIA

AUSTRIA

SWEDEN

NORWAY

DENMARK

Berlin

Dresden

GERMANY

SWITZERLAND

ITALY

SICILY

CORSICA

MEDITERRANEAN SEA

LIBYA

Tripoli

TUNISIA

ALGERIA

Algiers

MOROCCO

Casablanca

Gibraltar

SPAIN

PORTUGAL

FRANCE

Vichy

Paris

Compiègne

BELGIUM LUX.

HOLLAND

Dunkirk

GREAT BRITAIN

IRELAND

ATLANTIC OCEAN

A U.S. battleship suffers a direct hit at Pearl Harbor, December 7, 1941. Within a few days of the attack, the U.S. was fully committed to the war, both in Europe and in the Pacific.

United States fleet at Pearl Harbor, Hawaii, and on U.S. installations in the Philippines, Guam, and the Midway Islands. The Japanese also attacked the British possessions of Hong Kong and Malaya. The following day, December 8, the United States declared war on Japan. In his address to Congress requesting the declaration of war, President Roosevelt began:

• • • *Yesterday, December 7, 1941—a date which shall live in infamy—the United States of America was suddenly and deliberately attacked by the naval and air forces of the Empire of Japan. The United States was at peace with that nation and, at the solicitation of Japan was still in conversation with its government and its Emperor looking toward the maintenance of peace in the Pacific.*[4]

The surprise attack and loss of American lives galvanized American public opinion. On December 11, Germany declared war on

---

[4] James MacGregor Burns, *Roosevelt the Soldier of Freedom* (New York: Harcourt Brace Jovanovich, 1970), p. 165.

the United States, an act which enlarged the war into a worldwide conflict. American entry into the war supplied the Allies with the industrial capacity and manpower that they badly needed in order to continue the war.

Turning the Tide in the Pacific. Although the Japanese surprise attack was successful in its short-term objectives of acquiring bases in the western Pacific, it did not strike a fatal blow to America's Pacific navy, as Japan had intended. After the Japanese conquered Hong Kong, the Philippines, the Dutch East Indies, Burma, and Malaya, the Japanese navy steamed toward Australia and New Zealand, intending invasion and conquest of the British possessions. But the Japanese fleet was intercepted and stopped by Allied naval and air forces in May 1942. A month later, a Japanese naval loss at the Battle of Midway marked the turn of the tide in respect to Japanese control of the Pacific. In August 1942, the United States began a counteroffensive with the capture of the Solomon Islands.

After two years of hard fighting, U.S. and British Commonwealth troops had regained control of most of the Pacific islands and were within striking distance of Japan itself.

WAR IN THE WEST

In 1942, the United States responded to its allies' pleas to enter the European theater of operations. The Soviet Union, which was occupied with the defense of Stalingrad, expected the U.S. and Britain to invade France in order to remove some of the pressure from the eastern front. The Allies were not yet prepared for such an invasion, but they did launch an intensive bombing campaign against Germany itself. As a result of this bombing, which continued throughout the war, 50 German cities were devastated; 300,000 German civilians were killed, and nearly a million rendered homeless.

FIGHTING IN NORTH AFRICA

While the Battle of Britain was raging in the west, Italian troops moved into Egypt. British forces were sent to repel the Italians, and in February 1941 they pushed the Italians back to their colonies in Libya and East Africa. Hitler, alarmed at the Italian defeat, sent one of the Reich's finest generals, Erwin Rommel, to North Africa with a body of crack German troops who became known as the *Afrika Korps*. Under Rommel's general-

ship, the British were forced back into Egypt. Throughout 1941 and early 1942, the two armies see-sawed back and forth across the Libyan-Egyptian border. The campaign was seen as vital, for if Rommel succeeded in conquering Egypt, the Germans would control the Suez Canal.

In June 1942, Rommel's forces reached the town of El Alamein in Egypt. Britain and the United States sent troops to reinforce the British line. When Rommel launched a major attack on August 31, the British general Bernard Montgomery managed to hold his ground. Other German attacks failed, and on October 23, Montgomery began a counterattack that eventually forced Rommel back to Tripoli and Tunisia.

In November 1942, an Anglo-American amphibious force landed in Morocco and Algeria, and within months had seized control of the entire North African coast, freeing the Mediterranean for Allied shipping and exposing Italy to invasion.

The invasion of Italy began in June 1943 with an Allied landing in Sicily, followed by an assault on the Italian peninsula. In those circumstances, the Italians overthrew Mus-

British troops approach a German stronghold near El Alamein, Egypt. The desert campaign was seen as critical to the Allied war effort.

solini's government, and in September Italy surrendered. German troops rescued Mussolini and moved into northern Italy to defend against the northward advance of the Allies. In April 1945, Italian partisans who were fighting with the Allies captured Mussolini and shot him.

VICTORY IN EUROPE

Worldwide, the tide of war had turned by mid-1943. The victories at Midway, Stalingrad, and El Alamein had shown that the Axis war machine was not invulnerable. By early 1944, the Axis powers were on the defensive everywhere.

ORGANIZING FOR VICTORY

Even more than in World War I, contributions by civilians in what was known as "the home front" were vital to the war effort. Industry, science, and agriculture had become vital parts of modern warfare. All the warring nations put their production facilities on a war basis.

In Germany Albert Speer planned industrial production, using Slavs, Jews, and other "inferior" peoples as slave labor. But Hitler was not as interested in the industrial and scientific plans as he was in the search for a military or technological breakthrough that would guarantee a quick victory. He devoted money toward rocket research in the hope of defeating Britain from the air. Indeed V-1 and V-2 rockets were developed and used by the Germans during the Battle of Britain, but were never produced in sufficient quantity to become a major factor.

The Allies' greatest asset was the industrial strength of the United States. U.S. factories supplied not only their own troops, but also those of Russia, Britain, China, and the other Allies. From about 1943, the Germans and Japanese suffered crippling losses that their factories could not replace. But U.S. industries continued to operate at full strength and served, in Franklin Roosevelt's phrase, as the "arsenal of democracy."

Scientific research produced countless developments that were part of the Allied victory. New types of textiles, more accurate bombsights, and such wonder drugs as penicillin all contributed to the war effort. The most spectacular development—with enormous consequences for the postwar world—was the development of the atomic bomb. At the urging of the German refugee scientist Albert Einstein, President Roosevelt ordered a crash program called the *Manhattan Project* to build a nuclear weapon. Though some of the scientists working on it privately expressed doubts about the possible consequences of their work, they believed in the necessity of eradicating the evil of Nazism.

THE SECOND FRONT

In early June of 1944, American General Dwight Eisenhower, commander of Operation Overlord, gave the order for the D-Day invasion of Europe to begin. For months, troops had been assembled at secret sites in Britain in preparation for the attack. At 2 A.M. on June 6, paratroopers landed on the beaches of Normandy in France. Four and one-half hours later, the tanks and troops landed. By the end of the day, a beachhead had been established in Hitler's Europe. Ironically, General Rommel, now in command of the troops assembled to ward off the expected invasion, had left the area, feeling that bad weather would make a landing impossible.

By June 26, the port of Cherbourg was taken, enabling supplies to be landed. On August 5, a second Allied landing in southern France took place. The Allies entered Paris on August 25, and swept through occupied France toward Germany.

The Generals' Plot. In the wake of the Allied success, some German generals believed that defeat was now inevitable. Hoping to surrender before Germany was devastated, several top officers plotted to assassinate Hitler. In July 1944, Colonel Klaus von Stauffenberg placed a briefcase containing a bomb

By July 1944, Hitler's capital city of Berlin lay in ruins, and German armies were on the defensive throughout Europe.

under a conference table where Hitler stood. The subsequent explosion killed several of those present, but Hitler was only slightly wounded. Most of the plotters, including Stauffenberg, were caught and executed.

Closing the Ring. By the autumn of 1944, Allied troops had entered parts of Germany. On October 21, Aachen fell; by November, Metz and Strausbourg were in Allied hands. The Germans launched a counteroffensive in December, and succeeded in breaking a hole in the Allied lines when bad weather kept the Allied air support from flying. Because the German advance produced a bulge in the line, this episode is known as the Battle of the Bulge. When the weather cleared, air support helped to halt the German advance, and the American general George S. Patton led tank divisions to the rescue.

General Eisenhower directed the advance toward the German fortifications called the Siegfried Line. It took four weeks of fighting before the Allies broke the line and advanced to the Rhine River. With the Ruhr valley in Allied hands by April, the center of German industrial might was denied the Third Reich.

The Russian Front. On the eastern front, Soviet forces began the final offensive in early summer of 1944; by August, the Russians were on the outskirts of the Polish capital of Warsaw. With their apparent rescuers so near, the Poles within the city began a rebellion against the German occupying force. But the Russian army failed to enter the city and join them. For two months the Poles fought alone. Only after Polish resistance was broken by the Germans did the Russians take the city. This cruel policy was intentional, for Stalin's government planned to establish a communist regime in Poland after the war, and wanted to eliminate any Polish resistance to it.

Hitler's Defeat. By the spring of 1945, Allied armies drew near to Berlin from both west and east. In April, the Russian general Georgi Zhukov began an assault on the German capital. Hitler ordered Germans to fight to the death of the last man. Fighting raged from block to block with German civilians—some old men, some as young as 12—and soldiers battling to hold the city.

On April 18, the Russian and American troops linked up at the Elbe River. Allied forces had stopped there, awaiting the Russian conquest of Berlin, as had been decided previously by the Allies.

As Berlin crumbled, Hitler was hiding in a bunker below the chancellery. With Russian troops just blocks away, he committed suicide on April 30. His mistress Eva Braun died with him, as well as his faithful propagandist Joseph Goebbels and his family.

The next day, May 1, it was announced to the German people that Hitler had died in defense of his country. Hitler's death ended most German resistance. At last, on May 7, 1945, the German government under the provisional leadership of Admiral Karl Doenitz surrendered unconditionally to the Allied forces. The war in Europe was over.

THE HOLOCAUST

As Allied troops advanced through Europe, they discovered the terrible deeds of the Third Reich. Concentration camps in towns whose names would haunt the world held emaciated prisoners who had been used as slave labor or subjects of bizarre medical research. The camps were piled high with corpses of Jews and other victims of the Nazi doctrine of racial supremacy.

In 1942, the outright murder of Jews had begun with Hitler's adoption of "the final solution to the Jewish problem," bureaucratic jargon for genocide. The death camps—Dachau, Auschwitz, Bergen-Belsen, and Buchenwald—horrified the world.

The camp commander at Auschwitz explained the final solution at his postwar trial:

• • • The "final solution" of the Jewish question means the complete extermination of all Jews in Europe. I was ordered to establish extermination facilities at Auschwitz in June 1941. . . . I estimate that at least 2,500,000 victims were executed and exterminated there by gassing and burning, and at least another half-million succumbed to starvation and disease.[5]

The precise death toll of the "final solution" can not be known, but many experts put the Jewish victims at six million. In addition, Hitler murdered at least six million other people who resisted his regime or were identified as being of "inferior" race.

[5] T. L. Jarman, *The Rise and Fall of Nazi Germany* (New York: Signet Books, 1956), p. 276.

As Allied armies proceeded across Europe, the full horror of the Nazi concentration and death camps was revealed to the world. In April 1945, a grim General Eisenhower and troops under his command toured a camp in Gotha, Germany.

The atomic bomb produced a devastation never before experienced. A view of central Nagasaki after the explosion reveals its force: all buildings and their inhabitants have been obliterated.

THE END OF THE WAR IN ASIA

In the Pacific, the United States pursued an island-hopping strategy, capturing key Pacific islands step by step. A major turning point occurred in August 1944, when the U.S. conquest of the Mariana Islands put its air force in range for bombing attacks on the Japanese home islands. From that point on, U.S. B-29 Superfortresses pounded Japan.

With the end of the war in Europe, the United States prepared for its final defeat of Japan. The March 1945 firebombing of Tokyo incinerated a major part of the city and killed at least 100,000 people. As intensive bombing raids of Japanese cities continued, the Allies prepared invasion plans, estimated to involve two million troops and thousands of casualties. On July 26, 1945, the U.S., Great Britain, and China demanded that Japan surrender unconditionally, but the Japanese failed to respond.

Unknown to all but a few, the United States was in the final stages of developing the atomic bomb. Without prior warning, the U.S. bomber, the *Enola Gay*, dropped an atomic bomb on the Japanese city of Hiroshima on August 6, 1945, killing thousands of people and obliterating the central areas of the city. Two days later, the Soviet Union declared war on Japan. On August 9, the U.S. dropped a second bomb on Nagasaki, bringing a Japanese offer to surrender.

On August 14, Japan accepted unconditional surrender terms; the formal document was signed on September 2, 1945. The most extensive and destructive war humankind had ever experienced was ended at last, six years and one day after it began. Worldwide joy and exaltation followed, but in retrospect, the ominous mushroom cloud of the atomic bomb hovered not only over the cities of Hiroshima and Nagasaki but over the rest of the world as well.

THE BIG THREE

Many of the most important decisions of the war were made by the leaders of the Soviet Union, Britain, and the United States, known as the *Big Three*. The decisions made at the conferences they attended would have a major effect on the postwar world.

THE TEHERAN CONFERENCE, 1943

Cooperation among the Allies was apparent at Teheran, Iran, in November 1943, when Churchill, Roosevelt, and Stalin met in conference for the first time. Although primarily occupied with planning war strategy, the three signed a declaration expressing their spirit of cooperation and their determination to work for a lasting peace once hostilities had ended. But the source of future conflict was already present, for the war had brought about a number of territorial changes. The apparent spirit of cooperation was made possible by an agreement between Stalin and Roosevelt to wait until the war's end to discuss territorial resettlements. Churchill had opposed this decision—pressing for an early discussion of boundary issues—but he was outvoted by the other two.

THE YALTA CONFERENCE, FEBRUARY 1945

Stalin, Churchill, and Roosevelt met again at Yalta, a seaside town in the Crimea, from February 4 to 11, 1945. The end of the war in Europe was in sight, and the three leaders began to grapple with the question of Germany's future. This issue was obviously a highly charged one for all those who had survived the war: in the view of many people, Germany had to be prevented from rising from defeat ever again. The three leaders reached two significant decisions concerning Germany's future. First, they agreed that Germany should be disarmed, demilitarized,

The "Big Three"—Winston Churchill, Franklin Roosevelt, and Joseph Stalin—met at Yalta in February 1945 to settle the issues of postwar boundaries and economic recovery.

and dismembered. Secondly, the conditions of peace were to include Germany's payment of $20 billion in reparations, in the form of equipment from existing German industries and annual deliveries of goods. Fifty percent of these reparations were to go to the U.S.S.R. in compensation for the losses it had suffered during the German invasion of 1941.

The war with Japan was also discussed at Yalta. Though the U.S.S.R. was party to a neutrality pact with Japan, Stalin did not intend to honor this agreement. Instead, he promised to enter the Pacific war on the Allied side within three months after the European war ended. In return, the Soviets were given territory that the Japanese had acquired in 1905 as a result of the Russo-Japanese War. These territories included the southern half of Sakhalin Island, the Kurile Islands, and Port Arthur. In addition, two Chinese railroads were to be placed under joint Soviet-Chinese companies, and the Soviet Union and China were to conclude a pact of friendship and alliance. These terms relating to China were reached without consultation with Chiang Kai-shek, the leader of the Chinese Nationalist government.

Critics of the Yalta agreements have castigated Roosevelt for his concurrence in the clauses which strengthened the Soviet position in Asia. Defenders of the president respond that, at the time, it was estimated that the final defeat of Japan would cost many thousands of American casualties. Thus, the promise of Soviet assistance was seen as a vital factor in the concluding battles of the Pacific war. Although Russian participation did not contribute to the final victory in the Pacific—the war was instead ended through the deployment of the atomic bomb—the Yalta agreement enabled the Russian army to enter Manchuria and to share in the division of Korea.

ESTABLISHING THE UNITED NATIONS

At Yalta, the Allies agreed to send envoys to San Francisco, California on April 25, 1945 to establish the United Nations Organization as a successor to the League of Nations. In the succeeding months, a basic framework for the organization was agreed upon. As was the case in the League of Nations, the new organization was to have an Assembly in which all nations were represented. In addition, a Security Council was created to deal with substantive decisions. This council was to have 11 members, of which five— the U.S., the U.S.S.R., Great Britain, France, and Nationalist China—were permanent, and would each possess a veto power.

THE POTSDAM CONFERENCE, JULY–AUGUST 1945

The Yalta Conference was the last meeting of Churchill, Stalin, and Roosevelt. At the next meeting, held at Potsdam, Germany, in July 1945, Stalin was the only remaining member of the original Big Three. Harry Truman had succeeded Franklin Roosevelt, who died of a stroke in April. A few days after the conference began, Churchill was defeated in the British general election and replaced by the new prime minister, Clement Attlee.

At this juncture, Germany had surrendered, and the Soviet army was occupying all of eastern Europe, including East Germany. The new postwar allies—Britain, France, and the United States—were each occupying zones of West Germany. The four powers were able to agree on these temporary occupation zones, but never reached agreement in regard to permanent borders. In Romania and Poland, the Soviets established local communist governments in power, and wanted them to be formally recognized. This the allies refused to do, since free elections had not been held. In Germany, the allies were willing to withdraw their occupation troops once elections had been held, but the U.S.S.R. would not relinquish its control of East Germany. Thus, the question of a settlement for Germany remained unresolved.

SUMMARY

World War II was the most destructive war in human history. At war's end, the cities of Germany and Japan were reduced to rubble. Both Europe and Asia were in chaos. The population losses reached staggering proportions. In Europe, 6 million Jews had been murdered by the Nazis, and 19 million military personnel and nearly 15 million civilians had died in combat. In Asia and the Pacific the dead numbered over 5 million military and nearly 16 million civilians. The combined losses reached nearly 54 million dead. Of those, nearly 20 million were Russians, and 7 million Germans. Countless others were wounded or homeless. After the war, millions of refugees struggled to return to their homelands. In liberated countries like France, Holland, and Belgium, the population was often divided by the effects of enemy occupation, and those who had resisted hunted down those who had collaborated with the enemy.

QUESTIONS

1 What were the underlying causes of the war in Europe?
2 What was the effect of the Nazi-Soviet Nonagression Pact? Why would the U.S.S.R. enter into such an agreement?
3 Why did the French offer so little resistance to the Germany army?
4 What were the war aims of Germany? Of Italy? Of Japan?
5 What agreements were reached by the Allies during the war? On what issues did they fail to come to a decision?
6 Compare the organization and goals of the League of Nations and the United Nations.

BIBLIOGRAPHY

CALVOCORESSI, PETER and GUY WINT. Total War: Causes and Courses of the Second World War. Harmondsworth, England: Penguin, 1979. A long monograph full of details about the battles, the strategies, and the politics of the war.

LIFTON, R. J. Death in Life: Survivors of Hiroshima. New York: Random House, 1967. A psychologist's study of the survivors of the atomic bombing of Hiroshima; their physical and psychological lives.

PLIEVIER, THEODORE. Stalingrad. New York: Time, Inc., 1966. An account from the perspective of the defenders of Stalingrad details the events that led to one of the turning points of the war.

SABUREO, IENAGA. The Pacific War: World War II and the Japanese. New York: Pantheon, 1980. A monograph by a Japanese historian who lived through the war years. The author's primary purpose in this work was to enlighten Japanese readers concerning the government's fascistic policies, and to warn them against a recurrence.

SCHOENFELD, MAXWELL P. Sir Winston Churchill: His Life and Times. Hinsdale, Ill.: Dryden Press, 1973. This brief biography gives the reader a sense of the great man who led his nation during the critical days of World War II.

TOLAND, JOHN. The Rising Sun. New York: Random House, 1970. A detailed popular history of the war in the Pacific for those who like to read about battles.

URIS, LEON. Exodus. New York: Doubleday, 1958. This novel describes the creation of Israel by the Jewish survivors of Hitler's Europe.

WEINBERG, GERHARD L. World in the Balance: Behind the Scenes of World War II. Hanover, N. H. and London: University Press of New England, 1981. Of particular interest in this work is the discussion of Hitler's misunderstanding of American attitudes and policies.

UNIT LVI

The Post-War World

● *You cannot shake hands with a clenched fist.*
INDIRA GANDHI

● *Today every inhabitant of this planet must contemplate the day when this planet may no longer be habitable. Every man, woman and child lives under a nuclear sword of Damocles, hanging by the slenderest of threads, capable of being cut at any moment by accident or miscalculation or madness.*

JOHN F. KENNEDY

● *God said this is our land, land in which we flourish as a people. . . . We want our cattle to get fat on our land so that our children grow up in prosperity; and we do not want the fat removed to feed others.*

JOMO KENYATTA

● *Politics is war without bloodshed; war is politics with bloodshed.*
MAO TSE-TUNG

● *If peace, he thought (as he had often thought before), only had the music and pageantry of war, there'd be no more wars.*

SOPHIE KERR

● We look with confidence to the day when all the peoples of the world may live full lives untouched by tyranny and according to their varying desires and their own consciences.

THE TEHERAN CONFERENCE

25

The Soviet Union and the United States in the Postwar World

The death, damage, and dislocations of World War II changed human society unalterably. Out of the ashes of the war arose new nations, new alliances, and new enemies. Among other effects was the destruction of the prewar balance of power. The traditional role of Europe as a dominant power in world affairs, both politically and economically, had been shattered. Into this power vacuum stepped the two major victors of the war— the United States and the Soviet Union— who, in the process of reconstructing the world, emerged as the postwar *superpowers*.

Together with their allies, the United States and the Soviet Union have dominated the world in the subsequent decades. These superpowers have been engaged in an ideological struggle which has had an impact upon every nation of the world. For the Soviet Union, Marxist ideology, by now considerably modified, has mandated the exportation of Soviet-style socialism and with it Soviet influence. The United States, too, has abandoned its prewar policy of isolationism and developed a commitment to international leadership. In its role as the world's most powerful democracy, the U.S.

has sought to support and inspire other democratic nations.

The relationship between the two superpowers in the postwar period can be divided into four stages: the *Cold War*, from 1945 to 1956; the *Thaw*, when Soviet leaders announced a policy of peaceful coexistence, 1956–1964; *Détente*, a period when tensions were relaxed, from 1964 to 1980; and the *Chill*, a period of renewed tension, from 1980 to the present.

THE COLD WAR   The term *Cold War* was first used by the journalist Walter Lippmann to describe the period between 1945 and 1956, when the superpowers seemed on the brink of war, a prospect more terrifying than ever before with the advent of nuclear weapons.

Almost as soon as victory over Nazi Germany was achieved, the Grand Alliance, crafted by the western Allies and the Soviet Union and implemented through conferences of its leaders, had begun to crumble. By the time of the Potsdam meeting in July 1945, the necessity of maintaining a united military front had all but disappeared. Allied harmony was replaced by an atmosphere of mutual distrust and suspicion as the Soviet Union and the western Allies jockeyed for power in Europe and maneuvered to carve out their own spheres of influence.

EARLY FRICTION BETWEEN THE SUPERPOWERS

In the opinion of many historians, the Cold War began at the Potsdam conference. From the point of view of the Western allies, the decision taken at the conference to postpone territorial settlements until the war had ended proved to be a mistake. Victory over Germany put Soviet troops in occupation of all of eastern Europe, including more than one-third of Germany. A new era of imperialism by the Soviet Union had begun.

Although the West had exacted vague agreements from the Soviet Union on self-determination for the peoples of Europe— particularly free elections in Poland—the Western allies had not been able to loosen the Soviet hold on eastern Europe. Determined to create a buffer area to protect its western borders and with a puppet state firmly in place in Poland, the Soviet Union saw little need to make concessions to Western ideas of democracy.

For their part, the Western allies, in particular the United States, became convinced that cooperation was no longer possible and that a tough stance was the only approach to the spread of Soviet power. Thus, the conflicting interests and goals of the two sides split the alliance. Instead, two competing superpowers emerged, each determined to follow its own path of self-interest. In his famous "Iron Curtain" speech in March 1946, Winston Churchill acknowledged the division of Europe into East and West:

● ● ● *Nobody knows what Soviet Russia and its Communist international organization intends to do in the immediate future, or what are the limits, if any, to their expansive and proselytising tendencies. . . . From Stettin in the Baltic to Trieste in the Adriatic, an Iron Curtain has descended across the Continent. Behind that line lie all the capitals of the ancient states of Central and Eastern Europe . . . in what I must call the Soviet Sphere, and all are subject in one form or another, not only to Soviet influence but to a very high and, in many cases, increasing measure of control from Moscow.[1]*

Prior to World War II, only one nation, the U.S.S.R., had adopted communism, although communist movements existed in several countries, including China and Indochina. Today more than half the world is under some form of Marxist rule. Some of the explanation for the rapid spread of communism can be found in the events immediately following the war. Between 1945 and 1949, the Soviet Union seized political control of all of eastern Europe, putting into power pro-Russian regimes in Poland, Czechoslovakia, Albania, Romania, Bulgaria, Hungary, and East Germany. In Yugoslavia, Marshal Tito's communist party independently installed a Marxist government.

The Truman Doctrine. This rapid spread of communist power, Russian threats toward Turkey, and the civil war in Greece between communists and noncommunists led President Harry Truman to adopt the policy of *containment*, the idea that Soviet expansionism could be checked or "contained" in places where it threatened democracy. The policy of containment was enunciated through the Truman Doctrine, which the President promulgated in 1947:

● ● ● *I believe that it must be the policy of the United States to support free peoples who are resisting attempted subjugation by armed minorities or outside pressures.[2]*

Under the Truman Doctrine, the United States provided $400 million in aid to Tur-

---

[1] Charles L. Mee, Jr., *Meeting at Potsdam* (New York: M. Evans & Co., 1975), pp. 301–02.

[2] Richard Current, *American History: A Survey*, 4th ed. (New York: Knopf, 1975), p. 750.

In a speech before a joint session of Congress, President Truman proposed a new policy of containing communism by offering economic aid to struggling democratic nations.

key and Greece and thus prevented communist takeovers.

Soon the Truman Doctrine was extended to the rest of Europe in the form of the European Recovery Program (ERP), also referred to as the Marshall Plan, because it was initially proposed and drawn up by George Marshall, Truman's secretary of state. As Marshall stated: "Our policy is not directed against any country or doctrine, but against hunger, poverty, desperation and chaos." In providing aid to 16 western European nations, the Marshall Plan not only bolstered Europe's economic recovery but also helped restore stability. Marshall regarded this stability as "the emergence of political and social conditions in which free institutions can exist."[3] The plan, which was in effect from December 1947 to 1953, cost the United States $20 billion.

Berlin Blockade. The Western allies and the Soviet Union could reach no real accord on Germany's future. The Soviets were determined to see a divided Germany that would never again pose a threat to Russia's

[3] Jack Sproat, Richard Curry, Kenyon C. Cramer, *The Shaping of America* (New York: Holt, Rinehart and Winston, 1972), p. 669.

borders. The United States wanted a revived, economically sound, and democratic Germany. Although discussions on Germany's future continued through 1947, it was apparent that the disagreements were irreconcilable. The Soviets proceeded to strip their eastern zone of its industrial power, while the Western allies focused their attention on building up West Germany's economy.

The conflict over Germany's future widened with the Soviet Union's imposition of the *Berlin Blockade*. The blockade represented one of the critical episodes of the Cold War. At the Potsdam conference, the Western powers had been assigned sectors of Berlin to administer, even though the city was totally within the Soviet zone. In January 1948, the Soviets began a gradual blockade of the city to prevent Allied entrance to their zones. The Western response was an airlift—"Operation Vittles"—to supply the needs of the two million inhabitants of the western zones. The United States airlifted one million tons of cargo before the Soviets ended the blockade in April 1949. Some historians have observed that Stalin backed off finally not because the airlift was so successful but because he decided that the United States, which had sent some atomic bombers to England, would go to war to preserve its control in Germany.

Two Germanies. In September 1948, at the height of the crisis, a constituent assembly of 65 delegates from the three western zones met at Bonn under the leadership of Konrad Adenauer to draw up the Basic Law, a provisional constitution for West Germany. This constitution was adopted in May 1949 when the Federal Republic of Germany was proclaimed. The Basic Law begins with a declaration of rights, comparable to the American Bill of Rights, and establishes a parliamentary democracy.

After the blockade was lifted, the eastern (Soviet) zone followed suit by setting up its own government. In May 1949, the Communist Party in the Soviet zone of occupa-

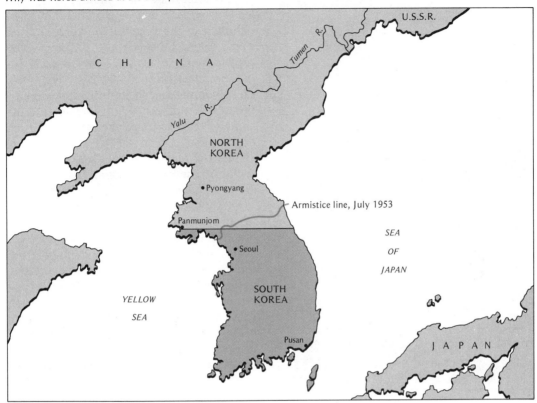

tion provided the voters a list of candidates for a "people's congress" which subsequently adopted a constitution "for the whole of Germany." The German Democratic Republic (GDR) was proclaimed in October 1949. Thus, the wartime Allies' inability to reach a settlement culminated in the establishment of two Germanies.

THE KOREAN WAR

The resolution of the German problem did not, however, end the Cold War. It was in fact only an event in a series of conflicts, one of which turned to actual battle. The world was again brought to the brink of world war in 1950 with the outbreak of fighting in Korea.

Background. Korea had been under Japanese domination since the Sino-Japanese War of 1894–95, and the victorious allies at the end of World War II agreed to a temporary military occupation. The U.S.S.R. was to occupy the territory north of the 38th parallel, and the U.S. the area to the south. Attempts at a permanent settlement foundered in December 1945, and gradually each occupying power allowed the emergence of separate governments.

In late 1946, a South Korean legislature assembled and took over the government, while the United States continued to provide advisers and financial aid. At the same time, a Russian-trained and -aided communist party established a government in North Korea. What had been intended as a temporary military occupation had by 1947 evolved into a creation of two semi-independent states.

Soldiers advance toward an enemy position in Korea. Although the war was fought with conventional weapons, 200,000 Koreans were killed and 5 million were rendered homeless during the year of fighting.

crossed the 38th parallel, claiming that South Korea had attacked first. Since the United Nations had supervised the establishment of the Republic of Korea, its Security Council met the next day and voted (in the absence of the U.S.S.R.) that the fighting should cease. When the directive failed, the UN implemented its police powers. Although 15 nations sent token forces, the United States assumed the primary burden of the war.

The UN forces were put under the command of American General Douglas MacArthur. Quickly, the fighting spread across Korea; at one stage, the Northern forces captured the Southern capital at Seoul. At another juncture, UN forces reached the Yalu River, the boundary between Korea and China. At that point, the Chinese Communist government intervened with 200,000 "volunteer" forces, and forced the UN army south of the 38th parallel. In July 1951, truce negotiations began, and two years later, in July 1953, a truce was finally signed, restoring the status quo of before the war, that is, two Koreas divided at the 38th parallel.

ATTEMPTS AT ARMS CONTROL

The Korean War represented the peak of tensions in the Cold War, a confrontation made more ominous by the possibility of nuclear war. As a step toward preventing the spread of nuclear power, the General Assembly of the United Nations in 1947 established the Atomic Energy Commission (AEC) to propose international control of atomic energy. The American statesman Bernard Baruch proposed to the UN a plan which included the creation of an International Atomic Development Authority (IADA) with absolute control over the use of atomic energy and with power to supervise peaceful, scientific, and economic uses of the atom. Although accepted by the General Assembly, the Baruch Plan was vetoed in the Security Council by the Soviet Union. The U.S.S.R. viewed an inspection system as interference in its in-

In an effort at reconciliation, the United Nations agreed to send a commission to Korea to assist in the formation of a government for all of Korea. When North Korea refused to cooperate, a constituent assembly was elected in the South. In May 1948, the South adopted a constitution and in June, Syngman Rhee was elected president of the Republic of Korea. In December 1948, the United Nations recognized this government as the only legitimate government of Korea, and the United States announced a three-year $300 million aid program.

The communist regime of North Korea responded by proclaiming the Democratic Peoples Republic of Korea, which also claimed authority for all of Korea.

The Korean War. War broke out on June 24, 1950, when the North Korean army

ternal affairs, and insisted on the right to veto any IADA actions.

In August 1949, the U.S.S.R. exploded its first atomic weapon. In response, President Truman early in 1950 introduced a crash program for the development of the more powerful hydrogen bomb, first successfully tested by the U.S. in November 1952. In June 1953, the U.S.S.R. tested its first hydrogen bomb. This segment of the arms race occurred during the same years as the Korean War, contributing to worldwide tensions between 1950 and 1953. The fear that conventional warfare could escalate to a nuclear conflict terrified many citizens of the world. Both superpowers, however, exercised restraint, even as the nuclear race between them intensified. By June 1953, each side had arrived at the potential to destroy the other, and subsequent stockpiling of weapons is now a matter of overkill—each side now having the potential to destroy the other at least 25 times over again.

THE THAW The end of the Korean War coincided with the beginning of the end of the Cold War, for Joseph Stalin died in March 1953. On March 9 he was eulogized, and several months later his embalmed corpse, outfitted in a military uniform, was laid to rest open to public viewing next to Lenin's in the marble tomb in Red Square. Stalin's death ushered in a new era of relations between the superpowers.

THE EMERGENCE OF KHRUSHCHEV

One of the flaws of the Soviet regime is that it has no mechanism for orderly succession of power. For the next three years, the various rivals to succeed Stalin jockeyed for power behind the scenes. One of them was the head of the secret police, Lavrenti Beria, who attempted to seize power forcibly and was shot in December 1953. The ultimate victor of the power struggle, Nikita Khrushchev (1894–1971), emerged triumphant by the same method Stalin had used in the

1920s—seizing control of the Communist Party. Acquiring the position of first secretary in the party in 1953, Khrushchev had placed his own supporters in positions of authority throughout its structure, and by 1956 was in control. Since the Soviet Union has only one legal political party, he then controlled the government as well.

De-Stalinization. The first indication that Khrushchev had won the power struggle came in February 1956 when he addressed the 20th congress of the Communist Party and bitterly denounced Stalin. In his "de-Stalinization" speech, Khrushchev detailed the dictator's crimes, including mass repression and terror, errors in Stalin's conduct of the war, and "the cult of personality" Stalin had erected around himself. This extraordinary speech signaled the end of the first stage of the postwar period of international relations, and introduced the second stage, the *Thaw* between the superpowers.

Peaceful Coexistence. De-Stalinization was closely linked in Khrushchev's speech with a new policy of *peaceful coexistence* with the Western powers. The policy did not mean a change in the ultimate aim of international victory for the communist movement. It meant instead a change in tactics. As Khrushchev described it:

• • • We communists, we Marxist-Leninists, believe that progress is on our side and victory will inevitably be ours. Yet the capitalists won't give an inch and still swear to fight to the bitter end. Therefore how can we talk of peaceful coexistence with capitalist ideology? Peaceful coexistence among different systems of government is possible, but peaceful coexistence among different ideologies is not.[4]

In Khrushchev's new policy of peaceful coexistence, war with the capitalist West was to be avoided, replaced by the peaceful strug-

---

[4] Edward Crankshaw, ed., *Khrushchev Remembers* (Boston: Little, Brown, 1970), p. 512.

The events of Nikita Khrushchev's term in office included the building of the Berlin Wall, the launching of Sputnik, and the Cuban missile crisis. In retrospect, the Khrushchev era was seen as a period of liberalization.

gle of ideas. Although this speech was intended for the inner circles of the party, the details of the text leaked to the rest of the world.

Liberalization. One reason for Khrushchev's change in policy was his desire to introduce reforms within the Soviet Union to eliminate the clumsiness and waste of the bureaucracy. He embarked on a program of reforming industry and agriculture, and of developing science and technology. Under his leadership Soviet industry grew by 70 percent; the first artificial satellite, *Sputnik*, was launched; and an unmanned satellite reached the moon, marking the beginning of the race in outer space. Khrushchev encouraged the production of consumer goods, and prodded the Soviet construction industry into better and faster ways of building. Cultural exchanges were fostered, and Soviet

society became somewhat more relaxed and liberalized.

Symbolic of this new liberalization of the dictatorship was the publication in the Soviet Union of Alexandr Solzhenitsyn's *One Day in the Life of Ivan Denisovich*. This book describes life in a Stalin-era slave labor camp. Also published in the Soviet Union in the 1950s was Vladimir Dudintsev's *Not by Bread Alone*, an attack on the effects of bureaucracy. On the other hand, when Boris Pasternak won the 1958 Nobel Prize for his novel *Dr. Zhivago*, he was denied permission to travel abroad to accept his award.

REVOLT IN THE SOVIET EMPIRE

Although Khrushchev's policies eased the conflict between the superpowers, the thaw in international relations encouraged dissent within the satellite states controlled by the Soviet Union. These states had in 1955 signed the *Warsaw Pact*, a treaty of "friendship, cooperation, and mutual aid": the participants in the pact were the U.S.S.R., Poland, Albania, Czechoslovakia, East Germany, Romania, and Bulgaria. Within each of the states the denunciation of Stalin's regime led to liberalization and cultural revolt.

Poland. In Poland, for example, the Soviet liberalization led to a revolt in June 1956, when workers and citizens of the industrial city of Poznan protested against the government. In the Poznan revolt, more than 50 people were killed and over 300 wounded. The demonstration of proletarian discontent with the "workers' government" brought some reforms in Poland. But although the idea that there should be some independent development—"the Polish road to socialism"—was recognized, Poland remained under Russian control.

The Hungarian Revolution, 1956. In October 1956, Hungarian students led a demonstration which rapidly spread, threatening to become a full-fledged revolution. When the Hungarians announced their intention to create a multi-party political system and to

A statue of Stalin was one of the casualties during the Hungarian student demonstrations of 1956. The nationalist movement was suppressed by the Russian army.

withdraw from the Warsaw Pact, the Soviets intervened with tanks and troops and forcibly ended the revolt.

From this episode, three major conclusions can be drawn. First, despite the thaw, the Soviet government would not allow its satellites to drift away from the Soviet system. Second, no Western nation was prepared to risk war with the U.S.S.R. on the question of freedom in eastern Europe. And finally, the Soviet Union kept control of its satellites only by military force. Although revolt in the satellite countries brought a measure of refreeze, the Soviets did not return to the harsh policies of the Stalinist dictatorship.

KHRUSHCHEV AND THE UNITED STATES

Khrushchev was an inveterate traveler, and voyaged around the world with his message of peaceful coexistence, trade, and extravagant promises of aid to developing countries. He toured Asia, Africa, and the satellite nations of eastern Europe. In 1959, he visited the United States. His cross-country tour included a stop at an Iowa farm, where he discussed corn crops with a prosperous Iowa farmer. He traded quips with Pittsburgh steel workers and visited a Hollywood film set. He carried out friendly discussions with Eisenhower on easing tensions in Germany and addressed the United Nations on his scheme for all nations to destroy their weapons permanently. At the end of his visit, he and Eisenhower agreed to hold a summit conference to discuss their differences. But in spite of the attempts of Khrushchev and American leaders to establish closer ties, several incidents threatened the development of better relations.

The U-2 Incident. The so-called *U-2 Incident* wrecked the planned Paris summit conference between Khrushchev and Eisenhower. On May 1, 1960, a high-flying reconnaissance plane, a U-2, was shot down over Soviet territory. Its pilot, Gary Powers, was captured, and confessed that he was on a mission to photograph Russian installations. On May 5 Khrushchev reported the incident, but did not say that Powers was a prisoner.

In response, the U.S. released a cover story saying that the U-2 plane was a weather plane that had strayed over Russian territory by mistake. Two days later, Khrushchev released the full details of Power's confession, trapping the U.S. government in its lie. In embarrassment, the U.S. made a full statement, explaining that its espionage activities were necessary because of Russian secrecy concerning its military capability. The Paris conference began as scheduled, but Khrushchev demanded an apology and punishment for those responsible. Eisenhower refused to meet his demands, and the conference collapsed.

The Bay of Pigs. Of particular embarrassment to the United States was the Bay of Pigs fiasco in Cuba shortly after John F. Kennedy became president in 1961. Two years earlier, the revolutionary leader Fidel Castro had deposed the corrupt Cuban government and had begun drifting toward Marxism. In response to the growing numbers of Cuban refugees who wanted to return to Cuba and overthrow Castro's regime, the U.S. Central Intelligence Agency (CIA) provided military training for them. In April 1961, the CIA assisted the landing of some 1500 men at the Bay of Pigs. Although wary of the operation, which was planned under his predecessor, Kennedy finally approved the invasion. It proved to be a disaster, as most of the invading forces were killed or captured. Relations with Cuba continued to deteriorate, and in December 1961, announcing that he was a convert to Marxism, Castro moved Cuba into the Soviet bloc.

The Berlin Wall. Closely following the Bay of Pigs incident, Kennedy and Khrushchev met in Vienna to discuss their differences over West Berlin. The immediate problem was that thousands of Germans from East Berlin were pouring into the Western sector of the city in search of freedom and economic opportunity. Khrushchev took a hard-line attitude with the new president, and Kennedy responded with a troop buildup in Germany. At a seeming impasse, the Soviets constructed the Berlin Wall, preventing East Germans from fleeing to the West.

The Cuban Missile Crisis. The next conflict in Soviet-American relations in the early 1960s, the *Cuban missile crisis*, was the most dangerous one. Beginning in June 1962, American aerial reconnaissance of Cuba revealed construction of nuclear missile installations. In September, missiles with nuclear warheads began to arrive from Russia. American experts calculated that the bases would be complete by November 1962. The Soviet decision to aid the Cubans provoked American concern, for since the enunciation of the Monroe Doctrine in 1822, American governments have viewed foreign intervention in any part of the Western Hemisphere as a direct threat to the United States.

Generally, Soviet policy since World War II had avoided such involvement. The Soviet decision to provide nuclear weapons to Cuba

During the Cuban missile crisis, U.S. Forces throughout the world were put on alert. Shown is a test launching of the Minuteman Inter-Continental Ballistic missile, one of the weapons in the U.S. nuclear arsenal.

led President Kennedy to announce on October 22, 1962, a naval *blockade*, or quarantine, of Cuba to be in effect until the missiles were withdrawn. At the same time, U.S. forces worldwide were put on military alert. Khrushchev warned that the U.S. was risking catastrophic consequences of nuclear war. However, on October 28, after the United States promised not to invade Cuba, the Russians withdrew the missiles. It had been a frightening confrontation, and Kennedy had forced Khrushchev to back down.

KHRUSHCHEV'S DECLINE

Although Khrushchev had advanced economic and political reforms in the Soviet Union, by 1964 his leadership was in trouble. His agricultural schemes to increase grain acreage in eastern Russia had failed. As a result, Russia had to import 11 million tons of grain in 1963. Domestic failures such as this, and defeats such as the retreat in the Cuban missile crisis, brought about Khrushchev's downfall.

In October 1964, the leadership of the party deposed Khrushchev. He was accused of fostering a "cult of personality" and of "erratic behavior," but no charges were filed against him and there was no purge of his followers. Instead, he was allowed to live undisturbed in retirement until his death in 1971. His successors represented an era of collective leadership, with Alexei Kosygin (1904–1980) named the head of the government and Leonid Brezhnev (1906–1982) named the secretary of the Communist Party.

DETENTE Khrushchev's era represented a thaw in relations between the superpowers, punctuated by occasional confrontations—at the Berlin Wall and on the question of Cuba. By the time he was deposed, each superpower had begun to adopt a policy of *détente*—a process of seeking better relations through diplomacy. Henry Kissinger, secretary of state under Presidents Richard Nixon and Gerald Ford, once described détente as a "process of managing relations with a potentially hostile country in order to preserve peace while maintaining our vital interests."[5] And a Soviet specialist characterized it as a procedure that "sets limits on what each side can do without risking war and gets officials concerned—Soviet and American—talking with each other."[6] This period of détente, from 1964 to 1980, was characterized by increased instances of cooperation between the superpowers, and U.S. retrenchment and Soviet expansionism.

The era of détente is also characterized by what is known as *multipolarity*; that is, the end of total dominance by the two superpowers (bipolarity). During this era, China deserted its former ally the Soviet Union, and western European states like France and Germany attempted to exert their own influ-

In one of his independent diplomatic initiatives, French president Charles de Gaulle visited Cracow, Poland, in 1967. He urged his listeners to work for peace and a united Europe.

ence. From the Western perspective, communism was no longer viewed as a monolithic force; that is, a single policy under the control of the Soviet Union.

Multipolarity had its origins in France under President Charles de Gaulle, who sought to end the dominance of the superpowers by introducing a third force, a militarily independent France. Chancellor Willy Brandt of Germany soon followed de Gaulle's example. In his search for ways to end the division of Germany, he began to negotiate with the Soviet Union directly (Chapter 26).

THE SINO-SOVIET SPLIT

One major factor in the détente between the superpowers was the split between the Soviet Union and China in 1960, and the subsequent easing of tensions between China and the United States.

---

[5] Irving Gordon, *American Studies: A Conceptual Approach* (New York: Amsco School Publications, 1975), p. 679.

[6] *Ibid.*, p. 679.

A new era in U.S.-China relations began in 1972, with the visit of President and Mrs. Nixon to the Chinese mainland. Prior to this visit, the U.S. had officially recognized only the government established by Chiang Kai-shek on Taiwan.

China had fallen to the communist rebels led by Mao Tse-tung in 1949 (Chapter 27), and since 1950 China and the Soviet Union had been bound in a treaty of alliance. By the late 1950s, however, the two allies had begun to quarrel, and by 1960 the rift became apparent when the Soviets withdrew their technicians from China. In the spring of 1962, the first border clash between China and the Soviet Union occurred.

The sources of conflict began with the rivalry between the Russians and the regime of Mao Tse-tung for leadership of world communism. The Russian Marxists took a paternalistic view toward China, viewing themselves as the leaders of the world communist movement. On the other hand, Mao Tse-tung was imbued with the centuries-old Chinese concept of superiority, and expected the Russians to defer to him.

The Sino-Soviet split also emanated from the Soviet policy of peaceful coexistence adopted by Khrushchev. By contrast, Mao Tse-tung strongly opposed any compromise with the capitalist world.

China and the Soviet Union have thousands of miles of common border and have historically disagreed over their territorial boundaries. During the period of increased tension in the late 1960s, the Soviet Union massed large military forces equipped with nuclear weapons along China's frontiers and the Chinese feared a preemptive nuclear strike. An important event in the growing rift between the two powers came with the *Brezhnev Doctrine*, enunciated when the Soviet Union invaded Czechoslovakia. Brezhnev asserted the U.S.S.R.'s right to use military force to prevent a socialist state from deviating from Marxist-Leninist doctrine. Given the doctrinal disagreements already apparent between the two, Chinese fears of a Soviet invasion were intensified. In 1969 and 1970, military clashes began to occur between troops stationed on the Sino-Soviet border.

Gradually, China turned to the West, and U.S. President Richard Nixon responded in February 1972 by journeying to Peking to negotiate with Mao Tse-tung and other Chinese leaders. Although the tangible results were modest, the significance of the journey was two-fold. First, it extended *de facto* recognition to Red China; in others words, the president's trip in itself implied that the U.S. government recognized the existence of the communist government. Moreover, the trip signified to the Chinese an important concession, an act of respect. Relations between the two powers continued to improve, and in 1978 President Jimmy Carter extended full diplomatic recognition (what is known as *de jure* recognition) to the People's Republic of China. The diplomatic revolution was complete.

U.S.-SOVIET DÉTENTE

During the presidency of Lyndon Johnson the U.S. began negotiations with the Soviet Union to ease tensions between the two countries. One result was the relaxation of travel restrictions, allowing increased numbers of American tourists to visit the Soviet Union. Détente also resulted in increased trade between the Soviet Union and its satellites, on the one hand, and the United States and western Europe on the other. This increased trade included western European export of high technology and manufactured goods in exchange for raw materials and energy supplies, including natural gas.

To enable the Soviet bloc countries to pay for their trade, Western banks made hard currency loans to Eastern nations. The result has been increasing Eastern indebtedness and increasing economic interdependency between the two sides.

SALT I and II. The policy of détente culminated in two major agreements signed during Nixon's trip to the Soviet Union in May 1972. The first agreement, a five-year military treaty known as SALT I, was the result of Strategic Arms Limitations Talks which began in 1969. Under this SALT agreement, a cap was placed on the number of ICBMs (Inter-Continental Ballistic Missiles) the U.S. and the U.S.S.R. could deploy over the following five years. The agreement also included a freeze on the construction of SLBMs (Submarine Launched Ballistic Missiles), and limits on ABMs (Anti-Ballistic-Missile Systems).

Although SALT I was an important breakthrough in the concept of an arms agreement between the superpowers, the Soviet maintained superiority in the total number of missiles covered in the agreement. At the same time, the two powers remained about equal in overall military capability, considering the U.S. superiority in a variety of weapons not covered by the SALT I agreement.

This agreement expired before talks began on its successor, SALT II. President Jimmy Carter cancelled SALT II talks in June 1977 as a result of Soviet buildup of weapons not covered under the original agreement. Talks were, however, resumed the next year and the SALT II treaty was signed in June 1979. SALT II set new ceilings on missile launchers and allowed each country to develop one new kind of missile and to modernize its arsenal within certain restrictions. SALT II has never been ratified by the U.S. Senate, the result primarily of the Senate's worries concerning Soviet expansionism.

Although tensions between the U.S. and the U.S.S.R. were somewhat reduced as a result of the SALT agreements, each continued to believe that any expansion in the influence of the other posed a direct threat to its own interests. As a result of such concerns, the United States engaged in the destructive and ultimately unsuccessful Vietnam War. The U.S.S.R., meanwhile, continued to build its conventional military forces and to develop its alliances with key nations in the Middle East.

War in Vietnam. After the French left Indochina in 1954 (Chapter 27), the United States began to play a more direct role in the ongoing struggle between the communist government of North Vietnam and the non-communist regime in the south. This involvement increased with the introduction of American military advisers and troops to South Vietnam in the early 1960s. At the

Mikhail Gorbachev meets with Tip O'Neill, Speaker of the U.S. House of Representatives. In his travels to the West, the Soviet leader has emphasized his commitment to arms control and world peace.

height of American involvement, the U.S. had over half a million troops in Vietnam.

The war in Vietnam pitted the world's greatest power against a ragtag guerrilla force supplied by China and the Soviet Union. Nevertheless, the U.S. was unable to achieve victory, and withdrew from Vietnam in January 1973, at the beginning of Nixon's second term. Two years later, when Cambodia and Laos fell to the communists, the United States took no action.

Soviet Expansion. During the period of détente, the Soviets also attempted to prevent the Western powers from extending their sphere of influence. One aspect of this policy was the growth of Soviet naval power. The Russian fleet began to patrol the Mediterranean in 1964, and expanded into the Indian Ocean in 1968. In the Middle East, the Soviets dominated Somalia and supplied various forms of aid to Libya, Iraq, and Syria. The most direct Soviet intervention was carried out in December 1979, when Russian troops invaded Afghanistan to prevent that nation from overthrowing its communist government. Like the U.S. in Vietnam, how-

ever, the Soviets have been unable to defeat the opposition guerrilla army.

THE CHILL   The era of détente ended in 1980 with the beginning of a period of more hostile relations, know as *the Chill*. The immediate cause of the shift in relationship between the superpowers was the Soviet invasion of Afghanistan, the first time in the post-World War II period that the Soviet Union used its own forces rather than those of client states to impose a communist government on another people. In response, President Carter withdrew American athletes from the summer Olympics held that year in Moscow, and imposed an embargo on the sale of American grain to the Soviets.

Underlying that immediate incident, however, was growing American realization of the Soviet expansion that had taken place during the previous decade. The election of Ronald Reagan as president in 1980 was in part a result of growing conservatism within the United States. As president, Ronald Reagan activated the policy of a chill in U.S.-Soviet relations, most noticably by returning to the rhetoric of the cold war and by massive increases in the U.S. defense budget. During Reagan's term in office, the United States began to support anti-communist groups in such places as Angola and in Nicaragua, where pro-Marxist governments are in power. It also aided the rebels in Afghanistan.

The emergence of a new generation of Soviet leadership began in 1985 when Mikhail S. Gorbachev became Secretary of the Central Committee of the Communist Party at the age of 54. Gorbachev's removal in July 1985 of Andrei Gromyko, foreign secretary of the Soviet Union for nearly three decades, is an indication that he is putting his own stamp on Soviet foreign policy. He has visited western Europe to meet with European leaders and in 1986 met with Ronald Reagan to discuss the question of arms control, with the promise of future meetings to resolve their differences.

SUMMARY

The superpowers, the United States and the Soviet Union, have dominated world politics in the four decades since the end of World War II. The relationship between them has progressed through four stages: the Cold War, the Thaw, Détente, and the Chill. Although the confrontations between them have occasionally neared the brink of conflict, the advent of the nuclear age has served as a deterrent to full-scale conflict.

QUESTIONS

1 Why did the United States and the Soviet Union emerge as superpowers at the end of the war?
2 What were the origins of the Cold War?
3 What was the significance of the Berlin Blockade?
4 What is the significance of revolts in the Soviet-bloc countries since 1945? What has been American policy toward the nations of East Europe?
5 What caused the Sino-Soviet split? What have been the results of this break?
6 What was détente? Why have postwar attempts at nuclear arms control failed?

BIBLIOGRAPHY

DE PORTE, ANTON. *Europe Between the Superpowers.* New York: Yale University Press, 1979. *This monograph traces the development of the Cold War, with a particular emphasis on the ongoing problem of a divided Germany.*

FEIS, HERBERT. *From Trust to Terror: The Onset of the Cold War, 1945–1950.* New York: Norton, 1970. *This work analyzes the breakdown in relations between the U.S. and the U.S.S.R.*

LINDEN, CARL A. *Khrushchev and the Soviet Leadership, 1957–1964.* Baltimore: Johns Hopkins Press, 1966. *Writing about Soviet history is made difficult by the limited Western access to primary sources. Linden relies on published Russian sources to reconstruct the years of Khrushchev's rule.*

MEDVEDEV, ROY A. and ZHORES A. MEDVEDEV. *Khrushchev: The Years in Power.* New York: Norton, 1978. *This biography was written by two Soviet dissidents. It attempts a balanced—even favorable—portrait of Khrushchev in the 1950s and 1960s. Especially useful are the insights into some of the men, little known to Americans, who advised and supported Khrushchev.*

SCHAPIRO, LEONARD. *The Government and Politics of the Soviet Union.* New York: Random House, 1965. *A useful handbook on the formal structure of the U.S.S.R., clarifying the role of the Communist Party and its control over government operations.*

SMITH, HEDRICK. *The Russians.* New York: Ballantine, 1976. *One of several recent books which describe life in the Soviet Union today. Smith lived in Moscow for three years as New York Times bureau chief, and writes at length about the Russians as he saw them.*

SPANIER, JOHN. *American Foreign Policy Since World War II.* New York: Holt, Rinehart, and Winston, 1980. *A useful survey of American foreign policy, from the beginnings of the Cold War through the era of détente.*

26

● *Happiness is a bank account with a million yen.*
MODERN JAPANESE SAYING

Europe and Japan: 1945–1987

It is an irony of 20th-century history that Japan and Germany, the losers of World War II, have emerged as two of the most politically stable and prosperous nations in the postwar world. During the same period, England and France, stripped of their empires, have lost much of their earlier power, prestige, and relative prosperity.

The postwar experiences of both the winner and loser nations had many similarities. The four nations had suffered significant destruction, in terms of population losses, bombed cities, and damaged economies. Each nation experienced reconstruction—political, economic, social, and intellectual recovery—with the help of American aid. In turn, all supported the United States in its confrontation with the Soviet Union. Yet, each nation faced unique problems and developed its own solutions.

RECONSTRUCTION IN EUROPE   The countless military operations of World War II had left roads, bridges, railroad lines, communications systems, and factories throughout Europe in ruins. Millions of displaced persons were on the move, either trying to return home, or seeking new homes. Among these refugees were thousands of prisoners of war and survivors of Nazi concentration camps.

Many Europeans in 1945 were near starvation as a result of the destruction and disorder. The most urgent problem was to rebuild and revitalize the economies of Europe. In the process of this reconstruction, the states of Europe began to cooperate with each other to a greater extent than they had before the war. Once again the dream of a united Europe surfaced, but as before, nationalism and economic competition prevented its fulfillment.

WEST EUROPEAN ECONOMIC COOPERATION
The economic recovery of the western European states was subsidized initially by the *Marshall Plan*, beginning in 1948. This plan infused billions of dollars into the economies of western Europe and contributed to their recovery. By 1962, the total output of goods and services in western Europe was double what it had been in 1948.

The Marshall Plan was successful in both its economic and its political goals. As the Cold War developed, the economic recovery of western Europe ensured the development

One of the first tasks of postwar reconstruction was to build housing for several million displaced Europeans. At the time, experts estimated it would take 40 years to rebuild Berlin.

of stable democracies friendly to the United States. The revival of western Europe was further aided by agreements among the separate nations to cooperate in certain economic affairs. This cooperation included the elimination of national tariffs which so often in the past had produced economic conflict and political tensions.

The first successful step toward elimination of protectionist policies in trade occurred when the Benelux countries—Belgium, the Netherlands, and Luxemburg—agreed to allow a free movement of goods between their countries. Even more significant was a proposal put forth in 1950 by the French foreign minister, Robert Schuman, outlining the integration of the French and German coal and steel industries. The *Schuman Plan* was put into effect under the leadership of another Frenchman, Jean Monnet, who fathered the European Coal and Steel Community. Founded in 1952, this organization, composed of France, Germany, Italy, and the Benelux countries, provided for the end of tariffs and quotas in iron ore, coal, coke, and steel. It also established a standard tariff on imports from other nations. This successful collaboration inspired another, the European Atomic Energy Community, established in 1957, which oversaw the development of peaceful uses of atomic energy.

The Common Market. The most significant of all agreements between the European countries was the creation in March 1957 of the Common Market. The original members of the Common Market were France, Germany, Italy, and Benelux; Great Britain, Denmark, and Ireland joined in 1973; and Greece in 1981. The Common Market provided for the gradual elimination of all restrictions on trade. By 1968, all tariffs between member nations were eliminated. The result of this policy was to stimulate competition and to lower prices: once protective tariffs were eliminated, producers could find a much wider market for their goods, and consumers could buy products at the lowest available prices. Free trade played a significant role in the "economic miracle" that Europe experienced in the 1950s and 1960s. In France and West Germany, average *per capita* income doubled over a 20-year period.

PER CAPITA INCOME IN DOLLARS		
	1957	1977*
France	3365	7177
West Germany	4151	8371
Japan	1423	6017
United States	5593	8715
* adjusted for inflation		

EUROPEAN MILITARY COOPERATION

The Soviet Union's expansion into eastern Europe after the war seemed to threaten western Europe as well. In response to these events, the North Atlantic Treaty Organization (NATO) was founded under the leadership of the United States in June 1949. Besides the U.S., membership included Great Britain, France, Belgium, the Netherlands, Luxemburg, Canada, Norway, Iceland, Denmark, Portugal, and Italy. Later, Greece, Turkey, and West Germany also joined. The stated purpose of NATO was:

• • • *To safeguard the freedom, common heritage, and civilizations of their peoples founded on the principles of democracy, individual liberty, and the rule of law.*[1]

Essentially a military alliance, NATO bound its members to come to each other's defense in case of attack by a hostile power.

NATO experienced one major problem when France refused to allow NATO bases on its territory, having decided to rely upon its own defense system. Nevertheless, even though the NATO alliance has never been tested, it remains another source of cohesiveness among western European states and between them and the United States.

WAR CRIMES TRIALS

The Allied victor nations agreed on the need

[1] *Encyclopedia Americana* (Danbury, Conn.: Grolier, 1980), Vol. 20, p. 421a.

to bring to justice those guilty of war crimes and, if possible, to eliminate all traces of Nazi ideology. Accordingly, in November 1945 the International Military Tribunal was established by the U.S., the U.S.S.R., Great Britain, and France to prepare for the Nuremburg war crimes trials. The accused were charged with three categories of crimes: *crime against peace*—in other words, responsibility for beginning the war; *war crimes*, or actions contrary to the accepted rules of war—specifically the murder or ill treatment of military prisoners or civilians; and the most serious category, *crimes against humanity*, including the murder or persecution of people based on their race or political beliefs. Included among the crimes in this latter category was the Nazi policy of genocide of the Jews of Europe.

Brought to trial were the remaining high-ranking German civilian and military leaders, including Hermann Goering, head of the Luftwaffe, Joachim von Ribbentrop, the foreign minister, Generals Wilhelm Keitel and Alfred Jodl, and Admiral Karl Doenitz.

The lengthy trials brought to the attention of the world the extent of the atrocities perpetrated by the Nazi regime. Perhaps most importantly, the German people were pro-

Hermann Goering, former chief of the Luftwaffe, takes the witness stand during the Nuremberg trials.

The trials of Nazi officials throughout Germany revealed the ghastly details of Hitler's administration. Here, participants in a trial visit a crematorium where Nazis disposed of their victims.

vided irrefutable evidence of the brutality of their leaders. Evidence presented at the trials included films which showed the thousands of emaciated corpses found at the concentration and extermination camps.

At the conclusion of the trials, 12 of the defendants were sentenced to death by hanging. One prominent leader, Hermann Goering, cheated the executioner by committing suicide. Four were sentenced to life imprisonment, four to lesser terms, and three were acquitted. In addition to the political and military leaders, the leaders of the Nazi party, the S.S., and the Gestapo were found guilty. Moreover, each of the Allied powers tried various categories of war criminals within its own occupation zone.

In addition to trying the war criminals, the victor nations believed that they should attempt to screen former Nazis to prevent their return to political power. This policy, known as *denazification*, was carried out by each of the occupying powers in different ways and with varying degrees of enthusiasm. The Allies' efforts in this area were limited by a number of practical considerations. For example, to prevent all former party members from ever holding office would cripple German recovery, for many of these people were key technicians and participants in German society. All in all, the Allies probably succeeded in identifying the most enthusiastic Nazis, but many others escaped public exposure.

WEST GERMAN RECOVERY

With the establishment of the two Germanies in 1949, the Allied-occupied portion, West Germany, began the slow path to recovery. West Germany became a federal republic composed of ten states, and its capital was moved to Bonn. Under the constitution of the Federal Republic, the legislative branch of its government contains two houses, the *Bundestag* and the *Bundesrat*. The president is elected by the Federal Assembly, composed of members of the Bundestag plus representatives of each of the ten states. The office of the presidency is largely ceremonial. The real executive is the chancellor, who is appointed by the president and confirmed by the Bundestag.

Konrad Adenauer, affectionately referred to as *Der Alte* ("the old one"), became the first chancellor of West Germany and was the most important figure of the early postwar years. Adenauer had been mayor of Cologne before the war, and was imprisoned by the Nazis—good credentials for a postwar German leader.

One of the most important questions regarding postwar Germany was whether the long authoritarian tradition could be replaced by a democratic one. During Adenauer's 14 years as chancellor, a stable democratic government was established and continues to function effectively. The stability of West Germany's government is also based on the existence of two major political parties, the Christian Democratic Union and the Social Democratic Party, which have alternated in control in the past 40 years.

THE ECONOMIC MIRACLE

Adenauer presided over the *Wirtschaftswunder*, the economic miracle of the postwar period. The economic recovery of West Germany was aided by several factors: American aid, the prewar industrial base, the German people's capacity for thrift and hard work, and the creation of new factories with modern equipment. Most important of all was the revival of industrial productivity, for Germany has a limited agricultural base and must import some of its food and raw materials. The economic miracle included the tripling of the *gross national product* (GNP)—a measurement of the total goods and services produced by the nation—between 1960 and 1973. In 1982, West Germany ranked fourth in the world in GNP, at $828 million.

One of the important by-products of German economic revival has been an increase in the standard of living, for most West Germans are prospering. This distribution of wealth has created a large, stable middle class whose prosperity is linked to the successful democratic system.

RECONCILIATION WITH THE WEST

Under Adenauer, the German Federal Republic joined the European Common Market. In 1955, the nation joined NATO. Germany developed good relations with its longtime enemy, France, cooperating in the steel and coal community, and eventually in a treaty of friendship. Although there have been quarrels on specific issues including rearmament, West Germany remains in the Western camp and retains close ties with the United States.

Largely due to the efforts of Konrad Adenauer, a stable federal republic was established in West Germany, and the national economy recovered and prospered.

The Goal of Reunification. Westpolitik (close relations with the West) was the basis for German foreign policy under the chancellorship of Adenauer. In 1973, Chancellor Willy Brandt began to develop a complementary policy toward the Soviet Union known as *Ostpolitik* (Eastern policy). The policy of Ostpolitik derives in part from Germany's precarious geographic position in the middle of Europe—the need to maintain good relations on both sides. It is also motivated by an urge to seek reunification with the German Democratic Republic. The Federal Republic continues to pursue a policy that will, on the one hand, retain close ties with the West, and at the same time lead to German unification.

GREAT BRITAIN AFTER THE WAR

The war had longlasting effects upon Great Britain. In addition to the massive destruction of its population and territory through aerial bombings, Britain lost its empire in the Mediterranean and in India. Without the possibility of reviving its former colonial trade and commerce, Britain's economy would necessarily be much more restricted in the postwar years.

The Labor Party, 1945–1951. The war served as a watershed in Britain's political and economic life. At war's end, the Labor Party won its first clear-cut electoral victory since its inception in 1900. The size of the electoral margin—Labor's 392 seats in Parliament compared to the Conservatives' 216 seats—convinced the new prime minister, Clement Attlee, that he had received a mandate for sweeping economic reforms.

The new Labor government passed through Parliament an unprecedented 84 pieces of legislation in its first 15 months in power. The effect was to create an economy which embodies many of the features of socialism. Through the National Health Service Act (1948), the government became responsible for providing nearly free medical and dental care to its citizens. A related mea-sure, the National Insurance Act, provided additional benefits for the elderly, the ill, and the unemployed. Another drastic reform was the nationalization of Britain's basic industries, including coal, steel, gas, electric power, and railroads. This sweeping nationalization was combined with an austerity program intended to bring about rapid economic recovery.

The Labor Party's program met with some successes: the standard of living increased, and the economy continued to improve. But Britain's unfavorable balance of payments—the result of foreign debts, and a greater volume of imports than exports—has kept the economy in a weakened condition. It has never fully recovered from the war.

The Conservative Party, 1951–1964. In 1951, the British public returned the Conservatives and Winston Churchill to power. The results of the election of 1951 suggest that a majority of the British people wanted no further progress toward socialism, and wished to take a firmer stance in regard to the Soviet Union. Nevertheless, the Conservatives retained most of the social legislation of the previous years.

Since 1964, political control has fluctuated between the two parties. In 1979, the Conservative leader Margaret Thatcher became Britain's first woman prime minister.

FRANCE AFTER THE WAR

Throughout the past two centuries, French politics have frequently been chaotic. This situation certainly prevailed at the end of World War II, when France faced a number of critical decisions concerning its future course. The leading politicians of prewar France were defeated at the polls by new leaders who had arisen in the resistance movement. Most of these new leaders blamed the prewar government for the failures of the 1930s, and called for radical changes.

The Fourth Republic. When France was liberated by the Allied armies in 1944,

Throughout his career, General Charles de Gaulle embodied the ideal of a free and self-sufficient French nation. This photo was taken during World War II, when de Gaulle represented the Free French forces in exile from occupied Europe.

Charles de Gaulle, leader of the Free French government based in England, became a national hero. Under de Gaulle's leadership, the *Fourth French Republic* was established in 1946, with a new constitution which created a parliamentary system and a figurehead premier. The real power of government resided in the National Assembly, which appointed a cabinet to serve as the executive branch. The existence of numerous political parties, none of which could command a clear majority in the Assembly, caused political instability in the years following the war. Coalitions were formed, only to collapse when policy disagreements emerged. The largest single party was the French Communist Party. This party controlled one-fourth of the deputies in the Assemby but could never put together a large enough coalition to control the government.

The Fifth Republic. The loss of France's Asian empire (Chapter 27) was quickly followed by difficulties in Algeria, where revolt broke out in November 1954. In 1956, as the French government appeared to be willing to grant Algerian demands for independence, the French army in Algeria attempted to take matters into its own hands. In May 1958, it was rumored that the army intended to overthrow the French government. Faced with this crisis, the government turned to former premier Charles de Gaulle for help. De Gaulle was given dictatorial powers for a period of six months in order to supervise the writing of a new constitution.

In September 1958, the *Fifth French Republic* came into being. The new constitution gave wide powers to the office of the president, who was to be elected for a seven-year term. In November, de Gaulle was elected to this post. Once in power, he acted decisively. He brought the army under control by purging its leaders, and granted independence to Algeria (1961) and other parts of the former French empire.

During his term as president, de Gaulle sought to preserve a strong position for France in the wake of its loss of empire. After failing to get access to U.S. nuclear secrets, de Gaulle began to develop France's own *force de frappe*—nuclear striking force. De Gaulle resigned from public office during his second term as president, in 1969. Although he had been responsible for creating a stable political system, neither he nor his successors could restore France to its former position as a world power.

Economic problems, especially inflation, plagued France in the 1970s and increased public support for the parties of the left, the socialists and communists. In 1981, François Mitterand was elected president and his Socialist Party received a majority of the seats in the National Assembly. But although his political philosophy is radically different from that of his more conservative predecessors, Mitterrand fared little better in his efforts to find solutions for the persistent problems of inflation and unemployment.

Nevertheless, the nation has developed a strong industrial base and enjoys relative prosperity and a balanced economy. It ranks fifth in the world in annual GNP. Today, France continues to follow an independent foreign policy while remaining on good terms with the United States.

OTHER NATIONS OF WESTERN EUROPE

In the other nations of western Europe, economic and political problems have encouraged the emergence of extremist groups which threaten the stability of these struggling societies.

Italy. In 1947 the Italian people adopted a new constitution which established a parliamentary form of government. As in other democratic societies, the parliamentary system has created problems, for no single party has been able to command a clear majority. Lacking a leading party, the elected legislature must forge coalition cabinets which represent several parties. Coalitions are inherently unstable, for the issues which divide the various parties inevitably surface during the cabinet's rule. As a result, Italy has experienced considerable political turmoil: there have been more than 45 governments since the end of the war. For this reason, among others, the Communist Party in Italy has assumed more influence than its numbers would justify.

Although Italy has industrialized since the war's end, continuing poverty, especially in southern Italy, has contributed to the country's instability. Radicalism across the political spectrum has become an aspect of contemporary society. One dramatic instance was the kidnapping and murder of the prominent politician Aldo Moro in 1978. This action was carried out by a leftist group known as the Red Brigade. Terrorism in Italy, as in most other parts of the world, has produced few concrete results, but tests the stability and resolve of the governments called upon to deal with it.

Portugal and Spain. Italy's economic and political problems are echoed in the Iberian peninsula, for Portugal and Spain have continued to suffer both economic underdevelopment and political instability. Although a republic since 1910, Portugal was ruled by the dictator Antonio de Oliveira Salazar from 1932 to 1968. In 1974, a group of army officers overthrew the government, and two years later a socialist government and a democratic constitution emerged. Nevertheless, Portugal has continued to experience problems stemming from its limited industrial base, a rapid population growth, and an unsuccessful military effort to retain the colonies of Angola and Mozambique.

In Spain, the long dictatorship of Francisco Franco, who had come to power during the Spanish Civil War of the 1930s, ended in 1975. His appointed successor, Prince Juan Carlos, established a constitutional monarchy, and encouraged liberal reforms. Although an attempted army coup against Juan Carlos failed in 1981, Spain continues to face threats to its regime. Among these is the separatist movement of Basque nationalists, whose terrorist activities include the assassination of the prime minister in 1974. Yet continued economic growth and modernization may lead to the stabilization of Spanish society.

Greece. The politics of Greece were of immediate concern to the Allies in the postwar period, for that nation experienced a civil war with communist guerrillas beginning in 1943. In fact, the threat that Greece would align itself with the Soviet Union precipitated the *Truman Doctrine* of 1947. Truman's strategy was to supply American aid to the noncommunist political parties of Greece—and of any other nonaligned country where a communist takeover appeared imminent. With American aid, the communist guerrillas were defeated by 1949. Greece then became a member of NATO, further strengthening the Western alliance.

Since 1974, when a republic was established and a new constitution promulgated,

Greek politics have been dominated by the Socialist Party and its leader, Andreas Papandreou. As in the cases of Italy, Spain, and Portugal, economic underdevelopment continues to contribute to political and social instability.

EASTERN EUROPE

Since the emergence of the United States and the Soviet Union as superpowers, each has sought to export its own political and economic ideology to the rest of the world. Those nations allied with or friendly to the United States would, it was assumed, choose democracy and some form of capitalism, while those in the Soviet camp would adopt the Marxist principles of the dictatorship of the proletariat and radical socialism. In the decades since the war, another pattern has emerged as well. The nations allied to the United States now include most of the world's developed industrial powers. Within the Soviet sphere of influence, on the other hand, the Soviet Union itself is the only fully industrialized nation.

THE COMMUNIST BLOC

The nations most closely tied to the Soviet Union—the communist-bloc countries—include Yugoslavia as well as the eastern European nations occupied by the Russian army at the close of World War II: East Germany, Poland, Czechoslavakia, Hungary, Bulgaria, Romania, and Albania. The political and economic systems of these states are determined by the Soviet Union and reinforced by Soviet military power.

In response to the formation of the Common Market and NATO, the Soviet Union formed two similar organizations of its own. The first was an economic alliance known as COMECON (Council for Mutual Assistance), which was formed in 1949 to coordinate the economic affairs of its satellite countries. In 1955, the Soviets sponsored the *Warsaw Pact*, a military alliance between itself and the eastern European countries.

In terms of industrialization, the nations of the communist bloc are characterized as developing nations. Poland ranks 16th in the world in terms of *gross national product*, and East Germany and Czechoslavakia are slightly lower on the scale. Yugoslavia, Romania, Hungary, and Bulgaria rank far below them. The contrast between a fully industrialized nation and a developing one is significant: the GNPs of the United States and of the Soviet Union, the two most developed nations, are measured in trillions of dollars, while those of developing nations may be measured in millions.

THE SOVIET INFLUENCE

The U.S.S.R. depends on its satellites to supply raw materials for Soviet industries and to serve as a market for Soviet goods—much in the same way that the 19th-century imperialists relied on their colonies. This system often has an adverse impact upon the development of the satellites. The nature of the Soviets' planned or *command* economy has also led to friction with the satellite countries. Because Soviet economic planners have emphasized industrial growth at the expense of consumer goods, there are often severe shortages of food, housing, and other products. In the face of such shortages, economic planners have sometimes raised the prices of certain staple items to reflect the real cost of producing them. Such price rises, in turn, have an immediate negative impact on the standard of living of the average worker. The demonstrations and rioting in Poland in 1968 and in 1981 were directly inspired by rises in the price of staple food items.

As a result of the perceived deficiencies in the Soviet economic system, several of the Soviet bloc states have sought to develop a degree of independence from the policies of the Soviet Union—i.e., the freedom to develop their own "road to socialism." Several of them have achieved some success in this area. Nevertheless, the political system of

POSTWAR EUROPEAN ALIGNMENTS

How did Allied military decisions in World War II affect the postwar boundaries of the U.S.S.R.?

each satellite is still governed by its Communist Party, which must maintain close ties and act in concert with the Soviet Union. Withdrawal from the Soviet orbit is prevented by Russian military power, which has been evidenced several times in recent decades: in the invasion of Hungary in 1956, the 1968 invasion of Czechoslavakia, and the implied threat of force in Poland in 1981.

CZECHOSLAVAKIA

In Czechoslavakia, the minority Communist Party seized control of the government in 1948 and introduced a Soviet-style dictatorship. In 1968, the communist leader Alexander Dubcek attempted to relax the stringent controls which his predecessors had imposed on the Czech people. In a brief period known as the *Prague Spring*, it seemed that Dubcek might realize his promise of creating a communist government "with a human face." But the leaders of the Soviet Union feared that Dubcek's policies would inspire demands for liberalization in other satellite countries, or even lead to their withdrawal from the communist bloc. Without warning, the Russian army invaded Czechoslovakia in August 1968 and removed Dubcek from power. The Soviet premier Leonid Brezhnev then issued the "Brezhnev Doctrine" in which he asserted that the U.S.S.R. would use military force to prevent any socialist state from deviating from Marxist-Leninist principles.

Eurocommunism. The Soviets' use of military force in one of its own satellite states embarrassed the local communist parties of western Europe. From their chagrin came the emergence of *Eurocommunism*, in which party leaders sought to disassociate themselves from Moscow's repressive policies. In Spain and Italy, in particular, communist party leaders promised that they would respect Western democratic traditions if they came to power. But this promise was seen as insincere, for it contradicted the fundamental principles of Marxism. As a result, the would-be Eurocommunist movement quickly died out in western Europe.

HUNGARY, ROMANIA, AND YUGOSLAVIA

Although the Eurocommunist movement never received popular support in western Europe, it had a direct impact in three Soviet-bloc countries, Hungary, Romania, and Yugoslavia. In the 1970s and early 1980s, these satellite states sought nonconfrontational ways to loosen the Soviet Union's control over them.

In Hungary, after the unsuccessful revolution of 1956, the Soviet-backed regime of Janos Kadar relaxed some of the authoritarian measures that his predecessors had adopted. He instituted a more liberal agricultural policy, and increased trade with the West. Likewise, Romania under the leadership of Nicolae Ceausescu has attempted to preserve an independent foreign policy and to raise its citizens' standard of living through extensive trade with the West.

In Yugoslavia, the wartime communist movement under Marshal Tito had won control of the government without the aid of the Soviet Union in 1945. Because of Tito's victory—and the fact that Yugoslavia has no common border with the Soviet Union—Yugoslavia has become the most independent of the communist-bloc states. In 1948, Tito broke with Stalin's regime as a result of economic disagreements. Tito's acceptance of American aid provided him leverage in pursuing a "Yugoslav road to socialism."

Relations between Yugoslavia and the Soviet Union were patched up in 1955 when Khrushchev apologized to Tito for Stalin's dogmatism. Khrushchev's relative liberalism encouraged the revolutions in Poland and Hungary in 1956, which the Soviets quickly suppressed. But the Soviets have continued to allow a freer national development in Yugoslavia. For Yugoslavia, Eurocommunism fit well with prior historical policy, and the nation has benefited from its extensive trade with the West.

THE CASE OF POLAND

After being partitioned by Russia, Austria, and Prussia in the 18th century, Poland did not reemerge as an independent nation until the end of World War I. During World War II, Poland was again partitioned by the occuping armies of the Nazis and Soviets.

The Marxist government established in Poland after the war was not received enthusiastically by the Poles, nor did it bring prosperity to the nation. In June 1956, worker demonstrations in the industrial city of Poznan led to a brief period of reforms. The Soviets agreed to end their policy of forcible collectivization of land, and eliminated some of the strictures they had imposed upon the Roman Catholic Church.

In 1970, a new party leader, Edward Gi-

Steelyard workers hold a demonstration behind improvised barricades in Nowa Huta, Poland. Authorities have often used water cannons and tear gas to break up such gatherings.

erek, took power and attempted to overcome worker dissatisfaction by stabilizing prices and increasing the availability of consumer goods. At the same time, the Communist Party increased its control over the country by centralizing its administration.

Between 1970 and 1980, Poland continued to experience serious economic decline, including a drastic increase in its foreign debt. Real wages for the workers declined. At the same time, the privileges accorded to the leaders of the Communist Party increased: they benefited from special health care and retirement benefits, access to resorts and Western consumer goods, tax loopholes, and housing privileges.

The inequities of the Soviet system and the shortages of food and housing for the

Lech Walesa, a steelyard worker, organized and led the workers' union that evolved into a national movement.

workers led to the emergence of an illegal workers' union, *Solidarity*, which was led by Lech Walesa and commanded the loyalty of most workers in Poland. In 1980 and 1981, the members of Solidarity carried out a series of workers' strikes which paralysed the country. The government of Poland, fearing a Russian invasion, declared martial law and through military means brought an end to the workers' rebellion.

TRADE WITH THE WEST

During the period of the *Thaw* in relations between the United States and the Soviet Union (Chapter 25), trade between East Europe and the West began to revive. Such trade between the capitalist countries and the communist bloc has had mixed results. On the one hand, the communist countries are no longer seen by the West as a menacing, monolithic force, as they were in the 1940s and 1950s. On the other hand, trade with the West has led to economic dependence and indebtedness on the part of the eastern European countries—a combined debt in 1981 of $62 billion. These loan commitments to Western banks have had a negative impact on the economies of these states, and portend problems should they have to default on their loans. Also, despite the relaxation of controls in regard to trade, all of East Europe remains within the Warsaw Pact and under Soviet domination.

JAPAN AFTER WORLD WAR II By May of 1945, Japan's industrial productivity was in rapid decline and Germany had recognized defeat. Nevertheless, the Japanese continued to fight on, for the Allies' terms of surrender, in which the losers would have no voice in the terms of the peace settlement, seemed humiliating and threatening. It was only after the two devastating atomic bomb raids on Hiroshima and Nagasaki in August that they agreed to accept the victors' terms.

THE OCCUPATION

Japan's formal, unconditional surrender occurred on September 2, 1945, and American occupation of the country immediately followed. Japan's postwar fate was in the hands of the American general Douglas MacArthur, the supreme commander of the Allied forces in the Pacific.

The policies which MacArthur initiated during the occupation and recovery are important factors in explaining Japan's rapid reconstruction. Rather than putting political control in the hands of the occupying army, MacArthur operated through the Japanese government. Emperor Hirohito was retained as a figurehead, and Japanese ministers implemented the reforms through which the Americans intended to transform Japan's militaristic and authoritarian government into a democracy.

The New Japanese Constitution. Among the reforms initiated during the occupation was the development of a democratic constitution, enacted in 1947. The opening lines of the constitution express the new democratic ideal:

• • • We, the Japanese people . . .
determined that we shall secure for ourselves and our posterity the fruits of peaceful cooperation with all nations and the blessings of liberty throughout this land, and resolved that never again shall we be visited with the horrors of war through the action of government, do proclaim that sovereign power resides with the people and do firmly establish this Constitution.[2]

The constitution instituted a parliamentary system of government, with the executive branch, a cabinet, responsible to the new two-house legislature. Women were given the vote, and the voting age was set at 20. The Japanese people were guaranteed tra-

---

[2] Edwin Reischauer and Albert M. Craig, *Japan: Tradition and Transformation* (Boston: Houghton Mifflin, 1978), p. 280.

ditional freedoms in a Bill of Rights. The first general election after the publication of the constitution was held in April 1947.

War Crimes Trials. To prevent the succession to political or military power of those who were judged responsible for the war, nearly 600,000 Japanese were screened by occupation authorities. Military conscription was abolished, and 80,000 former military personnel were prohibited from holding public office. Moreover, those suspected of war crimes were placed on trial by the International Military Tribunal for the Far East. Thousands of officers and military men were tried and hundreds executed. Among the major wartime figures brought to trial were 2 premiers, 13 generals, an admiral, and several ministers and ambassadors. All but two were found guilty of "conspiracy to wage aggressive war," and those condemned to death were convicted of "breaches of the laws and customs of war."

Democratic Reforms. In addition to establishing a democratic government, the occupation authorities required reforms in the organization of industry, labor, and agriculture. The school system was reformed so that it would develop democratic traditions among the young. Economic reforms included the dissolution of the giant prewar military-industrial complex, the Zaibatsu, to eliminate the concentration of economic power in the hands of a few companies. Land was distributed to former tenant farmers to create a more equitable and productive agricultural system. All in all, these various reforms laid the foundation for a democratic political system and a stable economy.

The Peace Treaty. The final peace treaty with Japan was signed on September 8, 1951, and military occupation was ended in April 1952. The treaty deprived Japan of all of its overseas empire, and contained a pledge that Japan would honor the United Nations Charter. It also obligated Japan to negotiate reparations payments to countries who had suffered damages from the war. At the same time, Japan signed a separate treaty with the United States in which the U.S. committed itself to the defense of Japan. The peace settlement with Japan was generous, and reflected a constructive attitude toward America's former enemy.

JAPANESE ECONOMIC RECOVERY

The economic recovery of Japan began during the period of American military occupation, aided by American dollars and foodstuffs for the underfed population. The Korean War (Chapter 25) provided Japanese industry with orders for military equipment worth around $4 billion. Industrial revival followed, aided by the invention of the transistor, an electronic device with many useful applications. Japan soon came to be one of the world's leading producers of consumer items such as cars, radios, television sets, and cameras. The impressive rebirth of Japanese industry is reflected in the growth of Japan's GNP. In 1946, the Japanese GNP was little over $1 billion; in 1972, it reached nearly $300 billion. In 1982, Japan ranked third in the world with a GNP of $1 trillion, nearly that of the second-place nation, the Soviet Union.

A number of different factors have contributed to the miraculous recovery of Japan's economy. Because Japan had been a major industrial power before the war, it had the basic foundations on which to rebuild its economic structure. Also, as in the case of Germany, the Japanese were able to turn wartime destruction to their advantage. While American steel mills, for example, are today hampered by their continued use of old equipment, Japanese factories have incorporated the latest technological advances.

Japan's recovery has also been aided by its ability to adopt—and improve upon—the technology and methods of the Western world. In the realm of labor relations, for example, the Japanese have combined their

A modern Japanese automobile plant. Due to innovative technology and management techniques, Japanese products have won a commanding share of world markets.

own cultural traditions with Western methods to produce a unique style of management. In contrast to labor practices in most of the Western world, Japanese companies make a lifetime commitment to their employees, assuring them not only of permanent employment, but also sponsoring the concept of the company as a community. In return, employees are willing to make personal sacrifices for the good of their companies. It was this spirit of sacrifice for the common good which first enabled Japan to take its commanding lead in the world marketplace. By keeping labor costs low while producing high quality products, the Japanese achieved a healthy economy. And once general prosperity had been achieved, the Japanese themselves became among the most avid consumers of the goods they produced, further stimulating the nation's economy.

The economic successes of Japan have also been abetted by government policies. In the early postwar years, tariffs and import quotas were extensively used to protect key Japanese industries from foreign competition. In latter years—in response to protests from Japan's trading partners—such tariffs have largely been eliminated. Nevertheless, Japanese exports continue to compete easily in foreign markets due to their relative low cost and high quality.

The Japanese government has also taken an active role in supporting industrial growth. The demilitarization imposed by the occupation forces enabled it to allocate its resources to consumer industries rather than defense spending, and it provided important aid to Japanese businesses in the form of credit and investment loans. Even after the ban against militarization was lifted, government leaders resisted the idea of creating a full-scale defense industry, preferring to devote Japan's resources to more productive pursuits.

SUMMARY

In the decades following World War II, the polarization of Europe into American and Soviet spheres of influences has been modified by the evolvement of different political and economic institutions within each camp. In eastern Europe, the satellite states have begun to seek ways to pursue their own best interests while avoiding direct confrontation with the Soviet Union. In western Europe, most nations have established stable, economically developed democracies, but Spain, Portugal, Italy, and Greece continue to struggle with economic and social problems. It remains to be seen whether the four struggling western European countries—as well as the newly decolonized nations of Asia and Africa—will follow the example set by the U.S. and other economically developed nations, or will turn to instead to the radical socialism of the U.S.S.R.

QUESTIONS

1 What have been the goals of European cooperation since the war? What results have been achieved?
2 What are the advantages of belonging to the Common Market?
3 What special problems are faced by Italy, Spain, Portugal, and Greece? Why have these countries been less successful than others in developing stable democracies in the postwar period?
4 Why have Germany and Japan, the losers of the war, recovered so successfully?
5 To what extent has the U.S.S.R. allowed independent development in its satellite states?

BIBLIOGRAPHY

ASH, TIMOTHY GARTON. *The Polish Revolution: Solidarity.* New York: Vintage Books, 1985. *An analysis of the rise and fall of the Solidarity movement in Poland. An excellent discussion of Poland and of Soviet policy toward its satellite states.*

CHAMBERLAIN, MURIEL E. *Decolonization: The Fall of the European Empires.* New York: Basil Blackwell, 1985. *A recent book which describes the end of European dominance in the post-World War II period.*

LEDWIDGE, BERNARD. *De Gaulle.* New York: St. Martin's, 1983. *A recent highly readable biography of de Gaulle, with coverage of the postwar culture of France.*

PRITTIE, TERENCE. *The Velvet Chancellors: A History of Post-War Germany.* London: Frederick Muller, 1979. *This book considers the policies of the first five chancellors after World War II, including Adenauer's role in the creation of West Germany, Brandt's Ostpolitick, and the postwar economic miracle.*

REICHAUER, EDWIN and ALBERT CRAIG. *Japan's Tradition and Transformation.* Boston: Houghton Mifflin, 1978. *Reichauer remains one of the best authors on modern Japan. In this volume, he examines Japan's modernization and postwar success.*

WERTH, ALEXANDER. *De Gaulle: A Political Biography.* New York: Simon & Schuster, 1966. *A popular biography which surveys the career of this dynamic leader, from his early years through 1965.*

27

> For my own part I have made my choice. I will not leave South Africa, nor will I surrender. Only through hardship, sacrifice and militant action can freedom be won. The struggle is my life. I will continue fighting for freedom until the end of my days.

NELSON MANDELA

The Developing World

The civilization of western Europe dominated global history for nearly five centuries—from the age of overseas exploration and conquest which began in the late 15th century until the end of World War II. This domination took many forms, ranging from the cultural influences of missionaries and traders to the direct political control exerted over colonial empires. Today, European domination of non-European peoples has nearly ended, although economic dependencies continue. But European colonization has left a complex legacy: the foundations for political, economic, and social development but also for significant problems. These problems form the backdrop for contemporary history, for many of the over 170 nations in the world today are ex-colonies of European powers, and most are underdeveloped.

PROBLEMS OF DEVELOPING NATIONS

Although economic progress is usually the barometer by which we measure modernization, political and social development are also necessary components of the modern state. The revolutions that have taken place in the developed world during the past two centuries have resulted in political and social institutions which uphold the principles of human equality, freedom, and the full development of human potential. But most developing nations lack the economic stability necessary to evolve such institutions.

ECONOMIC ISSUES

One of the critical decisions facing a developing nation is the choice of a system to govern the society's economic life. Many have looked to socialism as their model. This may take the radical form evolved in the U.S.S.R., where the state owns all means of economic production, or it may involve communal or collective ownership on a smaller scale—at the community level. Socialism is an attractive economic model to non-Western societies for several reasons. First, state ownership of key industries is the expedient way to bring about rapid change. Also, capitalism, the other dominent economic system, often has undesirable connotations because it was the system that motivated European imperialists. In addition, capitalism implies competition and individualism, whereas many cultures have developed traditions of community and of cooperation.

Command Economy. One of the central features of the radical socialism practiced in the Soviet Union is a *command economy;* that is, an economy controlled and directed by the political leadership. For example, if a goal is development of steel mills and other heavy industries, the state can, through planning, concentrate the nation's economic resources upon that target. The industrialization of the Soviet Union followed such a model in the 1920s and 1930s, when the wealth of the state was used to develop key industries, and consumer items, including housing, were neglected.

In the Soviet Union's command economy, now in effect for nearly 75 years, the state has become industrialized, but the standard of living for Russian citizens has remained low compared to that of the Western industrialized states. While the GNP of the U.S.S.R. ranks second only to that of the United States, the nation's average income per capita is less than half that of the U.S. The disparity is largely accounted for by the fact that the Soviet Union allocates a large portion—about 10 percent—of its annual GNP to military spending.

Market Economy. The opposite of a command economy is the market economy which governs the private sector of a capitalistic economy. Inherent in the market system is competition. If a manufacturer of television sets, for example, cannot compete in price or quality with other manufacturers, consumers do not buy the product and the company goes out of business. In a market economy, change is slow to occur, for it must await the impact of supply and demand. The advantage of such a system is that the incentive of individual profit tends to increase the overall productivity of a society. But as a nation industrializes, a pure, or unregulated, market economy may bring about great inequities in the distribution of wealth, as occurred in 19th-century England (Chapter 13). For this reason, all of the Western democracies have evolved ways to regulate

their economies through laws and regulations. Through government controls on the supply of money, tax rates, employment practices, and many other matters, the extreme imbalances of a free market economy can be corrected.

TECHNOLOGICAL DEVELOPMENT

The fundamental flaw of underdeveloped nations is the lack of technology. These nations are subject to a series of dilemmas in their efforts to bring about industrial transformation. In the first place, they need to acquire machine tools in order to manufacture the equipment used in key industries—for example, to build the tractors required to till the soil more efficiently. The most likely way to acquire such tools is to trade—to sell enough commodities to pay for them. But since underdeveloped nations typically do not produce manufactured goods for sale and export, they must trade in agricultural commodities. The dilemma here is that the absence of modern technology—tractors and commercial fertilizers—keeps their agricultural productivity low, and they rarely produce a surplus beyond the needs of their own citizens. Moreover, the economies of many nations operate so close to the subsistence level that a drought or other act of nature can cause mass starvation.

Capital Funding. An alternative to foreign trade as a means of acquiring capital has been foreign loans and foreign aid—frequently offered by both the United States and the Soviet Union in their competition for the allegiances of nonaligned nations. But foreign loans and aid frequently come with strings attached. The receiving nation may be requested to supply the trading partner with certain valuable minerals, for example, or to allow a military base to be installed upon its territory. As a result of such requirements, many developing nations seek to retain their nonaligned status and the independence to find their own solutions to their problems.

In developing countries, farming and industries are highly labor intensive, rarely producing a surplus of commodities for sale. Shown is a coal-mining operation in India and rice-winnowing in South Vietnam.

Roads and Communications Systems. In addition to the need for industrial machinery, developing nations must also build modern transportation and communications systems in order to exploit whatever economic potential they may have. Roads or railroads are needed to transport commodities to urban markets or to ports for foreign trade. In addition, more rapid forms of communications such as telephones are useful in conducting the everyday transactions of manufacturing and transportation. To illustrate the disparities between the capabilities of developed and nondeveloped nations: while the United States has 1032 miles of roads for every thousand square miles, Chad has only 1 mile per thousand. And while the United States has 77 telephones for every 100 persons, Ethiopia has only 3.

The Problem of Illiteracy. Modernization, industrialization, and democracy require a literate population. The literacy rate in many developed nations is 95 percent or higher, but in developing countries it may be as low as 15 percent. Bringing about an increase in literacy is difficult for an underdeveloped nation. It requires money to build and maintain school buildings, to provide books, and to pay teachers. To keep children in school also requires doing without their labor—a luxury only a wealthy society can afford. In the United States, 78 percent of the school-age population (ages 5 to 24) are in school; in Kenya, 39 percent; and in Ethiopia, 8 percent. Yet without an educated and trained work force, industrialization is impossible, and capable administrators and leaders will also be in short supply.

Health and Overpopulation Problems. The lack of hospital facilities and trained medical personnel obviously affect the health and productivity of a society, and when combined with inadequate food supplies, will have even more serious consequences. One characteristic of underdeveloped nations is a high rate of infant mortality. In Botswana, for example, there are 175 deaths for every thousand live births; in India, 139; and in Kenya, 83. In the United States, by contrast, there are about 11 infant deaths for every thousand live births. Yet despite their high rates of infant mortality, developing nations continue to experience a rapid population growth; that is, babies being born at a greater rate than people dying. While the United States has a 7 percent population growth, such nations as Kenya, Ethiopia, Iraq and El Salvador have growth rates four or five times as high. Rapid growths in population, then, are occurring in precisely those nations whose economic resources are most limited. The result is the very low standard of living prevalent in these countries.

POLITICAL ISSUES

As we have seen, a command economy implies at least a degree of political dictatorship, for the state must have the ability to force or command economic change. By contrast, the government of a democratic capitalistic society incorporates the peoples' will—in theory, at least. Because citizens of a democracy demonstrate their political views through the ballot, change is slow. A new idea must be introduced, explained, and defended until the majority accepts it.

One Party Rule. Most developing and underdeveloped nations are in a hurry to bring about change and unwilling to wait for popular acceptance. This is one reason why most have adopted some form of political dictatorship, or one-party rule. Other circumstances have also contributed to the prevalence of such governments. Independence from the colonial powers was usually achieved through a mass movement organized by nationalists, often by military means. With victory achieved, these leaders remained in power, not only because of their military strength, but also because they had won the allegiance of the people. Although many of these leaders have promised or even carried out elections, a true democracy requires a literate population and reliable transportation—conditions nearly unattainable in an underdeveloped society.

Problems of National Identity. Most boundaries in colonial territories were created by the imperialist powers for their own purposes and do not reflect natural divisions. In many cases, such as Nigeria, national boundaries bisect tribal areas, a fact which has contributed to internal dissension. The Ibo peoples of Nigeria, for example, see themselves as members of a tribe with its own political, social, economic, and cultural cohesiveness; they do not view themselves as Nigerians.

Leaders of the newly independent developing countries have had to find ways to forge a national identity for their peoples. One of the methods they have used is to encourage the hatred of an outside group. In the Middle East, for example, the unifying self-concept of many Arab states has been animosity toward Israel.

Religious Conflict. In some areas, different religious factions within a new nation have created civil wars. For example, India before independence was torn by Hindu-Moslem rivalries, which climaxed at the time of independence in 1947 and resulted in the creation of two separate nations. Lebanon today is torn by similar religious conflicts—among various Christian sects and Moslem sects, and between Christians and Moslems. The differences between them are based on centuries-old tribal and religious issues.

DECOLONIZATION

Although World War II was the watershed period in the process of decolonization, the roots of independence movements reach back into the 19th century. As nationalism became a primary force for change in Europe, its seeds were transplanted into the non-Western world as well. At first, such indigenous nationalist movements were stifled by the military might and economic influence of the European colonial powers. By the end of World War II, however, the European states had lost much of their will to rule and their power to do so. Some, like Britain, bowed graciously to the inevitable; others, like France and Portugal, clung tenaciously to their possessions until the forces of rebellion overwhelmed them.

THE BRITISH EX-COLONIES British imperialist policy was always pragmatic; that is, the government traditionally adapted its colonial policy in accordance with local needs and demands. In 1931, the British parliament enacted the Statute of Westminster, which ended legislative control over the mostly white-populated British Dominions—Canada, New Zealand, and Australia. The former dominions became equal partners in a new entity called the *British Commonwealth*. At this time, British leaders contemplated extending *dominion* status, which entailed a limited self-government, to Britain's non-white colonies. But the nationalist movement in India accelerated more rapidly than they expected.

THE INDIAN NATIONALIST MOVEMENT

The nationalist movement in India had coalesced in 1885, when the Indian National Congress was formed. The Congress provided a means by which Indian leaders could communicate their concerns to the British government and press for reforms. A second organization, the Muslim League, was formed in 1906. This group provided a

Through nonviolent methods, Mahatma Gandhi forced Britain and the world to think about the issue of native rule in India. In this demonstration, in 1930, Gandhi and his supporters marched to the sea to collect salt in violation of a British law which required Indians to pay a tax on this item.

forum for Muslim nationalists who felt that the Hindu-dominated National Congress did not address their needs.

Mahatma Gandhi. In the 20th century, the nationalist movement was revitalized by the Hindu leader Mohandas Gandhi (1869–1948). Gandhi had been trained as a lawyer in England and lived for 20 years in South Africa, where he campaigned against racial laws that discriminated against Indians and other minorities. Shortly before the outbreak of World War I, Gandhi returned to India, where he joined the National Congress and adopted the simple lifestyle of the poorest class of Indian.

In his long struggle for a peaceful separation of India from the British Empire, Gandhi originated the tactics of *civil disobedience* and *nonviolent resistance*. He orchestrated campaigns in which Indian demonstrators singled out a particular colonial law and disobeyed it in a peaceful way. When the British authorities reacted, Gandhi and his followers submitted to arrest, imprisonment, and even beatings without returning the violence. Gandhi soon became known as the *Mahatma,* or Holy One.

In 1919, as a result of India's contributions to the war effort, the British Parliament introduced reforms which allowed Indian ministers to administer certain bureaus of the government. These reforms were not enough, however, and Gandhi, Jawaharlal Nehru, and other Indian leaders were jailed again in 1930 for their continuing civil disobedience campaign. In 1935, the British Parliament passed the Government of India Act, which provided for limited self-government, and in 1943, the British government promised to grant India full independence at the end of World War II.

The Partition of India. Complicating the issue of independence were the rivalries between Hindus and Moslems, which degenerated into episodes of violence in 1946. The last viceroy of India, Lord Mountbatten, was faced with the task of enacting India's independence while averting a civil war between Hindu and Moslem nationalists. He proposed the partition of India into the Hindu state of India and the Moslem state of Pakistan, a solution which the Muslim League had been demanding since 1940. In the face of continuing violence between the two factions, Gandhi and other leaders reluctantly agreed, and the proposal was enacted in August 1947. But the settlement was fraught with problems, including the resettlement of thousands of Hindus and Moslems into their respective areas, and the added complication of an East and West Pakistan on either side of India.

Following the partition, conflicts continued to occur. Among the victims of religious warfare was Gandhi himself, assassinated in January 1948 by a Hindu who resented his conciliatory attitude toward the Moslems. The Moslem leader Mohammed Ali Jinnah died the same year.

In Pakistan, a series of military coups ensued. Moreover, conflict developed between the relatively prosperous West Pakistan and the poverty-stricken East Pakistan. In 1971, with India's aid, East Pakistan separated from West and established the independent state of Bangladesh.

Modern India. Like Pakistan, India faced serious difficulties upon independence, including overpopulation, agricultural underproduction, and disunity. Jawaharlal Nehru, who had been Gandhi's most prominent supporter in the fight for independence, served as prime minister from 1947 to 1964. Nehru attempted to solve India's problems by modernizing its agricultural methods, introducing new industries, and encouraging the use of birth control methods. In spite of some success, however, the growth of India's population cancelled most of the gains made in agricultural and industrial production. Moreover, the press for modernization often came into conflict with the ancient Indian traditions and lifestyles that Gandhi himself had glorified.

471

THE PARTITION OF INDIA

Did the partition of India resolve the conflicts between Moslems and Hindus?

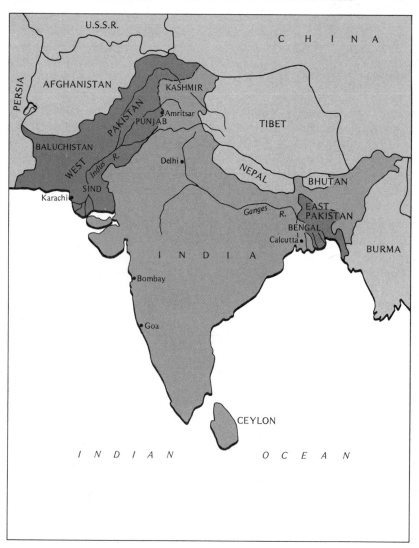

Nehru's problems were complicated by a Chinese invasion of Indian territory in 1962. This action forced India to abandon its policy of peaceful nonalignment, for it became necessary to organize an army to protect India's borders. Eventually, India diverted enough resources from other programs to create its own nuclear deterrent.

After Nehru's death in 1964, the prominent politician Lal Bahadur Shastri was elected prime minister. In 1966, he was succeeded in office by Nehru's daughter, Indira Gandhi. During her term in office, cultural and religious conflicts within India were intensified as she continued her father's programs of modernization and introduced a controversial new family planning program. In 1984, she was assassinated by members of the Sikh faction, a religious sect which combines elements of both Hinduism and Islam.

In 1947, Jawaharlal Nehru became the first prime minister of India. Nehru led a struggle to modernize India and alleviate its poverty, while Gandhi had represented the nation's traditional way of life.

Kwame Nkrumah (center) was elected prime minister of Ghana in 1957. Faced with problems caused by tribal rivalries and an economic depression, Nkrumah gradually established a police state. He was deposed by an army coup in 1966.

BRITAIN'S AFRICAN COLONIES

Britain's African colonies acquired independence in a relatively brief period, from 1951 to 1964. The leadership of both major political parties in Britain recognized the inevitability of the loss of the empire, and usually refrained from engaging in protracted military struggles against the revolutionaries.

BRITAIN'S AFRICAN COLONIES—DATES OF INDEPENDENCE

1957	Ghana (Gold Coast)
1960	Nigeria
1961	Sierra Leone
	Tanganyika (Tanzania '64)
1962	Rwanda
1963	Zanzibar (Tanzania '64)
	Kenya
1964	Nyasaland (Malawi)
	Northern Rhodesia (Zambia)
1965	Gambia
1966	Basutoland (Lesotho)
	Bechuanaland (Botswana)
1968	Swaziland

Ghana. The first of the African colonies to achieve independence was the Gold Coast, now the nation of Ghana. The nationalist movement was led by Kwame Nkrumah, who pressed the British governors of the colony to allow free elections. In 1951, Nkrumah's demand was granted, and his workers' party received a clear mandate in national elections. The next year, he became head of the new state of Ghana. Full independence was granted in 1957.

Kenya. In the British colony of Kenya, the nationalist movement at first centered on the fact that European settlers had appropriated much of the colony's land. In 1952, a terrorist movement known as the Mau Mau mounted a rebellion and killed a number of white settlers. The British were unwilling to allow this form of protest, and after four years of fighting, finally succeeded in quelling the

When the principle of majority rule was instituted in Kenya, Jomo Kenyatta quickly emerged as a national leader. He maintained a firm hold on the economic and political life of Kenya until his death in 1978.

lius Nyerere, wanted to create a more egalitarian state than that of Kenya—a government controlled by the common people rather than by a wealthy clique. To this end, he encouraged the growth of village communes—based on African tribal traditions of cooperation as well as socialist models. Because Tanzania does not attract substantial outside investment, it remains a poorer country than Kenya, but its political institutions have ensured a more democratic form of government.

Nigeria. One of the wealthiest of Britain's colonies, oil-rich Nigeria, received independence in 1960, but soon experienced civil war between its three major tribes. Beginning in 1967, the tribal leader Colonel Ojukwu led a movement to establish an independent Ibo state to be known as Biafra. After three years of bloody civil war, this independence movement was suppressed by the Hausa-dominated Nigerian government, and the country was reunited. In 1979, a one-party republic was established in Nigeria,

Mau Mau movement in 1956. The nationalist leader Jomo Kenyatta was imprisoned during this period, although he denied involvement with the Mau Maus. After his release from prison, Kenyatta negotiated for the institution of free elections and black national rule. In 1963, he was elected prime minister of the newly independent state of Kenya.

During Kenyatta's term as prime minister, internal dissent was repressed, and a few wealthy men controlled the government. The economy of Kenya benefited—and continues to benefit—from the substantial investments of European and American businesses in its industries.

Tanzania. Zanzibar was granted independence in 1963—the same year as Kenya—and joined with the former colony of Tanganyika to form the new state of Tanzania. The nationalist leader of Tanzania, Ju-

During the bitter civil war in Nigeria, thousands of Biafrans starved to death after Ojukwu's forces were surrounded and cut off from the outside world. Here, concerned Americans display a poster in front of the White House to call attention to the crisis.

BIAFRA POSTCARD

474

A black township in South Africa. Under the policy of apartheid, native South Africans must live in areas separate from the white population, work at poorly paid jobs, and attend separate schools. Nevertheless, their labor is an essential part of the nation's economy.

but in 1983 a coup reestablished a military government. While the nation's oil riches have provided a measure of economic prosperity, periodic drops in world oil prices have threatened the country's stability.

South Africa. The thorniest of problems continue to plague the former British colony of South Africa. The population of South Africa today is rigidly segregated into four categories: the dominant whites, descendants of the original British and Dutch colonists; the racially mixed "coloreds;" Asians; and native Africans. Each group has a sharply defined and separate status, and the governing white minority have enforced a variety of discriminatory and unfair laws upon them. As one example, native Africans are not allow to settle in the cities where many of them work, forcing them to spend several

hours a day commuting to their homes in the largely uninhabitable wasteland areas.

The white government has enforced its policy of segregation, or *apartheid,* through military means. The whites' rigid suppression of the human rights of the majority of South Africans has incurred worldwide disapproval and varying degrees of political and economic pressure from other nations. These pressures have included divestiture of stocks in companies which do business in South Africa, sanctions, and public protestation.

The determination and resolve of such black leaders as Nelson and Winnie Mandela, and Bishop Desmond Tutu, crystallized black opposition to the white regime in South Africa, and rendered it only a matter of time until South Africa could join the rest of the continent as a native-ruled country.

The white minority government of South Africa has used its police and military power to prevent public demonstrations against its policies. Such suppressions of basic civil rights have isolated the government from the rest of the world.

COLLAPSE OF THE FRENCH EMPIRE

The French controlled the second largest colonial empire after Britain's, with possessions in Indochina and in most of north and central Africa. Divestment of these colonies did not begin until a decade after World War II had ended, for the French government made a determined military effort to retain its possessions.

THE VIETNAM WAR

Even before the outbreak of World War II, nationalist movements had sprung up in the French colony of Indochina, now known as Vietnam. In the 1920s, Ho Chi Minh (1890–1969), a young Marxist revolutionary, began to organize opposition to the French, and in 1930 he founded a communist party as a focus for nationalist activities. During the years of the Japanese occupation of Vietnam (1941–1945), Ho formed the *Vietminh* movement, a league dedicated to the independence of Vietnam. With Japan's defeat in 1945, the Vietminh took control of northern Vietnam and established the Democratic Republic of Vietnam under Ho Chi Minh's leadership. When the French returned to Vietnam, they recognized Ho's republic in the north, but tried to resume their control of the south.

At the end of 1946, war broke out between North and South Vietnam, a conflict that would continue for 29 years. The Soviet Union and its allies, including China, supported Ho's regime, while the U.S. and its allies supported the French in the south. After eight years of fighting, the French lost a disastrous battle in May 1954 and withdrew from Vietnam.

An international conference was held in Geneva in 1954 to decide Vietnam's future. A truce line was established at the 17th parallel. By now, the United States was supporting the government in the south. The conference agreed that elections were to be held in 1956 to establish a government for the entire country. However, the United States did not sign the accords, and the elections were never held.

Gradually, U.S. aid to South Vietnam increased; financial aid and weapons were followed by military advisers, and under President Lyndon Johnson, the U.S. sent troops to help in the fighting. The North Vietnamese, aided by guerrillas in the South called the *Viet Cong*, proved to be formidable enemies. During the Johnson administration, American forces rose to 500,000 troops, and massive bombing raids devastated parts of both the North and South—all to no avail.

The Vietnam War became a serious drain on U.S. resources, and an anti-war movement arose in the United States. President Richard Nixon was elected in 1968 after promising to end the war. When negotiations with the North failed, the war spread into neighboring Laos and Cambodia, which the communists were using as supply routes and staging areas.

Finally, in 1973, the Paris Peace accords were signed, providing for American withdrawal on the understanding that communist troops would remain in place. However, the South Vietnamese government, even with massive American aid, was unable to keep the communists from violating their promises. In 1975, the North Vietnamese conquered the South and established a government over the entire country.

The effects of the war included the collapse of noncommunist governments in

A scene from the Vietnam War: an American soldier guards a prisoner suspected of being a Viet Cong. The war was waged for 29 years and claimed the lives of more than a million Vietnamese.

Cambodia and Laos. In Cambodia, the triumphant Khmer Rouge communist forces renamed the country *Kampuchea* and carried out a ghastly campaign of extermination against their own people. In 1978, Vietnam invaded Cambodia to establish order, but faced opposition from China, which feared the growth of a powerful Vietnam on its borders. China invaded northern Vietnam briefly in 1979. The spectacle of communist forces fighting each other demonstrated that, in this instance, the forces of nationalism were stronger than communist ideology.

Between 1975 and 1980, more than 800,000 refugees fled the fighting throughout Southeast Asia. Around 300,000 left Vietnam to escape communist rule there. Many of these refugees were accepted into the United States. The war, which was the longest in American history, claimed the lives of 56,000 Americans as well as the lives of at least one million Asians and cost $150 billion. The disaster led to widespread reluctance among the American people to further commit American troops to oppose communist forces.

FRANCE'S AFRICAN COLONIES

The nature of France's colonial administration complicated the question of independence in many of its colonies. In most French colonies, massive programs had been undertaken to impart a knowledge of French language and culture to the natives, for it was intended that the colonies would eventually become integrated into France's own political and social structure. In 1946, French citizenship was extended to all of the inhabitants of French colonies. However, there were many irregularities in the elections and local governments that were established, and this measure did little to dampen nationalist movements for independence. The Arab nationalist leaders of Tunisia, Morocco, and Algeria would accept nothing less than full independence, and the weakness of France after the Second World War ensured that they would eventually succeed in their goal.

Algeria. In Algeria, an ardent group of Arab nationalists led by Ben Bella declared war on France in 1954. Bella's organization of about 20,000 men operated secretly and used terrorist tactics to achieve its goal of evicting the French from Algeria. The French government was forced to commit half a million soldiers in its effort to counter Bella's movement. But although many French citizens began to think that the cost of retaining Algeria had become too high, the approximately one million *Colons* in Algeria, descendents of the original French settlers, insisted that France must ensure their right to live in Algeria through force.

In 1958, French army forces sympathetic to the *Colons* organized a revolt against the government of the Fourth Republic in 1958. In this crisis, General Charles de Gaulle was elected, receiving the vote of many Algerians who thought he would oppose the independence movement. Instead, de Gaulle granted Algeria's independence in 1962, ending the Algerian war.

Tunisia and Morocco. In both Tunisia and Morocco, as in Algeria, conflicts broke out between French colonists and Arab nationalists shortly after World War II. Both nations achieved independence in 1956. Since independence, Tunisia and Morocco have pursued relatively moderate foreign policies, avoiding permanent alliances with either the West or the Soviet bloc.

THE FRENCH COLONIES: DATES OF INDEPENDENCE	
1956	Morocco
	Tunisia
1958	Guinea
1960	Malagary Republic (Madagascar)
	Dahomey
	Niger
	Upper Volta
	Ivory Coast
	Central African Republic
	Chad
	French Congo
	Gabon
	Mali
	Senegal
	Mauritania
1962	Algeria

In Algeria, nationalist issues were complicated by the fact that several generations of French colonists had looked upon Algeria as their home. Terrorist acts such as this car bombing were carried out by desperate colons as independence approached.

OTHER INDEPENDENCE MOVEMENTS

Like Britain and France, the other European colonial powers, the Netherlands, Belgium, and Portugal, were unable to retain their empires following World War II. With the independence of their colonies in Africa and Asia the colonial era finally came to an end.

INDONESIA

The Dutch East Indies, later known as Indonesia, was occupied by the Japanese during the war period. Because of this occupation, Indonesians were all the more unwilling to submit to the return of a Dutch colonial government. After four years of bloody conflict, the Dutch government recognized the independence of its island empire in 1949.

Indonesia was ruled by Achmed Sukarno, the nationalist leader who had led the movement for independence, until 1966. In that year, his dictatorship was overthrown by General Suharto. As the superpowers contested each other for influence in Asia, Indonesia declared its allegiance by joining ASEAN, a nonmilitary alliance of Southeast Asian Nations which works to prevent the spread of communism in that area. (This organization replaced an American-dominated group, SEATO, which was dissolved in 1977.) The other members of ASEAN are Malaysia, Thailand, Singapore, and the Philippines.

THE BELGIAN CONGO (ZAIRE)

The Belgian Congo, later renamed Zaire, is about seven times the size of its colonial ruler. Nevertheless, Belgium was able to retain control of this colony until 1960. Soon after independence, Zaire experienced civil war when Moise Tshombe led an effort to make the rich province of Katanga (now Shaba) an independent nation. Through the intercession of Belgium, the United States, and the United Nations, this secession movement was finally suppressed in 1963.

In 1965, an army coup brought to power General Joseph-Desire Mobutu Sese Seko, who established a one-party regime. Since then, invasions by Soviet-backed Angola have been repelled with the aid of Belgian and French troops. The Western powers, including the United States, have also supplied economic support to prevent the collapse of the Mobuto government.

ANGOLA AND MOZAMBIQUE

The Portuguese were the first Europeans to explore Africa, and the last to relinquish their African colonies. Both Angola and Mozambique received their independence in 1975, and each established a Marxist regime. In Angola, Jose Eduardo dos Santos established a one-party regime which accepts aid from the Soviet Union and the support of Cuban troops. A rebel movement, supported by the Union of South Africa, is in control of some parts of the country.

Across the continent lies the other former Portuguese possession, Mozambique. In its policy toward South Africa, Mozambique works closely with Zimbabwe (formerly the British colony of Rhodesia), which established a black majority government in 1979.

THE MIDDLE EAST

Current events in the Middle East are a collage of religious conflicts, historic animosities, Soviet and American influence, and oil. Most nations in the Middle East and in Arab North Africa were also targets of European imperialism.

THE BRITISH-FRENCH MANDATES

After World War I, the territories of the defeated Ottoman Empire—the modern states of Israel, Jordan, Syria, and Iraq—were assigned as mandates to Britain and France. Through their trusteeship, the British and French hoped to control trade routes through the Suez Canal and the Persian Gulf, and to develop the region's oil resources. For the most part, both countries yielded to local independence movements when they arose, and maintained only indirect control over their territories: by 1932, Britain had recognized the legitimacy of Arab governments in Iraq, Transjordan (now Jordan), and its former protectorate of Egypt, while France had sponsored the development of constitutional governments in Syria and Lebanon. The one exception to this policy of indirect control was Palestine (now Israel). Because of a promise made in 1917 by Arthur Balfour, the British foreign secretary, Britain was committed to the establishment of a homeland for the Jewish people. For this reason, Palestine could not be granted independence as long as the majority of its citizens were Arabs.

TURKEY AND IRAN

In both Turkey and Iran, nationalist movements led to the expulsion of the imperialist powers. These movements differed from those in the other areas of the Middle East, however, for their leaders did not consider Islamic religion and culture to be the primary unifying force of their nations. Instead, they elected to follow Western models in modernizing their countries.

Turkey. In 1919, as the Ottoman Empire was being divided among the victorious Allies, Greece sought to regain the territory in Asia Minor which had once belonged to the ancient Greek Empire. The Greek invasion of the Turkish homeland of Anatolia was supported by the Allies, who intended to share in its division. Between 1919 and 1923, the Turkish nationalist leader Mustapha Kamal—later known as Ataturk, or "father of the Turks"—led the Turkish battle for survival as a nation.

Surprisingly, the Turks succeeded in repelling the invasion, and Ataturk was recognized as supreme ruler of Turkey in place of the Sultan. In the following decades, he began to modernize his country in defiance of religious fundamentalists: nearly all of his reforms violated the tenets and customs of

Ataturk led the Turks in their fight to retain Anatolia after the Ottoman Empire was dissolved. To the dismay of many of his supporters, he then restructured Turkey as a modern, industrialized republic.

Islam. The practice of polygamy was abolished; women were given equal rights with men; and Turks were ordered to adopt a Western-style alphabet—violating the Islamic law that the Koran must be read in Arabic. Moreover, the education system was remodeled along western European lines, and the process of industrialization was begun. Within a few years Turkey had evolved from the defeated capital of an outmoded empire to a modern, self-sufficient republic.

Iran. The nation of Persia, how known by its ancient tribal name of *Iran*, had never been directly controlled by a colonial power, but Britain had important investments in the region's oil resources through the Anglo-Persian Oil Company, and Russia had also established a presence in the area.

In 1925, Reza Khan, a nationalist reformer, seized control of the government and evicted both British and Russian troops from the country. He proclaimed himself to be Shah of Iran. Like Ataturk, he believed that the best way to deal with the Western nations was to achieve equality with them. He began a program to modernize the country along Western lines, concentrating upon education and industrialization. Many of his rulings—for example, a proclamation that women need not veil their faces in public—contradicted Islamic law.

In 1951, a new group of nationalists seized control of the Iranian government, and began to follow an anti-Western foreign policy. The Western powers, fearing that Iran might align itself with the Soviet bloc, helped the Shah, Mohammed Rezi, to return to power in 1953. From that time on, the Shah ruled as an autocrat. The infamous *Savak*, a secret police organization, enforced the Shah's policies and eliminated all internal dissent. With the vast wealth of Iran's resources and economic aid from the U.S., Iran was able to establish an industrial base and completely reform its agricultural system by 1970. As a result of these measures, living conditions for all Iranians improved, while the gap between rich and poor also became more visible. But although Iran was viewed as a stable, properous nation by the outside world, the forces of dissent were at work within the country.

In 1979, the Shah was deposed by a political and religious revolution led by Ruhollah Khomeini, a prominent *ayatollah*, or religious leader of the Shiite sect of Islam. After establishing his fundamentalist government, Ayatollah Khomeini depicted the United States as the enemy of Islam because of its long support of the Shah. In November 1979, Iranian militants seized control of the American embassy in Teheran and kept the embassy's staff hostage for more than a year, effectively breaking diplomatic relations with all of the Western powers. Many of the moderate Islamic leaders of Iran—including several who had participated in Khomeini's

The Ayatollah Khomeini became the focus of the 1979 revolution which deposed the shah of Iran. Under his leadership, Iran has undertaken a messianic role, attempting to export its fundamentalist revolution throughout the Middle East.

revolution—were executed, and the Shiite regime undertook a complete reorganization of Iranian society. All Western influences were denounced as "evil" or "satanic," and traditional Islamic laws—including the rule that women must hold veils over their faces in public—were reinstated. Foreign policy, too, reflected the missionary zeal of the fundamentalist Shiites. In Lebanon, Khomeini sponsored terrorist actions to enhance Shiite influence in that country, and also undertook a major war against neighboring Iraq.

ISRAEL

By the end of World War II, hundreds of thousands of Jewish refugees had emigrated to the British mandate of Palestine as a result of Hitler's persecutions in Europe. The British at first tried to limit this emigration in response to the protests of Arab Palestinians. But the Balfour Declaration of 1917 had committed Britain to the idea of establishing a Jewish state in Palestine, and widespread sympathy for the sufferings of the Jewish people during the war increased the force of this commitment.

Unable to reconcile the demands of the Arabs and Jews in Palestine, and becoming daily more unpopular with each faction, the British handed over responsibility for the Palestinian problem to the United Nations. A UN committee suggested the partition of Palestine into separate Jewish and Arab states, but this plan was rejected by the Arabs. In May 1948, when the British withdrew from the area, the Jews of Palestine took matters into their own hands and declared the formation of the state of Israel.

The formation of a Jewish state in the predominately Arab Middle East created long-lasting problems and conflicts. Nearly one million Arab Palestinians were forced to emigrate from the area and were placed in relocation camps, pending their resettlement in other Arab states. The question of their future has become one of the most central and irresolvable questions in the contemporary Middle East.

EGYPT AND THE ARAB WORLD

In 1952, the corrupt government of King Farouk of Egypt was overthrown by a group of nationalists led by Colonel Gamal Abdel Nasser. Nasser's goals were to establish a republic in Egypt, and to make Egypt the center of the Arab world.

Adopting a policy of nonalignment with either of the superpowers, Nasser sought economic aid from both, especially to finance his Aswan High Dam project. When the Western powers withdrew their aid in 1956, Nasser seized control of the Suez Canal. This action precipitated an international crisis when Israel, supported by Britain and France, invaded Egypt to regain control of the canal. Major war was avoided when the United States and the United Nations insisted upon the withdrawal of these troops. But the episode led to two more major conflicts between Egypt and Israel.

ARAB/ISRAELI CONFLICT

In recent years, Arab nationalist leaders in the Middle East have formed several effective coalitions. These alliances have helped

Jewish survivors of Hitler's concentration camps began to arrive in Palestine at the end of World War II. In recognition of their desperate plight, British quotas governing immigration were waived.

Gamal Abdel Nasser became the recognized leader of the Arab world after defying the Western powers during the Suez Canal crisis. Sunken ships were used to block the canal.

the Arab nations to promote their common economic interests and to avoid dependence on either of the superpowers. However, the essential unifying factor behind them has been animosity toward the state of Israel.

The first coalition among the Arab states was the Arab League, formed in 1945 by Egypt, Iraq, Syria, Lebanon, Saudi Arabia, and Yemen. This alliance was put into action during the Palestine War of 1948, when the Arab states helped the Palestinians to mount a war against the newly formed state of Israel. Despite overwhelming odds, however, the Israelis defeated the Arabs.

The PLO. In 1964, Palestinian refugees formed the *Palestinian Liberation Organization* (PLO), a group dedicated to reclaiming Palestine from the Israelis. Leadership of the PLO was quickly assumed by Yasir Arafat, a guerrilla fighter who had been organizing attacks on Israel from bases in Syria, Jordan, and Lebanon. The PLO came to be the focus of Arab attempts to defeat Israel, as Arafat worked closely with Nasser and other Arab leaders to formulate a common policy.

The Six Days' War. In 1967, Nasser called upon the Arab states to mount a war against Israel. In response, Jordan, Syria, and Iraq promised to join Egypt in invading Israel. However, the Israeli general Moise Dayan convinced his government that Israel must strike first. On June 5th, the Israelis launched a surprise attack, destroying the Egyptian air force on the ground. During the next five days, the Israeli army captured the Sinai peninsula, the West Bank of the Jordan, and the Golan Heights. The war represented a resounding defeat for Nasser and his allies, and Israel retained control of the territory it had captured.

The Yom Kippur War. Nasser's successor as president of Egypt was Anwar Sadat (1970–1981), a moderate leader who hoped to negotiate a solution to the Arab-Israeli conflict. When, after two years, he was unable to persuade Israel to cede the territory

Anwar Sadat, Jimmy Carter, and Menachem Begin successfully negotiated an Egyptian-Israeli peace treaty in March 1979. Although many territorial issues remained unresolved, the treaty represented a major step in stabilizing relations between the two nations.

it had captured in the 1967 war, Sadat ordered a surprise attack upon Israel. The attack occurred on October 6th, 1973, as Israelis were observing the solemn festival of Yom Kippur. Egyptian, Syrian, and Iraqi forces, supplied by the Soviets, attacked Israel on two fronts. But Israel, which had a superior army and was equipped with weapons supplied by the U.S., quickly regrouped its forces after the surprise attack and defeated the Arab forces within two weeks. The war left the territorial boundaries of Israel unchanged.

After the failure of the Yom Kippur War, Sadat decided to satisfy the Israelis' primary condition for the return of territories by recognizing the existence of Israel. In 1977 he met with Menachem Begin, the prime minister of Israel. These preliminary talks led to a meeting with Jimmy Carter in 1979, in which the three leaders formulated an Egyptian-Israeli peace treaty. But while most Egyptians applauded the treaty, Sadat's initiative alienated Islamic fundamentalists, and isolated Egypt in the Arab world. In October 1981, a group of Islamic extremists as-

sassinated Sadat. His successor, Hosni Mubarak, has continued to follow a moderate policy.

Further Conflicts. Although the Egyptian-Israeli peace treaty ended the threat of an Egyptian invasion of Israel, the PLO continued to carry out terrorist attacks on Israel from bases in Lebanon. The anarchy prevailing in Lebanon—which had been the scene of a bitter civil war between various Moselm and Christian factions since 1975—provided an ideal background for guerrilla activities. Moreover, many thousands of Palestinian refugees, the pool from which PLO fighters were drawn, had settled in the area.

In response to PLO activities, the Israelis invaded Lebanon in 1978 with 20,000 troops. This encounter proved to be indecisive. In 1981, the Israelis began bombing PLO base camps in Lebanon and in 1982 invaded Lebanon again, forcing most PLO military forces out of that beleaguered country. With the withdrawal of the Palestinians, the Shiites, supported by Iran and other allies, became the most powerful Moslem faction in Lebanon.

Since 1975, Lebanon has been the battleground for many of the political and religious conflicts of the Middle East. Shown is a group of Shiite militiamen on patrol; a young victim of a bomb planted near a school in Christian East Beirut; and destruction caused by Israeli bombing of a Palestinian-controlled area in 1982.

What geo-political interests do the Western world and the U.S.S.R. have in the Middle East?

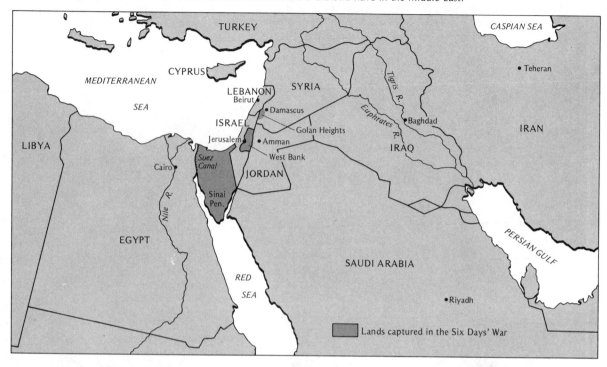

Lands captured in the Six Days' War

OPEC AND ARAB NATIONALISM

The Egypt-Israel conflicts in 1967 and 1973 caused intense concern in diplomatic circles throughout the world. The industrialized nations of the world considered the Middle East to be of vital strategic importance, since the area at the time supplied about 60 percent of the crude oil they consumed. Moreover, both of the superpowers had been closely involved in these conflicts through their supply of military equipment and other aid to the various Middle Eastern factions.

In 1961, the oil-producing countries of the Middle East formed the Organization of Petroleum Exporting Countries (OPEC) to coordinate marketing strategies for their product. As political conflicts with Israel and the superpowers developed, the members of OPEC began to use sales of crude oil as a political weapon. In 1973, OPEC protested Western support for Israel by restricting oil exports to Israel's allies, creating a quadrupling of oil prices in 1973 and 1974. This measure had immediate repercussions, causing inflation, unemployment, and other economic problems in the U.S., western Europe, and Japan. But the high price of oil also made it economically feasible to develop other sources of crude oil, notably in Britain and the U.S. Within a few years, Western oil production began to influence world markets, and the price of oil again plummeted.

The OPEC action of 1973 altered the political balance of the Middle East, bringing to prominence the two foremost oil-producing states, Saudi Arabia and Libya.

Saudi Arabia. In the mid-1920s, Ibn Saud consolidated his control over the Arabian peninsula and was recognized as the legitimate ruler of this territory by the British. Since that time, Saudi Arabia has continued to be governed by a monarchy and represents one of the most stable forces in the Middle East. The nation's oil riches have been used to develop an industrial base and to provide social services for its inhabitants. While

maintaining generally good relations with the West, the monarchs of Saudi Arabia have also played a leading role in Arab affairs. Because the holy cities of Mecca and Medina both lie within Saudi Arabia, the Saudi king is viewed as a central figure in the Moslem world. The Saudis have also provided substantial economic aid to Egypt and other poorer Arab countries, lessening their dependence upon the superpowers.

Libya. Libya, once an Italian colony, achieved its independence in 1951. From that time until the present, this sparsely populated nation has been ruled by one-man regimes. Until 1969, the conservative king, Mohammed Idris, maintained good relations with the West, even allowing the U.S. and Britain to establish military bases in the country. This situation was completely changed by a military coup in 1969, which established the regime of Colonel Qaddafi, a radical Arab nationalist. In 1970, Qaddafi forced the evacuation of the American and British bases in Libya and nationalized all foreign businesses. Since that time, Qaddafi has been a fervent supporter of the Palestinian cause, using his nation's oil wealth to aid terrorist groups and to build up a stockpile of advanced military weapons.

THE PHILIPPINES

The United States' only significant colony, the Philippines, received its independence in 1946. The new nation successfully followed a democratic path until the election of Ferdinand Marcos in 1965. Reelected overwhelmingly in 1969, Marcos moved to increase his power in the face of a communist insurgent movement. In 1972, he declared martial law and arrested hundreds of political opponents and journalists. The following year he proclaimed a new constitution.

While poverty plagued the Philippine population, Marcos and his wife amassed an immense fortune for themselves. Political opposition to their regime grew, and in 1986 the moderate Corazon Aquino was elected president. Aquino's husband, a prominent opponent of the Marcos regime, had been assassinated by Marcos forces, and her election represented the triumph of the liberal ideals that they had fought for. Although the U.S. had supported the corrupt Marcos regime in return for the right to station military bases in the Philippines, American recognition of the Aquino electoral victory has laid the basis for good U.S.-Philippine relations.

COMMUNIST CHINA

After years of civil war, China became a communist state on October 1, 1949, with the formal declaration of the People's Republic of China. Mao Tse-tung, the leader of the communist movement in China, was a pragmatic thinker who adopted Marxist theory to fit the particular circumstances of his country. Mao identified the peasants as the oppressed class in China, and first achieved recognition as a leader by organizing a successful peasant rebellion against the landlords. Although China was an agricultural nation, Mao proclaimed that industrialization could be brought about under the authority and direction of a Marxist government.

MAO'S AGRARIAN POLICY, 1949–1958

Once in power, Mao sought various means to convert China's agrarian society into an industrial one. To accomplish his aim, he first planned to increase agricultural productivity—to create the surplus of agricultural goods necessary to support an industrial revolution. As a preliminary step in this process, Mao introduced the slogan, "Land to the tillers." Like Mao's previous actions, this program was intended to inspire the co-operation of the peasants. In 1949 and 1950, peasants were encouraged to eliminate the last vestiges of feudal China by murdering their former landlords. Thousands enthusiastically responded.

Having achieved success in the first stage of his program, Mao introduced the second stage—the collectivization of agriculture. By 1952, 40 percent of China's rural households had complied with Mao's order to create joint farms or *producer cooperatives* by pooling their land, labor, and equipment. Mao then undertook another experiment in collective agriculture, the formation of *state farms*. Under this plan, initiated in 1955, land owned and managed by the state was tilled by peasants working for wages. This program, however, failed to receive enthusiastic support, and was incapable of satisfying the agricultural needs of nearly one billion Chinese—much less to act as a source of surplus capital.

THE GREAT LEAP FORWARD, 1958

Mao launched the Great Leap Forward campaign in 1958. Utilizing the slogan, "Walk on two legs," the Great Leap Forward was an attempt to bring about industrialization within gigantic, self-sufficient peasant communes: in these communes, peasants would not only produce agricultural products, but would manufacture steel as well. In accordance with this plan, more than 500 million Chinese peasants were placed in about 260,000 communes. Each commune of about 5000 families was organized along military lines, with peasants divided into squads to accomplish particular tasks. The Great Leap Forward proved to be a colossal failure. Bad harvests, peasant opposition, and the inferior steel produced in backyard steel furnaces were the products of this system. In 1961, the Maoist government again changed direction, breaking up the large communes into smaller economic units.

After overcoming the forces of the Kuomintang, Mao proclaimed the establishment of the People's Republic of China on October 1, 1949.

A mass rally of Red Guards in Peking. During the Cultural Revolution, all symbols of authority and prestige came under attack: universities were closed, ancient art works destroyed, and thousands of people—including high officials of the Communist Party—were sent to the countryside to perform manual labor.

THE GREAT PROLETARIAN CULTURAL REVOLUTION, 1965–1969

The last year of the Great Leap Forward experiment, 1960, coincided with conflicts between China and the Soviet Union (Chapter 25). As a result of these two factors, a major policy disagreement emerged within the Chinese Communist Party (CCP), centered on the question of economic systems. Out of these policy debates and subsequent tensions came the Great Proletarian Cultural Revolution (GPCR), launched in 1965.

The GPCR was Mao's solution to China's problems. The essence of the quarrel within the Chinese Communist Party was whether to bring about economic and political change gradually—the position advocated by the premier, Chou Enlai, or to quickly restructure the entire society—the position advocated by Mao. In Mao's view, Chinese society was infected by moderates, or "backsliders," who should be either converted to the ideals of the communist revolution or eliminated.

Beginning in 1965, the youth of China, or-

ganized into the Red Guard, went on a rampage. Rallies and demonstrations were held, in which readings from Chairman Mao's "Little Red Book" of collected thoughts played a prominent part. The Red Guard then went into factories, universities, and rural areas, seeking and identifying "capitalist roaders " and "bourgeois elements."

During the GPCR, the quality of being "red," or ideologically dedicated to communist principles, became the sole criterion in awarding government offices, university professorships, and other posts. The enemy during this period was "the expert," one who put technical or scientific knowledge above politics. The effect of the GPCR was complete national upheaval for nearly four years. Thousands of people were killed, and many more were imprisoned or sent to agricultural communes to reform themselves through hard manual labor and self-criticism. It was a unique experience, a revolution and a virtual civil war, begun not by rebels but by the government itself.

Mao's rationale for instigating the GPCR appears to have been, first of all, his attempt to win the power struggle within the Communist Party. By providing the youth of China—the Red Guard—with a focus and a visible enemy, Mao effectively preempted the forces of revolt. The ideal of a continuing communist revolution also implied reverence of Mao as the founder of the original revolution, and kept any other privileged class from emerging.

The End of the GPCR. In 1969, the Chinese regular army—the People's Liberation Army—brought an end to the national disorder. Gradually, the moderate elements within the Communist Party reasserted power over the army and the nation, and Mao's revolution was denounced as too extreme. Although Mao remained as party chairman, he was now an old man, and he increasingly came under the influence of his third wife, Chiang Ching, an ex-movie actress who was later charged of having antiproletarian leanings.

China after Mao. In 1976 both Mao and Chou Enlai died. Mao's death marked another turning point for China, for he had personified the communist revolution. In retrospect, it appeared that Mao had made little progress in attaining his goal of industrialization. At the same time, he had instituted a vast totalitarian regime which enforced conformity of thought, action, and even physical appearance.

Mao was briefly succeeded by the "Gang of Four," a coalition led by his widow. After this group was defeated and brought to trial, a more moderate regime came to power. The current leader, Deng Ziao-ping, was at one time a victim of the GPCR. His reputation was restored in the 1970s, and he is now introducing a wide variety of reforms. The most dramatic reform has been the introduction of a limited capitalism, in which peasants are allowed to sell a percentage of their surplus production for profit. The results have been impressive. Although most peasants' income remains at the subsistence level, an increasing number are prospering, and are able to purchase consumer goods for the first time.

CONTEMPORARY LATIN AMERICA Although most Latin American countries have been independent for over 150 years, they remain underdeveloped or developing nations, struggling with the same problems that afflict the newly independent nations—economic disparities between privileged and nonprivileged classes, repressive one-party dictatorships, and foreign interference.

Both Cuba and Nicaragua have adopted Marxist governments. El Salvador continues in the throes of civil war, with a significant Marxist guerrilla movement. In Chile, the socialist government of Salvador Allende, a popular leader, was toppled by a military coup in 1973: there have been allegations of U.S. involvement in Allende's assassination. His successor, General Augusto Pinochet, is a dictator with a record of state-directed brutality and contravention of human rights.

Except for Argentina, the other major states of Latin America are all governed by dictatorships. In Argentina, Britain's victory in a war over the offshore Falkland Islands brought about the downfall of the military dictatorship which had sponsored the war. The nation is now governed by a more representative civilian government.

U.S. Policy in Latin America. In general, U.S. policy toward its neighbors to the south is embodied by the Monroe Doctrine of 1823 and the Roosevelt Corollary of 1904. These documents established the principle that foreign involvement in Latin America constitutes a direct threat to U.S. security and provides a rationale for interference in Latin American affairs. Under recent presidents, the U.S. has supported right-wing regimes, despite their violations of human rights, in an effort to prevent the spread of communism. Nevertheless, the poverty of most Latin American nations makes them prime targets of radical political activists.

SUMMARY

The disparities between the rich and poor of the world contribute both to international tensions and to internal conflicts. The peoples of most new nations experienced a period of rising expectations as independence approached, believing that they would immediately share in the prosperity of developed nations. But such hopes were almost always disappointed. In addition, independence often aggravated ancient tribal and religious rivalries, as each group strove to achieve a dominent position in the new nation.

The process of modernization and industrialization—the only way to achieve economic sufficiency—is a slow, painful, and uneven one. Yet for the first time in history the means—the technology and expertise—are at hand. Each of the struggling new nations has had to determine its priorities and find its own path to development.

QUESTIONS

1 Summarize the problems that developing countries face. Which are the result of colonialism? Which can be attributed to other factors such as geography, climate, and cultural traditions?
2 Why is the socialist model attractive to the leaders of developing countries? What are the weaknesses of socialist economic policy?
3 Before granting independence, Britain and France established parliamentary democracies in nearly all of their former colonies. Yet few of these governments have survived. What are the requirements of a successful democracy? Why have so many developing countries failed to develop representative governments?
4 What is apartheid? How has it affected South Africa's relations with its neighbors and with the rest of the world?
5 Why is the Middle East considered a vital strategic area by the Western powers and the Soviet bloc?

BIBLIOGRAPHY

CHESNEAUX, JEAN. *China, The People's Republic, 1949–1976.* New York: Pantheon, 1979. *A recent survey of the regime of Mao Tse-tung, including an analysis of the Great Proletarian Cultural Revolution.*

DEAN, VERA MICHELES. *The Nature of the Non-Western World.* New York: Mentor Books, 1966. *The author analyzes the important historical and cultural roots of non-Western nations, discusses their present status, and analyzes the cultural factors that may impede future development.*

FRASER, JOHN. *The Chinese: Portrait of a People.* New York: Summit Books, 1980. *A personal account of life in contemporary China by the bureau chief of the Toronto Globe, who lived in China between 1977 and 1979. The author has captured the character of the Chinese people as they faced the changes brought about after the death of Mao.*

PATON, ALAN. *Cry, The Beloved Country.* New York: Harper & Row, 1951. *Paton's novel, set in South Africa, depicts the tragedy of apartheid in that country.*

SEGAL, RONALD. *African Profiles.* Baltimore: Penguin Books, 1963. *Biographical sketches of more than 400 politicians who influenced and led the independence movements of the African states between 1945 and 1963.*

WARD, BARBARA. *Five ideas that Change the World.* New York: Norton, 1959. *An analysis of the impact of nationalism, industrialism, colonialism, communism, and internationalism in the modern world.*

WARD, BARBARA. *Rich Nations, Poor Nations.* New York: Norton, 1962. *An overview of the economic disparities between nations and a plea to the Western nations to aid the poorer ones.*

28

● *The old order changes, yielding place to new.*
ALFRED, LORD TENNYSON

Postmodern Times

We live at the dawn of a new age and witness changes as profound as those that occurred during the two most significant eras in human history. The first, the Neolithic revolution, which began in the Middle East some 9,000 years ago, transformed human beings from food gatherers to food producers. This transformation marked the beginning of civilization as we know it. As they learned to cultivate grains and domesticate animals, humans were able to form permanent settlements—villages, towns, and eventually great cities—which led in turn to the development of complex social, political, and economic institutions.

The second radical transformation was the Industrial Revolution, which began in England in the 18th century. This shift from a predominantly agrarian to a predominantly industrial economy came about as humans learned to harness the forces of nature. It was characterized, as we saw in Chapter 10, by the replacement of small handcraft workshops with large mechanized factories, by major population shifts from rural to urban areas, and by the rise of a new economic structure based on capital and labor.

The present transformation is many-fac-

eted and—for us who are living in the midst of it—difficult to characterize with a single term. It is in part a scientific and technological revolution that has enabled humans—with the help of computers—to explore both the vastness of outer space and the intricacies of subatomic particles. It is in part a cultural revolution that has led to the creation of new methods and new forms in philosophy and the arts. And it is in part a political and social revolution that is redefining warfare and extending the concepts of human rights and participatory democracy to include increasing numbers of minority and previously disenfranchised groups.

POSTMODERN SCIENCE AND TECHNOLOGY

In the last half of the 20th century we have witnessed scientific and technological developments of revolutionary proportions taking place on four major fronts: in the use of atomic energy, in space exploration, in computer design, and in biomedical engineering. On each front, the potential to enhance human existence is precariously balanced with the potential to inflict harm—even, in the case of nuclear power, the potential to annihilate all life forms on the planet.

THE ATOMIC AGE

The *atomic age* was inaugurated in 1942 when the first nuclear chain reaction was produced at the University of Chicago. The United States, by then deeply involved in World War II, gave top priority to the Manhattan Project—the military application of this new power source. On July 16, 1945, the first atomic bomb was successfully detonated at a test site in New Mexico. Three weeks later, atomic bombs were dropped on Hiroshima (August 6) and Nagasaki (August 9), killing more than 100,000 Japanese, most of them civilians. While this act succeeded in bringing about the end of the war, it forever altered the strategic implications of "hot" war as a solution to conflicting national claims. Within five years, the Soviet Union had detonated its first atomic bomb, and the Cold War era was well under way. Great Britain, France, China, and India soon joined the "nuclear club."

Today's nuclear warheads, which yield up to 10 megatons of explosive force (1 megaton = 1 million tons of TNT), are some 500 times more powerful than the bomb that was dropped on Hiroshima. It has been estimated that the United States and Russia alone have enough warheads to destroy one another's population 20 times over. Although no sane person wants to use these weapons, debate is heated between those who feel nuclear weapons secure the peace by assuring the "other side" will not attempt a preemptive strike, and those who feel that peace would be better secured by dismantling nuclear arsenals entirely. Meanwhile, the possibility exists that an error in military communications systems could lead to an unintentional first strike, or that terrorist groups could acquire a nuclear weapon.

Peaceful Applications of Atomic Power. The peaceful applications of atomic energy have included extensive use of nuclear power as a cheap source of energy. Of the more than 200 nuclear power plants currently in operation throughout the world, nearly 100 are in the United States. France, West Germany, and Japan also rely heavily on nuclear power, and the Soviet Union has nearly 50 plants.

Despite the efficiency of nuclear power plants in providing "clean" energy, many people have reservations about their safety. These reservations have been intensified by major accidents such as those at Three Mile Island in the United States, and at Chernobyl in the Soviet Union.

The Chernobyl accident, which occurred on April 25, 1986, involved a graphite fire in the reactor which released radioactive particles into the atmosphere and threatened to produce a total meltdown at the facility. Although the Soviets initially made no announcement of the accident, its effects soon became evident in high radiation levels over much of Europe. In addition to two workers killed by the initial explosion, another 30 plant employees died of radiation-induced illness within the next four months. While 40,000 persons in the area immediately surrounding Chernobyl were being evacuated to Kiev, warnings were issued in Poland, more than 300 miles to the west, against drinking contaminated milk. To the north, by the fol-

The nuclear reactor at Chernobyl in the Soviet Union. A fire at this plant nearly resulted in an uncontrolled nuclear chain reaction.

A Polish scientist tests milk for radioactivity. For several weeks after the Chernobyl accident, grass and other crops consumed by animals contained dangerously high levels of radiation.

lowing winter, the reindeer-based economy and traditions of the Lapps appeared to be on the verge of collapse as reindeer became so contaminated that their meat could not be eaten or sold. Longer-term effects of Chernobyl are projected to include 24,000 deaths from radiation-induced cancer.

The fear of another Chernobyl, coupled with known problems in closing down old plants and disposing of their radioactive waste materials, has led to many protests against the building of additional nuclear plants. Some protestors argue that world power needs could be met by harnessing other sources of energy, such as solar and tidal energy, or by hastening the development of a cost-effective nuclear fusion technology.

THE SPACE AGE

The *space age* began in October 1957 when the Soviet Union launched *Sputnik*, the first human-made satellite. This Soviet success stimulated the American space effort by rallying popular support for a massive and ex-

pensive program. The Space Act of 1958 created the National Aeronautics and Space Agency (NASA), which quickly developed the Mercury and Gemini programs. In 1961, the young American president, John F. Kennedy, made a commitment to land an American on the moon by the end of the decade—the Apollo project. Neil Armstrong fulfilled that promise when he became the first human on the moon on July 20, 1969. His statement as he set foot on the moon, "That's one small step for a man . . . one giant leap for mankind," summarized the impact of this achievement.

Since then, the United States and the Soviet Union have continued to develop an increasingly more sophisticated space effort. In 1975, the two rival superpowers set their differences aside long enough to execute an in-space linkup on a joint *Apollo 18/Soyuz 19* mission. U.S. and Soviet astronauts ate meals together, conducted experiments, and held a joint news conference.

The Soviet astronaut Yuri Gagarin was the first man to travel beyond the earth's atmosphere. His voyage, in April 1961, lasted 108 minutes.

Buzz Aldrin became the second man to walk on the moon during the Apollo II space mission of 1969.

Thereafter, a major focus of the NASA program was the development of a reusable space shuttle vehicle. In April 1981, the shuttlecraft *Columbia*, piloted by Robert Crippen, became the first such vehicle to complete its mission and return to earth intact and ready—after repairs—to be used on future missions. The *Columbia* was soon joined by three other shuttlecraft, *Challenger*, *Discovery*, and *Atlantis*.

Meanwhile, in the 1960s and 1970s, NASA had also invested in a program of unmanned missions to other planets. *Mariner* spacecraft flew close to Venus, Mars, and Mercury and returned thousands of photos and other data that greatly increased our knowledge of the solar system. In 1975, *Viking 1* was successfully landed on Mars where it continued to function for more than six years. In September 1977, *Voyager 2* was launched on an ambitious transplanetary journey to Jupiter, Saturn, Uranus, and Neptune, and beyond. When the *Voyager* craft encountered Uranus on January 27, 1986, and began transmitting data back to earth, NASA officials were elated by its success.

Their elation quickly turned to grief, however, on the following day, January 28, when the shuttlecraft *Challenger* exploded 73 seconds after lift-off, killing all seven astronauts aboard. Among the seven was a young schoolteacher and mother, Christa Mc-Auliffe, who had been selected as the first private citizen to travel in space.

During the investigation that ensued, there was much debate over the growing U.S. emphasis on manned versus unmanned missions. Critics of the shuttle program claimed that unmanned missions are safer, less expensive, and provide scientists with more varied and useful data. Supporters claimed that manned missions are necessary for developing and studying human adaptation to space conditions and that, because they are of more interest to the general public, they help garner financial support for the space program as a whole. As this debate continued, a chastened NASA worked to correct flaws in the shuttle's booster rockets and to resume the shuttle program with the aim of constructing a permanent station in space.

Peaceful Applications of Space Technology. The conquest of space and the ongoing experiments in space laboratories have already had practical application. Orbiting satellites have improved weather forecasting and serve as transcontinental telephone and television relay stations. Experiments in space-based labs have focused on subjects ranging from the human vascular system to the development of composite metals that can withstand extreme heat. Gravity-free space manufacturing processes have produced small batches of specialty products such as ultrapure drugs and perfectly round ball bearings. Studies of the effects of radiation, of weightlessness, and of the influence of gravity on humans, plants, and animals are currently in progress. On-ground research in support of the space missions has led to the development of widely accepted consumer products, including Tang breakfast drink, ultrathin but thermally efficient "space blankets," and Velcro fasteners.

Futurists see space vacations on the horizon, when technology will make possible a trip to the moon in 48 hours. Permanent factories and laboratories in space are already feasible, based on experiments aboard the shuttle orbiters. Eventually, humans may settle permanently in space colonies constructed to replicate earth's ecological system. Intergalactic travel may become possible as well. Some people believe that outer space will help earth deal with her exploding population by providing alternative sources of energy, raw materials, and even food grown on other planets. One space dreamer projects lengthened life expectancy in the zero-gravity environment, which requires less effort by the heart.[1]

Military Applications of Space Technology. From the outset, the space age has taken on the overtones of a military contest between the United States and the Soviet Union. The use of photoreconnaissance via satellites has enabled each of the superpowers to learn much about the other's military installations and activities. Satellites can also be used as early warning devices in the event of nuclear attack. Recently, the United States has embarked on a more advanced program, formally known as Strategic Defense Initiative (SDI), with the avowed aim of providing a virtual "shield" to intercept and destroy enemy missiles in space. The Soviets have argued that such a shield would destabilize the balance of power between the two rivals since it would permit the United States to make a first strike without fear that retaliatory Soviet missiles would reach American soil. Critics on both sides fear that if the SDI system is deployed, the Soviets will develop a system to counter it, and that once these two systems are in place they may precipitate a nuclear exchange with disastrous consequences on earth and in space. Thus, SDI is often referred to as "Star Wars."

THE COMPUTER REVOLUTION

The exploration of space in manned and unmanned vehicles, the deployment and use of satellites, and the management of complex military defense systems was made possible by revolutionary developments in computer technology. Initially developed for these and other government projects, computers have now become prevalent in every area of postmodern life. They are found in factories, of-

---

[1] See Ben Bova, *The High Road* (Boston: Houghton Mifflin, 1981) for descriptions of life and work in outer space.

fices, homes, hospitals, churches, and schools, and their presence often challenges the very humans they were designed to aid.

A Brief History of Computers. Although we tend to think of the computer as a purely 20th-century invention, its origins can be traced back to the abacus, which was used by the Chinese over 5,000 years ago. Like today's computers, the abacus enabled users to perform computations more rapidly and more accurately. The next significant development in mechanizing mathematical computation came in 1642, when Blaise Pascal invented the first adding machine. Two centuries later, Charles Babbage (1791–1871), who is often considered the father of the modern computer, helped to invent a machine that could solve polynomial equations. The product of his theories about a mechanical calculator was a model of the difference engine, although he never built one that actually worked. His collaborator was the Countess of Lovelace, Ada Augusta Byron, the daughter of the English poet Lord Byron. A computer language currently in use, Ada, is named for her.

Although Babbage and Lady Byron did not succeed with their difference engine, they did provide the theoretical foundations for the work of Herman Hollerith, who invented a tabulating machine to aid the U.S. government in counting the population after the 1890 census.

The next calculators were the Mark I, the invention of Harvard professor Howard Aiken, and the ABC or Atanascoff Berry Computer, both built in 1944. These experiments with computers coincided with the invention of the ENIAC during World War II; its purpose was rapid calculation of artilery projections. The ENIAC was extremely large—it occupied 1,500 square feet of floor space and weighed 30 tons—and, by today's standards, extremely slow—it could handle only 300 numbers per second. Moreover, it had to be rewired for each new program, a time-consuming step. However, its devel-

opment set the stage for the invention of the UNIVAC in 1951, which is usually viewed as the beginning of the *computer age.*

UNIVAC was also large and, like earlier machines, it relied on vacuum tubes—thousands of them. The tubes helped to account for the size of the computer and, because they have a life span of less than one hour of running time, for its frequent down time. Moreover, UNIVAC's memory capacity was only 4,096 characters.

The so-called *second generation* of computers began in 1959 with the invention of the *transistor*—a device 100 times smaller than a vacuum tube that permitted faster, more reliable calculation, and expanded memory capacity to 32,768 characters. Moreover, computers using transistors were less expensive to build and operate.

The *third generation* of computer technology began in 1965 when transistors were replaced with miniature integrated circuits on silicon chips. The small size of the chips, less than one-eighth-inch square, has ena-

The miniaturization of circuits on tiny silicon chips has greatly expanded the practical uses of computers. Here, a student at the U.S. Naval School demonstrates a miniature recorder created for the space shuttle program.

bled the calculating power of a 30-ton ENIAC to be contained in a portable computer small enough to fit in a briefcase. The miniaturization of computers, in turn, has allowed them to be sent aloft in spacecraft and satellites, to be taken underwater in submarines and deep-sea robots (like ALVIN, who investigated remains of the sunken *Titanic*) and to perch on millions of desktops around the world.

These advances in computer design were accompanied by the creation of *computer languages*, which are necessary for translating human instructions into machine language, and by the development of highly sophisticated and user-friendly software.

Computer Applications. Aside from the scientific and military uses already mentioned, computer technology is now being applied to almost every facet of human life. In hospitals and laboratories, computers assist in research and diagnostic activities. Computer graphics can be used to illustrate the composition of DNA, the body's basic building block. Computerized brain scanners are used to study the brains of those suffering from mental illness. The CAT scan (computerized axial tomography) improves medical diagnosis by providing pictures of cross sections of the body.

Computers play an increasingly important role in business, where they are able to provide complex data bases for decision makers as well as perform routine operations in areas such as payroll, accounting, inventory control, and sales analysis. Factory operations have been streamlined via computer-aided design (CAD) and computer-aided manufacturing (CAM). The factories of the future will be almost completely automated as manufacturing processes become computer-programmed and controlled.

In elementary and high schools, computers provide programmed instruction that can be tailored to the needs of individual students. In colleges and universities, computers maintain library catalogues, schedule courses, and assist in theoretical and applied research activities.

Indeed, on a typical day in countries like Japan and the United States virtually every citizen is likely to interact with some form of computer-controlled device—whether a word processor, a video game, or an automated bank teller or supermarket checkout.

Artificial Intelligence. Many theorists are now investigating the artificial-intelligence (AI) capabilities of computers—that is, the extent to which computers can replicate the thought processes of the human brain. Whether or not actual replication can be accomplished, research in this area has already stimulated study of the processes of the human mind, including its use of language. AI programs are currently being used to help in problem solving by suggesting new approaches and new avenues of investigation.

Sociological Effects. The tremendous amount of data produced by computers has created what John Naisbitt calls *the information society*, a new order that is replacing the industrial society. In Naisbitt's words, "We now mass-produce information the way we used to mass-produce cars."[2] He suggests that control of knowledge will be the new source of power in technologically advanced societies.

At the same time, there is concern that our increasing reliance on computers and computer-generated information will undermine the value of the human being. People who are used to exchanging a few words of greeting with their bank teller or supermarket clerk may feel alienated as these workers are replaced by electronic devices. As computers take over manufacturing processes, massive numbers of factory workers are displaced. While many displaced workers succeed in retraining for other jobs, others are forced out of the labor market entirely. Some

---

[2] John Naisbitt, *Megatrends* (New York: Warner Bombay, 1982), p. 16.

people worry that, if future developments in artificial intelligence enable computers to "think" like human beings, humans will be reduced to mere consumers in a computer-run society.

BIOMEDICAL ADVANCES

Beginning with Alexander Fleming's discovery of the "miracle drug" penicillin in 1928, the 20th century has witnessed remarkable advances in pharmacology and disease control. In the industrialized nations, widespread use of antibiotic agents has virtually eliminated diseases such as tuberculosis. Worldwide smallpox vaccination programs have been so successful in eradicating this disfiguring disease that the miniscule risk associated with receiving the vaccine is now greater than the risk of going without it; therefore, the vaccination programs have recently been discontinued. The use of phenothiazine derivatives and lithium salts has enabled many people with severe mental diseases, which in past decades would have required long-term hospitalization, to function normally in their communities. The discovery in 1975 that the brain itself produces pain-killing endorphins stimulated further research into the chemistry of the human body and ways that it could be manipulated—with or without drugs—to affect health, behavior, and mental status. As a result, bio-feedback, imagery, and relaxation techniques are now employed to alleviate migraines, to assist in cancer treatment, and to reduce stress and the incidence of stress-related disease. On the surgical front we have seen advances in organ transplant procedures and, beginning in 1982, the experimental use of artificial hearts.

Another area in which revolutionary progress has been made is genetic research and engineering. Physicians are now able to diagnose and treat genetic diseases in the fetus prior to birth—or, when such diseases cannot be treated, to provide detailed genetic counseling to would-be parents about the

The Nobel Prize-winning scientist Dr. Maurice Wilkins demonstrates a model of the molecular structure of DNA, the material which encodes the genetic characteristics of all living organisms. By splicing and recombining DNA from different organisms, scientists are now able to create new forms of life.

risks they may face in having children. Meanwhile, success with in vitro fertilization techniques has enabled previously infertile couples to bear their own children—or even to employ another woman's womb for this purpose.

Experiments with recombinant DNA have taught scientists how to combine genetic materials in ways that result in new forms of life. Practical applications include the creation of a bacteria that can absorb oil spills and of cells that are efficient producers of helpful substances such as insulin.

Biomedical Concerns. While these and other biomedical advances have been of great benefit to human beings, they have also raised many concerns. For example: the widespread use of antibiotics has produced

499

strains of bacterial and viral organisms so resistant to medication that increasingly large doses are required to combat them. Although the incidence of diseases such as tuberculosis, polio, and smallpox has been greatly reduced, the incidence of a fatal new disease, acquired immune deficiency syndrome (AIDS), is reaching epidemic proportions and challenging the capabilities of the biomedical establishment. Mental patients who are released from hospitals with their symptoms well controlled by medication frequently neglect to continue taking these drugs and are found wondering aimlessly on the streets of large cities, unable to care for themselves. Controversial new life-prolonging measures, such as the artificial heart, have caused many people to question whether the added months or years of life can really make up for a greatly diminished quality of life.

Concerns over genetic engineering run especially deep. Fears have been raised that a mad scientist could concoct a monstrous being—or, perhaps more likely, that a newly created bacteria could escape from the laboratory and destabilize the ecological balance on earth. The ability to predetermine the sex of offspring and the potential for cloning genetically exact copies of a human being threaten to alter the traditional and natural course of propagation. Indeed, the use of in vitro fertilization, surrogate mothers, and stored embryos has already raised difficult legal and moral issues.

ISSUES IN SCIENTIFIC RESEARCH

As we have seen, many of the scientific and technological achievements of the past several decades have raised critical moral and ethical questions. Does the scientist have the moral right—or the obligation—to pursue research wherever it leads, regardless of the social and ethical implications? Should atomic physicists have refused to participate in the Manhattan Project, knowing the destructive use to which their nuclear fission device would surely be put? Or did Hitler and his Third Reich scientists pose an even greater threat that demanded this project be carried out? Should even one nuclear power plant have been built before scientists had discovered a safe way to dispose of radioactive wastes? Or was it more desirable to meet today's energy needs today and leave it to the more advanced technology of our children's generation to deal with those wastes? Should the *Challenger* have been sent aloft on a cold January morning, despite doubts about its safety, in order to meet tight research schedules? Or should the entire shuttle program have been shut down when it was discovered to have life-threatening safety flaws? Should experimental biomedical procedures such as artificial heart implantation be halted on the grounds that they turn patients into virtual guinea pigs? Or is such research the fastest road to tomorrow's cures?

Who should determine which scientific projects are selected for research? Should, or can, a theoretical scientist control the applications of his or her theory? Most research projects are enormously expensive and require external sources of funding; one of the most common sources is government contracts—often with military implications. Should the theoretical scientist conduct research only on subjects that will contribute to human well-being? Can the scientist differentiate—especially in the early stages of research—between those projects that will result in constructive applications and those that will result in destructive applications? Are there, in fact, projects that have no potential for destructive use? These and other ethical considerations will continue to challenge the human community.

POSTMODERN CULTURAL DEVELOPMENTS

Burgeoning advances in science and technology—and the perplexing questions they have raised—are reflected in every facet of postmodern culture. Philosophy, literature, the visual and performing arts, and the popular media of television and films—all are attempting to grapple in some way with the predicaments and opportunities of postmodern times. And all have been influenced by the increasing interconnectedness of the human community.

CONTEMPORARY PHILOSOPHY

To the degree that philosophy aims to analyze and explain the human condition, the events of the 20th century have provided it with an often overwhelming challenge. The effect of two world wars, the Holocaust, and the unleashing of nuclear energy has been to shatter conventional beliefs and produce a deep skepticism and despair among many people. A philosophical movement that clearly reflects this doubt, *existentialism*, flourished in Europe in the years following the end of World War II. Building on the work of Sören Kierkegaard (1813–1855), who had described the despair that results when one realizes the antithesis between existence and truth, French existentialists like Jean-Paul Sartre (1905–1980) and Albert Camus (1913–1960) proclaimed the world to be absurd and meaningless. They urged humans in despair to create value and meaning for themselves—to take responsibility for their own existence and commit themselves to a search for meaning and human dignity.

In Germany, Karl Jaspers (1883–1969) proposed a transcendent "encompassing" reality in which human existence is enclosed. Concerned with the situation of individuals, he believed that philosophy should spring from the individual's own existence within this "encompassing," and should address itself to other individuals to increase their understanding. Thus Jaspers objected to abstract or general philosophical principles and declined to identify himself with the existential movement.

Another German who declined the existential label despite his influence on the movement was Martin Heidegger (1889–1976). Heidegger was deeply influenced by the *phenomenology* of Edmund Husserl (1859–1938), which held that the data of consciousness, e.g., a centaur or a white raven, are as real as objective facts and that one can discern the structure of experience through the study of consciousness. In his later years, Heidegger became more interested in *ontology*, the study of being, and the way in which being is related to time. He proposed that the crisis in Western civilization had resulted from a mass "forgetfulness of being."

In Britain and the United States, philosophers tended to focus on questions concerning the meaning of language rather than questions concerning the meaning of existence. *Logical Positivism*, *linguistic analysis*, and *structural linguistics* were some of the movements based on these questions, many of which were first posed by Ludwig Wittgenstein (1889–1951). Wittgenstein tried to show that the forms of language, thought, and reality bear a direct correspondence to one another; thus, philosophy must concern itself with the analysis and correct use of language. His suggestion for "doing" philosophy is quite thought-provoking:

● ● ● *The correct method in philosophy would really be the following: to say nothing except what can be said, i.e. propositions of natural science—i.e. something that has nothing to do with philosophy—and then, whenever someone else wanted to say something metaphysical, to demonstrate to him that he had failed to give a meaning to certain signs in his propositions. Although it would not be satisfying to the other person—he would not have the feeling we were teaching him philosophy—this method would be the only strictly correct one.*[3]

[3] Ludwig Wittgenstein, *Tractatus Logico-Philosophicus*, trans. D. F. Pears and B. F. McGuinness (Atlantic Highlands, N.J.: Humanities Press, 1974), pp. 73–74.

A recent development in philosophy has been the blending of Eastern and Western modes of thought. As Buddhist, Taoist, Vedantic, and yogic teachings have spread to the West, Westerners have discovered they are based on well-developed philosophical systems that grapple with the nature of reality, the meaning of existence, and the correct methods of enquiring into these matters.

CONTEMPORARY LITERATURE

The literary trends of the late 20th century arose out of the same events that influenced philosophy and were shaped by the political situations that prevailed in different nations. In the Soviet Union, for example, writers were expected to adhere to the party line—a line that changed periodically. Thus Alexandr Solzhenitsyn was able to publish his first novel, *One Day in the Life of Ivan Denisovich* (1962), because its description of life in a concentration camp was in line with the de-Stalinization process then underway. However, his subsequent novels were banned. When the first volume of *The Gulag Archipelago* appeared in Italy in 1973, Solzhenitsyn, who had been awarded the Nobel Prize in 1970, was sent into exile. Another Soviet writer whose work was acclaimed abroad but banned at home was Boris Pasternak (1890–1960). When his epic novel of the revolution, *Doctor Zhivago*, was published in Italy in 1957, it earned him the Nobel Prize. But government officials prevented Pasternak from traveling to Stockholm and forced him to decline the award. As a result of these and other political pressures on Soviet writers, an active underground press now reproduces and distributes banned writings in clandestine *samizdat* editions.

In Germany, where Nazism severely interrupted the development of literature and sent a whole generation of writers into exile, contemporary writers have tended to be deeply interested in social and political issues. In his early novels, written in the 1950s, Heinrich Böll portrayed the problems of a nation afflicted by guilt and defeat. Recently, the Nobel Prize-winning author has focused on topics of more international concern, such as terrorism, a theme in *The Safety Net* (1979). While Böll is noted for his realism, his compatriot Günter Grass, an outspoken socialist, is noted for his use of humor and experimental forms in novels such as *The Flounder* (1977).

In France, writers reacted to the midcentury shattering of traditional values by inventing the *nouveau roman*, the "new novel" or "antinovel," which eliminated the traditional novelistic features of plot, character, and chronological sequence. According to Alain Robbe-Grillet (b. 1922), the old forms created a stultifying illusion of order and meaning, whereas the new novel, by dispensing with technique and narrative interpretation, is able to foster change.

Among recent trends in the United States is the emergence of ethnic—Jewish and black—and feminist literatures. The two U.S. writers who received Nobel Prizes in the 1970s were both Jewish: Saul Bellow and Isaac Bashevish Singer. Bellow's protagonists, like the title character of *Herzog* (1964), tend to be characterized by a driving intensity as they confront crises, often with comic overtones, and attempt to reconcile themselves to flawed emotional and social conditions. Singer, a rabbi's son who writes in Yiddish, portrays Polish Jews in various times and settings. His stories in particular are colored with fantasy, humor, and tints of the mystic and supernatural.

James Baldwin is a sophisticated and prolific black writer of novels, short stories, essays, and plays that examine human dilemmas and the situation of American blacks from a number of perspectives. Alex Haley won a 1977 Pulitzer Prize for *Roots*, his account of the history of his forebears from the time they were taken from Africa into slavery. When *Roots* was dramatized in one of television's first miniseries, it generated widespread interest in black history and inspired Americans from all ethnic groups to learn more about their own ancestors.

The feminist movement that began in the 1960s has inspired many novels on the theme of women breaking free from traditional roles and expectations. *Fear of Flying* (1973) by Erica Jong was an important early work in this genre. While writers like Joyce Carol Oates and Joan Didion do not deal explicitly with feminist themes, their novels often focus on women caught up by disturbing social forces. In Oates' novels, such as *them* (1969), the women tend to be portrayed as highly passionate, and society as grotesquely violent. In Didion's novels, such as *Play It as It Lays* (1970), the women are more likely to suffer acute depression and breakdown, reflecting the disintegration of the society in which they are cast adrift.

VISUAL ARTS

Painting. We have seen how many postwar philosophers turned away from the traditional content of philosophy in order to focus on the existential situation of the philosopher and the linguistic process involved in doing philosophy. In a similar fashion, American artists in the late 1940s and 1950s turned away from the traditional content of painting in order to focus attention on the painter's activity and the process of painting. Their method of painting became known as *action painting* while the term *Abstract Expressionism* was given to the movement they inspired. The success of this movement was instrumental in relocating the "art capital" of the world from Paris to New York. Jackson Pollock (1912–1956) was a leading figure in Abstract Expressionism and his paintings typify the movement as a whole. He used enormous canvases and—dispensing with notions of background and foreground—filled every square inch with flowing streams and ribbons of paint. The paints were dripped rather than brushed on, or even squeezed directly from tubes, creating

The artist Jackson Pollock at work. Pollock's "action paintings" caused a sensation in the art world, and helped to establish New York as the new art capital.

rhythms and patterns that were largely spontaneous and accidental. The deeply textured surface that resulted was charged with energy and drew attention to itself. When the work was completed, it was essentially a visual record of the artist's activity and an expression of his feeling as he engaged in that activity.

By the end of the 1950s a reaction had set in to the seriousness and inward intensity of Abstract Expressionism, giving rise to a new movement called *Pop Art*. Pop artists tried to build a bridge between high culture and popular culture by depicting everyday images (e.g., comic strip characters, soup cans, Coke bottles) and by using the techniques of sign painters and commercial artists. Andy Warhol (1930–1987) was a leader of this movement. For his multi-image silk-screen portrait of Marilyn Monroe, he employed a low-resolution newspaper photo, whose enlarged dots are a distinctive "pop" feature of the finished work. The mass production of this and other Warhol paintings, including the famous Campbell's soup can, was also in accordance with Pop Art principles.

Today we are witnessing a trend toward *neo-realism* and *photorealism*, in which the artist depicts figures and scenes from real life but presents them as they would appear to the camera's lens rather than the artist's personal vision.

Earthworks. The late 1960s and 1970s saw the creation of a new art form known as *earthworks*, in which the artist injects intentional elements into natural forms. Earthworks are often, of necessity, located in remote areas and so massive in scale that they can be viewed in their entirety only from the air. As such, they are a form well suited to mass culture and to its advanced technology for transmitting images. They also reflect the changes and uncertainties in postmodern life, in that they are subject to rain, wind, and other natural forces that will alter and eventually obliterate them.

MUSIC

The status of music among the general public has been greatly enhanced by recent technological advances, many of them emanating from Japan, in recording and playback equipment. Long-playing high fidelity and stereo records have enabled music lovers to hear complete selections from virtually every period in muscial history. The tape recorder, an outgrowth of World War II defense efforts, has permitted in-home duplication of favorite pieces from records and radio broadcasts, as well as complex overdubbing and editing in commercial recording studios. The latest innovation, the compact disc (CD), holds up to 75 minutes of digitally encoded sound which is read out by laser beams. Meanwhile, playback equipment, along with its power source, has been miniaturized to the point where it will fit into a shirt pocket. As a result of these developments, the production of recordings has reached an all-time high. The 1987 *Schwann Catalogue*—a compedium of all the classical, jazz, popular, electronic, and spoken-word recordings commercially available in the United States—listed more than 80,000 titles that could be had in record, cassette, and/or CD format.

An important trend in composition has been the blending of Western and non-Western styles. *Minimalist* composers like Steve Reich and Philip Glass have studied and incorporated elements of the music of India, Asia, and Africa. Their works have enjoyed wide acceptance despite (or perhaps because of) their emphasis on repetitive rhythms with little harmonic variation.

Rock music, a distinctive feature of postmodern times, also relies heavily on rhythm or beat to convey its powerful energy. Americans Bill Haley (1927–1981) and Elvis Presley (1935–1977) were early rock innovators. The Beatles, a group from Liverpool, England, popularized soft rock in the 1960s. Since then, various subspecies of rock have emerged—including hard rock, folk rock, jazz rock, acid rock, and punk rock—and rock groups have been formed in many other countries, including the Soviet Union. The introduction of music videos in the mid-1980s has stimulated rock artists to additional creativity in the field of visual effects.

Since many adults find rock music too loud and too harsh to enjoy, it has become the special province of energetic young people for whom it often serves as a symbol of protest against establishment values. But rock has also played a notable role in addressing world problems: Beginning in the mid-1980s many rock artists contributed their talents to internationally televised concerts to raise money for charitable purposes. "Live Aid," for example, was broadcast to 152 countries in July 1985, and raised an estimated $70 million to provide food to Ethiopian refugees.

TELEVISION

The mass medium of television has served to shape postmodern culture as well as to transmit its content. As satellite relays have enabled televised programs and events to be instantly transmitted around the world, the world has become more of a *global village*—a place where everyone knows what everyone else is doing. And as peoples of various nations become more familiar with one another, we learn that what we have in common is stronger than what divides us. The fact that people have laughed at *I Love Lucy* in more than 50 languages is one evidence of this commonality. Moreover, transnational telecasts of space conquests (and disasters), Olympic competitions, sporting events, operas, royal wedding ceremonies, and live rock concerts—as well as "space bridge" conversations between U.S. and Soviet citizens—serve to increase our interconnectedness as we share these new experiences together.

But television, with its propensity to focus on violent and catastrophic events, also has the potential to make us insensitive to violence. When highlights of the Vietnam War could be viewed daily in people's homes, it was difficult to remember that it was not "just a movie." While the depiction of repeated acts of violence on popular prime-time programs helps some viewers let off vicarious steam, it may teach others that violence is a socially acceptable solution to a multitude of problems.

Television has had far-reaching effects on political processes as well. Beginning with the televised debates between U.S. presidential candidates John F. Kennedy and Richard M. Nixon in 1960, it became clear that the more telegenic the candidate, the better his or her chances of being elected. Today's political campaigns are often characterized by schedules designed with the evening news in mind and by overly simple messages and slogans that will fit conveniently in a 30-second commercial slot. Nearly all candidates now employ public relations experts to advise them on such subjects as mannerisms and dress as well as political tactics.

POSTMODERN POLITICAL AND SOCIAL TRENDS

As we watch current events unfold on our television screens, we become more aware of emerging trends in the political and social arenas. We can detect patterns emerging that engender hope for the planet's future—the gains that are being made in self-determination and democratic participation, and the attention that is being focused on human rights and social equality issues. But other patterns, like the increasing frequency and brutality of terrorist incidents, arouse our anger and concern.

TRENDS IN WAR AND CONFLICT RESOLUTION

We have seen how the development of nuclear weapons has made the notion of all-out war between nations unacceptable—that such weapons are built and stockpiled with the primary intention (however rational or irrational) of preventing the need for their use. Moreover, even the notion of "conventional ground warfare" seems increasingly to be a thing of the past. Virtually none of today's armed conflicts involve regular troops from opposing sides confronting one another on a well-defined battlefield. Instead, we are witnessing a trend toward guerrilla warfare and terrorism as the most prevalent means of violent conflict.

Guerrilla Warfare. Although guerrilla tactics have figured in armed conflict since the American War for Independence, they were a particularly prominent feature of the Vietnam War. Like the Viet Cong in that war, guerrillas are irregular troops who operate in areas nominally controlled by the enemy. They specialize in the sneak attack as opposed to mass confrontation of forces. They are especially effective in irregular terrains, preferably forested, in which they can hide. Local guerrillas, moreover, are likely to be much more familiar with the strategic features of their territory than the occupying enemy—especially a foreign enemy.

Guerrillas also depend on the support of

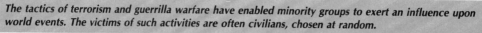

The tactics of terrorism and guerrilla warfare have enabled minority groups to exert an influence upon world events. The victims of such activities are often civilians, chosen at random.

the local population, from whom they receive food, shelter, and other necessities. Additional supplies, including weapons, may be ordered from a supporting power via radio and brought in on aircraft. In some cases guerrillas are well integrated with the local populace; they are the sons and brothers of village dwellers in whose homes they take their meals. If they are not, they may need to use propaganda and terrorist tactics to compel local support. As a result, enemy actions against guerrilla strongholds often succeed in killing as many or more civilians as they do combatants.

In addition to its prevalence in Vietnam and other parts of Southeast Asia, guerrilla warfare was a prominent feature of Algeria's war for independence from France (1954–1962) and of Fidel Castro's struggle against Fulgencio Batista for control of Cuba (1956–1959). Castro's success led to widespread use of guerrilla campaigns in other Latin American conflicts, including those in El Salvador and Nicaragua. Since the late 1960s, guerrilla tactics have been used by the Palestinians in their struggle for a homeland in the Middle East, and, since 1979, by the Afghan *mujahidin* in their resistance to the Soviet-backed government in Kabul.

Terrorism. Like guerrilla warfare, with which it is closely associated, the use of terrorism has roots that go far back in history. Modern terrorist tactics have included kidnapping and hostage taking, killing, hijacking, and bombing of property and persons. Often, several of these tactics are combined in a single incident.

Terrorist acts differ from other, similar acts of violence (e.g., kidnapping a child with the intention of extorting money from wealthy parents) in that they are politically motivated. Although terrorists may also demand ransom money, their intention is to use these funds to achieve their political aims. Often, instead of money, they demand the release of prisoners held by their enemies. Other terrorist acts, like the killing of two Israeli athletes at the 1972 Munich Olympics by Palestinian terrorists appear to be primarily retaliatory in nature.

Whatever the intention of specific acts, terrorism in general is a kind of psychological warfare aimed at producing public shock and drawing attention to the terrorists' grievances. Victims are usually private citizens, with whom other citizens can easily identify, often Americans. The U.S. State Department has estimated that some 30 to 35 percent of international terrorist incidents are aimed at U.S. citizens or property. Israel is another frequent target of terrorism.

In response to the increasingly brutal wave of terrorism that began in the 1980s, the U.N. General Assembly unanimously adopted a resolution in December 1985 condemning international terrorism as criminal in nature. Even so, terrorist activities are expected to remain a prominent and disturbing feature of international politics for the rest of the century.

TRENDS IN GOVERNMENT AND DEMOCRATIC PARTICIPATION

In recent decades we have witnessed a movement toward self-government and democratic participation that has affected organizations ranging in size and significance from small corporations and tiny nations to large superpowers and multinational bodies.

National Independence and Self-Rule. The push for national independence and self-rule has largely succeeded in dismantling the final remnants of the old colonial empires. As of 1986, 159 self-governing nations had become members of the United Nations. The small size of some of these nations, who collectively control the General Assembly, indicates what deep inroads the movement toward self-rule has made. Among the five countries that joined in the 1980–1981 period, only one, Zimbabwe, had

a population of more than 200,000 people.

At the same time, other groups have struggled unsuccessfully to assert their claims to self-government. In some cases, such as the threat of French-speaking Quebec to leave the Canadian confederation, these claims were probably more a matter of political strategy than serious intent. In other cases, however, they were backed by violence and bloodshed. In Northern Ireland, for example, bombings, shootings, and other terrorist activities have caused more than 2,000 deaths as the Catholic minority has battled the British-supported Protestant government.

The Overthrow of Unpopular Regimes. Elsewhere the struggle for self-determination was not between competing religious or ethnic groups but between the citizenry as a whole and a ruling power they perceived as failing to represent their interests. In the Philippines, for example, when the people perceived that Ferdinand Marcos had rigged the 1986 presidential election, they banded together and used "people power" to drive Marcos into exile and inaugurate Corazon Aquino, the candidate for whom the majority had voted.

While the Filipinos achieved their aim quickly and with a minimum of bloodshed, the struggle of the Afghan people against a Soviet-imposed government has been more violent and protracted. As of 1987, more than 2 million Afghans had been forced to flee to neighboring Pakistan where they constitute one of the largest refugee populations in the world.

Extension of Voting Rights. In virtually every democratic nation, voting rights have been extended to all citizens, regardless of race, sex, color, or creed. In the United States, the Voting Rights Act of 1965 succeeded in tearing down the last barriers to voting by blacks. Even the People's Republics of the Communist bloc subscribe to universal franchise, although the opportunity to vote is almost meaningless since no choice of candidates is offered. In 1987, Soviet leader Mikhail Gorbachev suggested that the U.S.S.R. was willing to experiment with "democratization" by allowing more than one candidate to compete for certain offices. All candidates, however, continue to be selected by party officials.

Democracy in the Workplace. It is worth noting that democratic participation is increasing at the corporate level as well as at national and international levels. Beginning in the late 1960s and early 1970s, manufacturers such as Volvo in Sweden initiated experiments in taking workers off the assembly line and giving them responsibility as a group for deciding how the product should be assembled. More recently, corporate leaders in the United States, noting the high productivity of workers in Japan and South Korea, have attempted to introduce some of the participatory management methods used in those countries. The result—a greater emphasis on worker participation in decision making, and on management participation in day-to-day operations and worker welfare—has tended to reduce the tension between management and labor that exists in highly authoritarian organizations.

TRENDS IN HUMAN RIGHTS AND SOCIAL EQUALITY

A distinctive and welcome feature of postmodern society is its renewed emphasis on human rights and its trend toward social equality for minority groups and women.

Human Rights. The concept of human rights, a product of the Enlightenment, was given new impetus on December 10, 1948, when the U.N. General Assembly adopted and proclaimed the Universal Declaration of Human Rights. The 30 articles of this document define rights ranging from "the right to life, liberty, and security of person" to "the right to freely participate in the cultural life of the community, to enjoy the arts and to share in scientific advancement and its benefits." The Declaration seeks to assure equality before the law, freedom of movement and residence, freedom of conscience and expression, and access to adequate food, clothing, housing, medical care, and education. It forbids enslavement, torture, arbitrary detention, invasion of privacy, and discrimination in pay. All in all, this document represents a remarkably advanced vision of a planet whose social and international order would permit all such rights to be fully and universally realized.

The reality of the decades since then, however, has shown how far we have yet to travel in order to actualize this vision. In the United States, homeless people are found sleeping on the streets of cities in which great wealth is displayed. In the Soviet Union, thousands languish in prisons because they have engaged in unauthorized worship activities. In Cambodia, whole populations have been driven from their homes and enlisted in forced labor brigades to clear forests and jungles. In South Africa, the press is forbidden to report on government actions against blacks. In Ethiopia, refugee camps are filled with bone-thin children who feel themselves fortunate if they are given the opportunity to wait in long lines to receive a small scoop of cereal. Each of these cases represents a serious violation of human rights.

But alongside this often dismal picture, there are areas in which the issues of human rights and social equality are being addressed and progress is being made. Prominent among these are the drives for minority rights and rights for women.

Minority Rights. Virtually no large nation is without its minorities—populations who by virtue of belonging to a different racial, religious, ethnic, or linguistic group suffer from low political status. The United States has large black, Hispanic, and Asian populations. The Soviet Union embraces ethnic Turkic, Tadzhik (Iranian), and a host of other minorities, many of them Moslems, who collectively will soon outnumber its Russian majority, now only 52 percent of the population. China's minorities include the

Dr. Martin Luther King utilized Mahatma Gandhi's tactics of nonviolent confrontation in his fight to end segregation and bring about equal job and educational opportunities for American blacks.

Uygurs (a Turkic Moslem group) and the Tibetans. India has confronted militant Moslem and Sikh minorities within its predominantly Hindu culture.

But in each of these, as well as other nations, the notion of minority rights has gained at least a small foothold as minorities have organized themselves and exerted their collective power. Whether this power is expressed violently—as the Sikhs have done in India—or nonviolently—as U.S. blacks have done under the leadership of Dr. Martin Luther King (1929–1968)—it has forced the majority to realize it is in its own best interest to begin to share the rights they enjoy.

The Feminist Movement. The term *feminism* refers to the principle that women should have political, economic, and social rights equal to those of men. Thus, men as well as women who hold to this principle can legitimately be called *feminists*.

The feminist movement arose mainly in Britain and the United States. Since the 19th century, when U.S. feminists and abolitionists worked side by side, advances in women's rights have been closely associated with advances in minority rights. Indeed, in movement leaders like Lucretia Mott (1793–1880), born only a year after the publication of Mary Wollstonecraft's ground-breaking feminist document, *A Vindication of the Rights of Woman*, the feminist and the abolitionist were combined in the same person. Ironically, some 19th-century feminists, like Elizabeth Cady Stanton (1815–1902), argued that giving the vote to women would offset the effects, distasteful to many Southerners, of black male voting. Once women's suffrage had been achieved in 1920, the feminist movement became quiescent as attention shifted to the growing crisis in Europe. Meanwhile, feminist ideas had spread from Britain eastward as far as Russia, where they were incorporated into the revolutionary communist program. As as result, Soviet women achieved certain rights such as equal employment opportunities before their sisters in the West.

The entry of large numbers of women into the labor force during World War II marked the initial stirrings of the "second wave" of feminism, which came to be known as the Women's Liberation movement. Inspired by the Civil Rights struggles of the 1950s and 1960s, and by the publication in 1963 of Betty Friedan's *The Feminine Mystique*, women began to form small consciousness-raising groups in which they identified the many ways—both blatant and subtle—in which they had suffered discrimination. The foundation of the National Organization for Women (NOW) in 1966 provided a nationwide structure to help women in the fight

509

While the status of women has generally improved during the 20th century, there have also been exceptions. Below: In 1980, women were included in the graduating class of the West Point Military Academy for the first time. Right: A rally in support of Ayatollah Khomeini. Under the Shiite regime, Iranian women have accepted a diminished status.

for abortion rights, maternity leave, day care centers, equal pay for equal work, and access to jobs and promotions traditionally reserved for men. Feminist leaders influenced Congress to pass the Equal Rights Amendment (ERA) bill in 1972 and for the next ten years struggled to achieve its ratification by the Constitutionally mandated three quarters majority of the states. In 1982, however, the bill expired, having been ratified by only 35 of the requisite 38 states, and feminists stepped back to analyze the causes of their defeat and devise new strategies for the future.

Meanwhile, the feminist movement has moved into the international arena. At recent international conferences on women's issues, women have addressed problems ranging from the most local (e.g., the sexual mutilation of young girls in certain African societies and the imposition of the veil on women in conservative Arab nations) to the most universal (e.g., population control, hunger, and the threat of nuclear war).

SUMMARY

The term **modern** *(or* **modernus,** *the Latin word from which it derives) has been used since the 6th century to describe the events that are taking place "just now." When we label our times as* **postmodern,** *we suggest that the "just now" is tied to and is in some special way a portent of future developments. The events of the last several decades have led us to expect startling new developments in space travel, atomic physics, computer intelligence, and biomedical engineering—and also to fear that human life could be drastically altered or destroyed by the forces that science has unleashed. We can look forward to an increasing internationalization of culture as communications satellites and jet-speed transportation enable peoples of all nations to share their art, their music, and their ideas. We hope to witness the expansion of human rights and democratic participation to the point where they are enjoyed equally by everyone. When and if such a world comes to pass, we sense that terrorists, having no further grievance, would cease their activities, that nuclear arsenals would be dismantled, and that humankind would at last find great meaning and joy in its existence.*

QUESTIONS

1 What is the nature of the contemporary scientific revolution?
2 What are some of the ethical issues that have been raised as a result of new scientific developments?
3 What is existentialism?
4 What effect has nuclear technology had upon the politics and culture of the postmodern world?
5 What problems do women, regardless of their nationality, confront?

BIBLIOGRAPHY

THOMAS HACKEY and RALPH WEBER. *Voices of Revolution: Rebels and Rhetoric.* Hinsdale, Ill.: The Dryden Press, 1972. *Selections from the writings of 29 revolutionaries, from Thomas Paine and Thomas Jefferson to Robespierre and Emma Goldman, with accompanying photographs.*

ROBERT JACKSON, ed. *Global Issues 85/86.* Guilford, Conn.: Dushkin, 1985. *A survey of the critical issues facing the world today, including useful analyses of problems of over-population and depletion of natural resources.*

MARY KINNEAR. *Daughters of Time: Women in the Western Tradition.* Ann Arbor: University of Michigan Press, 1982. *A survey of the history of women in the Western world.*

TATYANA MAMONOVA. *Women and Russia.* Boston: Beacon Press 1984. *A collection of essays written for the samizdat (underground) press reveals the small but insistent feminist movement in the Soviet Union today.*

JOHN NAISBITT. *Mega Trends: Ten New Directions Transforming Our Lives.* New York: Warner Books, 1984. *An updated work which analyses the most important sociological issues facing contemporary society.*

AGNES SMEDLEY. *Portraits of Chinese Women in Revolution.* New York: The Feminist Press, 1976. *First-person accounts of women revolutionaries who joined Mao Tse-tung primarily in protest against traditional women's roles in China.*

MICHELE WENDEN ZAK and PATRICIA A. MOOTZ. *Women and the Politics of Culture.* New York: Longman, 1983. *A collection of essays on the nature, origin, and themes of the feminist movement.*

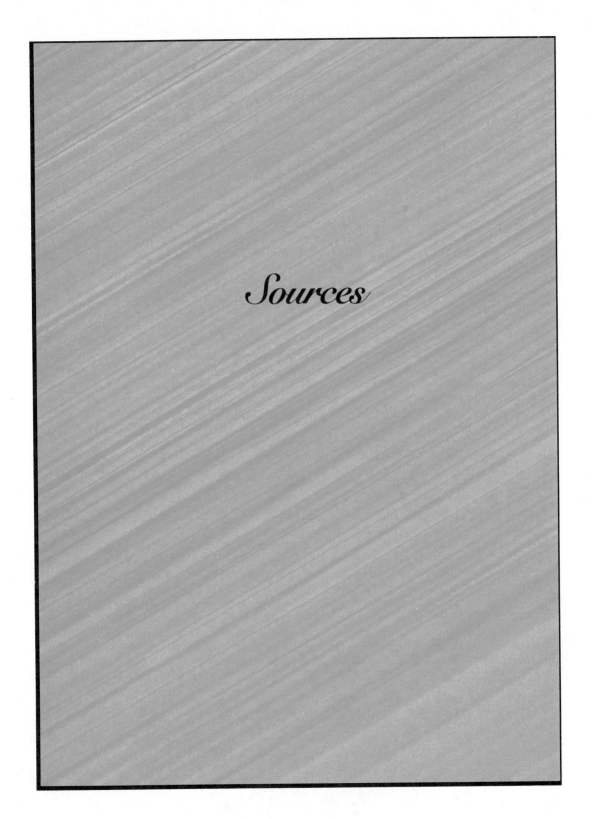

Sources

The Renaissance was a time of creative and rapid change. Events and ideas were moving at a faster pace than the society that spawned them. These two readings reflect the platitude that the more people change the more they remain the same. Excerpts from Baldassare Castiglione's (1478–1529) Book of the Courtier (a Renaissance book of etiquette for the upper classes) is followed by the Florentine humanist Leon Battista Alberti's (1404–1472) account of the daily activities of the wife of a Renaissance merchant.

Standards for an Ideal Renaissance Courtier

I wish, then, that this Courtier of ours should be nobly born and of gentle race . . . for noble birth is like a bright lamp that manifests and makes visible good and evil deeds, and kindles and stimulates to virtue both by fear of shame and by hope of praise. . . .

I am of opinion that the principal and true profession of the Courtier ought to be that of arms; which I would have him follow actively above all else, and be known among others as bold and strong, and loyal to whomsoever he serves.

Therefore, let the man we are seeking be very bold, stern, and always among the first, where the enemy are to be seen; and in every other place, gentle, modest, reserved, above all things avoiding ostentation and that impudent self-praise by which men ever excite hatred and disgust in all who hear them. . . .

Then coming to the bodily frame, I say it is enough if this be neither extremely short nor tall, for both of these conditions . . . are gazed upon in much the same way that we gaze on monsters. . . . I would have him well built and shapely of limb, and would have him show strength and lightness and suppleness, and know all bodily exercises that befit a man of war: whereof I think the first should be to handle every sort of weapon well on foot and on horse, [and] . . . to understand the advantages of each.

There are also many other exercises, which although not immediately dependent upon arms, yet are closely connected therewith . . . [such as] . . . the chase, because it bears a certain likeness to war. . . . It is fitting also to know how to swim, to leap, to run, to throw stones. . . . Another admirable exercise, and one very befitting a man at court, is the game of tennis, in which are the disposition of the body, the quickness and suppleness of every member. . . .

I would have the Courtier strive, with all the thoughts and forces of his mind, to love and almost to adore the prince whom he serves, above every other thing, and mold his wishes, habits and all his ways to his prince's liking. . . . He will not be an idle or untruthful tattler, nor a boaster nor pointless flatterer, but modest and reserved, always and especially in public showing that reverence and respect which befit the servant towards the master.

SOURCE: Baldassare Castiglione, *Book of the Courtier*. In *Great Issues In Western Civilization*, 3rd ed., eds. Brian Tierney, Donald Kagan et al. (New York: Random House, 1976), Vol. 1, pp. 457–60.

The Merchant's Wife

After my wife had been settled in my house a few days, and after her first pangs of longing for her mother and family had begun to fade, I took her by the hand and showed her around the whole house. . . . I showed her where things needed for the table were kept, and so on, through the whole house. At the end there were no household goods of which my wife had not learned both the place and the purpose. Then we returned to my room, and, having locked the door, I showed her my treasures, silver, tapestry, garments, jewels, and where each thing had its place. . . .

Only my books and records and those of my ancestors did I determine to keep well sealed. . . . These my wife not only could not read, she could not even lay hands on them. I kept my records at all times . . . locked up and arranged in order in my study, almost like sacred and religious objects. I never gave my wife permission to enter that place, with me or alone. I also ordered her, if she ever came across any writing of mine, to give it over to my keeping at once. To take away any taste she might have for looking at my notes or prying into my private affairs, I often used to express my disapproval of bold and forward females who try too hard to know about things outside the house and about the concerns of their husband and of men in general. . . .

[Husbands] who take counsel with their wives . . . are madmen if they think true prudence or good counsel lies in the female brain. . . . For this very reason I have always tried carefully not to let any secret of mine be known to a woman. . . . Furthermore, I made it a rule never to speak with her of anything but household matters or question of conduct, or of the children. Of these matters I spoke a good deal to her. . . .

[I said to my wife] . . . I shall be most pleased if you do just three things: first . . . see that you never want another man to share this bed but me. . . . She blushed and cast down her eyes. . . . Second, I said . . . she should take care of the household, preside over it with modesty, serenity, tranquillity, and peace. . . . Third . . . she should see that nothing went wrong in the house.

Never, at any moment, did I choose to show in word or action even the least bit of self-surrender in front of my wife. I did not imagine for a moment that I could hope to win obedience from one to whom I had confessed myself a slave. Always, therefore, I showed myself virile and a real man.

SOURCE: Leon Battista Alberti. In *Not In God's Image*, eds. Julia O'Faolain and Lauro Martines (New York: Harper & Row, 1973), pp. 187–89.

1. *What in each of these portrayals would be just as true today as when they were written five hundred years ago?*

2. *Are the characteristics of Castiglione's courtier the same kind of qualities that are desirable in those who serve today's political leaders? If you were writing a similar book, what characteristics for an ideal public servant would you add or delete?*

3. *According to Alberti's merchant, what types of affairs are strictly the concern of men? Why should these affairs be kept secret from wives? What can we infer about the wife's education before she married—e.g., can she read or write?*

The Reformation begins with Martin Luther's (1483–1546) verbal attack against the selling of indulgences by the monk Johann Tetzel (1465?–1519) in the vicinity of Wittenberg in the year 1517. Excerpts from one of Tetzel's sermons help to explain Luther's anger. Selected passages from the "Ninety-Five Theses" provide the rationale for his wrath. The Reformation movement, however, was not limited solely to those leaving the Roman Catholic Church. Excerpts from the constitution of the Society of Jesus (Jesuits), founded by Ignatius Loyola, describe how one of the more militant arms of the Catholic Church planned to regain lost territory and spread the faith beyond the confines of Europe and around the world.

Johann Tetzel's Sermon on Indulgences

You may obtain letters of safe conduct from the vicar of our Lord Jesus Christ, by means of which you are able to liberate your soul from the hands of the enemy, and convey it by means of contrition and confession, safe and secure from all pains of Purgatory, into the happy kingdom. For know, that in these letters are stamped and engraven all the merits of Christ's passion there laid bare. Consider, that for each and every mortal sin it is necessary to undergo seven years of penitence after confession and contrition, either in this life or in Purgatory.

How many mortal sins are committed in a day, how many in a week, how many in a month, how many in a year, how many in the whole extent of life! They are well-nigh numberless, and those that commit them must needs suffer endless punishment in the burning pains of Purgatory.

But with these confessional letters you will be able at any time in life to obtain full indulgence for all penalties imposed upon you, in all cases except the four reserved to the Apostolic See. Thence throughout your whole life, whenever you wish to make confession, you may receive the same remission, except in cases reserved to the Pope, and afterwards, at the hour of death, a full indulgence as to all penalties and sins, and your share of all spiritual blessings that exist in the church militant and all its members.

Do you not know that when it is necessary for anyone to go to Rome, or undertake any other dangerous journey, he takes his money to a broker and elsewhere he may receive again his funds intact, by means of the letters of this same broker? Are you not willing, then, for the fourth part of a florin, to obtain these letters, by virtue of which you may bring, not your money, but your divine and immortal soul, safe and sound into the land of Paradise?

SOURCE: Johann Tetzel. In *Western Civilization: Images and Interpretations*, ed. Dennis Sherman (New York: Knopf, 1983), Vol. 1, pp. 280–81.

Martin Luther on Indulgences

The revenues of all Christendom are being sucked into this insatiable basilica. The Germans laugh at calling this the common treasure of Christendom. Before long all the churches, palaces, walls, and bridges of Rome will be built out of our money. First of all we should rear living temples, next local churches, and only last of all St. Peter's, which is not necessary for us. We Germans cannot attend St. Peter's. Better that it should never be built than that our parochial churches should be despoiled. The pope would do better to appoint one good pastor to a church than to confer indulgences upon them all. Why doesn't the pope build the basilica of St. Peter out of his own money? He is richer than Croesus. He would do better to sell St. Peter's and give the money to the poor folk who are being fleeced by the hawkers of indulgences. . . .

Papal indulgences do not remove guilt. Beware of those who say that indulgences effect reconciliation with God. The power of the keys cannot make attrition into contrition. He who is contrite has . . . remission of guilt and penalty without indulgences. The pope can remove only those penalties which he himself has imposed on earth, for Christ did not say, "Whatsoever I have bound in heaven you may [let] loose on earth."

The saints have no extra credits. . . . If there were any superfluous credits, they could not be stored up for subsequent use. The Holy Spirit would have used them fully long ago. Christ indeed had merits, but until I am better instructed I deny that they are indulgences. His merits are freely available without the keys of the pope. . . . Therefore I claim that the pope has no jurisdiction over purgatory. . . .

Indulgences are positively harmful to the recipient because they impede salvation by diverting charity and inducing a false sense of security. Christians should be taught that he who gives to the poor is better than he who receives a pardon. He who spends his money for indulgences instead of relieving want receives not the indulgence of the pope but the indignation of God. . . . Love covers a multitude of sins and is better than all the pardons of Jerusalem and Rome. . . .

Peace comes in the word of Christ through faith. He who does not have this is lost even though he be absolved a million times by the pope, and he who does have it may not wish to be released from purgatory, for true contrition seeks penalty. . . .

SOURCE: Selected passages from Martin Luther's "Ninety-Five Theses." In Roland H. Bainton, *Here I Stand: A Life of Martin Luther* (New York: Abingdon-Cokesbury Press, 1950), pp. 30–83.

From the Constitution of the Society of Jesus, 1540

He who desires to fight for God under the banner of the cross in our society—which we wish to distinguish by the name of Jesus—and to serve God alone and the Roman pontiff, his vicar on earth, after a solemn vow of perpetual chastity, shall get this thought before his mind, that he is a part of a society founded for the especial purpose of providing for the advancement of souls in Christian life and doctrine and for the propagation of faith through public preaching and the ministry of the word of God, spiritual exercises and deeds of charity, and in particular through the training of the young and ignorant in Christianity and through the spiritual consolation of the faithful of Christ in hearing confessions; and he shall take care to keep first God and next the purpose of this organization always before his eyes. . . .

All the members shall realize, and shall recall daily, as long as they live, that this society as a whole and in every part is fighting for God under faithful obedience to one most holy lord, the pope, and to the other Roman pontiffs who succeed him . . . whatever the present Roman pontiff, or any future one, may from time to time decree regarding the welfare of soul and the propagation of the faith, we are pledged to obey without evasion or excuse, instantly, so far as in us lies, whether he send us to the Turks or any other infidels, even to those who inhabit the regions men call the Indies; whether to heretics or schismatics, or, on the other hand, to certain of the faithful.

SOURCE: Western Civilization: Images and Interpretations, ed. Dennis Sherman (New York: Knopf, 1983), Vol. 1, pp. 287, 288.

1. *Based on the preceding documents what can be said about the "temper" of the times and the nature of the conflicting issues in the Reformation era?*
2. *How would Tetzel defend himself against the criticism that he was abusing his authority to distribute indulgences?*
3. *Summarize the three major points made by Martin Luther in his condemnation of the selling of indulgences. Does he overstep the bounds of propriety by today's standards? Was his statement considered heretical in his own day?*
4. *What in the Constitution of the Society of Jesus might help to explain the order's considerable success in combatting heresy and spreading the Catholic religion around the world?*
5. *If indulgences became a public issue today, would there again be a firestorm of protests? What religious issues exist in contemporary society that enlist the same kind of fervor and loyalty?*

THE SPANISH ARMADA

That the defeat of the Spanish Armada in 1588 was a momentous event in European and world history is hardly a topic of controversy—although its significance and impact on the future course of world events still is open to debate. The choice of the following excerpts, however, is not for the purpose of throwing more light on any historical debate as much as it is an attempt to understand the thought processes and conclusions of historians as they go about analyzing a specific event in the past. All three passages describe the events of the actual battle and/or the results.

A 19th-Century Account

On the afternoon of July 19, 1588, a group of English captains was collected at the bowling green on the Hoe, at Plymouth, whose equals have never before or since been brought together. . . . There was Sir Francis Drake, the first English circumnavigator of the globe, the terror of every Spanish coast in the Old World and the New; there was Sir John Hawkins, the rough veteran of many a daring voyage on the African and American seas and of many a desperate battle; there was Sir Martin Frobisher, one of the earliest explorers of the Arctic seas in search of the northwest passage. Another of our Elizabethan sea-kings, Sir Walter Raleigh was at that time [in] Cornwall [helping] to raise and equip the land forces [for the coming battle].

A match of bowls was being played, in which Drake and other high officers of the fleet were engaged, when a small armed vessel was seen running before the wind into Plymouth harbor with all sails set. Her commander landed in haste, and eagerly sought the place where the English lord admiral and his captains were standing. . . . and he told the English officers that he had that morning seen the Spanish Armada off the Cornish coast. . . . the captains began to hurry down to the water, and there was a shouting for the ships' boats; but Drake coolly checked his comrades, and insisted that the match should be played out. He said that there was plenty of time both to win the game and beat the Spaniards. . . .

It was on Saturday, July 20th, that [the British fleet] first came in sight of [their] formidable adversaries. The armada was drawn up in form of a crescent, which from horn to horn measured some seven miles. There was a southwest wind, and before it the vast vessels sailed slowly on. The English let them pass by, and then, following in the rear, commenced an attack on them. A running fight now took place, in which some of the best ships of the Spaniards were captured; many more received heavy damage, while the English vessels, which took care not to close with their huge antagonists, but availed themselves of their superior celerity in tacking and maneuvering, suffered little comparative loss. . . .

The armada lay off Calais, with its largest ships ranged outside, "like strong castles fearing no assault, the lesser placed in the middle ward." . . . on the night of the 29th [the English Admiral] sent eight fire ships among them. . . .

The Spaniards cut their cables and put to sea in confusion. One of the largest galleasses ran afoul of another vessel and was stranded. The rest of the fleet was scattered about on the Flemish coast. . . . Now was the golden opportunity for the English to assail them . . . and nobly was that opportunity used.

SOURCE: Sir Edward Shepherd Creasy. In *The Great Events by Famous Historians*, ed. Rossiter Johnson (The National Alumni, 1905), Vol. 10, pp. 251, 252, 253, 269, 272.

Churchill on the Armada

The nation was united in the face of the Spanish preparations. While the Armada was still off the coast of England Queen Elizabeth reviewed the army at Tilbury and addressed them in these stirring words. ". . . Let tyrants fear. I have always so behaved myself that, under God, I have placed my chiefest strength and safeguard in the loyal hearts and goodwill of my subjects; and therefore I am come amongst you, as you see, resolved, in the midst and heat of the battle, to live or die amongst you all, to lay down for my God, and for my kingdom, and for my people, my honour and my blood, even in the dust. I know I have the body of a weak and feeble woman, but I have the heart and stomach of a king, and of a king of England too, and think foul scorn that . . . any prince of Europe should dare to invade the borders of my realm. . . . I myself will take up arms, I myself will be your general, judge and rewarder of every one of your virtues in the field."

. . . The Channel passage was a torment to the Spaniards. The guns of the English ships raked the decks of the galleons, killing the crews and demoralising the soldiers. The English suffered hardly any loss. . . . . Yet Howard (the English Admiral). . . scarcely realized the magnitude of the victory. "Their force is wonderful great and strong," he wrote on the evening after the battle, "yet we pluck their feathers by little and little.". . .

But to the English people as a whole the defeat of the Armada came as a miracle. For thirty years the shadow of Spanish power had darkened the political scene. A wave of religious emotion filled men's minds. One of the medals struck to commemorate the victory bears the inscription "Afflavit Deus et Dissipantur"—"God blew and they were scattered."

With 1588 the crisis of the reign was past. England had emerged from the Armada year as a first-class Power. She had resisted the weight of the mightiest empire that had been seen since Roman times. Her people awoke to a consciousness of their greatness, and the last years of Elizabeth's reign saw a welling up of national energy and enthusiasm focusing upon the person of the Queen. . . .

SOURCE: Winston S. Churchill, *A History of the English Speaking Peoples*, Vol II, *The New World* (New York: Dodd, Mead, & Company, 1956), pp. 126, 129, 130, 131, 133.

Mattingly on the Armada

Historians agree that the defeat of the Spanish Armada was a decisive battle, in fact one of the Decisive Battles of the world, but there is much less agreement as to what it decided. It certainly did not decide the issue of the war between England and Spain. . . . the English enterprise [against] Portugal in 1589 ended in disastrous failure, and thereafter the war dragged itself out for nearly fourteen years more, as long, in fact, as Queen Elizabeth lived, and ended in no better than a draw. Some historians say that the defeat of the Armada "marked the decline of the Spanish colonial empire and the rise of the British." It is hard to see why they think so. By 1603, Spain had not lost to the English a single overseas outpost, while the English colonization of Virginia had been postponed for the duration. Nor did the Armada campaign "transfer the command of the sea from Spain to England." English sea power in the Atlantic had usually been superior to the combined strengths of Castile and Portugal, and so it continued to be, but after 1588 the margin of superiority diminished. The defeat of the Armada was not so much the end as the beginning of the Spanish navy. . . .

Nevertheless, the defeat of the Spanish Armada was in one sense, a decisive event. Less for the combatants than for the onlookers. . . . For the spectators of both parties, the outcome, reinforced, as everyone believed, by an extraordinary tempest, was indeed decisive. The Protestants of France and the Netherlands, Germany and Scandinavia saw with relief that God was, in truth, as they had always supposed, on their side. The Catholics of France and Italy and Germany saw with almost equal relief that Spain was not, after all, God's chosen champion. From that time forward, though Spain's preponderance was to last for more than another generation, the peak of her prestige had passed. . . .

Meanwhile, as the episode of the Armada receded into the past, it influenced history in another way. Its story, magnified and distorted by a golden mist, became a heroic epilogue of the defense of freedom against tyranny, an eternal myth of the victory of the weak over the strong, of the triumph of David over Goliath. It raised men's hearts in dark hours, and led them to say to one another, "What we have done once, we can do again." In so far as it did this, the legend of the defeat of the Spanish Armada became as important as the actual event—perhaps even more important.

Garrett Mattingly, *The Armada* (Boston: Houghton Mifflin, 1959), pp. 397, 400, 401, 402.

1. *Is there anything in the backgrounds (heritage and careers) of the authors that might effect their interpretations of the defeat of the Spanish Armada? (Sir Edward Creasy was a 19th-century English writer who specialized in military subjects, and Mr. Mattingly is a contemporary American historian.) Does the climate of the times in which they lived help to explain similarities and/or differences in their written accounts?*
2. *Look at one of the recently published accounts of the Vietnam War and compare it to what Churchill and Mattingly had to say about the defeat of the Spanish Armada. Are there any major differences in style and attitude toward military events? How do you explain the differences?*
3. *Which one of the three writers is the best historian? Give reasons for your choice.*
4. *What roles did Frobisher, Drake, Hawkins, and Raleigh play in discovering and settling the New World? What is a galleass, and in what ways were the British warships superior to their Spanish counterparts.*

> ***The first two selections are brief observations by European explorers and trader-adventurers at the dawn of the Age of Exploration in the 15th and 16th centuries. The third excerpt describes the initial experiences and perceptions of an Indian visitor to England during the 19th century, and the fourth is a comment upon British racial attitudes by a 20th-century Englishman.***

Columbus Discovers the New World

Sir . . . I write you this letter, whereby you will learn how in thirty-three days' time I reached the Indies . . . where I found very many islands thickly peopled, of all which I took possession without resistance, for their Highnesses by proclamation made and with royal standard unfurled. To the first island that I found I gave the name of San Salvador, in remembrance of His High Majesty, who hath marvellously wrought all these things to pass; the Indians called it Guanaham. . . . [Another island I called Juana]. . . . I found . . . so large that I thought it must be the mainland—the province of Cathay [China]. . . . [However] . . . I had learned from some other Indians whom I had seized, that this land was certainly an island. . . .

[The inhabitants] never refuse anything that they possess when it is asked of them, on the contrary, they offer it themselves, and they exhibit so much loving kindness that they would even give their hearts; and, whether it be something of value or of little worth that is offered to them, they are satisfied. . . . I gave away a thousand good and pretty articles which I had brought with me in order to win their affection; and that they might be led to become Christians, and be well inclined to love and serve their Highnesses and the whole Spanish nation, and that they might aid us by giving us things of which we stand in need. . . . I took by force, in the first island that I discovered, some of these natives, that they might learn our language and give me information in regard to what existed in those parts. . . . All Christendom ought to rejoice, both for the great exaltation which may accrue to them in turning so many nations to our holy faith, and also for the temporal benefits which will bring great refreshment and gain, not only to Spain, but to all Christians.

Pizarro's Conquest of the Incas

It was not long before sunset when the van of the royal procession entered the gates of the city. . . . Elevated high above his vassals came the Inca Atahuallpa, borne on a sedan or open litter, on which was a sort of throne made of massive gold of inestimable value. . . . Round his neck was suspended a collar of emeralds of uncommon size and brilliancy. . . .

Pizarro saw that the hour had come. He waved a white scarf in the air, the appointed signal. The fatal gun was fired from the fortress. Then, springing into the square, the Spanish captain and his followers shouted the old war-cry of "St. Jargo and at them." It was answered by the battle-cry of every Spaniard in the city, as, rushing from the avenues of the great halls in which they were concealed, they poured into the plaza, horse and foot, each in his own dark column, and threw themselves into the midst of the Indian crowd. The latter, taken by surprise, stunned by the report of artillery and muskets, the echoes of which reverberated like thunder from the surrounding buildings, and blinded by the smoke which rolled in sulphurous volumes along the square, were seized with a panic. . . . Nobles and commoners—all were tramped down under the fierce charge of the cavalry, who dealt their blows, right and left, without sparing; while their swords, flashing through the thick gloom, carried dismay into the hearts of the wretched natives, who now for the first time saw the horse and his rider in all their terrors. . . . Though the massacre was incessant, it was short in duration. The whole time consumed by it, the brief twilight of the tropics, did not much exceed half an hour; a short period, indeed—yet long enough to decide the fate of Peru and to subvert the dynasty of the Incas.

An Indian Visitor to England

The first and greatest defect I observed in the English is their lack of faith in religion, and their great inclination to philosophy [atheism]. The effects of these principles, or rather want of principle, is very clear in the lower class of people, who are totally dishonest. . . . They are ever on the watch to take for themselves the property of the rich, who, on this account, are obliged constantly to keep their door shut, and never permit an unknown person to enter them. . . . The second defect most conspicuous in the English character is pride, or insolence. . . . Their third defect is a passion for acquiring money and their attachment to worldly affairs. These . . . sordid and illiberal habits are generally found to accompany avarice and parsimony, and, consequently make these English contemptible. . . .

The Question of Race in India

Especially after the Indian Mutiny [1857], the fatal doctrine of racial superiority came more and more to dominate the imaginations of the British in India. Perhaps the deterioration in this respect can be made concrete from the records of my own family. During the 18th and 19th centuries two of my ancestors . . . married what the late-19th century British would, so offensively, have called native women. In each case, so far as the family records go, these marriages did not excite the least adverse comment or injure their careers in any way. How unthinkable such alliances would have been to my great-uncles . . . who were members of the Governor-General's Council in the 1870s.

SOURCE: *Readings In World History*, ed. Leften S. Stavrianos (Boston: Allyn and Bacon, 1962), pp. 122–25, 128–30, 140–41, 604–06.

1. *What evidence of ethnocentrism is there in each of these accounts?*
2. *List the motives for European interest in exploration and settlement. Arrange your list in the appropriate order of importance, with the most significant cause coming first.*
3. *What judgments can be made about the Indian visitor to England? For example, what class or caste would he most likely have represented back in India?*

Life in 17th and 18th century Prussia and Russia was harsh and austere even by the standards of the times. Frederick William the Great, Elector of Prussia (1640– 1688), was among the most successful rulers of his day when it came to consolidating political power into his own hands. In a private letter to his son and heir, Frederick William advises the boy to follow in his footsteps.

In tsarist Russia life was at best tolerable, and at its worst brutal and savage. Excerpts from the Law Code of 1649, Robert K. Massie's biography of Peter the Great, and Catherine the Great's "Instructions" to her 1767 commission on legal reforms illustrate the worst and the best that Muscovy and its rulers had to offer the Russian people.

Advice to a Son and Successor

It is necessary that you conduct yourself as a good father to your people, that you love your subjects regardless of their religious convictions, and that you try to promote their welfare at all times. Work to stimulate trade everywhere, and keep in mind the population increase. . . . Take advantage of the advice of the clergy and nobility as much as you can; listen to them and be gracious to them all, as befits one of your position; recognize ability where you find it, so that you will increase the love and affection of your subjects toward you. But, it is essential that you always be moderate in your attitudes, in order not to endanger your position and lose respect. With those of your own station in life, be careful never to give way in matters of precedence and in all to which you are entitled; on the contrary, hold fast to the eminence of your superior position. Remember that one can lose one's superior position if one allows too great pomposity and too great a show upon the part of members of the court.

Be keenly interested in the administration of justice throughout your land. See to it that justice is maintained for the poor as well as for the rich without discrimination of any kind. . . .

Seek to maintain friendly re'ations with the princes and the nobility of the Empire. Correspond with them frequently and maintain your friendship with them. Be certain not to give them cause for ill-will; try not to arouse emotions of jealousy or enmity, but be sure that you are always in a strong position to maintain your weight in disputes that may arise. . . .

It is wise to have alliances, if necessary, but it is better to rely on your own strength. You are in a weak position if you do not have the means and do not possess the confidence of the people.

SOURCE: Frederick William. In *Western Civilization: Images and Interpretations*, ed. Dennis Sherman (New York: Knopf, 1983), Vol. 2, pp. 7–8.

The Law Code of 1649

If a member of another faith, regardless of which faith, or a Russian, should blaspheme our Lord and Savior Jesus Christ, or His mother the Holy Queen, Mary, the Virgin Mother of God, or the honorable cross, or its holy servants . . . the blasphemer of God should be burned at the stake.

Should anyone think maliciously about the sovereign's health, and should another person report him concerning this malicious thought . . . such person upon investigation, should be executed.

Wives and children of traitors, if they were aware of their treasons, should be executed.

And if someone should reveal the state of the Sovereign's health, or if they should disclose information about people whom they serve, or, if they be peasants, to whom they belong, and if such reports are not convincing, they should not be believed. After they have been severely punished for spreading lies, through merciless whipping with a knout, [they will then be] returned to those persons to whom they belong. . . .

Whoever should initiate mass discontent or a conspiracy against his Tsarist Majesty or his boyars, or his high assistants, or members of the boyarskaia duma . . . or other officials of the central government in provincial cities . . . those persons who initiate it should be condemned to death without mercy.

And should someone wish to travel for trade purposes or other private matters from the Muscovite state into a foreign country which is on peaceful terms with the Muscovite state, such person in Moscow must petition the Tsar, and in [other] cities petitions are to be addressed to the local official for a travel permit.

SOURCE: *Medieval Russia: A Source Book 900–1700*, ed. Basil Dmytryshyn (Hinsdale, Ill.: The Dryden Press, 1973), pp. 294–300.

The Use of Torture in Peter the Great's Russia

Torture in Russia in Peter's day was used for three purposes: to force men to speak; as punishment even when no information was desired; and as a prelude to or refinement of death by execution. Traditionally, three general methods of torture were used in Russia: the batog, the knout and fire.

The batog was a small rod or stick about the thickness of a man's finger, commonly used to beat an offender for lesser crimes. . . . Two men applied batogs simultaneously to the bare back. . . . The two punishers wielded their sticks rhythmically in turn, "keeping time as smiths do at an anvil until their rods were broken in pieces." . . .

More serious punishment or interrogation called forth the knout, a savage but traditional method of inflicting pain in Russia. The knout was a thick, hard leather whip about three and a half feet long. A blow from the knout tore skin from the bare back of a victim and, when the lash fell repeatedly in the same place, could bite through to the bone.

Torture by fire was common. . . . In its simplest form, interrogation by fire meant that the victim's "hands and feet are tied and he is fixed on a long pole, as upon a spit, and he has his raw back roasted over the fire and he is examined and called upon to confess." . . .

In general, executions in Russia were similar to those in other countries. Offenders were burned to death, hanged or beheaded.

SOURCE: Robert K. Massie, *Peter the Great: His Life and World* (New York: Knopf, 1981), pp. 249–51.

Catherine's Instructions for Composing A New Code of Laws

1. The Christian Law teaches us to do mutual Good to one another, as much as possible we can.

9. The Sovereign is absolute; for there is no other Authority but that which centers in his single Person, that can act with a Vigour proportionate to the Extent of such a vast Dominion.

210. Proofs from Fact demonstrate to us, that the frequent Use of capital Punishment never mended the Morals of a People. Therefore, if I prove the Death of a Citizen to be neither useful nor necessary to Society in general, I shall confute those who rise up against Humanity. I repeat here, to "Society in general;" because the death of a citizen can only be useful and necessary in one Case; which is, when, though he be deprived of Liberty, yet has such Power by his Connections, as may enable him to raise Disturbances dangerous to the publick Peace. . . .

211. It is not the Excess of Severity, nor the Destruction of the human Species, that produces a powerful Effect in the Hearts of the Citizens, but the continued Duration of the Punishment.

212. . . . . It is a general Rule, that rapid and violent Impressions on the human Mind, disturb and give Pain, but do not operate long upon the memory. . . .

526. But as no perfect Work was ever yet composed by Man; therefore, if the Commissioners should discover, as they proceed, that any Rule for some particular Regulation has been omitted, they have Leave, in such a Case, to report it to Us, and to ask for a Supplement.

SOURCE: Catherine the Great. In *Readings in Russian Civilization: Imperial Russia, 1700–1917*, ed. Thomas Rita (Chicago: University of Chicago Press, 1969), pp. 252–55.

1. *What measures advocated by Frederick William could have led to an improvement of conditions in Russia?*

2. *Given the condition of the times, and the nature of the political system in Germany, what other advice might the son need in order to build upon and continue the success of his father?*

3. *Why was Catherine deserving of the respect given to her by Voltaire and other great thinkers of the Enlightenment? Define the term, "Enlightened Despot." By your definition, was Catherine the Great a successful "Enlightened Despot?"*

THE PEASANTS IN LOUIS XIV'S FRANCE

Peasants at the time of Louis XIV were the most numerous and the poorest group in France. In addition to the traditional feudal obligations they owed to local seigneurs and to the king, peasants were also subject to the extortions of various other officials— law court judges, the clergy, bailiffs, and the many officers in charge of collecting their rents and taxes.

The working of the land was wholly in the hands of the peasants which— allowing for a good deal of regional variation—owned less than half of it. Except for the very few remaining freeholds, peasant property was not of the "Roman" type but manorial, that is to say that it was never independent. It is fashionable among royalist historians to assert the peasant's right to sell, lease, exchange, give or bequeath his land and this was true up to a point, but only with the consent of his overlord and after payment of what were frequently crippling dues and bearing in mind the fact that the seigneur always could, and often did, withdraw his consent. (It was quite within his rights to substitute himself as purchaser and at the same price.) It is further maintained nowadays that the peasants' feudal dues, which had been fixed for a long time, had dwindled into insignificance with the decline in the value of money. This is true of the old financial payments made in direct rents but false as regards all other dues which were often levied in kind and in particular of rentes and champarts; the last alone currently amounted to a tenth and sometimes a third of the crop. The feudal nature of his holding was to the peasant at the same time an annoyance and a burden, aggravated by the amazing variation in local conditions.

It seems probable that the small part of French territory which did belong to four-fifths of its inhabitants was divided extremely unfairly. The few serious studies which have been made of some provinces lead to the following conclusions. Not many peasants were altogether landless. About a tenth possessed the few hectares (varying from one region to the next) which meant economic security for their families. [One hectare is approximately two and a half acres.] The vast majority had only a few scattered plots, often the poorest land in the district, and were compelled to find other means of livelihood. The peasants who were really high and powerful were those who farmed great estates and manors who were to some extent the overseers and agents of the great landowners. These conclusions are valid at least for the Ile-de-France and Picardy, though they have still to be confirmed elsewhere. A village of a hundred families would include one or two big farmers whose ploughs, teams, holdings and credit make them powerful men in the locality, a dozen or so more or less independent labouring men and the same number of poor souls whose only possessions were their hovel, their patch of ground and their ewe or who were frankly beggars. The remainder, farm hands, casual labourers, vineyard workers, woodmen and weavers were all humble folk scraping a meagre living from tiny holdings and trying their hand to any trade that came their way. The tools, livestock and employment on which the entire village depended for a livelihood, at least in good years, were in the hands of the dozen or so "big men" and even, in some cases, of a single "cock" of the village. Nothing could have been less egalitarian than a French village community. "Jacques Bonhomme" never existed except in the minds of novelists and pamphleteers. Village administration, which was more energetic and effective than that of modern councils, was naturally in the hands of the farmers and labouring men who formed the "better part" of the local assemblies. The village community levied taxes from all its members towards the upkeep of the church, priest's house, graveyard, schoolhouse and teacher, and for the communal shepherd, or shepherds, and wardens and keepers to watch over the crops or vineyards. In many cases the local village community was combined with the religious one of the parish to form a basic administrative unit of the kingdom in matters concerning bailliages, elections, salt stores and control of woods and forests and so forth. More rarely it was identified with the seigneurie.

This, with the village and the parish, constituted the third social group to which the peasant belonged. As we know, the seigneur, whether individual or collective, nobleman or roturier [commoner], clergy or layman, enjoyed a great many rights, honorary or otherwise, which varied endlessly from place to place and were persistently confused with the privileges of nobility. (A fact extremely convenient for the faux nobles, seigneurs of long standing who probably formed the bulk of the French nobility.) These seigneurial dues might be slight or they might be ruinous and were generally substantial but they were invariably a burden, the extent of which varied according to the region, the seigneur and his collector. In the long sequence of peasant revolts which go to make up the history of rural France in the seventeenth century it is as common to find the peasants allied with the seigneur against the king—as for instance, in Auvergne—as it is the opposite—notably in Brittany and Picardy. Even as absentee seigneur often made his authority felt through the severity and unlimited powers of his collectors, intendants, judges, bailiffs, seneschals, clerks and fiscal attorneys, who were not always remarkable for their honesty. Insufficient study has been devoted to the seigneurial courts which were numerous, busy and basic to an understanding of rural life. They clearly served a useful purpose to their clients but sometimes at the cost of substantial fees and the imposition of large fines for trivial offenses. . . .

There were four interested parties preying on the labour and income of the peasants: the local community, the Church, the seigneur (lord) and the king. The last of these was the most diverse and also the most oppressive, varying from simple, direct methods such as the taille, the gabelle and a number of additional taxes, to the more complex and equally burdensome host of indirect levies, the most loathed of which were the aides on liquor. In theory these were an extraordinary and purely temporary measure, as were the dues paid for the food and lodging of military personnel, although even these were not so harsh as the actual billeting of a swaggering, thieving soldiery which was dreaded almost as much as the plague and had turned up all too often in the past twenty-five years.

The levies raised in kind, whether they were collected or required to be delivered, difficult as they were, were the easiest to manage. For the rest, money had to be found somehow by dint of piece work, day labouring and the marketing of small items such as a calf, a few fleeces, some lambs or a clutch of eggs or chickens if these could be raised. The poorer peasants borrowed to raise the money, always from the same people: the better-off labourer, the tax collector or any scrivener, court official or tradesman prepared to advance the price of a piece of cloth or a few dozen nails. The debt remained to be paid, entered on a scrap of paper, with interest added in advance, and registered officially in the presence of a notary or before a court of law. The debtor did his best to pay it back in kind and the partial or complete repayment of these small IOUs was often his chief reward. One bad harvest, a visitation by soldiers, an epidemic or the death of a cow or a few sheep could mean a swift rise in the amount of the debt and eventual foreclosure. Anyone who has gone through the inventories compiled after the deaths of labourers of the time finds the monotonous repetition of the same lists of liabilities, cutting into or even wiping out the assets, becoming an obsession. In order to satisfy the collectors of rents and taxes, the peasants fell victim to a host of creditors, some local but more often townsmen, a few in the church but the majority belonging to the bourgeoisie. When times were particularly hard, as they were during the Frondes, this system resulted in the wholesale dispossession of country folk by their creditors and in the passage of numerous smallholdings into wealthy hands to form the basis of large estates, especially in the vicinity of prosperous towns and abbeys. In this way a considerable portion of the income earned by the peasants of the kingdom was swallowed up simply in paying back loans.

SOURCE: Pierre Goubert, *Louis XIV and Twenty Million Frenchmen*, trans. Anne Carter. Copyright © 1969 by Anne Carter. Reprinted by permission of Pantheon Books, a Division of Random House, Inc., and Allen Lane, the Penguin Press, London.

1. *Who comprised the Third Estate in France? What percentage of the total French population were peasants in the 17th century?*
2. *What remained of the feudal system in France by 1700?*
3. *What were the rights and privileges of the seigneurs (lords)?*

THE ENGLISH BILL OF RIGHTS, 1689

The "Glorious Revolution" of 1688 transferred the crown from James II to William and Mary. The Bill of Rights as an Act of Parliament serves to legitimize the succession, to place limits on royal authority, and to preserve the powers of Parliament and Protestantism. At the same time, it did not democratize the English system.

Whereas the . . . late King James the Second having abdicated the government and the throne being thereby vacant, his Highness the Prince of Orange (whom it has pleased almighty God to make the glorious instrument of delivering this kingdom from popery and arbitrary power) did (by the advice of the Lords Spiritual and Temporal and divers principal persons of the Commons) cause letters to be written to the Lords Spiritual and Temporal being Protestants, and other letters to the several counties, cities, universities, borough and cinque ports, for the choosing of such persons to represent them as were of right to be sent to Parliament, to meet and sit at Westminster upon the two and twentieth day of January in this year, in order to such an establishment as that their religion, laws and liberties might not again be in danger of being subverted, upon which letters elections having been accordingly made.

And thereupon the said Lords Spiritual and Temporal and Commons, . . . being now assembled in a full and free representative of this nation, taking into their most serious consideration the best means for attaining the ends aforesaid, do in the first place (as their ancestors in like case have usually done) for the vindicating and asserting their ancient rights and liberties declare:

That the pretended power of suspending of laws or the execution of laws by regal authority without consent of Parliament is illegal.

That the pretended power of dispensing with laws or the execution of laws by regal authority, as it has been assumed and exercised of late, is illegal.

That the commission for erecting the late Court of Commissioners for Ecclesiastical Causes, and all other commissions and courts of like nature, are illegal and pernicious.

That levying money for or to use of the crown by pretense of prerogative without grant of Parliament, for longer time or in other manner than the same or shall be granted, is illegal.

That it is the right of the subjects to petition the King, and all commitments and prosecutions for such petitioning are illegal.

That the raising or keeping a standing army within the kingdom in time of peace, unless it be with consent of Parliament, is against the law.

That the subjects which are Protestants may have arms for their defense, suitable to their conditions and as allowed by law.

That election of members of Parliament ought to be free.

That the freedom of speech and debates or proceedings in Parliament ought not to be impeached or questioned in any court or place out of Parliament.

That excessive bail ought not to be required, nor excessive fines imposed, nor cruel and unusual punishments inflicted.

That jurors ought to be duly impanelled and returned, and jurors which pass upon men in trials for high treason ought to be freeholders.

That all grants and promises of fines and forfeitures of particular persons before conviction are illegal and void.

And that for redress of all grievances, and for the amending, strengthening and preserving of the laws, Parliament ought to be held frequently.

And they do claim, demand and insist upon all and singular the premises and their undoubted rights and liberties, and that no declarations, judgments, doings or proceedings to the prejudice of the people in any of said premises ought in any wise to be drawn hereafter into consequence or example; to which demand of their rights they are particularly encouraged by the declaration of his Highness the Prince of Orange as being the only means for obtaining a full redress and remedy therein.

Having therefore an entire confidence that his said Highness . . . will perfect the deliverance so far advanced by him, and will still preserve them from the violation of their rights which they have here asserted, and from all other attempts upon their religion, rights and liberties, the said Lords Spiritual and Temporal and Commons assembled at Westminster do resolve that William and Mary, Prince and Princess of Orange, be and be declared King and Queen of England, France, and Ireland and the dominions thereunto belonging, to hold the crown and royal dignity of the said kingdoms and dominions to them . . . during their lives and the life of the survivor of them, and that the sole and full exercise of the regal power be only in and executed by the said Prince of Orange in the names of the said Prince and Princess during their joint lives, and after their deceases the said crown and royal dignity . . . to be to the heirs of the body of the said Princess, and for default of such issue to the Princess Anne of Denmark, and the heirs of her body, and for default of such is due to the heirs of the body of the said Prince of Orange. And the Lords Spiritual and Temporal and Commons do pray the said Prince and Princess to accept the same accordingly. . . .

Now in pursuance of the premises the said Lords . . . and Commons . . . do pray that it may be declared and enacted that all and singular the rights and liberties asserted and claimed in the said declaration are the true, ancient and indubitable rights and liberties of the people of this kingdom, and so shall be esteemed, allowed, adjudged, deemed and taken to be; and that all and every the particulars aforesaid shall be firmly and strictly holden and observed as they are expressed in the said declaration, and all officers and ministers whatsoever shall serve their Majesties and their successors according to the same in all times to come.

And the said Lords . . . and Commons . . . do hereby recognize, acknowledge and declare that King James II having abdicated the government, and their Majesties having accepted the crown and royal dignity as aforesaid, their said Majesties did become . . . and of right ought to be by the laws of this realm our sovereign liege lord and lady, King and Queen of England, France and Ireland and the dominions thereunto belonging, in and to whose princely persons the royal state, crown and dignity of the said realms with all honors, styles, titles, regalities, prerogatives, powers, jurisdictions and authorities to the same belonging and appertaining are most fully, rightfully and entirely invested and incorporated, united and annexed . . . And the said Lords . . . and Commons do in the name of all the people . . . most humbly and faithfully submit themselves, their heirs and posterities forever, and do faithfully promise that they will stand to, maintain and defend their said Majesties, and also the limitation and succession of the crown herein specified and contained against all persons whatsoever that shall attempt anything to the contrary.

And whereas it has been found by experience that it is inconsistent with the safety and welfare of this Protestant kingdom to be governed by a popish prince, or by any King or Queen marrying a papist, the said Lords . . . and Commons . . . do further pray that it may be enacted that all and every person and persons that is, are or shall be reconciled to or shall hold communion with See or Church of Rome, or shall profess the popish religion, or shall marry a papist, shall be excluded and be forever incapable to inherit, possess or enjoy the crown and government of this realm . . . or to have, use or exercise any regal power, authority or jurisdiction within the same; and in all and every such case or cases the people of these realms shall be and are hereby absolved of their allegiance; and the said crown and government shall from time to time descend to and be enjoyed by such person or persons being Protestants as should have inherited and enjoyed the same in case the said person or persons so reconciled, holding communion or professing or marrying as aforesaid, were naturally dead; and that every King and Queen of this realm who at any time hereafter shall come to and succeed in the imperial crown of this kingdom shall on the first day of the meeting of the first Parliament next after his or her coming to the crown, sitting in his or her throne in the House of Peers in the presence of the Lords . . . and Commons . . . therein assembled, or at his or her coronation before such person or persons who shall administer the coronation oath to him or her, . . . make, subscribe and audibly repeat the declaration mentioned in the statute made in the thirtieth year of the reign of King Charles II entitled, An Act for the More Effectual Preserving the King's Person and Government by Disabling Papists from Sitting in Either House of Parliament. . . .

SOURCE: Statutes of the Realm (London: Her Majesty's Stationery Office, 1810–1828), VI, 143–45.

1. *Why did the Parliament state that James had abdicated (rather than being deposed)?*
2. *In what ways does this document perpetuate the principle of divine right? In what ways does it limit the principle?*
3. *How does this document safeguard English Protestantism?*
4. *How does it strengthen and preserve the powers of Parliament?*
5. *To what extent did the authors rely on precedent as the authority for their actions?*

THE MARK OF A GOOD GOVERNMENT

In his early writings, the French philosopher Jean Jacques Rousseau (1712–1778) enumerated the deficiencies of existing political systems. Later, he outlined the means of creating a radically new type of society. His most famous work, **The Social Contract,** *begins with the declaration: "Man is born free, and everywhere is in chains," and expounds the revolutionary principles of liberty, equality, and a free society guided by the "general will" of its members.*

The question "What absolutely is the best government?" is unanswerable as well as indeterminant; or rather, there are as many good answers as there are possible combinations in the absolute and relative situations of all nations.

But if it is asked by what sign we may know that a given people is well or ill governed, that is another matter, and the question, being one of fact, admits of an answer.

It is not, however, answered, because every one wants to answer it in his own way. Subjects extol public tranquility, citizens individual liberty; the one class prefers security of possessions, the other that of person; the one regards as the best government that which is most severe, the other maintains that the mildest is the best; the one wants crime punished, the other wants them prevented; the one wants the State to be feared by its neighbours, the other prefers that it should be ignored; the one is content if money circulates, the other demands that the people shall have bread. Even if an agreement were come to on these and similar points, should we have got any further? As moral qualities do not admit of exact measurement, agreement about the mark does not mean agreement about valuation.

For my part, I am continually astonished that a mark so simple is not recognized, or that men are of so bad faith as not to admit it. What is the end of political association? The preservation and prosperity of its members. And what is the surest mark of their preservation and prosperity? Their numbers and population. Seek then nowhere else this mark that is in dispute. The rest being equal, the government under which, without external aids, without naturalization or colonies, the citizens increase and multiply most is beyond question the best. The government under which a people wanes and diminishes is the worst. Calculators, it is left for you to count, to measure, to compare.

SOURCE: Jean Jacques Rousseau, "The Mark of a Good Government." In *Readings in Western Civilization*, ed. James Dodson (Hinsdale, Ill.: Dryden Press, 1972), pp. 190–91.

1. *How would Louis XIV have answered Rousseau's question? How do modern democratic societies answer it?*
2. *To what extent does Rousseau's argument in this early essay reflect the concepts developed by Hobbes and Locke?*
3. *What is Rousseau's conclusion regarding the mark (sign) of a good government?*

THE DECLARATION OF THE RIGHTS OF MAN AND THE CITIZEN

One of the first acts of the National Assembly in France was the Declaration of Rights of Man and the Citizen, adopted on August 26, 1789.

The Representatives of the people of France, formed into a National Assembly, considering that ignorance, neglect, or contempt of human rights, are the sole causes of public misfortunes and corruptions of Government, have resolved to set forth, in a solemn declaration, these natural, imprescriptible [inviolable], and unalienable rights: that this declaration being constantly present to the minds of the members of the body social, they may be ever kept attentive to their rights and their duties: that the acts of the legislative and executive powers of Government, being capable of being every moment compared with the end of political institutions, may be more respected: and also, that the future claims of the citizens, being directed by simple and incontestible principles, may always tend to the maintenance of the Constitution, and the general happiness.

For these reasons, the National Assembly doth recognize and declare, in the presence of the Supreme Being, and with the hope of his blessing and favour, the following sacred rights of men and of citizens:

I.   Men are born, and always continue, free, and equal in the respect of their rights. Civil distinctions, therefore, can be founded only on public utility.

II.   The end of all political associations is the preservation of the natural and imprescriptible rights of man; and these rights are liberty, property, security, and resistance of oppression.

III.   The nation is essentially the source of all sovereignty; nor can any Individual, or any Body of Men, be entitled to any authority which is not expressly derived from it.

IV.   Political Liberty consists in the power of doing whatever does not injure another. The exercise of the natural rights of every man has no other limits than those which are necessary to secure to every other man the free exercise of the same rights; and these limits are determinable only by the law.

V.   The law ought to prohibit only actions hurtful to society. What is not prohibited by the law, should not be hindered; nor should any one be compelled to that which the law does not require.

VI.   The law is an expression of the will of the community. All citizens have a right to concur, either personally, or by their representatives, in its formation. It should be the same to all, whether it protects or punishes; and all being equal in its sight, are equally eligible to all honours, places, and employments, according to their different abilities, without any other distinction than that created by their virtues and talents.

VII.   No man should be accused, arrested, or held in confinement, except in cases determined by the law, and according to the forms which it has prescribed. All who promote, solicit, execute, or cause to be executed, arbitrary orders, ought to be punished, and every citizen called upon, or apprehended by virtue of the law, ought immediately to obey, and renders himself culpable by resistance.

VIII.   The law ought to impose no other penalties but such as are absolutely and evidently necessary: and no one ought to be punished, but in virtue of a law promulgated before the offence, and legally applied.

IX.   Every man being presumed innocent till he has been convicted, whenever his detention becomes indispensable, all rigour to him, more than is necessary to secure his person, ought to be provided against by the law.

X.   No man ought to be molested on account of his opinions, not even on account of his religious opinions, provided his avowal of them does not disturb the public order established by the law.

XI.   The unrestrained communication of thoughts and opinions being one of the most precious rights of man, every citizen may speak, write, and publish freely, provided he is responsible for the abuse of this liberty in cases determined by the law.

XII.   A public force being necessary to give security to the rights of men and of citizens, that force is instituted for the benefit of the community, and not for the particular benefit of the persons with whom it is entrusted.

XIII.   A common contribution being necessary for the support of the public force, and for defraying the other expenses of government, it ought to be divided equally among the members of the community, according to their abilities.

XIV.   Every citizen has a right, either by himself or his representative, to a free voice in determining the necessity of public contributions, the appropriation of them, and their amount, mode of assessment, and duration.

XV.   Every community has a right to demand of all its agents, an account of their conduct.

XVI.   Every community in which a separation of powers and a security of rights is not provided for, wants a constitution.

XVII.   The right to property being inviolable and sacred, no one ought to be deprived of it, except in cases of evident public necessity, legally ascertained, and on condition of a previous just indemnity.

SOURCE: Thomas Paine, *Rights of Man: Being an Answer to Mr. Burke's Attack on the French Revolution* (London, 1791), pp. 116–19.

1. *What do the authors believe are the natural rights of human beings?*
2. *To what extent is this document comparable to the United States Bill of Rights?*
3. *What was the French revolutionaries' definition of freedom in this declaration?*
4. *What did they mean by equality?*
5. *To whom was the principle of equality before the law extended? Who was not included?*
6. *Which clauses can be described as conservative, that is, tending to preserve a status quo?*

NAPOLEON'S RUSSIAN CAMPAIGN

Napoleon's invasion of Russia in 1812 was initially successful, but before final victory could be attained, the city of Moscow burned to the ground. After some delay, in December Napoleon ordered a retreat of the Grand Army, but the winter snows reduced the once mighty army to a band of stragglers. Of the nearly 700,000 men who entered Russia in June, about 100,000 survived. The following account was written by one of these survivors.

On the sixth of December, the day following the departure of the Emperor, the sky became still more terrible. The air was filled with infinitesimal ice crystals; birds fell to the earth frozen stiff. The atmosphere was absolutely still. It seemed as if everything in nature having movement or life, down to the very wind, had been bound and congealed in a universal death. Now not a word, not a murmur broke the dismal silence, silence of despair and unshed tears.

We drifted along in this empire of death like accursed phantoms. Only the monotonous beat of our steps, the crunch of the snow, and the feeble groans of the dying broke the vast mournful stillness. Among us was heard neither raging nor cursing, nothing that would imply a trace of warmth: we have hardly enough strength to pray. Most of the men fell without a word of complaint, silent either from weakness or resignation; or perhaps because men only complain when they have hopes of moving someone to pity.

The soldiers who had been most resolute until then lost heart completely. At times the snow opened up under their feet. Even where it was solid, its ice-coated surface gave them no support, and they slipped and fell, and got up to fall again. It was as if this hostile earth refused to carry them any longer, laid snares for them in order to hamper them and retard their flight, and so deliver them up to the Russians, who were still on their trail, or to their terrible climate.

When exhaustion compelled them to halt a moment, the icy hand of winter fell heavily on its prey. In vain the miserable victims, feeling themselves grow numb, staggered to their feet, already without voice or feeling, and took a few steps, like automatons. Their blood was freezing in their veins, like water in a brook, and slowing up their hearts. Then it rushed to their heads, and the dying men reeled along as if they were drunk. Actual tears of blood oozed from their eyes, horribly inflamed and festered by loss of sleep and the smoke of campfires. Their chests were racked by deep sighs. They stared at the sky, at us, at the earth with a wild, frightened look in their eyes; this was their farewell to a merciless nature that was torturing them, perhaps also a reproach. Before long they fell to their knees, then forward on their hands. Their heads wagged stupidly from side to side for a little while, and a gasping rattle issued from their lips. Then they collapsed in the snow, on which appeared the slow-spreading stain of blackish blood—and their suffering was at an end.

Their comrades passed them without taking a single step out of their way, lest they should lengthen their journey by a few feet—without so much as turning their heads, for their beards and hair were bristling with icicles, and the least movement was painful. They did not even feel pity for those who fell; for what had they lost by dying? What were they leaving? We were suffering so much! . . . In this confusion, in the violent and continuous movement of a life filled with action, danger, and pain, it [death] seemed a mere transition, a slight alteration, one more change of place, and it no longer shocked us.

Such were the last days of the Grand Army: its last nights were still more frightful. The groups of soldiers, overtaken by darkness far from any human habitation, halted at the edge of the forest. There, they lit their fires around which all night long they sat, stiff and motionless as ghosts. They could not get enough of this heat. They drew so close to it that their clothing took fire, as well as their frozen extremities, which the flames scorched. Soon the dreadful pain forced them to lie down—a fatal move—and the next morning they tried in vain to get up again.

Meanwhile those with whom winter had left nearly intact, who still preserved a remnant of courage, were preparing their sorry evening meal. This was composed, as it had been since Smolensk, of some slices of broiled horsemeat, and rye meal made into gruel with snow water or rolled into pancakes which the men, having no salt, seasoned with powder from their cartridges.

All night long the light of these fires attracted other specters whom the first comers did not allow to approach. These miserable creatures wandered from one fire to another until, overcome by cold and despair, they gave up altogether and lay down in the snow behind the circle of their more fortunate companions, and breathed their last. Some of the men, without tools or strength to cut down the tall firs of the forest, tried in vain to set fire to their trunks. Death caught them in all sorts of attitudes around those trees.

Even greater horrors were seen in the spacious barns and sheds dotted here and there along the way. Soldiers and officers alike poured into them until they were filled to bursting. There, like so many cattle, they crowded together around two or three fires. The living, unable to drag the dead away from the circle, lay down on them and died in their turn, and served as deathbeds for still other victims. . . .

And this was the army that had issued from the most civilized nation in Europe, that army once so brilliant, victorious over men up to the last moment, and whose name still inspired respect in so many conquered capitals! Its most glorious warriors, those who had borne themselves so heroically on the world's great battlefields, had now lost all their noble bearing. Covered with rags, their feet naked and torn, they staggered along, supporting themselves on branches cut from fir trees; and all the strength and perserverance they had once put to the service of victory, they now employed in running away.

SOURCE: Count Philippe-Paul DeSegur, *Napoleon's Russian Campaign* (New York: Time Life Books, 1958), pp. 268–71.

1. *What events led up to Napoleon's decision to invade Russia?*
2. *What were Napoleon's alternatives to retreat in the depths of winter? Why did he not choose one of the alternatives?*
3. *What was Napoleon's military objective in the invasion of Russia?*
4. *To what extent did Napoleon's failure in Russia contribute to his national defeat?*
5. *What lessons did Napoleon's defeat hold for future would-be conquerors of Russia, like Adolf Hitler? What lessons did it hold for future defenders of Russia?*

The role of the family in society, and that of women and children in particular, have undergone significant changes—albeit very slowly until recent times. In the first selection the social historian Peter Laslett describes the structure of the family a century and a half before the Industrial Revolution. The next document graphically portrays living conditions in early Victorian slums.

During the Industrial Revolution, attention also focused on abuses such as child labor that had existed in rural areas for centuries but had gone virtually unnoticed. With the growth of extensive slums in urban industrial centers, the public at large began to demand reform. Ultimately, both men and women as well as children were the beneficiaries of this new public awareness and reform-minded spirit.

The Early Modern Family

In the year 1619 the bakers of London applied to the authorities for an increase in the price of bread. They sent in support of their claim a complete description of a bakery and an account of its weekly costs. There were thirteen or fourteen people in such an establishment: the baker and his wife, four paid employees who were called journeymen, two apprentices, two maidservants and the three or four children of the master baker himself. . . .

The only word used at that time to describe such a group was "family." The man at the head of the group, the entrepreneur, the employer, or the manager, was then known as the master or head of the family. He was father to some of its members and in place of father to the rest. There was no sharp distinction between his domestic and his economic functions. His wife was both his partner and his subordinate, a partner because she ran the family, took charge of the food and managed the women-servants, a subordinate because she was woman and wife, mother and in place of mother to the rest.

The paid servants of both sexes had their specified and familiar position in the family, as much part of it as the children but not quite in the same position. At that time the family was not one society only but three societies fused together: the society of man and wife, of parents and children and of master and servant. But when they were young, and servants were, for the most part, young unmarried people, they were very close to children in their status and their function. . . .

Apprentices, therefore, were workers who were also children, extra sons or extra daughters (for girls could be apprenticed too), clothed and educated as well as fed, obliged to obedience and forbidden to marry, unpaid and absolutely dependent until the age of twenty-one. If apprentices were workers in the position of sons and daughters, the sons and daughters of the house were workers too. John Locke laid it down in 1697 that the children of the poor must work for some part of the day when they reached the age of three. The sons and daughters of a London baker were not free to go to school for many years of their young lives, or even to play as they wished when they came back home. . . .

We may see at once, therefore, that the world we have lost. . . was no paradise or golden age of equality, tolerance or loving kindness. . . . The coming of industry cannot be shown to have brought economic oppression and exploitation along with it. It was there already.

SOURCE: Peter Laslett, "The World We Have Lost: The Early Modern Family." In *Western Civilization: Images and Interpretations,* ed. Dennis Sherman (New York: Knopf, 1983), Vol. 2, pp. 21–22.

Early Victorian Slums

. . . . I attended a family of thirteen—twelve of whom had typhoid fever, without a bed in the cellar, without [even] straw [to lie down on]. . . . I have sometimes checked myself in the wish that men of high station and authority would visit these abodes of their less fortunate fellow-creatures; and witness with their own eyes the scenes presented there. . . . They have only to visit the Zoological Gardens and to observe the state of society in that large room which is appropriate to a particular class of animals, where every want is relieved, and every appetite and passion gratified in full view of the whole community. In the filthy and crowded streets of our large towns and cities you see human faces retrograding, sinking down to the level of these brute tribes, and you find manners appropriate to the degradation. . . .

SOURCE: A medical officer from West Derby Union. In *Documents of English History: 1832–1950*, ed. W. A. Barker et al. (London: A. & C. Black, Ltd., 1954), p. 30.

A Child Miner's Testimony

How old were you when you went into the mine?—Going [on] nine years.

At what age do they usually go into the mine?—There is some that is five or six years of age.

Do these children do the same work as you?—What the little [one] can't manage himself the others help. . . .

Do the boys and girls work exactly in the same way?—Yes, both exactly in the same way.

Do they ever get crooked with bending?—Yes; there is some as grows crooked as goes in pits, and some as does not.

How are they crooked?—Some in their backs and some in their legs. . . . When they grow into men, about thirty or forty years of age, then they starten a growing crooked.

What is the weight of the basket you draw?—About four hundred weight.

Have sometimes two little children under six such a basket to draw between them?—Yes; in an easy place. . . .

Is the greater part of the mine dry?—I don't know any place that is dry. . . .

How high is it where you work?—It is about three-quarters of a yard, [and] some is about thirty inches or so.

Do you work barefoot?—Some with clogs and some barefoot, boys and girls the same; they take all their clothes off except breeches. . . .

SOURCE: Testimony Describing Child Labor in the Mines. In *Documents of English History: 1832–1950*, ed. W. A. Barker et al. (London: A. & C. Black Ltd. 1954), p. 25.

1. Compare the condition of the family in contemporary American society with its counterparts in preindustrial and mid-19th century English society. What problems have been solved? What new problems have emerged?

2. How does the baker's family differ in organization and responsibilities from a family in the last quarter of the 20th century?

THE OPIUM TRADE IN CHINA

A British missionary provided the following description of a Chinese opium den. In 1839, the opium trade led to a war between Britain and China.

While we have been sauntering around, we have noticed one particular kind of building that differs from all the others about it. . . . Its front is not open like those next door to it so that the public can see what is going on inside. Its aim, indeed, seems to be to conceal from the passers-by the movements of the people within, whilst at the same time intimating that anyone that likes to enter may do so freely. . . . As we stand speculating . . . a man approaches in a furtive manner, with head cast down as though he were ashamed, and glides in a ghostlike manner into the opening behind the screen and vanishes into the dark interior. . . . His clothes were greasy and dilapidated-looking, and his face wore a leaden hue as though his blood had been transmuted by some chemical process into a colour that nature would never recognize as a product of her own. . . .

Our curiosity is excited. . . . We feel we must investigate, and so we cautiously get within the screen and peer into a dimly lighted room that lies right in front of us. . . . We advance into the room and the fumes are so dense that we feel inclined to retreat, but we are inquisitive, and we should like to have a glimpse at what at the present moment may be called the curse of China. We find the owner seated in front of a little desk where he keeps the opium all ready for the use of his customers. . . . His face is thin and emaciated and his Mongolian high cheekbones jut out like rugged cliffs that have been beaten bare by the storms. His fingers are long and attenuated and stained with the dye that the opium has put into them, and they are deftly measuring out into tiny little cups, in anticipation of coming customers, the various amounts that he knows by experience each man may need.

With a ghastly smile that would have suited a corpse he invited us to be seated, for he knew at a glance that we were no opium smokers. . . . We noticed that the three men had already curled up, each one on his own particular bench, busily manipulating the opium and with infinite pains thrusting it with a knitting-like needle into the narrow opening in the bowl of his pipe. He then held it close to the flame of a small lamp, and as it gradually melted, he drew a long breath, and the essence of the opium traveled in a cloud to his brain, while at the same moment he expelled the smoke from his mouth. . . .

"Opium," the owner said, "is an imperious master and treats its subjects like slaves. It first of all comes with gentle touch as though it were full of the tenderest love for man. Then in a few weeks, when it has got its grip upon the man, it shows itself to be the cruellest taskmaster that ever drove man to a lingering death. . . . By the way," he added suddenly, "is it not true that opium was brought to China by you English? How cruel of you people . . . to bring such wretchedness upon a nation that never did them any wrong!"

SOURCE: Roger Pelissier, *The Awakening of China, 1793–1949* (New York: G. P. Putnam's, 1967), pp. 59–61.

1. Why did the British initiate the opium trade? Why did the Chinese blame the British government, rather than private merchants, for their opium problem?

THE INDEPENDENT LABOR PARTY

The Independent Labor Party was established in Great Britain in 1893.

Object: The object of the Party is to establish the socialist state, when land and capital will be held by the community and used for the well-being of the community, so as to secure the highest possible standard of life for the individual. In giving effect to this object it shall work as part of the international social movement.

Method: The party, to secure it objects, adopts:

1. Education Methods, including the publication of socialist literature, the holding of meetings, etc.
2. Political Methods, including the election of its members to local and national administrative and legislative bodies

Programme: The true object of industry being the production of the requirements of life, the responsibility should rest with the community collectively; therefore: The land, being the store house of all the necessaries of life, should be declared and treated as public property.

The capital necessary for industrial operations should be owned and used collectively. Work, and wealth resulting therefrom, should be equitably distributed over the population. As a means to this end, we demand the enactment of the following measures:

1. A maximum forty-eight hours' working-week, with the retention of all existing holidays, and Labour Day, May 1, secured by law.
2. The provision of work to all capable adult applicants at recognized trade-union rates, with a statutory minimum of sixpence per hour.

In order to remuneratively employ the applicants, parish, district, borough and county councils to be invested with power to: (a) Organize and undertake such industries as they may consider desirable. (b) Compulsorily acquire land; purchase, erect or manufacture buildings, stock or other articles for carrying on such industries. (c) Levy rates on the rental values of the district, and borrow money on the security of such rates for any of the above purposes.

3. State pensions for every person over fifty years of age, and adequate provision for all widows, orphans, sick and disabled workers.
4. Free, secular, moral primary, secondary and university education, with free maintenance while at school or university.
5. The raising of the age of child labour, with a view of its ultimate extinction.
6. Municipalization and public control of the drink traffic.
7. Muncipalization and public control of all hospitals and infirmaries.
8. Abolition of indirect taxation, and the gradual transference of all public burdens onto unearned incomes, with a view to their ultimate extinction.

The independent Labour Party is in favor of adult suffrage, with full political rights and privileges for women, and the immediate extension of the franchise to women on the same terms as granted to men. . . .

SOURCE: William L. Sachs, *English History in The Making* (New York: John Wiley, 1970), Vol. 11, pp. 254–55.

1. How much of the Labor Party program was enacted in Great Britain by 1987? In the U.S.?

2. What is unearned income? Why do the authors of this program want to eliminate it?

THE NARODNIKI MOVEMENT

The Narodniki movement represented an attempt to bring about social and political reforms in tsarist Russia from "below"—by educating the peasants. Catherine Breshkovsky (1844–1934) was one of the young idealists who went out among the people in the 1870s. She is sometimes known as the "grandmother of the Russian Revolution," but in fact she disapproved of the direction that the revolution took and spent the rest of her years in exile. The following excerpts are taken from her memoirs.

Having disposed of our former belongings, Mashenka and I rose with the sun one day early in June, donned our peasant dresses . . . and went down to the steamer that would take us down the Dnieper. . . . We spoke the language of the region, and we planned to explain our manners and education by the fact that we had belonged to the house-serfs and had lived with our masters and had learned much from them. . . . We opened our dying workshop and became acquainted with some girls and young women. . . .

We had brought with us several copies of appeals to the people in the form of proclamations, leaflets, tales, and legends. . . . [At the appointed hour] some twenty people filled the hut. They listened attentively. When I had finished, one of the workers asked, "Where did you learn to read so well?" . . . In one of the villages I gave away my last illegal leaflet and then decided to write an appeal to the peasants myself. I did this because when I spoke to the peasants they always said, "If you would write down these words and spread them everywhere, they would be of real use, because the people would know then that they were not invented." In those terribly ignorant times when the only written papers in the villages were the orders issued by the authorities, their faith in a written word was great, all the more so since there was no one in the villages who could write even moderately well. . . .

One one fine Sunday as I was returning home . . . I was stopped. My coat and my kerchief, tied "Russian fashion" under my chin, had distinguished me from the Little Russian [Ukrainian] crowd. The Commissar took maps and written sheets from my sack. He began to read aloud; his face became flushed with exultant joy. Scores of peasants of all ages had in the meantime gathered in the hut. The peasants stood around bareheaded. They had taken off their caps at the reading of the "edict." Again the proclamation was read distinctly, solemnly, in a loud voice. The peasants made the sign of the cross and the hut grew ever more crowded. . . .

The magistrate soon appeared. He was older and was stern and silent all the time. The inspector had his clerk read the proclamation aloud a third time, to the great satisfaction of the audience, who with heads bared made the sign of the cross. I was also pleased. We had not worked in vain. The proclamation was being read to a large audience very distinctly so that everyone could understand it.

SOURCE: Catherine Breshkovsky, *The Little Grandmother of the Russian Revolution: Reminiscences and Letters of Catherine Breshkovsky*, ed. Alice Stone Blackwell (Boston: Little, Brown, 1918), pp. 329–30.

1. *What difficulties did the populists face in their rural campaigns?*
2. *What mistakes did Catherine make that led to her arrest?*

MANIFESTO OF THE PROVISIONAL GOVERNMENT OF RUSSIA, MARCH 1917

The Provisional Government which replaced the government of the tsar was composed primarily of liberals in the Duma. Soon after they took power, the leader of the Provisional Government issued this manifesto.

Citizens! The Provisional Committee of the Members of the State Duma, with the aid and sympathy of the troops and population of the capital, has triumphed over the dark forces of the Old Regime to such an extent that it can now proceed to organize a more stable executive power. Toward this end the Provisional Committee of the State Duma has appointed as ministers of the first public cabinet the following men whose past public and political life assures them the confidence of the country. [A list of members follows.]

In its immediate work the Cabinet will be guided by the following principles:

1. An immediate general amnesty in all political and religious cases, including terrorist acts, military revolts, agrarian offenses, etc.

2. Freedom of speech and press; freedom to form labor unions, to assemble, to strike. These political liberties should be extended to the army in so far as war conditions permit.

3. The abolition of all class, religious and national restrictions.

4. Immediate preparation for the calling of a Constituent Assembly—elected by universal, equal, direct and secret ballot—which shall determine the form of government and draw up a constitution.

5. The replacement of the police by a popular militia, with elected officers and subject to the organs of local self-government.

6. Elections to the organs of local self-government based on universal, direct, equal, and secret suffrage.

7. Military units which have taken part in the revolutionary movement shall not be disarmed or removed from Petrograd.

8. While strict military discipline is to be maintained in the lines and in the fulfillment of military service, soldiers shall have the same public rights granted to other citizens. The Provisional Government considers it necessary to add that it has no intention of using the war conditions to delay the realization of the above-mentioned reforms and measures.

SOURCE: *Readings in Russian Political and Diplomatic History: the Soviet Period*, ed. Alfred Erich Sunn (Homewood, Ill.: The Dorsay Press, 1966), pp. 19–20.

1. *Which clauses of this manifesto played into the hands of the Bolsheviks?*
2. *What problems did the Provisional Government face in putting into effect article 4?*
3. *List three causes of the failure of the Provisional Government.*

THE REPRESENTATIVE OF THE PEOPLE ACT, 1918

The extension of the vote to women was achieved in England in 1918, by the Representative of the People Act. In this legislation, the voting age for women was established at 30, while men were eligible to vote at age 21. By a subsequent act in 1928, the voting age for women was lowered to 21.

A woman shall be entitled to be registered as a parliamentary elector for a constituency (other than a university constituency) if she has attained the age of thirty years and is not subject to any legal incapacity and is entitled to be registered as a local government elector in respect of the occupation in that constituency of land or premises (not being a dwelling-house) of a yearly value of not less than 5 pounds, or dwelling-house, or is the wife of a husband entitled to be so registered.

A woman shall be entitled to be registered as a parliamentary elector for a university constituency if she has attained the age of thirty years and either would be entitled to be so registered if she were a man, or has been admitted to and passed the final examination, and kept under the conditions of any university forming, or forming part of, a university constituency which did not at the time the examination was passed admit women to degrees.

Every person registered as a parliamentary elector for any constituency shall . . . be entitled to vote at an election of a member to serve in Parliament for that constituency; but a man shall not vote at a general election for more than one constituency for which he is registered by virtue of a residence qualification, or for more than one constituency for which she is registered by virtue of any other qualification.

A person shall not be disqualified from being registered or from voting as a parliamentary or local government elector by reason that he or some person for whose maintenance he is responsible has received poor relief or other alms.

SOURCE: William L. Sachs, *English History in the Making* (New York: John Wiley, 1970), Vol. 11, pp. 269–70.

1. *What were the conditions under which women were determined eligible to vote?*
2. *What effect did World War I have upon the suffrage movement? To what extent was this legislation a logical product of the 19th-century reform movement in England?*

THE RACIST THEORIES OF ADOLF HITLER

The racist theories of Adolf Hitler were based on his notion of Aryan superiority. Although the "Aryan race" itself cannot be clearly traced, Hitler assumed that most Germans were Aryans. In his warped mind, Jews were engaged in a satanic plot to adulterate the "pure blood" of the Germans.

All the human culture, all the results of art, science, and technology that we see before us today, are almost exclusively the creative product of the Aryan. This very fact admits of the not unfounded inference that he alone was the founder of all higher humanity, therefore representing the prototype of all that we understand by the word "man." He is the Prometheus of mankind from whose bright forehead the divine spark of genius has sprung at all times, forever kindling anew that fire of knowledge which illumined the night of silent mysteries and thus caused man to climb their path to mastery over the other beings of this earth. Exclude him—and perhaps after a few thousand years darkness will again descend on the earth, human culture will pass, and the world turn to a desert.

If we were to divide mankind into three groups, the founders of culture, the bearers of culture, the destroyers of culture, only the Aryan could be considered as the representative of the first group. From him originate the foundations and wills of all human creation, and only the outward form and color are determined by the changing traits of character of the various peoples. He provides the mightiest building stones and plans for all human progress and only the execution corresponds to the nature of the varying men and races.

Blood mixture and the resultant drop in the racial level is the sole cause of the dying out of old cultures; for men do not perish as a result of lost wars, but by the loss of that force of resistance which is contained only in pure blood.

All who are not of good race in the world are chaff. And all occurrences in world history are only the expression of the races' instinct of self-preservation, in the good or bad sense.

With satanic joy in his face, the black-haired Jewish youth lurks in wait for the unsuspecting girl whom he defiles with his blood, thus stealing her from her people. With every means he tries to destroy the racial foundations of the people he has set out to subjugate. Just as he himself systematically ruins women and girls, he does not shrink back from pulling down the blood barriers for others, even on a large scale. It was and it is Jews who bring the Negroes into the Rhineland, always with the same secret thought and clear aim of ruining the hated white race by the necessarily resulting bastardization, throwing it down from its cultural and political height, and himself rising to be its master.

And so he tries systematically to lower the racial level by continuous poisoning of individuals.

SOURCE: Adolf Hitler, *Mein Kampf,* (Boston: Houghton Mifflin, 1971), pp. 290, 296, 325.

1. *Who were the Aryans?*
2. *What historic factors accounted for the acceptence by many Germans of Hitler's master race theory?*

THE NAZI – SOVIET NONAGGRESSION PACT

On August 23, 1939, Germany and the Soviet Union signed a ten-year pact.

ARTICLE I: Both High Contracting Parties obligate themselves to desist from any act of violence, any aggressive action, and any attack on each other, either individually or jointly with other powers.

ARTICLE II: Should one of the High Contracting Parties become the object of belligerent action by a third power, the other High Contracting Party shall in no manner lend its support to this third power.

ARTICLE III: The Governments of the two High Contracting Parties shall in the future maintain continual contact with one another for the purpose of consultation in order to exchange information on problems affecting their common interests.

ARTICLE IV: Neither of the two High Contracting Parties shall participate in any grouping of powers whatsoever that is directly or indirectly aimed at the other party.

ARTICLE V: Should disputes or conflicts arise between the High Contracting Parties over problems of one kind or another, both parties should settle these disputes or conflicts exclusively through friendly exchange of opinion or, if necessary, through the establishment of arbitration commissions.

ARTICLE VI: The present treaty is concluded for a period of ten years, with proviso that, in so far as one of the High Contracting Parties does not denounce it one year prior to the expiration of this period, the validity of this treaty shall automatically be extended for another five years.

ARTICLE VII: The present treaty shall be ratified within the shortest possible time. The ratifications shall be exchanged in Berlin. The agreement shall enter into force as soon as it is signed.

Secret Additional Protocol: On the occasion of the signature of the Nonaggression Pact between the German Reich and the Union of Socialist Soviet Republics the undersigned plenipotentiaries of each of the two parties discussed in strictly confidential conversations the question of the boundary of their respective spheres of influence in Eastern Europe. These conversations led to the following conclusions: 1. In the event of a territorial and political rearrangement in the areas belonging to the Baltic States (Finland, Estonia, Latvia, Lithuania), the northern boundary of Lithuania shall represent the boundary of the spheres of influence of Germany and the U.S.S.R. In this connection the interest of Lithuania in the Vilna area is recognized by each party.

2. In the event of a territorial and political rearrangement of the areas belonging to the Polish state the spheres of influence of Germany and the U.S.S.R. shall be bound approximately by the line of the rivers Narew, Vistual, and San.

The question of whether the interests of both parties make desirable the maintenance of an independent Polish state and how such a state should be bounded can only be definitely determined in the course of further political developments.

SOURCE: Elfred Erich Senn, *Russia Political and Diplomatic History* (Homewood, Ill: Dorsey Press, 1966), Vol. 11, pp. 206–08.

1. *What were the primary terms of the agreement contained in articles 1 and 2?*
2. *What was the effect of the secret additional protocol?*

THE ATLANTIC CHARTER

In August 1941 the U.S. President Franklin Roosevelt met with Britain's Prime Minister, Winston Churchill, on board a naval vessel in the Atlantic. At the conclusion of this meeting, they issued the following declaration of principles.

Declaration of Principles, Known as the Atlantic Charter, by the President of the United States and the Prime Minister of the United Kingdom, August 14, 1941:

Joint declaration of the President of the United States of America and the Prime Minister, Mr. Churchill, representing His Majesty's Government in the United Kingdom, being met together, deem it right to make know certain common principles in the national policies of their respective countries on which they base their hopes for better future for the world.

First, their countries seek no aggrandizement, territorial or other;

Second, they desire to see no territorial changes that do not accord with the freely expressed wishes of the people concerned;

Third, they respect the right of all peoples to choose the form of government under which they will live; and they wish to see sovereign rights and self-government restored to those who have been forcibly deprived of them;

Fourth, they will endeavor, with due respect for their existing obligations, to further the enjoyment by all States, great or small, victor or vanquished, of access, on equal terms, to the trade and to the raw materials of the world which are needed for their economic prosperity;

Fifth, they desire to bring about the fullest collaboration between all nations in the economic field with the object of securing, for all improved labor standards, economic advancement and social security;

Sixth, after the final destruction of the Nazi tyranny, they hope to see established a peace which will afford to all nations the means of dwelling in safety within their own boundaries, and which will afford assurance that all men in all the lands may live out their lives in freedom from fear and want;

Seventh, such a peace should enable all men to traverse the high seas and oceans without hindrance;

Eighth, they believe that all of the nations of the world, for realistic as well as spiritual reasons, must come to the abandonment of the use of force. Since no future peace can be maintained if land, sea or air armaments continue to be employed by nations which threaten, or may threaten, aggression outside of their frontiers, they believe, pending the establishment of a wider and permanent system of general security, that the disarmament of such nations is essential. They will likewise aid and encourage all other praticable measures which will lighten for peace-loving peoples the crushing burden of armaments.

SOURCE: The Atlantic Charter. In *Readings in Western Civilization*, ed. James Dodson (Hinsdale, Ill.: Dryden Press, 1972), pp. 322–23.

1. *In what ways is this document similiar to Woodrow Wilson's Fourteen Points?*
2. *What were Roosevelt's four Freedoms?*

THE BREZHNEV DOCTRINE

The Brezhnev Doctrine was enunciated in 1968 to justify the Soviet Union's military interventions in Czechoslovakia, a satellite state which was attempting to liberalize the regime and loosen its ties to the U.S.S.R.

In connection with the events in Czechoslovakia, the question of the correlation and interdependence of the national interest of the socialist countries and their international duties acquire particular topical and acute importance.

The measures taken by the Soviet Union, jointly with other socialist countries, in defending the socialist gains of the Czechoslovak people are of great significance for strengthening the socialist community, which is the main achievement of the international working class.

We cannot ignore the assertions, held in some places, that the actions of the five socialist countries run counter to the Marxist-Leninist principle of sovereignty and the rights of nations to self-determination.

The groundlessness of such reasoning consists primarily in that it is based on an abstract, nonclass approach to the question of sovereignty and the rights of nations to self-determination.

The peoples of the socialist countries and Communist parties certainly do have and should have freedom for determining the ways of advance of their respective countries.

However, none of their decisions should damage either socialism in their country or the fundamental interests of other socialist countries, and the whole working class movement, which is working for socialism.

This means that each Communist party is responsible not only to its own people, but also to all the socialist countries, to the entire Communist movement. Whoever forgets this, in stressing only the independence of the Communist party, becomes one-sided. He deviates from his international duty.

Marxist dialectics are opposed to one-sidedness. They demand that each phenomenon be examined concretely, in general connection with other phenomena, with other processes.

Just as, in Lenin's words, a man living in a society cannot be free from the society, one or another socialist state, staying in a system of other states composing the socialist community, cannot be free from the common interests of that community.

The sovereignty of each socialist country cannot be opposed to the interests of the world of socialism, of the world revolutionary movement. Lenin demanded that all Communists fight against small nation narrow-mindedness, seclusion and isolation, consider the whole and the general, subordinate the particular to the general interest.

The Socialist states respect the democratic norms of international law. They have proved this more than once in practice, by coming out resolutely against the attempts of imperialism to violate the sovereignty and independence of nations.

It is from these same positions that they reject the leftist, adventurist conception of "exporting revolution," of "bringing happiness" to other peoples.

However, from a Marxist point of view, the norms of law, including the norms of mutual relations of the socialist countries, cannot be interpreted narrowly, formally, and in isolation from the general context of class struggle in the modern world. The socialist countries resolutely come out against the exporting and importing of counterrevolution.

Each Communist party is free to apply the basic principles of Marxism-Leninism and of socialism in its country, but it cannot depart from these principles (assuming, naturally, that it remains a Communist party).

Concretely, this means, first of all, that, in its activity, each Communist party cannot but take into account such a decisive fact of our time as the struggle between two opposing social systems—capitalism and socialism.

This is an objective struggle, a fact not depending on the will of the people, and stipulated by the world's being split into two opposite social systems. Lenin said: "Each man must choose between joining our side or the other side. Any attempt to avoid taking sides in this issue must end in fiasco."

It has got to be emphasized that when a socialist country seems to adopt a "nonaffiliated" stand, it retains its national independence, in effect, precisely because of the might of the socialist community, and above all the Soviet Union as a central force, which also includes the might of its armed forces. The weakening of any of the links in the world system of socialism directly affects all the socialist countries, which cannot look indifferently upon this.

NATO threat seen. The antisocialist elements in Czechoslovakia actually covered up the demand for so-called neutrality and Czechoslovakia's withdrawal from the socialist community with talking about the right of nations to self-determination.

However, the implementation of such "self-determination," in other words, Czechoslovakia's detachment from the socialist community, would have come into conflict with its own vital interests and would have been detrimental to the other social states.

Such "self-determination," as a result of which NATO troops would have been able to come up to the Soviet border, while the community of European socialist countries would have been split, in effect encroaches upon the vital interests of the peoples of these countries and conflicts, at the very root of it, with the right of these people to socialist self-determination.

Discharging their internationalist duty toward the fraternal peoples of Czechoslovakia and defending their own socialist gains, the U.S.S.R. and the other socialist states had to act decisively and they did act against the antisocialist forces in Czechoslovakia.

SOURCE: Reprinted from *Pravda*, 9/25/68. Translated by Novosti, Soviet Press Agency.

1. *How does Brezhnev justify the use of force in Czechoslovakia?*
2. *According to this doctrine, how much independence will the Soviet Union allow an Eastern European satellite state?*
3. *To what extent does the policy outlined in this doctrine resemble imperialism? How does Brezhnev define imperialism on the part of a Marxist-Leninist state?*

THE QUESTION OF AFRICAN UNITY

In the view of some African leaders, unity is the way to future strength of the Continent. One basis for unification may lie in the concept of "negritude" or the idea of the "African personality."

A major focus of the relations between African States as they have gradually become independent since 1958 has been the attempt to find some basis for unification. Without exception, the leadership of the new states has placed African unity in the forefront of the goals of foreign policy for their countries. On the surface it may seem somewhat paradoxical that these new states, having gone through the bitter struggle for self-identification and the attainment of sovereignty, should be so eager to surrender a part or even all of their newfound sovereignty to a larger body in which they would be but constituent units. Not all have been in favor of the kind of total unification and submergence within the federal structure that has been the theme of the leader of Ghana, Kwame Nkrumah. But all have been prepared to make at least some sacrifice of their complete independence in order to gain a greater measure of African unity and cooperation.

The commitment of the African leaders to unification stems from the feeling that only in this way can the ultimate objectives of the African revolution be accomplished. Although successful political action had brought independence to most of Africa by 1963, the African revolution in the eyes of today's leaders will not be finished until all of Africa is free and united. Full political equality for Africans in the eyes of the outside world will only come, it is argued, when Africa speaks with a united voice, although, it should be added, there is little inclination to sacrifice for unity the individual vote in the United Nations of each new state.

Reinforcing the political argument for unification is the cultural claim expressed in such terms as negritude and "African personality." Negritude, a term most closely associated with the writings of Leopold Senghor, the President of Senegal, has been defined, albeit from necessity vaguely, as a Weltanschauung, an expression of the innate emotional qualities which bind Negroes of the world together. One recent commentator insists that negritude is not . . . a preconceived doctrine, elaborated from a priori concepts. It claims to rest upon Negro-African realities from which it draws its substance and its being. It tries to translate on the basis of systematic philosophy the values of Negro-African civilization. . . .

The theory of negritude must be placed in the historical, economic and social context of the African world. The Negro is not radically different from the white man or the yellow man solely by the fact that he is black. It is the milieu in which he lives that conditions his reactions, that fashions his mind and his feelings; in a word, which gives a particular tone and expression to every manifestation of his being.

Some African writers see negritude as the African response to such foreign ideologies as Communism because it seeks to identify true Negro-African values; in itself it becomes a defense by the Negro-African world against Communism. "It is," says Doudou Thiam, "for the black world what pan-Arabism is for the Arab World."

The expression "African personality," on the other hand, tends to have a much more geographically confined content and specifically political significance than has negritude. As used by Kwame Nkrumah, it refers to those traits of character or personality which are specifically African and which imply an African way of political, social or economic organization which is distinct from that to be found elsewhere in the world. The psychological basis, then, of African unity derives from those aspects of personality which are common to all Africans. Closely related to this is the theme of an earlier unity of parts of Africa such as the old empires of the Sahara, the Ashanti federation and the Yoruba Kingdoms, which are cited as proof that there exists a historical basis for African regional unity predating European contact which can be revived as the basis for a larger contemporary union.

SOURCE: L. Gray Cowan, *The Dilemmas of African Independence* (New York: Waller & Co., 1964), pp. 56–58.

1. *Is there such a thing as a "national personality" or a "natural character?"*
2. *Does a federal system, comparable to that of the United States, offer positive solutions to African problem? How?*
3. *What problems would a federal African state create? Are they insurmountable?*
4. *What is the "African Way" of political, social, or economic organization?*
5. *Which problems facing independent Africa are the effect of the centuries of slave trade and Western imperialism in Africa?*

Index

Monck, George (general), 107
Monet, Claude (artist), 213
Money crop, 17
Mongols, 15, 16, 127
Monmouth, Duke of, 110
Monnet, Jean, 451
Monroe, Marilyn, 503
Monroe Doctrine, 320, 444, 490
Montaigne, Michel de (philosopher), 57
Montesquieu, Charles de Secondat, and
　the French Enlightenment, 153
Monteverdi, Claudio (composer), 156
Montezuma (Aztec emperor), 71
Montgomery, Bernard (general), 426
Moon, landing on, 494, 495
Morales, Jose, and independence of
　Mexico, 316
More, Thomas, 18, 20, 21, 38
Moro, Aldo (Italian politician), 457
Morocco, 311, 426, 478
Morris, William, and Marxist party in
　Britain, 250
Morse, Samuel F. B. (inventor), 195
Moslems. See also Shiite muslims and
　religious warfare in India, 471
Mosley, Oswald, and fascist movement
　in Britain, 393
Motion, laws of, 146
Mountbatten, Lord, and the partition of
　India, 471
Movable type, 10, 24
Mozambique, 312, 479
Mozart, Wolfgang Amadeus, 158, 211
Mubarak, Hosni (Egyptian president),
　484
Mujahidin, 506
Mukden Incident, 412–15
Multipolarity, 445
Munich Pact, 401
Muscovy, princes of, 127–28
Music
　atonal, 214
　baroque, 156–57
　classical, 157–58
　contemporary, 504
　French opera, 87
　jazz, 383, 384
　minimalist, 504
　post-WWI, 384
　rock, 504
Musical instruments, 157
Music hall, 214
Muslim League in India, 470–71
Mussolini, Benito, 387, 391, 392–93,
　401, 415
Mussorgsky, Modest (composer), 267
Mustafa, Kara (Grand Vizier), 118

Nagasaki, 430, 462, 493
Naisbitt, John (quoted), 498
Namibia, 312
Nana (Zola), 212
Nanking, fall of, 416–17
Napoleon, Louis. See Louis Napoleon

Napoleon Bonaparte, 170, 171–77, 218,
　219, 232. See also Napoleonic
　wars
　Egypt and, 308
　Latin America and, 316, 317
　Russia and, 422
Napoleon I. See Napoleon Bonaparte
Napoleonic Code, 172
Napoleonic wars
　Coalitions and, 173–74, 175
　Russia and, 176, 256–57
Napoleon III. See Louis Napoleon, as
　emperor of France
Narodniki movement, 265–66, 542
NASA. See National Aeronautics and
　Space Agency
Nasser, Gamal Abdel (Egyptian
　president), 482, 483
National Aeronautics and Space Agency
　(NASA), 494–96
National Assembly, in France, 164–65,
　324–25
National boundaries
　in Africa, 315
　after WWI, 355, 372
　Congress of Vienna and, 221–23
　in Latin America, 319
　political vs. ethnic, 327
　underdeveloped nations and, 469
　WWII and, 431
National Convention, French revolution
　and, 167
National Health Service Act (England),
　455
National independence, modern trends
　toward, 507–08
National Insurance Act (England), 455
Nationalism
　Arab, 486–87
　Balkan conflict and, 328
　communism and, 390, 477
　decolonization and, 469
　economic, 383
　in Germany, 273, 277–88
　imperialism and, 291, 308
　in Italy, 225, 273–77
　in Japan, 403
　19th-century Europe and, 197–98
　study of history and, 203
　war and, 338
　World War I and, 324–31
Nationalist Socialist German Workers
　Party. See Nazi Party
Nationalization, in Russia, 369
National Organization for Women
　(NOW), 509–10
National socialism. See Nazi Party
National Union of Women's Suffrage
　Societies, 253
National workshops, 231
Native culture, western influence and,
　292, 314
NATO. See North Atlantic Treaty
　Organization

Naturalism, 212
Natural law
　concept of, 142–43
　in economics, 199–200
　for society, 150–51
　for war, 149
Natural rights, 151
Naval power, pre-WWI Europe and, 331
Navigation
　in China, 64
　compass and, 65
Nazi death camps, 429
Nazi Party, 394, 396, 397, 399–400
Nazis
　atrocities of, 452–53
　postwar trials of, 452–53
Nazism, Marxism and, 420
Nazi-Soviet Nonaggression Pact, 419–
　20, 546
Nehru, Jawaharlal, 471–73
Nelson, Admiral Horatio, 175
Neolithic revolution, 492
Neo-Platonists, 21
NEP. See New Economic Policy
Nepotism, in Roman Catholic Church,
　28
Neptune (planet), 495
Netherlands, 17, 50. See also Spanish
　Netherlands
　African colonies and, 479
　Congress of Vienna and, 221
　European banking and, 183
　free trade and, 451
　German invasion of, 420
　Indonesia and, 301
　NATO and, 452
　southern Africa and, 312–13
Neva River, 337–38
Nevsky Prospekt, 337
New Atlantis (Bacon), 145
New Christianity (Saint-Simon), 201
Newcomen, Thomas (inventor), 187
New Economic Policy (NEP), in USSR,
　369, 390
New Lanark, Scotland, model
　community in, 201
New Order in East Asia, 417
New Spain, 74
New Testament. See under Bible
Newton, Isaac, 145, 146
New World
　colonization of, 71–77
　discovery of, 69–70
New Zealand, 470
Ney, Michel (general), 226
Nicaragua, 316, 490, 506
Nicholas II (tsar of Russia), 270, 331,
　359, 360–61, 364
Nicholas I (tsar of Russia), 245, 258,
　259, 266
Nietsche, Friedrich, influence of in pre-
　WWI era, 338
Niger, independence of, 478
Nigeria, 311, 469, 473, 474–75

NATO and, 452
Truman Doctrine and, 437–38
WWI settlement and, 357
Turks. *See* Ottoman Empire
Turner, William, and the Romantic
movement, 209, 210–11
Tutu, Desmond (bishop), 475
Twenty-one Demands of Japan (1915),
405
Two Treatises on Civil Government
(Locke), 151
Tzu-hsi (empress dowager of China),
299

U-boat, 349, 350, 351
U-2 Incident, 443
Ulyanov, Alexander (brother of Lenin),
365
Union of Fascists, in England, 393
Union of South Africa. *See* South
Africa
Union of Soviet Socialist Republics,
Bolshevik rule in, 366–70
Union of Soviet Socialist Republics
(USSR). *See also* Russia
atomic weapons and, 441, 493
Chinese communism and, 407, 445–
47
command economy in, 390–91, 458–
59
command economy in, 467
contemporary literature in, 502
creation of, 370
détente and, 445, 447–48
Genoa conference and, 379
human rights in, 508
Hungarian revolution and, 442–43
industrialization and, 390, 458
under Khrushchev, 441–42
liberalization in, 442
minorities in, 508
occupation of Eastern Europe by, 432
peaceful coexistence policy of, 441–
42
post-WWII friction with U.S. and,
437–38
power of soviets in, 389
purges of 1930 and, 391
revolt in empire of, 442–43
space age and, 494–96
under Stalin, 388–91
summit conferences and, 443
totalitarianism in, 388–91
and U.S., 1945–present, 436–48
Vietnam War and, 476–77
voting rights in, 507–08
WWII invasion of, 422
Yalta conference and, 431–32
Unions, in England, 238, 248–50
United Nations
Atomic Energy Commission and, 440
establishment of, 432
General Assembly in, 440, 507
Palestinian problem and, 482
Security Council in, 440

terrorism and, 507
Universal Declaration of Human
Rights and, 508
United Provinces of Central America,
316
United States
atomic bomb and, 427, 430
Bay of Pigs and, 444
Central Intelligence Agency, 444
Cold War period and, 436–41
contemporary literature in, 502–03
détente and, 445, 447–48
human rights in, 508
isolationism and, 383
Khrushchev and, 443–44
Korean War and, 439–40
Latin America and, 490
League of Nations and, 374–75
minorities in, 508
Mukden Incident and, 413–14
NATO and, 452
peace settlement with Japan and, 463
Philippines and, 487
post-WWI social change in, 383
relations with communist China,
446–47
Soviet expansionism and, 448
space age and, 494–96
summit conferences and, 443
support of anti-communist groups,
448
trade with China and, 296
Treaty of Paris and, 115
and USSR, 1945–present, 436–48
Vietnam War and, 477
WWI and, 350–51, 383, 423–25
WWII home front in, 427
Yalta conference and, 431–32
United States Constitution. *See also*
Equal Rights Amendment
Montesquieu's theories and, 153
19th Amendment to, 383
UNIVAC (computer), 497
Universal Declaration of Human Rights
(U.N.), 508
Unter den Linden (boulevard), 337
Unterseeboot. See U-boat
Upper Volta, independence of, 478
Uranus (planet), 495
Ursuline order, 40
USSR. *See* Union of Soviet Socialist
Republics
Usury, 32, 182
Utopia (More), 21–22
Utopian Socialists, 200
Uvarov, Sergius (minister of Nicholas I),
259

Vacuum tube, 497
Valla, Lorenzo (Renaissance scholar), 28
Valois, Georges, and fascist movement
in France, 393
Valois-Hapsburg Rivalry, 45–46
Van Dyke, Anthony (artist), 155
Van Eyck, Jan (artist), 23, 155

Van Gogh, Vincent (artist), 213
Vauban, Sebastien de (military expert),
93
Vega, Lopa de (dramatist), 51
Velasquez, Diego (artist), 155
Venetia, 276, 277
Venezuela, 317
Venus (planet), 495
Vermeer, Jan, and Dutch baroque
movement, 156
Versailles, palace at, 85–86
Versailles, treaty of. *See* Treaty of
Versailles
Vesalius, Andreas (anatomist), 146, 147
Vichy France, 421
Victor Emmanuel II (king of Piedmont-
Sardinia), 273–74, 276, 277
Victoria Falls, 308
Victorian Age, 242–43
Victoria (queen of England), 242–43,
247
Vida Es Sueno, La (Calderon), 52
Vienna, 335–36
Viet Cong, 477, 505
Vietminh, 476
Vietnam, 476–77
Vietnam War, 447–48, 476–77
Viking 1, 495
Vindication of the Rights of Women
(Wollstonecraft), 198, 251, 509
Vishinsky, Andrei (Soviet prosecutor),
391
Voitinsky, Gregory (Russian agent), 406
Voltaire, 94, 152–53
Von Moltke, Helmuth (general), 282
Von Ranke, Leopold (historian), 203
Von Richthofen, Baron ("Red Baron"),
346
Voting rights. *See also* Secret ballot
in Britain, 106–07, 194, 240, 244,
247, 248, 544
in communist bloc countries, 507–08
in Japan, 411
in 19th-century France, 226
postmodern extension of, 507–08
for women, 252–53, 352, 383, 509
Voting Rights Act of 1965 (U.S.), 507
Voyager 2, 495
Vulgate, 42

Wagner, Richard (composer), 211
Walesa, Lech, 461–62
"Walk on two legs" (slogan), 488
Wallachia, 245, 246, 259, 260
Wallenstein, Count (Czech soldier), 58
Walpole, Sir Robert, (British statesman)
113
War. *See also specific wars*
nationalism and, 338
nuclear weapons and, 505
postmodern trends in, 505–07
rules for, 149
War and Peace (Tolstoy), 268
War of the Austrian Succession, 97,
119, 124

572

War communism, 369, 389
War crimes trials
 Japan and, 463
 Nazis and, 452–53
Ward, Frederick, 297
War debt, 383, 392
War of Devolution, 92
Warhol, Andy, 503–04
War of Jenkins' Ear, 97
War of the League of Augsburg, 93–94
War of Liberation, 177
War of the Polish Succession, 119
War of the Roses, 13
Warsaw Pact, 442–43, 458, 459
War of the Spanish Succession, 94, 112
Wartburg Fest, 224
War of the Three Henrys, 56
Washington Conference, 376–77
Water frame, 189
Waterloo, 177
Watt, James, 186–88
Watteau, Antoine (artist), 157
Wealth of Nations (Smith), 199
Weapons, 331, 332, 345–46. *See also*
 Nuclear weapons
Webb, Beatrice, 250
Webb, Sidney, 250
Weimar Republic, 372, 394, 395–96
Wells, H. G., 250
Weltpolitik, 327, 331, 332
Wentworth, Thomas (parliamentary
 leader), 104
West Africa, colonization of, 311
West Bank of the Jordan, 483
Western Europe
 communist parties in, 460
 world domination by, 466
Westernizers, 261
West Germany. *See* Federal Republic of
 Germany
West Pakistan. *See* Pakistan
Westpolitik, 455
What is Property? (Proudhon), 230
Whigs, 109, 113, 238, *See also* Party
 system
"White man's burden," 293
Whites (Russian faction), 369, 390
"White terror," in the French
 Revolution, 170
Whitney, Eli (inventor), 189, 190
Wilberforce, William, 240
Wilhelm I (German kaiser), 280, 285,
 332
Wilhelm II (German kaiser), 327, 330
 abdication of, 354
Wilkins, Maurice (scientist), 499
Wilkinson, John (inventor), 188
William of Orange (Dutch ruler), 50
William of Orange (king of England),
 93, 110, 111–12
Wilson, Woodrow (U.S. president), 355,
 356, 374–75
 declaration of war and, 350–51
 Fourteen Points of, 353–54, 378

League of Nations and, 374–75
 quoted, 372
Windischgratz, Prince (military
 commander), 234
Winstanley, Gerrard, 106–07
Wirtschaftswunder, 454
Witchcraft, 147–48
Witte, Sergei (count), 269
Wittgenstein, Ludwig, and
 contemporary philosophy, 501
Wolfe, James (general), 98
Wollstonecraft, Mary, 198, 199, 251,
 509
Wolsey (Cardinal), 38
Women, 251. *See also* Feminist
 movement
 Chinese footbinding and, 405
 education of, in the Renaissance, 18–
 19
 French revolution and, 169
 industrialization and, 190, 193, 194,
 240
 political rights for, 198. *See also*
 Voting rights, for women
 property rights and, 172, 251
 in Russia, 266
 in 17th-century Russia, 130–32
 voting rights and, 252–53, 352, 383,
 509
 witchcraft and, 147–48
 in World War II, 509
 WWI war effort and, 352
Women's Liberation Movement. *See*
 Feminist movement
Wool industry, 17
Wordsworth, William, and the
 Romantic movement, 209
Working class, Russian revolution and,
 362–63
Working conditions
 in 19th-century Britain, 238, 240,
 248–49
 in Russia, 270
Workplace, democracy in, 508
World, circumnavigation of, 70–71
World Court, 374
World Economic Conference of 1931,
 383
World War I, 340–57
 alliance system and, 341–42
 battlefield conditions in, 345–47
 battle of the Marne and, 342–43
 casualties in, 355
 causes of, 324–38
 defeat of central powers and, 352–55
 economic effects of, 352, 355
 expansion beyond Europe of, 344
 fascist Italy and, 391–92
 Gallipoli campaign in, 344–45
 home fronts in, 351–52
 July diplomacy and, 341
 naval warfare in, 349–50
 postwar settlements and, 355–57
 post-war social change and, 383
 Russian withdrawal from, 368

in the East, 343–44
 in the West, 342–43
 United States and, 350–51, 383
 war guilt and, 357
 Wilson's Fourteen Points and, 353–
 54, 378
 women's suffrage and, 253
World War II, 419–32
 in Asia, 412, 415–17, 430
 Battle of Britain and, 421–22
 economic recovery from, 450–51,
 454–55, 456, 463–64
 fighting for France and, 420–21
 German invasion of USSR in, 422
 North Africa and, 426–27
 outbreak of, 419
 peace treaty with Japan, 463
 role of women in, 509
 roots of, 397–401
 in the Pacific, 423–25
 United States and, 423–25, 427, 430,
 463
 victory in Europe, 427–28
Wren, Sir Christopher (architect), 108
Wundt, Wilhelm, 207
Wyclif, John, and early Church reform
 movement, 27

Xavier, Francis (Saint), 41
Ximenes, Cardinal (Archbishop of
 Toledo), 39–40
X-rays, 206

Yalta conference, 431–32
Yang Kai-hui (wife of Mao), 409
Yeats, William Butler, 335
Yellow bile, and theory of four humors,
 147
Yemen, 483
Yermack (Cossack leader), 128
Yom Kippur War, 483–84
"Young Italy," 228
Young Plan, 382–83
Young Turks, 328
Yuan Shih-kai, 404–05
Yugoslavia
 German invasion of, 422
 independence of, 354
 Marxist government in, 437
 USSR and, 458, 460
Yusupov (Russian prince), 362

Zaibatsus, 411
Zaire, 479
Zanzibar, 473, 474. *See also* Tanzania
Zemski Sobor, 128
Zemstvo, 262
Zenjiro, Yasuda, 412
Zhukov, Georgi (general), 422, 428
Zimbabwe, 479, 507
Zimmerman telegram, 351
Zinoviev, Grigori, and Stalin's purges,
 391
Zola, Emile, 212, 326, 338
Zollverein, 278
Zwingle, Ulrich, 34

Acknowledgments /Credits

SOURCES OF CHAPTER-OPENING QUOTES
Page 10: Introduction to Contemporary
Civilization in the West, ed. by the Contemporary
Civilization Staff of Columbia College (New York:
Columbia University Press, 1960), p. 637. *Page 26:*
Roland H. Bainton, Here I Stand: A Life of Martin
Luther (New York: Abingdon-Cokesbury Press,
1950), pp. 185–6. *Page 44:* François Voltaire,
Voltaire's Alphabet of Wit, ed. Paul McPharlin
(New York: Peter Popper Press, 1955), pp. 19–20.
Page 63: Luis Vaz de Camoens, The Lusiads, trans.
William C. Atkinson (Hammondsworth, Eng.:
Penguin Books, 1973), p. 39. *Page 82:* The
Greatness of Louis XIV, ed. William F. Church
(Lexington, Mass.: D.C. Heath, 1972), pp. 8–9.
Page 100: F. Roy Willis, Western Civilization: An
Urban Perspective (Lexington, Mass.: D.C. Heath,
1973), p. 520. *Page 117:* Will and Ariel Durant,
The Age of Louis XIV, Vol. 8 of The Story of
Civilization Series (New York: Simon & Schuster,
1963), p. 39. *Page 160:* Charles Dickens, A Tale of
Two Cities (London: Dent, 1970), p. 1. *Page 179:*
S.C. Burchell and eds. of Time-Life Books, Age of
Progress (New York: Time-Life Books, 1966), p. 74.
Page 197: John Stuart Mill, On Liberty, The
Harvard Classics, ed. C.W. Elliot, Vol. 25 (New
York: Collier, 1937), p. 250. *Page 218:* Burton F.
Beers, World History: Patterns of Civilization,
(Englewood Cliffs, N.J.: Prentice Hall, 1983), p.
403. *Page 238:* G.K. Derry and T.L. Jarmon, The
Making of Modern Britain (New York: New York
University Press, 1956), p. 291. *Page 255:* Alexis
de Tocqueville, Democracy in America, ed.
Richard Heffner (New York: New American
Library, 1956), p. 142. *Page 273:* Theodore H.
White, In Search of History: A Personal Adventure
(New York: Harper & Row, 1978), p. 156. *Page
290:* Jerome H. Buckley and George B. Woods, eds.,
Poetry of the Victorian Period (Chicago: Scott,
Foresman, 1965), p. 903. *Page 304:* Quoted in
Daniel Mannix, Black Cargos: A History of the
Atlantic Slave Trade, 1518–1865 (New York:
Viking Press, 1962), p. 131. *Page 324:* The History
of the Times: The 150th Anniversary and Beyond,
Vol. 14, Part I (London, 1952), p. 168. *Page 340:*
Sidney Eisen and Maurice Filler eds., The Human
Adventure: Readings in World History, Vol. 2
(New York: Harcourt Brace Jovanovich, 1964), pp.
114–5. *Page 359:* "Bulletin of the Provisional
Government," March 7, 1917. Quoted in Robert V.
Daniels, ed., The Russian Revolution (Englewood
Cliffs, N.J.: Prentice Hall, Inc., 1972), pp. 16–18.
Page 372: Quoted in Annals of America, Vol. 14
(Chicago: Encyclopedia Britannica Co., 1968), p.
152. *Page 387:* Quoted in Stanley Payne, Falange:
A History of Spanish Facism (Palo Alto, Calif.:
Stanford University Press, 1961), p. 14. *Page 403:*
Quoted in Edwin Reischauer and Albert M. Craig,
Japan: Tradition and Transformation (Boston:
Houghton Mifflin, 1978), p. 218. *Page 419:*
William Shakespeare, Julius Caesar, Act III, Scene
i. *Page 436:* Quoted in Richard Current et. al.,
American History: A Survey, 4th ed. (New York:
Knopf, 1975), p. 733. *Page 450:* Quoted in Edwin
Reischauer and Albert M. Craig, Japan: Tradition
and Transformation (Boston: Houghton Mifflin,
1978), p. 286. *Page 466:* Nelson Mandela, The
Struggle is My Life (London: Inter-National Defense
and Aid Fund for Southern Africa, 1978), p. 115.
Page 492: Alfred Lord Tennyson, "The Passing of
Arthur," in The Oxford Book of Nineteenth-
Century Verse, ed. John Haywood, p. 523.